THE HISTORICAL ATLAS OF KNIGHTS & CASTLES

A CARTOGRAPHICA BOOK

This updated edition published in 2010 by
CHARTWELL BOOKS, INC
A division of BOOK SALES, INC
276 Fifth Avenue Suite 206
New York, New York 10001
USA

Reprinted in 2011

ISBN-13: 978-0-7858-2747-4
ISBN-10: 0-7858-2747-1

QUMHA14

This book is produced by
Cartographica Ltd
6 Blundell Street
London N7 9BH

Cartography:
Red Lion Mapping

Printed in Singapore by
Star Standard Industries Pte Ltd.

The Historical Atlas of Knights and Castles

By

Dr Ian Barnes

Contents

Map List

INTRODUCTION

The forerunner of the medieval knight, a Roman cavalryman, highly trained and amongst the most prestigious in the Roman Empire. He was equipped with an iron or bronze helmet, mail armor, a large oval shield with a spear and long sword. He could be regarded as the prototype for the mounted warrior who evolved into the knight of the early Middle Ages.

Geoffrey Chaucer (c. 1343–1400) is one of England's greatest poets who lived in the heart of high society, observing and eventually recording in verse aspects of medieval life. In 1357, he was a page to Elizabeth, Countess of Ulster and wife of Prince Lionel, Duke of Clarence, third son of Edward III. Chaucer married Philippa de Roet, a lady in attendance on the Queen, and sister to Catherine Swynford, third wife of John of Gaunt, the King's fourth son. He became squire to the King and went to war against France, later being captured near Rheims and ransomed, with Edward III paying part of it. His best remembered poem is *The Canterbury Tales*, a collection of stories narrated by pilgrims going to Canterbury to visit Becket's grave. The prologue to the poem contains the best description of a knight:

A PERFECT KNIGHT

"There was a knight, a most distinguished man,
Who from the day on which he first began
To ride abroad had followed chivalry,
Truth, honour, greatness of heart and courtesy.
He had done nobly in his sovereign's war
And ridden into battle, no man more,
As well in Christian as in heathen places,
And ever honoured for his noble graces.

He saw the town of Alexandria fall;
Often, at feasts, the highest place of all
Among the nations fell to him in Prussia.
In Lithuania he had fought, and Russia,
No Christian man so often, of his rank.
And he was in Granada when they sank
The town of Algeciras, also in
North Africa, right through Benamarin;
And in Armenia he had been as well
And fought when Ayas and Attalia fell,
For all along the Mediterranean coast
He had embarked with many a noble host.
In fifteen mortal battles he had been
And jousted for our faith at Tramiaaene
Thrice in the lists, and always killed his man.
This same distinguished knight had led the van
Once with the Bey of Balat, doing work
For him against another heathen Turk;
He was of sovereign value in all eyes.
And though so much distinguished, he was wise
And in his bearing modest as a maid.
He never yet a boorish thing had said
In all his life to any, come what might;
He was a true, a perfect gentle-knight."

Geoffrey Chaucer, c. 1390

Thus, the knight was characterized by his personal qualities, courage, and prowess, and was jealous of his honor. Most importantly he was dedicated to the service of an ideal, a code which dictated his behavior. He would always aid a maiden in distress and would never refuse a fight simply because the odds were greatly against him. No consideration of personal advantage could sway him from adherence to his beliefs and loyalties. Service to his sovereign lord was essential and his Christian faith shone forth especially when on crusade, whether in the Near East, Spain, or the Baltic. Excellence in combat and absolute integrity—these were the chief qualities of a paragon, the knight in shining armor, who embodies the ideal of chivalry through the ages to the 21st Century in films, fiction, cartoons, political posters, and advertisements.

This book seeks the reality behind this image. It is a reality that is difficult to identify, not least because in the Middle Ages the image of the noble knight was inspired almost from the first by the ideal of knighthood portrayed in the great medieval romances. These romances were pervasive, so that even those sources where one would normally expect to find facts rather than fantasy (histories, chronicles, biographies and so on) are, in the Middle Ages, flavored with the exotic spices of romance.

High standards of behavior were set, and history shows us that they were rarely attained in practice. Knights were primarily men who trained to fight and who inhabited a violent world. What distinguished a medieval knight from his predecessor, the mounted warrior of the early Middle Ages, was his consciousness of the ideal of knighthood including those aspects which were the hardest to live up to and, perhaps most important, his desire for honor. The concept of chivalry developed from a simple warrior's code into a sophisticated system of values. In this the principles of personal integrity, the duty to defend the weak from oppression, and the practice of knightly values such as generosity, compassion, a free and frank spirit, and courtliness, especially to women, combined with the more traditional virtues of loyalty and prowess. These qualities are stressed in medieval accounts, where the conduct of both real knights and fictional heroes is measured against this standard.

Fictional ideal and historical reality must be seen together. Medieval commentators were aware that there were bad knights who brought knighthood into disrepute. In romances, too, the hero knights encountered these sinister mirror images, the wicked knights who terrorized helpless peasants, dishonored women, even desecrated churches. Just as these dark knights certainly had their counterparts in real life among the robber barons, freebooters, and mercenaries of medieval Europe, so too it is clear that thousands of knights felt themselves contributing to a tradition of chivalry stretching back to the heroes of antiquity.

Additionally, this book describes the built environment of knighthood. The castle and fortress feature as households and as an instrument of domination and show of power often in a hostile world.

Complete armor for horse and man, c. 1530. By the end of the medieval period the elaborate suit of armor had reached its zenith. This Maximilian-styled fluted armor is particularly decorative, designating the wearer's social status, despite the fact that its military practicality had almost disappeared with the advent of firearms.

The Legacy of Rome

THE END OF THE ROMAN EMPIRE IN THE WEST ALLOWED LOCAL WARLORDS AND LANDOWNERS, WITH THEIR ARMED RETINUES, TO FLOURISH AND CONTROL THEIR LOCALITIES. THIS FRAGMENTATION OF POWER WAS SUBJECT TO ATTACKS BY ROVING BARBARIAN TRIBESMEN.

The tomb stone of a Roman auxiliary cavalryman, called Vonatorix, excavated near Bonn in Germany. He wears scale armor popular during the late Roman period, which could be polished to a high sheen; he was, indeed, the first "knight in shining armor."

The Roman Empire had a lasting influence on European history. Rome was noted for the excellence of its army, which acted as the main guarantor of the empire, and for its cultural, intellectual, and architectural achievements. Its language, Latin, has provided the foundation of the Romance languages: Italian, French, Friulian, Ladi, Romansch, Castillian, Catalán, Galego, Portuguese, and Romanian. Latin served as the language of European diplomacy, until it was replaced by French in the early 18th Century. It was the main instrument of scholarly activity in parts of Europe until the 19th Century and was used as the language of the Christian religion well into the 20th Century. The literature of Rome, alongside its language, has been the mainstay of traditional Classic European education until the 1950s.

The ruins of Roman settlements, works, and roads can be found from Britain to the deserts of Syria, from the Rhine to the upper Nile and Asia Minor. One of Rome's legacies, its laws, inspired and influenced many European and non-European legal systems. Despite the earlier persecution of Christians, Constantine the Great adopted the Christian faith at the time of the Battle of the Milvian Bridge in 312 and, under Theodosius, Christianity became the religion of state in 395. Christianity has remained, despite "barbarian" invasions, the dominant faith in most of Europe.

The architects and planners in the cities of the empire achieved exceptional standards in street planning, buildings, central heating, aqueducts, dams, plumbing, and sewage disposal. Rome's roads were crucial both to communications and to Rome's military needs across Europe and into Asia Minor and the Near East. Long and straight, the lines of these roads have provided the foundation for many roads still in use today.

Rome had dominated the Mediterranean, politically and militarily, during the last two centuries BC, and under Octavian (whose reign name was Augustus), Rome was transformed into an empire by the end of the 1st Century BC. Augustus gave Rome strong centralized government enabling it to prosper, stimulated by wealth and trade and an economic and political shift westward from Greece, Egypt, and Asia Minor. For the first two centuries AD Italy flourished, revealed by the remains of buildings, visual arts, jewelry, and other artifacts that archaeologists have unearthed.

Under Augustus the northern Iberian peninsula was conquered and the Danube became the frontier in the east. These conquests would continue throughout the 1st and 2nd Centuries, under Trajan (98–117) to Marcus Aurelius (168–180). Nevertheless, the 2nd Century became one of relative stability and consolidation; the period of great and gradual expansion came to an end. The golden age of Rome came with the Antonines: Antoninus Pius (136–161) and his adopted son, Marcus Aurelius. During this period, Rome reached its greatest geographical limit.

These bone tablets, excavated in Palestrina, in Italy, were carved during the 4th Century BC. They give a clear idea of the arms and crested helmets of the professional soldier élite of antiquity, the predecessors of the medieval knight.

The Pax Romana (the long period of relative peace experienced by the Roman Empire) spread from the Atlantic to the Persian Gulf. The empire had almost stable frontiers, apart from outbreaks of fighting in Asia against the Parthians and Persians, while the provinces were firmly controlled and protected with the *limes*, or frontier lines, from Hadrian's Wall to the Danube delta.

In the 3rd Century, Rome entered a period of unsteady decline, with the exception of the reign of Diocletian (285–305), who introduced reforms, restored efficiency to government, and laid the foundation of an empire in the east, which would last into the mid-15th Century. By the late 3rd and 4th Centuries, the eastern and western parts of the empire were growing apart. Failure to defend the west against barbarian attack at the beginning of the 5th Century was caused by the political, economic, and social weakness of western Roman society. Large areas of the west were rural and undeveloped and wealth lay in the hands of a few overmighty families. By contrast, in the east, wealth was based upon trade in the cities around the Mediterranean, which had prospered in a climate where a more egalitarian society had developed. The gentry in the east, unlike their western counterparts, provided well-educated civil servants for the administration in Constantinople, capital of the eventual Eastern Roman Empire (now with its modern Turkish name Istanbul). Likewise, the rural peasantry was more independent than their western peers, who had more or less become serfs.

After the reign of Diocletian, the Roman army began to suffer manpower shortages which led to the employment of barbarian troops as *foederati*. Whereas the barbarian element in the eastern army was about 28 percent, after the Battle of Adrianople in 378, it was as high as 60 percent in the western army. This led to a situation in which a Germanized army faced German invaders in the west—the Visigoths, Ostragoths, and Vandals—whereas, in the east, the army could draw upon Asia Minor for manpower. The Visigoths crossed the Danube frontier in 376, advancing upon Italy. The Vandals surged into Gaul and Spain between 406 and 409. Rome was sacked in 410 by the Visigoths and later in 455 by the Vandals and in 493 by the Ostrogoths. In the meantime, the Burgundians—an East Germanic tribe that may have originated on mainland Scandinavia—settled along the middle Rhône Valley after 430. Nevertheless, rather than being organized military campaigns, the barbarian invasions should be seen as great waves of economic migration, from the underdeveloped north to the rich lands around the Mediterranean. The conquering tribes were often divided against each other; their leaders wanted to become "Roman" and were quite prepared to desert their fellow tribesmen in order to achieve this. The barbarian invasions changed lifestyles in the west. By the late 5th Century, most western provinces were virtually lost to the empire.

During Emperor Constantine's reign Christianity became recognized as the official religion of the Roman Empire. Without this historically-important decision the concept of knighthood and chivalry, which is deeply connected to the teaching of Christianity, may never have evolved.

In the 6th Century, Justinian attempted to reunite the eastern and western parts of the Empire, inspired by the ideal of a Christian Roman Empire with the Mediterranean Sea as its epicenter. Although he reestablished Roman control over those Germanic peoples who had settled in Italy, France, Spain, and North Africa, Justinian was the last true Roman Emperor, and his reign (527–556) marks the end of the Late Roman period and the beginning of the Byzantine Empire. Built on Roman foundations, this would last until 1453, almost all the way through the period of chivalry and knighthood.

Hadrian's Wall, built in AD 122-126 was the northern frontier for the Roman province of Britannia. Its stone construction left a lasting influence in defensive architecture.

Below: Under the reign of Emperor Diocletian the Roman Empire was divided into two parts, each with its own capital and emperor. In AD 303 Diocletian initiated a program of persecution of the Christians.

Origins of Knighthood

At Poitiers in 732, Charles Martel turned back a Muslim raid by dismounting his cavalry, stiffening his infantry into that 'wall of ice' which repelled Arab cavalry assaults and missile attacks. Thus, Gaul remained free from Arab conquest.

By AD 732, just 100 years after the death of the Arab religious and political leader, the Prophet Muhammad, who established Islam, his Muslim followers had created a huge empire with astonishing speed. Egypt, Palestine, Syria, Persia, North Africa, and Spain had all fallen to them in succession. The Caliphs, islamic leaders, ruled over half the known world, and were eager to conquer the rest. Fanatical followers of the Prophet posed a grave threat to Christendom. The Muslim army that invaded Spain in 711 and killed Roderick, the last king of the Visigoths, had penetrated deep into the south of France. In 720 they occupied Narbonne as a base for raiding parties venturing into the neighboring Kingdom of the Franks (a confederation of west Germanic tribes). In 732 a raiding party sacked Bordeaux and was marching north toward Poitiers. However, on the way they were confronted by the Frankish army, led by Charles Martel, and they were totally destroyed.

An engraved bronze plaque dating from the 7th Century of a Lombard horseman. The horseman was often used as a symbol by wandering Germanic tribes. The armed and armored horseman was a person of military and social significance, an early manifestation of the knight.

Historians disagree about the military significance of this victory, but its consequences were crucial. The advance of the Muslim empire was halted and Charles Martel, Mayor (leader) of the Franks, gained such prestige and support that he became a respected and permanent ruler. He requisitioned many grants of land from the Church and used them to reward his followers. In return they swore to fight for him on demand, equipped with horse and spear as well as sword and shield. Charles' power base was secure enough to unify the various tribes and provinces of the Franks into a credible kingdom; after his death his son, Pepin

Enemy at the Gates
date of loss of territory by the Roman empire
475
450
446
431
400
Federates (allied to Rome)
border of the Western and Eastern Roman empire, 450
Anglo-Saxon homeland
expansion of Anglo-Saxon settlement
migration of Ostrogoths
migration of Visigoths
ATLANTIC OCEAN
CELTIC PEOPLES
ANGLO-SAXONS
TEUTONIC PEOPLES
FRANKS
EMPIRE OF THE HUNS
KINGDOM OF THE VISIGOTHS
KINGDOM OF THE SUEVES
WESTERN ROMAN EMPIRE
KINGDOM OF THE VANDALS
BURGUNDIANS
OSTROGOTHS from 454
Pannonia by 446 lost to the Empire of the Huns
Agri Decumates 260 given up
by 3rd century loosely held area given up
Angles
Saxons
Mediterranean
Eburacum
Deva
Lindum
Glevum
Corinium
Londinium
Rutupiae
Oesoriacum
Bagacum
Colonia Agrippina
Mogontiacum
Rotomagus
Remio
Lutecia
Augusta Treverorum
Argentorate
Turones
Bituriges
Vesontio
Aventicum
Curia
Augusta Vindelicum
Cambodunum
Lauriacum
Vindobona
Carnuntum
Aquincum
Virunum
Emona
Mursa
Siscia
Pannonia
Singidunum
Viminacium
Pictavi
Santones
Burdigala
Arverni
Lugdunum
Vienna
Mediolanum
Verona
Aquileia
Pollentia
Genoa
Ravenna
Florentia
Ancona
Tolosa
Arelate
Narbo
Massilia
Brigantium
Asturica
Legio
Bracara
Salmantica
Clunia
Caesarea Augusta
Barcino
Tarraco
Toletum
Olisipo
Emerita Augusta
Valentia
Corduba
Hispalis
Gades
Malaca
Carthago Nova
Tingis
Sala
Aleria
Rome
Scodra
Dyrrhacium
Barium
Neapolis
Tarentum
Caralis
Codenra
Messina
Panormus
Rhegium
Syracuse
Icosium
Saldae
Caesarea
Auzia
Sitifis
Hippo Regius
Utica
Carthago
Constantina
Lambaesis
Theveste
Hadrumetum
Thaenae
Oea
Sabrata
Leptis Magna
Berenice
Boreum
R. Seine
R. Loire
R. Ebro
R. Douro
R. Tagus
R. Po
R. Danube
R. Rhine
R. Elbe
R. Oder
50°
40°
30°
20°
0°
N
0 200 km
0 200 miles

the Short, succeeded him as mayor but ten years later was elected king. Pepin drove the Muslims out of their remaining strongholds in the south of France, and his son, Charlemagne (Charles the Great), was spectacularly successful in enlarging the Frankish Kingdom into the Carolingian Empire, which stretched northward to include Saxony, westward to Bavaria, and southward to northern Spain, Lombardy, and half of Italy.

An illustration of a Frankish warrior, fully equipped and prepared for his lord's call to war service, just as a knight would be obliged to serve his lord or King at a later date.

THE FRANKS

It was Charlemagne who can be credited with the development of the famous heavy cavalry of the Franks. The mounted warriors who formed these elite troops were necessarily drawn from among the Frankish nobility and landed gentry, as they had to provide themselves with horses, coats of mail, helmets, swords, and lances. Charlemagne ensured that his warriors were properly equipped. In 806 he wrote to one of his vassals:

> *You shall come to the Weser with your men prepared to go on warlike service to any part of our realm that we may point out; that is, you shall come with arms and gear and all warlike equipment of clothing and victuals. Every horseman shall have shield, lance, sword, dagger, a bow, and a quiver. On your carts you shall have ready spades, axes, picks, and iron-pointed stakes, and all other things needed for the host. The rations shall be for three months, the clothing must last for six.*

Building on that early success at the Battle of Poitiers in 732, the Franks employed the tactic of charging their enemies in close formation, spears bristling forward. When this terrifying onslaught had shattered the enemy ranks, the Franks dispatched them with their swords. The combination of Frankish superior numbers, their greater skill, and reputation for savagery overwhelmed most of their opponents, but there were occasions in which the cavalry was defeated by more lightly-armed troops. In 778, while Charlemagne was leading his victorious army back into France after a campaign against the Spanish Muslims, his baggage train, full of looted goods and provisions, was ambushed in the pass of Poncesvalles by soldiers from the ethnic group of Basques. By the time Charlemagne realised the peril and arrived with reinforcements, the loot had been stolen and all his rearguard slaughtered. The Basques had melted away into the woods and rocky terrain. One of the dead commanders was Count Roland of the Breton Marches, later to be immortalized in the great *Chanson de Roland*, which turned even this crushing defeat into a kind of victory. Only four years later, at the Battle of Suntelberg in 782, it seems that overconfidence in the technique that had so often proved their superiority led the Frankish commanders to disaster when, without the necessary discipline, they charged an armed camp of rebel Saxons. The Saxons—a group of tribes who had migrated from Scandinavia and northern Germany—were able to surround isolated units of cavalry and cut them down.

The empire created by Charlemagne did not, as he had hoped, form the basis for a united

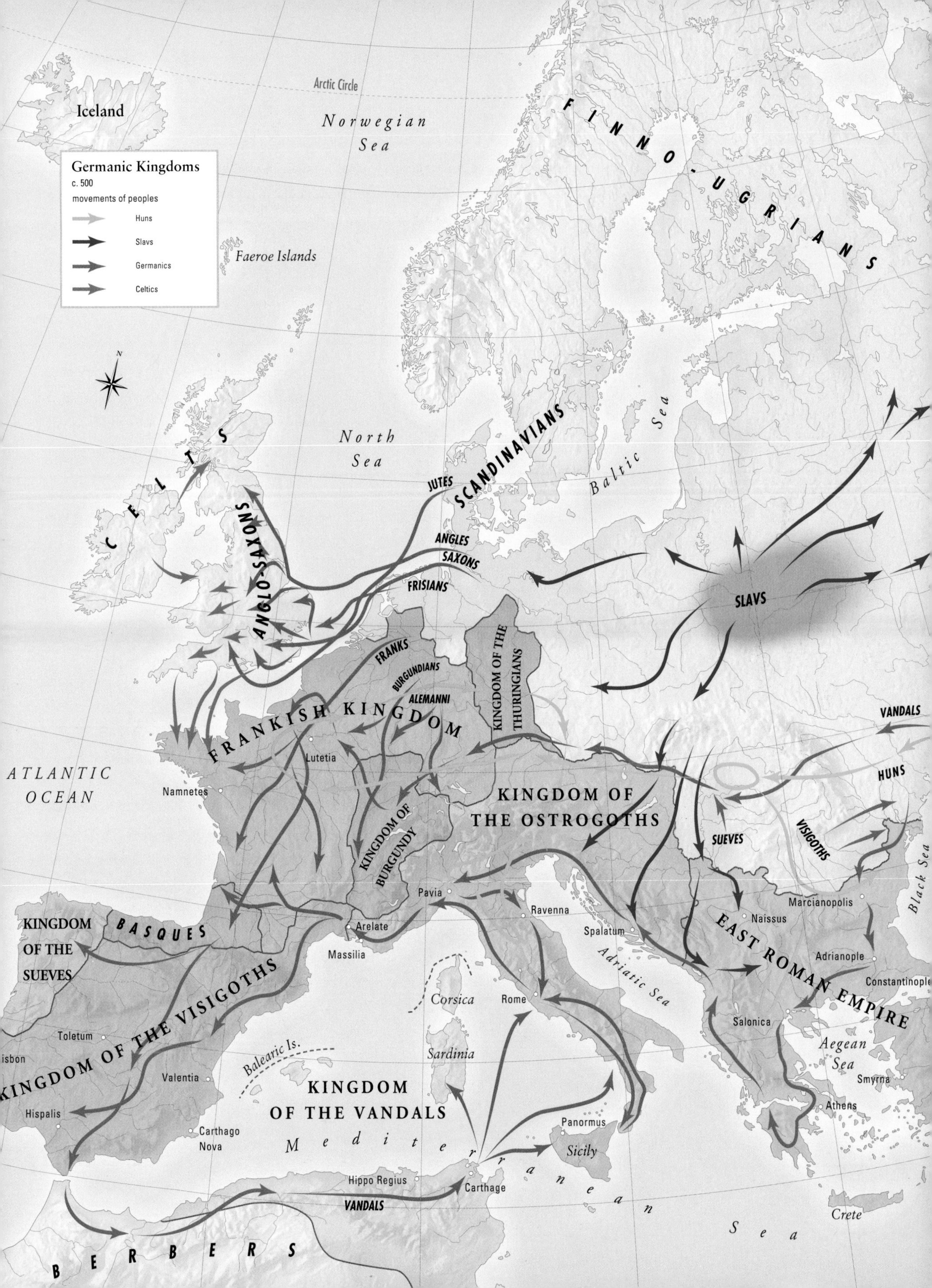
Germanic Kingdoms
c. 500
movements of peoples
Huns
Slavs
Germanics
Celtics
Arctic Circle
Iceland
Norwegian Sea
Faeroe Islands
FINNO-UGRIANS
North Sea
Baltic Sea
CELTS
SCANDINAVIANS
JUTES
ANGLES
SAXONS
FRISIANS
ANGLO-SAXONS
SLAVS
FRANKS
BURGUNDIANS
ALEMANNI
KINGDOM OF THE THURINGIANS
FRANKISH KINGDOM
Lutetia
ATLANTIC OCEAN
Namnetes
KINGDOM OF BURGUNDY
KINGDOM OF THE OSTROGOTHS
VANDALS
HUNS
SUEVES
VISIGOTHS
Black Sea
KINGDOM OF THE SUEVES
BASQUES
Pavia
Arelate
Massilia
Ravenna
Spalatum
Naissus
Marcianopolis
EAST ROMAN EMPIRE
Adrianople
Constantinople
Adriatic Sea
KINGDOM OF THE VISIGOTHS
Toletum
Lisbon
Valentia
Hispalis
Carthago Nova
Corsica
Rome
Sardinia
Balearic Is.
KINGDOM OF THE VANDALS
Salonica
Aegean Sea
Smyrna
Athens
Panormus
Sicily
Mediterranean Sea
Hippo Regius
Carthage
VANDALS
Crete
BERBERS

European state, a credible successor to the Roman Empire, in which military power would support strong central government. The empire was divided between his grandsons: quarrels between them and between their successors ensured the gradual decline of the Carolingian Empire. In the 10th Century a confederacy of duchies and counties, in which had been the Germanic western part of Charlemagne's dominion, developed into a unified German Kingdom. In 962 its King, Otto I, was

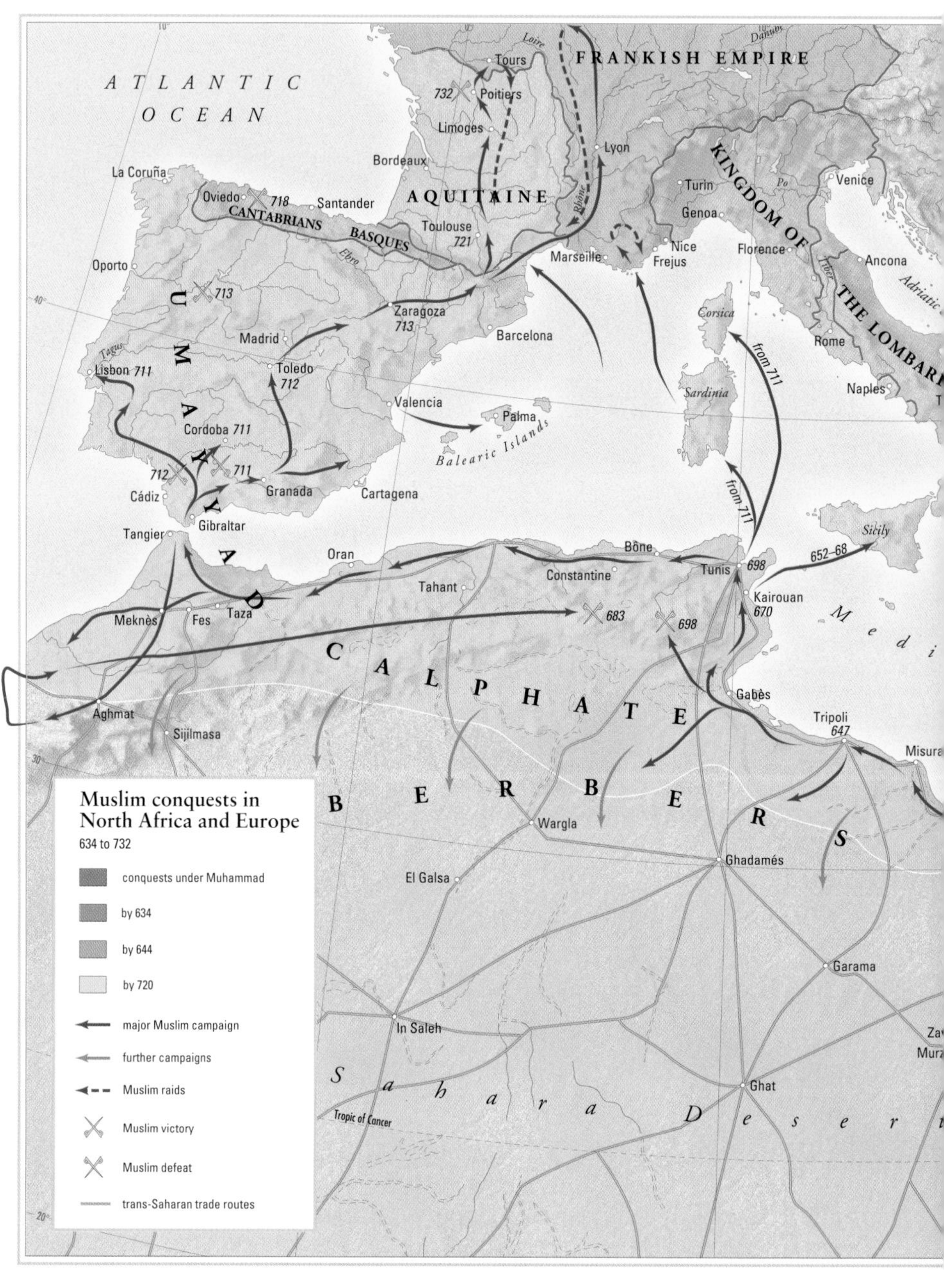

The greatest threat faced by Charlemagne's Empire was the expansion of Islam. After conquering Spain, Muslim armies advanced into the heartlands of the Franks. However they were defeated at the Battle of Poitiers in 732.

crowned Emperor of the Holy Roman Empire of the German Nation. Charlemagne had provided inspiration for Otto and successive medieval rulers in that his reign became a symbol of the ideal Christian state. Charlemagne, and some of his famous warriors, were honored and celebrated in stories and in art during the succeeding centuries as models for the rapidly developing feudal relationship of ruler and vassal.

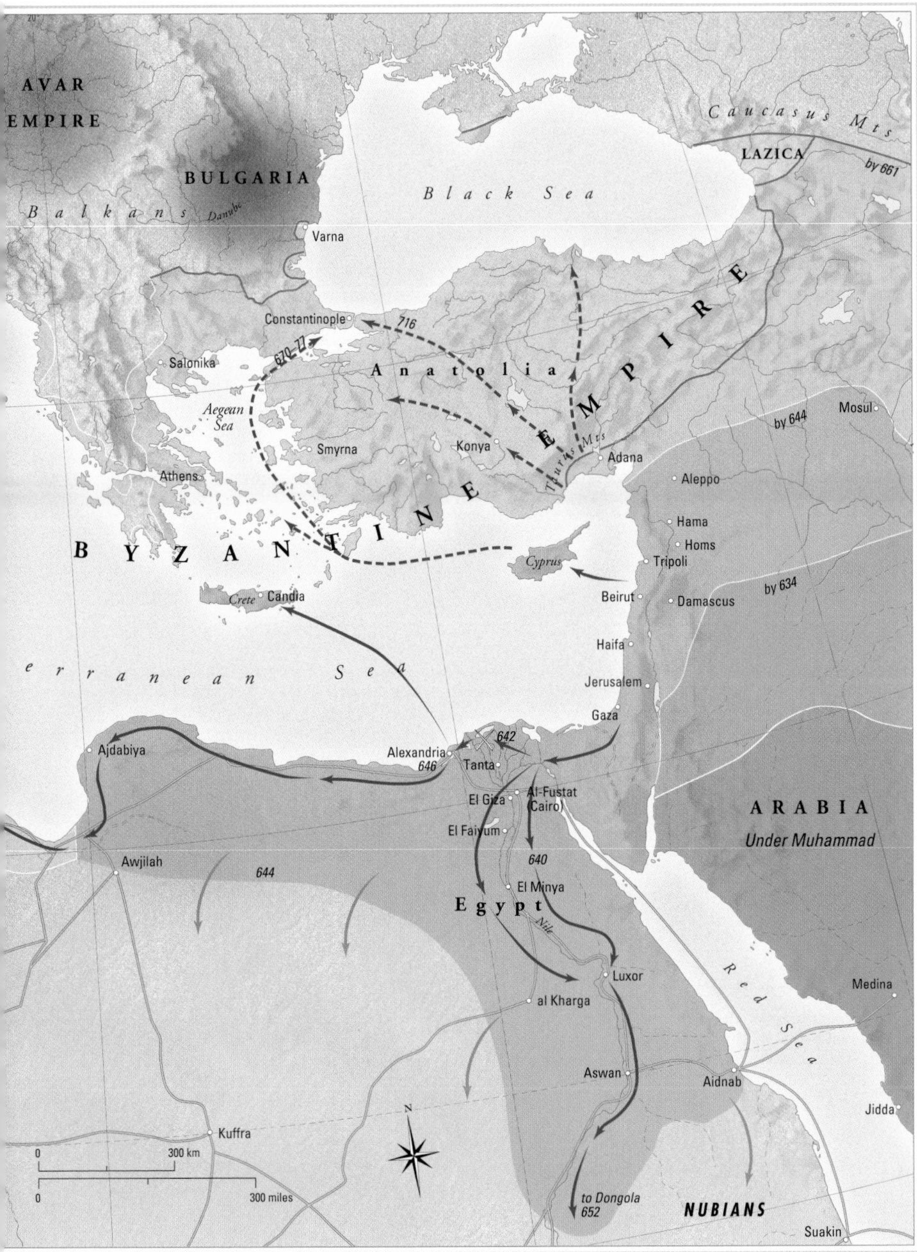

A detail from a medieval illustration showing the defenses of Constantinople. The largest and most important Christian city of the East, it was for centuries the bulwark of Christian Eastern Europe.

CHRISTENDOM

CATHOLIC BISHOPS, MONKS, AND MISSIONARIES COAXED PAGAN BARBARIANS INTO A SEMBLANCE OF CHRISTIAN BELIEF. MOST BARBARIANS ADOPTED THE HERETICAL, ARIAN FORM OF CHRISTIANITY AS OPPOSED TO THE ORTHODOX CATHOLIC CREED.

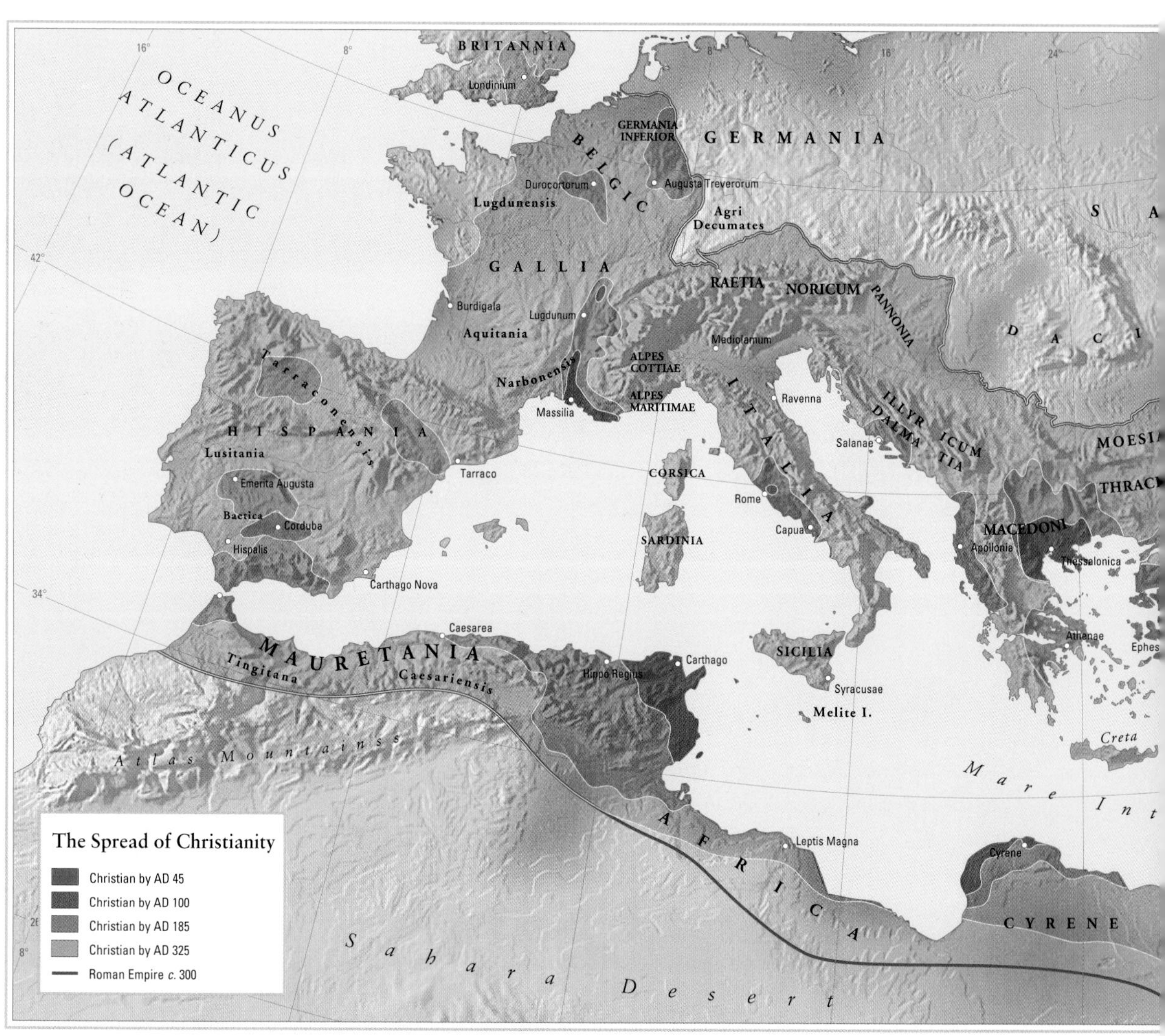

Prior to and after the conversion of the Roman Emperor Constantine (312–337), Christianity was less well established in the west than the east. The problem of the strength of paganism was exacerbated by the less urban, and therefore less controllable, nature of the west, plus lack of local clerical-pastoral institutions. The Church lacked a clear hierarchical organization. It was riven by theological divisions and faced increasing pressure from barbarian settlers, most of whom were pagan or Arian, following the conversion of the Goths by the Christian bishop and missionary Ulfila. Arian Christians believed that Jesus was not totally divine. The close alliance between Church and state in the east was not replicated in the west; the sack of Rome by the Visigoths in 410 led to a fierce dispute between Christian and pagan apologists. Nevertheless, Christianity did much to strengthen its hold in the west from the late 4th Century. The western

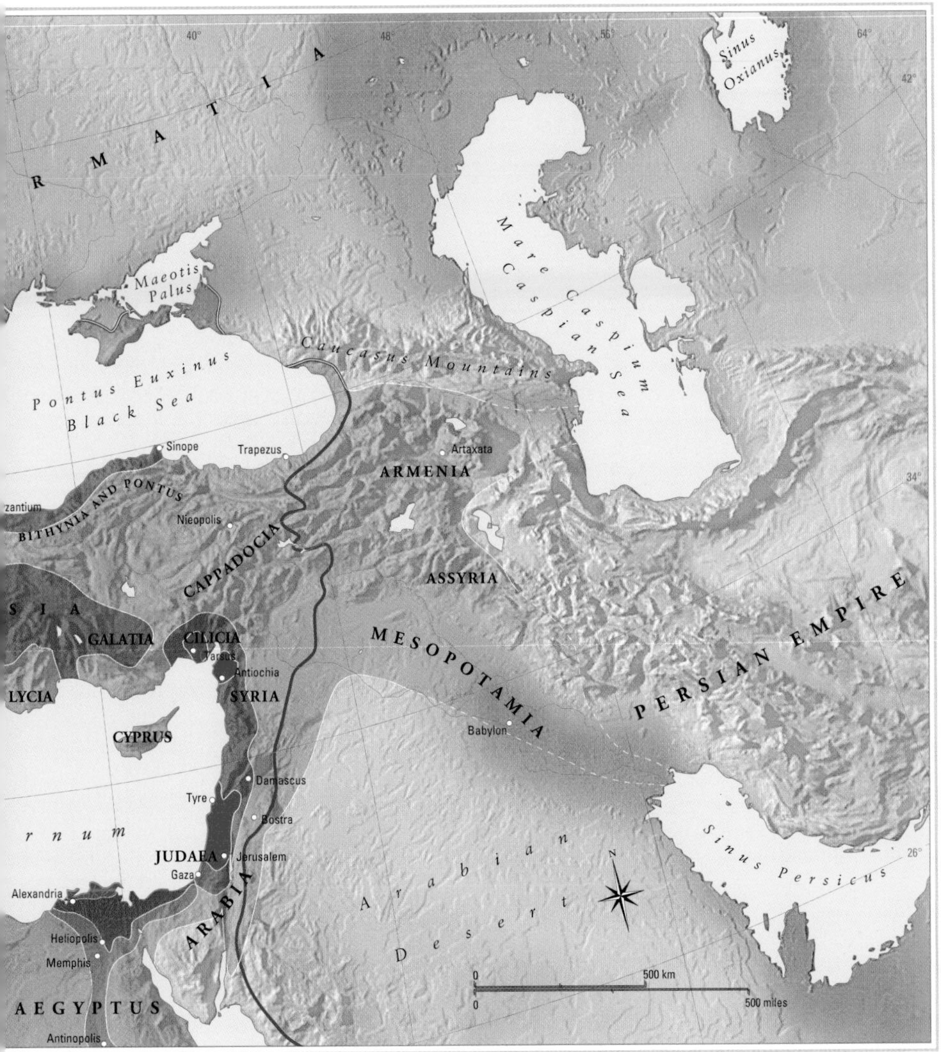

This mosaic shows Bishop Ambrose of Milan. Important clerics like him held immense power. In AD 390 Ambrose succeeded in making Emperor Theodosius do public penance.

THE SPREAD OF CHRISTIANITY
Christianity spread across the Roman Empire and by AD 200, was well established in many communities. Despite two major periods of persecution, AD 250 and 303, the religion survived to become recognized as the religion of state in AD 313.

Roman emperor, Theodosius I (379–395) opposed Arianism and paganism while a formidable number of Latin theologians such as Ambrose (d. 397) and Augustine (d. 430) strengthened the Church's doctrinal position, and the conservative senatorial aristocracy abandoned paganism in the early 5th Century. By the time of Pope Leo I the Great (440–461), the see (bishopric) of Rome had created a complex bureaucratic structure, becoming the mouthpiece of the west in disagreements with the east using its Petrine origins (of St. Peter, founder of the Church of Rome). It claimed authority in the west, including final ecclesiastical jurisdiction and the right to confirm clerical appointments.

The weakening of imperial institutions led to an increased political role for the bishops in Rome and other cities. Bishops took over social and charitable services in their cities and became the representatives of Roman communities in diplomacy with barbarian leaders while reinforcing their hold over their flocks by manipulation of ceremonies and the cult of saints (prayer to saints in the hope they will intercede on your behalf with God). The migration from the east of monastic leaders such as Athanasius and John Cassian helped spread monasticism. The latter had served as a monk in both Bethlehem and Egypt, and wrote influential Latin treatises on monastic life, founding two monasteries in Marseille, one for women. His monasticism differed from the eastern ascetic version, where a Syrian Holy Man called Simeon the Stylite achieved isolation by living on top of a 60-foot pillar for 30 years. Although they differed by being more aristocratic and urban, monastic figures such as St. Martin of Tours (d. 397) and St. Severinus of Noricum (d. c. 470) played a key role in the leadership of their local communities and in evangelizing the countryside.

Byzantium under attack. In this miniature taken from the Chronicle of St. John, a Byzantine cavalry force drives off a larger group of Bulgars, who had been besieging Salonika. It symbolizes the triumph of Christian soldiers over opposing faiths.

The fall of the empire led to a general extension of the Church's power, but its position in the 6th Century differed according to political circumstances. Southern Britain was one of the scarce areas where an almost complete disintegration of ecclesiastical institutions is evident. In Africa, Spain and Italy, the predominantly Arian regimes of the Vandals, Visigoths, Ostrogoths, and Lombards restricted the Church's influence, although complete persecution was rare. In the Celtic north-west, conversion of southern Scotland and of Ireland had been undertaken in the 5th Century by the missionary bishops Ninian and Patrick, but in the 6th Century the kin-based, nonurban nature of society led to the creation of a monastic form of church. In Europe new sees were founded, Church councils regularly convoked, and supervisory powers given to the heads of provinces, whether metropolitan in charge of a city bishopric or an archbishop in charge of all the bishops in a province. With the spread of monastic Rules such as St. Benedict's (d. 547), missionary work became the preserve of committed monks, such as the Irishman, Columba, who began the conversion of the Picts (an ancient people inhabiting northern Scotland), working from the island of Iona in the Inner Hebrides. St. Augustine was sent by Pope Gregory I the Great to convert the Anglo-Saxons in 597, and Columbanus established austere Irish foundation in Gaul and Italy extending the appeal of Christianity among Germanic aristocrats. Monks traveled vast distances: sailing in a leather boat, St. Brendan (d. c. 577) was blown so far off course that he is thought to have been the first European to reach the coast of what we now know as Canada. The extension and organization of the English Church was largely the work of monks, either Irish-inspired, such as Aidan at the island of Lindisfarne off the northeast coast of England, or Roman in alliance with Wilfrid of York. By the late 7th Century, Irish and Anglo-Saxon missionaries managed conversions and set up sees east of the Rhine, famous leaders being Willibrod and Boniface.

By 750, little success had been made in converting pagans outside the old Roman Empire. Notional Christians remained attached to traditional Germanic values and superstition remained widespread in the countryside, partly because local parish structures did not yet exist. However, by greatly improving its hierarchical organization, its texts and the quality of its trained clerics, the Church had achieved much in spreading its ideals.

The Byzantine Empire was the most powerful Christian state in the east and faced threats both from the north and the east. There had been little success in converting pagans outside the borders of the old Roman Empire. Thus Byzantium, Rome's successor, remained prone to pagan attack.

Byzantine Victory

- Byzantine Empire, c. 950
- Gained by Byzantium, 971
- Lost by Byzantium to Bulgaria, 986
- Samuel of Bulgaria attacks Larissa, 986
- Basil's unsuccessful attack on Sofia, 987
- Samuel attacks Basil retreating army, 987
- Basil attacks Bulgarian army, 987
- Byzantine Empire, 1025
- Under Venice influence

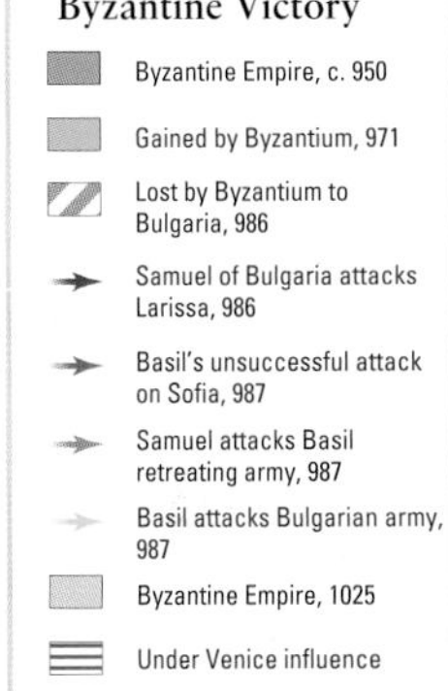

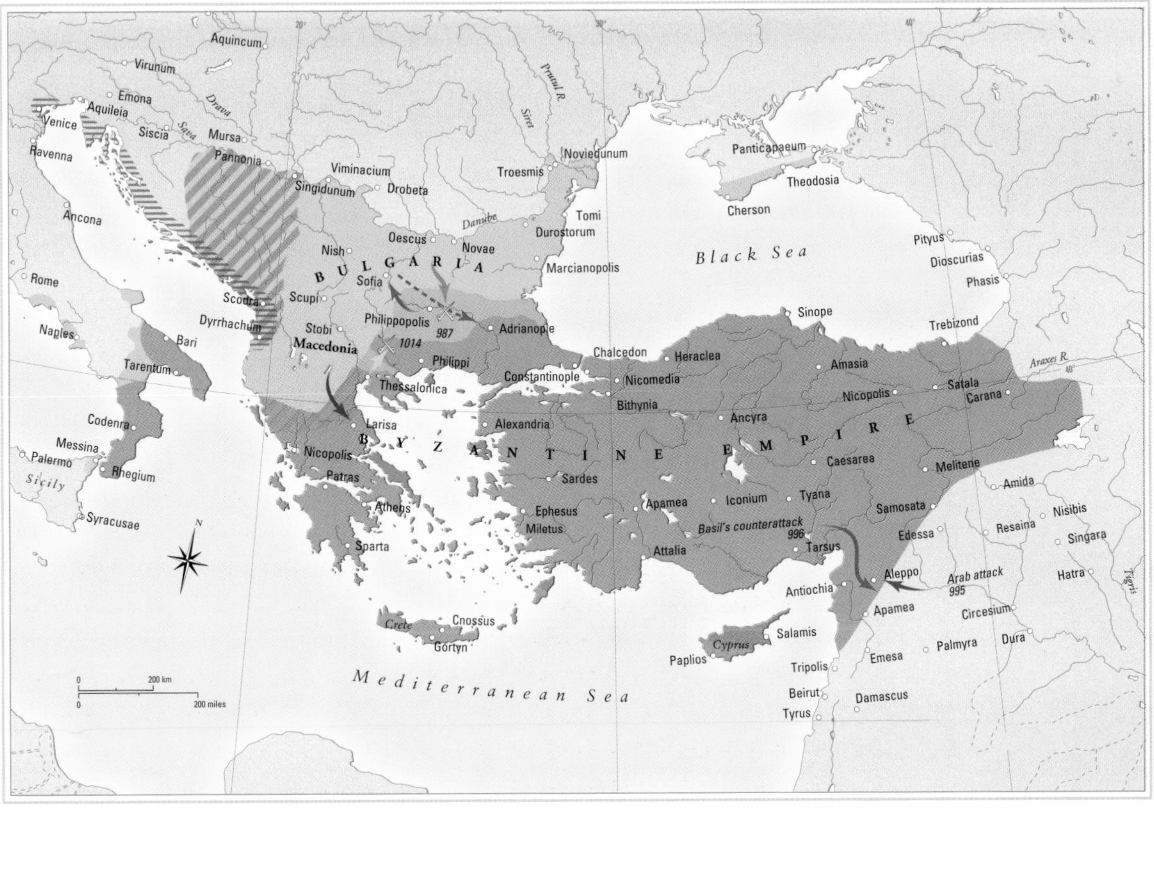

The Christian Empire

"YOU WILL GREET FOR ME THE MOST GLORIOUS AND GRACIOUS PEPIN OUR KING, AND GIVE HIM GREAT THANKS FOR ALL THE ACTS OF KINDNESS WHICH HE HAS DONE FOR ME..."

ST. BONIFACE, ARCHBISHOP OF MAINZ
TO THE ABBOT OF SAINT-DENIS

A decorated window from Freiburg in Germany showing the martyrdom of St. Sebastian.

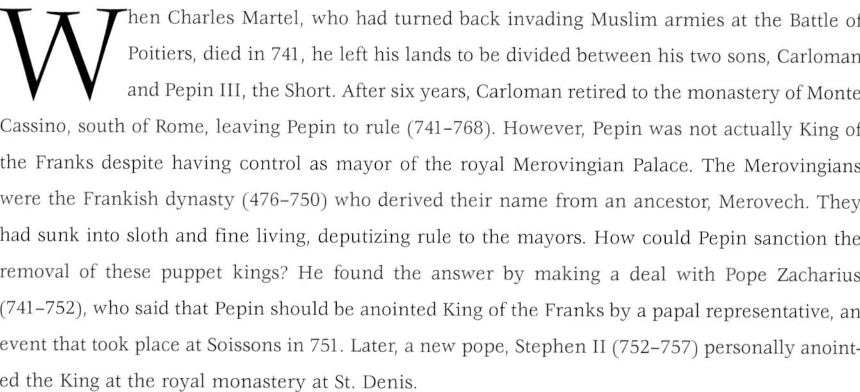

When Charles Martel, who had turned back invading Muslim armies at the Battle of Poitiers, died in 741, he left his lands to be divided between his two sons, Carloman and Pepin III, the Short. After six years, Carloman retired to the monastery of Monte Cassino, south of Rome, leaving Pepin to rule (741–768). However, Pepin was not actually King of the Franks despite having control as mayor of the royal Merovingian Palace. The Merovingians were the Frankish dynasty (476–750) who derived their name from an ancestor, Merovech. They had sunk into sloth and fine living, deputizing rule to the mayors. How could Pepin sanction the removal of these puppet kings? He found the answer by making a deal with Pope Zacharius (741–752), who said that Pepin should be anointed King of the Franks by a papal representative, an event that took place at Soissons in 751. Later, a new pope, Stephen II (752–757) personally anointed the King at the royal monastery at St. Denis.

These two popes had backed Pepin because they wanted his military support in Italy, where the Church sought to surround Rome with a temporal state, over which the pope would have civil as well as spiritual rule. They needed protection against the Lombards (Germanic people who had invaded Italy during the 6th Century) and could no longer rely on Byzantine help owing to the Byzantine Emperors' iconoclasm, the banning of statues and pictures of Christ and the saints. Iconoclasm was considered heresy and how could a pope rely on the soldiers of heretics? Geopolitically the pope was threatened when the Lombards conquered the "impregnable" city of Ravenna, seat of the Byzantine government in Italy. Pepin provided military support, defeating the Lombards, and gave some Lombard lands to the pope. This "Donation of Pepin" gave Pope Stephen

Pilgrimage was, and still is, an important expression of faith for many Christians. This medieval illustration shows pilgrims at the door to the shrine of St. Catherine of Alexandria at her monastery on Mount Sinai.

the territory he desired, which grew into the Papal States, Vatican City being the last remaining vestige of a great papal temporal state across the center of Italy. Thus the popes gave a spiritual sanction to the usurpation of the Merovingians by Pepin's Carolingians, legitimizing their rule. The Merovingians were pitched into a monastery, their long hair, a symbol of royalty, cut off. The papacy produced a forged document, the '"Donation of Constantine," that claimed Constantine, the first Christian Emperor, had given the pope the imperial crown. Although the pope returned the crown he asserted that the papacy had the power of governance. Pepin's alliance with the papacy was significant and would have repercussions on medieval kingship for generations.

Pepin realized the importance of religion as it dominated every activity of human life, personal and political. The popularity of pilgrimages existed alongside missionary activities in Europe, with mass conversions of peoples and the spreading of the Gospels by violence, fire, and sword. Ascetic hermits in isolation contrasted with the birth of monastic orders in the 10th Century. Along with a belief in miracles and millenarianism came superstitious fear of purgatory and the eternal fires of hell and damnation. Organized and centralized religion brought a sense of unity to western Christendom, enhanced by the usage of Latin in worship and legal processes. Linked with the religious climate was a growing cleavage between western Christendom and the Byzantine Empire. Latin Christianity and Orthodoxy grew further apart and broke with the Schism of 1054.

The Carolingian Empire reinforced the power of both Church and state with obligatory tithes, the banning of pagan ceremonies, the death penalty for the murder of priests, and a move toward centralizing political power. The link between the Pope and the western emperor was strengthened with the coronation of Charlemagne in 800. This event meant that there would be a Catholic Emperor in the west, independent of Byzantium, with an Orthodox Empire and emperor in the east. Now the pope would crown the western emperor. This lead to the Investiture Controversy—a dispute over who would control appointments of church officials—which might have been the single most important issue of the central Middle Ages, for both the contemporary and long-term effect it had upon Europe, especially with regard to the Italian and German lands.

Throughout Europe, the process of institutionalized Christianity continued. The first monastic order, centered on reform of the Benedictine Rule, was founded at Cluny in Burgundy in 910. A network of more than 300 monasteries was founded by the middle of the 12th Century. The more

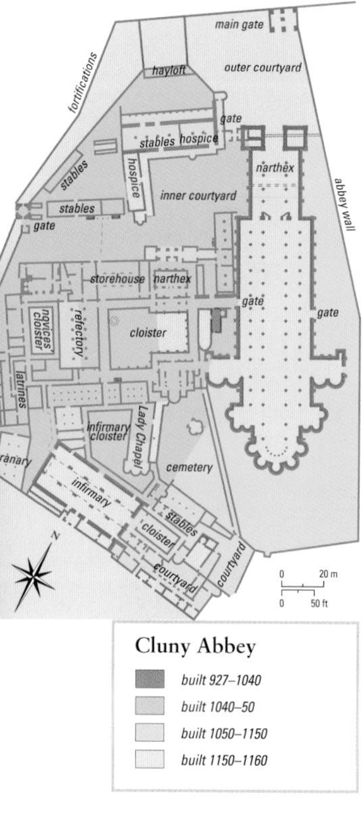

Cluny Abbey, founded by the Benedictines in AD 910. In the next 250 years over 300 monasteries would be founded, forming a Christian network across Europe.

austere Carthusian Order, based upon silence, contemplation, and closed cells, was founded in 1084 by St. Bruno at Chartreuse; in 1098 the Cistercian Order was established at Cîteaux in Burgundy.

The Saxon Kings, Henry II The Fowler (918–936), founder of the Saxon dynasty, and his son, Otto I The Great (936–973), were successors of the Carolingians. Under Otto the crown developed stronger links with the Church, which became a pillar of the monarchy. Monasteries were centers of imperial power throughout the German duchies. By conquering the Italian lands and acquiring the imperial title, Otto restored stability within Germany after the collapse of the Carolingians. He controlled the papacy. Popes had to swear allegiance to the emperor. His grandson, Otto II, became true successor to Charlemagne firming up the Holy Roman Empire, which lasted until 1804.

This detail of a mosaic shows Justinian I, 483–565, who was Byzantine Emperor from 527. He recovered North Africa from the Vandals, southeast Spain from the Visigoths and Italy from the Ostrogoths, largely owing to the skills of General Belisarius (c. 505–565), who led the imperial armies.

CHARLEMAGNE

CHARLEMAGNE, SON OF PEPIN WHO USURPED THE LAST MEROVINGIAN KING, BECAME SOLE KING OF THE FRANKS IN 771. HIS LONG REIGN WAS SPENT AT WAR, AMASSING LANDS IN WHAT BECAME A "CHRISTIAN EMPIRE."

A Frankish helmet dating from circa AD 600. This fine example has a mail neck guard and plate metal cheek protecters and was found in Germany.

Early in 772, Charlemagne commenced the Saxon wars, which lasted until 804. During these conquests the Saxons' sacred wood, the Irminsul, was destroyed and their nobility baptized en masse. The Christianization of the Saxons developed through the activities of bishoprics at Verdun, Bremen, Paderborn, and Hamburg. A Saxon March, or frontier, was established to keep the Danes in check, who were determined to capture German Baltic and north sea trading centers. Meanwhile, Charlemagne invaded the Kingdom of Lombardy, annexed it and assumed its crown (774), placing the papal states under Frankish protection. The Duchy of Spoleto, south of Rome, was acquired in 774. In 778, the Duchy of Bavaria was absorbed and the Bavarian policy continued of establishing tributary marches (borders protected in return for tribute or taxes) among the Slavic Serbs and Czechs.

The remaining power confronting the Franks in the east were the Avars—nomadic people from eastern Asia—but they were destroyed by a combined Franko-Bulgarian attack (796). Charlemagne acquired other Slav areas, including Bohemia, Moravia, Austria, and Croatia. His onslaught on the Umayyad Muslim caliphate in Spain achieved limited success, but a buffer Spanish March was established as a shield against a possible Muslim power revival. Charlemagne had built a mighty empire and in 800, Pope Leo III crowned him emperor, formalizing realities that all Christians in Europe, except the British Isles, owed allegiance to him. His position was recognized by Byzantine Emperor Michael I in the 812 Treaty of Aix-la-Chapelle (Aachen, in present day Germany) in exchange for Istria, Venice, and Dalmatia.

CHARLEMAGNE WARRIOR

This Carolingian warrior on patrol wears a chain mail hauberk that is slit at the sides. This suggests that he is accustomed to fighting on foot as well as on horseback. He wears a conical helmet, which is decorated. His lance has lugs beneath the blade, which indicate a thrust and parry style of fighting. Although his horse has a framed saddle and stirrups, the technique of charging with couched lance is still approximately 150 years or so in the future. He carries a round shield with a spiked boss in the center that could also be used as a weapon, and on his feet he wears leather shoes with a simple prick spur. His sword is of the early type with a rounded end to the blade, designed for cutting rather than for stabbing.

This reliquary bust of Charlemagne, the man who became the first Holy Roman Emperor, is from the cathedral treasury at Aachen.

Charlemagne placed his power and prestige in the service of Christianity. He encouraged monasteries and cathedrals to maintain schools, and invited to his court scholars and writers from Ireland, England, Spain, and Italy. Alcuin of York, later Abbot of St. Martin's of Tours, standardized writing, improving teaching and helping to revive Latin. These processes were useful in copying of manuscripts of classical works. The Church benefited from a better-educated clergy and scholarship and authors flourished; the historian Einhard wrote *Vita Karoli Magni,* a biography of Charlemagne. The emperor utilized bishops and abbots as agents of government and established a royal capital at Aix-la-Chapelle, where his Palatine Chapel was consecrated. He attempted to introduce vassalage (holding of land by feudal tenure on condition of homage and allegiance) as a system of government and marches comprised several counties as a means of controlling the tributary tribes inhabiting them. A major flaw in the empire was its personalized nature. Charlemagne's decision to divide his territories among his three sons was frustrated by only one surviving him. Third son Louis the Pious continued the scheme until the empire, renamed the Carolingian Empire, was fragmented into three kingdoms by the Treaty of Verdun (843), under the rule of his sons. Descendants of Carolingian magistrates and nobles identified with their localities, stressing a move toward feudalism. The empire was weakened by a minimalist administration and was damaged by Viking raids, which had begun during Charlemagne's lifetime.

Far right: EUROPE AT THE TIME OF CHARLEMAGNE
Between 722 and 812 Charlemagne built an empire stretching from Brittany in the west to Moravia and Dalmatia in the east, and from the shores of the Baltic in the north to the Mediterranean in the south.

Part of an account of Charlemagne's war against the Saxons, written by his biographer, Einhard. This account illustrates the manner of Charlemagne's military campaigns and reveals his concept of justice.

THE SAXON WARS

The Frankish loss was greater than mere numbers, for two of the ambassadors, Adalgis and Geilo, were killed, also four counts, and twenty other noble and distinguished men, together with those who followed them, because they would rather die with them than live without them.

When the King heard of this disaster he decided not to delay, but made haste to gather an army, and marched into Saxony. There he called to his presence the chiefs of the Saxons, and inquired who had induced the people to rebel. They all declared that Widukind was the author of the treason, but said that they could not produce him because after the deed was done he had fled to the Northmen.

But the others who had carried out his will and committed the crime they delivered up to the King to the number of four thousand and five hundred; and by the King's command they were all beheaded in one day upon the river Aller in the place called Verdun. When he had wreaked vengeance after this fashion, the King withdrew to the town of Diedenhofen for winter quarters, and there he celebrated the Nativity of our Lord and Easter as he was wont to do.

Europe
The Empire of Charlemagne
Arctic Circle
Norwegian Sea
FINNIO UGRIANS
SCANDINAVIANS
Kaupang
Birka
KINGDOM OF PICTS
SCOTTISH KINGDOMS
STRATHCLYDE
North Sea
Baltic Sea
BALTIC PEOPLES
DENMARK
Ripen
Hedeby
Lindisfarne
NORTHUMBRIA
York
IRISH KINGDOMS
Dnieper
Hamburg
Friesland
Saxony
Vistula
WELSH STATES
MERCIA
London
WEST WALES
WESSEX
SLAVS
Rhine
Aachen
Hessen
Mainz
Frankfurt
Bohemia
Dniester
France
Paris
Metz
Nordgau
Moravia
Britanny
Strasbourg
Bavaria
ATLANTIC OCEAN
FRANKISH EMPIRE
Alamannia
Carinthia
Pannonia
Danube
Geneva
Aquitaine
Lyon
Lombardy
BULGARIA
Bordeaux
Milan
Venice
Dalmatia
Turin
Burgundy
Genoa
Ravenna
Varna
Oviedo
Toulouse
Septimani
Florence
Nish
ASTURIAS
Marseille
Spanish March
Papal States
Adriatic Sea
Ragusa
Constantinople
Oporto
PRINCIPALITY OF BENEVENT
Corsica
Rome
VLACHS
Barcelona
Salonica
EMIRATE OF CORDOVA
Naples
Aegean Sea
Ushbunah
Balearic Is.
Otranto
BYZANTINE EMPIRE
Sardinia
Calabria
Smyrna
Athens
Qurtubah (Córdova)
Cartagena
Panormus
Sicily
Catania
Mediterranean Sea
Crete
ABBASIDS (AGHLABIDS)
IDRISIDS
RUSTAMIDS

Hostile Invasions

THE DISINTEGRATION OF THE CAROLINGIAN EMPIRE INTO FEUDAL UNITS WAS A RESPONSE TO AN ONSLAUGHT BY MAGYAR, VIKING, AND ARAB RAIDERS WHO TORE DOWN BORDERS AND RAIDED INTO THE HEARTLAND OF EUROPE.

This illustration goes some way to showing what a Magyar horseman might have looked like. They were mounted on small but strong horses from the steppe and were armed, chiefly, with bows and lances.

The relative peace and stability established during Carolingian rule ensured that most of western and east-central Europe was protected from outside raids. Christianity spread under pressure of missionaries from Ireland, and enforced conversion at sword point in places like Saxony facilitated the growth of churches and religious communities. The wealth of these institutions, together with that of merchant settlements, proved an attractive target for three marauding groups: Magyars, Muslims from North Africa and the eastern Mediterranean, and Vikings.

The Magyars were a Finno-Ugric people whose early history resided on the upper reaches of the Volga and Kama rivers. Based around the Lower Don Valley in the 9th Century, this federation of seven Magyar tribes were joined by three Khazar hordes (Kavars). Together, this group was known as On-Ogur (Ten Arrows). The year 900 witnessed attacks by Pechenegs, another seminomadic Turkic people from the steppe region, who drove the On-Ogur to the limits of the western steppes. In 892, Arnulf, the German Emperor, invited the Magyar tribes to help reassert authority over the Moravian Duke Sviatopulk, set upon expanding his territories to include Bohemia and parts of contemporary southern Poland. The On-Ogur federation crossed the Carpathian Mountains, destroying the Moravian Empire by 906, defeating a German defensive force, and occupying the Pannonian plain.

MAGYARS

Like their Hun and Avar predecessors, the Magyars raided and looted far and wide. In 899, they had assaulted villages along the Italian Po river and reached as far south as Otranto, on the east coast of the present day "heel" of Italy. In the year 900 the Magyars pillaged Bavaria, Germany receiving their attention, especially around Frankfurt, Cologne, and as far north as Bremen. After the year 917, northern France was regularly attacked and in 924 they made incursions into the area of Nîmes. Other forces pushed into Bulgaria, reaching into the Byzantine Empire, terrorizing but failing to capture, Constantinople. The Magyars were mainly horse archers, but also used javelins and lassoes. Like the earlier Huns, the nomadic Magyars comprised small loose groups rather than large formal armies. They were skilled in ambushes, sometimes feigning retreat before counterattacking. Their tactics were to confuse an enemy unit, weaken it with accurately fired arrows, then attack with a final destructive charge. These tactics were used brilliantly at the Battle of Brenta in 899. Some 5,000 Magyars had faced days of being chased by about 15,000 Lombard cavalry. The Magyars traversed a river, made camp, attempted to negotiate, then suddenly mounted fresh horses, launched an attack across the river at the resting Lombards, routing them and butchering most in pitiless pursuit.

Henry I of Germany built fortifications against the Magyars and his son, Otto I, gave frontier guards the duty of protecting the Holy Roman Empire from raids. Unlike Charlemagne, who had attacked the Avars with overwhelming force in Pannonia, little else was achieved. A Magyar attack in

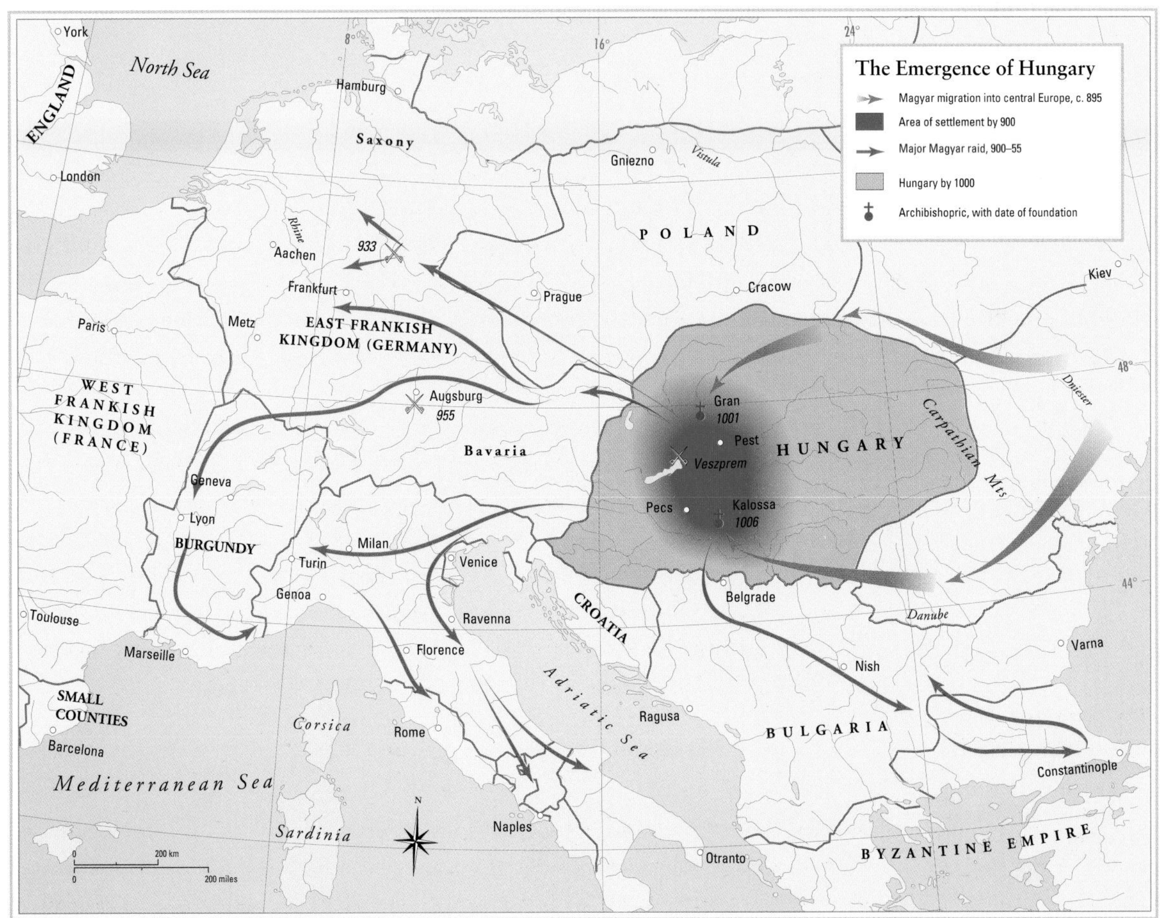

924 resulted in the capture of a Magyar prince enabling Otto to arrange a truce that lasted nine years. Later, Henry I defeated the raiders at Riade in Thuringia (in the year 933), while Otto I crushed them at the Battle of Lechfeld (Augsburg) in 955; Magyar marauders were caught returning home booty-laden, where a blocking force of 9,000 German cavalry forced the Magyars into a fruitless frontal attack. Furthermore, Otto's victory had seen a united German force of Saxons, Bavarians, Swabians, and Franconians cause great slaughter in the name of the Holy Roman Empire.

The year 995 seemed to mark the end of the period of Magyar raids, which had lasted less than a century. Domestic developments on the Pannonian plain reduced Magyar aggression, a medieval Hungarian state was beginning to develop. Succeeding his father, Taksony, as hereditary chieftain of the hordes in the year 972, Duke Géza sent an embassy to Otto II at Quedlinnburg in Germany, and in 975 he and his family were received into the western Christian Church. Conversions in Hungary followed under Bishop Pilgrin of Passau (971–991) and St. Adelbert of Prague. Géza's successor, St. Stephen (977–1038) crushed any eastern Christianization from Constantinople and any remaining paganism. He looked to the west, and later married a Bavarian princess. He called in Roman churchmen and Benedictine monks, and eventually broke the power of tribal chieftains. He was crowned Apostolic King in 1001 with a crown gifted to him by Pope Sylvester II, and was canonized in 1083. Meanwhile, Hungary received its own Metropolitan by Papal consent, thereby ending the rival religious claims of Passau and the Greek Church to the kingdom.

VIKINGS

Bands of Scandinavian Viking warriors, using ships of technically advanced design, began raiding western Europe in the final years of the 8th Century. Some Vikings were colonists, moving from Scandinavia into the Atlantic, reaching the northern islands of Britain early in the 8th Century and the Faroes one hundred years later. The mid-9th Century witnessed Norwegians organizing a lordship in Orkney (c. 800) before pushing on to Iceland (860), Greenland (settled in 986), and L'Anse aux Meadows in Newfoundland, the first Europeans to reach North America (c. 1000–1020). Others sailed south through the Hebrides to the Isle of Man (c. 850) and Ireland, settlements being established at Dublin (847), Wexford, Waterford, Cork, and Limerick. From Ireland, the Vikings reached Lisbon and Seville (844) in the Iberian Peninsula. Division within the Norse communities in Ireland plus effective Irish opposition led to the Viking expulsion from Dublin in 902. King Brian Boru won a great victory over the Vikings at the Battle of Clontarf (1014), subsequently Viking enclaves were assimilated into the native Irish political power structures. Several factors occasioned the Viking expansion. Population increases generated landless sons seeking their fortunes elsewhere. When kings

Viking expansion was made possible by their skill in shipbuilding. The shipbuilders' significance in Scandinavian society is demonstrated by their continuing appearance in poetry, art, and religious burial practices. Ships like this replica of the *Helge Ask*, a small Danish warship dating from around AD 1000, sailed the rivers of Russia, the Baltic, the Atlantic, the Irish Sea, the North sea and the Mediterranean.

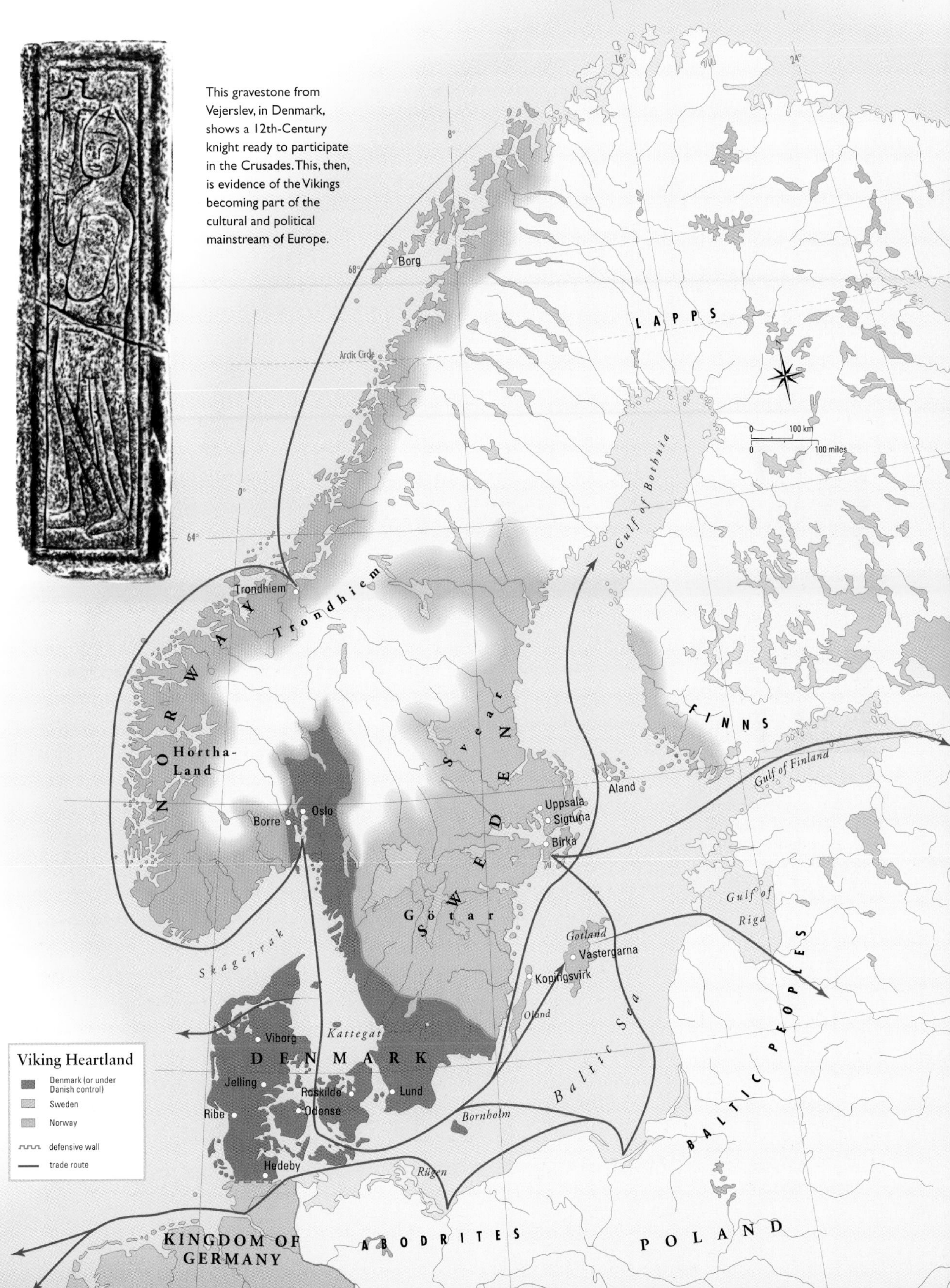

This gravestone from Vejerslev, in Denmark, shows a 12th-Century knight ready to participate in the Crusades. This, then, is evidence of the Vikings becoming part of the cultural and political mainstream of Europe.

began to exert their authority in Scandinavia, the resentful were driven out or left. The Viking dragonship, such as the Oseberg ship, might carry a crew of 40 to 100 warriors. Viking seamen attacked the coasts of northern Europe, shaking the very foundations of the Christian states attached. They penetrated rivers, using these routes to loot towns and monasteries, seize many captives who were sold as slaves in the markets of al-Andalus (the Muslim-governed parts of the Iberian Peninsula), the Russian states, the Mediterranean, the Middle East, and Central Asia. Irish captives reached Iceland, some ending up in Greenland. Most slaves seized by the Vikings were used by the Vikings themselves when settling in an area they had pillaged and then finally claimed as their own.

Especially favored targets were monasteries, defenseless and rich in gold, silver, and jewel-adorned books. The lust for silver was boundless, required for gifts, bride wealth, blood money, and general economic need. The requirement for a valued medium of exchange was a probable motor for political and social competition. When large Viking armies arrived in England, they were greatly interested in exacting tribute, the "Danegeld." Between 991 and 1014, the Vikings received more than 150,000 pounds weight of official silver, some 36 million coins. The Swedish Vikings moved from Finland at Old Ladoga down the Dnieper, Don, and Volga rivers to trade with Constantinople and Baghdad. More than 85,000 Arab coins have been found in Sweden, and contact with German and Slav areas, using the Oder and Vistula rivers was evident. In excess of 70,000 German coins have been uncovered in Sweden.

Thousands of Arab dirhems were found in a hoard on the Swedish island of Gotland. During the Viking age a huge amount of wealth poured into Scandinavia from the Atlantic coasts, the Mediterranean, Eastern Europe, and the Near East.

The Swedish Vikings or Varangians penetrated the Russian river systems and challenged Khazar control of the Constantinople-Black Sea trade. They established outposts at Polotsk, Smolensk, Kiev, Rostov, Murom, and south to the Crimea. The Byzantine emperors recruited a personal bodyguard unit called the Varangian Guard. A Swedish dynasty established itself at Novgorod, one of its princes capturing Kiev, which became the center of the well-organized, powerful state of Kievan Rus. By the middle of the 10th Century Kiev, under Prince Sviatoslav, had its Varangian population demographically swamped by the Slavs. Vladimir I, Prince of Kiev (980–1015), chose Eastern Orthodox Christianity for his state, submitting himself to the spiritual authority of the patriarch in Constantinople and opening his state to Byzantine influence, led by Basil II. Vladimir also agreed to marry Basil's daughter, thereby cementing cultural ties.

Eventually, raids by Viking bands turned into invasions of large armies. This resulted from the establishment of politically centralized Scandinavian states, especially in Denmark. The Danes savaged the Anglo-Saxon kingdoms in England, such as Mercia, until, in the 870s, only Wessex remained free of Danish control. In 878, King Alfred of Wessex beat the Danish Vikings at the Battle of Edington; this was also marked by Danish King Guthrum's acceptance of Christianity and the generation of a border from Chester to London, the northern part of England becoming the Danelaw. Subsequently, Alfred's descendants fought back to exterminate Danish control. By 924, Edward the Elder, Alfred's son (899–924), conquered the five Danish boroughs of Lincoln, Derby, Nottingham, Stamford and Leicester. His successors, Athelstan, Edmund and Eadred, exerted their authority over the north despite opponents such as Erik Bloodaxe. By the end of his reign, Eadred ruled a united England from Wessex. Only Scotland and Wales were independent under a blurred kind of vassalage. The Earldom of Orkney remained a Viking possession while the Vikings' places of origin were converted into the kingdoms of Norway, Sweden, and Denmark.

As the Danelaw became established, the English shire system merged into it using the Danish boroughs as a nucleus, often using men of Danish origin as administrators. The Thegns, aristocratic leaders, emerged as a professional warrior class and a system of semifeudalism developed whereby each man had a lord who was responsible for him by law. Great earldoms began to emerge, such as Wessex, Northumbria, East Anglia, and Mercia.

From the 830s to 910, the Vikings attacked Francia, the western part of the Carolingian Empire, (roughly present day France, Belgium, Netherlands, and Alsace-Lorraine). Raids reached the mouth of the Loire. From 840 the Vikings assaulted Nourmoutier, Antwerp, and Utrecht, and in 841 Rouen was sacked while in 843 the Loire was penetrated, Nantes torched and the Garonne Valley looted. Between 845 and 857, Bordeaux, Blois, Orleans, and Poitiers were damaged. Two years later, the Vikings sailed from the Loire down the Iberian coasts. Passing into the Mediterranean, North Africa was raided as were the Balearics and Barcelona. The Vikings wintered at the mouth of the Rhône near Marseille. The following year, southern France was raided as far north as today's Valence, while Pisa and Luna in Italy were attacked. Paris received special treatment from the Vikings, from bases like the island of Oiselle in the Seine near Rouen. In 845, the Vikings demanded 7,000 pounds weight of silver as ransom money. Paris was sacked in 857 and attacked yet again in 861 and 865 while Rouen was sacked in 885 as a precursor to the siege of Paris. The event was witnessed by a young monk, Abbo, from the abbey at St. Germain-des-Prés, and the story told in verse. Seven hundred ships, led by Siegfried, reached fortifications in the Seine on 24 November. Paris comprised a city on two islands, the Île-de-la-Cité and the Île-St-Louis. The biggest island was linked to the river banks by two fortified bridges and the Vikings could only advance by taking the bridges. The one leading from the Île-de-la-Cité to the right bank was defended by a tower that the Vikings attacked but could not capture or destroy. The Vikings used ballistae siege engines and also pickaxes to break down the walls but were defeated by normal weapons and by having hot liquid wax and pitch poured upon them. The defenders also used spear catapults to good effect. The Vikings used stone throwing engines, an interlocking shield testudo to fill the ditch, and siege towers on earthen ramps. The defenders used sorties to capture two towers and repulsed a breach in the wall with Count Odo, future King of West Francia, in the thick of the fighting. The Holy Roman Emperor, Charles the Fat, raised the siege by defeating the Vikings and with the payment of tribute. The Vikings were allowed upstream to plunder Burgundy, an enemy of Charles, but Odo forced the Vikings to carry their boats around Paris overland. They lost because they did not have enough men to surround the city, the bridge tower was too high to be overcome, and the defenders were determined opponents, despite suffering from plague.

Viking Invasion of the British Isles and France
c. 910

In west Francia, a Norse chieftain, Rolf (also known as Robert, Rollo or Hrolf the Ganger), had established a base settlement at the mouth of the River Seine. King Charles III the Simple of West Francia (c. 898–922) decided to turn Rolf's domain into a buffer zone against further Viking encroachment (911). The relationship was cemented by Rolf marrying Charles' daughter and converting to Christianity. The Treaty of St. Clair-sur-Epte gave Rolf lands around Rouen and Evreux. The territory was rich in pastures and forests, a prize that was territorially extended by Rolf's successors in an aggressive fashion. Fresh colonists were recruited from Scandinavia for nearly a century, generating a strong local identity. Yet, by 1000, this Duchy of Normandy used Norman

French and had rebuilt a Carolingian administration while working closely with the Church. Rolf gained middle Normandy (the Bessin, 924) and his son, William Longsword (927–942) won the Contentin and Avranches (933), including Bayeux and Mont St. Michel. Robert II used his warriors and the power of the church to control Normandy in both political and religious senses. As his power grew he became increasingly interested in foreign affairs, particularly under Longsword's grandson, William the Bastard, who would become King of England.

ARABS

BIRTH OF ISLAM

Islam is an Arabic noun from the verb *aslama*, to surrender oneself. In its primary sense the active participle "muslim" means someone who surrenders himself or herself to God as revealed through the teachings of the Prophet Muhammad (c. 570–632). Muhammad is believed by Muslims to have communicated God's revelation in the Koran, a text Muslims regard as the final revelation of God to humankind. Collected under the third of Muhammad's successors, the Caliph Uthman (reigned 644–656), the Koran is composed of 114 *suras*, or chapters. These are said to have been revealed in Muhammad's native city of Mecca, where he was a respected merchant, and suras also date from the period of his sojourn in Medina (622–632).

In Mecca—Islam's holiest site—the Koran's condemnation of the sins of pride, avarice, and the neglect of social duties, its warnings of divine judgement, and its attacks on pagan deities, brought Muhammad and his followers into conflict with the leaders of his own tribe, the Quraish. His fellow clansmen were boycotted, with Muslim converts subjected to persecution, and a number took refuge in Axum (Ethiopia). However, Muhammad's fame as a prophet and trusted man of God spread beyond Mecca. He was invited to act as judge and arbitrator between the feuding tribal factions of Yathrib, later renamed Madinat al-Nabi ("the city of the Prophet"), usually shortened to Medina, an oasis settlement about 250 miles northeast of Mecca. The *hijra* (migration) of the Muslims in 622 marks the beginning of the Muslim era. The passages in the Koran dating from the Medina period, when Muhammad was the effective ruler, contain some of the legislative material that would form the basis of what became Islamic law. After a series of campaigns against the Meccans, the Muslims emerged victorious. In the last year of his life Muhammad returned in triumph to Mecca, receiving the submission of the tribes along the way. He reformed the ancient ceremonies of the *hajj* (pilgrimage), discarding their animist aspects and reorienting them to what he believed to be the original monotheism (doctrine or belief that there is only one God) of Abraham. After further expeditions he returned to Medina. He died there after a short illness in 632.

Muhammad's death left the Muslim community without an obvious leader. One of his oldest companions, Abu Bakr (632–634), was acknowledged by several leaders as the first caliph, or successor. Under Abu Bakr and his successor Umar (634–644), the tribes, which had begun to fall away on the death of Muhammad, were reunited under the banner of Islam and converted into a formidable military and ideological force. The Arabs broke out of the peninsula, conquering half the Byzantine provinces as well as defeating the armies of Sasanian Persia. Ctesiphon, the Persian capital, fell in 637, followed by Jerusalem in 638. By 646, under Umar's successor Uthman (644–656), the whole of Egypt had come under Muslim Arab control. Acquiring ships from Egypt and Syria, the Arabs conducted seaborne raids, conquering Cyprus in 649 and pillaging Rhodes in 654. Religious differences between the Byzantine rulers and their subjects in Egypt and Syria ensured that the Muslims were met with indifference, or even welcomed by fellow monotheists embittered by decades of alien Byzantine rule. But secular factors were also important. The Arabs were motivated by desire for plunder, as well as religious faith. In previous eras nomadic predators would have taken the plunder or held onto land, dispersing as landlords or peasants among the conquered peoples. In a farsighted decision Caliph Umar encouraged the tribes to settle with a system of stipends paid from the common treasury, which used these tribes to control the conquered lands. The Arabs were kept apart from the population in armed camps that evolved into garrison cities such as Basra and Kufa in Iraq. Although the tensions over the distribution of booty would erupt into open civil war the overall control exercised by the fledgling Islamic government remained under dynastic rule. Though individual dynasties would often be challenged as ruling contrary to Islamic principles of equality and justice, the dynastic system of governance fitted the prevailing form of social organization, the patriarchal kinship group, and remained the norm until modern times. Under the Umayyads the remarkable expansion of Islam continued, with the Arab raiders reaching as far as central France and the Indus Valley. In southern Carolingia (the part of France with a mediterranean littoral) people prayed to God for protection against Muslim raiders: "Eternal Trinity, deliver thy Christian people from the oppression of the pagans." Christians referred to the Muslims as something "other," Saracens (heathen nomads) or infidels (people without faith), and endured their raids until almost the year 1000. This new Muslim project was different from that belonging to the settlers establishing al-Andalus. There, the Muslim state was a recognized, stable entity that traded and occasionally fought but was held in balance by Leon and Charlemagne's Spanish March. Now, a semi-independent Aghlabid emirate, notionally owing loyalty to the Abbasids who controlled large areas of Ifriqiyah, Tunisia, and eastern Algeria, went raiding, seen by Christians as a continuation of Islamic conquest. Crete had fallen in 824 while attacks were launched at Byzantine Sicily, an Arab base being established at Palermo. The Byzantine capital Siracusa, on the eastern coast of Sicily, held on until 878. Crete was kept from 827–861 while the control of Cyprus was shared. The Arabs plundered Thessalonica, Greece, in 904.

An Islamic banner captured at the Battle of Las Navas de Tolosa and bears the Arabic inscription "I take refuge in God... In the name of God, the Merciful, the Compassionate, God bless him and give him peace."

In 840, Bari in Italy was taken, becoming the capital of an extra Aghlabid emirate that terrorized southern Italy and the Adriatic. Bari was retaken by the Byzantines in 876, reducing Muslim pressure in the central Mediterranean. Elsewhere, Muslim shipping assaulted Christian shipping, looted coastal cities, and penetrated river valleys to raid inland communities. Bases were built on the southern coast of West Francia, then attacks launched up the Rhône to Upper and Lower Burgundy and the Kingdom of Italy. The Aghlabids moved into the Balearics, assaulting Sardinia and Corsica, and establishing colonies. They robbed, ransomed or raided monasteries and towns, including Rome, desecrating churches and stealing treasures. The Aghlabid fleet reigned supreme in the central Mediterranean. Expansion was prevented by the Byzantine Empire reviving its fleet and reducing the Muslim bases and by the Muslim states in Spain and North Africa disintegrating into internal war.

Western and central European monarchs underestimated Arab military strength and strategy whereas Byzantine forces came to know and respect them. The Arabs were great horsemen but they also used infantry. Arab light cavalry would torment their opponents and press home a charge with heavy horse if the opportunity arose. When the enemy appeared too strong, the cavalry would retire to their infantry support base. The infantry were drawn up into dense blocks with aisles for the cavalry to retreat through. These blocks constituted ranks of kneeling spearmen with their spear butts dug into the ground. Behind were archers and javelin men loosing their missiles overhead. The heavier javelins could damage armored cavalry. The infantry were disciplined to receive an attack and remain

Far right: EXPANSION TO AD 750
After AD 634 the Arabs broke out of the peninsula, conquering the eastern provinces of the Byzantine Empire and defeating the armies of Sassanian Persia. The whole of Egypt came under Muslim control. Acquiring ships from Egypt, the Arabs launched seaborne raids conquering Cyprus in 649 and attacking Rhodes in 654. Conquest followed along the north African coast and crossed into Europe via Spain in the 700s.

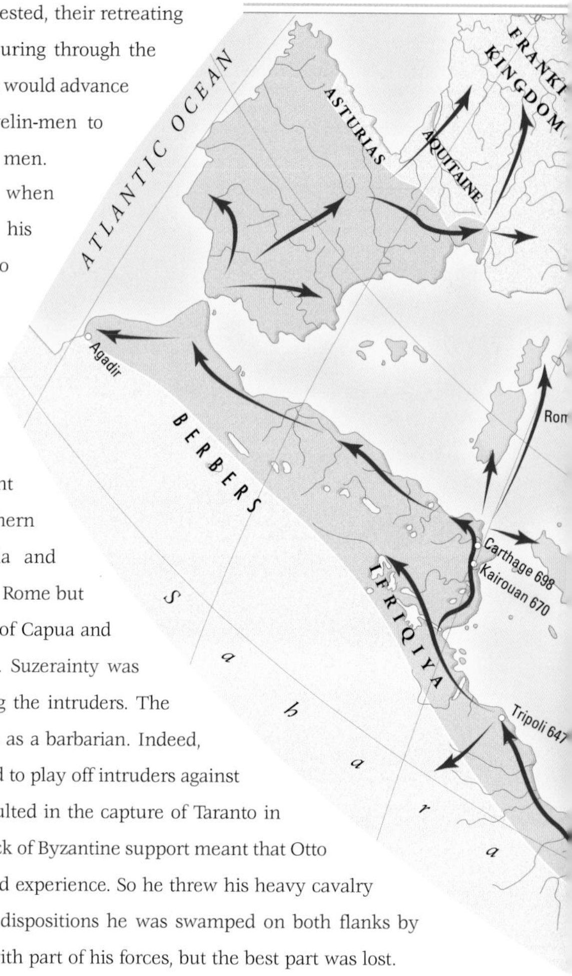

immovable. Once enemy cavalry were bested, their retreating forces would be hit by Arab cavalry pouring through the infantry aisles. Sometimes Arab bowmen would advance in skirmish order accompanied by javelin-men to protect the infantry from enemy missile men.

One Christian defeat occurred when Emperor Otto III decided to display his authority in Italy. His ambition was to succeed where his father had failed and unite the whole of Italy under his government. Byzantine Emperor John Tzimisces' death in 976 led to civil war and disorder, and Greek weakness gave Otto III the encouragement he needed to attack the Muslims in southern Italy to prevent Arab raids in Apulia and Calabria. The Emperor's forces moved to Rome but found their ally, Pandulf Ironhead, ruler of Capua and Benevento, dead and his lands usurped. Suzerainty was recovered only at the cost of recognizing the intruders. The Greeks failed to join Otto, regarding him as a barbarian. Indeed, the Greeks distrusted everyone but hoped to play off intruders against each other. Force against the Greeks resulted in the capture of Taranto in 982. Then the Muslims arrived and the lack of Byzantine support meant that Otto could not draw on their military skills and experience. So he threw his heavy cavalry at the Arabs. Failing to find the enemy dispositions he was swamped on both flanks by devastating attacks. Otto escaped north with part of his forces, but the best part was lost.

The Aghlabid emirs developed a brilliant civilization at their capital, Kairouan. An impressive court was based on oppressive taxes, while public works conserving and distributing water contributed to a prosperous, peaceful region. Notable amongst the emirs were: Ibrahim ibn al-Aghlabid (800–812) who received an embassy from Charlemagne; Ziyadat Allah I (817–838) who launched the attacks on Sicily; and Abu Ibrahim Ahmad (856–863), who commissioned many public works. The Arab conquests separated Sicily from Constantinople and from the Italian mainland. Arab Sicily became increasingly independent from Africa but passed from the Aghlabids to the Fatamids in 909. Sicily witnessed Arab immigration and conversions of Christians, making Sicily politically and culturally part of the Arab world, despite the Christian communities scattered across the island.

Southern Europe now defended itself with fortifications built by local warlords who established a feudal independence. Likewise, the Viking raids promoted the devolution of power to local élites who responded to Frankish and Byzantine weakness by sponsoring self-interested feudalism.

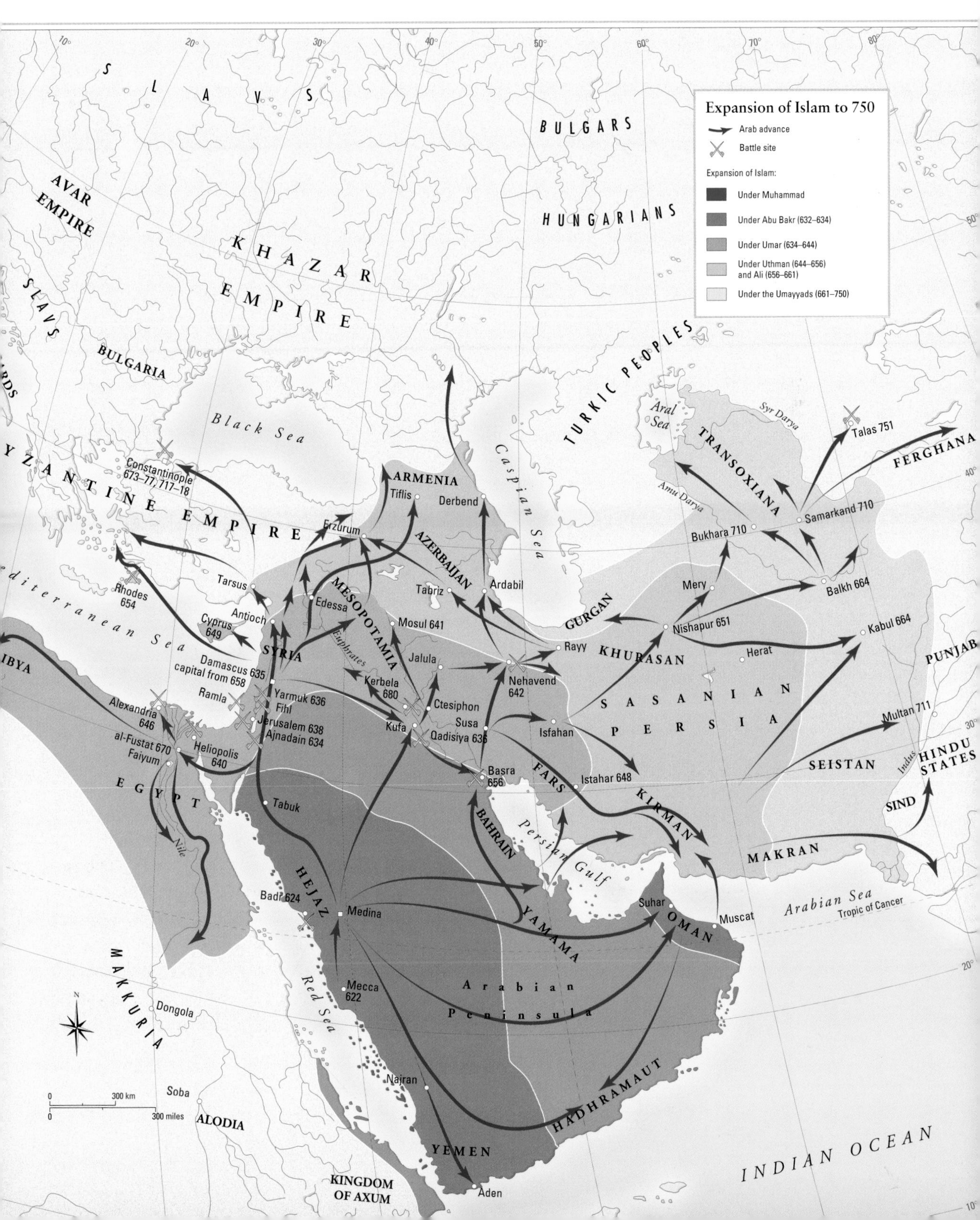
Expansion of Islam to 750
Arab advance
Battle site
Expansion of Islam:
Under Muhammad
Under Abu Bakr (632–634)
Under Umar (634–644)
Under Uthman (644–656) and Ali (656–661)
Under the Umayyads (661–750)
SLAVS
BULGARS
HUNGARIANS
AVAR EMPIRE
KHAZAR EMPIRE
BULGARIA
TURKIC PEOPLES
Black Sea
Caspian Sea
Aral Sea
Syr Darya
Amu Darya
Talas 751
FERGHANA
TRANSOXIANA
Constantinople 673–77, 717–18
BYZANTINE EMPIRE
ARMENIA
Tiflis
Derbend
Erzurum
AZERBAIJAN
Samarkand 710
Bukhara 710
Merv
Balkh 664
Tabriz
Ardabil
Tarsus
Rhodes 654
Edessa
MESOPOTAMIA
GURGAN
Nishapur 651
Kabul 664
Antioch
Cyprus 649
Mosul 641
Euphrates
Rayy
KHURASAN
Herat
PUNJAB
Mediterranean Sea
SYRIA
Damascus 635 capital from 658
Jalula
Nehavend 642
SASANIAN PERSIA
Kerbela 680
Ramla
Yarmuk 636
Fihl
Ctesiphon
Alexandria 646
Jerusalem 638
Ajnadain 634
Kufa
Qadisiya 636
Susa
Isfahan
Multan 711
al-Fustat 670
Faiyum
Heliopolis 640
Basra 656
FARS
Istahar 648
SEISTAN
Indus
HINDU STATES
EGYPT
Tabuk
KIRMAN
SIND
Nile
BAHRAIN
Persian Gulf
MAKRAN
HEJAZ
Badr 624
Medina
YAMAMA
Suhar
OMAN
Muscat
Arabian Sea
Tropic of Cancer
MAKKURIA
Red Sea
Mecca 622
Arabian Peninsula
Dongola
N
HADHRAMAUT
Najran
Soba
ALODIA
0 300 km
0 300 miles
YEMEN
KINGDOM OF AXUM
Aden
INDIAN OCEAN

Song of Roland

THE EARLIEST "CHANSON DE GESTE" TO SURVIVE IS THE MAGNIFICENT "CHANSON DE ROLAND" COMPOSED IN ABOUT 1100. THIS EPIC POEM RECOUNTS THE DESTRUCTION OF CHARLEMAGNE'S REARGUARD BY A BASQUE AMBUSH IN 778, WHICH WAS RECORDED BY HIS BIOGRAPHER, EINHARD, IN ABOUT 830.

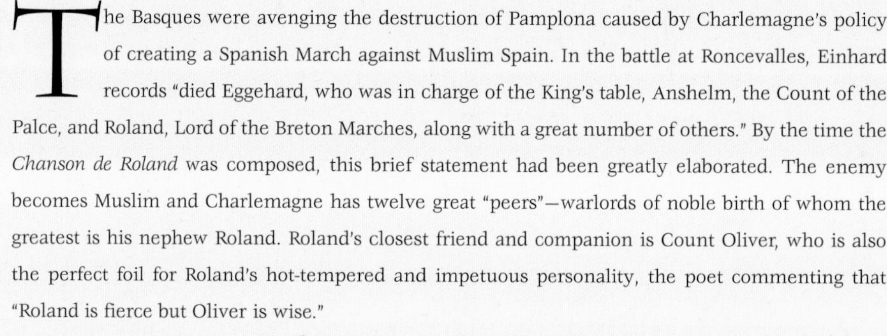

The Basques were avenging the destruction of Pamplona caused by Charlemagne's policy of creating a Spanish March against Muslim Spain. In the battle at Roncevalles, Einhard records "died Eggehard, who was in charge of the King's table, Anshelm, the Count of the Palce, and Roland, Lord of the Breton Marches, along with a great number of others." By the time the *Chanson de Roland* was composed, this brief statement had been greatly elaborated. The enemy becomes Muslim and Charlemagne has twelve great "peers"—warlords of noble birth of whom the greatest is his nephew Roland. Roland's closest friend and companion is Count Oliver, who is also the perfect foil for Roland's hot-tempered and impetuous personality, the poet commenting that "Roland is fierce but Oliver is wise."

Troubadours were lyric poets of southern France, Spain, and northern Italy singing in the southern Provençal language. They included lords and wandering minstrels.In this medieval drawing a troubadour sings a song of great deeds, known as a *chanson de geste*. The *Chanson de Roland* is an notable example of the genre.

Roland also has an enemy: his stepfather, Ganelon. Ganelon's enmity is aroused early in the poem, when Roland nominates him for a dangerous mission; he must be Charlemagne's messenger to the pagan King Marsile, who has just sued for peace. The last two ambassadors sent by Charlemagne were killed, and Ganelon sees his order as nothing less than an attempt on his life by Roland. He consequently devises a plan for revenge; he betrays his own king and country by plotting with Marsile to ambush the Carolingian rearguard as it crosses the Pyrenees on its return to France. Reunited with Charlemagne, Ganelon nominates Roland to lead the rearguard, which will protect the retreating army and its baggage through the narrow mountain passes. Everyone knows this is a position fraught with danger, but Roland reacts with characteristic pride; he swears that Charlemagne will not lose so much as a pack-mule, cannot be dissuaded from taking command, and refuses to accept reinforcements: the usual 20,000 soldiers will do.

This poem, like many epics, is tragic in the classical sense. Roland is a great hero, but his personality has a fatal flaw; his immense pride in his noble blood and in his personal reputation for bravery and prowess. When Oliver sees the pagan forces coming in arms against them, he points out that the French are outnumbered five to one, and begs Roland to summon help from Charlemagne by blowing his ivory horn, named Oliphant. But Roland refuses (see excerpt top right).

Battle is joined and described in bloodthirsty detail, with many cleavings down the middle with swords and thrustings through the body with lances. Roland, Oliver and the other Peers perform wonders of fighting, and the 100,000-strong Saracen host is cut down in thousands: "Of hundred thousand scarce two will fight again", the poet comments. But then King Marsile draws up with 20 more huge battalions. Battle is rejoined, but the French know that they are doomed. One by one the Twelve Peers fall; for each death Roland and Oliver exact a terrible revenge. The pagan Prince Grandoyne strikes down four of the Peers, then meets Roland (see excerpt below right).

The time has run out for the French. Four assaults have been withstood but the last 60 knights soon fall with Roland dying last, turning his face toward the enemy. Roland thus personifies knightly qualities: his prowess as a heroic warrior, his loyalty to Charlemagne, and his love for his companions. However, he has overweening pride and boastfulness, and gets an entire rearguard slaughtered. Even so, the song holds him up as someone to be emulated.

Female troubadours, attractive and musically gifted, were well-known and expressed a certain sexual immediacy in the presentation of their songs.

"Now God forbid," Roland makes answer wroth,
"That living man should say he saw me go
Blowing of horns for Paynim foe!
Ne'er shall my kindred be put to such reproach.
When I shall stand in this great clash of hosts
I'll strike a thousand and sev'n hundred strokes,
Blood-red the steel of Durendal shall flow.
Stout are the French, they will do battle bold.
Those men of Spain shall die and have no hope."

"The Prince Grandoyne was a good knight
and gallant,
Strong of his hands and valorous in battle;
Athwart him now comes Roland the great captain;
He'd never met him, but knew him instanter
By his proud aspect, and by his noble stature,
His haughty looks, and his bearing and manner.
He cannot help it, a mortal fear unmans him;
Fain would he fly, but what's the good? He cannot.
The Count assails him with such ferocious valour
That to the nasal the whole helmet is shattered,
Cloven the nose, and the teeth and the palate,
The jaz'rain hauberk and the breastbone
and backbone,
Both silver bows from off the golden saddle;
Horseman and horse clean asunder he slashes,
Lifeless he leaves them and the pieces
past patching.
The men of Spain fall a-wailing for sadness:
The French all cry: "What strokes! And what
a champion!"

These two passages express the epic nature of *Song of Roland* and the battle that took place at Roncevalles. This was part of Emperor Charlemagne's campaign to establish a March, or border territory, that would act as a buffer on the Empire's southern border.

Culture and the Church in Medieval Europe

The early Church's attitude to warfare was explicit: killing people, even in battle, was a sin and no Christian could be excused its consequences. In the first three centuries after Christ, this could mean a severe public penance lasting for several years.

In the 5th Century St. Augustine evolved the concept of the "just" war and thereafter, particularly in strife-torn medieval Europe, the Church recognized that there were circumstances in which homicide was not only excusable but every Christian's duty. Charlemagne and his successors exacted feudal levies from bishops and abbots, and it was not unknown for churchmen to fight in person; the ferocious Archbishop Turpin in the *Chanson de Roland* had his counterparts in real life, such as Geoffrey, Bishop of Coutances, and Odo, Bishop of Bayeux, who fought in the army of Duke William of Normandy at the Battle of Hastings in 1066.

This detail from a Flemish manuscript of the late 13th Century shows the three estates of medieval society. From left to right; those who pray, those who fight and those who work.

The consolidation and extension of ecclesiastical power during the 11th and 12th Centuries affected the knightly class as well as all other parts of society. The Church attempted over a long period to control the often brutal nature of knighthood, partly by law and sanction, more successfully by directing martial energies to ecclesiastical ends and by seizing the rituals and ceremonies of knighthood. On the whole, however, the knights resisted this process and continued to justify their existence and their activities in largely secular terms.

Consider the normal state of affairs between Church and knight. In the society of the Middle Ages, the two were closer to each other than the frequent fulminations of churchmen would lead us to suppose, for both had an interest in preserving the stable order of society. Knights throughout the Middle Ages regarded themselves as equal partners with the Church in performing the important tasks of local government and administration; it was their job to sit as judges in secular courts. No matter how bitter the quarrels between individual prelates and lords might be, they united immediately against the threat of social

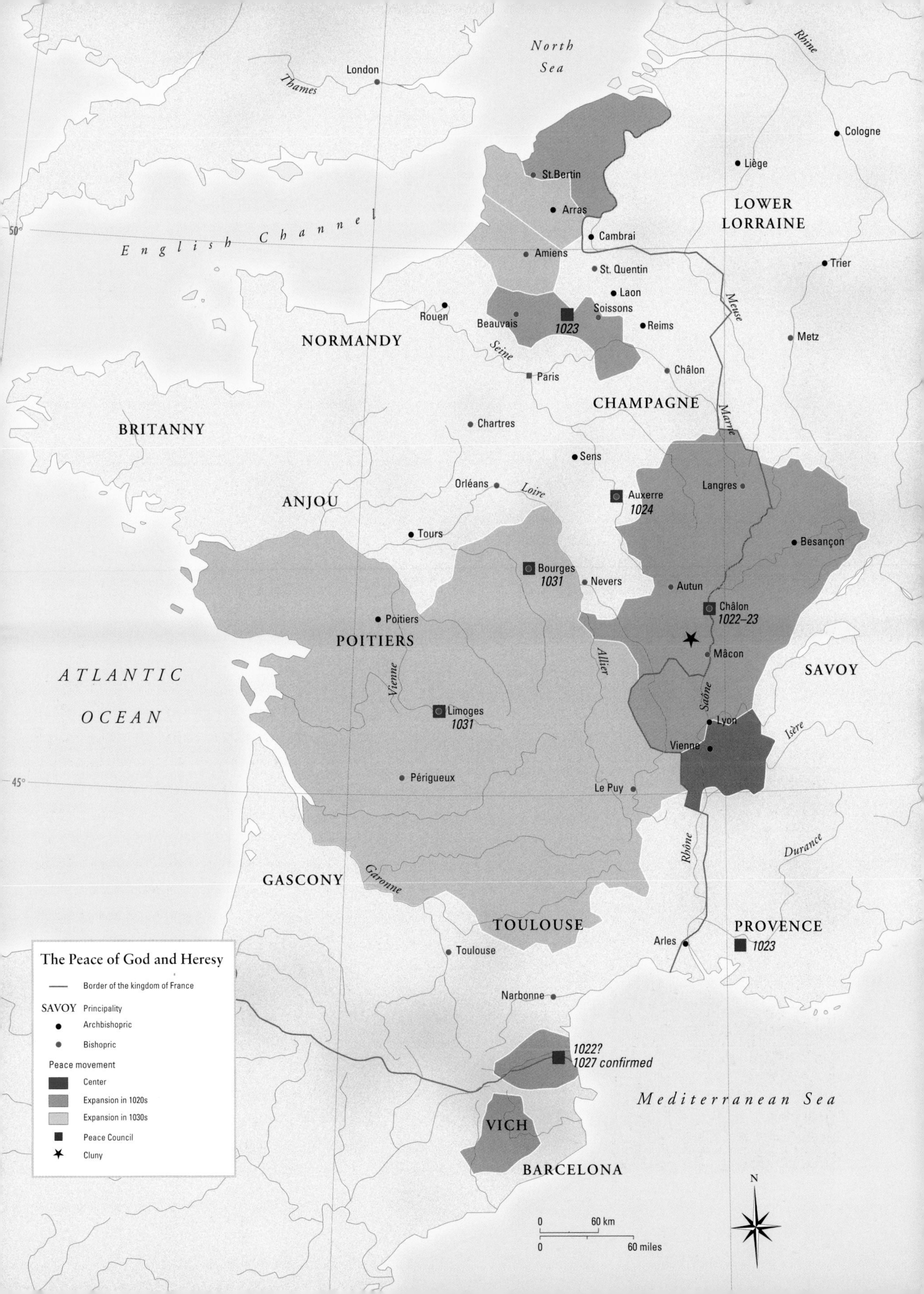

The Peace of God and Heresy
Border of the kingdom of France
SAVOY Principality
Archbishopric
Bishopric
Peace movement
Center
Expansion in 1020s
Expansion in 1030s
Peace Council
Cluny
North Sea
English Channel
ATLANTIC OCEAN
Mediterranean Sea
Thames
Rhine
Meuse
Marne
Seine
Loire
Vienne
Allier
Saône
Isère
Rhône
Durance
Garonne
London
Cologne
Liège
LOWER LORRAINE
St.Bertin
Arras
Cambrai
Amiens
St. Quentin
Trier
Laon
Soissons
Rouen
Beauvais
1023
Reims
Metz
NORMANDY
Châlon
Paris
CHAMPAGNE
BRITANNY
Chartres
Sens
Orléans
Langres
ANJOU
Auxerre
1024
Tours
Besançon
Bourges
1031
Nevers
Autun
Châlon
1022–23
Poitiers
POITIERS
Mâcon
SAVOY
Limoges
1031
Lyon
Vienne
Périgueux
Le Puy
GASCONY
TOULOUSE
PROVENCE
Arles
1023
Toulouse
Narbonne
1022?
1027 confirmed
VICH
BARCELONA
50°
45°
0 60 km
0 60 miles
N

insurrection from the laboring classes, on whom both depended for their livelihood.

The important officers of the Church were almost all drawn from the same class as knights, that is the landholders. Whether these were counts, dukes, princes, or simple families holding one estate with sufficient revenue to maintain the rank of knight, all land-holders had, essentially, the same interests and felt a class solidarity. The Church offered an honorable career for younger sons and for superfluous daughters of landholding families. Knights might often have one or more brothers in a monastery or in the priesthood, and history gives up many examples of great lords relying on their relatives, who held high ecclesiastical office, for support. An example is Stephen of Blois whose brother, Henry, was the powerful and influential Bishop of Winchester; the latter who usually worked for his brother's cause in the dispute with Empress Matilda over the throne of England.

It is difficult now for us to comprehend the religious sensibilities of a medieval person or to realize quite how important the Church was in everybody's lives. Particularly in the later Middle Ages, with the proliferation of religious orders, no one could walk far without coming across a church, monastery, friary, or priory. Every country parish had a church with its parish priest, every city its bishop. Prosperous towns supported a large number of religious communities, and in cities cathedrals were built more splendid than many princes' palaces. Almost all religious foundations had been granted their initial endowments by secular lords, and grew and thrived on continued gifts of money and land.

The Peace of God was intended to put an end to the endemic strife between petty lords, who were constantly ravaging their neighbors' lands. The church wanted to settle these local squabbles, which were normally aimed at territorial acquisition and enforce church rules over unruly lords and knights and end anarchy.

The Church had its own courts and laws, and a significant hold over education. By far the majority of literate people were clerics of some sort (hence the "benefit of clergy" rule, which meant that an accused man could exempt himself from trial in the secular judicial system if he could prove that he could read). The Church was heavily involved in local and national government. It wielded the power to enforce moral dictums, and its influence over the daily life of every member of medieval society was enormous. Even the most godless of lords were known to undergo sudden repentance and set off on pilgrimage barefoot, or to donate vast sums of money to their chosen monastery.

The Church was a great landlord; many knights held their lands from abbeys or monasteries, and their feudal overlords were abbots or bishops. The closeness and mutual benefit of the knights' relationship with the Church can be seen in surviving medieval churches, where tomb effigies, stained glass windows, family monuments with banners and achievements, painted altar-pieces, all testify to the importance of piety in the knight's self-image. In addition, penitent or grateful knights donated gifts of plate to church treasuries, or sometimes paid for an entire chapel or for a new roof to the church.

Another important way in which the Church influenced knights was by the grandeur of church ceremonial, with its rich embroidered robes, incense, awe-inspiring solemnity, and sacred objects invested with spiritual significance. This was certainly an unconscious influence, since most of the complaints of churchmen against knights criticize them for their love of finery and the vanity of their self-aggrandizement. There can be no doubt that knights, like others in society, were fascinated by rich robes and solemn rituals. The rituals they devised for themselves (dubbing ceremonies, vowing ceremonies, ceremonial banquets, the ceremonies associated with tournaments) became more elaborate as time went by, but must initially have been inspired by the richness of high masses sung at cathedrals, or by state weddings and investitures that the knights themselves had witnessed.

The willingness of knights to cooperate with the Church's efforts to contribute to, and increasingly to control, its rituals were related to the Church's ability to enhance the honour of knighthood. Many knights were clearly extremely pious on the whole but they retained a strong sense of their own place and value in the scheme of things, independent of the Church's views.

THE PEACE OF GOD AND TRUCE OF GOD

The first evidence of a serious campaign by the Church to reform and control the knights of Europe is the ecclesiastical legislation known as the Peace of God and Truce of God. Enacted between 990 and 1049, these laws were made in response to social conditions that threatened the peace and stability of the community at large, including the Church. The principal source of this disruption was the endless petty wars between rival lords, mainly conducted as a series of guerrilla raids on the territories of their opponents. Parties of armed, mounted men would descend on a village, or even on a monastery, burn the buildings, kill anyone who resisted, and steal or slaughter their livestock. Even worse were the "robber barons," who held strongly fortified castles and simply extorted goods from the communities of the surrounding countryside by force.

The power of Church and state: in this 12th-Century manuscript Jesus is shown handing a key to the pope and a sword to the Holy Roman Emperor.

Growth of Feudalism

FEUDALISM WAS A SYSTEM OF MILITARY AND SOCIAL OBLIGATION TO THE KING THAT OPERATED AT ALL LEVELS OF SOCIETY. THE KNIGHT WAS A KEY INDIVIDUAL IN THE HIERARCHY, IN RETURN FOR MILITARY SERVICE TO HIS KING OR LORD HE WAS GRANTED LANDHOLDINGS THAT WOULD PROVIDE THE INCOME THAT WOULD EQUIP BOTH HIMSELF AND HIS FOLLOWERS.

The knight, an essential building block of feudal society, stood between the élite class and the peasants.

Feudalism, as it developed in early medieval France, was not new but evolved naturally out of the social conditions that had existed for hundreds of years in western Europe, where settled Christian states were almost always under threat; from invasion by hostile Norse or Muslim nations from north and south, or destructive raids by Slav and Magyar tribes from the east. The fundamental two-way contract of feudalism, in which a lord protected his people in exchange for services, was the obvious way to structure a society that was heavily rural and agricultural, where there were few towns, and "government" consisted of agreement between the most powerful noblemen in the land. The obligation of the lord to protect his society generally, and the people who worked his land and provided his wealth in particular, was desirable in such conditions. Just as the peasants were required to work on their lord's lands a certain number of days in the year, the lord himself was required to be a trained warrior, capable of turning out, ready and equipped to fight, at the command of the overlord from whom he held his lands. If the lord had an extensive holding, his obligation would extend to the provision of a number of trained fighting men in addition to himself, and the wealthier he was, the larger, better equipped, and more highly skilled the force he provided had to be.

Every lord held his lands in fief from an overlord, who in turn held his from a great and powerful noble family, who held their patrimony from the King. Each link in this chain had made an oath to the effect that his tenure of the land was conditional on the service he rendered his overlord. The relationship was symbolized by the act of homage, in which the lord would kneel and place his hands between the hands of his overlord and swear an oath to serve him.

In theory this system enabled a well-regulated kingdom to mobilize an efficient fighting force against a common enemy for the protection of society. In practice, particularly in France, where the authority of the monarchy was *weal* (the good of the community), the great nobles, counts of large regions such as Anjou and Blois, could mobilize efficient fighting forces against each other and

THE MEDIEVAL KING

The king owned all the land. He retained about 20 percent of this land for his own use, and granted the rest to the Church and the barons.

CHURCH	BARONS
About 25 percent of this land is granted to the Church. The bishops (tenants-in-chief) granted land to their undertenants. These men promised to supply knights when the king needed them.	About 55 percent of this land is granted to his barons. The barons (tenants-in-chief) granted land to their undertenants. These men promised to supply knights when the king needed them.
UNDERTENANTS	UNDERTENANTS
Undertenants granted land to the peasants. In return, the peasants provided rent or labor services.	Under-tenants granted land to the peasants. In return, the peasants provided rent or labor services.
PEASANTS	PEASANTS
In return for land, peasants provided labor services (serfs).	In return for land, peasants provided rent (free peasants).

Right: EARLY CAPETIAN FRANCE
After the collapse of the Carolingian rulers of France, the Capetian Duke of the Franks, Hugh Capet, became King. He ruled over great estates in central France and enjoyed church patronage and family connections across the country. However, to the west lands were beyond his control and were eventually united with the Plantagenet dominions.

conduct what amounted to private wars within the kingdom. The 10th and 11th Century legislation known as the Peace of God and Truce of God was an attempt by the Church to limit the sufferings caused by these wars.

Europe in the 13th Century was recognizably the same shape and size as Europe of today, stretching from the British Isles in the west to the kingdoms of Hungary, Bohemia, and Poland in the east, and from recently converted Scandinavian countries in the north to the Iberian peninsula in the south. What made it different from Europe of today was that all constituent countries felt as members of a unified Christian state. They acknowledged one faith, that of the Holy Roman Catholic Church, which wielded spiritual and temporal authority over the region, and in theory the overlordship of the Holy Roman Emperor. Divisive nationalistic movements and religious dissent did not occur until the later Middle Ages, when Europe fragmented into nations and Christendom into the different Christian theologies. In the 13th Century Christendom was united against the threat of Islam; this was the age of the crusades, when the Church could mobilize vast armies drawn from all parts of Europe against pagan enemies; the Turks or Egyptians in the Holy Land, the Prussians and Lithuanians in northern Europe, or, in the case of the Albigensian crusade, heretical sects within their own Christian community.

The people of the ruling class were members of a confederation of extraordinary mobility; they traveled widely to visit friends and relations or to go to war, and it was not uncommon for noblemen of one area to be invited to take up vacant thrones in another. They were known by the territory that was their main holding, such as Geoffrey of Anjou or Eleanor of Aquitaine, to knights who took their name from one village or estate. During the period covered by this book, and indeed during the 13th Century, there were many changes of boundary and fortune within Europe; the map (*right*), of medieval Christendom, will help to place some of the individuals named in this history.

The practical aspects of feudalism—the fact that a lord often trained and equipped his own body of fighting men—were mirrored in its ethos, which had developed from the loyalty of much earlier Germanic warrior societies. Compare the evidence of the Roman historian Tacitus, writing in the 2nd

Medieval barons frequently equipped their own armies and set about aggrandizing themselves and their estates. Theoretically they were vassals of their King, and therefore should not be fighting each other, but in practice powerful barons could hold almost as much power as their King.

Early Capetian France
Eastern frontier of Capetian France
French Royal domain
Ecclesiastical lands
Lands of fuedal lords
Lands acquired by the counts of Champagne as fiefs of the crown of France, or from the King of Germany, the Duke of Burgundy, and bishops
Place for which Royal charter issued
Archdiocese
Diocese where bishop appointed by King
Royal monastery
Castle of fuedal lord
North Sea
KINGDOM OF GERMANY
KINGDOM OF BURGUNDY
Flanders
Artois
Vermandois
Coucy
Vexin
Valois
Champagne
Normandy
Maine
Gatinais
Blois
Anjou
(part of) Anjou
Touraine
Sancerre
Nevers
Duchy of Burgundy
Berry
Poitou
Bourbon
La Marche
Angoulême
Aquitaine
Auvergne
Toulouse
Gevaudan
Rouergue
Gothia
Antwerp
Bruges
Ghent
Brussels
Liège
Guines
Cassel
Boulogne
St Omer
Thérouanne
Tournai
Lille
Fournes
Montreuil
St Pol
Douai
Arras
Cambrai
St Valery
St Riquier
Eu
Corbie
Somme
Amiens
St Quentin
St Michel-en-Thiérache
Ribémont
Nesle
Meuse
Fécamp
Laon
Noyon
Evergnicourt
Attigny
Breteuil
St-Leger-aux-Bois
Coucy
Rethel
Jumièges
Rouen
Beauvais
Compiègne
Soissons
St Thierry
Bayeux
Seine
Bèthisy
Liancourt
Mont-Notre-Dame
Reims
Verdun
Caen
Lisieux
Le Bec
Senlis
Crépy
Pontoise
Orry
Meulan
Argenteuil
Falaise
Evreux
Mantes
St Denis
Meaux
Marne
Châlons
Brevel
Poissy
St-Germain-en-Laye
Paris
Lagny
St Maur des Fossés
Faremoutiers
Vitry
Avranches
Dreux
Montfort
St Cloud
Mortain
Thimer
Châteaufort
Coulomos
Corbeil
Champeaux
Provins
Montier-en-Der
Rosnay
Mortagne
Aleçon
Chartres
Melun
Etampes
Brienne
Bellerne
Nogent-le-Rotrou
Morigny
Sens
Troyes
Bar-sur-Aube
Clairvaux
Le Puiset
Châteaudun
Pithiviers
Ferrières
Bar-sur-Seine
Le Mans
Langres
Joigny
Sablé
Fréteval
Orléans
Fleury
Auxerre
Tonnerre
Loir
Vendôme
Micy
St-Benoit-sur-Loire
Blois
St Sauveur
Rougemont
Flavigny
Angers
Chaumont
Amboise
Loire
Langeais
La Ferté
Bourgeuil
Tours
Pontlevoy
Dijon
Saône
Doubs
Saumer
Chinon
Cher
Sancerre
Montreuillon
Citeaux
Loches
Bourges
Thouars
Loudun
Châtillon
Issoudun
Nevers
Autun
Mirebeau
Châtellerault
Deols
Chalon
Parthenay
Tournus
Poitiers
Épineuil
Cluny
Lusignan
Mâcon
Niort
Semur
Charroux
Mozac
Thiers
Lyons
Limoges
Clermont-Ferrand
Vienne
Rhône
Isère
Brioude
Périgueux
Le Puy
Valence
Mende
Viviers
Lot
Cahors
Rodez
Milhau
Orange
Montauban
Albi
Avignon
N
0
100 km
0
100 miles

Century, with much later Germanic tribal groups in 9th and 10th Century England as described in the Anglo-Saxon Chronicles, a collection of writings by unknown Saxon authors, and the poem *The Battle of Maldon*, probably written by a monk shortly after the battle. These sources indicate that the loyalty between a chieftain and his *comitatus*, his group of personal household warriors, remained unchanged for a period of about 800 years. Tacitus wrote of the tribes inhabiting what the Romans called 'Germania' that:

Real distinction and strength belong to the chief who always has around him a band of chosen warriors to be a glory in peace and a protection in war... When the fighting begins, it is shameful for a chief to be outdone in bravery, and equally shameful for the followers not to match the courage of the leader: to survive one's chief and return from battle is a foul disgrace that lasts as long as life. To defend him, to support him, to turn one's own deeds to his glory, this is the main oath of their allegiance.

This relationship was fostered by bonds of tradition, of common upbringing between the young warriors, and often also by kinship within the small tribal group. It was a two-way relationship. To earn this devotion from his men, a good chieftain must be generous with gifts of weapons and armor, while the young warriors' eagerness for these gifts was not so much the desire to be rewarded as to be honored.

This picture, from the Froizart's Chronicles, depicts the capture of a lord on the battlefield, the ultimate disgrace. Apart from the shame of failure to carry out your feudal duty to your lord, to protect his life and honor at all costs, there was also the ransom that would have to be paid. This could cost the lord and his estates dearly.

The tribes referred to by Tacitus—the Saxons, Goths, Lombards, and Franks—settled in large areas of western Europe after the power of the Roman Empire had declined: the Saxons in England, the Goths in southern France and Spain, the Lombards in northern and central Italy (Lombardy), and the Franks in huge areas of what is now northern and central France and the Low Countries. The values of their society, in which government was based on oaths of personal loyalty and service sworn by men to their lord, were central to the developing feudal systems of these lands.

Tacitus' remark that it is a foul disgrace to return alive from a battle in which your chief has been killed is borne out by two examples, one historical, one literary, from Anglo-Saxon England. In 757, the Anglo-Saxon Chronicles tells the story of a feud between Cynewulf, the King of Wessex, and Cyneheard, a prince whose brother Sigeberht had been King of Wessex until he was deposed and banished by Cynewulf "for unlawful actions." Cyneheard discovered that Cynewulf intended to banish him too, and ambushed the king one night when he had gone with only a small retinue of men to visit his mistress. Cynewulf was attacked in the bedchamber by Cyneheard and his men and he was killed. His small band of men was woken by his mistress's screams and they rushed to attack the superior force of Cyneheard's men, as described in the Anglo-Saxon Chronicles:

...and the prince offered each of them money and life, and none of them would accept it, but they all went on fighting continuously until they all lay slain.

In the morning, the tables were turned when the dead king's loyal thanes (warriors holding land from the king and owing military service in return), Osric and Wigfrith, arrived with the rest of the king's warriors and surrounded the house. Cyneheard offered them money and land if they would accept him as king, and he mentioned that he had with him some kinsmen of theirs, in the hope that they would not attack him if it meant killing members of their own families:

> *They replied that no kinsman was dearer to them than their lord, and they would never follow his slayer, and then they offered to let their kinsmen depart unharmed.*

But the kinsmen did not think highly of this suggestion, and refused to desert their lord "any more than your comrades who were slain with the King." The King's thanes then attacked the house and Prince Cyneheard and all his men were killed, except for one who was Osric's godson, and he, the chronicler relates, was badly wounded.

The poem *The Battle of Maldon* celebrates an event that took place in 991, when the Norwegian Anlaf, with 93 ships full of men, was raiding the coasts of Kent and East Anglia. The King at this time was Ethelred, the famously unready, but the coast was defended by the Ealdorman of Essex, Byrhtnoth. He caught the invading army at Maldon. The battle commenced favorably for the English, who were able to keep the stronger force at bay because they were defending a narrow split of land. But Byrhtnoth, "because of his pride," fell back to allow more Vikings to cross over and fight. The battle turned disastrously against the English when Byrhtnoth was decapitated. Despite the battle being a defeat for the English, the poem was written to celebrate the loyalty and bravery of a few of Byrhtnoth's men, who decided to fight by their fallen leader, even though this meant certain death:

> *"Byrhtnoth grasped his spear and spoke.*
> *He was an old companion. He brandished his ash-spear*
> *And with wonderful courage exhorted the warriors*
> *'Mind must be firmer, heart the more fierce,*
> *Courage the greater, as our strength grows less.*
> *Here lies out leader, dead,*
> *An heroic man in the dust.*
> *He who now longs for escape will lament forever.*
> *I am old. I will not go from here,*
> *But I mean to lie by the side of my lord,*
> *Lie in the dust with the man I loved so dearly."*

Thus we can see that, long before the appearance of knights as we know them today, there had been a tradition of a warrior élite whose idea of honorable conduct was bound up in a nexus of noble qualities, such as courage and prowess, stemming from the absolute loyalty and personal devotion they felt for their leader. These were important stepping stones toward the knight's sense of identity, both individually and as a member of an international band of like-minded brothers.

NORMANDY

WHEN ROLLO WAS MADE COUNT OF NORMANDY, HE FOUNDED A STATE IN WHICH THE AMALGAM OF VIKING SETTLERS AND THE LOCAL FRENCH POPULATION CREATED A VIBRANT MILITARY SOCIETY THAT LEFT A LASTING MARK ON THE HISTORY OF EUROPE.

A tough no-nonsense Norman foot soldier highly experienced in the arts of war. He would follow his lord to victories over large parts of western Europe.

Until the second half of the 10th Century, there are virtually no literary sources about Normandy and Viking rule there. The archaeological evidence is next to nothing. Place names in Normandy are hybrids. In northern England the Scandinavian settlements resulted in purely Scandinavian place-names, but in Normandy names tend to be Scandinavian with a Romanised suffix referring to someone's farm or villa, as in Tourville. What emerged here in the 10th and 11th Centuries was a Scandinavian élite ruling over a population who spoke French.

Viking raids up the Seine convinced King Charles III, the Simple, that he required a buffer territory to protect the mouth of the river from Viking incursions. Here he turned to Rolf, a Norwegian, who had established a base at the Seine's estuary. Nobody knows when Rolf arrived in west Francia. Eventually known as Rollo, later Icelandic sources identifying him with Hrolf the Ganger, son of Ragnvald, Earl of Moer, he went "a-viking" (raiding) before settling in Francia.

Nothing much is known about the Treaty of St. Clair-sur-Epte (911) except that land on the lower Seine, extending as far west as the mouth of the Seine on the coast and near the source of the Eure inland, was ceded as a buffer zone to Rollo, who cemented the relationship by marrying Charles' daughter, being Christened and taking the name Robert. A charter of Charles III dated 14 March 918 says that the land was given to "the Northmen of the Seine, for the defense of the kingdom." Rollo appears as a count in 911, with the traditional duties of a Carolingian count, protection and the administration of justice. Some sources claim that Rollo was a duke but others suggest that there was no Norman march before 960–966 and a dukedom only being created after Hugh Capet became King of France.

KNIGHT C. 1180
This knight carries a lance that he can couch to charge his opponents, and since it is not decorated with a pennon (long triangular or swallow-tailed flag) or banner he can also throw it, a technique equally favored at this date. His helmet, with round top and nasal bar, is of a style introduced around 1100. His main hauberk or byrnie (coat of mail) has been extended: it now incorporates a hoof or coif (metal skullcap); an aventail (loose flap hanging in front of his throat) can be pulled up and secured by thongs to helmet or brow to protect his face, and the sleeves are now lengthened into mittens. He carries the characteristic kite-shaped Norman shield, and rides in a saddle with raised pommel and cantle (behind) to give him an extra secure seat during combat. His shins are protected by mail greaves.

The 911 agreement was successful, although the Normans under Rollo carried out some raids in the Seine in 923. In 924, the King ceded Le Mans, Bayeux, L'Huernin, and Bassin. In 933 the Contentin and Avrachin, previously Breton lands, were ceded to William Longsword (927–942), Rollo's son. By 933, the area of Normandy corresponded with the archdiocese of Rouen with the seven cities of Rouen, Bayeux, Avranches, Evreux, Sees, Lisieux, and Coutances. Thus, the development of the Church and the Norman dukes were closely associated.

William Longsword married the daughter of Herbert of Vermandois, but his children were born of a Breton mistress. He supported Louis IV and it was his "protection" over Brittany that gained him the Contentin and Avrachin. William was murdered on the orders of Count Arnulf of Flanders, and his son, Richard, still a minor, succeeded him. Louis IV and Hugh the Great tried to grab Normandy, and Louis took young Richard. Louis then seized Rouen and Hugh took Bayeux. Richard escaped his imprisonment at Laon, recaptured Rouen, and then requested help from the Viking leader, Harald of the Bassin. Richard regained control over Normandy, kept the peace, and married Emma, daughter of Hugh the Great, now Count of Vermandois. They had no issue but Richard's mistress, Gunnor, a Dane, had several children. Richard II, son of Gunnor and Richard I, succeeded his father in 996 while another son, Robert, was archbishop of Rouen from 989 to 1037. Emma, a daughter, married Ethelred of England, becoming Queen there, a status she kept after his death when she married Canute. Gunnor's family became the heart of the new aristocracy that developed during the 11th Century.

The great bastion of Falaise Castle in Normandy, birthplace of William the Conqueror.

Normandy became wealthy from Richard I's reign, Rouen becoming a commercial entrepôt. Coins were minted under Richard I and examples of these have been found in Scotland, Denmark, Pomerania, Poland, and Russia. Normandy's political links were less with France than with England and Denmark.

Duke Richard II ushered in the period of Norman military power, being supported by his subordinates who now called themselves counts on his elevation in status. He began to play a role on Europe's political scene. He had linked himself dynastically to England yet allowed his ports to give shelter to those Vikings attacking England's coasts. His sons were short-lived: Richard III, a warrior; William who became a monk at Fécamp; and Duke Robert who commenced his eight-year reign by allegedly poisoning his brother and later going mad.

This was the inheritance of eight-year-old William, conqueror-to-be, when he took the ducal throne in 1035. William was surrounded by advisors selected by his father. The main four guardians were Archbishop Robert, Count Alan of Brittany, Osbern Herfasston, the steward, and Turold of Neufmarché. He was probably brought up in the Herfasston household with several other boys where his tutors trained him in Latin, castle-building and weaponry. His biographer, William of Poitiers, said of the youthful William: "It was both gratifying and awesome-inspiring to see the prince grasp the reins, scythe the air with his sword while his lustrous shield defended him, and to behold him as a warrior, terrifying in his gleaming helmet and death-dealing lance."

Norman territorial growth

- Granted to Rollo (Count of Normandy), *911*
- Acquired *924*
- Aquired *933*
- Norman attacks
- Added *1051*
- Unsuccessful Frankish attempt to reconquer Normandy
- Place name of Scandinavian origin

1066 Invasion of England

THE NORMANS YELLED THEIR WAR CRIES, ESPECIALLY "DIEU AIDE" (ASSIST US, GOD), BUT COULD MAKE LITTLE IMPRESSION. THE SAXONS WORKED OUT A KIND OF LAND SHANTY AS THEY WENT ABOUT THEIR GRISLY WORK; ANYONE GAINING A TOEHOLD ANYWHERE NEAR THE ADAMANTINE BARRIER OF SHIELDS WAS RUN THROUGH, THE CORPSE THROWN BACK WITH AN EXULTANT CRY OF "OUT, OUT!"

In this detail from the Bayeux Tapestry, Edward the Confesssor, an unsaintly and neurotic king, passed the English throne directly to Harold Godwineson on his death. Meanwhile, Duke William of Normandy claimed that he was promised the throne of England and that Harold was his sworn vassal. In the spring of 1066 William set about organizing his army to rectify this situation.

King Edward the Confessor's death in January 1066 left England without an heir of the royal blood line. Duke William of Normandy claimed that Edward had promised him the kingdom in 1051 and that Harold Godwineson, Earl of Wessex, had sworn to be William's vassal and help him acquire the English throne. Legend states that Harold had been tricked to swear his loyalty on hidden holy relics. Whatever the case, Edward gave Harold the kingship on his deathbed. However, there were other tenuous claimants to the kingship. The Scandinavian Kings were certain to cause trouble as Harald Hardrada of Norway did in September 1066, while Swein Estrithson of Denmark interfered after the Norman conquest. Another problem facing Harold Godwineson was his brother, Tostig, exiled in 1065, who joined Hardrada, hoping to regain his Earldom of Northumbria.

William of Normandy was not slow to summon his lords and commence collecting an army and building an invasion fleet. A skilled war captain, William acquired military experience at the Battle of Val-ès-Dunes (1047) where the French King helped him defeat rebellious Norman magnates. Later engagements at Mortemer-en-Bray (1054) and Varaville (1057) developed his skills, as did warfare against the Bretons and his acquisition of Maine (1063), added to conquests in Brittany and Ponthieu. To counter William, Harold stationed an army along the south coast with a fleet based off the Isle of Wight.

Harold maintained a watch on the English Channel until September when his army's food ran out leaving him to disband his levies and return to London. William's luck was in; the prevailing wind that had bottled him up in port during the summer changed, allowing him to invade England. Meanwhile, a Norwegian army landed in Yorkshire and defeated the Yorkshire earls, Morcar and Edwin, at Gate Fulford in a dire battle that left the victorious Vikings in control of York. There the men of the shire, many of Viking descent, agreed to help in the conquest of England. However, Harold surprised the Norwegians at their camp five days later. The day long fight at Stamford bridge left Hardrada and Tostig dead and the Norwegians routed.

The seal of Harold, Earl Godwineson, the symbol of his dynastic power.

The Great Seal of William the Conqueror shows him as an armored warrior mounted on a war horse.

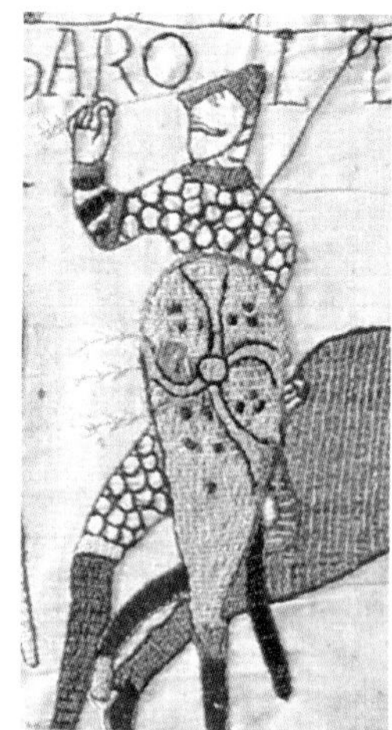

The death of King Harold, killed by an arrow in the eye, or so the Bayeux Tapestry portrays it. This medieval embroidery depicts the Norman Conquest of England and is displayed in Bayeux Cathedral.

While celebrating his victory, Harold learnt that William had landed at Pevensey on 28 September with his army of Normans, Flemings, and Bretons. Harold rushed south covering 190 miles to London, raised more troops and traveled a further 50 miles to Hastings, ready to fight the nearby Normans, and all in 13 days, as well as pacifying the north. If Harold had taken more time, he would have faced William with a larger force. As it was, some reinforcements arrived the night after the battle. Apparently Harold wished to surprise William, but Norman scouts reported the English advance and 14 October witnessed the Anglo-Norman engagement at the ridge at Senlac Hill in Kent.

The English dismounted and formed a shield wall with their axemen, perhaps some 7,000 men with the county levies. The Normans had larger forces with about 5,000 infantry, including crossbowmen and archers, and some 2,000 knights. Battle commenced at 9.00 am and lasted all day with repeated cavalry charges that failed to break the shield wall, again proving that disciplined infantry can defeat knights on horse. Reports of the battle differ but many agree that a feigned retreat by the Normans caused the shield wall to disintegrate as some soldiers rushed forward only to be scythed down by the returning cavalry. The English forces reorganized but Harold's brothers, Leofwine and Gyrth were killed. According to the Bayeaux Tapestry, Harold lay dying at dusk from an arrow in the eye. There is no evidence to suggest he was hit by that mythical arrow. Records state that his body was hacked to pieces. Their king dead, Harold's housecarls (bodyguard) fought to the death, swinging their bearded axes which could chop a man clean in half. The English suffered 4,000

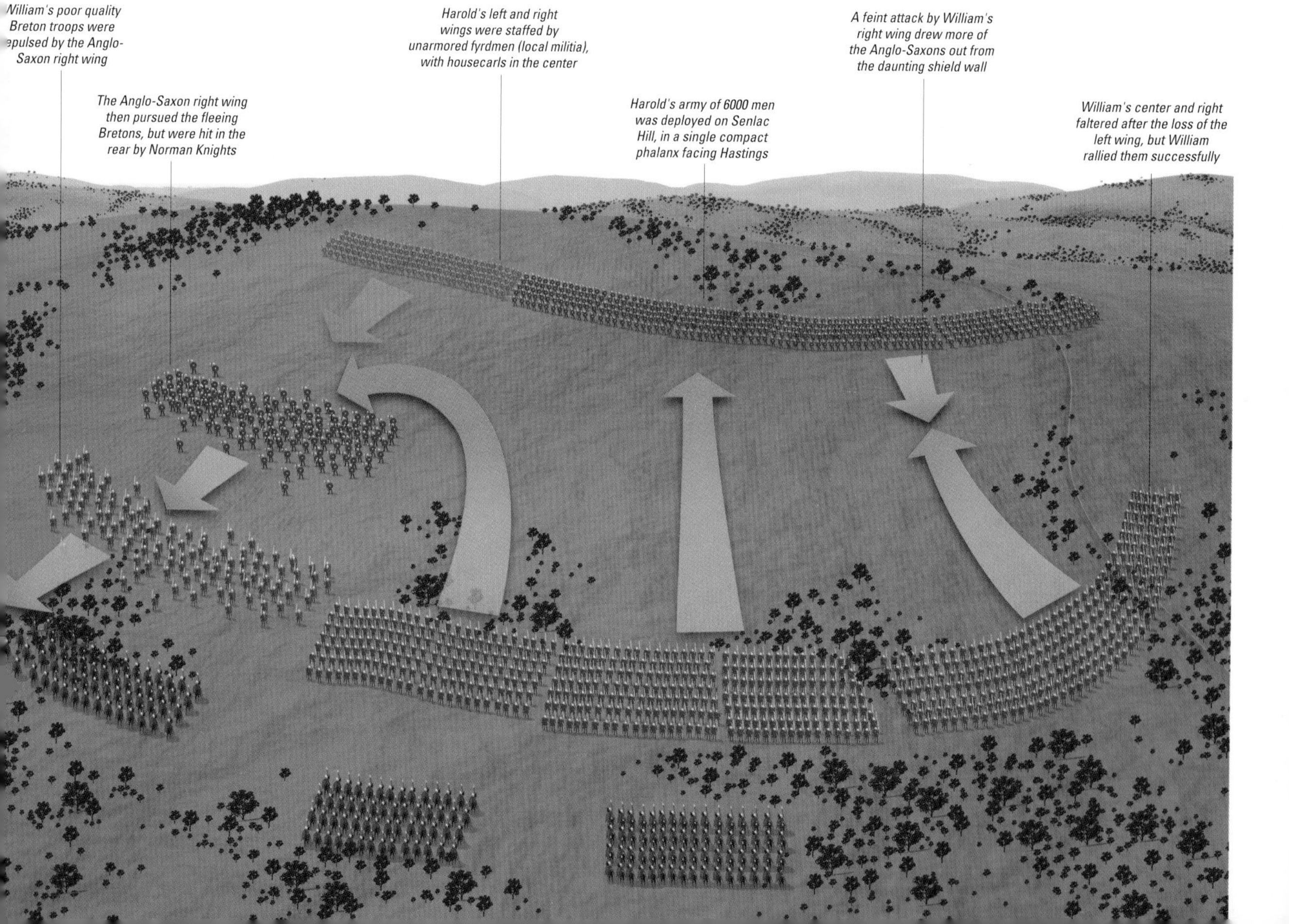

William's poor quality Breton troops were epulsed by the Anglo-Saxon right wing

The Anglo-Saxon right wing then pursued the fleeing Bretons, but were hit in the rear by Norman Knights

Harold's left and right wings were staffed by unarmored fyrdmen (local militia), with housecarls in the center

Harold's army of 6000 men was deployed on Senlac Hill, in a single compact phalanx facing Hastings

A feint attack by William's right wing drew more of the Anglo-Saxons out from the daunting shield wall

William's center and right faltered after the loss of the left wing, but William rallied them successfully

Conquest of England
1066–69
Abbey whose tenant may have fought for Harold at Hastings
Tenant recorded to have died at Hastings
Towns where castles were built by William
Army emcamped for several days
Rebellions 1067–68
Rebellions early 1069
Fleet anchorage
Battle sites
Areas heavily ravaged by Norman army
Tostig, April–May 1066
Harold, May–September 1066
Harald Hardrada
Harold, October 1066
William's arrival, 1066
William's route October–December 1066
William, December 1067–late March 1068
William, summer 1068 first northern campaign
William, February–April 1969 Second northern campaign
Campaigns of rebellion against William
Arrival of Danish fleet, August 1069
SCOTLAND
Durham
Northumbria
Wharfe
25 Sept 1066
York
Stamford Bridge
Fulford
20 Sept 1066
Tadcaster
Riccall
Irish Sea
North Sea
ublin
Doncaster
Derwent
Don
Lincoln
Trent
ENGLAND
The Wash
Derby
Nottingham
Burton-on-Trent
Crowland
Thorney
Shalgrave
Norwich
Leicester
Peterbrough
Mercia
Ramsey
East Anglia
Coventry
Ely
Huntingdon
Cambridge
Warwick
Hemmingford
Dagnorth
WELSH PRINCIPALITIES
Hereford
Bedford
Ipswich
Cavendish
Buckingham
Colchester
Little Berkhamsted
Berkhamsted
Abingdon
Wallingford
Bristol
London
Sheppey
Southwark
Thames
Rochester
Brockton
Canterbury
Sandwich
Kent
Farnham
Guildford
Dover
1067
Winchester
Wessex
Sussex
Romney
Montacute
16 Oct 1066
Boulogne
Hastings
Pevensey
Exeter
Isle of Wight
English Channel
St. Valerv-sur-Somme
N
0
50 km
50 miles
Ronen
Dives-sur-Mer
Normandy

casualties, other troops having fled the field into the woods of the Weald, while the Normans received 2,500 casualties. The battle had been a close thing but William could view the slaughter of nearly all the Anglo-Scandinavian nobility as a precursor to their replacement with a new layer of European aristocracy. William next needed to coerce the English into surrender. Raids and threatening marches followed with reinforcements landing at Chichester, capturing Winchester, the capital of old Wessex and home of the treasury, then marching along the Thames to meet other Norman spearheads at Wallingford. William was apparently unable to force London Bridge so burnt Southwark instead. Raids deep into the current counties of Surrey and Hampshire, followed by a vast raid north of the Thames, occasioned the surrender of many English leaders. On Christmas Day 1066, William was accepted and crowned King of England, but in reality he had only defeated the forces of southern and central England. The next few years would see revolts in the West Country, Mercia, Yorkshire, and Northumbria. Only their suppression would see Norman power consolidated.

CONQUESTS OF ENGLAND AND THE REBELLIONS IN THE NORTH

The Normans were regarded as the most professional and best equipped warriors in western Europe. The knights, shown above, wore helmets and chain mail and used the lance thatbecame their distinguishing mark. Their horses were equipped with stirrups, making it harder to unseat their riders. The English, who almost exclusively fought on foot, found it difficult to defeat the Norman cavalry on the battlefield.

The Norman invasion was a turning point in history. William brought to England new political élites, new techniques of warfare, and a different language. Norman rule was imposed slowly, fighting against internal as well as external threats. Twenty years of struggle ensued between a few Normans and their allies as they tried to hold down a relatively large territory while being outnumbered.

Some historians explain Norman success through castle building. At Pevensey in 1066 William built his first castle, clearly shown in the Bayeux Tapestry. Castles were then placed at strategic points on road junctions, fords, and in large centers of population where they would dominate and intimidate the defeated English. A traditional picture emerges of the early timber and earth fortifications that hoped to make use of natural, if not man-made features. Often the castle comprised a motte, or mound, topped by a wooden palisade and a surrounding bailey, or enclosure. These fortifications could be built rapidly, William erecting two at York in eight days. However, Norman castles or fortifications were legion in their types.

The primary task of a castle was an offensive one, a base for raids in surrounding territory that could be controlled by fast-moving cavalry stationed inside the castle. The fortification would be designed to be impregnable although this could never be guaranteed. After 1066, castles were often erected at the sites of Anglo-Saxon burhs (fortified towns). William's Norman and Flemish companions were rewarded with land and some 600 castles were constructed in the Welsh marches, although many were abandoned after conquest. Generally, early fortifications were enclosures with outer ditches with sheer scarps, the spoil making earth ramparts surmounted with timber palisades. Not all earthen and timber castles were motte and baileys. Many were large baileys enclosed by a

Conquest of England
1069–86
Norman castles built by 1086
Rebellions Autumn 1069
Rebellions 1070
Battle sites
Areas deliberately devastated by William, January–March 1070
Count Brian
William's Lieutenants
William's route, September – to early April 1070, 3rd Northern Campaign
William's route 1072
Campaigns of rebellion against William
Danish fleet September 1069
Danish fleet 1070
SCOTLAND
Abernethy
1070 King Malcolm of Scotland
Norman Fleet
Northumbria
Cumbria
Newcastle
Durham
Tyne
Tees
Richmond
Northallerton
North Sea
Man
(to Earldom of Orkney)
Wharfe
York
Skipsea
1069
Spring 1070 King Swen
Irish Sea
Penworthan
Pontefract
Dublin
Isle of Axholme
Derwent
Don
Lincoln
Trent
Rhuddlan
Chester
ENGLAND
The Wash
Welsh Principalities
Stafford
Nottingham
Belvoir
Tutbury
Edric the Wild
Shrewsbury
Bytham
East Anglia
Norwich
Peterbrough
Rockingham
Stanton Holgate
Dudley
Montgomery
Mercia
Ely
Eye
Huntingdon
Wigmore
Richard's Castle
William Fitz Osbern
Warwick
Cambridge
Eardisley
Ailey
Worcester
Clifford
Hereford
Ipswich
Ewyas Harold
Goodrich
Buckingham
Bishop's Stortford
Colchester
Monmouth
Gloucester
Oxford
Berkhamsted
Hertford
Chepstow
Caerleon
June 1070 Danes depart
Rayleigh
Wallingford
LONDON
Bristol
Bishop Geoffrey
Thames
Windsor
Rochester
Midsummer 1069 Harold's sons
Wessex
Canterbury
Kent
Dover
Dunster
Salisbury
Winchester
Sussex
Montacute
Bramber
Arundel
Lewes
Hastings
Pevensey
Boulogne
Exeter
Carisbrooke
Tavistock
Count Brian
Corfe
Isle of Wight
Tremanton
English Channel
N
0
50 km
50 miles
Barfleur
Normandy
56°
54°
52°
50°
4°
0°

ditch, rampart, and gate. Within this ring would be placed buildings needed by the new lord, his retainers, household, and garrison. Sometimes there would be mottes without baileys, baileys without mottes, ramparts topped with palisades, ramparts with masonry walls, multiple ditches, artificial mounds. Others were sited on cliff tops, promontories or on defensible river banks such as Chepstow Castle in England, built 1067–75. Carisbrooke Castle on the Isle of Wight was built on the site of a Roman fort that had defended the Saxon shore.

Resistance to Norman authority began in 1067 with a rising in Herefordshire under Edric the Wild, followed by one in Kent. In 1068 the uprising in Exeter was subdued followed that year by the submission of the southwest of England, with castles being placed at Trematon, Dunster, Exeter, and Montacute. The strength of the Normans there, especially Bristol, prevented King Harold's illegitimate sons from winning support when they mounted an expedition out of Ireland.

Real trouble exploded in 1069 in the north of England, which had little experience of Norman rule. A general rising took place headed by Edgar the Atheling, grandson of King Edmund II Ironside, the monarch of the Wessex royal line who had fought so hard against Danish Cnut. King Swein Estrithson sent a fleet to help, the combined forces capturing York before moving into north Lincolnshire. Edgar eventually swore fealty to William and served him. Resistance stiffened elsewhere and Edric the Wild's rebellion spread toward Chester and Stafford in the northwest. Other revolts occurred in Dorset and Somerset in the southwest, and Harold's sons launched another expedition.

William retaliated in a brutal and harsh fashion. He sent his minions to crush the south and west while he marched north, cutting a swathe of destruction around York and forcing the rebels to retreat to ships in the Humber estuary. The "Harrying of the North" was followed by systematic destruction during the height of winter. The Norman forces marched north to the Tees, crossed the Pennine hills to crush Chester and Stafford, then returned south. The Danish fleet sailed from the Humber to join a Lincolnshire thegn (English 'thane'), Hereward the Wake, who conducted a legendary rebellion from the fens in the Isle of Eley. The joint forces sacked Peterborough but 1070 saw the Danes withdraw from the fray and Hereward's island defenses were eventually overrun. The heroic defender is said to have surrendered or escaped, such is myth. Another story claims he swore fealty to William but there is no recorded evidence.

In 1086, the Domesday survey analyzed landholdings and wealth in a systematic fashion so that William could ascertain his royal revenue. It listed all the tenants and their lords, secular and clerical, thereby ensuring that all oaths of allegiance could be made in an irrevocable manner. The book demonstrates the dispossession of the Anglo-Saxon-Scandinavian nobility in favor of the Normans and their allies. Many Englishmen retained their lands but only two magnates survived. Earls Morcar and Edwin were found in William's retinue; other Englishmen offered submission, receiving their lands back from William. 1071 saw Edwin's fall from grace, and dispossessions continued after the 1069–70 rebellions with Norman lordships established throughout the south, southwest, Cheshire, Shropshire, the Midlands, and East Anglia. The north followed later.

An interesting case of the English experience lies in Earl Waltheof who, in 1065, received an earldom comprising the shires of Huntingdon, Northampton, Bedford, Rutland, and Cambridge. He submitted to William in 1067, joined the northern rebels in 1069, but was restored to favor and married William's niece, Judith. However, he joined another rebellion in 1075, was condemned as a traitor and executed in May 1076. His daughter, Matilda, married King David I of Scotland, making Earl Waltheof an ancestor of the Kings of Scotland.

ANGLO-NORMAN EMPIRE 1066–1154

After 1066, William the Bastard was King of England, Duke of Normandy, and Count of Maine, but he owed fealty to the King of France for Normandy, a situation which he tended to ignore while he exercised all royal powers within his domains. William used his English title in Europe to show his status was equal to that of the King of France, despite the latter being his overlord for Normandy.

The Anglo-Norman Empire was very compact, unlike the holdings of so many other European princes. William's lands also made him a threat to the French king, since Norman borders were only 20 miles from Paris. The empire was also linked together by the English Channel. Many people view the sea as a barrier but, in a time where roads were poor, traveling on the water was often the quickest method available. Ports at Southampton, Portsmouth, Barfleur, and Dieppe meant a courier ferry service could operate with the added benefit of William owning the sanctuary of the Channel Islands (*Iles Anglo-Normandes*) if ships were blown off course. Yet the empire had permeable borders. English kings claimed overlordship over Scottish and Welsh princes. The Welsh princes resented this, reacting by raiding livestock, resulting with the marcher lords countering in exactly the same fashion. Marcher counties like Ponthieu and Anjou gave concern to the Norman duchies borders, while the King of France wanted desperately to weaken this potential northern danger to his realm.

A problem facing the empire, like other family holdings, was that the conglomerate of lands was held by a family, similar to a joint-stock company. The Norman Duchy, unlike most other political entities, had developed the tradition of impartibility, whereby an inheritance would be passed on undivided to the first-born male of the duke who had the right of succession, whether he be a bastard or legitimate. However, all family members thought they had some type of claim to an inheritance or patrimony. Thus, when a ruler died, the heir had to fight off rival family claimants to ensure others' shares were minimalized. A ruler's death could spark off wars of succession. The Normans had not considered a custom developed by the Turks of murdering all possible rival claimants, brothers especially, to facilitate a smooth transition of power.

The Anglo-Norman Empire fell foul of this situation when William the Conqueror died in 1087. The eldest son, Robert, became Duke of Normandy, William Rufus was crowned King of England and Henry Beauclerc was given £5,000 and no land. When Henry died there was warfare between claimants from two residual female lines. At this time, many lords, secular and clerical, held lands both sides of the Channel and looked for political stability, desiring a monarch capable of uniting all lands.

William Rufus was harsh like his father, but also capricious. Factor this into a scenario when those lords holding lands in both Normandy and England now owed feudal allegiance to two sovereigns. The baronage played both lords against each other and were inclined to baronial rebellions. Rufus was condemned by many for his peculiar morals and his financial exactions and it was not perhaps

The White Tower, the central building of the Tower of London, was started by William the Conqueror and completed by his sons and successors around 1087. The White Tower was the home of the medieval Kings of England, their court, and center of government.

strange that he was shot dead by a random arrow while hunting in the New Forest; his brother Henry was in the hunting party but his association with the death in 1100 was never proved. However, Henry immediately hurried to Winchester to acquire the royal treasury.

The feckless Robert of Normandy had previously left on the First Crusade, having pawned Normandy to Rufus for 10,000 marks.

As Henry I, the new king granted a charter guaranteeing the rights of the baronage and the Church while the English were promised the justice and laws of Edward the Confessor. Thus, Henry made a pitch for the support of all races in his empire. His marriage to Matilda, niece of the last surviving Saxon claimant to the English throne and descendant of the old English royal line, was an astute political move. Robert returned in 1100 and feudal rebellion broke out in England, which took Henry several years to quell. In 1105, he crossed the Channel to destroy Robert's power. In September 1106, the two contestants joined battle at Tinchebrai. Both commanders dismounted their knights to stiffen their infantry but Henry had many English axemen, whose shield wall would be invincible. Henry kept a flanking cavalry force under his vassal, Helias of Maine, a distance from the battlefield. When the forces were closely engaged, Helias led his force to attack the Norman rebels under Robert, who was soundly defeated. The Saxon contingent regarded the victory as revenge for Hastings. Robert was imprisoned for the rest of his 80 years while his son, William Clito, became the focus of two rebellions against Henry, a threat removed by his death in 1128.

The defeat of the French king at Brémule in 1119, regained Henry's border principalities of Boulogne, Bellême, Maine and Brittany under his authority, which Robert had lost. Only the Vexin remained lost. Power was also consolidated by Henry's daughter, Matilda, being married to the German Emperor while his only legitimate son, William, was married to the Anjou heiress; his nephew, Stephen, was Count of Blois and Chartres. Most of Wales was controlled and the Scots King reduced to client status. Then William, traveling in the White Ship, was drowned when the vessel hit a rock. Reputedly, Henry never smiled again.

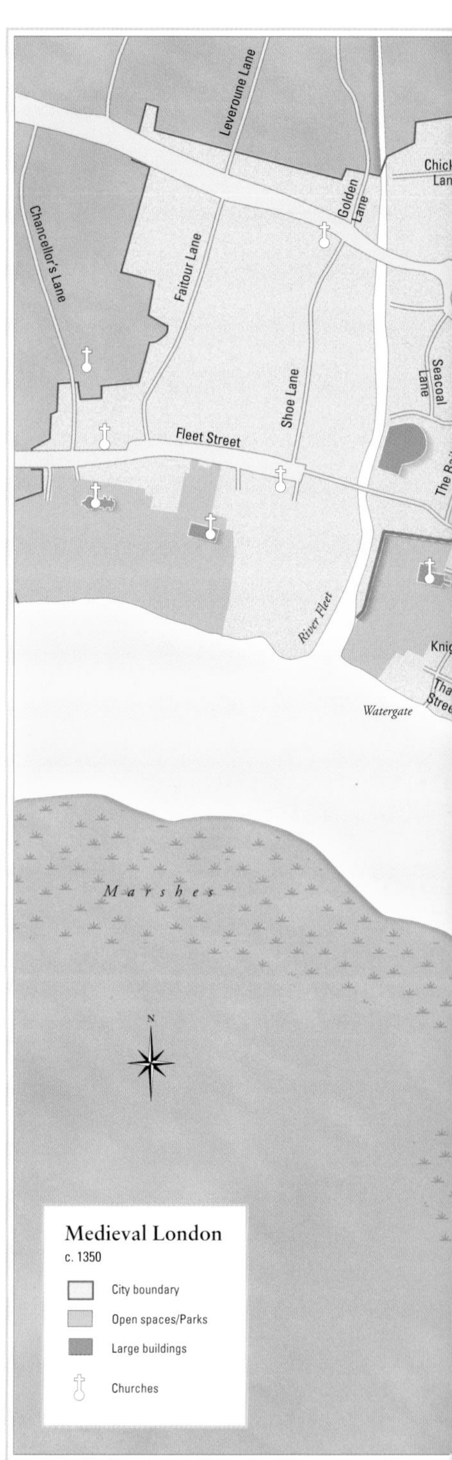

Medieval London was dominated by its Norman buildings, notably the Tower of London, the King's residence and the Seat of Government.

The Norman Periphery

NORMAN PENETRATION INTO WALES AND SCOTLAND BEGAN WITH MARAUDING BARONIAL ARMIES IN WALES, AND WITH KING DAVID I OF SCOTLAND MODELING HIS STATE UPON ENGLAND BY THE INTRODUCTION OF NORMAN KNIGHTS AS TENANTS.

Medieval rulers sought to spread their power and influence beyond their borders to create client states as a buffer against potential enemies, and the early Norman rulers of England were no exception. Norman relations with Scotland fluctuated between violence and friendship. King Malcolm III Canmore remembered when Scotland controlled Cumbria and Northumberland, now part of the Kingdom of England, and sought to regain land by border incursions. Provoked, William I The Conquerer, launched an expedition by land and sea in 1072, meeting Malcolm at Abernethy. Malcolm, instead of giving battle, performed homage for Scotland recognizing William as his lord and handing over one of his sons as hostage. He invaded England again, renewing his homage after William mounted another expedition, and was killed on his fifth raid in 1093 by forces of King William II of England, known as Rufus, the "Red One."

Hermitage Castle, Scotland, a typical motte and bailey structure. There has been a castle on this site since the late 12th Century. One of the earliest tenants was the Baron de Soulis, who proved to be a cruel and unjust lord. After much suffering, his tenants captured him while he was out hunting and boiled him alive in a vast cauldron.

Norman influence penetrated Scotland by stealth. Malcolm III's second wife was Margaret, sister of Edgar Atheling (c. 1050–1130), Anglo-Saxon prince and grandson of English King Edmund II Ironside (981–1016); three of her six sons ascended the Scots throne. After the death of Malcolm III, he was succeeded by his brother Donald Ban. Margaret's son, Edgar, ousted him in 1097. Another son, David I (1124–53), supervised a virtual Norman conquest. His reign saw introduction of a coinage and construction of Norman-style motte and bailey castles with which to dominate Scotland. Norman infiltration was encouraged by David, who spent many of his early years at the Norman court in England. There he married in 1113, making close friends with his brother-in-law, future King Henry I, and gained the earldom of Huntingdon from his wife. From 1170, with Anglo-Norman aid from his brother, King Alexander I, David acquired Cumbria, Strathclyde, and Lothian.

In his earldom and his Scottish court, David gathered around him a number of Anglo-Normans, tenants from Huntingdon, and they Normanized southeastern Scotland; Norman-Scottish barons

Europe 1095
Holy Roman Empire
Border
Probable border
After the Norman conquest of England, this militarily-successful people moved to where opportunities presented themselves. They were particularly active in Wales, Ireland, Scotland and in southern Italy.
Norwegian Sea
North Sea
Baltic Sea
ATLANTIC OCEAN
Mediterranean Sea
Adriatic Sea
NORWAY
SWEDEN
FINNS
ESTONIANS
LIVS
LITHUANIANS
DENMARK
POMERANIA
SLAVS
POLAND
SCOTLAND
IRISH KINGDOMS
WELSH STATES
ENGLAND
KINGDOM OF GERMANY
KINGDOM OF BOHEMIA
HUNGARY
FRANCE
Normandy
Brittany
Aquitaine
Gascony
KINGDOM OF BURGUNDY (ARLES)
KINGDOM OF ITALY
VENETIAN REPUBLIC
PISA
PAPAL STATES
NORMAN PRINCIPALITIES
BYZANTINE EMPIRE
NAVARRE
ARAGON
CATALAN COUNTIES
MUSLIM STATES
CID
LEÓN-CASTILE
MUSLIM KINGDOM OF MALLORCA
EMPIRE OF THE ALMORAVIDS
Corsica
Sardinia
Sicily
Rhine
Vistula
Danube
Nidaros
Bergen
Oslo
Stockholm
Åbo
Aarhus
Roskilde
Malmö
Scone
Glasgow
Edinburgh
York
Dublin
Cork
Hereford
Oxford
Wells
London
Hamburg
Bremen
Hanover
Amsterdam
Rotterdam
Poznan
Wroclaw
Cracow
Cologne
Prague
Mainz
Frankfurt
Rouen
Rheims
Metz
Paris
Strasbourg
Vienna
Pozsony
Esztergom
Buda
Munich
Salzburg
Orléans
Nantes
Tours
Zurich
Innsbruck
Graz
Dijon
Bern
Szeged
Pécs
Geneva
Limoges
Lyon
Trieste
Zágráb
Temesvár
Milan
Verona
Venice
Belgrade
Bordeaux
Turin
Genoa
Bologna
Zara
Naissus
Corunna
Oviedo
Bayonne
Toulouse
Avignon
Nice
Pisa
Florence
Spalato
Mostar
Marseille
Perugia
Oporto
Saragossa
Salamanca
Barcelona
Rome
Salonica
Bari
Naples
Taranto
Janina
Tuledo
Lisbon
Valencia
Caralis
Qurtubah (Córdova)
Ishbiliyah
Cartagena
Palermo
Messana
Qadis
Malaqah
Catana
Algiers
Tunis
56°
52°
48°
44°
40°
36°
N

were used to rule Cumbria. David ruled with a cosmopolitan knighthood, succeeding in feudalizing Scotland. This was a basis for centralized land tenure—feudal knight service—whereby knights given land gained revenue from the land and in return fought for their lord, garrisoned his castle, and were present at rituals. Of the new settler families given extensive land grants, many had names originating in Normandy, or were soldiers of William I who moved to Scotland. Amongst these, in their current spellings are Bruce, Stewart, Comyn, and Oliphant. David fulfilled a king's role by giving grants to land-hungry knights from any country. Not only did he gain greater control over his turbulent kingdom but also he created a cavalry force that had not existed previously.

The development of the Scottish Church by David continued his mother's work and saw the growth of territorial dioceses, grants of land to new religious orders including Tironensians, Cistercians, and Premonstratensians from France; abbots and bishops of the Scottish religious institutions bore Norman names, although these disappeared in the next century.

David's loyalty to Henry I of England continued through his daughter, Matilda, during the English war of succession after Henry's death. He fought against King Stephen of England, hoping to gain Northumberland. In 1136, he made peace with Stephen and gained Cumberland, while his son acquired Huntingdon by transfer, becoming Earl Henry. David was defeated at Northallerton, the Battle of the Standard, in 1138. The peace terms gave Northumberland to Earl Henry as a fief from Stephen. In another campaign David knighted Matilda's son, Henry Plantagenet, who later became King Henry II of England.

Compared with Scotland, Norman relationships with Wales were turbulent. Wales had been an anarchy of petty kingdoms but, by the time of the Conquest, four major kingdoms emerged: Gwynedd in the northwest, Powys in the northeast, Deheubarth (Dyfed) in the southwest and Glywysing (Morgannwg) in the south. Their size and influence changed but they were core leaders of Welsh resistance from 1066 to the Statute of Rhuddlan in 1284 (when King Edward I of England turned conquered Wales into an English principality). After Gruffudd ap Llywelyn became the first ruler of all Wales using Viking and English mercenaries, an English army was dispatched to Wales, defeating and killing Gruffud in 1063. Thereafter, north Welsh kings were appointed first by the English then the Normans, although the nature of the overlordship was scarcely defined.

After 1066, William I created the great palatine earldoms of Hereford (William Fitz Osbern), Shrewsbury (Roger de Montgomery), and Chester (Hugh d'Avranches): counties where lords had powers normally reserved by the crown. Taking advantage of the disunity of the Welsh Princes, they launched offensives against any Welsh ruler too weak to resist. Territories were passed on to their descendants as Marcher lordships. William II also encouraged the Marcher lords to penetrate eastern Wales. Every ford, bridge, and mountain pass was guarded by a castle, some 600, providing a tight-knit defensive system. The Normans introduced laws and culture into their territories administering justice and authority over a population effectively denied royal

The Great Seal of King Alexander II, 1214–1249, son of William I of Scotland. It portrays him as a knightly figure clutching a sword, astride his charger.

The Borders
1500–1600
English–Scottish border
Scottish border marches
English border marches
Castle
English royal castle
Main area of Reiver activity
Major Scottish campaign
Major English campaign
Debatable Land area
Main border crossing
HALLS Prominent border families
SCOTLAND
ENGLAND
North Sea
Solway Firth
Scottish East March
Scottish Middle March
Scottish West March
English East March
English Middle March
English West March
Palatinate of Durham
Edinburgh
Berwick (English from 1482)
Coldstream
Norham
Home
Etal
Bamburg
Peebles
HUMES
Smallholm
Kelso
Flodden
9 Sept 1513
Selkirk
Dunstanburgh
Cessford
Hawick
Ferniehurst
Alnwick
Branxholme
Warkworth
Hermitage
Harbottle
Coquetdale
Redesale
Sanquhar
OLIVERS
SCOTTS
CROSERS
TEITS
MILBURNS
ELIOTS
NIXONS
HALLS
FORESTERS
CHARLTONS
ROBSONS
MILBURNS
DODDS
ARMSTRONGS
Liddesdale
Teviotdale
Eskdale
Annandale
Tynedale
Morpeth
BEWCASTLE WASTE
FENWICKS
Dumfries
Lochmaben
GRAHAMS
MAXWELLS
JOHNSTONES
HETHERINGTONS
Bewcastle
Chipchase
Prudhoe
Newcastle Upon-Tyne
Caerlaverrock
Solway Moss
24 Nov 1542
Askerton
South Tyne
Hexham
Derwent
Threave
Carlisle
Naworth
CARLETONS
Durham
Eden
Wear
Kirksowald
Tees
Penrith
Brougham
Cockermouth
Appleby
Brough
Egremont
Kendal
Tweed
N
20 km
20 miles
3°30'
3°
2°30'
2°
1°30'
1°
56°
55°30'
55°

protection. The Marcher lords were brutal, acting like monarchs in their palatine lands, conquering and colonizing in a virtual imperial expansion, carving out "petty kingdoms" by the sword.

Elsewhere in Wales, native rulers continued to survive. Bleddyn ap Cynfyn, King of Gwynedd and Powys, died in 1075 and was succeeded by Gruffudd ap Cynan. Despite intense Norman military pressure he created a kingdom extending from Anglesey in the north to the Vale of Clwyd and south to the borders of Deheubarth. Dying aged 82 years, he was succeeded by his son, Owain Cyfeiliog. Rhys ap Tewdwr, last independent King of Deheubarth, was killed by the Normans in 1093 and succeeded by his son, Gruffudd, who made peace with Henry I, dying in 1137.

Norman control remained in the lowlands. The resilience of the Welsh princes, tested in mountainous terrain suited to guerrilla warfare, allied to the deadly Welsh longbow, prevented any further Norman conquest. This longbow was an early type of war bow, a precursor of those that English archers used to shoot down French knighthood in the Hundred Years War. The Marcher lords built castles as part of William The Conqueror's defensive plans for England, the first being Wigmore Castle. By the end of the 12th Century, the Normans were resident in south Wales, taking tribute from local populations and bringing English, Flemish, and Norman settlers into the south in Glamorgan, Gwent, the Gower, and Pembroke.

Wigmore Castle, a motte and bailey structure built by Marcher Lord William FitzOsbern between 1068–72. The castle was passed to Ralph de Mortimer, the most powerful Marcher Lord, when FitzOsbern's sons rebelled against King William I in 1075. This reconstruction shows the castle while under the ownership of Ralph de Mortimer's descendants.

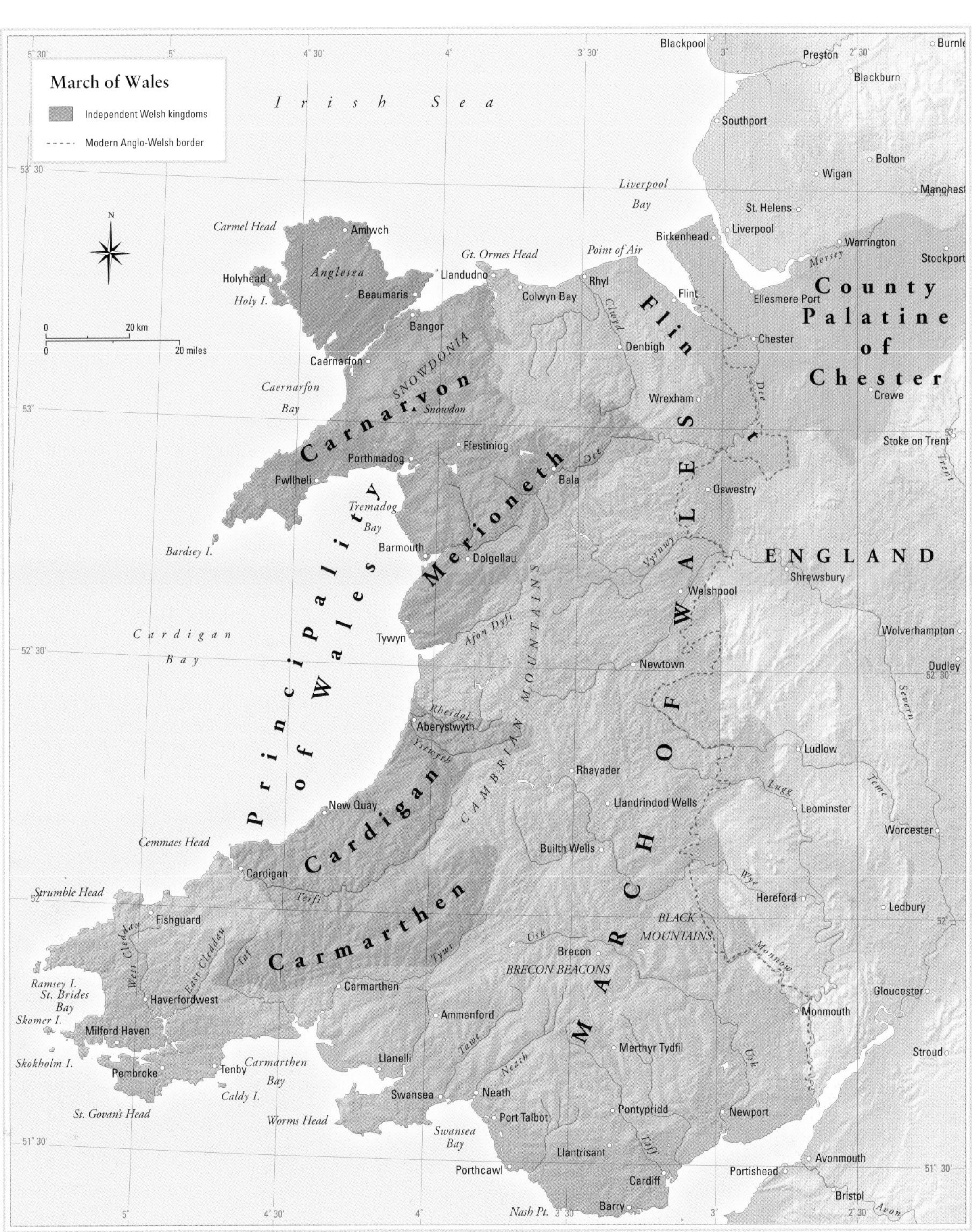
March of Wales
Independent Welsh kingdoms
Modern Anglo-Welsh border
Irish Sea
Liverpool Bay
Carmel Head
Anglesea
Holy I.
Gt. Ormes Head
Point of Air
Caernarfon Bay
SNOWDONIA
Snowdon
Carnarvon
Merioneth
Tremadog Bay
Bardsey I.
Principality of Wales
Cardigan Bay
Cardigan
Carmarthen
CAMBRIAN MOUNTAINS
Flint
MARCH OF WALES
County Palatine of Chester
ENGLAND
BLACK MOUNTAINS
BRECON BEACONS
Cemmaes Head
Strumble Head
Ramsey I.
St. Brides Bay
Skomer I.
Skokholm I.
St. Govan's Head
Carmarthen Bay
Caldy I.
Worms Head
Swansea Bay
Nash Pt.
Blackpool
Preston
Blackburn
Southport
Bolton
Wigan
St. Helens
Liverpool
Birkenhead
Warrington
Stockport
Amlwch
Holyhead
Beaumaris
Llandudno
Colwyn Bay
Rhyl
Flint
Ellesmere Port
Chester
Bangor
Caernarfon
Denbigh
Wrexham
Crewe
Ffestiniog
Porthmadog
Pwllheli
Bala
Oswestry
Stoke on Trent
Barmouth
Dolgellau
Shrewsbury
Welshpool
Tywyn
Wolverhampton
Newtown
Dudley
Aberystwyth
Ludlow
Rhayader
Llandrindod Wells
Leominster
New Quay
Worcester
Builth Wells
Cardigan
Hereford
Fishguard
Ledbury
Brecon
Carmarthen
Haverfordwest
Gloucester
Ammanford
Monmouth
Milford Haven
Merthyr Tydfil
Stroud
Llanelli
Pembroke
Tenby
Swansea
Neath
Port Talbot
Pontypridd
Newport
Llantrisant
Avonmouth
Porthcawl
Portishead
Cardiff
Bristol
Barry
Mersey
Clwyd
Dee
Trent
Vyrnwy
Afon Dyfi
Rheidol
Ystwyth
Severn
Lugg
Teme
Wye
Teifi
Usk
Tywi
Taf
East Cleddau
West Cleddau
Monnow
Tawe
Neath
Taff
Avon
0 20 km
0 20 miles
N

Conquest of Ireland

Diarmait MacMurchada's expulsion from Ireland in 1166 set in train a series of events that within ten years saw the kings of Ireland accept the King of England as their lord. Vast parts of the island fell into the hands of the Norman barons.

Wealth in the Middle Ages depended on good agricultural practice and bringing more land under the plough. Knights required revenue and rents from land to arm themselves and feed their households. As the population grew in the medieval west, knights raised more sons but only one would inherit; this was certainly so in England. Landless sons who became knights would only gain land as a gift from an ambitious lord, who would give his followers fiefs from conquered territories. Ireland was ruled by a pack of squabbling, tawdry little kings and in constant political ferment. It was, therefore, a ripe fruit fit for plucking by the Anglo-Norman knights. These ultimately victorious barons then had to fight to retain their territorial booty.

The Seal of Richard FitzGilbert de Clare, Lord of Pembroke, alias Strongbow. The Norman Marcher lord and leader of a group of Norman warrior knights was originally based in the Welsh border lands.

The year 1171 witnessed English King Henry II's intervention in Irish affairs by preventing an independent Irish-Norman Kingdom being established by Richard "Strongbow" FitzGilbert de Clare, Earl of Pembroke. Strongbow had seized the Kingdom of Leinster, plus the towns of Waterford, Wexford, and Dublin and part of the Kingdom of Meath. Henry II landed with his army at Waterford and Strongbow then offered to hold Leinster as a fief. The Kingdom was formally granted to him in return for homage, fealty, and the service of a hundred knights, while the king kept the city and Kingdom of Dublin and all seaports and fortresses. Meath was given to Hugh de Lacy (c. 1125–86), grandson of Walter de Lacy who fought at Hastings, who had accompanied Henry II's army to Ireland. De Lacy was decapitated by an assassin while pulling down a monastery to build a castle at Derrow. While traversing Munster to Dublin, the English King

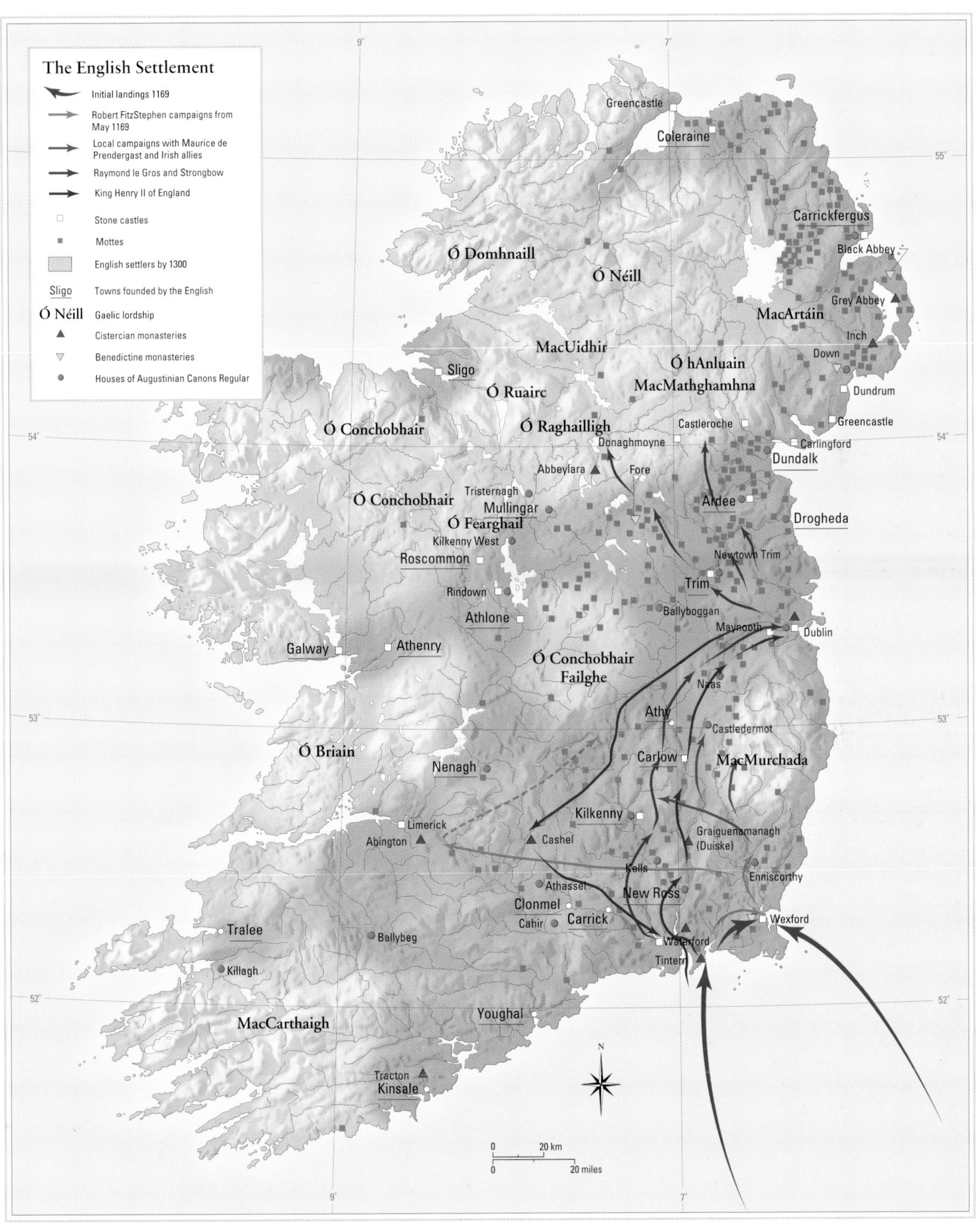

The English Settlement
Initial landings 1169
Robert FitzStephen campaigns from May 1169
Local campaigns with Maurice de Prendergast and Irish allies
Raymond le Gros and Strongbow
King Henry II of England
Stone castles
Mottes
English settlers by 1300
Sligo Towns founded by the English
Ó Néill Gaelic lordship
Cistercian monasteries
Benedictine monasteries
Houses of Augustinian Canons Regular
Greencastle
Coleraine
Carrickfergus
Black Abbey
Grey Abbey
Inch
Down
Dundrum
Greencastle
Carlingford
Dundalk
Ó Domhnaill
Ó Néill
MacArtáin
MacUidhir
Ó hAnluain
MacMathghamhna
Sligo
Ó Ruairc
Ó Raghailligh
Ó Conchobhair
Castleroche
Donaghmoyne
Abbeylara
Fore
Tristernagh
Mullingar
Ó Conchobhair
Ó Fearghail
Kilkenny West
Ardee
Drogheda
Roscommon
Newtown Trim
Trim
Rindown
Athlone
Ballyboggan
Maynooth
Dublin
Galway
Athenry
Ó Conchobhair Failghe
Naas
Athy
Castledermot
Ó Briain
Carlow
MacMurchada
Nenagh
Kilkenny
Limerick
Abington
Cashel
Graiguenamanagh (Duiske)
Kells
Enniscorthy
Athassel
New Ross
Clonmel
Cahir
Carrick
Wexford
Tralee
Ballybeg
Waterford
Tintern
Killagh
MacCarthaigh
Youghal
Tracton
Kinsale
N
0 20 km
0 20 miles
9°
7°
55°
54°
53°
52°

Giraldus Cambrensis (Gerald of Wales), the great historian of the English invasion of Ireland, warned of the Irish that "From an old and evil custom they always carry an axe in their hand as if it were a staff... Wherever they go they drag this along with them. When they see the opportunity, and the occasion presents itself, this weapon has not to be unsheathed as a sword, or bent as a bow, or poised as a spear. Without further preparation, beyond being raised a little, it inflicts a mortal blow. At hand, or rather in the hand, and ever ready, is that which is enough to cause death."

received submission and hostages, as well as promises of tribute, from seven Irish Kings. A church synod recognized his overlordship, a logical reaction since Pope Adrian IV, an Englishman, had granted Henry II and his successors with the right to rule Ireland.

The invading forces followed standard Norman practice in enemy territory and built motte and bailey fortifications, such as that at Clonard, Meath. This defensive settlement would be the focus for raids upon local Irish chieftains to destroy their power while rustling their cattle. Once the local Irish "king" was defeated from the Normans' easily defended forts, then the best Irish land could be sequestered and subdivided among the owner of the fort's minions in a process of subinfeudation. Other types of defenses were ringwork castles, like de Lacy's built at Trim.

The Anglo-Norman zone expanded and all Irish kings, except those of the northwest, recognized Henry II's supremacy. New Norman lordships were created in Ulster under John de Courci and in Munster under de Cogon, de Braose, and others. The 1175 Treaty of Windsor saw Ruaidrí Ua Conchobhair (Rory) O'Connor, the High King of Ireland, accepting Henry as his overlord and restricting his own title to just King of Connacht. Now that military conquest had been completed, the invaders pursued economic exploitation. The Anglo-Normans invested in imported agricultural systems, based on the economically efficient English manor home with its mixture of arable and pastoral farming. The Irish peasantry was not dispossessed, but labor was scarce; English peasants and artisans were recruited to colonize the land, tempted because land was at a premium in England and many were promised new farmland and better conditions of tenure.

Anglo-Norman economic development resulted in increased commercial activity as shown by the foundation of new towns by the ruling élite, such as Kinsale, Tralee, Galway, Sligo, Trim, Carrickfergus, Athlone, Athy, and Dundalk. New towns were accompanied by city walls and castles, as defenses and exercises in imperial and architectural domination. Apart from the new towns, castles were built at existing population centers. Woodland was cleared, arable land developed, crop rotation introduced. The agricultural surplus created increased domestic and foreign trade. A network of small market towns moved goods, especially in eastern Ireland, to provincial centers, then to ports and onward to England and continental Europe.

The failure of Rory O'Connor to resist Strongbow after he captured Dublin, and the loss of his army together with the submission of Irish Kings and Church to Henry II, did not mean that Irish resistance ended. However, savage reprisals ensured against armed resistance. This ruthless intimidation helped suppress raids against the new towns and settlements. O'Rourke, King of Bréifne, was murdered at the instigation of de Lacy on his way to negotiations in 1172. His head and decapitated body were placed on display on Dublin's walls. Thus, Kings who survived the Anglo-Norman juggernaut now knew that they had to work with the new ruling power to survive.

In many parts of England and Ireland mottes were raised on which were built defensive forts. This example is at Clonard, Meath, near to the existing monastic settlement.

Accommodation did not last. The 13th Century witnessed uncoordinated English territorial advances, despite promises of the English Kings that this would not happen. By the 1250s, the Irish reacted; in 1258 the chief Irish Kings challenged Anglo-

Norman rule by acclaiming Brian O'Neill (descendant of Rory) as High-King of Ireland. In 1260, his forces were defeated by the English at the Battle of Down, O'Neill's head being sent to publicly decorate the Tower of London as a warning.

King John visited Ireland in 1210 and established a civil government independent of the feudal lords. An Irish exchequer had been created in 1200, and a chancery followed in 1232. Ireland was divided into administrative counties, English law introduced, and attempts made to diminish the feudal "liberties" of the Anglo-Norman lords (lands held in personal control of aristocratic families and the Church). Parliament commenced and 1297 saw peers and prelates joining county representatives; in 1350 towns also sent members. The institution only represented the Anglo-Irish; the native Irish—in Ulster under the O'Neills and O'Donnells, and southwest Munster under the MacCarthys—were unrepresented.

English colonists failed to settle in large numbers and the Anglo-Normans failed to eradicate the most powerful Irish kings. Total conquest of Ireland was problematic. However, Anglo-Norman ambitions could not be extinguished and the late 1230s saw a large-scale invasion of Connacht

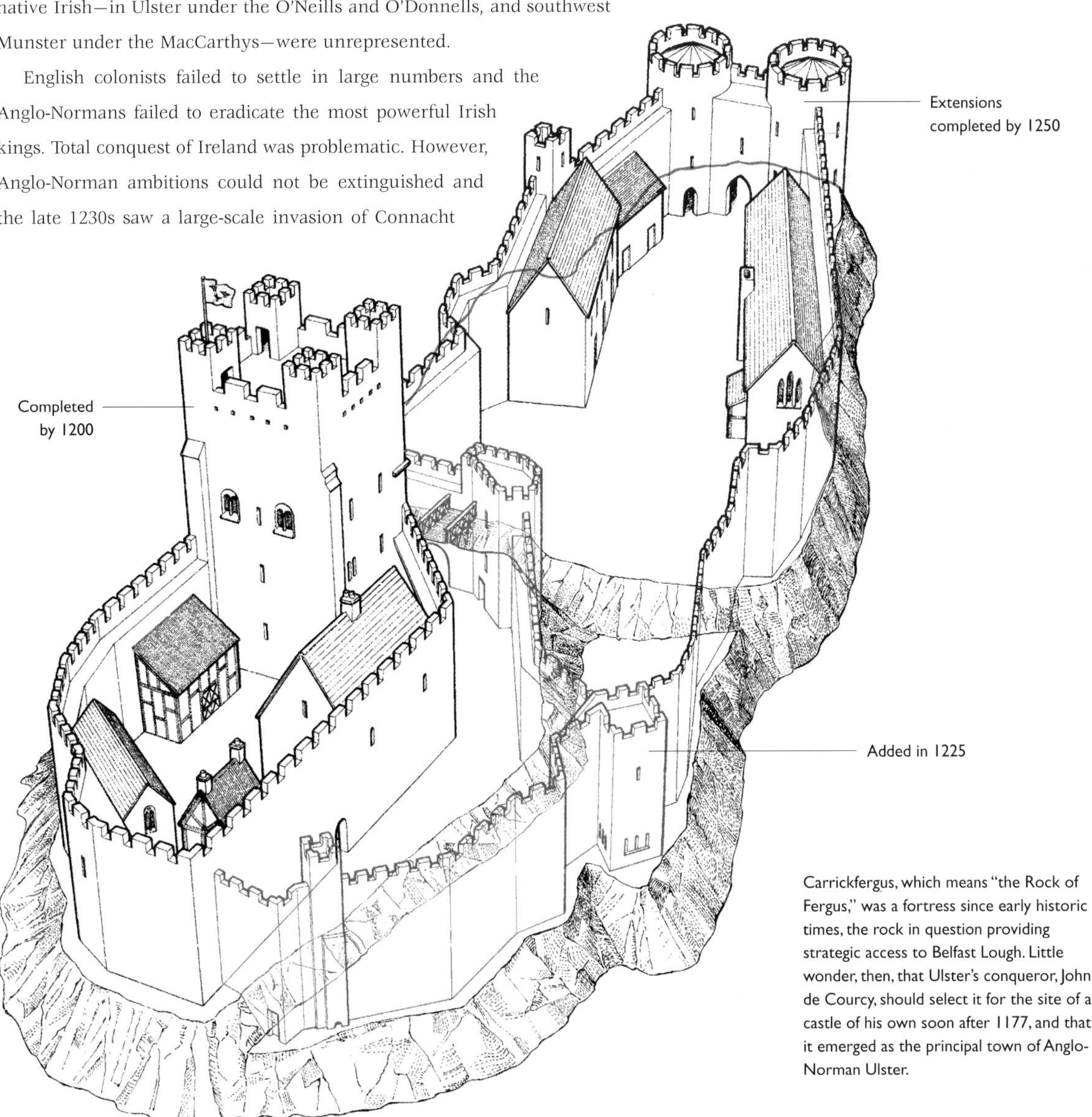

Carrickfergus, which means "the Rock of Fergus," was a fortress since early historic times, the rock in question providing strategic access to Belfast Lough. Little wonder, then, that Ulster's conqueror, John de Courcy, should select it for the site of a castle of his own soon after 1177, and that it emerged as the principal town of Anglo-Norman Ulster.

resulting in the creation of English colonies in places as remote as Mayo. This expansion could not continue because many able Anglo-Norman leaders in the 1240s left no sons to inherit their territorial dreams. Additionally, the MacMurroughs of the Wicklow Mountains, from the 1270s, attacked up to the walls of Dublin, the center of English royal government in Ireland. The 1297 parliament reported that settlers were beginning to lose their culture and take on that of the native Irish.

Ireland was threatened by Edward Bruce, brother of King Robert I of Scotland, who invaded Ulster in 1315, joining the O'Neills in an attempt to drive out the English settler population. Despite failing to win unanimous Irish support, Bruce defeated English forces several times and almost captured Dublin. The Scots threat was ended with the defeat and death of Bruce at the Battle of Forbart in 1318.

During the Bruce wars, a decisive battle occurred at Athenry in August 1316. Felim O'Connor (King of Connacht 1310–16) wanted to make himself Supreme King of Connacht and kick out the Anglo-Normans to win back lands lost in 1232. He was joined by the petty Kings of Meath, Bréifne, Annelly, Leney, Ui Maine, Ui Tiachrach Muaidhe, and Munster. Some 20,000 men faced the Connacht Normans and their main leaders, Richard de Burgh, Earl of Ulster, and Lord Bermingham of Athenry. The Irish suffered 10,000 casualties, including five kings killed, mown down by archers and the armored might of mounted knights, leaving Connacht in Norman hands.

A stylized image of an Anglo-Norman knight. He is Thomas de Cantwell in Kilfane church, County Kilkenny, Ireland.

The Bruce invasion and defeat revealed the latent strength of the English presence. The settlers were united against the Bruce onslaught despite Bruce's bullying tactics to loosen their allegiance to the English king. The settlers considered themselves superior to the "barbarian" Irish. Facing this conquering self-esteem, the Irish waited for further opportunities to improve their condition. English control was augmented by the creation of three new Anglo-Irish earldoms: Kildare, given to the head of the Leinster Fitzgeralds; Ormonde, granted to the head of the Butlers who held lands around Tipperary; and Desmond, gifted to the head of the Munster Fitzgeralds.

The Irish economy was weakened by the Bruce wars, famine between 1315–1317, and the arrival of the Black Death in 1348–49. Absentee landlords and the resident nobility caught up in feuds, and large numbers of skilled peasants returning to England enabled the Irish to reconquer frontiers. Another major Irish weapon was a cultural victory. So worried were the English that Edward III's son, Lionel, Duke of Clarence, viceroy from 1361–1367, passed the Statutes of Kilkenny. The English were forbidden to speak Irish or marry Irish. Irish outside the obedient Pale were dubbed enemies holding land through usurpation. Other statutes forbade the wearing of Irish clothes or hair styles, selling food or horses to the Irish in time of war and weapons in times of peace. In reality the Irish were feared, attacks against and beleaguered English outposts were occasionally bought off by payments in gold.

English defensiveness responded to a resurgent Gaelic culture seeking to recoup its losses since 1170.

This contemporary illustration shows a meeting between the representatives of Richard II and Diarmait MacMurchada, the king of Leinster. The English, led by the Earl of Gloucester, are depicted heavily armored, the Irish King considerably less so.

By the end of the 13th Century, educated Gaelic families began a cultural journey writing poetry, legal commentaries, translations of European medical treatises, and works of genealogy and Irish history. In some ways, the Irish revival was nostalgic seeking to provide links with the archaic past and a continuity with the present. Gaelic culture became so strong that it appealed to leading Anglo-Norman families like the de Burghs, Butlers, and Fitzgeralds.

During the years 1360 to 1369 the English Crown poured time and money into Ireland. Edward II's son, Lionel of Clarence, was viceroy for five years and Richard II of England visited Ireland twice in the 1390s. Richard was deposed in 1399 and his successors were not interested enough in Ireland to invest money in it. Instead, the Crown became reliant on aristocratic families; the Butlers of Ormond and the Fitzgeralds of Desmond and Kildare, they to steer parliament, represent the Crown's interests, and defend the Anglo-Norman settlement. The knight had his feudal duties to perform across the whole of Ireland except the Gaelic lands of the north and west.

The Great Seal of the town of Athenry, Galway, shows two severed heads thought to represent the heads of Irish kings who were slain in battle.

Southern Italy and Sicily

THE WARRIOR-ARISTOCRACY OF NORMANDY FOUGHT IN MOST EUROPEAN THEATERS OF WAR. POPULATION PRESSURE, GREED AND ADVENTURE DROVE WARRIORS INTO DISTANT LANDS IN THE 10TH CENTURY, EVEN INTO THE SOUTHERN ITALIAN PENINSULA AND SICILY WHERE, OPPORTUNITIES BECKONED.

Norman knights followed their lords on any opportunity that could lead to lands and wealth to call their own, driven not by chivalry but the pursuit of power.

Daring landless Norman knights penetrated deep into southern Italy and Sicily. At the beginning of the 11th Century, Byzantium regarded southern Italy as part of its territory but reality was different. Greeks ruled in southern Italy, Apulia and Calabria but Sicily was a Saracen-controlled island with a mixed Christian and Muslim population. Amalfi, Naples, and Gaeta were independent city states, developing through trade links with north Africa and mainland Europe. Salerno, Capua, and Benevento were Lombard principalities owing to Byzantium, so the Greeks thought. Southern Italy was anarchic, fertile ground for Norman adventurers.

In 1016 a few Norman pilgrims returning from Palestine via Italy witnessed the Prince of Salerno fighting against the Muslims, and saw that Melo, Duke of Apulia, required recruits for his private wars. The Normans were hired as reinforcements, becoming mercenaries and later bandits who terrified Greeks, Muslims, Lombards, and Italians alike. They acquired

Roger II, King of Sicily 1130-54. Born in 1095, the son of Count Richard I of Sicily, he defeated the papal forces at the battle of Benivento and became Duke of Apulia in 1128. On becoming king he introduced a series of new laws and established a strong central government creating in Sicily a major regional power.
Here we see Richard dressed more as a Byzantine king than his Norman knightly roots.

Alongside the knights went foot soldiers, who in return for loyal service might hope for elevation to the knighthood or at least a living within the lord's private army.

a permanent base at Aversa in 1030, seizing Melfi in 1041. Prominent amongst the Normans were three sons of Tancred de Hauteville, a minor Norman baron, who won many battles. They were outshone by the eldest son of Tancred's second marriage, Robert Guiscard, determined to create his own principality. The year 1053 was a turning point in Robert's life. The strongest of the Hauteville brothers died leaving Robert as the main Norman leader in Italy. At the same time the Normans had begun conquest of Apulia and Calabria from the Byzantines, who appealed to the pope for help. Pope Leo IX was defeated and captured by Robert's troops at the Battle of Civatate the same year. Although outnumbered two to one, Robert's cavalry charge caused most of the pope's infantry to flee; the remaining battle was a mop-up operation against the papal cavalry.

Political forces realigned in Italy. In 1059, Pope Nicholas II, at the Investure of Melfi, granted Robert Guiscard with Calabria, Apulia, and Sicily, and Richard Count of Aversa with Capua. Robert was now empowered to conquer southern Italy from the Byzantines and Sicily from the Muslims. Calabria fell in 1060 with the capture of Reggio, although the conquest of Apulia was delayed until 1071, when the local Byzantine capital, Bari, fell. Robert Guiscard gave his brother, Roger, the task of conquering Sicily. A bridgehead was established at Messina in

Norman Campaigns in the Mediterranean
1053–1108

Byzantine Empire c. 1050
Muslim territory c. 1050
Town besieged, or blockaded with date
Land battle
Port
Trani 1063 Town conquered by Normans with date
Norman expeditions:
1061
1064
1071
1081
1084
1107
Sea battle, Venetian victory
Sea battle, Norman victory
Norman acquisitions:
to 1059
to 1085
to 1130
to 1154

1061 and troops ferried to Sicily despite the presence of an Arab fleet. Victory at Cerami in 1063 gave him control of Val Demone. He threatened Palermo, which surrendered in 1072, although Muslim resistance continued until 1091.

After Roger Guiscard's death in 1085, Sicily became the main source of Norman power, reaching its height under his brother Roger II in 1103. Meanwhile, Guiscard's son Roger Borsa misruled southern Italy while his brother, Bohemond, joined the First Crusade (1099–1100), becoming Prince of Antioch. Roger II was a child when his father died, but his father had created a strong state which survived into his son's majority in 1112. His mother, Adelaide del Vasto, left for Palestine in 1113 to marry King Baldwin I, becoming Queen of Jerusalem. This left Roger II in effective control of Sicily.

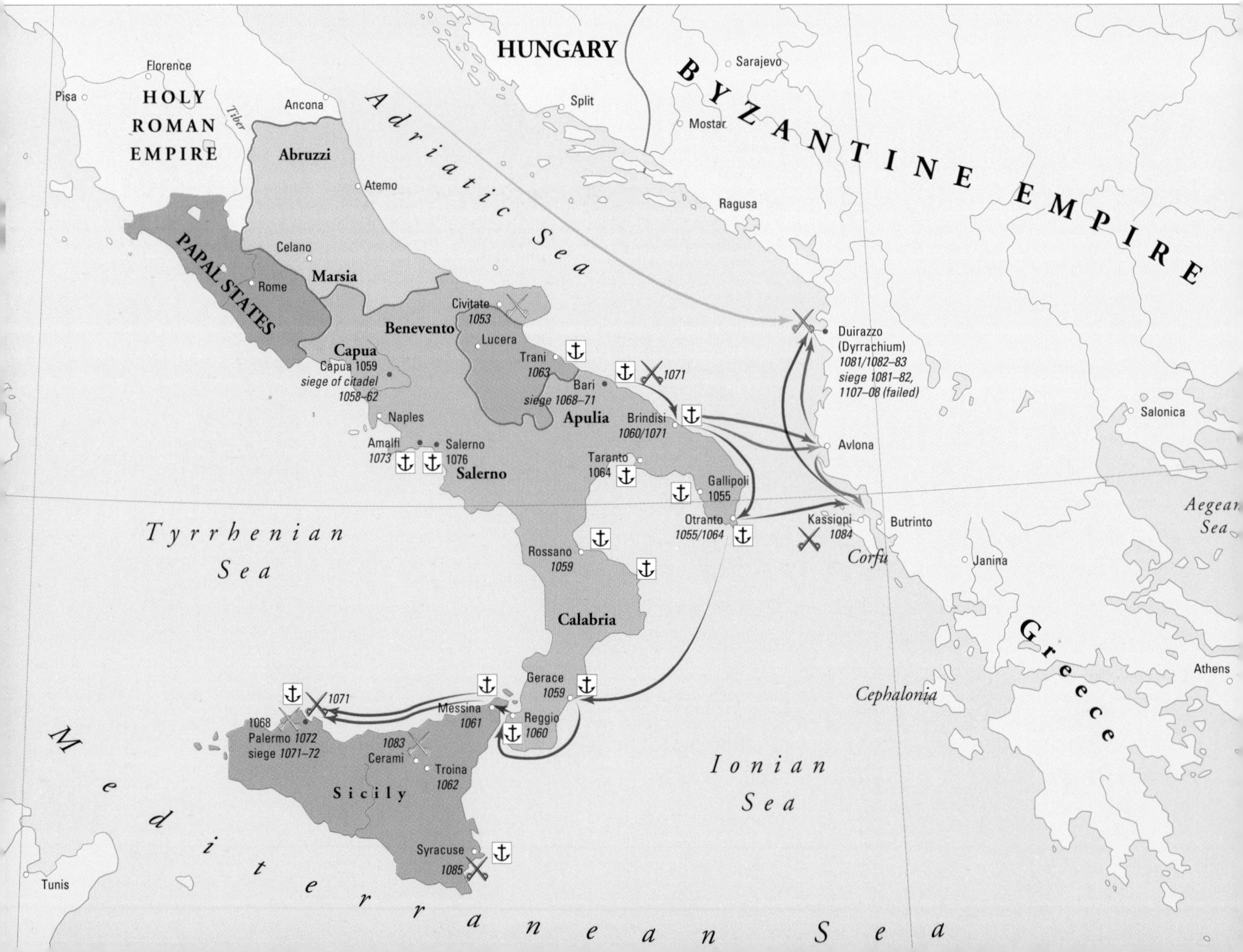

Roger, born in the Mediterranean region, appreciated the many facets of his subjects, whether Greek, Sicilian, Norman, or Muslim. Greeks were used as administrators and Muslims formed the core of his army. The descendants of the Norman Guiscards requested aid from Roger II to control their rebellious baronage in Apulia and Calabria. His military might was bought with their mainland territories. By 1122, Roger had Calabria and in 1127, when Duke William of Apulia died without issue, Roger laid claim to the Duchy. Control took many years and Roger backed the antipope Anacletus in the Papal Schism,

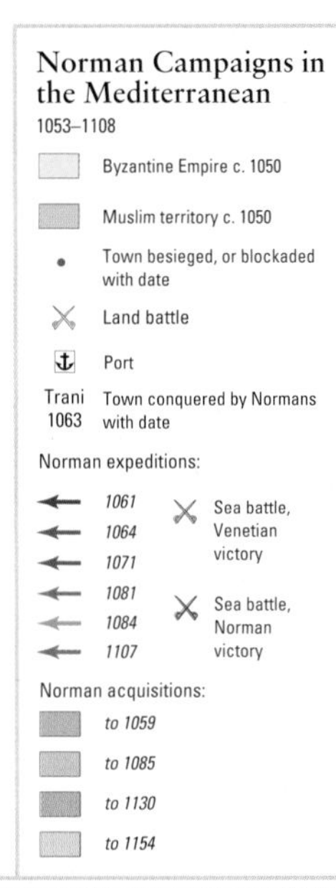

being given the title of King of Sicily and of the duchies of Apulia and Calabria. In 1137, he was ousted from the mainland by rebellious barons allying with the Holy Roman Emperor Lothar. The Emperor died that year and Anacletus the next. Pope Innocent II took the field against Roger but was defeated and captured at Galluccio in 1139. The pope was then forced to confirm Roger as King of Sicily with a mainland overlordship of all Italy south of the Garigliano River.

King Roger II was an unusual man, head of a multilingual state, who believed in the autocratic divine right of monarchy; he ensured a stable Sicily by allowing only small, scattered fiefdoms. A guide to his character can be found in the mosaic in the Church of Martorana, where he is shown in Byzantine robes being symbolically crowned by Christ. His state was run with great financial efficiency, the king himself checking the exchequer account rolls. He created a civil service based upon Norman, Greek, and Arabic models. Eventually, Arabs were left to finance, while the navy was mainly Greek. Its head was called the Emir of Emirs, from which is derived the naval rank of admiral. The king's fleet protected Sicily but was to acquire much of contemporary Tunisia in a short-lived African Empire. Roger seized Corfu and had his fleet kidnap Theban silk workers to found a court silk workshop in Palermo. Sicily was the only place in Europe where a student could study both Greek and Arabic, the latter being the scientific language of the day. Sicily kept out of the Second Crusade, Roger being tolerant with both his Christian and Muslim subjects. By his death in 1154, Sicily was a prosperous kingdom with a unique political and religious climate wherein all races, creeds, and cultures enjoyed almost complete equality, ruled over by the descendent of a Norman adventurer knight who considered himself a kind of Mediterranean King.

The Italian and Sicilian story best exemplifies the qualities of ambitious, landless knights: go out into the world with sword and lance seizing and holding foreign lands in company with like-minded knights; "enfeoff" your followers (give freehold land or property in return for pledged service) and rule with an iron hand; use the best characteristics of your knightly band and conquered peoples to blend a new society open to cosmopolitan ideas and faiths.

Pope Innocent III, born c.1160 of noble parents, was educated at Bologna and Paris and when only 37 years old was elected Pope. Unlike previous Popes he believed strongly in the supremacy of the papacy and consistently promoted the theory of Papal Power. He saw himself as the judge of all men but judged by none, and was the first to assume the title of Vicar of Christ. He sought to reinvigorate the papacy both politically and spiritually. He challenged the greatest of European powers, and excommunicated King John of England following his refusal to accept the papal nominee as Archbishop of Canterbury. It was this powerful individual who turned his gaze on the Norman Kingdoms of southern Sicily and Italy, seeking to reassert papal influence and bringing the local Norman lords to heel.

THE ANGEVIN EMPIRE 1154–1204

THE 17-YEAR-OLD FULK NERRA OF ANJOU, FRANCE, COMMENCED A LIFETIME OF VIOLENCE WITH HIS MIXTURE OF BRUTALITY, UNSCRUPULOUSNESS, CHRISTIAN HUMILITY, AND REPENTANCE. HE MADE HIS CAPITAL AT ANGERS AND FORTIFIED HIS DOMAINS WITH STONE-BUILT CASTLES AND DEFENSE TOWERS.

The Castle of Loches, built by Fulk III Nerra in the 11th Century. The rectangular donjon (tower), standing 121 feet (37 meters) tall, dominates the area and was designed to defend the southern borders of Anjou.

A key figure in the history of Anjou, the home of the Angevin dynasty, was Fulk III Nerra (c. 970–1040). A powerful ruler, Fulk fought with the Celtic Bretons to secure his western borders, coming into conflict in the east where he faced Eudes II, Count of Blois. Success against this enemy brought him control of Saumur in 1026. No stereotypical knightly qualities existed in Fulk's character but, although he burnt and looted monasteries, he felt need for penance, making pilgrimages to Palestine. He founded and restored several abbeys, notably at Angers, Saumur, and Loches. Fulk became well known for building stone castles rather than timber and earth types. He opened up the unoccupied fertile river valley in Anjou, moving in surplus populations from Angevin villages and defending these lands with castles. Again, this exemplifies how knights depended on agricultural revenue. Extra castles meant that more knights could be employed as troops. Land, wealth and security were inextricably linked.

The fortunes of Fulk Nerra's County of Anjou began to suffer after 1060 when its count, Geoffrey Martel (1006–60), died without issue, causing civil war between his two nephews, Geoffrey the Bearded (d. 1096) and Fulk the Surly (1043–1109). Fulk won, becoming count Fulk IV, but Anjou was so weakened that the King of France seized the Gâtinais, William VIII recovered Saintonge and William of Normandy grabbed Maine. The count's son, Fulk V The Young (1089-1143) became count in 1109, keeping quiescent with Anjou and Touraine, seeming content with his southern borders on the Loire. Recovering Maine from Normandy was his ambition and he acquired part, Le Mans, in 1110. He remained loyal to the King of France in the hope that his lord would help him regain the rest of Maine.

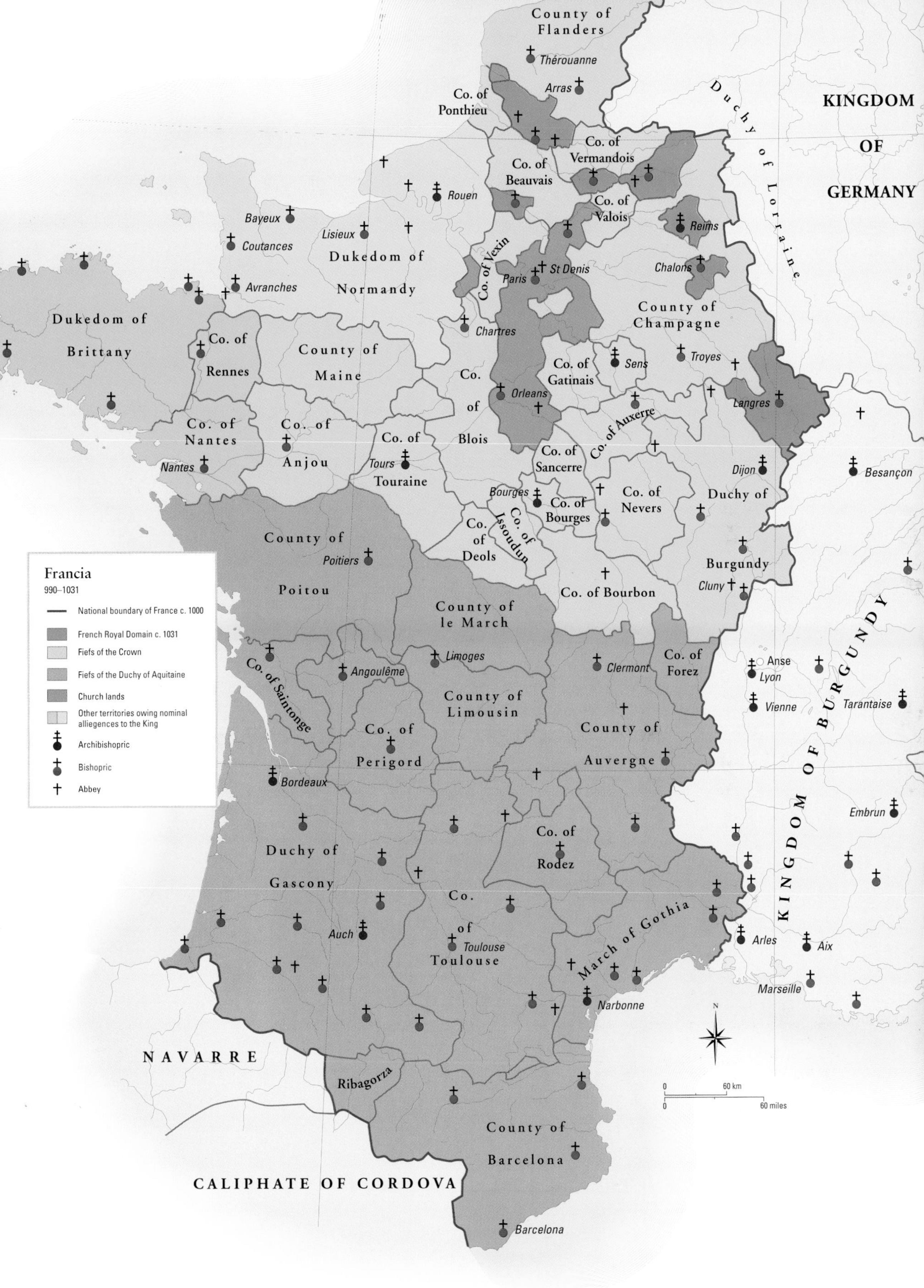

Francia
990–1031
National boundary of France c. 1000
French Royal Domain c. 1031
Fiefs of the Crown
Fiefs of the Duchy of Aquitaine
Church lands
Other territories owing nominal alliegences to the King
Archibishopric
Bishopric
Abbey
County of Flanders
Thérouanne
Arras
Co. of Ponthieu
KINGDOM OF GERMANY
Duchy of Lorraine
Co. of Vermandois
Co. of Beauvais
Co. of Valois
Rouen
Reims
Bayeux
Lisieux
Coutances
Dukedom of Normandy
Co. of Vexin
St Denis
Paris
Chalons
Avranches
Dukedom of Brittany
County of Champagne
Chartres
Co. of Rennes
County of Maine
Co. of Gatinais
Sens
Troyes
Co. of Blois
Orleans
Langres
Co. of Auxerre
Co. of Nantes
Co. of Anjou
Co. of Touraine
Tours
Nantes
Co. of Sancerre
Dijon
Besançon
Bourges
Co. of Bourges
Co. of Nevers
Duchy of Burgundy
Co. of Deols
Co. of Issoudun
County of Poitou
Poitiers
Cluny
Co. of Bourbon
County of le March
KINGDOM OF BURGUNDY
Co. of Saintonge
Angoulême
Limoges
Clermont
Co. of Forez
Anse
Lyon
Vienne
Tarantaise
County of Limousin
County of Auvergne
Co. of Perigord
Bordeaux
Embrun
Co. of Rodez
Duchy of Gascony
Co. of Toulouse
Toulouse
Auch
March of Gothia
Arles
Aix
Marseille
Narbonne
N
NAVARRE
Ribagorza
0
60 km
60 miles
County of Barcelona
CALIPHATE OF CORDOVA
Barcelona
5°

Far right: This contemporary illustration shows Henry II, King of England from 1154, who ruled for 35 years. Born in Le Mans, France in 1133, Henry became Duke of Normandy in 1150, and Count of Anjou and Maine a year later. Henry married Eleanor of Aquitaine in 1152, making him one of the most powerful men in France. King Stephen of England recognised Henry as his heir in 1153.

In 1127, Henry I of England and Fulk V of Anjou renounced their enmity, forming a marriage alliance: Henry's son, William, would marry Fulk's daughter. However, William drowned sailing to France in 1120. King Henry had a daughter, Matilda, who had married Holy Roman Emperor Henry V. When Henry died childless in 1125, Matilda was summoned back to England. King Henry's barons were persuaded to recognize her as their future sovereign. Her marriage to Fulk's son and heir, Geoffrey of Anjou, was arranged and consummated in 1128. This left Fulk free to go on pilgrimage, leaving his county in Geoffrey's hands. Fulk later married the daughter of the King of Jerusalem, Baldwin II, succeeding his father-in-law as King of Jerusalem in 1131.

Civil war was raging in England between King Stephen of Blois and Matilda over the succession after the death of Henry I; the Count of Anjou supported his wife seizing Normandy, which he gave to his son, Henry. His lands, however, were invaded by Louis VII of France in support of Stephen. Henry lost the Norman county of Vexin, including Gisors after a French campaign against him. In the English civil war lawlessness was rife: bands of knights roamed the countryside spoiling for a fight and loot; many illegally built castles as defenses against robber knights and unfriendly neighbours. These castles were often reduced by siege by King Stephen, a successful siege commander.

Meanwhile, Louis VII went on crusade accompanied by his wife, Eleanor of Aquitaine, who scandalized Europe by taking along 300 women dressed as Amazons. Suspected of licentious behaviour and infidelity, Eleanor enjoyed brief reconciliation with her husband, producing a second daughter. In 1151, when Henry of Normandy was in Paris signing the agreement to hand over Vexin, he attracted Eleanor's attention, causing King Louis to become so jealous that he had the

Orford Castle, Suffolk, England, built in 1165 on a coastal site personally selected by Henry II. At £1,400 it was the most costly of his building projects to date. The stone for its outer facing was brought from Caen in Normandy.

marriage annulled. Eleanor moved to Aquitaine and met Henry, who had succeeded his father as Count of Anjou. They married in 1152, causing Aquitaine to pass from the French crown to unite with Anjou.

Rather than allying with King Stephen in England, King Louis arranged a truce between the warring sides allowing Henry to land in England, where he persuaded Stephen to accept him as his heir. In October 1154 Henry became Henry II, King of England, Duke of Aquitaine, Duke of Normandy, Count of Anjou, Maine, and Tourraine, with more extensive territories than the King of France.

Henry II strengthened his power further in the typical medieval way: force, inheritance claim, and by marriage. Henry desired Brittany with its extended Channel coast. His brother Geoffrey gained lordship of Nantes, an important Breton city, in 1156. He died childless in 1158, thereby providing Henry II the opportunity to claim succession and suzerainty over Brittany, a move sanctioned by King Louis of France. In 1173, Count Raymond of Toulouse paid homage to Henry and Eleanor's son, Richard. Aquitaine was augmented by the acquisition of the Auvergne and Henry gained a controlling position in Berry too. In 1177 he purchased the county of La Marche.

Planned marriages gave Henry II influence in the courts of Europe. In 1168 his eldest daughter, Matilda, married Henry the Lion, Duke of Saxony; his second daughter, Eleanor, married King Alfonso VIII of Castile; and in 1177 Joan, the youngest, married King William II of Sicily. Henry hoped the engagement of his son, John, to the heiress of Humbert III of Savoy might offer up opportunities for Angevin meddling but she died before the marriage. Henry II was in a stronger position in France and more influential in Europe than was the King of France. Like all sensible rulers, he attempted to increase his territory to acquire more wealth and grant fiefs to increase his knight force. A marital network gave him influence abroad. Power and money meant everything.

The Rise of Anjou and Henry II

THE VAST DISPARATE ANGEVIN TERRITORIAL HOLDINGS WERE KEPT TOGETHER AT THE COST OF CONTINUOUS VIGILANCE AND HIGH EXPENDITURE. THE FRENCH KINGS COULD MAKE NO INROADS ON THIS DYNASTIC "EMPIRE," DESPITE THEORETICALLY BEING OVERLORDS OF THE EUROPEAN COMPONENTS.

Henry II's domains were disparate in type and heritage. Hence, in Aquitaine he ruled as a customary duke while in Anjou as a count. So, the empire was built on politically different territories not on political unity. In England, he enjoyed a certain stability and was not faced with the constant rebellions confronting him on mainland Europe.

Historians recognize that Henry was an intelligent man who desired to improve England after the 25 years of anarchy under Stephen. He presided over an economic boom and growth of urbanization. Henry was literate and spoke to scholars, being interested in developing the legal system of common law, administered by royal courts whose authority superseded the jurisdiction of local or baronial courts; he aimed not just at law but justice. He grasped the problem of land tenure, stating that the disputes between the king's tenants-in-chief should come under the jurisdiction of the king's court. Here, he wished to end the knightly banditry plaguing England during the civil war and crush the normal territorial squabbles between rival lords and knights.

Henry's legal decrees grounded England in the judge and jury system, which became customary and gradually eradicated trial by combat and ordeal as a method to obtain a legal verdict. The move towards a monarchical bureaucracy transcended the feudal monarchy, especially with use of scutage (money paid by a vassal to his lord in lieu of military service) and the royal courts for private legal suits. Henry was a transitional figure in a move toward the vestiges of a parliamentary system. This was having a fundamental effect on the feudal system and the place of the knight in society. Henry used his friend and chancellor, Thomas Becket, to rein in the turbulent baronage, slighting castles

The Plantagenet Empire
1151–1226
Boundary of Plantagenet Empire in France 1154
Lands ruled by Stephen to 1154
Lands ruled by Henry of Anjou before 1151
Lands aquired by Henry II on his father's death
Lands aquired by Henry II by marriage to Eleanor of Aquitaine 1152
Extensions to the domain under Henry II 1154–1189
Territory disputed between Henry II of England and Louis VII of France
Boundary of Plantagenet Empire in France 1226
County of Toulouse
Archdiocese
Diocese
Important monastery
Major Plantagenet castle
SCOTLAND
IRELAND
1171 overlordship of Henry II reconnized
ENGLAND
Northern Counties
1157 Henry II recovers land from Malcolm IV of Scotland
Brittany
Came under Henry II's control in 1171 by marriage of his son Geoffrey to Constance of Brittany
North Sea
English Channel
ATLANTIC OCEAN
Bay of Biscay
Ulster
Connaught
Meath
Leinster
Munster
Normandy
Maine
Anjou
Touraine
Poitou
La Marche
Limousin
Aquitaine
Saintonge
Perigord
Gascony
Armagnac
Agenais
Quercy
Toulouse
Flanders
Hainault
Vermandois
Champagne
Gatinais
Nivernais
Burgundy
Bourbonnais
Auvergne
Ventadour
Turenne
Velay
Gevaudan
Foix
Bigorre
Brabant
Castile
Navarre
Kelso
Ayr
Roxburgh
Dumfries
Newcastle
Carlisle
Durham
Richmond
Armagh
Lancaster
York
Granard
Pontefract
Tuam
Athlone
Dublin
Rhuddlan
Deganwy
Conisbrough
Beaumaris
Chester
Lincoln
Caernarvon
Hawarden
Nottingham
Conway
St Asaph
Birr
Timahoe
Athy
Limerick
Shrewsbury
Litchfield
Norwich
Leighlin
Leicester
Cashel
Ardfinnan
Aberystwyth
Coventry
Ely
Bury St Edmunds
Lismore
Waterford
Builth
Worcester
Cardigan
Evesham
Cork
Hereford
St Davids
Oxford
Colchester
Pembroke
Gloucester
St Albans
London
Thames
Llandaff
Bath
Canterbury
Rochester
Dover
Wells
Salisbury
Winchester
Chichester
Southampton
Exeter
N
0 150 km
0 150 miles
Boulogne
Tournai
Amiens
Cherbourg
Barfleur
Rouen
Oise
Reims
Château Gaillard
Bec
Bayeux
Caen
Lisieux
Evreux
Paris
Marne
Tinchebrai
St Pol de Léon
Treguier
St Milo
Avranches
Sées
Mt. St Michel
St Brieuc
Dol
Troyes
Le Mans
Rennes
Quimper
Orléans
Loire
Blois
Vannes
Angers
Tours
Fontevrault
Chinon
Bourges
Nantes
Issoudun
Poitiers
St Savin
La Rochelle
Clermont-Ferrand
Limoges
Saintes
Angoulême
Perigueux
Le Puy
Souillac
Bordeaux
Conques
Mende
Cahors
Bazas
Agen
Garonne
Maissac
Rodez
Albi
Lodeve
Aire
Dax
Auch
Toulouse
Bayonne
Beziers
Carcassonne
Agde
Lescar
Tarbes
Conserans
Narbonne
Oloron
Comminges
Elne
Mediterranean Sea

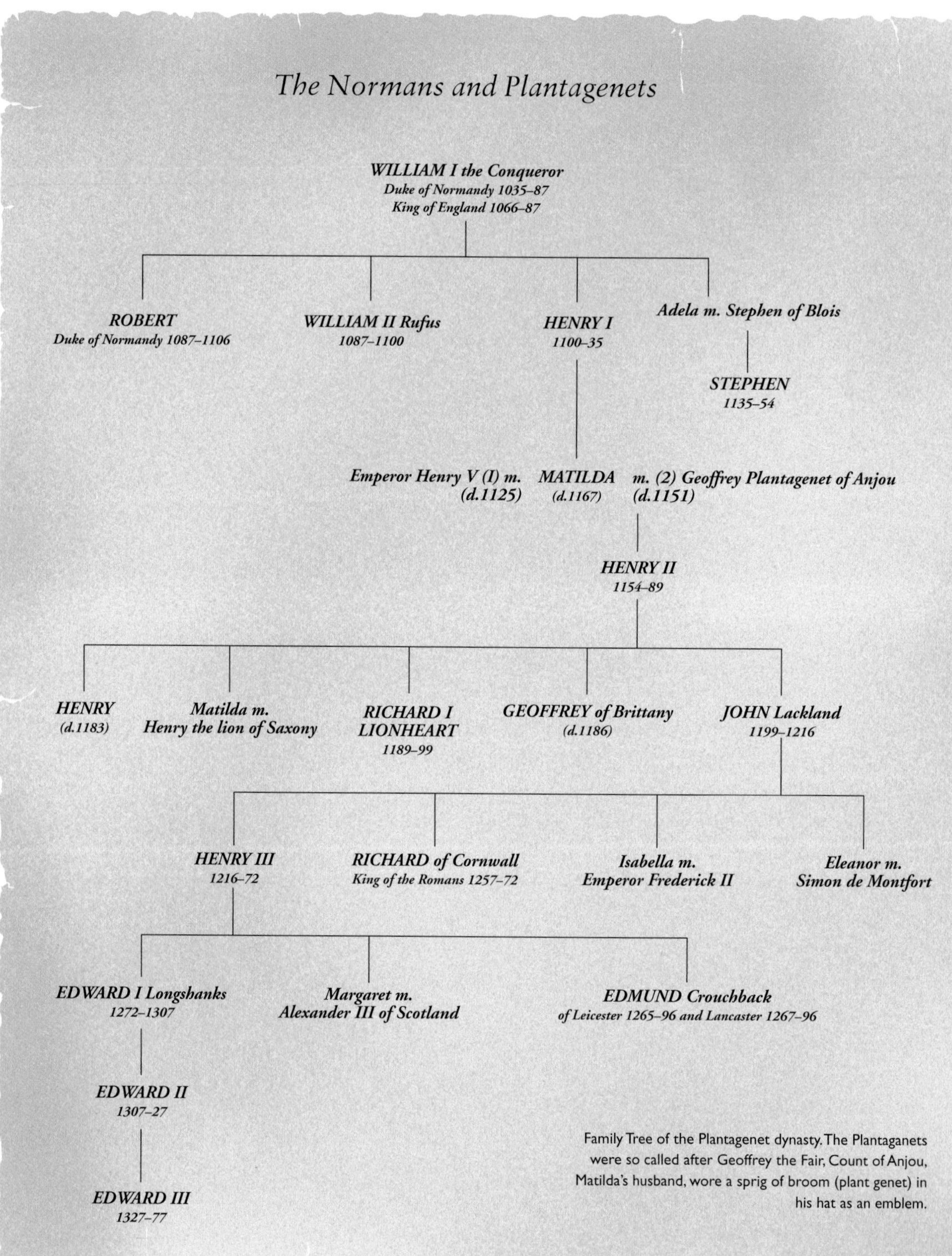

Family Tree of the Plantagenet dynasty. The Plantaganets were so called after Geoffrey the Fair, Count of Anjou, Matilda's husband, wore a sprig of broom (plant genet) in his hat as an emblem.

(razing parts so they become indefensible) and generally restoring order. His system of government was based upon Anglo-Norman institutions, which provided the necessary organization and bureaucracy to run the state. The king had a council of barons with an inner group being the judges and accountants who ran the Exchequer, the receptacle for taxes due from the shires paid over by the royal local representative, the shire-reeve (sheriff). The king was fortunate in his barons, some of whom were great civil servants, such as Robert of Beaumont, Earl of Leicester; Nigel, Bishop of Ely; and Ranulf de Glanville, the chief justiciar (administrator of justice).

In 1164, the Constitutions of Clarendon were promulgated that claimed to reassert the old rights of the king over the Church in matters such as clerical immunity, appointment of bishops, custody of vacant sees, excommunication, and appeals to Rome. Becket, who had become archbishop in 1161, refused to accept these demands and in the resulting battle neither would give way. Henry's concern was the country's judicial system and his program laid down in the 1166 Assize of Clarendon, which established a new jury system, judicial circuits, and swift justice based upon a fee. The conflict with Thomas Becket over legal jurisdiction was ended by the archbishop's murder at the altar of Canterbury Cathedral in 1170, a crime of sacrilege. Becket became a martyr and was canonized, with Canterbury becoming a pilgrimage center, described by Chaucer in *The Canterbury Tales*. Henry had not ordered the murder, even though his anger had prompted it. Nevertheless, he performed penance, walking barefoot through the streets of Canterbury and submitting to a ceremonial flogging. Although humiliated, he achieved most of his aims. He won control of appointments to Church offices in England, and by the end of his reign royal justice had made major inroads on the jurisdiction of Church courts. Centralization was being achieved.

This enamel reliquary shows the scene of the martyrdom of St. Thomas Becket.

The Angevin Empire was an economic and cultural empire too. Prosperous communities lined the valleys of the Seine, Loire, and Garonne rivers ensuring that surplus crops and goods could be grown and moved by river. Centers of learning art, architecture, poetry, and music were established; Eleanor was a patron of the latter in the culture of courtly love and the troubadour. Western France was home to production of wine and salt, which could be exchanged for English wool. Profits accrued to the lord ruling these domains. Commercial ties were aided by the growth of ports at London, Southampton, and Bristol in England, and Rouen, La Rochelle, Bordeaux, and Bayonne in France. Marine technology produced the cog, a large, roundish ship suitable for carrying considerable amounts of cargo.

The reigns of Henry II and his son, Richard I Lionheart (Coeur de lion), demonstrate the importance and wealth of the Angevin Empire. Assistance was given to the Kingdom of Jerusalem, ruled by a cadet line of the Angevin royal house. Henry subsidized his cousins, showing his influence throughout the world and the significance of family connections. Richard organized the Third Crusade (1189–92). As war leader, he took a fleet and army not just over the Channel but to the Levant, a feat of remarkable organization. Richard saw national or political borders as having little significance. Affairs between the Angevin Empire and France assumed primary importance as did Mediterranean issues. Political links with Scandinavia were cut and well run lands could look after themselves. Henry and Richard imposed stability on their lands, especially England, fully realizing its necessity for a commercial economy to develop. Kings became facilitators for the growth of early capitalism, which underpinned the lifestyles of both monarchs and knights. When Richard went abroad he left behind two regents to operate on his behalf: William Longchamp, Bishop of Ely, and Walter of Coutances, Archbishop of Rouen.

ANGEVIN DECLINE

THE ANGEVIN DOMAIN'S SURVIVAL WAS DEPENDENT ON DYNASTIC CIRCUMSTANCES, SINCE THE LANDS CONCERNED LACKED ANY REAL POLITICAL COHERENCE. THE EARLY DEATH OF RICHARD I LEFT A DISPUTED SUCCESSION BETWEEN ARTHUR OF BRITTANY AND JOHN, VICTORIOUS IN 1200.

By virtue of his various titles, Henry II had inherited the claims of his predecessors over neighbouring lands, which led to expeditions into Wales in 1157, 1163, and 1165 to ensure the continuation of homage and fealty to the King of England. Diplomacy gained the homage of Malcolm IV, King of Scotland, at Chester in 1157 and the restoration of Northumberland, Cumberland and Westmoreland, which had been occupied by the Scots king. Later in his reign, homage was exacted from Malcolm's brother and successor, William the Lion. In Ireland, Henry allowed an expedition by south Wales barons to establish Anglo-Norman supremacy in Leinster (1169), which the King extended in 1171.

Despite these successes over England's immediate neighbors, there were weaknesses in an Empire that stretched from Scotland to the Pyrenees. The Empire was a collection of several principalities differing one from another in customs, political government, and racial characteristics. These differences were shrouded when a masterful ruler like Henry imposed his will over them, but the flimsy nature of the linkages was demonstrated when Henry made his adult sons his lieutenants over some principalities. The sons constantly quarreled and resented their father for allowing them so little initiative, because he reserved the real authority for himself alone.

Far right: ANGEVIN DECLINE
The Angevin Empire was in decline due to the failure of king John of England's foreign policy. Also, the French monarchy was increasing in strength because it gradually imposed its power over previously semi-independent vassals.

Queen Eleanor of Aquitaine bore Henry eight children, the surviving sons being Henry, Geoffrey, Richard, and John. In 1170, the King crowned his eldest son, Henry, as co-regent with himself but gave his son no powers. Young Henry opposed his father's proposals to find territories for John, at the expense of Geoffrey. Richard joined the argument supported by his mother. At this point—when Henry II was hated for the murder of Thomas Becket and some recent taxation—a revolt of the

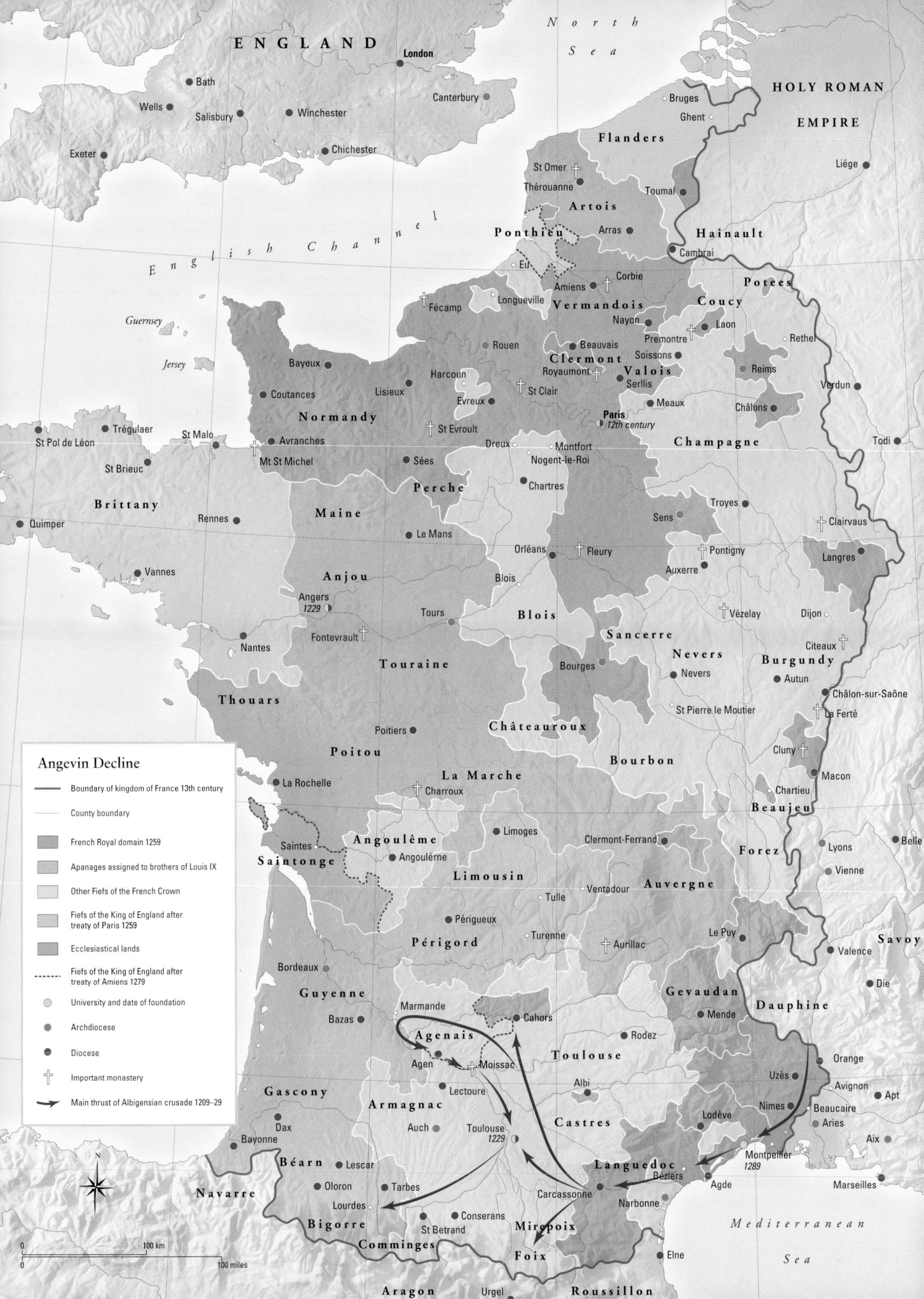
North Sea
ENGLAND
London
Bath
Wells
Salisbury
Winchester
Canterbury
Exeter
Chichester
HOLY ROMAN EMPIRE
Bruges
Ghent
Flanders
Liége
St Omer
Thérouanne
Toumal
Artois
English Channel
Ponthieu
Arras
Hainault
Cambrai
Eu
Corbie
Amiens
Potees
Longueville
Fécamp
Vermandois
Coucy
Guernsey
Nayon
Laon
Premontre
Rethel
Jersey
Rouen
Beauvais
Soissons
Bayeux
Clermont
Reims
Harcoun
Royaumont
Valois
Lisieux
St Clair
Serlis
Coutances
Evreux
Verdun
Meaux
Châlons
Normandy
Paris
12th century
St Evroult
Trégulaer
St Malo
St Pol de Léon
Avranches
Dreux
Montfort
Todi
Champagne
Mt St Michel
Nogent-le-Roi
St Brieuc
Sées
Perche
Chartres
Brittany
Troyes
Maine
Rennes
Sens
Clairvaus
Quimper
Le Mans
Orléans
Fleury
Pontigny
Langres
Auxerre
Vannes
Anjou
Blois
Angers
1229
Tours
Vézelay
Dijon
Blois
Fontevrault
Sancerre
Citeaux
Nantes
Nevers
Touraine
Burgundy
Bourges
Nevers
Autun
Thouars
Châlon-sur-Saône
St Pierre le Moutier
La Ferté
Poitiers
Châteauroux
Poitou
Cluny
Bourbon
La Rochelle
La Marche
Macon
Charroux
Chartieu
Beaujeu
Limoges
Saintes
Angoulême
Clermont-Ferrand
Lyons
Belle
Saintonge
Angoulérne
Forez
Vienne
Limousin
Ventadour
Auvergne
Tulle
Périgueux
Le Puy
Savoy
Turenne
Périgord
Aurillac
Valence
Bordeaux
Die
Guyenne
Gevaudan
Marmande
Dauphine
Bazas
Cahors
Mende
Agenais
Rodez
Toulouse
Agen
Moissac
Orange
Uzès
Lectoure
Albi
Avignon
Gascony
Apt
Armagnac
Nimes
Beaucaire
Castres
Lodève
Dax
Auch
Toulouse
1229
Aries
Bayonne
Aix
Montpellier
1289
Béarn
Lescar
Languedoc
Béziers
Agde
Oloron
Tarbes
Marseilles
Navarre
Carcassonne
Lourdes
Narbonne
Conserans
Mediterranean Sea
Bigorre
St Betrand
Mirepoix
Comminges
Foix
Elne
Aragon
Urgel
Roussillon
0
100 km
0
100 miles
N
Angevin Decline
Boundary of kingdom of France 13th century
County boundary
French Royal domain 1259
Apanages assigned to brothers of Louis IX
Other Fiefs of the French Crown
Fiefs of the King of England after treaty of Paris 1259
Ecclesiastical lands
Fiefs of the King of England after treaty of Amiens 1279
University and date of foundation
Archdiocese
Diocese
Important monastery
Main thrust of Albigensian crusade 1209–29

baronage in England and Normandy occurred, supported by Louis VII of France and William the Lion of Scotland. Henry reacted vigorously, crushing problems in Normandy and Brittany before crossing the Channel to settle matters in England. In July 1174, the Scots king was captured at Alnwick, while Henry suppressed the rebellion in England three weeks later. Henry pardoned his sons but Eleanor remained in custody for 16 years until his death. A second rebellion broke out in 1181 after a quarrel between young Henry and Richard over the government of Aquitaine. Young Henry died in 1183. In 1184 Richard and John quarrelled, the latter having been ordered to take Aquitaine from the former. Son Geoffrey died in 1186 and Henry's attempt to find an inheritance for John led to a campaign against him by Richard allied to King Philip II Augustus of France, succeeding Louis. Henry was defeated and some say his death, in 1189, was hastened when he heard that John had joined his enemies.

Left: A medieval town suffers siege. Local and national rivalries brought ruin and destruction to many towns and cities. Henry II was noted for his ruthless suppression of rebellions in England and Normandy.

When Richard I became king (1189–1199) the empire was attacked by the French king while he was on crusade. On return he campaigned to retrieve lands captured in Normandy and Touraine until only the castle of Gisors remained in French hands. The loss of this bastion was compensated by the building of Château Gaillard, key to Normandy's defenses. He was killed while besieging Châlus, a castle belonging to the Vicomte of Limoges. While away from his domains, administration fell to Eleanor, who helped her son John when he became king, until she died in 1204.

When Richard died the baronage of the Empire preferred different heirs. The barons of England and Normandy chose John; Anjou, Maine, and Touraine wanted Arthur of Brittany, Geoffrey's son; Eleanor held Aquitaine on John's behalf. King Philip's support for Arthur was withdrawn after the cession of the Vexin and Evrecin by the 1200 Treaty of Le Goulet. French pressure was relentless and the leading lords of Anjou and Poitou rebelled while others were disgusted with John, believing the well founded rumor that he had Arthur murdered. The impregnable Château Gaillard was besieged and taken (1203–04). By 1204, John had fled to England having lost Normandy, Anjou, Maine, Touraine and all of Poitou except La Rochelle. In 1206 and 1214, John led campaigns in Poitou but the defeat of Otto IV of Brunswick—the Holy Roman Emperor supporting rebellious French princes against Philip II of France with English troops and their allies at the Battle of Bouvines (July 1214)—meant that John's European strategy had failed.

Château Gaillard, built by Richard the Lionheart in 1196. It defended the approaches to Normandy built high on the escarpment overlooking the River Seine, and was considered impregnable.

The king's defeat caused disquiet in England. The baronage sought an alternative king but there was no real candidate with Arthur dead and Henry's sons were too young. Some thought Philip Augustus' son, Louis, was a possibility. Reform was urgently needed and John was forced to sign the Magna Carta at Runneymede in June 1215. The settlement was made impossible by militant lords and John appealed to the pope for support. This granted, John ravaged the northern counties and the Scottish border. Prince Louis of France landed in England at the request of certain barons. On John's death in 1216 peace was patched up, rebels were restored to their lands, Louis withdrew from England and John's son became king as Henry III. By 1224, only Gascony remained to England in France, plus the Channel Islands.

The family structure of Angevin land holdings shows how feudalism could fail. Any lord or knight wanted a degree of sovereignty and this could lead to feuding. Any father wanted to secure an inheritance for his sons. A king, however, had to provide duchies and treat all sons equally. Henry II failed as a parent and Angevin territories suffered until King John lost northern France to the French king.

Hundred Years' War

THE HUNDRED YEARS' WAR WITNESSED MASSIVE CHANGES IN MILITARY TECHNOLOGY AS THE MOUNTED CAVALRY OF FRANCE WAS LAID LOW BY THE SOCIALLY INFERIOR BOWMEN OF ENGLAND. THIS WAS COUNTERED BY THE INCREASING USE OF FRENCH ARTILLERY ON THE BATTLEFIELD AND IN SIEGE.

This carved effigy, dating from 1347, gives a good indication of the knight's equipment in both English and French armies.

The Hundred Years' War commenced in 1337 and lasted for 116 years, with lengthy periods of truce interspersed with the most brutal and savage warfare. In some ways, the war was a continuation of previous hostilities involving the loss of most of the Angevin Empire. Included within and overlapping the Anglo-French war was a sub-war between Scotland and England, Scotland being an ally of the French. King Edward III, King John's grandson, hoped to weaken this alliance by attacking Scotland. Consequently Edward III went adventuring in Scotland to support Edward Balliol in his quest for the Scots throne. In 1333, the Earl of Douglas led an army to relieve Berwick-upon-Tweed, which was besieged by Edward. At Halidon Hill, the Scots schiltrons (hedgehog-like formations of pikemen, defended on all sides) and mounted knights were slaughtered in an arrow storm, the survivors being charged by men-at-arms while being enfiladed by English archers. When routed, the Scots remnant was attacked and pursued by mounted knights. Scots losses were so grievous that their ally King Philip VI of France would not go on crusade until Edward desisted in his conquest of Scotland. Philip insisted that any peace to sort out border disputes with Aquitaine must include peace with Scotland or Aquitaine would be open to confiscation.

In May 1337 Philip formally confiscated Aquitaine, sending troops across the border to seize his vassal Edward's castles. French fleets harried the southern English coast, ravaging Jersey, Folkestone, Dover, Portsmouth, Southampton, Hastings, and the Isle of Wight. French ships entered the Thames. A number of English ships were captured, including Edward's great ships, the cogs *Edward* and *Christopher*. England feared a French invasion and Edward strengthened his coastal defenses.

The threat to Aquitaine was serious since a flourishing wine trade had grown with the export of

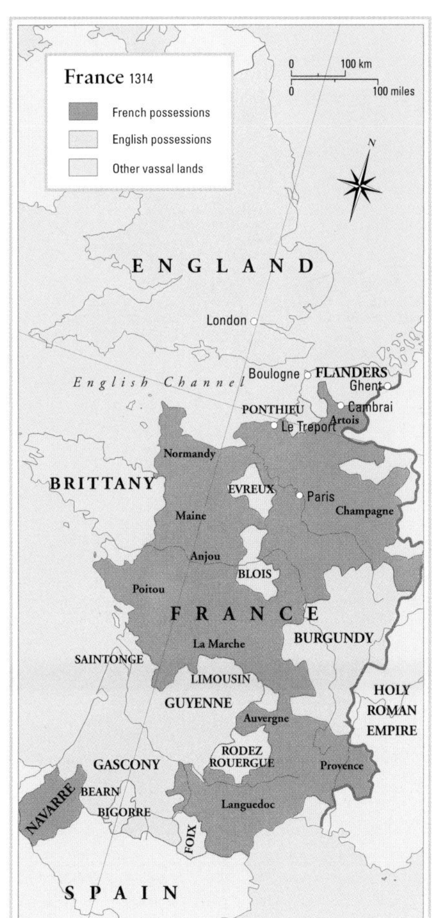

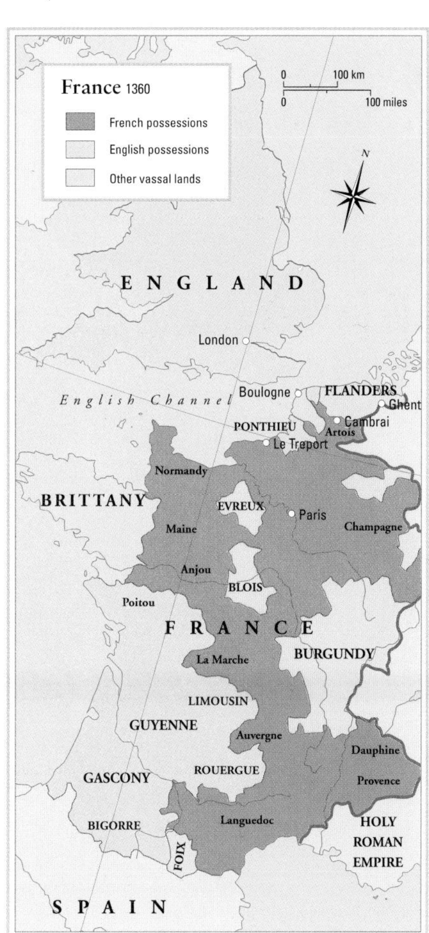

KNIGHTS OF THE GARTER
Edward III wearing the robes of the Order of the Garter, which he founded c. 1348 as "a society, fellowship and college of knights." It was, and still is, the highest order of knighthood. The original statutes required that each member was already a "knight bachelor." One legend that explains the origin of the Order involves Joan of Kent, the Countess of Salisbury. While dancing with King Edward at Eltham Palace, her garter slipped from her leg to the floor. When nearby courtiers sniggered, the King is said to have picked up the garter, tied it to his own leg, and exclaimed, '*Honi soit qui mal y pense*' (Shame on him who thinks evil of it). The phrase becomes the motto of the Order. In another legend, during the 12th-Century Crusades, King Richard I was said to have been inspired by St. George the Martyr to tie garters around the legs of his knights, who then won in battle. King Edward III was said to have recalled the event in the 14th Century when he founded the Order.

Bordeaux wine to England. Issues of trade were also pertinent to Flanders, coveted by Philippe of France. The English wool trade with Flanders formed the staple of English exports, and was probably the sole form of wealth generated above the resources of agriculture. The Flemish towns achieved a high level of economic development, based upon weaving cloth and depending upon English wool for their prosperity. The counts of Flanders and their nobility nursed French sympathies and regarded the burghers as dangerous and subversive of the correct social order. The counts placed restrictions on the wool trade, angering Flemish burghers and the mercantile element in the English Parliament, who were already incensed with constant sea-fights with French ships in the Channel.

In 1336, Edward retaliated, placing an embargo on all exports of English wool, thus provoking a crisis in the Low Countries. The townspeople rebelled against the feudal aristocracy, and produced a warlike leader, Jacques Van Arteveldt from Ghent. The rebellious townsfolk gained control of much of the urban areas of Flanders and looked to England for aid lest their aristocracy seek revenge with French help. Thus, the commercial interests of England and the Flemish bourgeoisie

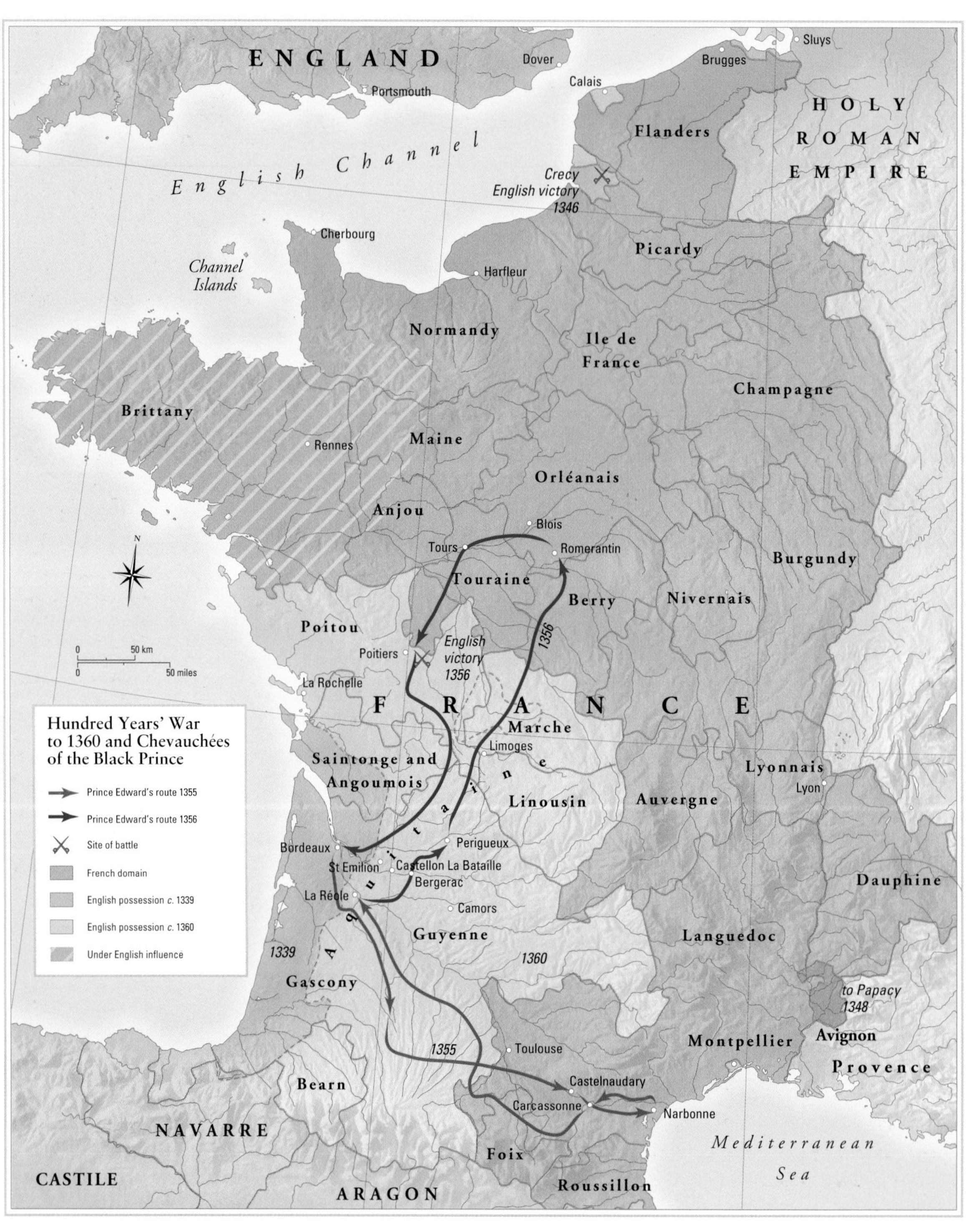
ENGLAND
Dover
Calais
Brugges
Sluys
Portsmouth
Flanders
HOLY ROMAN EMPIRE
English Channel
Crecy
English victory
1346
Cherbourg
Channel Islands
Picardy
Harfleur
Normandy
Ile de France
Champagne
Brittany
Rennes
Maine
Orléanais
Anjou
Blois
Tours
Romerantin
Touraine
Berry
Nivernais
Burgundy
Poitou
Poitiers
English victory 1356
1356
La Rochelle
FRANCE
Marche
Limoges
Saintonge and Angoumois
Aquitaine
Linousin
Auvergne
Lyonnais
Lyon
Bordeaux
Perigueux
St Emilion
Castellon La Bataille
Bergerac
La Réole
Camors
Dauphine
Guyenne
Languedoc
1339
1360
Gascony
to Papacy 1348
Avignon
1355
Toulouse
Montpellier
Provence
Bearn
Castelnaudary
Carcassonne
Narbonne
NAVARRE
Mediterranean Sea
Foix
CASTILE
ARAGON
Roussillon
0 50 km
0 50 miles
Hundred Years' War to 1360 and Chevauchées of the Black Prince
Prince Edward's route 1355
Prince Edward's route 1356
Site of battle
French domain
English possession c. 1339
English possession c. 1360
Under English influence

merged. Profit and politics became a powerful motive for war.

A major cause of war was the question of the French royal succession. In 1328, Charles IV of France died without heirs. Edward III of England had the best claim to the French throne through his mother, Isabella of France, who was Charles' sister. However, Philip of Valois had a plausible claim through his father, Charles' uncle. The French would never countenance an English King, however legitimate, and their nobility revived an ancient law of the Salian Franks (precursors of the Carolingians) that the right to inherit could not pass through a woman. Considering how aristocratic landholdings were increased through marriage, the law was a nonsense. Nevertheless, Valois became Philip VI. Edward III initially accepted this decision but in 1337 used it as a pretext for war.

Monarchs always had difficulty waging war because war was so expensive. In England, Parliament voted annual subsidies to fuel the war with Scotland and these were increased in 1337. A tenth of all cash was to be handed over in addition to a fifteenth of the value of all lands, secular or clerical. Religious institutions had to sell their silver plate, lords handed over some of their receipts, towns taxed traders, royal jewels were pawned and the assets of foreign merchants seized. A half of the annual wool crop was sequestered and sold on the open market for Edward.

On All Saints' Day 1337, the Bishop of Lincoln, Henry Bergersh, arrived in Paris and gave Edward's challenge to Philip and withdrew Plantagenet allegiance for Aquitaine (Guienne). The French attempted to capture this embassy while it was returning to England but failed, leaving the French to shelter on the island of Cadsand in the River Scheldt's delta. These were attacked by Sir Walter Manny of Hainault with 500 men-at-arms and 2,000 archers. They defeated the 5,000 French, capturing their commander Sir Guy, Bastard of Flanders. Before invading France in 1339, the English sacked Le Treport in the spring and in 1340 entered Boulogne harbor where they burnt 30 French ships, hanging their captains and burning part of the lower town in retaliation for the torching of the English south coast towns.

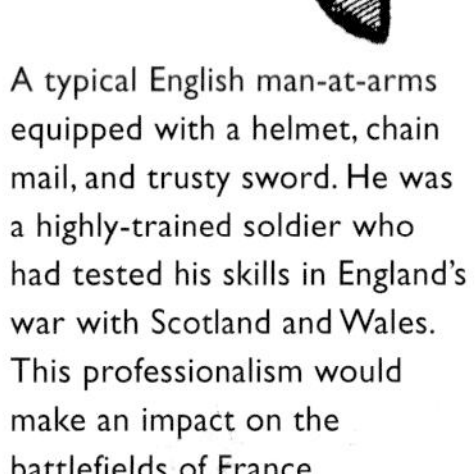

A typical English man-at-arms equipped with a helmet, chain mail, and trusty sword. He was a highly-trained soldier who had tested his skills in England's war with Scotland and Wales. This professionalism would make an impact on the battlefields of France.

This English warship of the type used at Sluys, shows clear Viking influence in the design of its hull. Its huge, square central sail provides its motive power; when becalmed several large oars could be used to maneuver the vessel. Unlike its Viking predecessors, small structures have been built at each end of the ship; from these platforms soldiers armed with bows or crossbows would engage enemy ships.

SLUYS

The years 1339 and 1340 saw failed attempts by Edward to invade northern France despite assistance from German allies, mercenaries, and the Duke of Brabant. The Duke of Brabant had become prosperous from the English wool industry and his help was partly motivated out of a desire to protect this. Edward marched across Artois seizing Cambrai and harrying the towns of the Thiérache. The armies of England and France faced each other at Buironfosse but Philip refused battle. Instead, the French King had planned an invasion of England but his fleet was scattered by a storm in 1339. After this reverse, trouble broke out in the Genoese galleys hired by France. Their admiral tried to steal the crew's pay, resulting in internecine strife. Some mutinied and sailed for home. Philip lost two thirds of his fleet and much of the rest was destroyed in that Boulogne raid of 1339. The French fleet was now reduced to armed merchantmen, the "Great Army of the Sea," leaving Philip with a defensive force now designed to block any English invasion. Normandy was taxed heavily to make them ready for war and to hire crews.

Elsewhere, Edward had collected some 160 ships, coerced into service from private hands. On 22 June 1340, with Edward in command, the English fleet sailed, now some 250 ships, finding the French fleet at the mouth of the River Zwyn on 24 June. The French fleet, including the great cog *Christopher*, was deployed in three lines stretched across the river's estuary. Hugh Quiéret and Nicholas Béhuchat, the two French admirals, doubted the quality of their ships so had them chained together. Equipped with fighting platforms, the fleet looked like a row of tiny castles. Maybe, they found it difficult to gain control of their Castilian and remaining Genoese allies. The

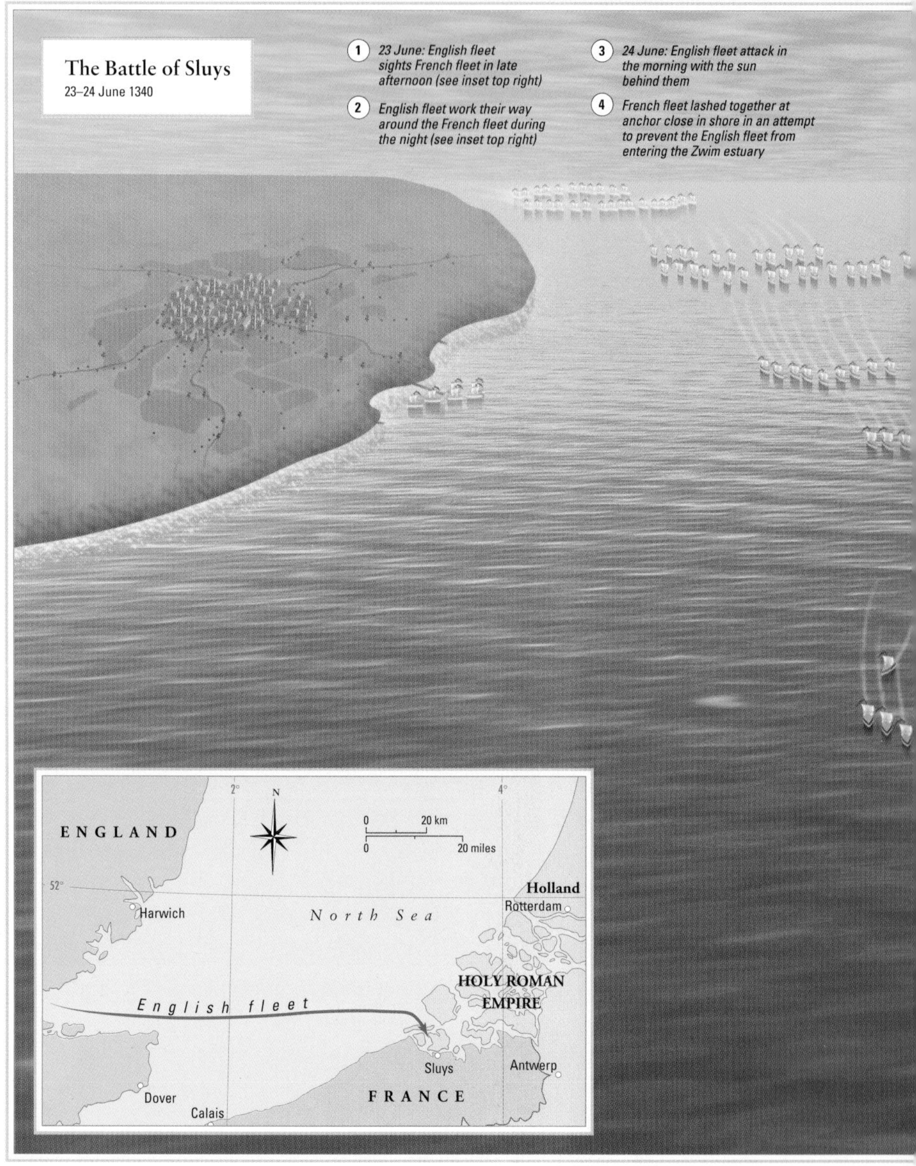

THE BATTLE OF SLUYS
The English fleet sailed around the Schelde Estuary approaching from the east with the sunrise. Meanwhile, the French fleet had chained themselves together presenting the attacking English with what looked like a row of small castles. As the English ships approached, archers firing from their raised platforms swept the French ships with deadly and accurate fire. The English ships then closed on the French fleet, boarding and capturing many ships.

French had no room to maneuver and were subject to the vagaries of tidal flows. Some ships fouled others and disorder followed as ships cut themselves loose.

The English sailed into this growing chaos in early afternoon when the sun was no longer in their eyes, also taking advantage of wind and tide. Sir Reginald Cobham and Sir John Chandos were sent ashore to make contact with the Flemings who were prepared to fight any French troops who left their ships. Edward sent his ships into the fray in units of three. Two ships were full of archers who swept enemy decks with a hail of arrows from their fore and stern castles, allowing the men-at-arms

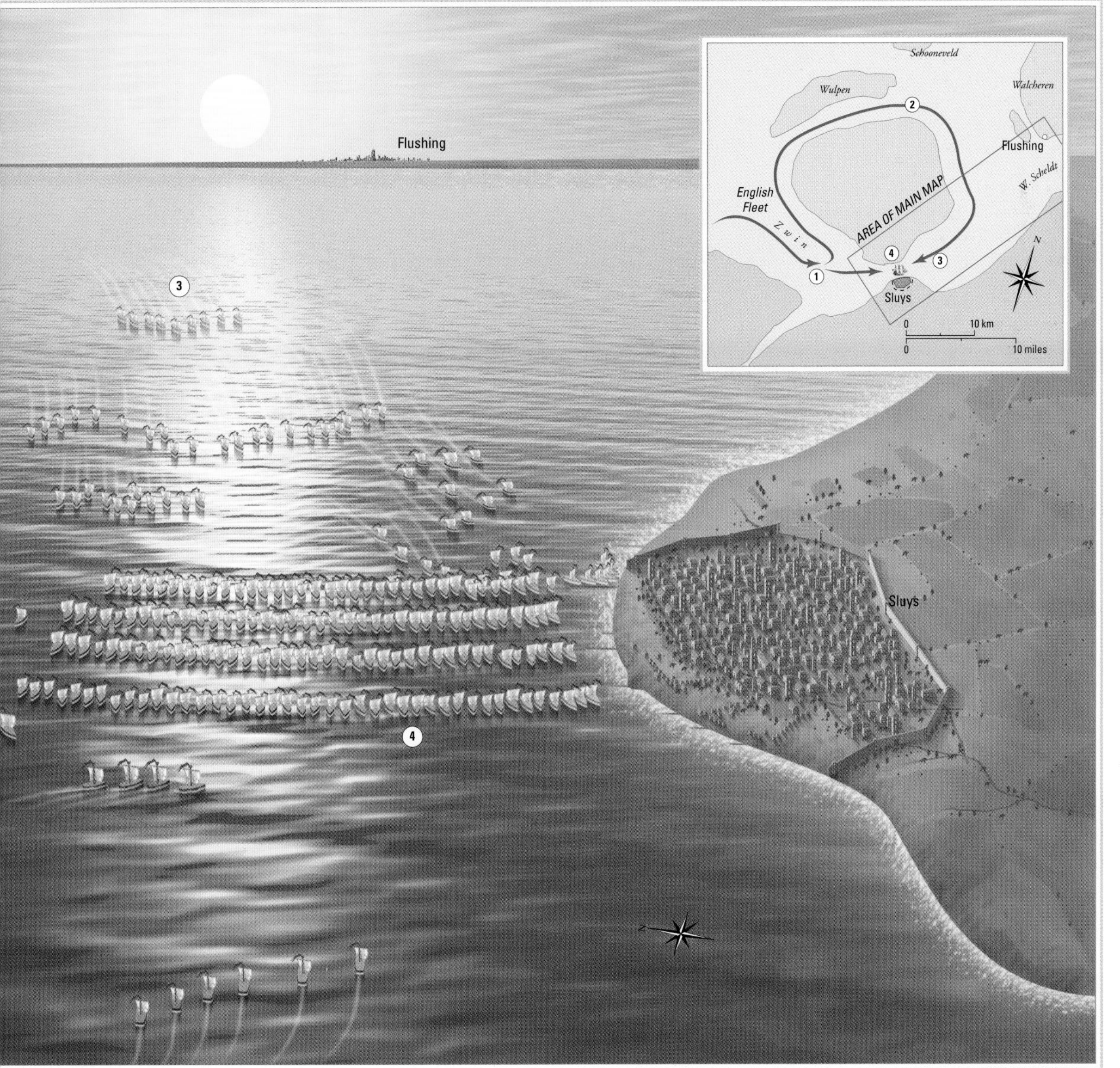

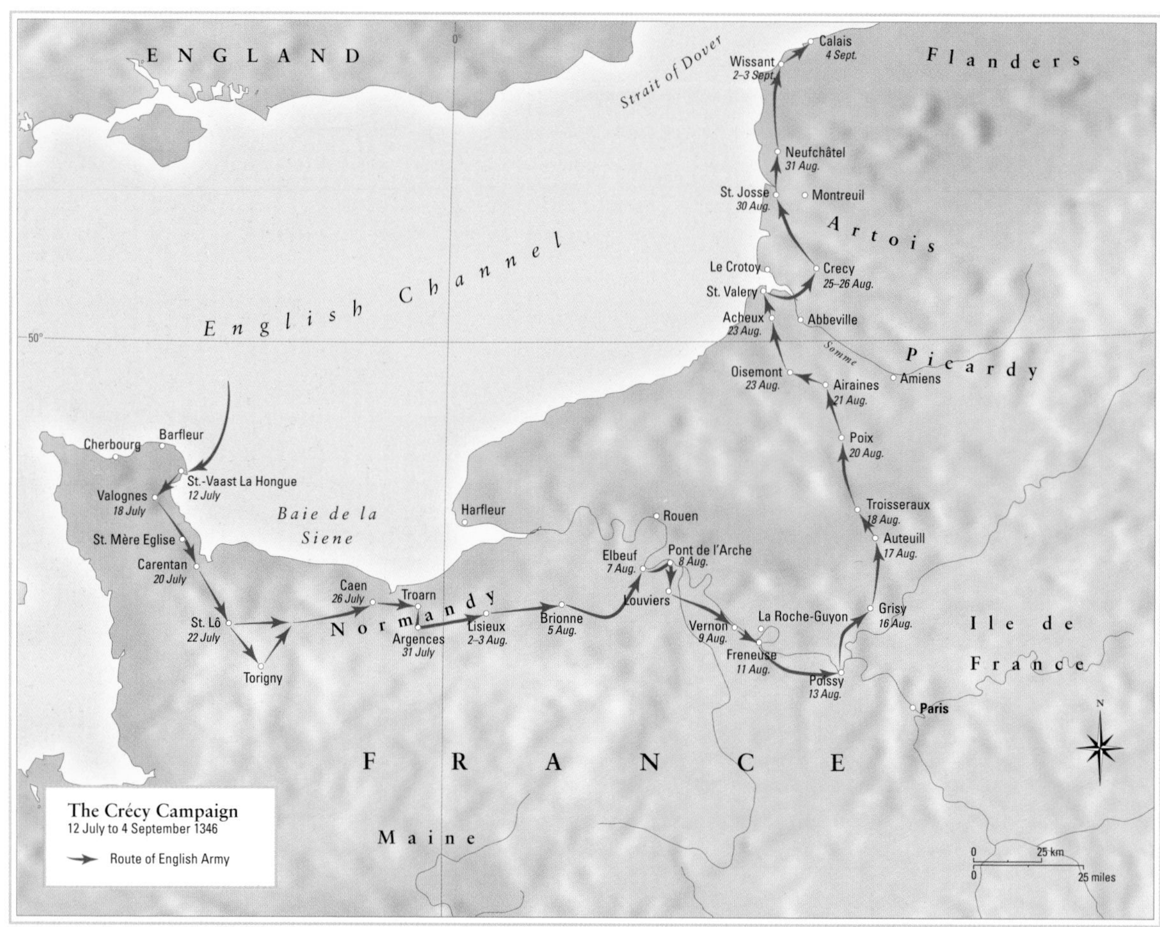

THE CRECY CAMPAIGN
The fleet that arrived at dawn on 12 July 1346, was the largest amphibious operation of the Hundred Years' War and caught the French completely by surprise.

from the third ship to board and overwhelm the remaining crew. The French crossbowmen were no match for the English archers, whose rapid firepower was devastating. The lines of French ships fell apart, drifting in knots of brutal fighting. The battle went on all day and into the night, with Edward being wounded in the thigh by a crossbow bolt.

The Fleming allies killed any French who swam ashore. Between 16,000 and 18,000 French soldiers were killed in the battle. Béhuchat was killed in the fighting while Quiéret was seized for ransom. When Edward found that Quiéret had been responsible for the assaults on the English coast, he had him strung up from his own yardarm.

The victory did not give England command of the Channel but invasion had been prevented. Edward marched to Tournai with 9,000 archers, several thousand Flemish pikemen and thousands of Dutch and German mercenaries. This huge force achieved little and Philip of France arrived and dug his army into a defensive position, while ambushing English foraging parties and refusing to give battle in fear of incurring heavy losses. The Duke of Brabant and Count of Hainault defected to the French, and Edward left for England with huge debts and a foul temper.

In 1341, Duke John III of Brittany died leaving the succession in dispute between Charles of Blois, who had won the right to succession by marrying its heiress, Countess Jeanne, Philip VI's niece and Count John de Montfort, the deceased Duke's half-brother. John captured the Duchy but when Charles gained Philip's support, he offered his fealty to Edward III, recognizing him as King of France. The English King saw the Breton situation as advantageous since a friendly Brittany would be less likely to attack English shipping out of Gascony. English troops aided John in what became a Breton civil war. Siege was laid to Rennes, Nantes, and Vannes. Jogn, Duke of Burgundy and Philip's heir, tried to lift the sieges but stalemate resulted.

The English now had a base in Brittany and helped its Countess, a woman who wore armor and led cavalry attacks against her enemies. Helped by Sir Walter Manny's troops she recaptured many castles and towns from Charles. In 1342, the Constable of England, William de Bohun, landed a force at Brest, traversed Brittany, defeating a French army under Charles de Blois at Morlaix. Sickness damaged the English troops and Vannes was retaken by the French. The Breton civil war then turned into a guerrilla war of ambush and skirmish to no side's advantage.

CRECY AND POITIERS

In 1346 and 1356 English-led armies under King Edward III and then Edward, Prince of Wales (1330–1376), who was just sixteen when first campaigning with his father, engaged in *chevauchée* against the French; these large scale raids were designed to ravage large areas of France by burning villages and crops, killing the people and stealing as much booty as possible. These terror tactics intimidated local populations and damaged the economy, thereby undermining French wealth. The sacking of towns and cities accentuated this process and captured French burghers could be held for ransom. Young Edward proved to be a brilliant campaigner, eventually known as the Black Prince because of the black armor he wore.

King Edward III's army landed at Saint-Vaast on the north coast of the Norman Cotentin Peninsula, immediately looting the small towns and villages in the area, from Barfleur to near Cherbourg, this town being too strongly fortified to take. Edward had originally intended to aid Henry of Lancaster in Aquitaine but was persuaded to attack Normandy because it was rich and peaceful. The army commenced marching south through Valognes, Sainte-Mère-Eglise, Saint-Côme-du-Mont, Carentan, Saint-Lô to Caen, which was sacked after a brief defense by the Constable of France. Edward moved to Lisieux and the River Seine, which he managed to cross at Poissy near Paris. French resistance stiffened with mounted troops attacking English foraging parties. The English realized that French King Philippe VI was pursuing with an army out of Paris and they had to reach the sea and safety. The Somme was the next barrier and the only ford defended by 3,500 French knights and crossbowmen. The English vanguard crossed the river driving off the French troops, chasing them towards Abbeville.

Archers would make up a fundamental offensive element of English armies operating in France. Trained since childhood in the use of the longbow, and experienced in England's interminable wars with Scotland and Wales, it was their ability that would give the English armies an offensive power that the French chivalric army could not answer.

Right: LIVING OFF THE LAND
The *chevauchée* meant living off the land and destroying the enemy's economic base. In fact, this meant burning and pillaging villages and communities in the line of march.

Edward III had hoped to force battle on the French and chose a ridge between the town of Crécy and village of Wadicourt—these settlements defending his flanks—while the French would have to advance up a slope to attack the English troops. Edward had some 15,000 men, half of whom were Welsh and Cheshire archers, defended by several thousand fully-armored knights and men-at-arms, supported by Welsh spearmen. The right flank was commanded by the Prince of Wales, aged 16 years, but supported by the Earls of Warwick and Oxford and Sir John Chandos, a well-known warrior. The left flank was under the Earl of Northampton and the center under the king. The flanks and the gaps between the divisions were filled with archers in arrowhead formation, which enabled them to fire front and flank. The Welsh spearmen were in three ranks behind the men-at-arms of the three main divisions. The archers were all well-trained in the use of the war bow (longbow), being able to loose 15 arrows a minute, creating an arrow storm through which an enemy must advance.

The French army comprised some 30,000–40,000 men including approximately 6,000 Genoese crossbowmen. The numbers are inexact but the English forces were outnumbered three or four to one. Philippe VI's army included elements from Germany, Bohemia, Flanders, Hainault, and Savoy, filled with arrogant and eager aristocrats, jealous of each other, and keen to get to grips with the hated English. The French marshals managed to create some order amongst the mass of French troops on the open ground before the slope. Eight divisions or battles were cajoled into formation, the advance guard being commanded by the John The Blind, King of Bohemia (son of the Holy Roman Emperor Henry VII), the Count of Flanders and the Duke of Alençon. The central guard was commanded by the Duke of Lorraine and the Count of Blois, while the king commanded the rearguard, accompanied by the exiled King of Majorca and Prince Charles of Luxembourg (blind John's son, emperor elect to the Holy Roman Empire who signed himself King of the Romans).

The Genoese crossbowmen were ordered to advance, commencing the attack. However, they had left their pavises behind. These large shields were set up to protect the men as they reloaded their bows. Despite having a longer range than the longbow, the crossbow took a long time to reload. After the first bolt shower, the English archers returned fire, darkening the sky and flailing the Genoese, who died or sought refuge amongst the French cavalry behind them. The French cavalry became entangled with the Genoese, cutting at them with their swords, accusing them of cowardice. As confusion spread, the English archers advanced, pouring in arrows, turning the first French formation into an uncoordinated mess as it moved up the slope toward the English men-at-arms. These hurled themselves into the fray, absorbing the French pressure, then sent it reeling back into the second French division seeking to attack the English left flank. English archers ran to the left flank of their men-at-arms and shot an enfilading fire into the French unshielded right side, causing chaos and mayhem to both men and horses. Edward III's five cannon were brought into play adding their stone balls to the fray. The French were driven back leaving heaps of dead and wounded. The battle continued in the same vein with repeated French assaults breaking on the English men-at-arms while being winnowed by constant arrow fire. Attacks continued with 12 to 15 attempts between 6 pm and midnight. Well-trained infantry and over half a million arrows had destroyed the French army as a fighting force for the moment. The blind King of Bohemia ordered his knights to tie their bridles to his so he could charge the English line. He was found dead

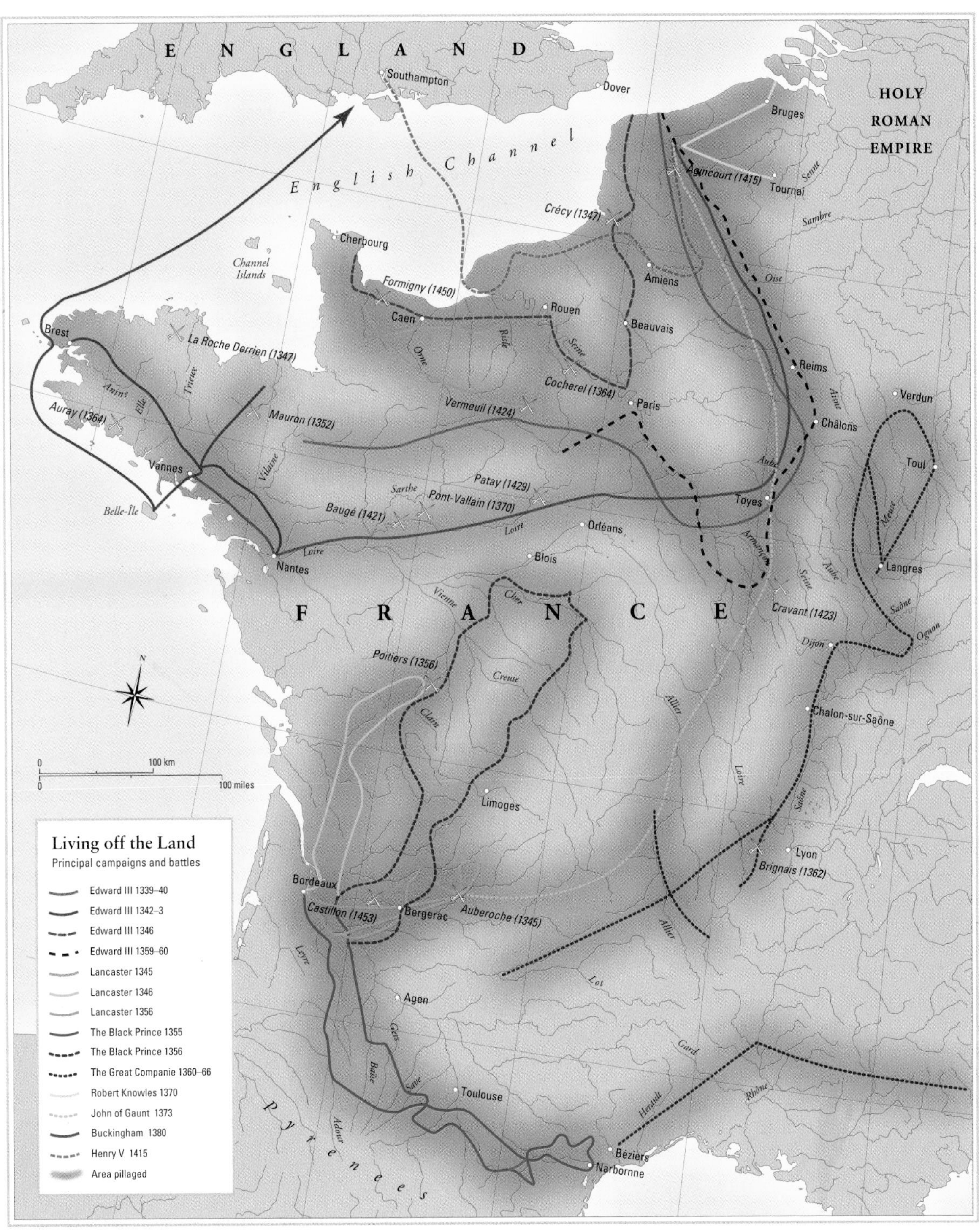

ENGLAND
Southampton
Dover
HOLY ROMAN EMPIRE
Bruges
English Channel
Agincourt (1415)
Tournai
Crécy (1347)
Cherbourg
Channel Islands
Amiens
Formigny (1450)
Rouen
Caen
Beauvais
Brest
La Roche Derrien (1347)
Reims
Cocherel (1364)
Verdun
Paris
Vermeuil (1424)
Auray (1364)
Mauron (1352)
Châlons
Toul
Vannes
Patay (1429)
Pont-Vallain (1370)
Toyes
Belle-Île
Baugé (1421)
Orléans
Blois
Langres
Nantes
FRANCE
Cravant (1423)
Dijon
Poitiers (1356)
Chalon-sur-Saône
100 km
100 miles
Limoges
Lyon
Brignais (1362)
Bordeaux
Castillon (1453)
Bergerac
Auberoche (1345)
Agen
Toulouse
Pyrenees
Béziers
Narborne
Living off the Land
Principal campaigns and battles
Edward III 1339–40
Edward III 1342–3
Edward III 1346
Edward III 1359–60
Lancaster 1345
Lancaster 1346
Lancaster 1356
The Black Prince 1355
The Black Prince 1356
The Great Companie 1360–66
Robert Knowles 1370
John of Gaunt 1373
Buckingham 1380
Henry V 1415
Area pillaged

next morning with his men. The Prince of Wales took his badge of three ostrich feathers and his motto *Ich Dien* (I serve) as his own out of respect.

The next morning, 27 August, the English heralds counted some 1,500 lords, knights, squires, and lesser lords amongst the dead, including the Counts of Blois and Flanders and the Dukes of

THE BATTLE OF CRÉCY
This marked the moment when infantry returned to importance on the battlefield after centuries of domination by heavily-armored cavalry, the knights. Opposite the English position, potholes had been dug to hinder the approach of the French cavalry. The initial attack was opened by Genoese crossbowmen advancing the firing on the English line. However, they were out-ranged by English longbowmen who also could fire at a faster rate. Under this withering fire, the Genoese broke and fled, although few escaped. The impatient French cavalry charged forward cutting down any Genoese in their path. As the French Cavalry approached the English line, once again the archers took a terrible toll. The handful that did reach the English line were quickly despatched by the men-at-arms. As more French reinforcements reached the battlefield, more uncoordinated charges were made against the English lines. All failed. The flower of European chivalry lay dead and dying across the battlefield.

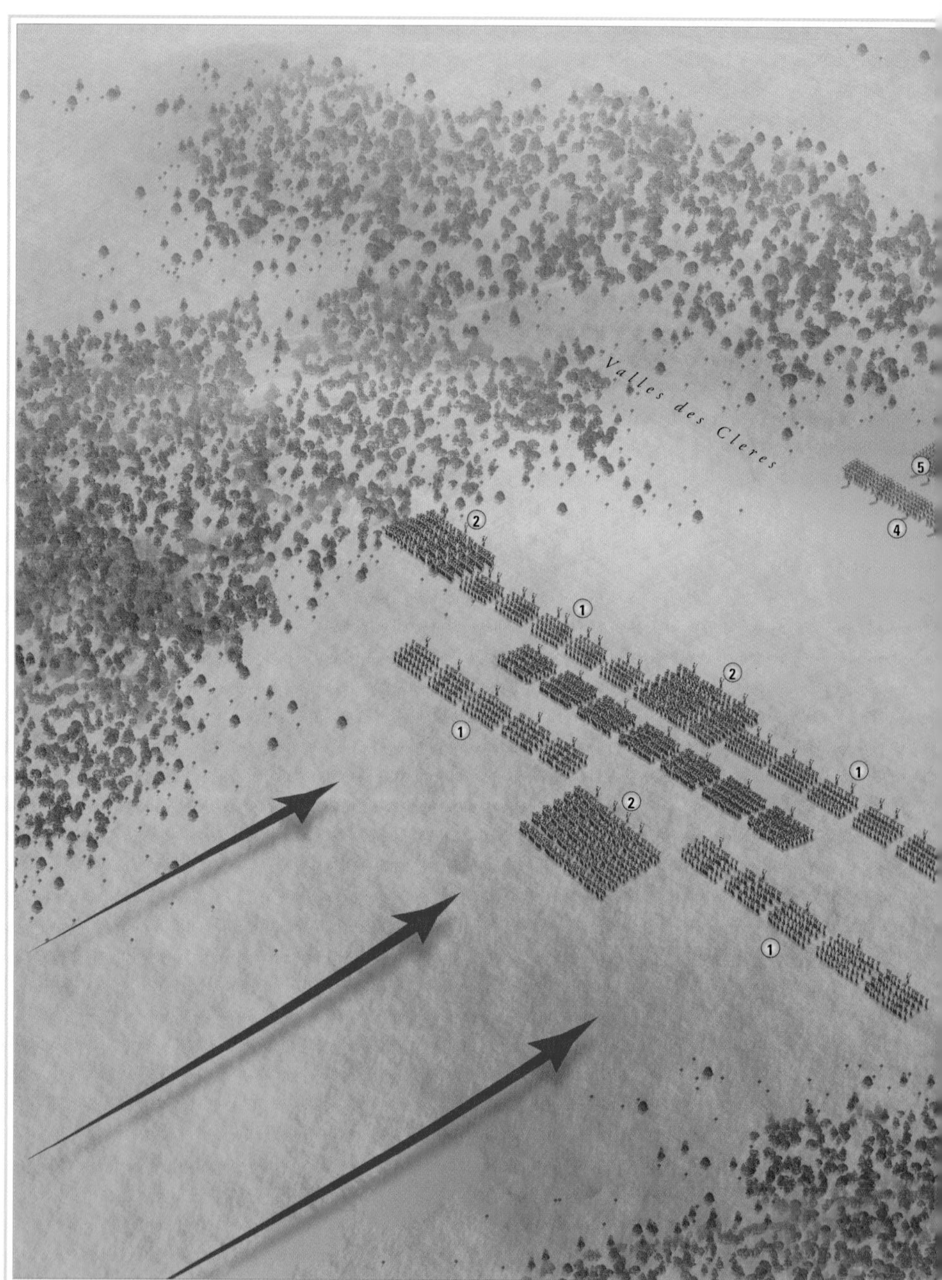

Alençon and Lorraine. French losses exceeded 10,000 while the English allegedly lost only 500. Despite victory, the English forces were too few to attack Paris and there were other French units converging on Edward III, so he marched north to besiege Calais, worried that the French cavalry might regroup. The siege lasted almost a year, until August 1347. The French garrison surrendered,

its officers being ransomed, and the town was repopulated with English traders and their families, becoming the only English port for the wool trade into Flanders and the Empire. Eventually, English tin, lead, and cloth entered Europe.

Edward III's campaign had secured a victory, emptied his treasure chests, and gained him a town. In September 1347, Edward concluded an eight-year truce with Philippe. Luckily, the English had enjoyed better success elsewhere. Henry of Lancaster had reoccupied the Duchy of Aquitaine and cleared the borderlands of Poitou returning to Bordeaux with loot and prisoners galore. He then joined his king outside Calais. Elsewhere, to relieve pressure on France, the Scots under King David II invaded Northumbria, meeting an English army under the Prince-Bishop of Durham and the Wardens of the border, Lords Percy and Neville of Raby, at Neville's Cross on 17 October 1346. The English arrow storm wiped out a third of the Scots and their wounded king was captured and sent to the Tower of London. The Tower, originally a castle to dominate Saxon London, later became a palace where important prisoners could be placed under house arrest and where traitors could be held until execution.

War had been turned on its head. The mounted cavalry of France and its friends had been smashed by dismounted knights and massed bowmen. Armored mounted might would gradually succumb to this military revolution where the archer, a common man, could kill a lord with his war bow.

In 1348, the plague known as the Black Death reached Europe from China, killing a third of the population while decimating social, economic, and military structures. War was on hold, apart from a few encounters, such as Sir John Beauchamp's victory at Taillebourg, constant skirmishes in Brittany, and the Battle of Mauron where 90 knights of the French new Order of the Star were killed or captured.

In 1356, serious warfare broke out again when Duke Henry of Lancaster left Brittany, invading Normandy. Simultaneously, the Prince of Wales marched out of Aquitaine crossing the Dordogne, traversing Poitou into Touraine, aiming for the Loire in order to link up with Henry of Lancaster. However, the French King John prevented the merger, hurrying south with his forces, gathering new units as he marched into Blois. The Prince of Wales decided that he would return to Bordeaux with all his plunder. The enemy armies' scouting parties encountered each other on 17 September. A captured French knight told the prince that his king's forces were waiting for the English.

Prince Edward found a good defensive position on a long wooded ridge nine miles southwest of Poitiers, close to the small village of Nouaille-Maupertius. King John's large army occupied Poitiers and spread into the surrounding fields. On Sunday 18 September, a holy day when fighting was disallowed, Cardinal Talleyrand de Périgord tried to make peace. Prince Edward was asked to surrender all his plunder, himself, and 100 knights; needless to say, he refused this invitation, in addition to the idea of French knight Geoffrey de Charny that the battle should be settled by combat between 100 French and English knights.

Edward's forces comprised 7,000 English and Gascon troops, the latter being mainly men-at-arms. The left was commanded by the Earl of Warwick, the right by the Earl of Salisbury, and the center by the prince. Across the front of the English position was a thick hedge, a potential obstacle to the

French attacking force. The French, over 30,000 men, were divided into three "battles" (the medieval term for "divisions"), the first commanded by the dauphin, the second by the Duke of Orléans and the third by King John.

THE BATTLE OF CRÉCY
English archers defeat the armored chivalry of France. Wave after wave of French cavalry were brought down by volleys of deadly arrows. This contemporary illustration shows a body of archers driving off a French cavalry attack. While in the background men-at-arms and dismounted knights prepare to move forward toward the disorganized French ranks.

Among the French was a Scot contingent led by Sir William Douglas, who persuaded King John not to repeat the tactics of Crécy. Instead, the French knights were to dismount and were armed with swords, axes and shortened lances. The French had the novel idea of using a small, well-armored force to charge into the English archers to open a breach for the French knights. These 300 were led by two Marshals of France, Clermont and Audrehem, who charged the center of the English line receiving an arrow storm from archers hidden in the hedgerow. Nearly all were killed or captured; Clermont was killed by an arrow and Audrehem made prisoner.

Dauphin Charles led the 2,000 men of the first French battle, surviving the arrows virtually intact and crashing into the Anglo-Gascon line. The archers dropped their bows and joined the engagement, wielding swords, axes and mauls. After half an hour, the Dauphin's troops broke into Orléans' second division causing a rout, his troops not making contact with the prince's forces. However, King John's battle—8,000 strong—marched up the slope accompanied by the Oriflamme, the French battle flag. The French shield wall must have looked frightening but the prince switched tactics. Leaving the archers to hold the line, he withdrew his knights, mounted them and led them in line to the hedge while a small mounted force under the Captal de Buch, the Gascon lord Jean III de Grailly, circled the French, hidden behind a small hill, ready to take them in the flank.

The 2,000-strong English knight force charged the French while the Captal took them in the flank. The French were compacted, an easy target for arrows as the archers came running to help the battle. The French fought hard but eventually broke, making for Poitiers where the gates remained firmly shut and allowing the English to slaughter them. King John remained on the field with his fourteen-year-old son, Philippe, and fought until exhausted, eventually surrendering to Sir Denis de Morbeque.

The English acquired the gold, silver, and jewels from the French camp and the ransoms of not just King John and his son, but from 17 great lords and five viscounts. Two thousand French knights lay dead on the field. France was devastated.

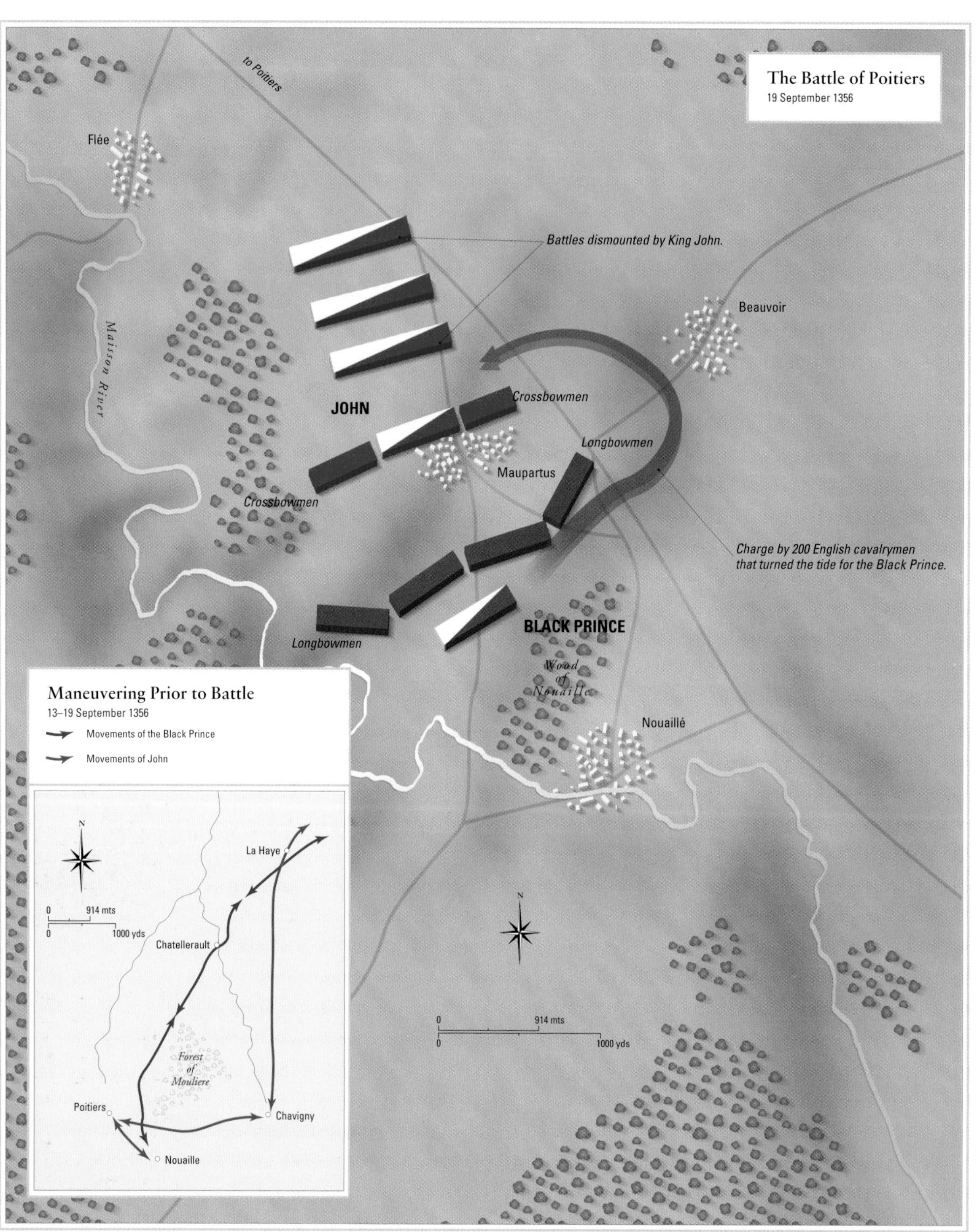
The Battle of Poitiers
19 September 1356
to Poitiers
Flée
Battles dismounted by King John.
Beauvoir
Maisson River
JOHN
Crossbowmen
Longbowmen
Maupartus
Crossbowmen
Charge by 200 English cavalrymen that turned the tide for the Black Prince.
Longbowmen
BLACK PRINCE
Wood of Nouaillé
Nouaillé
N
0 914 mts
0 1000 yds
Maneuvering Prior to Battle
13–19 September 1356
Movements of the Black Prince
Movements of John
N
La Haye
0 914 mts
0 1000 yds
Chatellerault
Forest of Mouliere
Poitiers
Chavigny
Nouaille

Without a king, France faced internal division. Charles of Navarre, who held lands in Normandy and was a grandson of Louis IX (leader of the 7th Crusade), claimed the French throne and seized control of Paris. Dauphin Charles raised troops from the Ile-de-France and crushed the Navarrese forces and their Parisian allies. Next, the French peasants rose in rebellion, the Jacquerie, north of the Seine, burning castles and towns. Harshly taxed, their crops robbed by marauding soldiers, providing ransom money for captured lords, and looted by roving bands of mercenaries, the peasants had reason for anger. However, peasant excesses united knight and burgher in a slaughter that ended the rebellion in August 1358.

Negotiations for the freedom of the French king dragged on. In January 1358, the first Treaty of London was signed. The king's ransom was four million gold ecus, 600,000 being the payment needed for release, the rest to follow. In territorial terms, England demanded the cession in full sovereignty of the Duchy of Aquitaine, and the counties of Bigorre, Poitou, Rouergue, Saintonge, and Quercy. When added to English lands held in Ponthieu and the Pale of Calais, Edward III would hold one third of France. However, Edward III became greedy and demanded a new, second treaty of London with the addition of further territory. He demanded all territory north of the Loire, west of the Ile-de-France to the Channel coast, plus Touraine, Anjou, Maine, and Normandy, with a coastal strip between the Somme and Calais; half of France was to be England's. The Dauphin refused and Edward III despatched an army to Calais, which raided through to Rheims although achieved little while a French fleet threatened the English south coast. During this military interlude, an English squire named Geoffrey Chaucer was captured by the French and English Queen Philippa paid his ransom.

England was forced to the negotiating table and the Treaty of Brétigny was signed in 1360. The territorial demands were reduced to the coastal strip from the Somme to Calais, Ponthieu, and an enlarged Aquitaine running from the Auvergne to the Pyrénées including Poiyou, Saintonge, Quercy, and the Agenais. The King's ranson was reduced by one million ecus. In return, Edward dropped his claims to the French throne. Ratification of the terms would occur at Calais when the first ransom payment arrived when the two Kings would mutually agree to renounce their claims on titles and territories. Renunciations never took place and the released French King sent some French royal Princes to England as hostages where they were incarcerated in Calais. Unfortunately, King John's second son, Louis of Anjou, broke his parole and escaped to see his wife who he had not seen for a year. On his refusal to return, King John gave himself up to the Captain of Calais and he returned to England to stay in honorable captivity under the full payment of his ransom. On 8 April 1364, King John died in captivity.

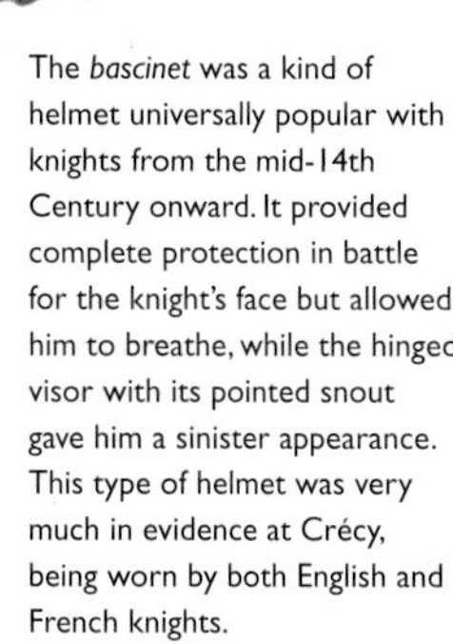

The *bascinet* was a kind of helmet universally popular with knights from the mid-14th Century onward. It provided complete protection in battle for the knight's face but allowed him to breathe, while the hinged visor with its pointed snout gave him a sinister appearance. This type of helmet was very much in evidence at Crécy, being worn by both English and French knights.

Left: THE BATTLE OF POITIERS
In many ways this battle was a rerun of the Battle of Crécy, as English archers destroyed the armored French army, both mounted and on foot. This assault was followed by vicious hand-to-hand fighting. The King of France was captured during the battle. His ransom, demanded by the English, was twice the entire annual income of the French crown.

Impact of Black Death

WHEN THE PLAGUE REACHED EUROPE IN 1347, IT FIRST ATTACKED SICILY, SARDINIA, AND CORSICA, APPEARING IN PARIS IN 1348. THE FOLLOWING YEAR, THE MEDIEVAL WEST WAS DEVASTATED, WITH IMMENSE SOCIAL AND MILITARY IMPLICATIONS.

The Black Death, or bubonic and pneumonic plague, first appeared in China in 1346, after which it surged along the trade routes, appearing in Sicily and Italian ports in 1348. The sickness bypassed quarantine regulations: the doors of infected houses were boarded up by town authorities and a red cross painted on the door; the occupants would stay there to die or live but could not get out to infect others. However, the fleas could move via rats. Western Europe was hit in 1348. The disease bacillus (*Pasteurella pestis*) lives in the blood of the flea, (*Xenopsylla cheopis*), which in turn lives on the rat, (*Rattus rattus*). When the plague killed the rats on board ships, the fleas jumped on to the crew who then infected the crowded seaports of Europe. During 1348–49, the plague spread rapidly in Europe, killing between a fifth and a third of the populations of France and England, with similar losses in other European countries.

Burying the dead in the city of Tournai. When this illustration was made in 1349, there was still time to make coffins for the dead.

The disease killed nearly half of the clergy, savaging monasteries in particular. Clerics shriving the dying (hearing confessions) would easily contract the sickness; monasteries, being closed communities, were unable to escape the flea. As ploughmen and shepherds died, fallow land turned to waste, flocks roamed freely, crops rotted in the fields and the entire social fabric fractured, damaging feudalism irrevocably. As people died, rents were not paid, money failed to circulate, slowing down economies. In the winter, famine affected England and France, with whole villages wiped out. Medical knowledge was inadequate to deal with the problem. Jews became scapegoats for ignorant Christians needing someone to blame for something they did not understand. Pogroms were

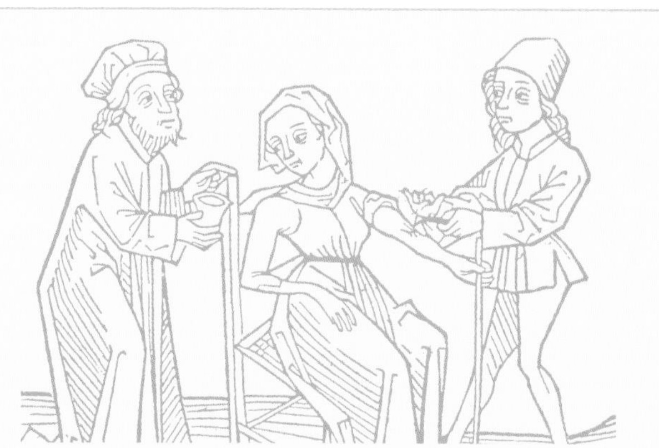

In this woodcut, the unfortunate patient is being bled, a common method of treatment in the Middle Ages. This could either be done by cutting a vein or by applying leeches to the skin. Medieval medicine failed to discover any cure, or even alleviation, for Bubonic Plague—"the Black Death."

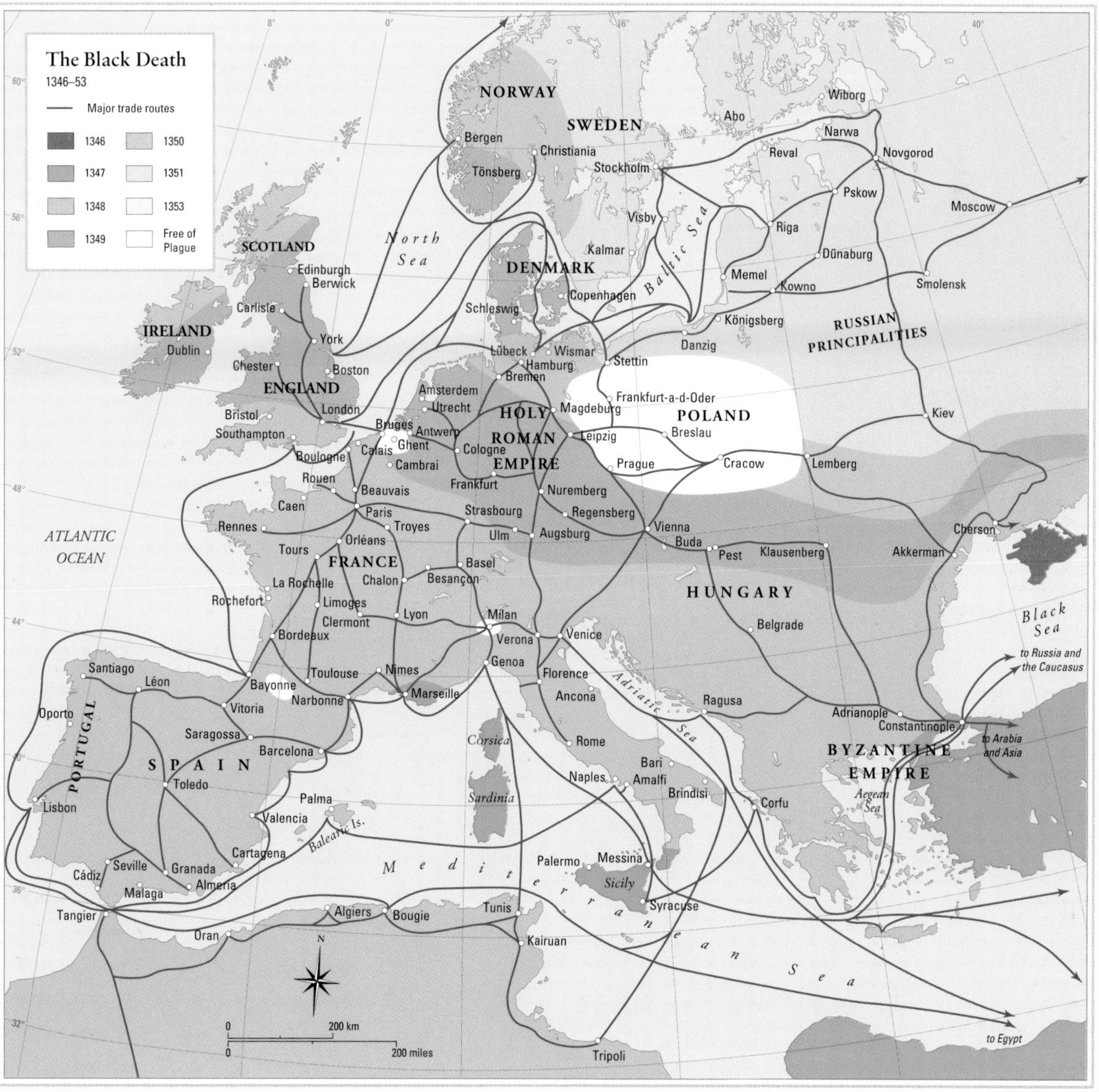

In this tapestry, dating from the 1370s, death rides his pale horse to collect the souls of the living. Death was constantly on the minds of Medieval men and women, especially at times of war, plague, and famine. Images of death were common, serving as dire warnings of what fate would befall those who did not repent and seek absolution.

unleashed to such an extent that 2,000 Jews were butchered in Strasbourg, and those of Frankfurt and Mainz were exterminated.

The nature of the plague was so disgusting that family members deserted each other. Burial pits were often so shallow that dogs would pull the bodies out and devour them. The plague revisited Europe in 1369, 1374–75, 1379, 1390 and 1407 and then every decade during the 15th Century. Those who were born in between plague years died off more rapidly because they had no inbuilt immunity. During the first exposure young women and children were vulnerable, which meant that populations took a long time to recover and warfare declined.

The chronicler of St. Denis stated that 50,000 people died in Paris, one-third of the city's population. People were advised to avoid swamps and chill air lest the disease was spread by miasma. Hand and mouth washing with vinegar was thought to be a deterrent, as was the stink of the latrines!

The Black Death was transported to England from Gascony arriving at Melcombe in Dorset, sweeping through the country in months. Winchester saw the death of 40 percent of its population, 4,000 souls. New cemeteries were opened in London but many bodies were tossed into the Thames, spoiling the water for those downstream.

The sickness was not respectful of rank. Eleanor, Queen of Peter IV of Aragon, and King Alfonso XI of Castile died, and Joan, daughter of Edward III passed away at Bordeaux while on the way to wed Alfonso's son. Two archbishops of Canterbury succumbed, John de Stratford and Thomas Bradwardine. The population of England in 1400 was probably half of what it had been a century earlier and more than a thousand villages disappeared. About 25 million people died in Europe and, arguably, its population failed to reach its pre-1348 level until the start of the 16th Century.

The impact of the Black Death was momentous in other ways. Trade slumped for a while. More fateful, the acreage of land under cultivation was reduced owing to the deaths of so many laborers. Many landowners were ruined. The labour shortage forced many landowners to substitute wages or money rents in place of feudal labor service in an attempt to keep tenants. There was a universal rise in wages for peasants and artisans. Edward III tried to keep wages low by a Statute of Laborers but this failed. Philip VI tried the same in vain. Laborers knew that they could leave their masters and find work anywhere where new needy employers would protect them. Men left for the towns or went soldiering with Free Companies of mercenary soldiers. Social stratification broke down into a more fluid system.

For the religious community, the plague was catastrophic. The reduced number of clerics were too few to provide spiritual guidance for all in a time of crisis. The Dominicans and other religious orders were so decimated that they had to recruit priests with little education and culture. The quality and intellectual strength of the Church declined so much that the plague might be responsible for the increase in superstitious practices and the birth and growth of so-called heresies.

For monarchs, parishes could not pay their taxes, manor lands remained unploughed, and national resources and revenues shrank. The shortage of money curtailed military plans but war was much needed for ransom money and so on. Fortunately for England, the capture of King John of France at Poitiers solved some problems.

The plague was seen by many Christians as Divine Punishment for their sins, which could only be cured by penitence, self-punishment, and strict religious observance. In this 15th-Century German illustration Christ is depicted showering arrows onto the bodies of sinners, while clerical figures pray for their souls.

Henry V in France

"WE FEW, WE HAPPY FEW, WE BAND OF BROTHERS;

FOR HE TODAY THAT SHEDS HIS BLOOD WITH ME

SHALL BE MY BROTHER; BE HE NE'ER BE SO VILE,

THIS DAY SHALL GENTLE HIS CONDITION:

AND GENTLEMEN IN ENGLAND NOW A-BED

SHALL THINK THEMSELVES ACCURSED THEY WERE NOT HERE,

AND HOLD THEIR MANHOODS CHEAP WHILES HE SPEAKS

THAT FOUGHT WITH US UPON ST. CHRISPEN'S DAY."

SHAKESPEARE'S HENRY V

Henry V, King of England from 1413–22, was a celebrated military leader, dedicated to expanding his domains.

Right: The rich lands of northern France and the Low Countries sat astride vital trade routes, especially the routes connecting England's wool trade with its customers in Continental Europe. The ownership of these territories yielded vast sums in taxes.

Henry V was the son of Henry IV, who had usurped the throne from Richard II in 1399 and then established the Lancastrian dynasty on firm foundations in England. Henry IV also won international acceptance for his position, as evidenced by a series of alliances in Germany, Scandinavia, Brittany, and Burgundian Flanders. Henry V ascended to the throne in 1413, cherishing dreams of conquest in France, a country with weak kingship and a disunited nobility.

Henry sailed his army to Harfleur, laying siege to that city. He had 12,000 men in a ratio of three archers to one man-of-arms and possessed a siege train of cannon. The siege took longer than thought possible but the city fell on 22 October 1415, providing him with a springboard into France. He left Harfleur on 6 October on a *chevauchée* to Calais. Not expecting any trouble on the 160-mile journey, the army had only eight days' rations. However, a large French army was assembling hoping to cut off the English from Calais. Henry's hungry troops only crossed the Seine on 19 October at the fords of Bethencourt and Voyenes. The road to Calais was blocked and Henry was forced to fight a battle at Agincourt on 25 October, securing a brilliant victory.

Agincourt

Before the Battle of Agincourt, Henry V received intelligence from French prisoners that his enemies planned a new strategy of attacking the archers with special units of barded warhorses (armored breast and flanks). Consequently, the King ordered every archer to make himself a six

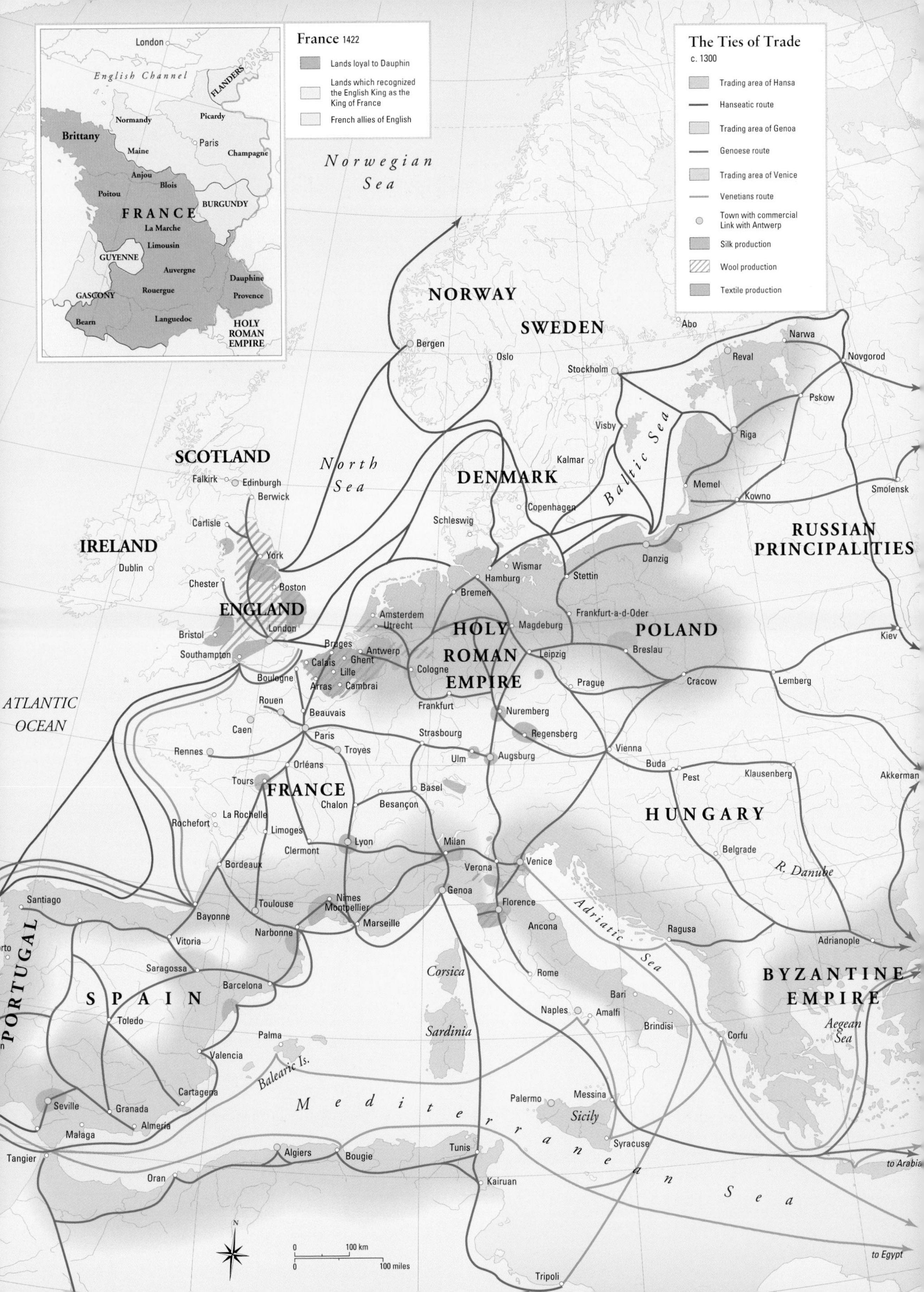
France 1422
Lands loyal to Dauphin
Lands which recognized the English King as the King of France
French allies of English
London
English Channel
FLANDERS
Normandy
Picardy
Brittany
Paris
Maine
Champagne
Anjou
Blois
Poitou
BURGUNDY
FRANCE
La Marche
Limousin
GUYENNE
Auvergne
Dauphine
GASCONY
Rouergue
Provence
Bearn
Languedoc
HOLY ROMAN EMPIRE
The Ties of Trade
c. 1300
Trading area of Hansa
Hanseatic route
Trading area of Genoa
Genoese route
Trading area of Venice
Venetians route
Town with commercial Link with Antwerp
Silk production
Wool production
Textile production
Norwegian Sea
NORWAY
SWEDEN
Bergen
Oslo
Abo
Stockholm
Narwa
Reval
Novgorod
Pskow
Visby
Baltic Sea
Riga
Kalmar
North Sea
SCOTLAND
DENMARK
Falkirk
Edinburgh
Berwick
Memel
Smolensk
Kowno
Copenhagen
Schleswig
Carlisle
RUSSIAN PRINCIPALITIES
IRELAND
York
Danzig
Dublin
Wismar
Hamburg
Stettin
Chester
Boston
Bremen
ENGLAND
Frankfurt-a-d-Oder
Amsterdem
Utrecht
HOLY ROMAN EMPIRE
Magdeburg
POLAND
Bristol
London
Kiev
Bruges
Antwerp
Breslau
Southampton
Calais
Ghent
Leipzig
Lille
Cologne
Boulogne
Arras
Cambrai
Prague
Cracow
Lemberg
ATLANTIC OCEAN
Rouen
Frankfurt
Beauvais
Nuremberg
Caen
Strasbourg
Regensberg
Paris
Troyes
Rennes
Vienna
Ulm
Augsburg
Orléans
Buda
Pest
Klausenberg
Akkerman
Tours
FRANCE
Basel
Chalon
Besançon
HUNGARY
La Rochelle
Rochefort
Limoges
Lyon
Milan
Clermont
Belgrade
Bordeaux
Venice
Verona
R. Danube
Genoa
Santiago
Nimes
Montpellier
Toulouse
Florence
Adriatic Sea
Bayonne
Marseille
Ancona
Ragusa
Vitoria
Narbonne
Adrianople
PORTUGAL
Saragossa
Corsica
Rome
BYZANTINE EMPIRE
Barcelona
SPAIN
Bari
Naples
Amalfi
Toledo
Brindisi
Sardinia
Aegean Sea
Palma
Corfu
Valencia
Balearic Is.
Cartagena
Palermo
Messina
Seville
Granada
Mediterranean Sea
Sicily
Almeria
Malaga
Syracuse
Tunis
Tangier
Algiers
Bougie
to Arabia
Oran
Kairuan
100 km
100 miles
to Egypt
Tripoli

Campaigns 1415 – 1419

1415
- English movements
- French movements

1417
- Henry V movements
- Other English movements

1418
- Henry V movements
- Other English movements
- Burgundian movements

1419
- Dauphinist movements
- Castles captured with dates
- Major English victory

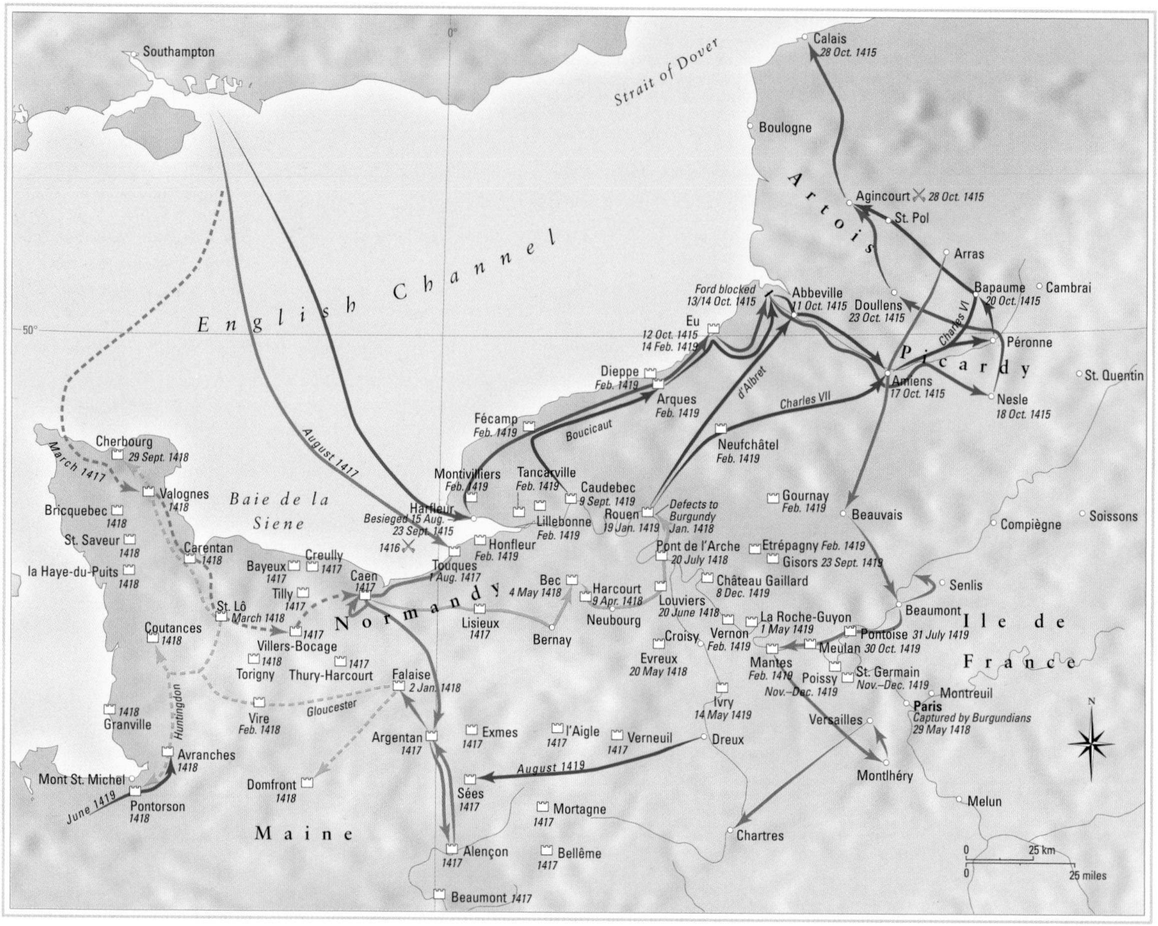

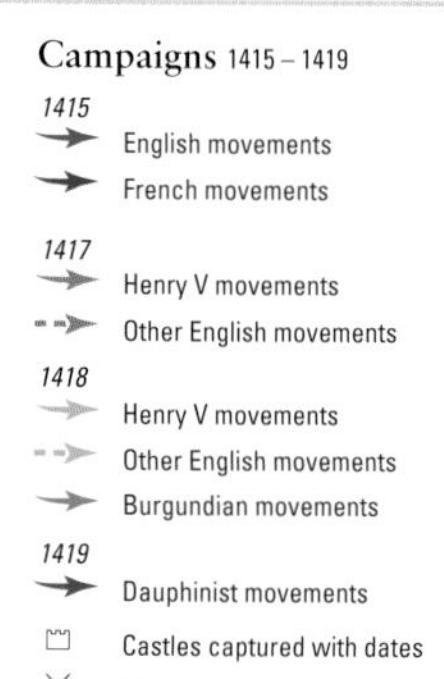

foot long stake sharpened at both ends so that they could be shoved into the ground with one sharpened end directed at an oncoming cavalry charge in order to impale the horses.

The French forces deployed a first battle of 6,000 dismounted men-at-arms with a planned 4,000 crossbowmen in front as skirmishers with cavalry forces on each flank, 1,600 on the left and 800 on the right. The second battle comprised 6,000 more men-at-arms with a third battle of about 8,000 cavalry behind them.

The battlefield was advantageous to Henry. It was very narrow, being 3,000 feet (915 m) wide between the villages of Agincourt and Tramecourt. Each village was surrounded by thick woods which funneled the vast French forces into such a constricted area that they could not deploy properly. Important, too, was the soggy nature of the ploughed land, lashed by the October rains. A virtual bog, no cavalry charge could gain impetus up its slope toward the English lines. The dismounted French knights made heavy weather of walking through the clinging clay and were led by the inexperienced Dukes of Alençon and Orléans. Meanwhile, Henry V marshalled his men in the normal English manner. Orthodox history states that his dismounted men-at-arms comprised three battles each with a forward projecting flank of archers. Where these projections met, they created a hollow outward pointing wedge-shaped formation, and before and within this wedge were planted the stakes creating a defensive field. The existence of three battles was notional. There were so few men at arms that they formed a solid line with three banners flying at intervals showing the position of the various commanders.

When the two armies faced each other, they remained watching each other for hours. The French front rank sat down, sending their pages for food. Henry V decided to disturb this picnic, advancing his forces complete with stakes to the narrowest part of the field within a bowshot of the French army. The archers pushed stakes into the ground, then pulled their bowstring and sent thousands of arrows hurtling into the close-packed French. The deep-toned pluck of the bowstrings was known descriptively as "devil's harp music."

The French reacted badly, rashly using their flank cavalry to attack, but these consisted of only 150 each because the poorly disciplined knights had not formed up according to plan. The narrow battle front meant they could not outflank the English archers, while the boggy ground slowed them down as they met the arrow storm. Some were impaled on stakes, some were catapulted out of their saddles and were killed while lying on the ground. A few reached the English lines but the rest fled crashing in to the advancing dismounted French. The French crossbowmen were not used to being behind the vanguard they were supposed to support. The men-at-arms, tired by trudging through the mud and damaged by arrow fire, crashed into the fresher foe and were repulsed.

Some mounted French knights formed in column and swerved out to attack the English flanks but the archers ran out to either side and took them in both flanks, shooting volleys of arrows into their horses. The French second battle did push the English back a little and Henry V had some florets of his golden crown knocked from his helmet. The archers were turned loose; lightly armed, they could dance across the boggy ground and hunt down French soldiers in packs. The French dead were reportedly piled three deep, their leaders butchered or captured. Seeing the total carnage, the third French battle ran away. Meanwhile, the English roamed the battlefield, killing the wounded and taking prisoners for ransom.

The battle was not complete. The French Count of Merle and the Lord of Fauquemburges collected together a force of several hundred men-at-arms, launching a final attack. Witnessing this and a flank attack by the local lord, Isembert d'Azincourt, usually described as an assault on the English baggage, Henry V feared for his small forces. He realized that he could not fight while guarding so many prisoners, and ordered his knights to kill them. Their refusal induced the king to order 200 archers to kill the least wealthy prisoners, which they did with alacrity. Merle's charge was stopped and repelled.

No-one knows the full extent of French losses but they numbered at least 10,000 with six counts, 120 barons and 1,500 knights. They also lost the Dukes of Brabant and Alençon. English casualties were reputedly 300 including the Duke of York and the Earl of Suffolk. The English also took some 1,600 prisoners, all knights or nobles, including Marshall Boucicat, Arthur, Count of Richement, the Counts of Eu and Vendôme, and two royal Dukes, Bourbon and Orléans. The latter was a prisoner for 25 years, and Boucicaut died in captivity. Much ado has been made about the murder of the

Left: Henry V's campaign of 1415 began with the capture of the port of Harfleur. From there a *chevauchée* aimed at Calais, passing through parts of Normandy, Picardy and Artois. The French army decided to give battle at Agincourt; the victory that Henry V won there destroyed the cohesion of the French nobility, making his campaigns that followed in 1417 and 1419 much more effective.

Right: THE BATTLE OF AGINCOURT
Henry V's army of less than 6,000 men took on the superior might of 25,000 French soldiers, and triumphed in this decisive battle.

French prisoners but there had been no outcry. The French had killed 2,000 prisoners before the Battle of Nicopolis (1396). Each side could be ruthless in an age when chivalry was dying.

Henry V returned to a joyful England, his victory being sufficient to secure more loans for his French adventures. In 1416 he allied with Holy Roman Emperor Sigismund, and Duke John of Burgundy pledged his allegiance as Henry's vassal, recognizing him as King of France. Sigismund used his influence to detach Genoa from its naval alliance with France.

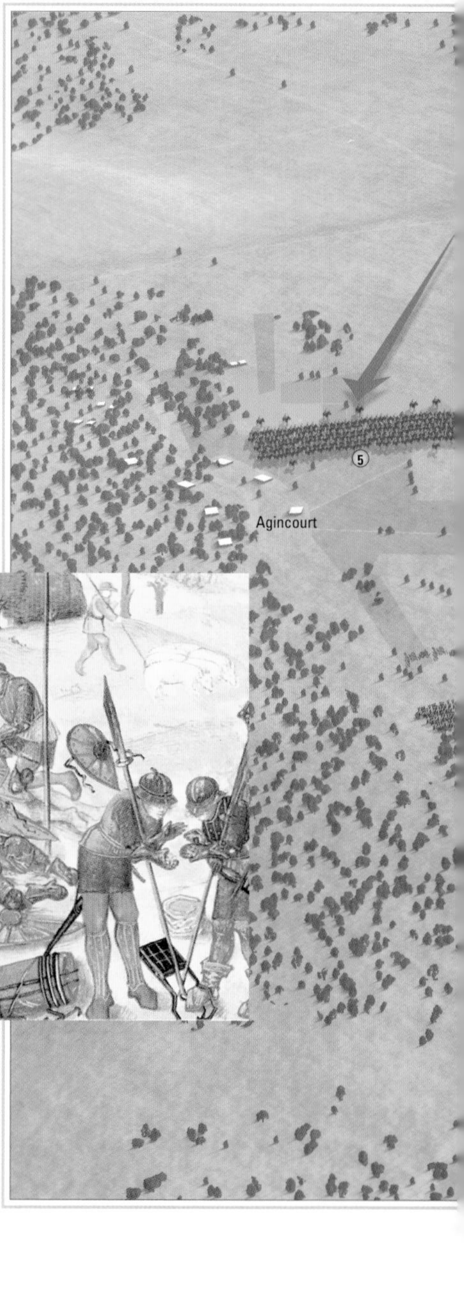

After securing the Channel by triumphing over a combined French-Genoese fleet blockading Harfleur, the Earl of Huntingdon, in 1417, destroyed the last of this fleet off Chef-de-Caux. Henry recrossed the Channel and took Caen, Bayeux, Argentan and Alençon by October. By 1418, Lower Normandy was taken, Caen becoming the administrative center of the recently seized territories. Cherbourg soon fell as did Rouen, after which Normandy collapsed by the summer of 1419. On payment of a few coins, Normans were given a certificate confirming their allegiance, loyalty, and homage to Henry as Duke of Normandy and King of France. The large landowners were dispossessed, being replaced by English nobility with an attempt to bring in English colonists. Some 4,500 troops were used to garrison Normandy.

A critical moment at the Battle of Agincourt. The order had been given by Henry V to kill the French prisoners. In this scene two English soldiers, below right, haggle over their spoils, while another strips a French knight of his valuable armor.

In 1418, Duke John of Burgundy seized Paris and was made King Charles VI. His murder by a rival Armagnac clan at Montereau caused the

Burgundian heir, Philip the Good, to support Henry V with a formal alliance. Philip wanted France for himself but he realized that the English would prevent this; however, an alliance with them would probably allow him to rule larger territories.

English success was crowned with the Treaty of Troyes (May 1420), ratified by Charles VI. Henry V became heir to the French King, and was to wed Charles' daughter, Catherine, immediately. Henry then besieged and took Montereau and Melun, returning to England in February 1421 to crown

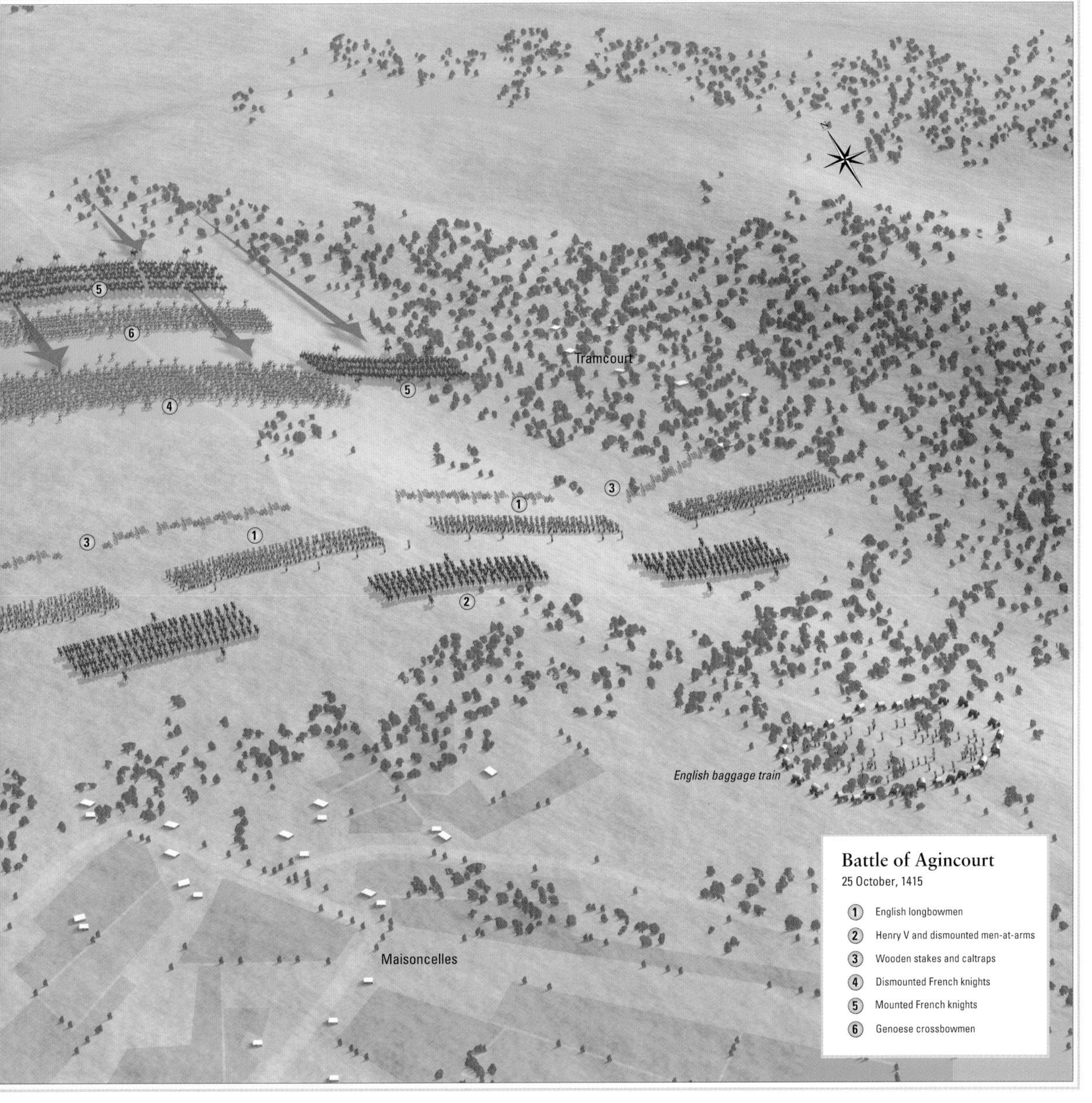

During the 1450s a new, confident French army had begun to reclaim territories taken during Henry V's reign. After years of defeat, they had learnt new methods of warfare, some inspired by their English enemies. In this colorful illustration the French besiege an English stronghold in Normandy.

Catherine as Queen. Returning to France, Henry captured Dreux, Vendôme, Beaugency and Meaux. The King then contracted dysentery at Meaux and died at Vincennes on 31 August 1422.

Henry had been a ruthless and cruel autocrat but a great general and was admired by all as a brave and honorable fighter. Chivalrous he was not. When taking the Armagnac Castle at Rougemont, he demolished the building and hung the garrison. After the surrender of Meaux, the French commander was beheaded and those who had mocked Henry during the siege were either killed or imprisoned in appalling conditions.

Before dying, Henry appointed his brother, the Duke of Bedford, as Regent of France and the Duke of Gloucester Regent of England. Henry V's son became Henry VI of England and Henry II of France. Bedford thought that the conquered territories should pay for themselves and embarked on further campaigns in Maine and Anjou. However, the French were inspired by Joan of Arc and the coronation of Charles VII. Breton and Burgundian allied support began to waver, the Normans resented their new masters, and the cost of garrisons and armies were enormously expensive, and the English Parliament found it difficult to raise money. The death of Bedford was a blow and Henry VI was a truly incompetent monarch. In 1449, the French invaded Normandy, clearing the duchy of the English by 1450. French forces then assaulted Gascony, these being lost to England by 1453, a really telling blow since these lands had been held by the English from the 12th Century. Calais was the only remnant of the English Empire in France. By 1471, Henry VI had lost his English realm, too, in dynastic clashes with the House of York, and he was murdered that year in the Tower of London.

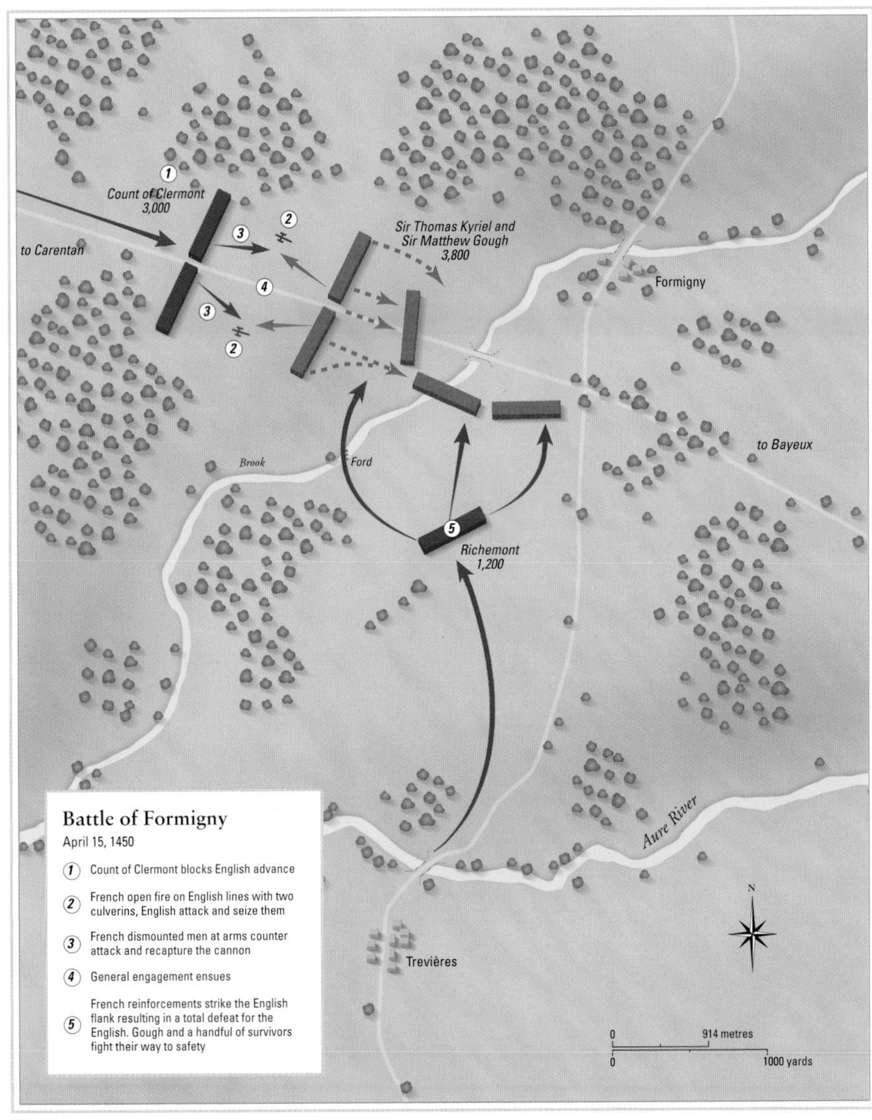

In 1449 King Charles VII of France launched a campaign to recapture Normandy, with a tactically and technically superior army, complete with cannon siege train. On 15 April the French met an English army at Formigny. The English commander, in tried and tested style, formed up his archers behind lines of stakes. The French, under Clermont, launched two probing attacks, both of which were repulsed. He then brought up two light guns that were able to disrupt the English archers, who then launched their own attack in an attempt to capture the guns. At this precise moment a fresh, French force, under the command of Richemont, approached from the south. The English formed a semicircle to face this new threat. The French then launched a concerted attack completely overwhelming the English army. Kyriell, the English commander, was taken prisoner, the rest of his army was either killed or captured.

The Perfect Knight

"On his head was placed a helmet, resplendent with many precious stones... very last of all a sword from the royal treasury was carried out to him. It had been preserved from long before, when it had been carefully crafted by that master, Weyland."

John of Marmoutier, Norman Chronicler

Ethos and Ideals of Knighthood

Far right: The Victorian painter Edmund Blair Leighton's intensely romantic portrayal of a dubbing, "The Accolade." The title refers to the blow on the neck—the *collée*—which actually conferred knighthood. In practice this was almost always done by another knight or a lord but certainly not by a woman. Later knighthood could only be conferred by a monarch including a female monarch (as in the painting) and the blow was made on the shoulders with a sword.

Pierre Terrail, seigneur de Bayard (1473–1524), was a great and lasting example of the ideals of knighthood and has become legendary as *le chevalier sans peur et sans reproche*, the fearless and blameless knight. His cheerfulness and kindness attracted another name from his contemporaries, *le bon chevalier*, the good knight.

Born at the Château Bayard in the Dauphiné, now the department of Isère in France, he became a page to Charles of Savoy, until Charles VIII of France promoted him to be one of his royal followers under the count of Ligry (1487) when aged 14. Evidently, he was admired for his looks, charming character, and skills in the tilt yard. In 1494, he accompanied Charles VIII into Italy, being knighted after the Battle of Fornovo, where he managed to capture an enemy standard. Charles' Italian adventure asserted his right to the kingdom of Naples, claimed as an Angevin inheritance. Later in the campaign, Pierre was taken prisoner entering Milan alone while pursuing the enemy. He was later freed by Ludovico Sforza, Duke of Milan, without ransom. In 1502, Pierre suffered wounds at the Battle of Canossa.

Pierre became a noted hero when, with 12 French knights, he fought against similar numbers of Germans. His bravery and unbounded energy permeated his activities throughout the period's Italian wars. Allegedly, he held a bridge at Garigliano, alone, against 200 Spaniards. This event prompted Pope Julius II to unsuccessfully entice Pierre into the papal service. He distinguished himself again at the siege of Genoa by Louis XII of France in 1508 after which the King made him captain of a company of cavalry and infantry.

His courage was seen again at the Siege of Padua but his reckless bravery in first scaling a parapet during the 1512 siege of Brescia caused him to be wounded. Before he was healed, he joined the French commander in Italy, Gaston de Foix, and was with him at the Battle of Ravenna (1512). The year 1513 witnessed Bayard in the French defeat by Henry VIII of England at the Battle of the

An expression of devotion; a knight kneels before his lady on a painted 15th-Century Flemish shield, designed for the parade before a tournament. Death hovers behind the knight, waiting for the moment when the knight's continual quest for danger leads him astray. The notch at the top left is for resting the lance on.

Spurs (1513). After failing to rally the French, he approached a resting English officer, demanding and accepting his surrender; he then surrendered to his captive. His bravery and gallantry so impressed Henry VIII that he released Bayard without ransom, merely demanding that he did not serve in the war for six weeks.

When Francis I became King of France he made Bayard his lieutenant-general in the Dauphiné (1515) and, after the French victory against the Swiss troops guarding Milan at the Battle of Marignano, Bayard dubbed his sovereign a knight. War broke out between Francis I and Charles V, the Holy Roman Emperor. Bayard, with 1,000 men, defended Mézières against a 35,000-strong enemy army. After six weeks the imperial forces withdrew, this resistance preventing an invasion of central France.

Bayard was made a knight of the Order of St. Michael in thanks. After stopping a revolt in Genoa, Bayard was sent to Italy with Admiral Bonnivet who was defeated at Robecco and wounded. He begged Bayard to take command and save his army. Bayard managed to repel the immediate pursuit but while in a rearguard action at Sesia was wounded by an arquebus ball. While dying amidst the enemy, he uttered his last words: "Pity me not. I die as a man of honor ought, in discharge of my duty. They indeed are objects of pity who fight against their king, their country, and their oath." Another account states that he died whilst reciting the Miserere (one of seven penitential psalms). Thus perished the epitome of chivalry, a skillful leader and a man disinterested in plunder. To his contemporaries, he was heroic, generous, kind, and devout: the Perfect Knight.

FEUDALISM

Knights were highly trained warriors whose duty was to kill and fight when their lord so decided. They lived in a world characterized by a virtual lack of political stability. However, for the knight, honor became more than courage and weapon skills. Cavalry forces were developed to oppose muslims, vikings, and magyars. The French term *chevalier* (horseman) and "knight," derived from Anglo-Saxon *cnight* (servant), came to have a common meaning. The ideal and ethos of knighthood and chivalry acquired the aura of a cult, a mystique, which honored aristocratic qualities, christian virtues, and the courtly, noble, love of women. Hence a knight should be a skilled and brave warrior, loyal to his lord, and generous to the poor and needy. A special virtue was to the join the crusades in the service of the pope and free the Holy Land. Southern France added the notion that a knight should serve a lady whom he would love passionately but fruitlessly, because in the romantic tales she would be betrothed to another.

Knighthood and its ideals developed in the aftermath of the collapse of the Carolingian Empire. The empire was then split into thousands of lordships without any overarching suzerainty. Such anarchy was chaos and a new system was needed to link political power and military defense into a coordinated system, a new institution known as feudalism. The new feudal lords with their military vassals managed to establish localized unity to drive off enemies and invaders. Its success encouraged monarchs to adopt it to centralize power and the countries they ruled.

"Pity me not. I die as a man of honor ought, in discharge of my duty. They indeed are objects of pity who fight against their King, their country and their oath."

Feudalism developed during the 11th, 12th, and 13th Centuries, originating in the area between the Rhine and the Loire but spreading under the Normans in the 11th Century into southern Italy and Sicily, and England under William the Conqueror. The 12th Century witnessed the spread of feudal institutions into Spain, northern Italy, southern France, and Germany but to a lesser extent than the original core home. The collapse of the Byzantine Empire during the Fourth Crusade saw feudalism introduced into the Latin states of Greece, while the crusades in general established feudal crusader states in the Near East. The chapter on Asian Knighthood shows the similarities and differences between European knights and Japanese samurai and the unique relationship between lords and vassals in Japan.

The main feature of western feudalism envisaged that all land belonged to a sovereign lord whether he was a king, duke, earl, or count, the lands being held by virtual divine right. In England all lands technically belonged to the king. The ruler gave fiefs to his chief retainers, barons, who rendered oaths of homage and fealty to him and were required to provide him with political and military service according to the term of the grant. When Richard de Clare, 2nd Earl of Pembroke, know as "Strongbow," was granted Leinster as a fief, Henry II demanded 100 knights in return. These barons might then act in the same fashion, granting parcels of their fief to knights who also swore homage and fealty to the barons and provided knight service as requested. For example, a baron given several seigneuries in return for 12 knights, could grant each a seigneurie to cover the king's knight service. Each knight might acquire more than one fief and would sub-grant to cover his service and so on. The result was a feudal pyramid caused by subinfeudation, providing a force of knights for the prince at the top.

Feudal service comprised a variety of tasks, military service in the field being just one facet. Vassals could be called to garrison a lord's castle and attend his court to render advice and become involved in judgment over cases concerning other vassals. Sometimes, a lord would demand money. The 12th and 13th Centuries saw many conflicts between

The medieval knight in all his glory, Sir Geoffrey Lutterill is armed by his wife and daughter, prior to setting off for a tournament, from the 14th-Century Luttrell Psalter.

lords and vassals over the exact nature of required services. In England, threat of civil war drove King John to sign the Magna Carta at Runnymede near Windsor in 1215. The document laid down certain rights: a freeman could not be imprisoned or dispossessed except by the lawful judgement of his peers or by the law of the land. Financial aid was never to be given, except for the occasion of the marriage of the king's eldest daughter, the knighting of his eldest son, or the king's own ransom. In France, it was customary to provide financial aid for a fourth event, a crusade. Vassals also demanded that if a lord made decisions about them, then they should be involved in the discussion about judgments over waging war, making alliance by marriage or with other lords, in peer legal judgements, and taxation generally.

An important aspect of feudalism was the contractual relationship between lord and knight. If a vassal refused required services, he could be charged in court before the other vassals, and if declared guilty, would forfeit his fief which would return to the lord's demesne. On the other side, if a lord failed in his duty to a vassal, then the lord could be defied, and the vassal might seek to defend his fief and offer it to another lord; this event would be unlikely because the vassal would need strong support from other vassals to succeed.

The feudal system established in northern and central France enabled its great lords, the counts and dukes who controlled large territories, to gain power at the expense of the monarchy. Fiefs were originally granted to a lord for his lifetime in return for service to the crown, and were supposed to revert to the crown on the lord's death. By the 11th Century, however, it had become accepted that both service and lands were hereditary. On the lord's death, his heir was entitled to take possession of his estates, provided that he acknowledged the overlordship of the king by doing homage. But in reality this meant that large areas of France, which had once been under the direct personal control of the king, had been alienated from him. His overlordship was in most cases merely a formality; he retained control only of a small area of central France. In the mid-12th Century the greatest landholder in France was, in fact, the King of England, Henry II.

In the German Empire, though the feudal system itself was essentially similar to that of northern France, this did not happen because successive emperors had been careful not to entrust key roles in their administrations to individual nobles and their families. Instead they had cultivated a close relationship with the Church, giving high office to bishops and abbots: men who had been appointed by the emperor in the first place (at least until Emperor Henry IV's great dispute with Pope Gregory VII over investitures in 1076). This meant that offices could not become hereditary, and the imperial family retained control of its own extensive territories.

The emperor and the men who served him in government needed reliable and efficient administrators to run their estates for them. These were the *ministeriales*, or 'serf-knights'. They were 'serfs' because technically they were unfree and tied to the lands of the lord they served. They could not marry outside their lord's domain or hold estates from other lords without his permission; their status was defined by the laws of the domain to which they belonged and they had no legal rights outside it. However, their service was like that of a knight to his feudal lord; they served him in hall, they administered his estates and, since they were mounted and trained in arms by the lord, they gave military service too. The serf-knights at any court would occupy the important positions of marshal, chamberlain, and seneschal (the steward in a great house).

By the mid-11th Century it had become generally accepted that *ministeriales* could own property, and many had acquired their own holdings, wealth, and status. Though the German aristocracy was more rigidly defined and stratified than elsewhere in Europe, the *ministeriales* managed to make the transition from "serfdom" to the lowest ranks as independent knights. During the investiture dispute and the civil wars which followed it they emerged as a crucial element of continuity and stability in enabling the Emperor to maintain control of his lands. They began to hold fiefs from, and do homage to, other lords as an ordinary member of the *Edelfreie* (lesser nobility) might. In the first half of the 12th Century they began to view themselves as a distinct social group; they held assemblies and acted collectively. Eventually they merged with other members of the lesser nobility to form the class of knights known as the Ritterstand.

William the Marshal—A Brilliant Career

William Marshal was probably born in about 1144. His father, John, was a minor landholder who held the hereditary office of marshal in the king's household. John Marshal substantially improved his family fortune by repudiating his first wife and marrying a lady of property whose brother became the Earl of Salisbury. William was the fourth of six sons so, though he was born into the knightly class, he had no money or property to inherit and had to make his own way in the world. We know much about William's life because he became so wealthy and famous that his biography was written within a few years of his death in 1219. Although the life story is in the form of a verse romance, it contains many fascinating and humorous details of a knight's life in the 12th Century.

England was in a state of civil war, following the death of Henry I and the accession to the throne of his daughter Matilda. Her cousin, Stephen of Blois, also claimed the throne with the support of about half the barons and lords of England. William had a narrow escape from death while still a child. His father, who was on the side of the Empress Matilda, was besieged by her rival, King Stephen. John Marshal had asked for a truce and the king had granted it in exchange for a hostage: William, who at this time was about eight years old. John broke the terms of the truce by using it to refortify the castle and Stephen threatened to kill the little hostage. William's father unfeelingly replied that he should go ahead, since he "still had the hammer and anvil on which to forge a better son than that one." One of Stephen's officers proposed putting William in a catapult and throwing him over the castle wall but Stephen was too kind-hearted to murder him and instead kept him prisoner for two months.

William was brought up from the age of about twelve in the castle of a family connection, William of Tancarville. There he learnt all the essential qualities of knighthood and was fond of listening to romances. He was knighted in 1164 on the eve of a battle at Drincourt. He acquitted himself well in the battle but unfortunately his horse was killed and he had to pawn the new robe that the lord of Tancarville had given him in order to buy another. Soon he was attending tournaments which, in William's day, consisted of two teams of knights attacking one another for sport over a wide range of countryside. The object was to take prisoner as many knights from the

The face of a hero: the tomb effigy of William Marshal in the Temple Church, London. William had joined the Knights Templar a few months before his death in the year 1219.

opposing team as possible, though it appears that knights were very often wounded and killed at these events. A captured knight forfeited his horse and possibly his armor too, and had to pay a ransom to be released. William was extremely successful and realized that he could make his fortune at tournaments. He entered into an agreement with a Flemish knight, Roger de Gaugi, in 1177, that they would travel from tournament to tournament together, helping each other to capture knights and splitting the ransom money equally between them. In ten months they took 103 knights prisoner.

William by this time had grown rich enough to equip his own team of knights, and the biographer records that he was generous with gifts to them. On one occasion he was dining with friends at an inn when he saw a knight fall from his horse in the street and break a leg. William rushed out and picked up the wounded man in his arms, armor and all, and carried him into the inn. There he presented him to his friends so that they could pay the bill with his ransom money. How the wounded knight felt about this act of chivalrous generosity is not recorded.

William was not immune to the dangers of tournaments. *The History of William Marshal* tells how one day some knights were seeking William after a tournament in order to give him the prize. They could not find him but at last he was spotted in the blacksmith's shop with his head on the anvil, having his helmet hammered back into shape so that he could get it off his head.

William's career really began to take off in 1167 when he had joined his uncle, the Earl of Salisbury, in a campaign to suppress a rebellion in Poitou. Their party was ambushed; the Earl was killed, William wounded and taken prisoner. William's courageous conduct in the campaign had, however, attracted the notice of Eleanor of Aquitaine, now Queen of England as well as the overlord of Poitou. She paid William's ransom and, in 1169, through her influence, William was placed in charge of her eldest son, Henry. William directed the prince's household and supervised his military training. In 1170, when the prince was 15 years old, his father Henry II of England, decided to crown him to ensure a peaceful succession, and from then on he was known as the Young King.

The Young King had inherited his father's ungovernable temper. Jealousy of his youngest brother, John, led him to rebel against his father in 1173. In preparation for a military campaign, the

Young King had himself knighted. He chose William Marshal to perform the crucial ceremony of girding on the sword and delivering the ritual blow. *The History of William Marshal* remains discreetly silent about William's part in the rebellion, but at its conclusion he was a party in the negotiations for the peace treaty, and retained his position.

His close relationship with the Young King was maintained until 1182, when he lost favor with both Henrys because of a malicious rumor that he was having an affair with the Young King's wife, Margaret of France. William challenged his accusers to single combat (then a legitimate legal process for determining the truth in a dispute) but the Young King forbade it and allowed William to leave the court unharmed.

So great was William's fame and prestige at this point that, as soon as it was known that he was no longer in the service of the Young King, three great lords offered him property and a pension if he would become their man. But William had no wish or need for their protection. He went on pilgrimage to Cologne instead, and waited until he could be reconciled with the Young King. This happened in 1183 when the Young King and his brother, Geoffrey, launched another rebellion against their father. The young Henry sent for William who joined him on his journey south, just in time to see his master die of a fever. On his deathbed, he asked William to discharge for him an unfulfilled vow to go on crusade to the Holy Land. William spent the next two years in Syria, returning home, it seems, just before the capture of Jerusalem by Saladin in 1187.

On return he was taken into service by Henry II and eventually was rewarded with the hand in marriage of Isabel de Clare, a rich heiress and daughter of the Earl of Pembroke. He remained at the center of political life throughout the reigns of Richard I and John, and one last story testifies to his absolute loyalty and honor. When King John died in 1216, his heir, Henry III, was a child of nine years. The country was in turmoil as large areas of the southeast acknowledged Prince Louis of France as King. An invasion by the French to subdue the rest of the kingdom was expected at any moment. The few nobles who had remained loyal to King John gathered together. On the initiative of the papal legate, Gualo, Henry was first knighted (by William) and then crowned King. William was then begged to become the king's guardian and protector. At first he refused, saying that he was too old (he was over seventy), but in the end he consented. The position, however, looked hopeless;

"They had entrusted me with an almost hopelesss governorship. The child has no money and I am a man of great age." Tears came into his eyes as he spoke and others wept too, out of pity. "Yes," said John de Erley, who had understood his way of thinking, "you have undertaken a task that must be carried through at all costs. But when we reach the end, I tell you that, even putting things at their worst, only great honor can come of it... No man will ever have earned such a glory upon earth."

"By God's sword," said William Marshal, "this advice is true and good. It pierces my heart. If everyone else abandoned the King, do you know what I would do? I would carry him on my shoulders, step by step, from island to island, from country to country, and I would not fail him, even if it meant begging my bread."

In this picture from the *Livre des Tournois du Roi René*, a squire prepares to display his knight's helm and colors before an appreciative audience prior to the beginning of a tournament.

The History of William Marshal records William consulting his friends for their advice:

"They have entrusted me with an almost hopeless governorship. The child has no money and I am a man of great age." Tears came into his eyes as he spoke, and the other wept too, out of pity. "Yes," said John de Erley, who had understood his way of thinking, "you have undertaken a task that must be carried through at all costs. But when we reach the end, I tell you that, even putting things at their worst, only great honor can come of it... No man will ever have earned such a glory upon earth."

"By God's sword," said William Marshal, "this advice is true and good. It pierces my heart. If everyone else abandoned the King, do you know what I would do? I would carry him on my shoulders, step by step, from island to island, from country to country, and I would not fail him, even if it meant begging my bread."

William captured and dismantled all the castles held by Louis in the east of England; Louis retreated to France in 1217 and the kingdom was secured for Henry III. William joined the military religious order of the Knights Templar (with whom he had served in Syria) shortly before he died in 1219 and was buried with great honor in the Temple Church in London.

PAGE, SQUIRE AND KNIGHTHOOD RITUAL

The son of a knight was under the charge of the women of the household for the first few years of his life. When he was about seven or eight, however, he was fostered out to the castellan (governor of a castle) to be brought up, together with the sons of other knights, in the castle. This was where he learnt the business of knighthood. At first he would serve as a page, learning how to serve at table and performing other simple household tasks. At this stage, like the youngest boys at a public school, his status was menial and he could be ordered about by other members of the household, sent on errands, or given cleaning tasks.

In his early teens, a boy would graduate to the next stage in the knightly hierarchy in the castle and become a squire. A squire had certain specific duties to perform, which included taking turns to serve his lord at table, look after his horses and harness, and, if he attended a tournament or went to war, take charge of his lord's equipment and armor, and to arm him before he went into action.

He would share sleeping quarters and take turns at these duties with a group of other squires like himself. During this period he would be trained to ride and to fight with a variety of weapons on foot and on horseback. Physical fitness was essential for a knight and squires had to develop the strength necessary to fight in chain mail which could weigh about 50 lbs (22.5 kg). Just to wear this for several hours at a stretch was tiring because the whole weight of the suit hung from the shoulders. In addition, the squire would have to learn to wield with ease the heavy sword which dealt the devastating blows we hear about in romance and chronicle, the even heavier lance and possibly also a battleaxe or club.

From contemporary pictures of the exercises undertaken by young squires in castle yards we can see that they learnt to handle weapons first on foot and without armor, performing tests of skill such as hitting targets with a lance carried at a run, or thwacking each other with swords. This also taught them how to use their shields effectively. They would then have to master the same skill while wearing armor, and finally while riding a horse. Squires trained together and this helped to reinforce the knights' sense of brotherhood and professional solidarity.

This brings up another important part of the chivalrous education a young squire received at a castle or court, his initiation into the finer aspects of courtly life: how to carve meat, how to serve his lord at table, how to dance, the exercise of courtly manners, the hunt, the banquet, and so on. He acquired a taste for courtly music and courtly literature, which included, as well as romances and books of instruction, treatises on hunting and warfare, the chronicles of his country and of the local noble family. He learnt about stately ceremony, fine clothes, weapons, and armor, as well as the rougher sports of knightly life. He may have learnt to read; he would certainly have learnt the rudiments of heraldry.

A knight rides to tournament wearing a surcoat (loose robe worn over armor) showing his colors, which are also emblazoned on his shield and his horse's coparision (horse's covering).

The squire was knighted, if he was in easy circumstances, on achieving a suitable age, usually the late teens or early twenties. If he did not have enough income to maintain the status of a knight and its attendant expenses, he might remain a "bachelor" for several years, or even not be knighted at all. There was an abundance of honorable employment for well-brought-up young men at courts and castles throughout Europe that did not require them to be knights; good squires were always valued, as were heralds and, for those of an intellectual bent, writers, whether they were historians or romancers.

The ceremony of dubbing to knighthood developed in its several varieties, from the stately ritual of mass-knightings at formal peacetime occasions, to the hurried conferring of the essential elements either on or shortly before taking to the field of battle.

By the late 13th Century, an elaborate ecclesiastical ritual for dubbing a knight is found in the pontifical of William Durandus of Mende. This ceremony was performed by a bishop; he took the sword and laid it on the altar, blessing it with a prayer being supplemented by a soldier's prayer from the Old Testament:

> "Blessed be the Lord God who formeth my hands for battle and my fingers for war. He is my salvation, He is my refuge, He setteth me free."

The bishop then put the sword into the knight's right hand, took it back, gave the knight the *collée* (blow) on the neck, as the knight knelt before him, and then girded the sword about the

Kings and nobles were addicted to hunting, when they could demonstrate their skill with weapons and their command of horsemanship. Hunting was considered the most civilized and manly of pastimes.

knight's waist. The knight rose and flourished the sword three times; he was then "marked with the character of knighthood." The bishop kissed him on the cheeks and admonished him to perform his duties faithfully and devoutly.

Not all knights were subjected to such an intensely religious ceremony. Many were knighted hurriedly before battles, without the benefit of clergy, but even those who were knighted at leisure during peacetime often created a ceremony equally elaborate but much more secular in its tone. From the evidence of chronicles and romances, it remained more important for the new knight to receive his knighthood from the hands of a knight, preferably a distinguished one, rather than from a priest or bishop. As the Middle Ages wore on, however, dubbing ceremonies became increasingly associated with the Church, they took place in a church rather than in the hall of a castle, and were performed in the presence of churchmen, if not actually by them.

Assuming that the new knight was not immediately able to settle on his estate and raise a family, he would be a "landless" knight, or one who would not inherit his patrimony for many years to come. Let us suppose that he gained employment at the court of a lord, and examine some of the peace-time activities that reinforced his sense of his knighthood and the honor of his calling.

THE HUNT

Hunting and hawking were important knightly activities. Hunting provided valuable additions to the medieval diet but for knights such considerations were secondary to its value as a sport. In northern and eastern Europe or Spain, where there were still huge areas of uncultivated land, including tracts of primeval forest, there was no need to restrict the access of peasants to the potential food source of wild animals. However, in densely populated and highly agricultural areas, such as England, France, and northern Italy, landowners, from kings to knights, valued their woods as game reserves and guarded them jealously against the depredations of poachers. The penalties for catching reserved animals, such as deer, were severe and included mutilation and flaying.

As land became scarce, hunting reserves could be enjoyed only by the richest and most powerful nobles and the knights in their household. Professional huntsmen were employed to look after the hounds and maintain the stocks of game. As a "noble" sport, hunting developed its own hierarchies and rituals over the years. A stag was the noblest quarry, followed by a boar, female deer, wolves, and bears. Foxes and hares were also hunted but were considered inferior species, while rabbits were left for the peasants to snare.

A gruesome description of the butchering of the dead animals ensues, which follows exactly the highly technical instructions for dismembering carcases given in contemporary hunting manuals, such as the *Livre de la chasse* written in 1387 (about the same time of the poem) by Gaston, *Count of Foix*, for his friend Philip, Duke of Burgundy. This treatise is the product of one man's lifelong enthusiasm. It is a medieval encyclopaedia of hunting, detailing the different hounds to be used for different quarry, the various methods of chase, the open and close seasons for all prey animals, different traps and baits, and incidental activities such as meals al fresco in the forest.

Deer could also be hunted with spears or swords instead of bows and arrows. It could thus be seen as another opportunity to exercise knightly qualities. Edward I was described by William Rishanger (a Benedictine monk and analyst known as "Chronigraphus") as a great lover of hunting, and he remarked how, as a young Prince, Edward hunted "stags, which he used to chase on horseback. When he had one cornered, he would strike down with his sword, rather than use a hunting spear." However bloodthirsty this practice may seem to the modern reader, it was considered a sign of great courage and spirit at the time. A later medieval commentator (Olivier de Serres, writing at the beginning of the 16th Century) pointed out the healthiness and practical usefulness of hunting.

From the earliest medieval times hawking had also been popular, and it, too, had great potential for development into a high art, or rather a science. Many manuals and treatises on hawking were written by knights and nobles from all over Europe, such as the *Treatise of Falconry* by Emperor Frederick II of Germany, with its beautifully detailed illustrations on the care and training of the birds. A 13th-Century treatise instructed the falconer to handle his bird as much as possible in order to tame it for training. Hawks and falcons were

Sir Tristan, fighting in a *mêlee* at court, watched by the Queen and her ladies. Sir Tristan was reckoned to be one of the five "dangerous knights," second only to Sir Lancelot. He is here fighting Sir Palomedes, who later became his friend.

very valuable and often given as prestigious gifts; then, as now, the penalties for stealing their eggs were severe.

Churchmen (and women) who were of noble birth were reluctant to relinquish their hunting of animals and birds. A bishop visiting nunneries in the south of England in the mid-14th Century found the nuns keeping greyhounds and indignantly wrote to them on the subject; not only was it against their rule to indulge in such pleasures as hunting, but the animals were eating up food which could have been given to the poor.

THE TOURNAMENT

The importance of the tournament to the culture of medieval knights cannot be overestimated. It provided an arena for the display of knightly virtues: *prouesse* in the combat, *courtoisie* to the watching and judging ladies, *largesse* to the crowds of minstrels, heralds, armorers, squires, and assorted hangers on. Also on display were knightly qualities such as the *franchise* and *debonnaireté* with which a knight should conduct himself in triumph and disaster (qualities that developed into the European gentlemen's sense of fair play), and the *pité* he should exercise to his defeated opponents.

It was regarded as a crucial training ground for young knights to practice handling their horses and weapons, the tactics of attack and defense, and of coordinating their actions with a team of companions, who would in real battle form a military unit. It was an opportunity for knights to win praise and glory, and to find employment with great lords who attended the tournaments and frequently recruited talented knights there. To this end the activities of the heralds were of vital importance, as they recorded the names and arms of those who took part in tournaments and the deeds they achieved. It was also a splendid occasion for sexual display. It is clear that ladies played a variety of active roles in the tournament; from hosting them, to encouraging individual knights, who competed wearing their 'favor' (a sleeve or other token), judging performances (before this role was taken over by heralds), giving prizes and, on occasion, being the prize themselves.

A knight could win considerable sums at tournaments, if he was successful; conversely, of course, he could also lose money. There can be no doubt that the prospect of winning valuable horses, armor, and ransoms contributed to the extreme popularity of tournaments all over Europe and all through the period. We have already seen from the history of William Marshal that it was possible for a knight who was good at tourneying to travel from tournament to tournament, accumulating a considerable fortune as well as a formidable reputation. There were also knights for whom the sport was an addiction, who returned time after time to tournaments although their losses might reduce them to bankruptcy and ruin. Jacques de Baudricourt relates a story about a relative of his, the Seigneur de Baudricourt, whose consistent bad luck at tournaments often required him to mortgage his estate, and even his household valuables, in order to pay his debts and losses. He wondered how it was that he always managed to pay off the mortgages and free his property for the next time, until he discovered that it was his wife whose financial prudence, caring for his estates and livestock, had saved him many times from ruin. When he returned home he confessed his wastefulness to his wife and she confessed her secret management and saving, and they forgave one another. She had never complained because, as she said, "all the honor that you win in the world I share with you."

The expenses of tourneying, though great, were much less serious than the physical dangers to which knights were inevitably exposed. In their early days, tournaments were fairly unregulated free-for-alls and they were so violent that the only distinction between them and a real battle was the fact that they were acknowledged to be waged in sport. Two teams of knights, usually from two different areas or towns, would attack each other with real weapons, ranging over a designated area of countryside, arming to take as many prisoners from the opposing faction as they could. Their only respite from the fighting was to go to the "neutral area" roped off outside the jousting area, where they could disarm and rest for a time.

Even after the introduction of regulations intended to make the sport safer, such as the use of blunted weapons, or the erection of barriers in jousting (when mounted knights charged each other using lances to try to unseat each other) to prevent the galloping horses from colliding, fatalities still occurred. As late as 1559, when tournaments had become stylized, ceremonious affairs, King Henry II of France was fatally injured jousting against his Constable, Montgomery, when a splinter from Montgomery's broken lance pierced his face through the visor of his helmet.

In time, rule books were drawn up for tournaments, which insisted on the use of blunted or 'bated' weapons, restricted the number of men who could accompany a knight, and ordained that

After the *melée*, or tournament, fell out of favor, considered too dangerous, the joust grew in popularity amongst the aristocracy. Single combat could be fought on foot or on horseback with a variety of weapons and usually ended with only serious bruising. This 13th-Century illustration shows combatants in action. During a joust a knight, unseated from his mount by a blunted lance (top), would lose the contest, while in a sword fight the outclassed knight surrendered his weapon to his victor (bottom).

foot soldiers and grooms should not be armed. The area in which the *mêlée* took place was strictly defined as the "lists," for the convenience of the spectators and judges; the mêlée was preceded by jousts between individual knights, the sporting equivalent of single combat. Knights taking part in a tournament then had to register and, in some places, to pay a fee; only knights, or those who bore arms (owned a coat of arms that could be displayed on the shield), were allowed to take part. Attacks were not permitted on, or by, knights who had surrendered themselves to captors.

CHIVALRY

Chivalry actually means the knightly class of feudal times in the Middle Ages, concentrating on the aspect of fully-armed fighting men based on the French word for horse, *cheval*. In England, "chivalry" meant the holding of land by knight's service. King Edward III inaugurated a court of chivalry with two judges, the earl marshal and lord high constable, who had summary justice over all alleged and

Left: This detail taken from a late 14th Century manuscript shows a knight receiving his sword from the King.

actual offenses of knights, generally associated with military matters. The 12th and 13th Centuries witnessed the development of the concepts of honorable and courteous conduct, this being accentuated by the Holy Crusades, with the earliest orders of chivalry, the Templars and Hospitalers. The 14th and 15th Centuries also saw a development of the tenets of chivalry, these being linked to aristocratic conspicuous display and public ceremony instead of military service. Evidence of such knightly rituals can be witnessed in the creation of the Order of the Garter in England and the Order of the Golden Fleece in Flanders, the highest status a knight could aspire to.

The popularity of chivalry continued at the end of the 15th Century when Raymond Lully's 13th-Century *Book of the Order of Chivalry* (1275), was translated into English by William Caxton. Lully, an aristocrat of Catalan-Majorcan origin, had been fascinated by knightly pursuits and wrote troubadour-style love poetry. After several religious visitations, he resolved to convert the Muslims living in Spain and North Africa. This, he asserted, should be achieved by arguing over religion in books, by training missionaries, and by his own missionary work.

Lully's overseas missions in 1292, 1307 and 1314 involved him in debating religion with other learned men. He was, however, imprisoned for six months when he publicly shouted in a Bugia market place that "the law of Christ is holy and true, and the sect of the Moors is false and wrong, and this I can prove!" He preached throughout Tunisia, where he was eventually beaten and stoned to death by an angry crowd at Bugia in 1316.

THE BLACK PRINCE

This tomb effigy in Canterbury Cathedral, England, is that of the Prince of Wales, the eldest son of King Edward II of England. A popular military leader, known as the Black Prince because of his distinctive armor, he was regarded by many of his contemporaries as the perfect knight: "The flower of chivalry of all the world" as described in Froissart's epitaph for the Prince.

Offense and Defense

THE ARMS AND ARMOR OF THE KNIGHT WERE DEVELOPED DURING THE CAROLINGIAN PERIOD, AND WERE CONSTANTLY ADAPTED TO CHANGING CONDITIONS ON THE BATTLEFIELD. DEVELOPMENTS THAT COULD BE APPLIED TO THE OFFENSE OR DEFENSE WERE APPLIED BY THE ARMORERS OF EUROPE.

A mail shirt from Scotland, this type of armor offered limited protection but more ease of movement when compared to plate armor.

Knights, their armor and weapons are associated with the period between the Viking invasions and the Hundred Years' War (1337–1453). This era witnessed the development of chivalry and is sometimes described as the Age of the Horse. Knights were cavalrymen, mounted shock troops, who were deployed by most European peoples. Over a period of time, the cavalry sought to protect itself with efficient armor and weaponry which evolved with technological changes.

The Normans and crusaders are archetypal images of the use of cavalry in their campaigns and battles, from Hastings to Arsuf. However, these are merely two examples of a general European use of horse soldiers as the key units in the armies of Byzantium, France, England, Italy, and the Holy Roman Empire. Other countries were not slow in following the lead of the Scandinavians, lowland Scotland, the Iberian kingdoms, Hungary, Poland, Lithuania, and Balkan lands.

In cavalry battles, knights or armored men had to possess great confidence, courage, discipline, and willpower to tackle an enemy. The confidence developed in hard training when young, from the protection afforded by armor, and the capacity to ride together in close formation. Cavalry also displayed wealth in the quality of the horse and the

An Italian suit of armor dating from the late 14th Century shows effective use of chainmail covering the areas of the body needing maximum flexibility.

modernity of the armor. A knight's armor was more than just protection against the more violent aspects of his lifestyle; it was intimately connected with his status as part of a military and social élite. Quality and craftsmanship in armor were valued by knights almost as much as efficiency; from the earliest days of the mail hauberk, armor was expensive and represented both a major capital investment and another opportunity to indulge the knightly love of finery. In the later Middle Ages particularly, armor became noticeably subject to the need to display wealth and keep up with the latest fashion. For this reason, many suits of armor, or "harness," that survive have been preserved as works of art.

When packed into a tight formation twenty horses wide, known as a "conroi," cavalry could move with immense force, like a tank on legs, an equine battering ram against which few infantry could stand. Well-trained, courageous infantry were not often found but did exist in Harold's housecarls (bodyguard) at Hastings, Scots schiltrons at Bannockburn, and the English at Agincourt. Therefore, battles were often cavalry engagements, but over time mixed forces of cavalry and infantry became the norm.

The successful use of cavalry was a function of leadership. Knights were known to be proud, independent, and sometimes rash, needing to be held in check. Hence, Richard I's victory at Arsuf was due to his handling of a cavalry force that was being constantly attacked by a force of light horse-archers. What is important to note is that when a feudal levy was called, it was a chaotic mass with men owing loyalty to their lords. A monarch needed to impose his will on his baronage to achieve any kind of battlefield order. The French were notorious in their inability to organize on the fields of Crécy, Poitiers, and Agincourt, falling foul of a disciplined enemy acting as infantry supported by archers with their immense fire power.

The medieval warrior was required to arm himself, feed and provision himself and any retinue, and fulfill his feudal obligations. However, there were never enough soldiers raised this way, so military leaders had to hire mercenaries or contract a leader to raise specified troops for a campaign, this situation being common in the 14th Century. Edward I faced this type of situation in 1300, when only 406 armored cavalry turned up for military service when summoned.

The knight's armor's first purpose was to protect the knight against his enemies in battle and developments in armor throughout the Middle Ages tended to be in response to new and better weapons. Chain mail, a crucial part of knights' armor for most of the period, was a good general protection but could not withstand a direct hit with a lance or arrow. This led first to the adoption of additional protective clothing, such as the metal-reinforced coat of plates, or the padded gambeson (though the latter was worn as much to keep mail from chafing the body as to stop weapons piercing it), and later to the development of armor constructed of solid metal plates, jointed for flexibility by smaller plates known as *lames* (hence the term laminated).

Plate armor weighed about the same as a complete chain mail suit (about 50 lbs or 23 kg) but, if properly made to fit its wearer perfectly, was more comfortable because the weight was distributed evenly over the body instead of being suspended entirely from the shoulders. The only period in which knights were so burdened by their armor that they could not get up if they fell, was during the mid-14th Century, a period of transition from full mail to full plate armor when it was customary to wear both.

German armor in the "Gothic" style, dating from about 1475-85. The horse armor was made for Waldemar VI, Duke of Anhalt-Zerbst.

Armor

BODY ARMOR DEVELOPED FROM EARLY SCALE AND LAMELLAR ARMOR, BASED ON ROMAN TRADITIONS, THROUGH CHAIN MAIL TO PLATE ARMOR. EARLY MEDIEVAL WARRIORS HAD TO BE WEALTHY TO AFFORD SUCH PROTECTION AND A FEW WELL ARMED MEN HAD A DISPROPORTIONATE IMPACT IN COMBAT.

A small 14th-Century wooden statue of St. George fighting the dragon. It depicts him wearing a bascinet, fully armored legs and a wooden targe or shield that would have been painted with a red cross on a white background.

CHAIN MAIL

Mail was the usual type of body armor during the early Middle Ages. It was formed by circular metal links, usually iron, arranged so that each link passed through two similar links in the row above and two in the row below. The Bayeux Tapestry depicts Norman cavalry wearing long mail shirts while the English infantry used knee-length shirts. The late 11th Century saw the addition of a mail hood to protect the neck and head while a mail flap was secured across the lower part of the face and mail mittens completed the ensemble. The mail shirt or hauberk was the preferred form of armor through the 12th and 13th Centuries with the addition of chausses (mail trousers), which covered the leg from foot to thigh, secured by straps to a belt under the shirt. Mail gloves replaced the mittens of the late 13th Century, while quilted cuisses were scale-lined thigh protectors. Knee-caps were also made from hardened leather, attached to the cuisses. Protectors called *besagews* were made for arms and armpits.

PLATE ARMOR

Armor of the 14th Century developed owing to the advent of the armor-piercing crossbow bolt and later to the hand-held gun. The élite heavily armored cavalry wore extremely sophisticated plate armor covering not only the head and body but the arms and legs too. While hardened leather was constantly used in the late Middle Ages, fully plated steel arms defenses were becoming

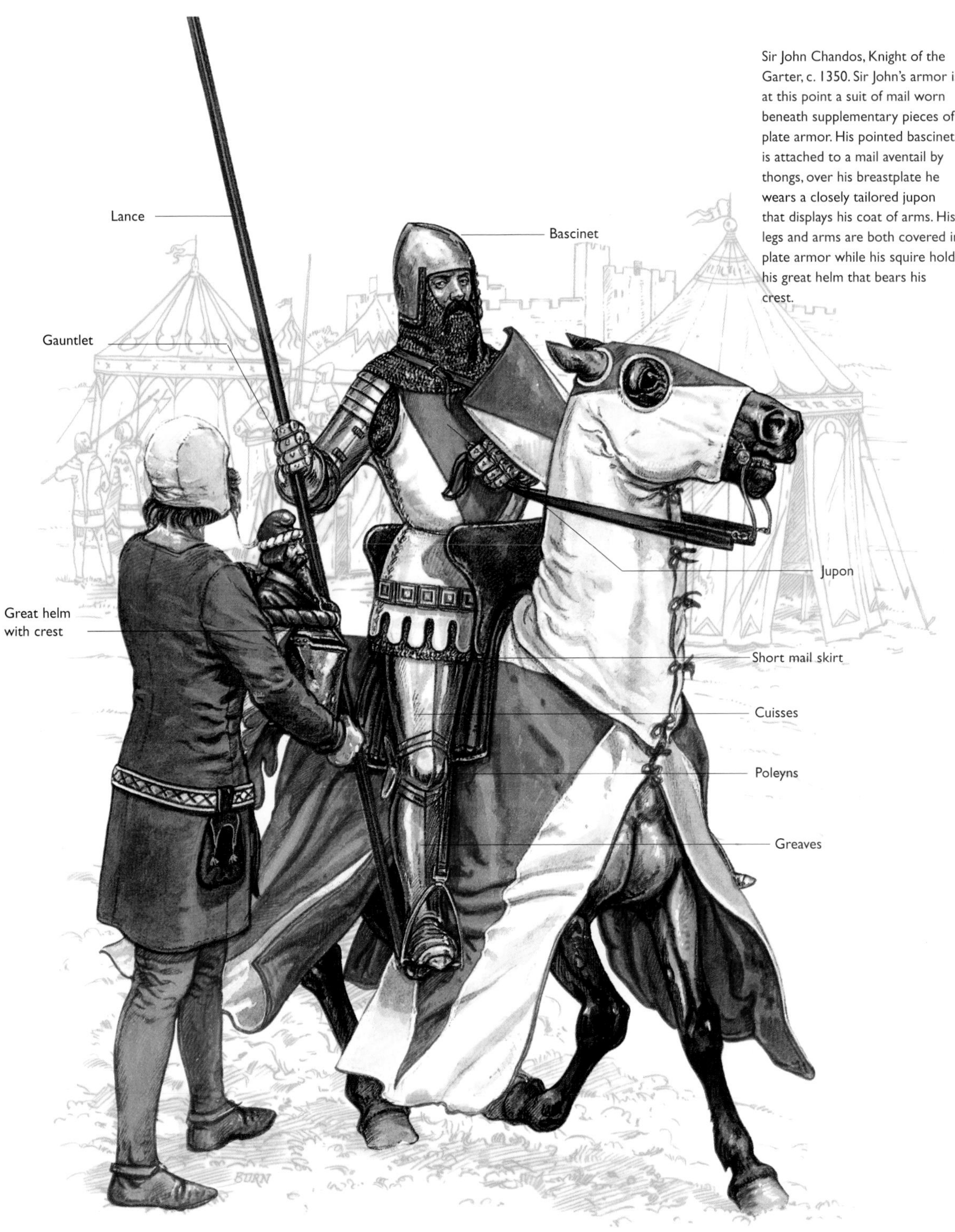

Sir John Chandos, Knight of the Garter, c. 1350. Sir John's armor is at this point a suit of mail worn beneath supplementary pieces of plate armor. His pointed bascinet is attached to a mail aventail by thongs, over his breastplate he wears a closely tailored jupon that displays his coat of arms. His legs and arms are both covered in plate armor while his squire holds his great helm that bears his crest.

ARMOR TERMINOLOGY AD 950–1550

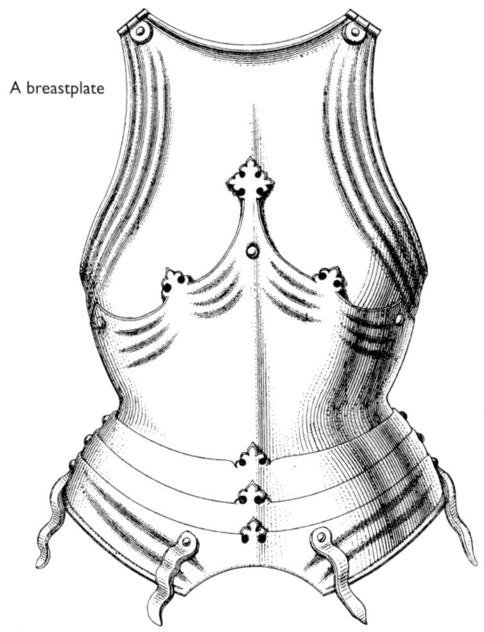
A breastplate

AILETTES	shoulder pieces for heraldic display
AKETON	quilted clothing worn beneath armor
ARMING CAP	padded cap worn beneath helmet
ARMING DOUBLET	alternative name for AKETON
AVENTAIL	a mail fringe attached to helmet edge
BALDRIC	sword belt
BARBOTE	alternative name for BEVOR
BESAGEWS	protection for armpits (see ROUNDEL)
BRIGANDINE	tight-fitting protective coat
CAMAIL	mail protection for neck, throat, and shoulders
CHAIN MAIL	another term for MAIL
CHAUSSES	mail leggings
CINGULUM MILITARE	broad hip belt
COAT OF PLATES	plates riveted inside a coat
COIF	mail hood
COUDES	elbow protection
COUTER	disc-shaped elbow protection
CUIRASS	back- and breast-plate
CUIR BOUILLI	hardened leather
CUISSES	padding for thighs
CYCLAS	over garment
ENARMES	straps on the inside of a shield
ESPALIER	padded shoulder protection
FAULD	protective skirt
GAMBESON	quilted protective garment
GAUNTLET	articulated plate gloves
GORGET	plate armour form of CAMAIL
GREAVES	protection for the lower leg
GUIGE	strap supporting a shield
HAKETON	padded protective garment
HAUBERGEON	a light form of hauberk
HAUBERK	mail shirt
JACK	infantryman's body protection
JAZERNEC	see HAUBERK

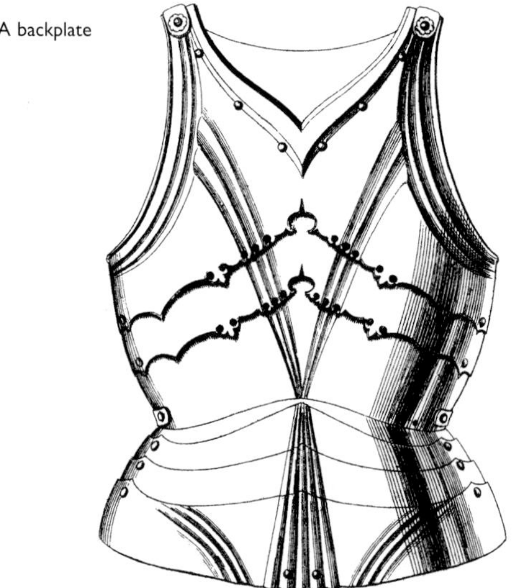
A backplate

In this late 14th-Century drawing, two knights in full plate armor joust with war hammers.

JUPON	short sleeveless tunic
LAMBREQUIN	see MANTLING
LAMES	thin metal plates
MAIL	armour formed of interlocking rings
MANTLING	protective cloth fixed to helmet
MUFFLERS	mail mittens
PAULDRON	shoulder guard
PLACKART	lower part of breastplate
POLEYNS	knee protectors
PONS	glove-like mail protection
POURPOINT	padded or quilted soft armor
REREBRACE	protection for upper arm
ROUNDEL	protection for armpits (see BESAGEWS)
ROWEL	star-shaped end of spur
SABATON	broad-toed mail foot armor
SOLLERETS	pointed metal shoes
SPAULDER	plate shoulder protection
SURCOAT	sleeveless cloth coat
TABARD	heraldic coat with sleeves
TACES	metal strips of skirt
TARGET	a circular shield
TASSETS	metal plates to protect thighs
TIPPET	neck and shoulder protection
VAMBRACE	protection for forearms
VENTAIL	a mail flap to protect the lower face

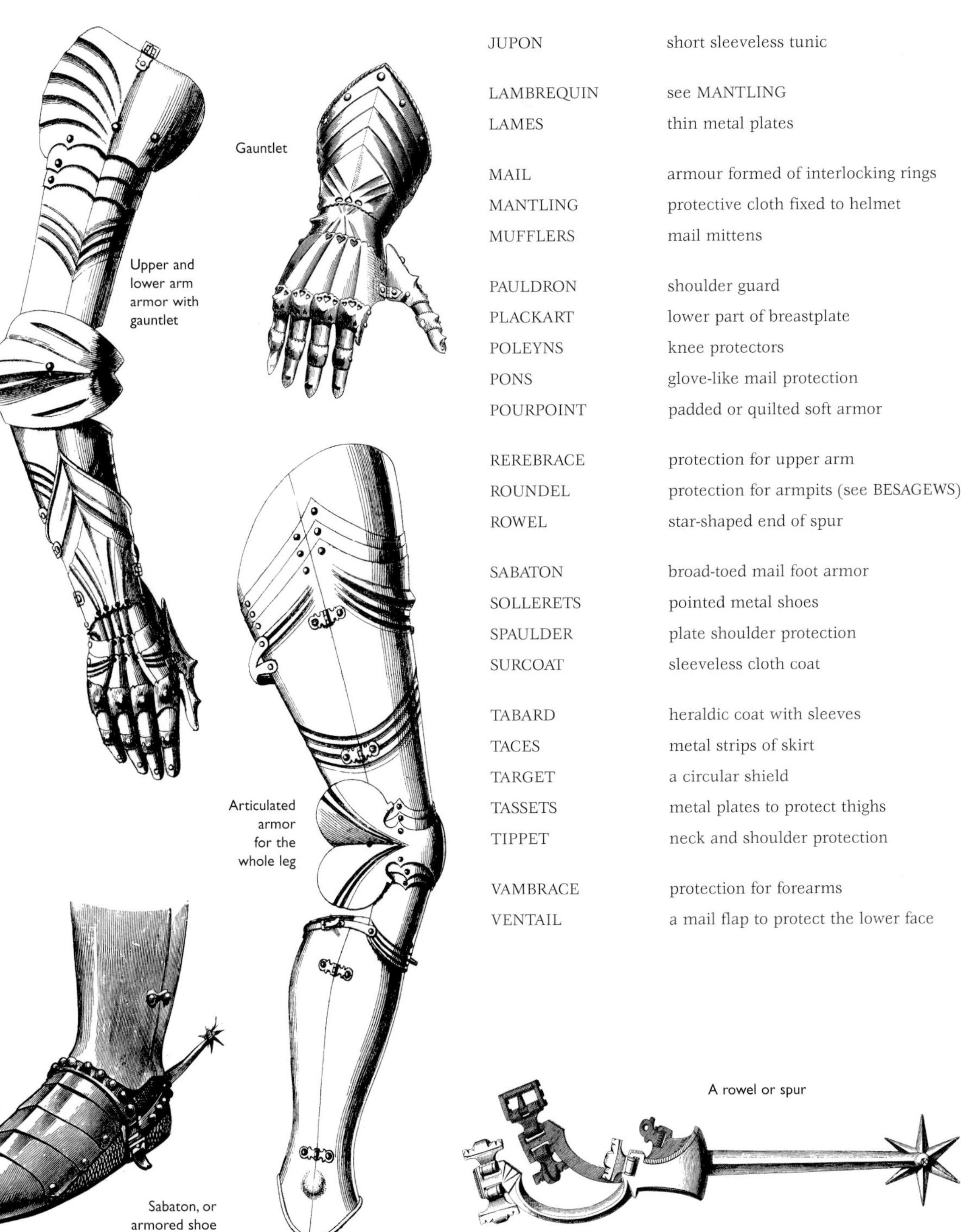
Gauntlet

Upper and lower arm armor with gauntlet

Articulated armor for the whole leg

Sabaton, or armored shoe

A rowel or spur

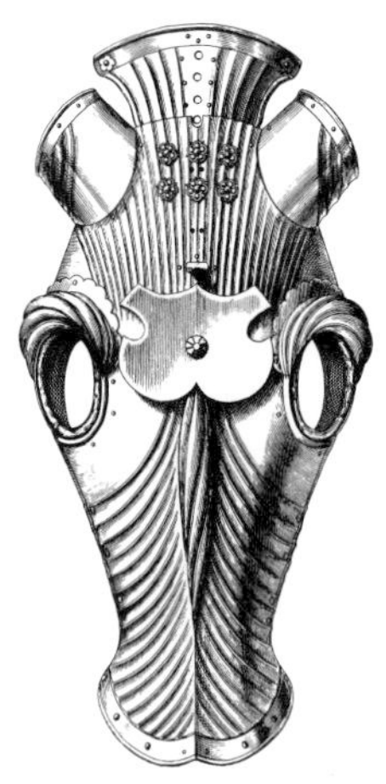

A horse face guard known as a shaffron, dating from about 1510-50 and made in the Maximilian style.

increasingly used by the mid-14th Century. These comprised the gauntlet for the hand and wrist, the vambrace for the lower arm, the couter for the elbow, the rerebrace for the upper arm, and the spaulder for the shoulder. By the end of the 14th Century the front of the shoulder was protected by a large plate pauldron, while the mail camail to protect the throat, neck, and shoulders was replaced by the gorget at the commencement of the 15th Century. Rigid pieces of leather leg armor were worn for thighs and shins beneath cuisses and chausses, but in the late 13th Century leg protection was improved. Greaves covered the lower legs, demi-greaves the shins, and metal plates called tassets protected the thighs; poleyns (knee protectors) and sabatons (segmented foot protection) were made of plate metal and eventually incorporated into complete suits of articulated armor, with a skirt (fauld) of steel hoops over the lower stomach.

The best quality armor was imported from Italy and Germany, the finest originating in the Missaglia workshop in Milan. Some armor was so well made that crafted contours reflected light so that the suit looked almost white. By the 15th Century, knights wore reasonably light suits of armor. Armor was sometimes painted black, for decorative and preservative purposes, and frequently blued, by controlling the heating of the metal. Some German armor of about 1520 imitated the pleated clothing of the time, the style called "Maximilian" after the German Emperor.

Plate armor was made of mild steel worked and shaped at 930°F (500°C). Sometimes a suit would be tested by firing a steel-tipped crossbow bolt at it. An estimate suggests that the average knight possessed an annual income of some $78 (£40) while a set of armor— bascinet (helmet), aventail, hauberk, breastplate, fauld, and leg armor—would cost $23 (£12). Armor could also be passed down through the family and extra armour acquired by capturing an enemy. Henry II's Assize of Arms in 1181 required that a knight should possess only a helmet, mail shirt, shield, and lance. The armor was light enough for a man to run or vault onto his horse. The joints were well articulated and the armor like a second skin and not much heavier than mail. One complete Italian-made suit found in Scotland weighs 55 pounds (25 kg) although special jousting armor might reach 83 pounds (38 kg).

A group of German mounted knights wearing full plate armor and sallet style helmets.

The infantry also wore protection, the norm being a brigandine (mail coat) or jack (leather or canvas sleeveless tunic strengthened with metal or horn plates). A kettle shaped, wide-brimmed metal hat was standard protection from the 12th Century. Low grade armor was also produced cheaply and archers and infantrymen had access to this. After a battle or skirmish, an infantryman or archer could also loot the dead and wounded and tie on what they found to their bodies.

Swiss knight, 1476. This knight is wearing a German harness, in characteristically angular style. His helmet, known as a sallet, has a long tail behind to protect his neck; its hinged visor, now in the upright position, only protects the upper part of his face. The chin and throat are protected by a bevor. His hand-and-a-half sword has a long blade with a sharp point for thrusting as well as cutting. He has no shield as full plate armor has made them obsolete.

NORMAN KNIGHT c. 1066

For hundreds of years the basic form of body armor consisted of the chain mail shirt, called a hauberk or byrnie. In one form or another, this was an essential piece of body defense until the late 15th Century. There is ample evidence in the Bayeux Tapestry of the equipment worn and carried by the Norman knights who rode to victory at Hastings. They had knee-length mail hauberks with elbow-length sleeves, split at front and rear for ease when riding, conical helmets with a nasal bar, and leather or padded cloth greaves. Only very high-ranking lords, such as Duke William or his brother, Bishop Odo of Bayeux, wore mail stockings to protect their legs and feet. Norman knights carried long, kite-shaped shields, decorated with swirling shapes like the one pictured, though there is no evidence that these decorations were associated with specific knights or families in the heraldic sense. Their main weapons were a sword and a long lance; the Saxons, by contrast, are often depicted wielding battle-axes and carrying smaller, round shields.

KNIGHT c. 1225–1250

The main development in the knight's equipment is the addition of the helm. This was originally a large, square-topped helmet that fitted over the top of a chain mail coif (show above resting on the knight's shoulders) and a padded arming cap. This was apparently worn either under or over the mail. For the first time the helm covers the whole face, with slits at eye-level for vision and perforations in front of nose and mouth for ventiliation. At about this time the mail mittens (mufflers) have developed into gloves with separate fingers. The padded gambeson is now reinforced with hardened leather—a cuirie (or *cuir boulli* if the leather had been hardened by boiling)—and the legs are protected by the addition of quilted cuisses on the thighs and the first sign of plate armor—poleyns to protect the knees.

TEUTONIC KNIGHT c. 1270

This Teutonic knight is one of the remnants of the Schwertbroder—the Brethren of the Sword, a rather disreputable minor military Order who had been instrumental in the conversion of Livonia (modern-day Latvia and Estonia). Most of the members were killed in a massacre when they were surprised on an expedition into Lithuania, and the survivors were incorporated into the Teutonic Knights in 1237. By 1270 knights' helms were once more domed over the crown of the head, since the curving surface deflected glancing blows. On top of the helm is a fitting where a crest can be attached. The hauberk is growing shorter and the gambeson is just visible beneath it. The shield is now much smaller and shaped like an iron (for this reason they are called "heater-shields"). The poleyns have been enlarged so that they completely cover the knee joint at front and sides. The sword has a new-style, wheel-shaped pommel.

SIR THOMAS CAWNE, c. 1360
Sir Thomas wears a typical 14th-Century combination of mail and plate. His arms and legs are increasingly protected by plate armor—cuisses on the thighs, greaves on the shins, poleyns on the knees, upper and lower cannons of the vambrace on the arms, with winged couters at the elbow, and characteristically bell-shaped cuffs on his gauntlets. The surcoat has now become a short, tight-fitting tunic called a jupon, which still displays the knight's coat of arms. Under it he is almost certainly wearing a coat-of-plates, or possibly a solid breast-plate, although it is not visible in the illustration. Underneath his plate armor, however, he is still wearing a mail habergeon (sleeveless coat), which shows beneath the jupon and at the joints in his limbs. His bascinet is inceasingly pointed in shape, with its mail aventail still in place. Sir Thomas also wears a typical belt of plates at his hips, to which are attached both his sword and his dagger.

ITALIAN KNIGHT c. 1400
The harness of this knight represents a late stage in the transition from mail to plate. His plate armour is more complete, but he still wears an aventail and a habergeon. His bascinet is fitted with the characteristic 'pig-faced' visor, which, when lowered, protects his face completely in battle. The breast-plate has been in use for some time and now has developed such refinements as a protruding socket at the right armpit on which the knight can rest his lance as he charges. His gauntlets are becoming bell-shaped. The fingers are made of canvas. Plate armour now covers the legs front and rear (although as yet he does not wear a back-plate); greaves and cuisses are in two parts, hinged at the inner leg seam. The winged plates on the poleyns and couters offer extra protection. The knight might still wear a jupon over his armour but with this amount of plate defence the shield is becoming obsolete.

JOHANN FRIEDRICH 1530
The style of armor that predominated during the first 30 years of the 16th Century, is usually called "Maximilian," after the famous German Emperor, especially when decorated with vertical fluting like this. It blended the Gothic with the Italian styles by having plates with burly, rounded shapes, decorated with bold fluting. The tassets have now been incorporated into the lower body armor, which is laminated for greater flexibility. The cunningly-jointed gauntlets each have separate armor-plated laminated fingers. The pauldrons on the shoulders have raised ridges, known as haute-pieces, which have extra protection to the neck. Close-helmets were universally worn at this time; following the contours of the head and face, they were hinged and fastened to an aventail of laminated plates at the top of the breast-plate. Close-helmets all had visors, which could be raised for better air and visibility when the knight was not actually fighting. The knight wears new, square-toed sabatons, in imitation of civilian fashion.

This drawing from 1482, shows Wilhelm of Ellrichshausen wearing the fashionable sallet-style helmet. In battle the wearer would pull the whole helmet forward, his chin and throat protected by a *bevor*, or throat guard.

HELMETS

The most well-known 11th-Century helmet is that worn by Norman cavalry with the face being protected by a nasal bar. These helmets were common in Europe but widespread use of crossbows led to an increase in the size of the nasal bar and the introduction of the coif, or mail hood. The great helm was introduced into France in the mid-12th Century; this cylindrical, flat-topped helmet had an eye slit. The year 1220 saw this *heaume* completely enclosing the head. There is written evidence suggesting that a visored helmet, *heaume à vissere* was present in the late 13th Century. The great helm is sometimes known as a pot helm owing to its cylindrical shape and flat top. Sometimes, a knight would use a *cervellière* beneath his great helm as double protection. This was a basic round helmet, a close-fitting cap worn by any soldier of any class, under or over a coif.

Eventually, the great helm was only used in tournaments where it developed into the tilting helm or tournament helm (permanently closed with an eye slit that could only be used when a rider was leaning forward in a tilting position while jousting). The 14th Century saw a variety of helmet innovations. The bascinet was a fairly lightweight close-fitting helmet giving protection to the neck and sides of the head. The bascinet was 13th Century Italian in origin later incorporating an aventail and a visor. This helmet is often described as hounskull or pig–face because it possessed a projecting scout with an eye-slit and ventilation holes being hinged at the sides of the helmet. For infantry the kettle hat and sallet were particularly favored.

Two south Germany sallets from the 1480s, also sometimes called a *salade*. This style of helmet became popular towards the mid-15th Century and were occasionally decorated, see example below. Instead of a visor, the whole helmet could be tilted backwards on the wearer's head when not in use.

German field armor in the Maximillian-style from about 1520. This style of armor, developed at the end of the 15th- and early 16th-Centuries, introduced fluting and decorative etching, differing from the plainer finish on earlier15th-Century armor. This era also introduced close-fitting helms.

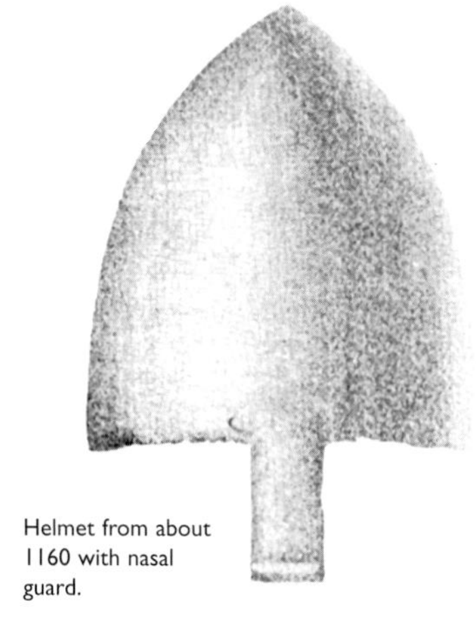

Helmet from about 1160 with nasal guard.

HELMET TERMINOLOGY

ARMET — helmet with cheek pieces and visor
ARMING CAP — padding worn beneath a helmet
AVENTAIL — a mail fringe attached to the edge of a helmet

BARBOTE — alternative name for a BEVOR
BARBUTE — helmet with a T-shaped opening at the front
BARREL HELM — see GREAT HELM
BASCINET — pointed steel helmet
BEVOR — plate armor to protect lower front of face
BURGANET — light helmet with cheek pieces (1th Century)

CAMAIL — mail protection for throat, neck, and shoulders
CERVELLIÈRE — close-fitting round helmet
CHAPEL DE FER — see KETTLE HAT
CHAPLET — an iron skull cap
CLOSE HELM — enclosed helmet with a movable visor
COIF — mail hood
CUIR BOUILLI — hardened leather

GORGET — plate armor form of CAMAIL
GREAT HELM — cylindrical helm with eye slit

A great helm from the 13th Century.

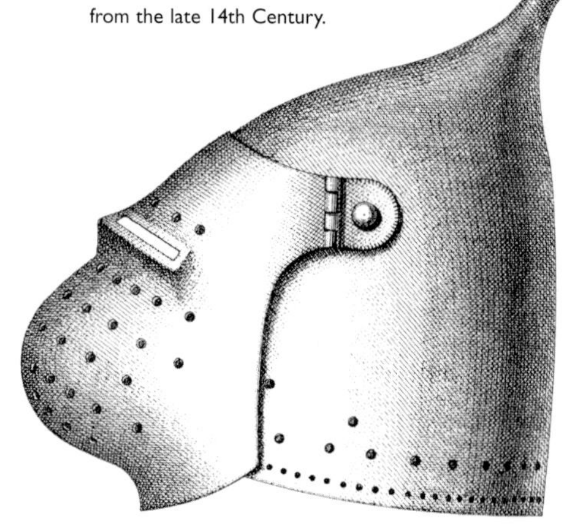

Bascinet with moveable visor from the late 14th Century.

The Kettle helmet, popular between the 12th and 14th Centuries, was most commonly worn by infantry. Its wide brim gave protection from above, such as cavalry swords.

HEAUME	see GREAT HELM
HELM	a basic helmet
HOUNSKULL	a snout-like visor on a BASCINET
KETTLE HAT	plate helmet with a broad brim
NASAL	protective nose bar
PANACHE	crest of feathers
PIG-FACE VISOR	see HOUNSKULL
POT HELM	early form of GREAT HELM
SALLET	domed helmet with neck extension
TILTING HELM	see TOURNAMENT HELM
TOURNAMENT	a close helmet for jousting
VENTAIL	a mail flap to protect the lower face
VISOR	hinged front-piece of helmet
WAR HAT	see KETTLE HAT

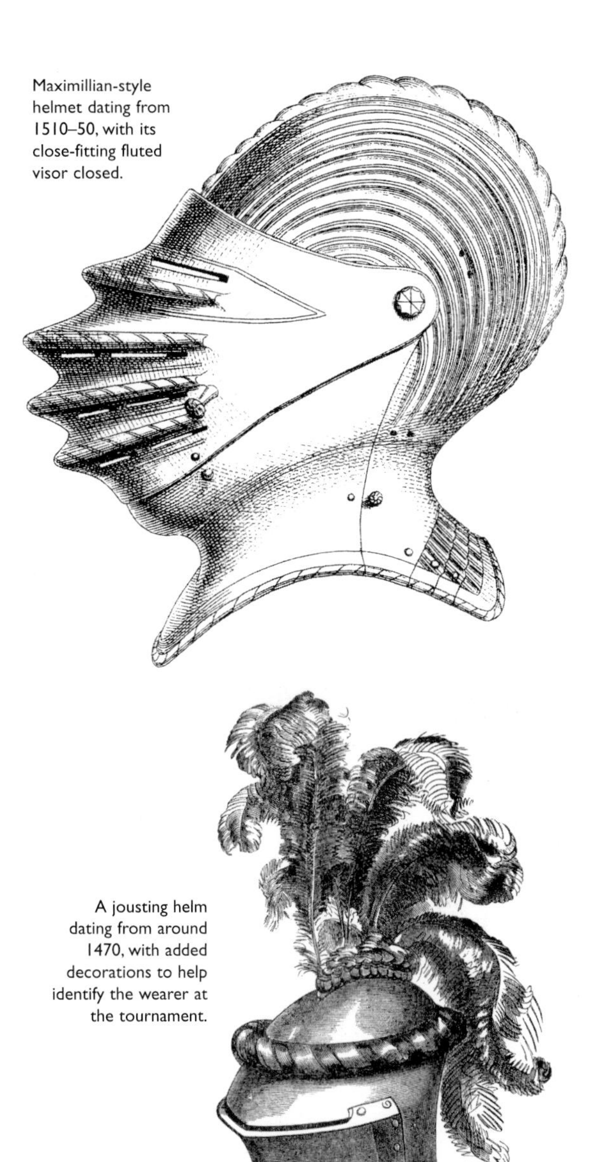
Maximillian-style helmet dating from 1510–50, with its close-fitting fluted visor closed.

A jousting helm dating from around 1470, with added decorations to help identify the wearer at the tournament.

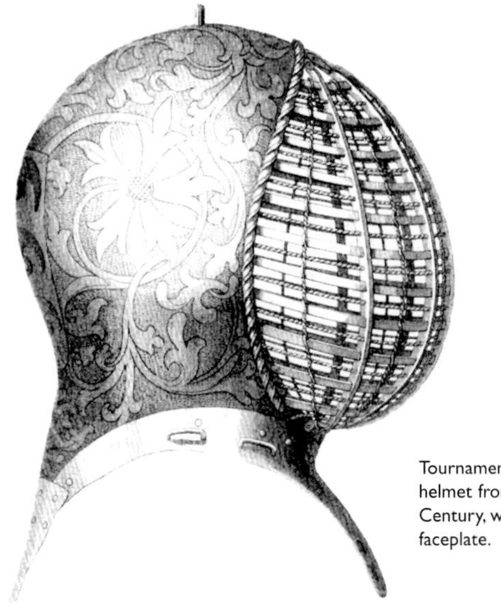
Tournament helmet from the 15th Century, with fixed faceplate.

SHIELDS

A variety of shields were used in the Middle Ages, ranging from the large round shield depicted being used by the English at the Battle of Hastings and common in Scandinavia and the Byzantine Empire, to pointed shields. The most famous of 11th Century shields was the long, narrow, kite-shaped shield that protected a Norman knight from neck to toe on his left-hand side. Made of wood covered with hard boiled leather, these were designed for use on horseback and had a rounded top. Kite shields were used by William the Conqueror's troops at Hastings or Senlac Hill, and are clearly seen in the Bayeux Tapestry. During the First Crusade any bosses or metal edges were often painted for decoration. In the 12th Century shields had flatter tops and armorial badges were commonly painted on.

Larger shields were known as targes (or target), and were made of leather-covered wood. A 12th-

A ceremonial shield from Florence made during the 15th Century.

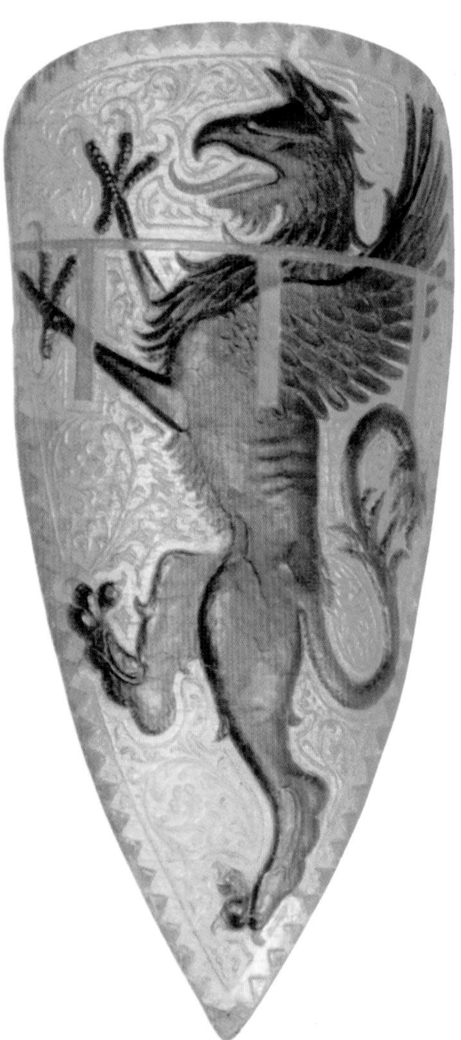

Century infantry soldier would sometimes use a very large shield called a talevas. By the 14th Century, shields had become much smaller and knights carried a heater shield shaped like a flat-iron, which is the shield widely used in heraldry. Another specialist shield was the pavise, often used by a two-man crossbow team. One man would hold the shield to cover himself and his comrade while his colleague was spanning (loading) the crossbow. Foolishly leaving these shields behind saw the slaughter of the Genoese crossbow troops at the Battle of Crécy. At the same time smaller handheld and sometimes metal bucklers were used, often being part of an archer's equipment. It could fend a blow or be used as a punching weapon. The increasing efficiency and power of the warbow and crossbow, together with the speedy development of plate armor, made the shield redundant for the knight. By the 15th Century, the shield was largely abandoned except in tournaments where the *à bouche* shield was used, which had a notch cut in the side to allow free movement of a lance during a joust.

A 13th-Century illuminated manuscript depicting cavalry combat. The knights use their shields on their unprotected, usually the left-hand side while wielding their swords with their right hand. Their shields bear their coat of arms identifying the owner in combat.

SHIELD TERMINOLOGY

À BOUCHE	having an indentation or notch to carry a lance
BUCKLER	small circular shield, normally wooden
ENARMES	carrying straps for the forearm
GUIGE	shoulder strap
HEATER	shaped like a flatiron
KITE-SHAPED	long, narrow shield
MANTLET	lightweight defensive hoarding
NORMAN SHIELD	as kite-shaped
PAVISE	large infantry shield
TALEVAS	large cavalry shield
TARGET/TARGE	large cavalry shield or circular infantry shield
TARGIAM	large form of cavalry shield

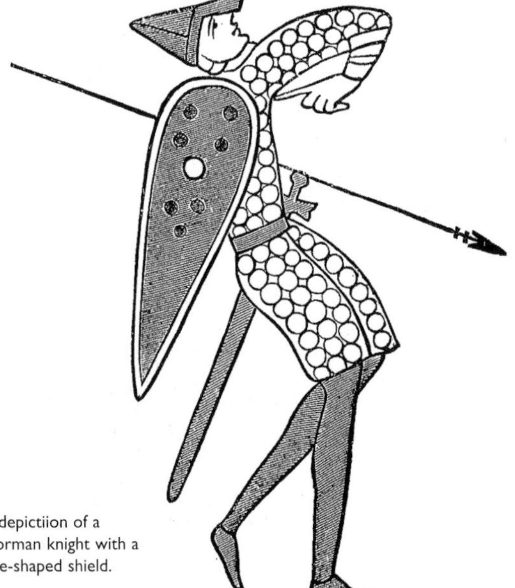

A depictiion of a Norman knight with a kite-shaped shield.

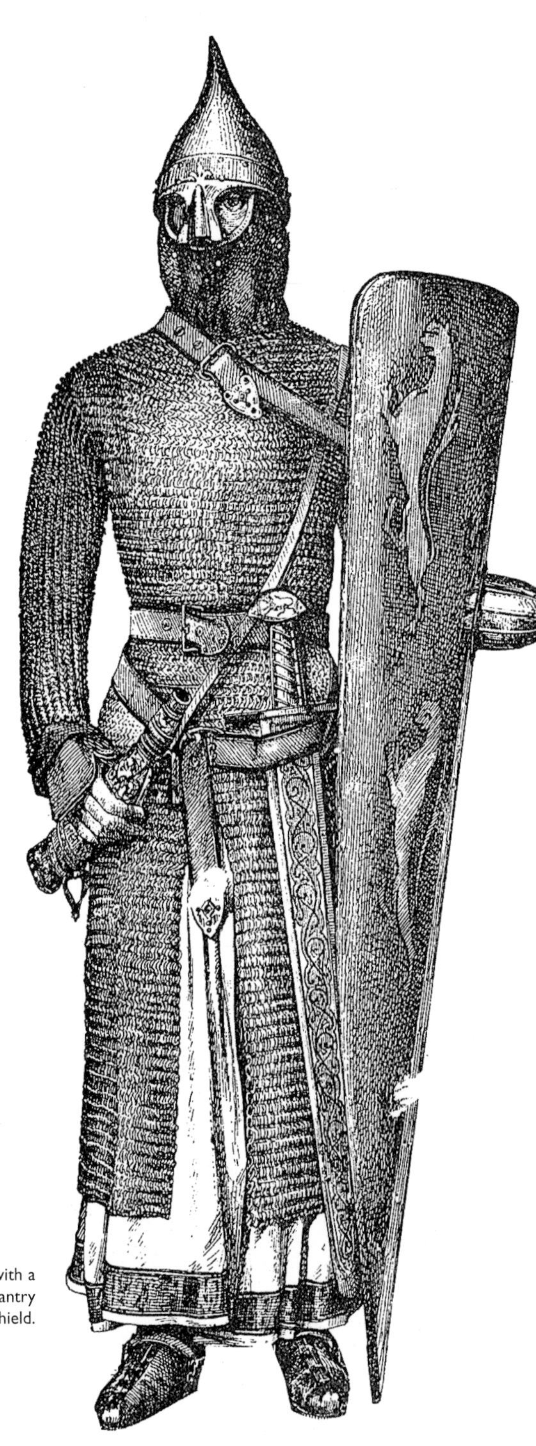

A soldier with a pavise infantry shield.

A heavily-decorated riding shield from 1280–98.

A Targe from 1480 made from wood with leather and canvas.

Front and side views of a Targe shield from 1440–80.

A Buckler shield from the 15th Century.

WEAPONS

THE SWORD WAS CONSIDERED TO BE THE MOST PRESTIGIOUS WEAPON DURING THE MEDIEVAL PERIOD BUT KNIGHTS USED LANCES, WAR HAMMERS, MACES, AND AXES, WHILE LOWLIER TROOPS USED SPEARS, JAVELINS, POLE ARMS, AND BOWS.

Horseman's war hammer originating from Germany, 16th Century. This weapon could deliver devastating concussion blows or, with the spike end, piercing blows that could penetrate both plate and chain armor.

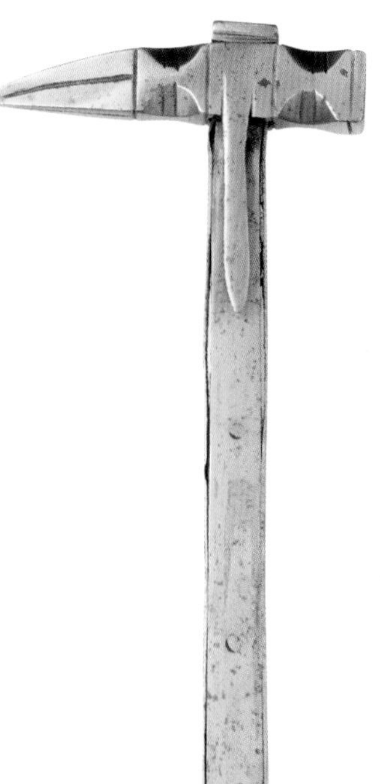

SWORDS, SPEARS AND AXES

A huge variety of weapons were used by knights and cavalry, and the number of weapons confronting them was likewise great. The symbol of knighthood par excellence is the sword originally based upon the Roman *gladius*. It became longer yet still light in the early Middle Ages, weighing between half a pound to just over three pounds (0.25 to 1.5 kg). It was primarily used for cutting and slashing. In the 11th and 12th Centuries they became longer and more pointed so they could be used for thrusting too.

Many types of swords existed. A particular favorite of archers was the falchion. This 13th-Century weapon had a single cutting edge with the blade broadening towards its point, giving it weight and penetrative power. It was particularly useful against unhorsed knights in a general melée after shattering a charge with an arrow storm. By the late 13th-Century the normal sword used by horsemen measured between 35–39 ins. (90–100 cm) with hilts being six to eight inches (15–20 cm); it weighed between half a pound to just over three pounds (0.25–1.5 kg). In the 14th Century the two-handed broadsword was six feet (1.8 m) long, yet a hand-and-a half sword, being designed for holding by one or two hands, had been used since Saxon times. A sword probably originating in the Palestine Crusader states was the baselard, an infantry short sword with an almost triangular blade and H-shaped hilt. All swords had a cross-guard, a pair of quillions, preventing the hand sliding down the blade. If the sword was reversed the quillions could be hooked around an opponent's knee or ankle to pull them off balance before delivering a telling blow. The hilt normally ended in a large pommel. This, too, was a weapon if a reversed sword was swung so the pommel hit someone between the eyes, a genuine medieval technique.

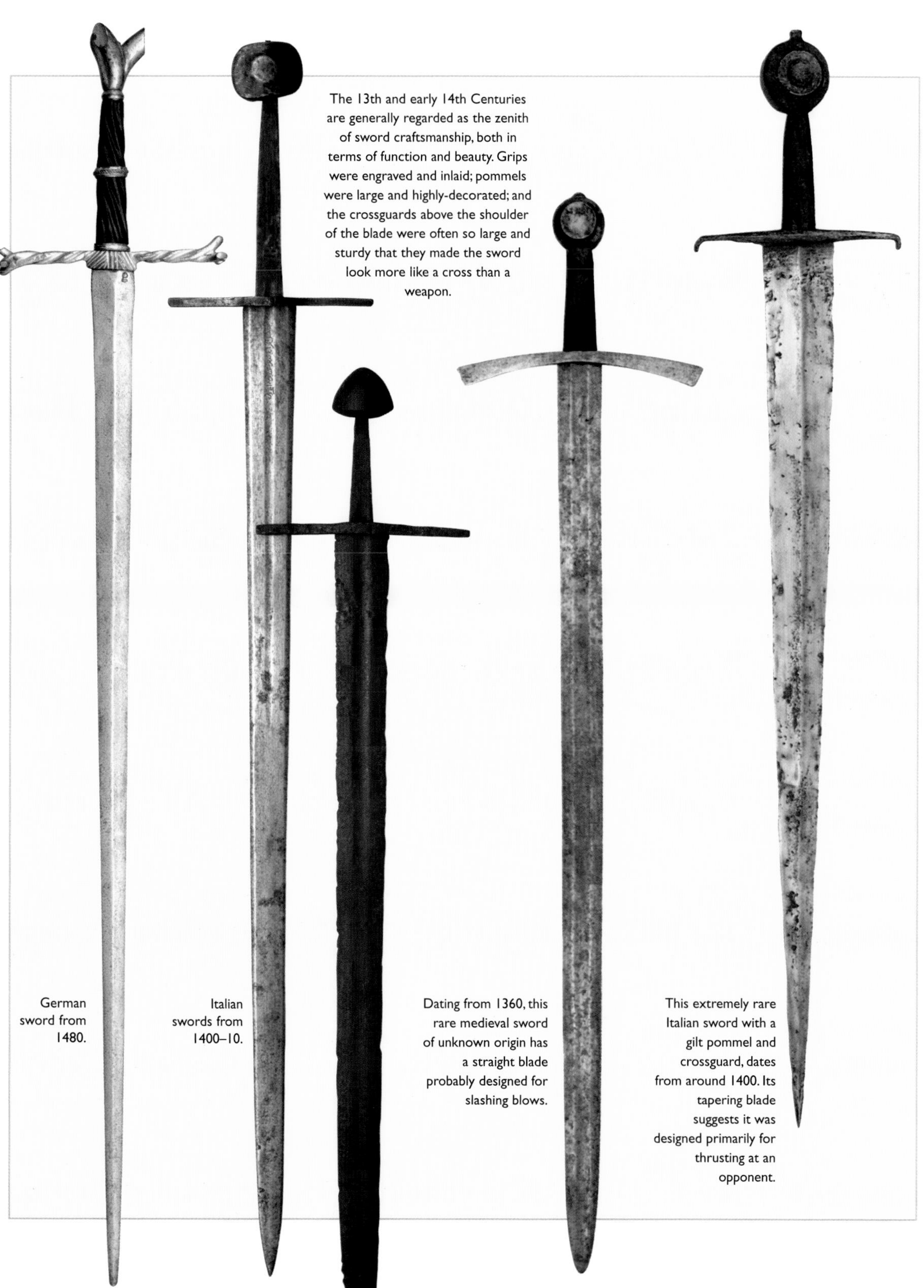

The 13th and early 14th Centuries are generally regarded as the zenith of sword craftsmanship, both in terms of function and beauty. Grips were engraved and inlaid; pommels were large and highly-decorated; and the crossguards above the shoulder of the blade were often so large and sturdy that they made the sword look more like a cross than a weapon.

German sword from 1480.

Italian swords from 1400–10.

Dating from 1360, this rare medieval sword of unknown origin has a straight blade probably designed for slashing blows.

This extremely rare Italian sword with a gilt pommel and crossguard, dates from around 1400. Its tapering blade suggests it was designed primarily for thrusting at an opponent.

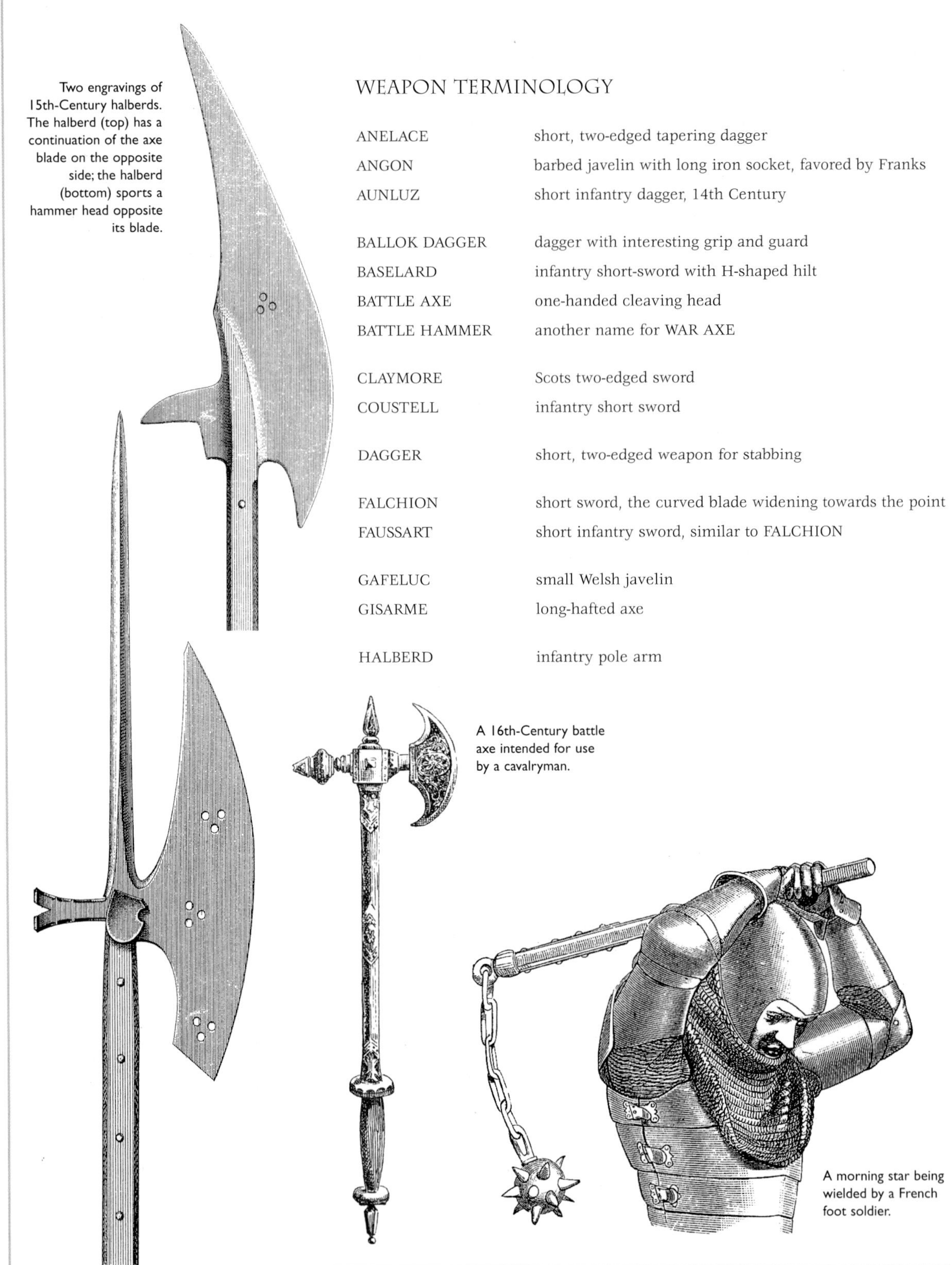

Two engravings of 15th-Century halberds. The halberd (top) has a continuation of the axe blade on the opposite side; the halberd (bottom) sports a hammer head opposite its blade.

WEAPON TERMINOLOGY

ANELACE	short, two-edged tapering dagger
ANGON	barbed javelin with long iron socket, favored by Franks
AUNLUZ	short infantry dagger, 14th Century
BALLOK DAGGER	dagger with interesting grip and guard
BASELARD	infantry short-sword with H-shaped hilt
BATTLE AXE	one-handed cleaving head
BATTLE HAMMER	another name for WAR AXE
CLAYMORE	Scots two-edged sword
COUSTELL	infantry short sword
DAGGER	short, two-edged weapon for stabbing
FALCHION	short sword, the curved blade widening towards the point
FAUSSART	short infantry sword, similar to FALCHION
GAFELUC	small Welsh javelin
GISARME	long-hafted axe
HALBERD	infantry pole arm

A 16th-Century battle axe intended for use by a cavalryman.

A morning star being wielded by a French foot soldier.

HAND-AND-HALF SWORD	sword capable of being wielded with one or two hands
JAVELIN	light spear
LANCE	long cavalry spear
MACE	single-handed club
MISERICORDE	thrusting dagger
MORNING STAR	type of mace
PIKE	long infantry spear used with both hands
POLE ARM	infantry weapon with cutting/thrusting blade
POLE AXE	combined cutting blade, hammer, and thrusting spike
POMMEL	rounded end of sword hilt
QUILLIONS	cross guard of sword grip
SPARTH	pole axe with upward curving blade
SWORD	weapon with long blade, hilt, and hand guard
WAR HAMMER	hammer-shaped mace
WYAX	double-headed axe

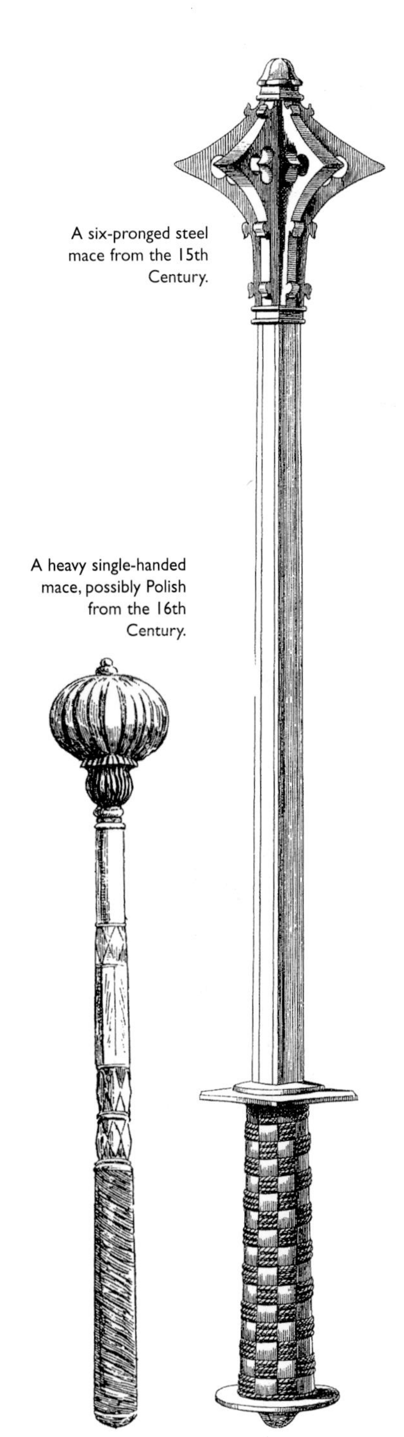
A six-pronged steel mace from the 15th Century.

A heavy single-handed mace, possibly Polish from the 16th Century.

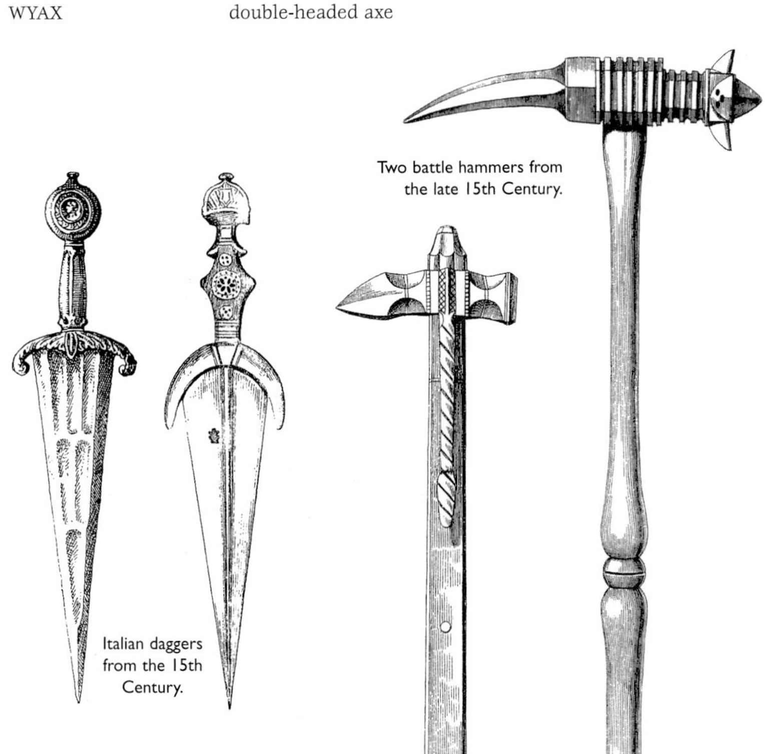
Two battle hammers from the late 15th Century.

Italian daggers from the 15th Century.

Spears were numerous in type. Javelins are often associated with Celtic and Anglo-Saxon forces but they were also used by Saracens and Catalan Almogavar light infantry. Infantry spears eventually graduated into longer pikes, used with two hands, most effectively by Scots schiltrons and by Swiss pike blocks, particularly when supported by crossbowmen and halberdiers. A range of weapons known as pole arms comprised a long pole terminating in blades and hooks, a glaive, for dragging a horsemen out of his saddle. The long-hafted bearded axe used in a Saxon shield wall developed into a gisarme itself replaced by the halberd. This comprised a pole arm terminating in an axe-blade, hammer, and thrusting pike.

The lance was originally the chief weapon of a knight. The Bayeux Tapestry depicts them being used as downward thrusting weapons and not necessarily couched. By the end of the 13th Century, the lance was eight feet (2.4 m) long and a century later ten feet (3 m). Lances were constructed from ash wood with an armor piercing spearhead.

Axes and maces were other weapons favored by knights. The battle axe was a one-handed cleaving weapon but the Viking axes had developed into not just halberds but the Scots Jeddart and Lochabar axes. Also well-known are the galloglass axe of Ireland and the sparth with its upward-curving blade. The 13th Century mace was a shaft terminating in a flanged head that would be used to crack helmets and plate armor. This was a cavalry and élite weapon, especially favored by fighting clerics (who would rather crack a skull than spill blood). The Morning Star was a mace

Soldiers armed with war hammers and axes loot a house looking for profit after the fighting was over. For many soldiers this was the real reason for signing-up for a great lord's campaign.

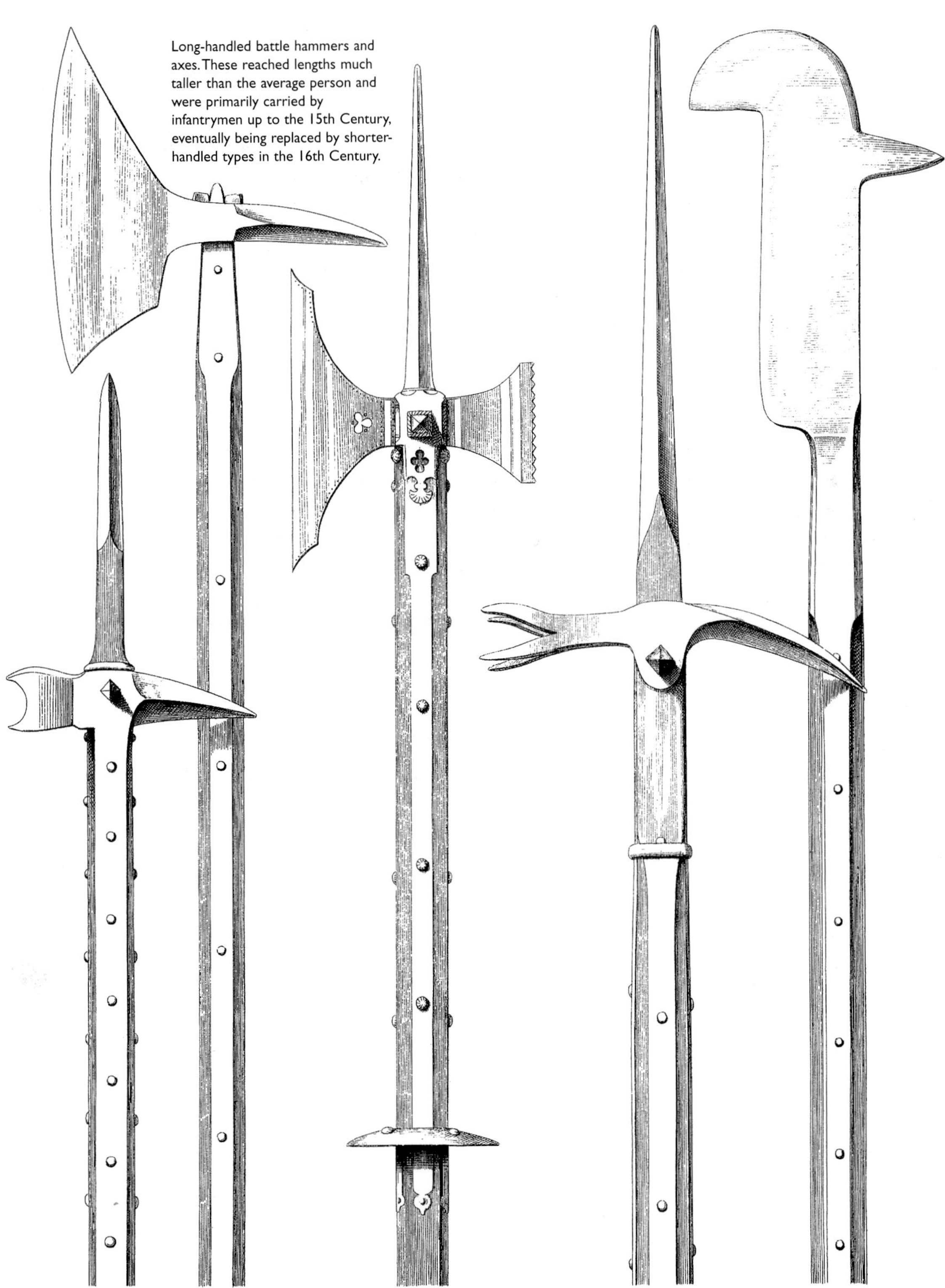

Long-handled battle hammers and axes. These reached lengths much taller than the average person and were primarily carried by infantrymen up to the 15th Century, eventually being replaced by shorter-handled types in the 16th Century.

Robert the Bruce kills Sir Henry de Buhun with his battle axe, fracturing the handle of the deadly weapon in the process.

A 15th-Century illustration of longbowmen with a sheaf of arrows through their belts.

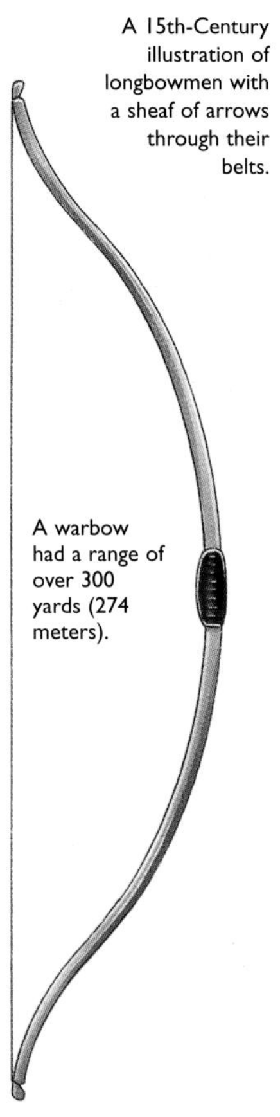

A warbow had a range of over 300 yards (274 meters).

with a spherical head with spikes projecting. Cavalrymen also liked the war hammer or battle hammer. These normally had a spike at the back of the hammerhead.

Most knights and infantry carried daggers. A wide variety of types existed but the following were common. The *dague à rouelles*, the rowel dagger, had a disc-shaped pommel and guard while the *ballok* dagger had a grip and guard resembling male genital organs. A popular dagger was the *anelace*, a short, two-edged tapering dagger. A much used weapon was the *misericorde* (from the Latin *misericordia*: mercy). This straight dagger possessed no guard, the blade being triangular section with one cutting edge. This weapon could be used to give a coup de grace by pushing it through a visor or worked in under a gorget to cut the throat.

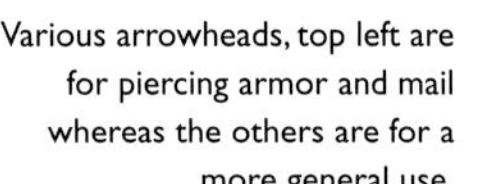

Various arrowheads, top left are for piercing armor and mail whereas the others are for a more general use.

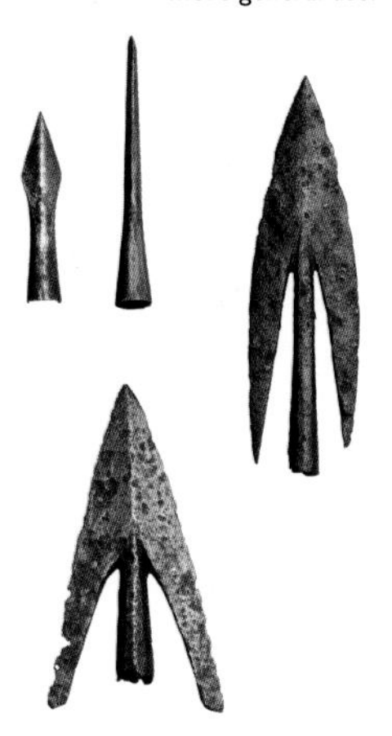

LONGBOW AND CROSSBOW

The long bow, or war bow, and the crossbow were used with devastating effect in the warfare of the Middle Ages. The famous bow of Crécy, Poitiers, and Agincourt could knock knights off their horses or slash into horse flesh. The bow was usually between five and six feet in length (1.5–1.8m), made by a bowyer from a stave of yew, and provided with a hempen string. Ordinary arrows were made from light aspen wood, but heavier 34 inch (83cm) armor-piercing arrows were made from ash, sometimes with the last few inches of oak scarfed into the shaft for added weight and punch on contact. The arrows had a bodkin point (very narrow with a triangular cross section) and were fletched with feathers, often goose. By the late 13th Century, arrows were sometimes barbed or spade-shaped, being useful to lacerate a horse's insides to bring it down and spill its rider. Such arrowheads could be three inches

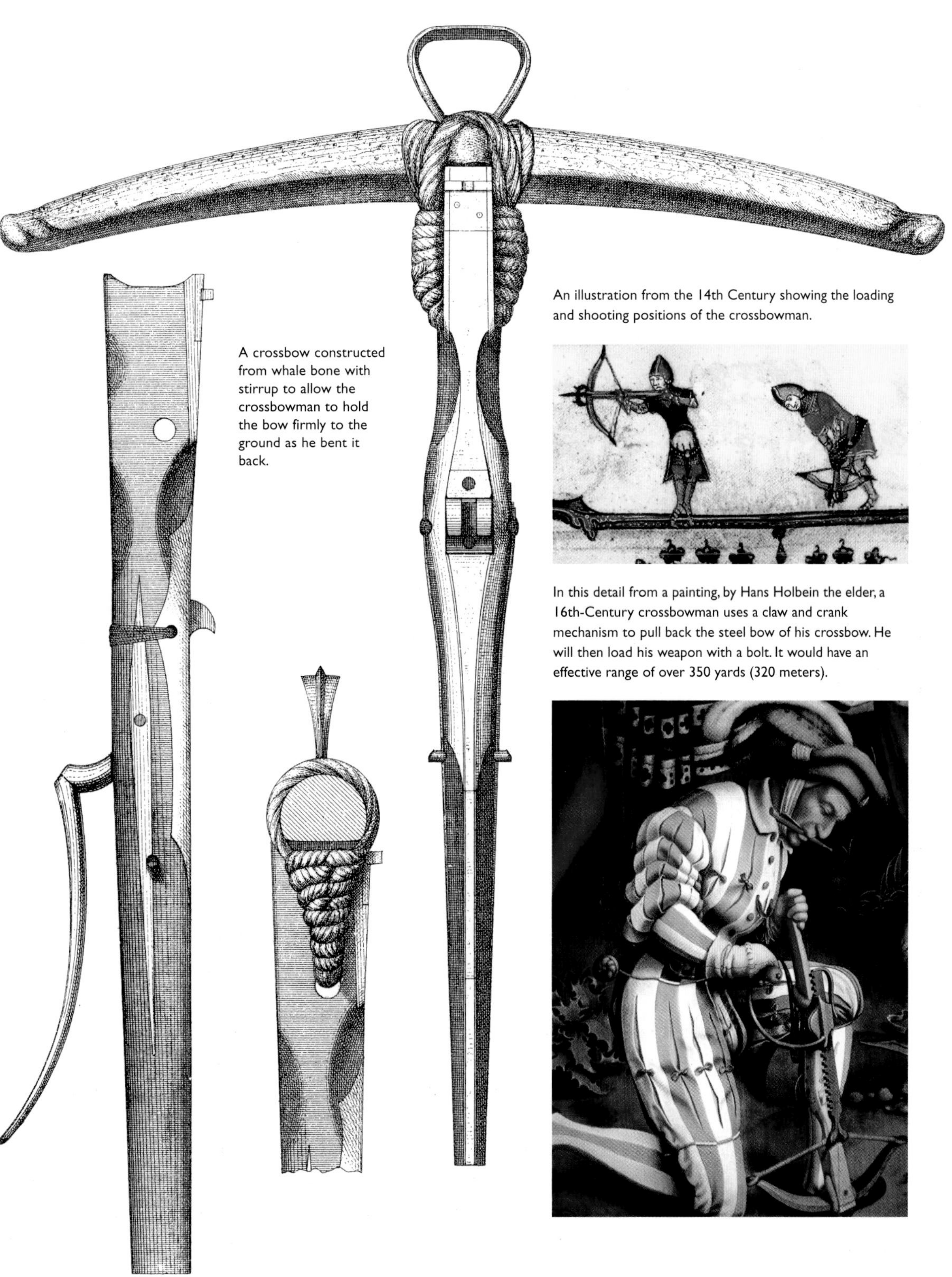

A crossbow constructed from whale bone with stirrup to allow the crossbowman to hold the bow firmly to the ground as he bent it back.

An illustration from the 14th Century showing the loading and shooting positions of the crossbowman.

In this detail from a painting, by Hans Holbein the elder, a 16th-Century crossbowman uses a claw and crank mechanism to pull back the steel bow of his crossbow. He will then load his weapon with a bolt. It would have an effective range of over 350 yards (320 meters).

(7.5cm) long and two inches (5 cm) broad. The nock taking the string was often protected with horn.

The bow was used throughout Europe, in France, Scandinavia, Poland, Bohemia, and Flanders, but only in England was this weapon used en masse with the monarchy demanding archery practice on the butts from all able-bodied men.

The English archer trained from boyhood and the constant drawing of the string could distort the boy's bones. The best English archers were hired by the great landed magnates who fought in France during the Hundred Years' War. They developed a volley-shooting technique that showered arrows, turning the sky dark as they rained down, creating carnage amongst the French cavalry, bringing horses down, and leaving the dismounted riders to be killed by both men-at-arms and archers. The high trajectory used—with each archer loosing fifteen arrows a minute—provided a formidable obstacle for any advancing troops. The archers had a technique of planting sharpened stakes into the ground to create thickets or *chevaux de fries* of six or seven rows, each row about a yard apart with the points angled toward the enemy. These stakes were designed to impale horses and reputedly archers stood in front of them, suddenly withdrawing into them at the last moment so enemy cavalry had no time to stop. All the time arrows would be pouring into the advance and when the chaos was great the infantry could join in. England had a complete system of weapons production and 1359 records show the delivery of 20,000 war bows and 850,000 arrows to the ordnance stores at the Tower of London. That number of arrows could be used by a 5,000-strong force of archers in eleven minutes.

The crossbow, arbalest or arblast, was a bow-arm fixed to a wooden stock with a mechanism to draw back the string and a trigger to release it. The crossbow entered into the military domain with the growth of siege warfare in the 11th Century. The crossbowmen were specialist troops, highly prized and highly paid, hailing from Genoa in north Italy or Gascony in southwest France. The swift development of protective armor in the 12th and 13th Centuries was undoubtedly a partial response to the effectiveness of the crossbow, which was more dangerous than the war bow against armor. The war bow's advantage was its rate of fire but the crossbow had a greater range.

By the late 13th Century crossbow arms possessed a composite structure made from yew wood, horn, sinew, and sometimes bone. They became increasingly powerful and hard to draw back, span, and eventually the most powerful bows used a windlass as a spanning device. The crossbow shot a bolt or "quarrel" some twelve inches (30 cm) in length with a tapered and flattened butt, weighing less than 3 oz (84g). The steel head or pile was normally a slender four-sided pyramid, similar to an arrow's bodkin point and the bolt was fletched with goose feathers or leather. The vireton bolt had a spiral flight causing the bolt to rotate and be more accurate.

A great crossbow was a large version of the ordinary type, made of yew and horn, about six feet (2m) long, being mounted on a frame-bench and spanned by an integral screw-winch system, useful on a castle parapet during a siege. A siege machine, the espringal, operated on the crossbow principle. A shipboard crossbow could be fitted onto a stand for greater stability while firing. The naval battle at Sluys saw French marine crossbowmen butchered owing to their low rate of fire compared with the English archers, although someone managed to fire a bolt into King Edward III's thigh. Crossbows were used in England and the records at the royal storehouse of St. Briavels Castle show 50,000 bolts being delivered at one time, probably from the notable production works in the Forest of Dean, Gloucestshire.

An illustration from a 15th-Century manuscript by Froissart, shows close ship-to-ship combat at the Battle of Sluys in 1340 that, in many ways, reflected land combat. Archers wore down the enemy's resistance, then the ship "closed" ready for hand-to-hand combat to decide the outcome of the battle.

Heraldry and Heralds

HERALDRY WAS CONCERNED WITH THE MANAGEMENT OF CEREMONIES AND DIPLOMATIC PROTOCOL AND ALSO WITH THE ORDERING AND RECORDING OF THE PERSONAL ARMORIAL DEVICES USED AT TOURNMENTS, ON SEALS, AND IN WARFARE. HERALDS WERE ATTACHED TO ROYAL AND MAGNATE HOUSEHOLDS.

Far right: A detail from a tapestry chairback in the House of Lords in London, representing the Royal Arms of England. In medieval tradition, the crest is a *lion stantant* (standing), *guardent* (front facing), above a royal crown on a gold helm with seven bars.

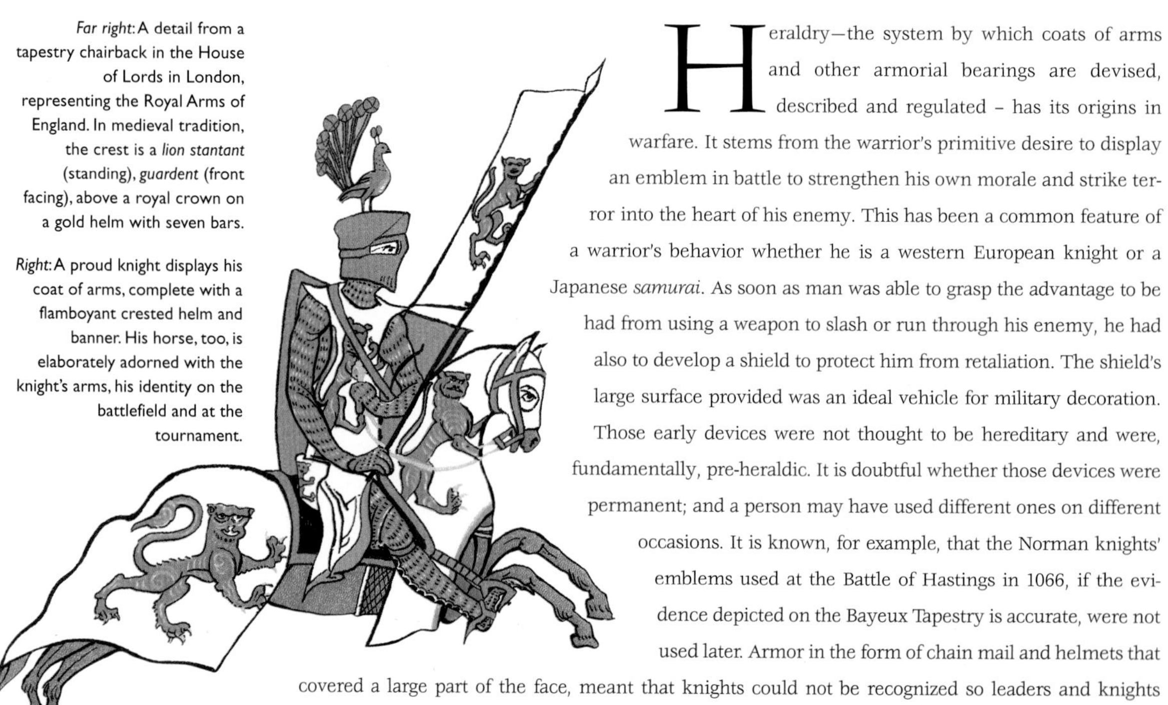

Right: A proud knight displays his coat of arms, complete with a flamboyant crested helm and banner. His horse, too, is elaborately adorned with the knight's arms, his identity on the battlefield and at the tournament.

Heraldry—the system by which coats of arms and other armorial bearings are devised, described and regulated – has its origins in warfare. It stems from the warrior's primitive desire to display an emblem in battle to strengthen his own morale and strike terror into the heart of his enemy. This has been a common feature of a warrior's behavior whether he is a western European knight or a Japanese *samurai*. As soon as man was able to grasp the advantage to be had from using a weapon to slash or run through his enemy, he had also to develop a shield to protect him from retaliation. The shield's large surface provided was an ideal vehicle for military decoration. Those early devices were not thought to be hereditary and were, fundamentally, pre-heraldic. It is doubtful whether those devices were permanent; and a person may have used different ones on different occasions. It is known, for example, that the Norman knights' emblems used at the Battle of Hastings in 1066, if the evidence depicted on the Bayeux Tapestry is accurate, were not used later. Armor in the form of chain mail and helmets that covered a large part of the face, meant that knights could not be recognized so leaders and knights required devices on their shields, flags, and standards by which they could be identified.

Seals were an identity on any national or international agreement and/or settlement of any disagreement.

The great feudal overlords also found it desirable to have some form of recognizable symbol with which they could authenticate documents and instructions that they issued to their largely illiterate subjects. Therefore, there came into use seals that depicted the overlord mounted on his horse, in battle armor, with a shield bearing his devices. Church establishments also used seals, with a picture of the bishop or abbot engraved upon them.

All land in Europe was nominally in the hands of the kings, who rewarded their followers by giving them land. Generally kings were wise enough not to give large, single blocks of land to one person, diminishing the risk of territorial magnates setting themselves up as rivals to the throne. Landowners held their estates in scattered parcels, and since they were unable to make frequent visits to them all, the need for seals was increased. Seals, carried by the lords' messengers, were marks of authority, badges of identification.

KNIGHT'S FEE

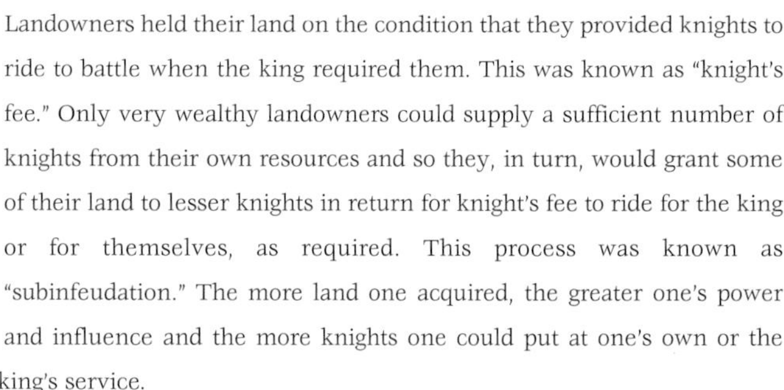

Landowners held their land on the condition that they provided knights to ride to battle when the king required them. This was known as "knight's fee." Only very wealthy landowners could supply a sufficient number of knights from their own resources and so they, in turn, would grant some of their land to lesser knights in return for knight's fee to ride for the king or for themselves, as required. This process was known as "subinfeudation." The more land one acquired, the greater one's power and influence and the more knights one could put at one's own or the king's service.

In the recurrent medieval feudal wars, when knights rode all over the country to fight on one side or another, it was necessary that each should wear a badge or symbol of his lord and on whose side he was fighting. Thus kings and lords adopted simple objects as a badge to distinguish their followers in the field. This practice gained wide acceptance in western Europe and during the crusades of the 11th, 12th, and 13th Centuries. The Angevin dynasty's use of the broom plant as a symbol gave them the name of Plantagenet and made them immediately known. The Holy Land, the birthplace of Christianity, was overrun by the Muslim Turks who cut off Christian access to it. The pope called on Christian leaders to take up arms and liberate the Holy Lands. The crusades were mounted from western Europe, with variable success. Men set forth under the sign of the Cross, emblazoned on their cloaks, shields, and banners, in different colors and different forms for each country and large contingent. Their swords were fashioned in the shape of crosses and engraved with pious emblems and inscriptions. The idea of a collective badge to identify a group took universal hold throughout Europe.

Stylized images of animals were the most popular heraldic device, with the eagle (*above*) and the lion leading the way. Clearly there was a desire in the medieval mind to invoke the power and presence of these animals.

ACCUMULATION OF LAND

Any ambitious lord sought to increase the amount of his land. One of the best strategies was to marry a lady who held land in her own right, either because she was a widow or because she was her father's heiress. As the number of young men who died in battle or from disease was high, and the number of wives who died in childbirth considerable, there was ample opportunity by judicious marriages to acquire large estates. A new husband would mark his authority over newly acquired lands by displaying on his seal the armorial bearings of the previous owners of this new acquisition. This meant that the mounted figure on the seals was soon dropped in favor of one shield showing all the arms belonging to the different people who had formerly held the land. Some seals also had the main arms engraved on a shield motif in the middle and the new ones on smaller shield motifs around the outside. The passing of arms from one person to another in this way inevitably led to them being passed from father to son. So heraldry, as we know it today, was born.

THE HERALDS

Heralds have been employed by kings and large landowners, principally as messengers and ambassadors, from very early times. They are believed to have come originally from the ranks of roaming troubadours and minstrels, who went from one place to another with their songs and tales. It seems clear that when they were acting as messengers or ambassadors heralds were free to come and go as they pleased, even across national frontiers. They typically wore a tabard (sleeveless jerkin) emblazoned with their master's arms while on official duty, and this was supposed to guarantee them protection. An attack on a herald who was wearing his master's arms was equivalent to an attack on his master. Most lords had land scattered about the country. Heralds were, therefore, traveling and meeting other heralds and other lords; in this way, they began to gather considerable knowledge of the armorial bearings of other people. This gave rise to their second important function, that of staff officer in battle.

Heralds were required to organize, announce, and referee the contestants at the tournament. They later became the only people employed to design recognized accredited heraldic emblems.

In medieval times many disputes were settled by force. Before embarking upon a dispute over borders with a neighbor, however, it was important to know how many knights he could put in the field against you. Heralds could easily discover this. During a battle they were also able to tell their lord, by recognizing the arms, who the opponents were, how many knights they could put into the field, and what men-at-arms they had under their command. They also reported who had left or joined the battle and what forces they had taken away or added. This last function was very important, since many of the combatants were involved only for what they could obtain for themselves; expected allies sometimes held back from the fray and joined it only when it was clear which side was going to win: not always the side with whom they had started out!

Something like this occurred at the 1485 Battle of Bosworth Field in England when the Earl of Northumberland held back from aiding his lord King Richard III, despite the king's numerical superiority, allowing Richard's forces to be defeated, thereby inaugurating the victor Henry as the first of the Tudor dynasty. Heralds quite often had to decide who had won a battle. At the Battle of Agincourt, the French and English heralds watched the day's events together and in the evening reported to King Henry of England that the "day was his."

Another important function was the identification of captives. Important people were held hostage for the ransom that could be gained, and ordinary people were sometimes just killed. During the Hundred Years' War, English knights recognized that campaigning in France could considerably increase their incomes by winning ransoms. Heralds also had the unenviable task of identifying the dead. This presented no great difficulty when men fought largely on foot and wore chain mail with open helmets made of iron. The slain could be easily recognized. Over their chain mail, knights wore a long, loose, padded coat, made of tough material, to help protect them from sword cuts, and they adopted the practice of painting their armorial bearings on these. This was called coat armor and is the derivation of the term Coat of Arms. If the face of the slain was not recognizable, it was possible to identify him by his Coat of Arms. The heralds, therefore, insisted that knights continue to wear a short surcoat, with their arms painted on them, so that mistakes could be avoided. The clash of hundreds of knights, at full charge and wielding every kind of dismembering weapon, must have been bedlam. Not only was it a question of identifying the dead, but a matter of finding all the right pieces, so the use of arms emblazoned on everything, including the crest of the helmet, enabled heralds to perform this grisly task.

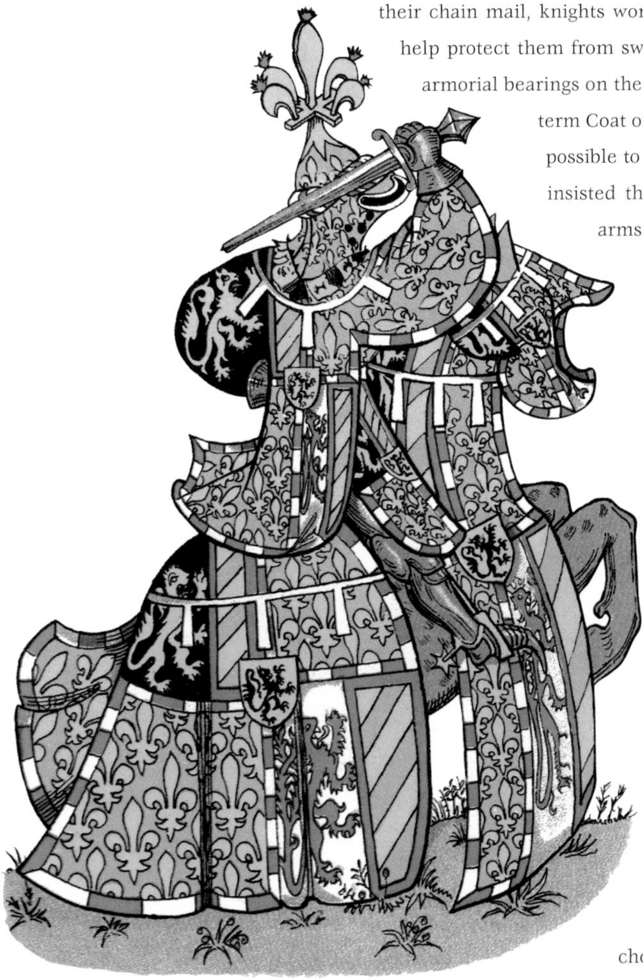

HERALDS AND TOURNAMENTS

Owing to their knowledge of armorial bearings, heralds were required to recognize and announce contestants at tournaments and it became their responsibility to organize and referee these events. Because of the social nature of the event and the desire by everyone to put on a good display, heralds were necessary to advise would-be contestants about the choice of armorial bearings that they could use. They were able to make sure that no one chose the arms of another, already in use. People came to them for advice on heraldic matters and they began to keep lists of all the armorial bearings used at different tournaments, gatherings, and battles and of the people who bore them. These lists were collected on long rolls of parchment and were called Rolls of Arms, or simply Rolls. Many of these have survived and they provide a valuable record of early heraldry. Because the heralds became so involved in the study and recording of Coats of Arms and in advising and adjudicating on matters relating to them, the business became known as Heraldry. In England heralds were incorporated by Royal Charter in 1484. The French acted likewise. Since people continued to assume Coats of Arms without having them registered and recorded at the College, disputes frequently arose over who was the actual owner of a Coat of Arms. Consequently, the heralds were required to tour the country to gather all heraldic information, so that they could be registered and disputes settled. Most of these "visitations," as they were called, took place in the 16th Century. They form the basis upon which ownership of arms is proved today. The records, however, are not complete, for those were stormy times in England, and in some instances people were unable to answer the call of the visiting herald, because they were confined to their place or residence by siege. The motive of the visitation may often have been political and not strictly for the well-being of heraldry. It was a worthwhile exercise for sovereigns to record their supporters and disqualify those who could not support them.

These two knights, dressed in their full chivalric regalia, prepare to do combat at a tournament. This was a great opportunity not only to show competence with sword and lance but also to put on the best display of their personal coats of arms.

ARMORIAL BEARINGS

In England, heralds had important duties as officers of the Crown, and they still exist today. Apart from these duties they were active in heraldic affairs. Their work fell into three categories.

Confirming arms: Any worthy person could apply for a grant of arms and the heralds would steer the applicant safely through the process. First it was necessary to check whether an aspirant armiger (person entitled to heralidic arms) was not entitled to an existing coat of arms. If he was not, it was then necessary to consider a possible new design and to check that it was not already held by someone. Once established and the design approved by all parties it could then be granted to the applicant as the sole right of him and his legal descendants. As well as private individuals, many commercial undertakings and corporate institutions applied for grants of arms.

Devising arms: The Heralds of Great Britain had jurisdiction only over subjects of the Crown. Although many people of British origin who are citizens of other countries wished to register coats of arms or varieties of arms belonging to their families to show their ancient lineage, the heralds were not able to grant arms to them. They could, however, following the proper searches, "devise" arms that could be used and register them in their records so that they would not be issued to others.

The heralds took great care to ensure that any arms, crests, supporters, mottos, badges, or standards were unique to the grantees. This is the point of the exercise: heraldry exists to identify individuals. There is no such thing as "Arms of a Name."

Heraldry employs a specialized technical language, a refinement of what was a medieval science. Its origins in western Europe occurred at a time when the predominant language was Norman French. Some of that language still survives in the heraldic terms used today, chiefly concerning the basics of design and color. When translating the meaning of the various elements of a coat of arms it is necessary to have an understanding of the herald's jargon.

With the invention of guns in the 14th Century, armor slowly began to fall into disuse, since it was no longer possible for a man to be mobile and to wear armor sufficiently strong to stop bullet and ball. It therefore became increasingly difficult to identify men on the battlefield and heraldic insignia ceased to be used for this practical purpose by the 17th Century. However, heraldic devices have continued to be used as an artistic and traditional way to identify a person; and shields, although they no longer serve a protective function, have remained the chief vehicle upon which to display armorial insignia. Insignia are commonly depicted on other accessories and devices besides the shield. The whole assemblage is known as "the Achievement," which is the correct term to describe the total collection of a person's heraldic accessories, also called 'appurtenances'. Different countries and customs dictate that Achievements contain different items. The shield holds the armorial bearings of a person which would otherwise be borne on his coat of arms, horse trappings, flags, banners, sail, or other items. It is from the coat of arms that was derived the name used to describe the shield, and what is displayed on it. In modern parlance "armorial bearings" has been shortened simply to "arms." An aspirant armiger would apply to the appropriate heraldic authority for a "grant of arms." At the same time, the other items to be included in the Achievement, as appropriate to the applicant's rank and circumstances, were assigned. To fully understand armorial bearings it is necessary to identify the types of shields depicted and the symbols and emblems displayed on the shield.

THE BLAZON

The "blazon" is the written description of a coat of arms, described in a technical language that is at first confusing. However, a well-written description is a masterpiece of concision that should enable any heraldic artist to draw correctly everything that is displayed on the shield. To blazon a coat of arms was to describe it in words. To "emblazon" it, was to paint or draw it in full color. Because the blazon always followed a strict pattern, it was painted on the shield in the same order.

THE SHIELD

The shield is the principal vehicle for the display of armorial insignia and is the only essential ingredient in an Achievement of Arms. The devices on the shield are the individual insignia—the armorial bearings—that mark one man from another. The shield is found in a variety of shapes and these are the outcome of different usages, fashions, and times. The principal shapes and styles are:

The long shield: Gives the most protection, and was used when men fought on foot. It afforded a protection against arrows as well as in closer combat.

The short or heater-shaped (flat iron) shield: This was specially devised for use in tournaments and was strong enough to withstand a hit with a lance. Its shape provided the most protection and deflected the lance from the bearer. It was also called the "target" or "targ," after the point at which a knight aimed in a charge at a tournament.

The square-shaped shield: This became popular when the custom developed of displaying more than one set of armorial bearings on one shield.

The horsehead shield: So-called because its shape is thought to have developed from the armor plate used to protect the head and face of a knight's horse. It was quite often used by ecclesiastical dignitaries when the military-style shield was felt to be inappropriate.

The lozenge and oval shield: Armigerous women customarily display their arms on an oval or a lozenge, since it was felt that it was inappropriate for a woman to display arms on a "military" shield.

Ornamental cartouches and other shapes: Once the practical use of the shield disappeared, arms began to be displayed on all kinds of ornamental shapes and designs of a perplexing variety. The square-shaped shield is used when several different armorial bearings are represented; the oval and the lozenge are used to display women's heraldic devices. But the shape of the shield is not sacred; it could be changed, due consideration being given to style and period, to any shape that best suits the design of the article upon which it is placed.

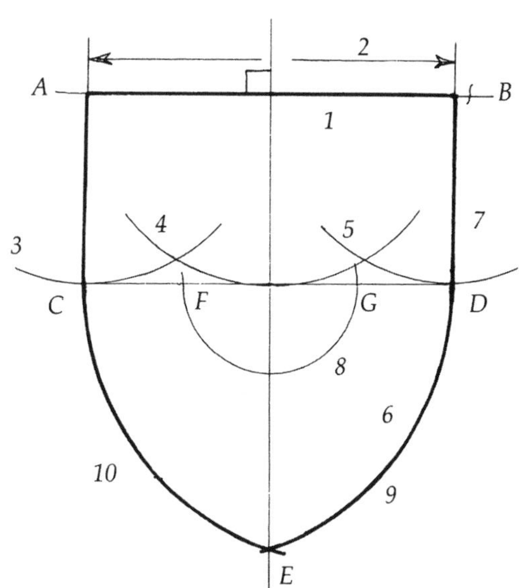

A simple method for how a quartered shield was drawn: two squares hang from the line A-B and from the points F and G respectively. Two arcs DE and CE are drawn. The proportions of the shield could then be varied by altering the positions of F and G.

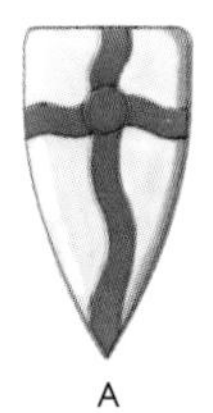
A

B

C

C

D

E

The principal shapes and styles of shields commonly found are as follows:
A—The long shield.
B—The short or heater-shaped shield.
C—The square-shaped shield (shown in two styles).
D—The horsehead shield.
E—The lozenge.

DESCRIBING THE SHIELD

There are two ways, apart from painting or drawing a detailed picture of the coat of arms, by which it could be described. The first is the blazon. All blazons follow a set pattern. Firstly, they describe the divisions of the field, if there are any, and the partition lines, if they are not straight. They consider next the main charge, then any secondary charges that may be placed either side of the main charge, and next any other charges that may be placed on the main charge.

The second is a method known as "the trick." This is a shorthand method of annotating a coat of arms, the sort of note that might be made to serve as a reminder of a coat of arms seen, for example, on a public building, in order to identify it later. This is the main use for the abbreviations in heraldry.

THE FIELD

Before any design was placed on a shield, that shield was painted a color, which could be one of the metals, colors, or furs. The base color was known as the "field." There are examples of Coats of Arms that consisted of a field with a plain tincture only: Bruget of Normandy bore a Coat of Arms and a shield "argent" (silver or white); the Duke of Brittany bore "ermine" (white with black tails); and Berrington of Chester bore "azure" (blue). Other colours or tinctures were "gules" (red), "sable" (black), "vert" (green), and "purpure" (purple). English heraldry also included 'murrey' (sanguine, a tint blended from gules and purpure); and "metalis" or (gold). There are other furs too: "ermine" (black field with white spots), "pean" (black field with gold spots), and "vair" (squirrel fur represented as alternated white and blue cup shapes). Notwithstanding all the items imaginable that might be placed on a blue shield, for example, it was soon necessary for differentiation to use two-colored shields, with one half red, for example, and the other white.

A field Semy, semé, strewn or powdered: Sometimes a field was strewn with many small "charges" (items placed on the field, see below) and these were usually of a stated color. Some of them had their own special terms: "*Semy de lis*" or "*semy of fleur de lis*" representing the lily, while "*crusiley*" meant that the field was strewn with little crosses. Other terms are "*of the roundels*," "*pomme*," '"*bezanty*," "*platy*," "*of the guttés*," and "*gutté d'or*."

The Divisions of the Field: The shield was divided in a variety of ways and the form of the division and the colors to be used were always mentioned first in the blazon. Each different form of division of the field has its own term. When describing a divided field, the color in the top dexter (right) corner from the bearer's point of view (i.e. left as depicted) was always given first.

The Lines of Partition: In all the examples shown on these pages, the divisions are made with straight lines. They may, however, be made with a variety of zigzag or wavy lines. In the blazon the order of description is as follows: the division of the field (if any), the configuration of the line (if not straight) and the colors, the top dexter being first.

DIVISION OF THE FIELD

PER PALE

PER SALTIRE

SALTIRE

QUARTERLY

GYRONY

MASONY

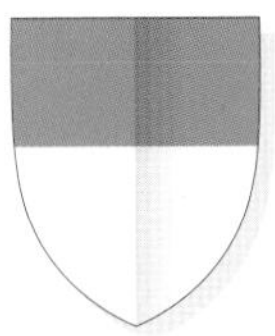
PER FESSE

PER BEND

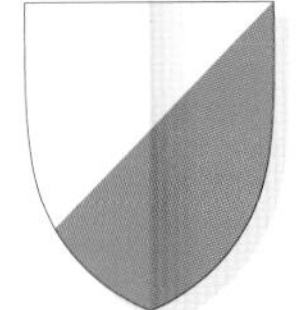
PER BEND SINISTER

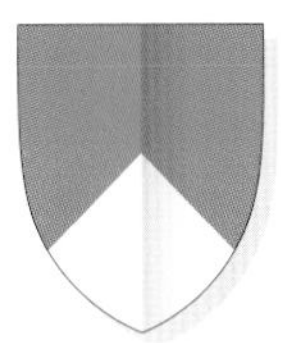
PER CHEVRON

TIERCED IN PAIRLE

BARRY

BENDY

BENDY SINISTER

PALY

LOZENGY

CHEQUEY

EXAMPLES OF LINE PARTITION

A FESS DANCY

A BEND WAVY

A FESSE EMBATTLED

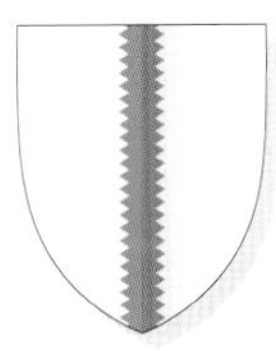
A PALE INDENTED

A SALTIRE ENGRAILED

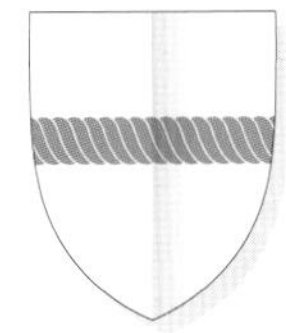
A FESSE WREATHY

EXAMPLES OF ORDINARIES

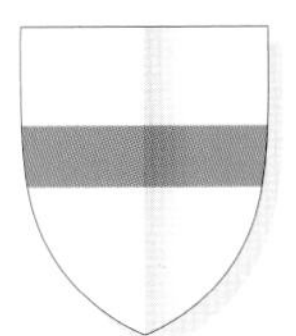
FESSE

BEND

CHEVRON

CHIEF

CROSS

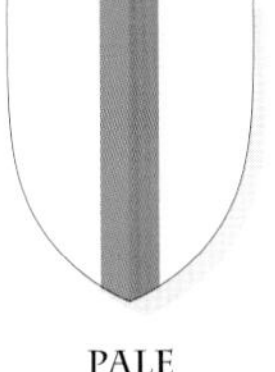
PALE

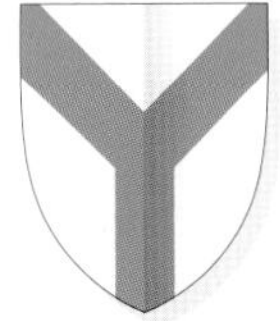
PALL

BEND SINISTER

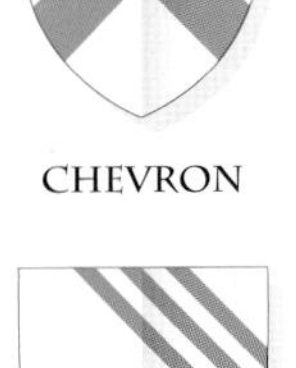
THREE BENDLETS ENHANCED

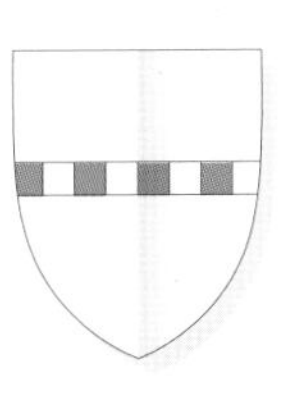
COMPONY

COUNTER COMPONY

CHEQUEY

EXAMPLES OF SUB-ORDINARIES

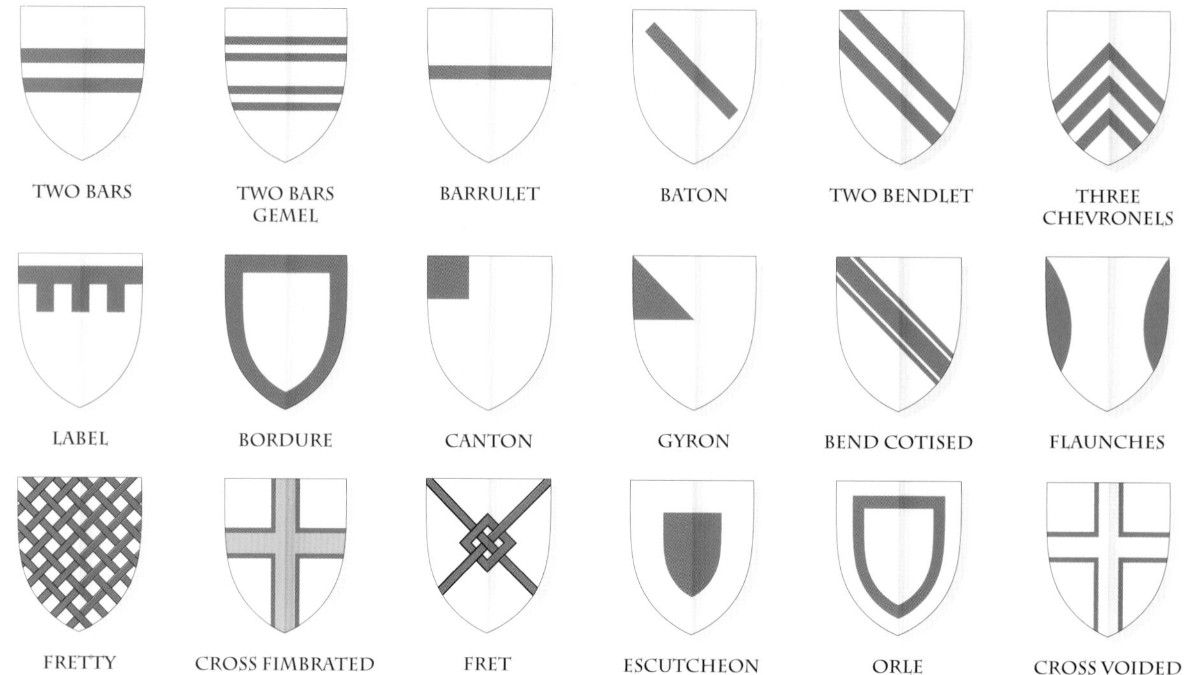

THE CHARGES

Any item placed upon the field of the shield is known as a "charge." If a shield has anything placed on it, it is said to be charged with that object. Similarly a lion with a rose on its shoulder is described as being "charged on the shoulder with a rose." It became the custom in an illustration of a coat of arms to show any charge placed upon the field as casting a shadow. As well as enhancing the artistic effect, the shadow showed that the item is not part of the field but was charged upon it. The light is always shown as coming from the dexter top. The provision of a shadow is, however, by no means a rule and in small works it was frequently omitted for the sake of clarity. Charges of all kinds could themselves be charged in never-ending successions and combinations.

The ordinaries: This main group of charges consists of geometric shapes placed upon a shield, stripes in different combinations and other shapes. An ordinary usually occupies about one-third of the area of the shield. An ordinary is not a division of the field but a charge placed upon it.

The subordinaries: These are smaller geometric charges, less frequently used, but no less important.

The roundel and gutté: The "roundels" appear as different colored circles each with their own name. A gold roundel is a "bezant," a silver roundal is called a "plate;" red, a "torteau;" blood-red, a "guze;" blue, a "hurt;" green, a '"pomme;" black, a "pellate," "ogress," or "gunstone;" purple, a "golpe;" orange, an "orange;" and when barry, wavy, argent or azure, a "fountain." "*Gutte*" (or "*gutty*," "*gouty*") means "strewn with droplets." Like the roundels, they have a different name for each color. "*Gutté d'or*"

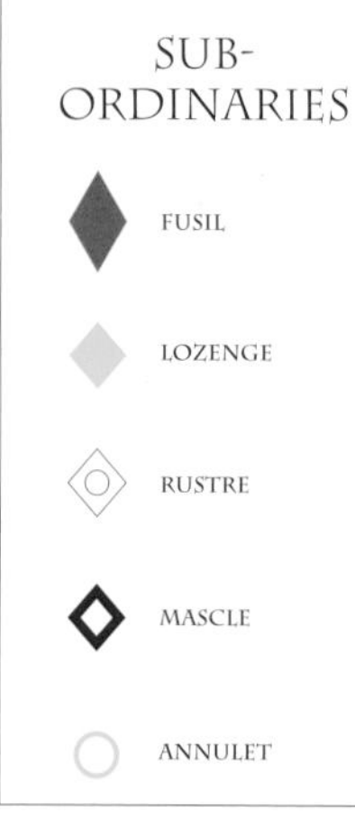

describes a field or charge strewn with gold drops; *"gutté d'eau,"* silver drops; *"gutté de sang,"* red drops; *"gutté de larmes,"* blue drops; *"de poix,"* black drops; and *"d'huile"* (or more rarely, *"d'olive"*), green drops.

Combinations: Combinations of these groups are frequently seen.

Counterchanging: This feature is quite often encountered, in which a charge is placed over a divided field and the colors reversed. Some exciting and exotic effects could be produced by this method.

Other charges: Any object may be placed upon a shield either on its own or in combination with the ordinaries, subordinaries or other unrelated objects. Charges may be of any color, including their own natural color, and they may be countercharged with the field or the ordinaries, subordinaries, or be themselves charges with other charges. The variety is endless, and needed to be, to ensure that each coat of arms was unique. The only limitations were those imposed by good taste and the rule of tincture concerning the use of color, metal, and fur.

Canting arms: Charges often related to the name of the bearer. This was a common practice but, unfortunately, with the gradual change of language over the centuries, the meaning of the allusion has often been lost.

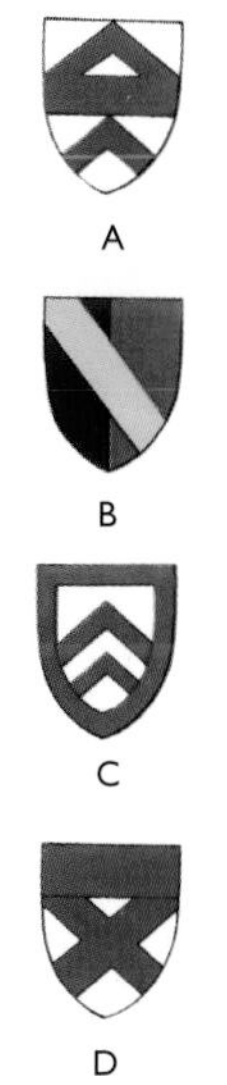

Four combinations of ordinaries and subordinaries are illustrated above, with the name of the arms bearer given in brackets:
A—Argent a fesse between two chevrons gules (Fitzwalter).
B—Per pale azure and gules overall a bend or (Langton).
C—Argent two chevrons with a bordure gules (Albini).
D—Argent a saltire and chief gules (Bruce).

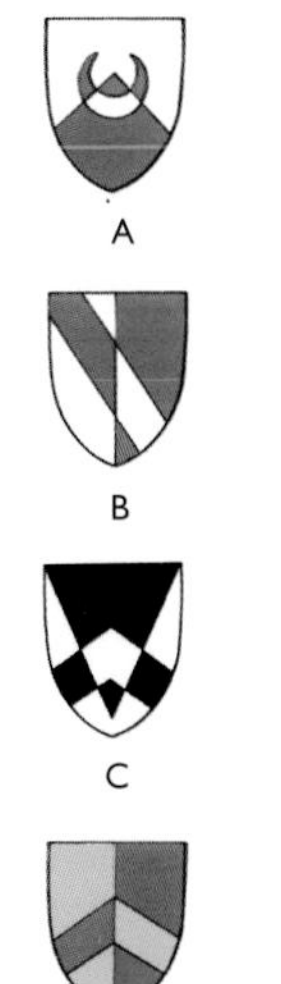

Counter-charging may be done in a number of ways. Illustrated here are four examples:
A—Per chevron argent and gules overall a crescent countercharged (Barker).
B—Per pale argent and gules overall a bend countercharged (Chaucer).
C—Argent a pile and a chevron countercharged.
D—Per pale and/or gules a chevron countercharged (Chambers).

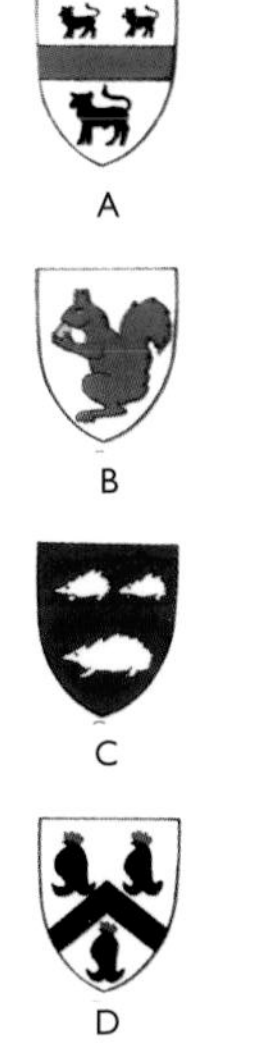

These four illustrations are examples of canting arms:
A—Argent between three calves sable a fesse gules (Calverly).
B—Argent a squirrel gules eating a gold nut (Squire).
C—Azure three hedgehogs argent (Harris).
D—Argent between three moorcocks a chevron sable (Moore).

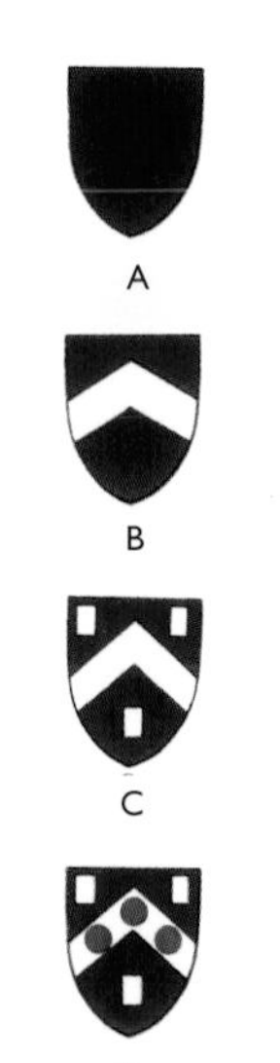

A shield had four main elements to be described in a blazon:
A—The color of the shield (azure).
B—The main charges (on a chevron).
C—The secondard charges (between three billets argent).
D—Any additional charges (three torteaux).

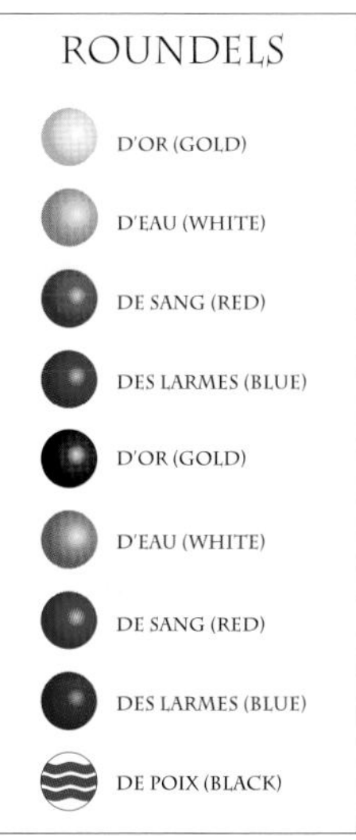

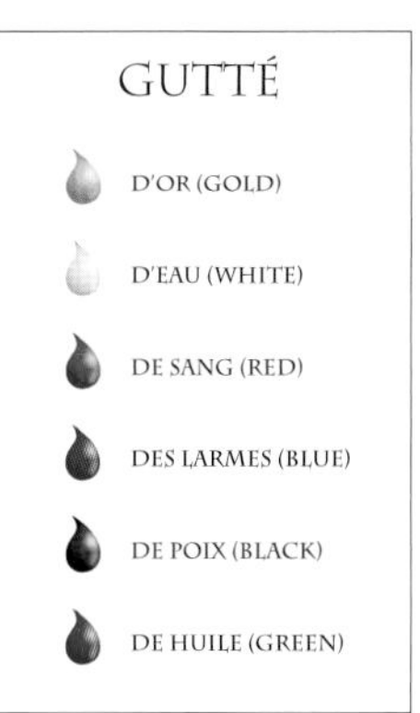

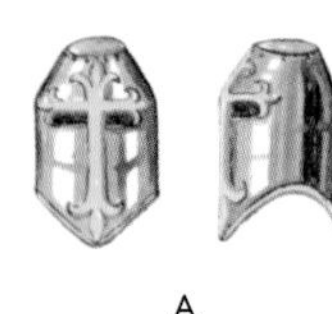

A

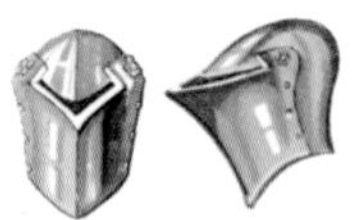

B

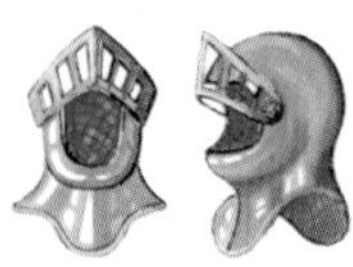

C

D

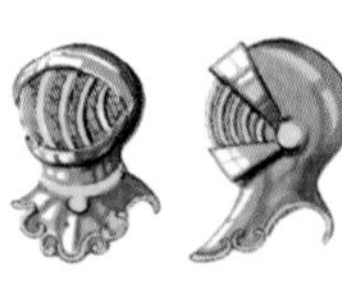

E

Various types of helmets are represented here:
A—The pot helm.
B—The tilting helm.
C—The helm with open visor and no bars.
D—The barred helm.
E—The armet.

HERALDIC ACCESSORIES

The Helmet

One of the prominent motifs used on a coat of arms is the knight's helmet. In the days of hand-to-hand warfare adequate protection for the head was provided by a simple iron cap or *bascinet*, which was sufficient to protect the wearer from sword blows. Later a noseplate and cheek plates were added. When cavalry was introduced, the helmet had to be much stronger and so the helmet that closed with a visor and which had a plate around the neck—a gorget—was introduced. Helmets with bars and grids across the face were also introduced.

Ceremonial helmets, usually of the type with bars, were made of softened leather and were richly decorated. They were used as vehicles to display the crest, especially in countries where whole families displayed the same armorial bearings on the shield and identify the individual only by a different crest.

In some countries it was the custom to depict different types and posture of helmet, or "helm" as it is more usually called, to differentiate men according to his social rank. This, however, is only a custom, not a rule, and it was often broken.

Pot helm: This, the oldest type of helm, was worn over the top of the small basinet and chain-mail gorget. Its use in heraldry is limited to gentlemen in Scotland and some families of ancient lineage, in Germany and Denmark.

Tilting helm: This helm was used by gentlemen and esquires in England, the Scandinavian countries, Germany and Poland, and (though less commonly) by persons of all ranks throughout Europe. Some members of the German, Austrian, Hungarian, and Polish nobility have used it to show that their armorial bearings are of more ancient lineage than those depicted by "newer men" on the more modern barred helm. It was also used in Italian Heraldry for non-titled ranks. Civic and corporate armorial bearings in England usually use this type of helm.

Helm with open visor and no bars: This type was more commonly used by British knights and baronets (hereditary knights) and Russian Leibkanpanez.

Barred helm: This helm, found in a variety of forms and types, was used all over Europe, usually to denote titled rank, although in Belgium, the Netherlands, and Spain it was used by untitled ranks as well. The posture of the helm depicted on the arms varies from country to country, and alterations in the number of bars and the artistic treatment are then used to signify distinctions of rank. An English peer of whatever rank, for example, used a five-barred helm facing to the left, as viewed. On the Continent this helm, whether facing the front or either side, was used by all ranks. In Italy and Spain the posture, the number of bars, and the amount of gold used, demonstrate the rank of the bearer. In Denmark and the Netherlands, a silver helm was used for non-titled persons, gold for peers.

Armet: This helm, with the visor open or closed and with or without bars, was used in Italian and Spanish Heraldry and, to a lesser extent, in France. Its style is quite different from that of the other helms used in European Heraldry, so that its use in an Achievement may give a good clue to the bearer's origins.

All the European sovereigns have used gold helms, facing the front and topped by a royal crown. In England the royal helm shows eight bars; others show a gold helm with the visor open.

Although the conventions that govern the use of helms are not rules (despite attempts to standardize the use of helms to indicate the rank of the wearer), there are discernible national styles that reveal the origin and rank of the wearer. But the helm alone is never conclusive evidence; it should be considered with caution and assessed in the context of the style of the other items of the Achievement.

The helm's crest

It will be seen from looking at any Achievement of Arms that shows a helmet that it is unusual for the helmet to have nothing placed upon it. Usually a helmet bears a crest. The crest is a product of the tournament, and because of the importance of pageantry and display in a tournament, the crest, which was proudly fixed atop the helm, became increasingly complicated and large. Every kind of emblem, carved of wood or made of leather and stiffened canvas and richly painted and gilded, was devised. Sometimes they repeated the devices on the armorial bearings, or a part of them; often they were any other thing, real or imaginary, that could be contrived to sit securely atop the helm.

A decorated shield and helm in the traditional medieval style utilizing animal and other symbols in the creation of a chivalric identity.

In England the practice has been for all members of a family to exhibit the same crest, but there are several instances of unrelated families displaying similar crests, so that the crest is not a reliable emblem of identification. When family ties and tradition are felt to be important, the crest is displayed on its own, especially on items such as rings, silver, china, and glass, that are likely to be handed down from one generation to the next.

On the Continent, where families display the same armorial bearings, each member sported a different crest by which he could be recognized. It is, therefore, a very personal emblem. It was often the practice before a tournament for helmets with their crest, to be displayed for inspection, especially by the ladies of the court. If a lady espied the crest of someone who had in any way wronged any of her number, she would touch the helm and it would be thrown to the floor by a herald. The owner was then unable to take part in the tournament and there was nothing for it but for him to pick up his helm and slink off in disgrace.

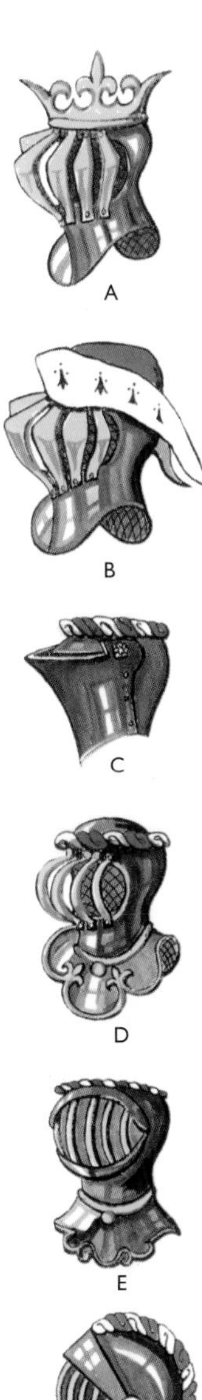

A—The crest coronet.
B—The chapeau.
C, D and E—The torso or wreath.
F—The Spanish torso.

MARSHALING OF ARMS

When two or more coats of arms are displayed on one shield, especially with respect to Royal heraldry, this was done to demonstrate sovereignty over territory. The first point to consider is that

A union of families resulted in an amalgam of arms in the growing identity of husband and wife in the identification of their unified estates.

heraldry is hereditary. Heraldic devices are passed down from one generation to the next. When a son came of age, he was entitled to display his father's coat of arms, bearing some small "mark of difference" so that it was possible to tell one from the other. When the father died, the first son, who had become the head of the family, removed his mark of difference and bore the "undifferenced" coat of arms of his father. Any other sons retained their marks of difference because their position in the family was unaltered, unless the first son died without his own heir, in which case the next son would take the place as the head of the family and bear the undifferenced coat. These Coats of Arms could be passed down through the generations in the respective families by the male heirs.

If a man had only daughters his arms could die with him, if none of his daughters married. If there was more than one daughter, they would be heiresses in heraldry of equal right and could display their father's arms after his death until they died, on a lozenge shaped shield. The arms would then cease to have anyone to bear them and become a matter of history. If, however, one or any of them married, the situation would different.

If an armigerous man married an heraldic heiress, he could display her arms on an "escutcheon" ("escutcheon of pretence") on his shield. He had no right to the arms, since he would only be preserving them for his heirs. His heirs may then quarter their mother's arms with those of their father. If the parent's arms were each a simple unquartered coat, the form was to divide the shield into four sections and place the paternal coat in the first and fourth quarter and the maternal coat in the second and third quarter. If the mother already had a quartered coat, these quarters would be included in the third and fourth quarter and more if necessary. If the father had a quartered coat, the new quarters came after the last of the father's quarters. It was not necessary to display all the quarters, if there were many, but if any were added the mother's paternal coat must be the first. There would always have to be an even number of quarters and so the paternal coat was repeated in the last quarter if necessary. If a daughter married a non-armigerous husband, she could display her father's arms until she died, but there was no vehicle for its continuance into the next generation and so the arms died with her. It would be incorrect for her children to display her arms. There was one course open and that was to apply to the College of Arms for a Grant of Arms to the husband in his own right. Once this was done, he could display the wife's arms on his own as an escutcheon of pretence and bear them forward for the next generation.

If a woman had brothers, she was not an heraldic heiress and she could not carry her paternal arms forward, this being already done by her brothers. However, her husband could "impale her arms" (place them side by side on the same shield) with his own. Such arms could not be carried forward by the next generation and the impalement ended with the generation for which it was done. It is still quite common to see arms impaled with civic arms or of other arms pertaining to an office, particularly with bishops, who display the arms of their see on the dexter side of their shield and their paternal arms on the sinister side. If they wished to display their wife's arms as an impalement they would be obliged to marshal together a second shield showing their paternal arms on the dexter side and their wife's paternal arms on the sinister side.

ORDERS OF CHIVALRY AND ENTITLEMENT TO ARMS

It has long been the custom for sovereigns to instigate orders of chivalry to honor the nation's most distinguished men and women. These orders have emblems that the members wear and which appear on their Achievements. Practice varies widely from country to country.

Circlet: European knights of an order often place a circlet around a shield. It is usually shown with a motto, as, for example, in the British Order of the Garter, which is blue with a gold edge and buckle and his the motto, "*Honi soit qui mal y pense*" (Evil be to he who evil thinks).

Chain: This is usually called a "collar," a gold chain worn around the arms, with the emblems of the order in alternate links with the badge of the order pendant, as, for example, in the Swedish Order of the Seraphim. People may display collars of more than one order.

Badge: The badge of an order is displayed by lower-ranking members of the order on a riband, below the shield.

Religious Orders of Chivalry

These are survivors of the crusades, when knights joined the military and hospital orders to fight for the Holy Lands and care for the sick and wounded soldiers and pilgrims. Some of these continue to exist for philanthropic purposes. They have their own arms and badges, known as crosses.

Grandmasters can show the arms of the order on their shields as a chief or quartering. Knights and dames of the order display the cross of their order behind the shield. Members can hang the cross of the order on a riband of the order below the shield.

Entitlement to Arms

Anyone today may apply for a new grant of Arms, but a person is entitled to existing arms only if they can prove that they are descended, in the male line, from someone to whom a grant of arms had previously been made. Some countries permit people to assume arms at will, but there is then no guarantee that the arms are unique.

Heraldry is essentially a European phenomenon. Because heraldic authorities in Europe have jurisdiction only over citizens of their own country, anyone wishing to enquire into their heraldic status should, of course, apply to the authority in their own country.

In the New World the position is slightly different. Many of the peoples of those countries are of European stock. If a person wishes to prove their right to an existing coat of arms, or even request a new coat of arms, they must apply to their country of origin, or that of their ancestors. Heralds of one country cannot grant coats of arms to citizens of another, though they can make "devisals of arms" to such people, which are then registered and recorded.

SIR ROBERT SETVANS, c. 1306. Sir Robert is wearing a blue surcoat over his hauberk, which displays his armorial bearings. These are also repeated on the ailettes, stiff leather plates attached to the shoulders presumed to have given protection against slashing blows at the neck. Through the slit in the surcoat the mid-thigh-length hauberk can be seen the padded gambeson just beneath it. Sir Robert has withdrawn his hands from the main mittens, which are now part of the sleeve of his hauberk, through the wrist holes allowing the mittens to hang down. His knees are protected by ornamental poleyns and his lower legs and feet by main chausses with prick spurs at the heels. Sir Robert would normally wear a padded arming cap prior to putting on his great helm, of the earlier, flat-topped shape, shown here at his feet without a crest.

OTHER USAGE OF HERALDRY

There are numerous ways in which heraldic bearings are displayed, with decorative functions and intriguing rules of form. The ownership of a coat of arms, whether it was one long in the family or one newly granted, was a matter of justified pride, a pride that could be expressed by displaying and using the arms in a wide variety of ways. These are just some of the ways in which heraldic bearings are displayed:

Below: THE CASTLE OF NUREMBERG, dating from 1050, includes a splendid painted door displaying the coat of arms of the castle's owner.

On Fabrics: Painted, printed, and sewn flags, banners, and standards; embroidered fire screens, stool and seat covers, and chair backs; painted and printed bedspreads; sewn spinnaker sails for yachts; and heraldic costumes.

On Glass: Engraved on table glass, doors and windows, table tops, and firescreens; stained-glass windows and hanging plaques; lamp windows.

On Jewellery: Engraved rings, seals, personal items; cast sculptured items; enameled and jeweled cuff links, badges, and brooches; pendants; enameled box lids and wall plaques.

On Leather: Embosses and gilded book bindings and covers, desk sets and chair backs, boxes, and belts.

On Paper and Vellum: Paintings of Heraldic Achievements, illuminated and calligraphic illustrations, family trees, and book plates.

On Wood: Wall plaques, carved and gilded or painted; carved newel posts; carved, painted and gilded books and panels on furniture; carved and painted or gilded shields.

Right: ST GEORGE'S CHAPEL, WINDSOR, ENGLAND
The banners of the present Knights of the Garter are seen here mounted above the choir stalls in this beautifully preserved church within the walls of Windsor Castle.

Languedoc and the Knight's Lady

LANGUEDOC, OR OCCITANIA, WAS THE HOME OF THE TROUBADOURS AND TROUVERES, MINSTRELS AND POETS, WHOSE LYRIC WORKS SANG OF LOVE BETWEEN A KNIGHT AND HIS BELOVED LADY, WHO HE COULD NEVER MAKE HIS OWN. THEIR WORK FLOURISHED IN THE COURT OF ELEANOR OF AQUITAINE.

PROVENÇAL CIVILIZATION

The historic province of Languedoc ranged from the Pyrenees Mountains to the French alpine border with Italy.

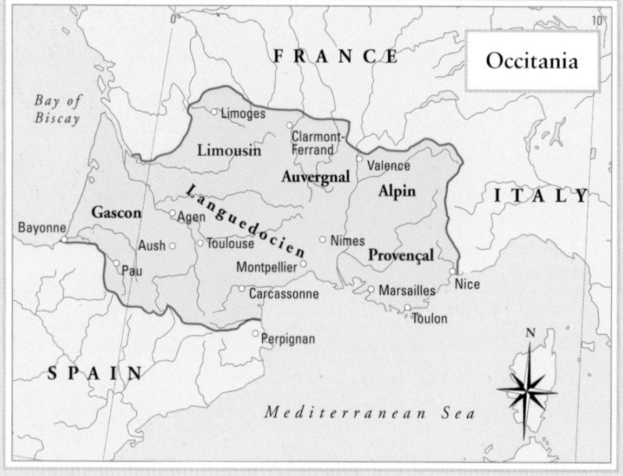

The former historic province of Languedoc, with its capital, Toulouse, has its heartland on the coastal plain towards Montpellier. This region was formerly the center of a vast Provençal area, known as Occitania, where the *langue d'oc* was spoken. *Oc* is 'yes' as opposed to the northern French *langue d'oil* (*oui*). Similar to Catalan, the *langue d'oc* is still spoken from Spain to northern Italy. The coastal plain has been a major trade route and the Romans came, making Narbonne the capital of the province Gallia Narbonnensis.

The Languedoc lands owed their loyalty to the Counts of Toulouse and the territories under their sovereignty were nearly as extensive as those giving their allegiance to the King of France. Languedoc was an independent region, a collection of provinces owning disparate loyalties. The count held some lands from the King of England while some of his vassals owed allegiance to the King of Aragon who himself held Montpellier and the viscounties of Carlat and Millau in the core of Languedoc. Arles belonged to the Emperor. The counts had little authority over their provinces, just like the French king over Toulouse. The counts of Foix remained independent in their mountain fortresses. The Trenceval family were hereditary viscounts of Béziers and Carcassonne, also possessing the area of Carcassès, Albigeois, and Razès, held in vassalage to the Kings of Aragon. Large ecclesiastical estates were determined to retain their independence too.

Even within their personal domains, the counts of Toulouse could not control their own vassals, or raise a military force, relying on mercenaries instead. In northern France, a lord's holding passed to his eldest son, ensuring its survival as a military unit. In the Midi, a fief was split equally among all a lord's children, the girls being bought off with a cash payment. A chateau or holding could belong to any number of *co-seigneurs* who by marriage couldbe co-seigneurs of other holdings. Consequently, holdings had a manager but had no real true lord.

The way to the Aude Gate in the medieval city of Carcassone, one of the great fortified trading centers of Languedoc.

The towns possessed their own independent spirit. The trade routes passing through Languedoc ensured the growth of prosperous towns. The burghers were a privileged class, being free men, citizens of a virtual urban republic and subject to its laws. Crimes committed outside the walls could only be tried by a city tribunal. The towns pursued the remnants of Roman law and were ruled by consuls, elected from the city nobility and the bourgeois class. The burgher was equal to a knight and rich burghers were equal to *grands seigneurs* who rigorously defended their liberties. In 1161, the citizens of Béziers murdered their viscount and thrashed their bishop inside his church.

The Church was rich in land and seemed more concerned with wealth than spirituality, being criticized by their congregations. The common priests were poorly regarded and many Catholics turned toward the Cathars, who cared for their flocks and stood out as a spiritual and regilious community.

The Languedoc civilization was unique in that villages were few, having been destroyed by Basque and Aragonese brigands. Peasants, many being free, tended to live in fortified *bourgs* and suburbs of cities. The numerous co-seigneuries meant that serfs were left to lead their own lives with no main seigneur around. The region was not only home to the troubadours but was so important in trade terms that burghers began to eclipse nobles' power, being the holders of wealth when capital was in short supply. Banking and money lending thrived. Wealth was also based upon textile and leather goods, the stocking of crusading armies, and the purchase and resale of crusading booty. Overseas trade was important with Spain, northern Italian cities, North Africa, Romania, and Egypt.

Contact with the Muslim world, with merchants and doctors, bred tolerance and respect. Jews became a powerful party of the community, Narbonne having some three hundred Jewish families in the late 12th Century. The spread of knowledge led to the creation of schools of medicine, philosophy, mathematics, and astrology, making Toulouse, Narbonne, Avignon, Montpellier, and Béziers university cities before the formal foundation of their universities. The intellectual life and culture of Languedoc was aided by an educated, literate nobility, forgetful of its military role, being more interested in trade, poetry, and music. The troubadour mentality, the use of Occitan, meant that the Languedoc became the southern home of a unique civilization, a manifestation of an open and truly catholic society.

TROUBADOURS AND TROUVERES

A young man expresses his love in verse showing his education and knowledge of romantic love.

In the southern part of France, society was not subjected to the stresses of invasion and strife to the same extent as the north. The legal and intellectual heritage of the Roman Empire was much stronger there, and peace and prosperity enabled a civilized courtly culture of considerable sophistication to develop. At these courts, from the late 11th Century onward, troubadours or *trouvères* created a new kind of poetry. Their poems present the first medieval treatments of "romantic" love, where the subject is the beauty and excellent qualities of the beloved lady, coupled with the agonies of unfulfilled love on the part of the poet.

Troubadours seem to have originated in a wide variety of social backgrounds, but the greater number of them came from the knightly class. More is known about troubadours than about the anonymous authors of the *chansons de geste*, because several of them had a short biographical sketch, known as a *vida*, added to manuscripts of their poems after their deaths. The troubadours, younger sons originally destined for the Church, or simply young men with a penchant for making verses, were educated, worldly, witty personalities who were highly valued at court and by their peers. Most were attached to the household of a lord, although some traveled from court to court in search of patronage. Occasionally a troubadour might be rewarded for his services with lands of his own, such as Perdigon who was awarded the status and maintenance of a knight by the Count of Auvergne, even though he was the son of a poor fisherman. Some troubadours were noble lords in their own right, such as Duke William IX of Aquitaine, Alfonso I of Aragon, Enric I of Rodez, William of Les Baux or Albert de Malespina. Even King Richard I of England, who lived for many years at the worldly and sophisticated courts of his mother, Eleanor of Aquitaine, tried writing poems. The *vidas* also record the existence of eight women troubadours, all beautiful, noble, and well-educated.

Courtly love themes were acquired from the writings of the Roman poet, Ovid, from Arabic literature from Arab Spain, and from the conditions of medieval aristocratic society. Young knights were often too poor to marry and the institution of marriage was normally based upon property contracts and land holdings rather than love.

The first troubadour whose poems have survived was Duke William IX of Aquitaine (1071–1127). He was a man who lived for his own pleasures and did not much concern himself with the strictures of the Church. Criticized by contemporary religious writers as godless and wicked, he kept a large number of mistresses, and his surviving poems often celebrate their charms in coarse language. By the mid-12th Century, poets such as Arnaut Daniel or Marcabru were writing complex lyrics in which the complexity of the verses was mirrored by their elaborately stylized sentiments.

Troubadours provide music and song to an audience of aristocratic dancers with their ladies.

The subject of these poems was almost always love, as a powerful motivating force, which refines and improves the good qualities of the lover until he has proved himself worthy to be granted the love of his lady. His lady is usually married, and normally somewhat above him in social status—the wife of a great lord. She is a distant, elevated being, beautiful and virtuous, and an expert in the manners and customs of courtly society. The poet always approaches his lady as an inferior, as a humble supplicant, who desires to serve her in order to be rewarded with her love.

The lady is sometimes kind and generous to her devoted lover, but sometimes cruel and capricious, being the dominant and more powerful partner. The poet/lover offers her worship and devoted love service; she can advance and reward or reject and spurn him. It is unlikely that many of the "loves" celebrated in the troubadours' poems were consummated in adulterous love affairs. Such a course would be extremely dangerous for the lover, since one of the greatest treasons any vassal could commit was to sleep with his lord's wife. However, physical consummation was undoubtedly the desired goal in many of the poems and, in this fictional world, rules were developed to regulate the behavior of lovers. This is the "Courtly Love" made famous by the 19th-Century French critic Gaston Paris, who assumed that the poems referred to a cult of adulterous love widely practiced in the courtly society of France.

"I would truly love to hold
My knight, naked in my arms one night,
And that he would consider himself in ecstasy
If only I would serve him as a pillow;
Fir I am more in love with him
Than was Floris with Blanchefleur:
I give him my heart and love,
My mind, my eyes and my life.

Dear friend, charming and good,
When shall I have you in my power?
If only I might lie with you one night
And give you a loving kiss!
Rest assured that I would have a great desire
To have you in place of my husband,
Provided that you would have sworn
To do everything that I might want."

Beatrice, Countess of Dia (d. c. 1175)

Modern writers prefer the view that the adoration of noble ladies expressed the social and emotional aspirations of the troubadour knights. Whether a literary convention or an account of real-life illicit love affairs, there can be no doubt that the cult of love and the quasi-religious worshipping of highborn ladies was to be immensely influential to the emergent literature of romance.Women troubadours agonize over love just like their male counterparts and sometimes are more forceful in their imagery. Beatrice, Countess of Dia (d. 1175) covered the issues of unrequited love, adultery, and secrecy but often expressed them in an outright sexual fashion.

THE RISE OF ROMANCE

The love story concerning Tristan and Iseult turned the medieval idea of morality on its head, but was a hugely successful story.

The manners and morals of a wealthy, leisured, sophisticated court society, having given birth to the troubadours, could not have offered greater contrast to the more rugged poetry and values celebrated in the *chansons de geste*. Troubadours were quickly imitated in northern France and Germany. From the mid-12th Century, however, a new kind of poetry began to be written, in which the knightly hero's martial prowess was complemented by refined manners and romantic motivations: the narrative verse romance.

The hero of a *chanson* had much in common with the hero of a *roman*, but there were also important differences. The epic hero is typically seen performing a role essentially related to the protection or advancement of his society, usually in warfare. His values are based upon a communal bond of loyalty, to his peers, to his country, to his God, and, overwhelmingly to his lord. This loyalty finds expression in his great courage and prowess in battle, and is absolute; no greater test can be imposed on it than that of fighting in the face of certain death against overwhelming odds. Epic writing often displays an attitude toward experience of a deeply fatalistic kind; the hero-warrior consents to his fate, displaying his superiority not necessarily by triumphing over his enemies but by embracing a glorious death.

In romance, however, the hero is essentially solitary and does not fight to protect his lord and society; instead, he seeks adventure in order to prove himself. He is conscious of living up to a standard of behavior, which embraces the refined qualities expressed in the term *courtoisie*, polished manners, a high moral sense, and knowledge and skill in the social arts of courtly life as well as in combat. Because the adventures befalling a romantic hero are often designed specifically to test some aspect of his knightly character, he tends to be successful in the end. He may fall short of perfection, or he may fail in his task and then learn from his mistakes, but he profits by experience and ultimately triumphs.

Whereas the epic world is one of military comradeship, where there is little place for women and love, the romance ensures Love is an important motivation for the hero. In the *Chanson de Roland*, romantic love is confined to a few lines describing how the sister of Oliver, Aude, who is betrothed to Roland, swoons and dies on hearing news of his death. In romances, the hero merely wishes to prove himself worthy of his lady's love.

Somewhere between 1155 and 1170 witnessed the writing of the earliest surviving version of the popular romance, Tristan. Here, the theme of noble characters torn by the conflicting demands of passionate love and feudal and moral duty is fully elaborated. Tristan, the nephew of King Mark of Cornwall, is sent to bring his uncle's bride, the Princess Iseult, from Ireland. On board ship they accidentally drink a love potion intended to ensure the happiness of the married couple. Unable to bear life apart from each other, the lovers resort to dishonorable tricks and stratagems to conceal their love from the elderly and jealous King Mark. The normal moral standards of life in feudal society are turned on their heads. Tristan and Iseult are admired for their goodness and loyalty to each other in maintaining an adulterous love, which leads them to lie and plot the deaths of those who would betray their secret. The barons who reveal their adulterous passion to the king are condemned as envious, spiteful, and wicked men.

This woodcut represents a medieval troubadour such as Bernard of Ventadour composing a song of love and romance. If the song was well received by his courtly audience, it could spread from Languedoc throughout Europe. The composer could earn considerable acclaim, if not wealth.

Most romances related stories from three great cycles of subject matter: the *Matter of France*, stories of Charlemagne and his twelve peers and their battles against the evil Saracens; the *Matter of Rome*, stories drawn from classical (usually Latin) authors, such as the stories of Troy, of Aeneas, and of Alexander the Great; and, the *Matter of Britain*, the most popular and often retold of all, the tales of King Arthur and his knights of the Round Table.

Knights, other than those of the Carolingian or Arthurian cycles, have their noble qualities or heroic exploits depicted. These have included national heroes, such as Richard Coer de Lyon or Chevalère au Cygne, the Knight of the Swan, a fictional hero of the First Crusade. Sometimes a story has been converted from a saint's life into a

BERNARD OF VENTADOUR (C. 1140–1190)

A celebrated and imitated troubadour, Bernard was a composer and a poet, creating both music and lyrics for his songs. Born to married servants at the castle of the viscount of Ventadour in southern France, he displayed great talent at an early age and was chosen for troubadour training by the viscount. However, the young man chose to cuckold the viscount and the minstrel fled and went to the court of Eleanor, Duchess of Aquitaine and Queen of England. He impressed that powerful patroness. Spending several years at her court creating songs, he achieved fame and wealth. Forty-four of his songs survive celebrating the joys and pain of romantic love.

Singing isn't worth a thing
If the heart sings not the song.
And the heart can never sing
If it brings not love along

Bernard eventually left Eleanor's court and joined the court of Raymond, Count of Toulouse, before ending his days in an abbey.

romance, as in the many versions of Sir Ysumbras, being based upon the life of St. Eustace. A story could tell a moral point as in *Amis e Amilun*, a tale of two faithful friends. One saves his friend's life by taking his place in a judicial single combat although a supernatural voice has told him that if he takes part in the fight, he will contract leprosy: the other then slaughters his own children so that his friend can be cured by bathing in their blood. Many short stories known as *Breton Lais* are based on ancient Celtic tales featuring supernatural characters and events. Some of the best of these were composed by the poetess, Marie de France, in about 1160–70. Such romances were soon superseded by the works of a medieval master.

CHRÉTIEN DE TROYES AND THE GOLDEN AGE OF ROMANCE

Bewteen 1170 and 1190, Chrétien de Troyes wrote his five surviving poems, *Eric et Enide, Cliqès, Yvain* (sometimes called *Le Chevalier au Lion*), Lancelot (sometimes called *Le Chevalier de la charette*), and Perceval, or *Le Conte du grail*, unfinished at his death. Nothing much is known about Chrètien except a prologue to Lancelot states that he was writing at the express wish of Marie, Countess of Champagne, so he was presumably attached to her court. He dedicated the unfinished *Perceval* to Count Philip of Flanders, a great patron of the arts.

All of these poems, long verse narratives, are subtle and complex explorations of the

Medieval minstrels—*histriones* in latin, *jongleurs* in French—sang and played musical instruments, as well as recounting stories. It seems likely that when reciting poems they did so to musical accompaniment. Here, two Spanish minstrels are playing a bowed instrument called a rebec, and a lute, an illustration taken from the Cantigas de Santa Maria.

difficulties of reconciling various ideals of behavior. They provide a depth of psychological analysis of their characters together with a vivid picture of aristocratic and courtly life and a richness of poetry that has rarely been equaled in any age. The two most influential poems were the *Lancelot* and the *Perceval*. Chrètien mentions that both the subject matter and treatment of it for the *Lancelot* were suggested to him by Countess Marie, something which he may have found creatively irksome since he left the poem to be finished by someone else. It was well known throughtout Europe but remained little known in England until Malory's *Morte d'Arthur* in 1485. Chrètien's work was incorporated into the vast compilation of French prose covering the rise and fall of the Round Table, known as the *Vulgate Cycle*.

Sir Lancelot was often seen as an archetype of the perfect knightly lover, and all subsequent portrayals of his character are derived from Chrètien de Troyes' poem. His *Lancelot* is a complex man whose passion for Queen Guinevere dominates his personality. In true troubadour fashion, he venerates Guinevere with a religious intensity which verges on blasphemy, while Guinevere alternates between tenderness and appalling cruelty.

At the opening of the poem, Guinevere, under the protection of the incompetent Sir Kay, is abducted by the evil knight Sir Meleagant. Sir Gawain, riding in hot pursuit, meets a nameless knight whose horse has been killed. The knight is Lancelot but his name is not revealed until half way through the poem, after 3,500 lines. Nor is his initial lack of identity merely accidental; it reflects the fact that the knight "has no strength or defense against love which holds him in its sway; his thoughts are such that he totally forgets himself, and he knows not whether he is alive or dead, forgetting even his own name, not knowing whither he is armed or not, or whither he is going whence he came." Lancelot has been brought to this state of near insanity by the abduction of the queen, and does not fully recover until the two are reconciled later in the poem.

The incident which gave the poem its other name—*The Knight of the Cart*—occurs not long after the appearance of the knight. After his second horse falls dead under him, Lancelot meets a hideous dwarf driving a cart. The dwarf offers to reveal news of the queen's whereabouts if the knight will ride in the cart. In those days, the narrator explains, it was a serious matter to be seen riding in a cart.

Whoever was convicted of any crime was placed upon a cart and dragged through all the streets, and he lost henceforth all his legal rights, and was never afterward heard, welcomed or honored in any court. The carts were so dreadful in those days that the saying was then first used "When you see and meet with a cart, cross yourself and call upon God, that no evil may befall you."

The knight is reluctant to associate himself, and his rescue of the Queen, with the shame and ignominy that will certainly follow if he rides in the cart. For two steps he hesitates, but then jumps in since this is the only way to get information about the queen. Through all his subsequent adventures, everyone greets him as the Knight who rode in the cart and he is taunted and despised as a man in disgrace.

Sir Gawain catches up with him again and before long the two learn that the land where the

Right: In this rare depiction of the Round Table, Sir Galahad is presented to the assembled knights.
King Arthur and his Knights grew to their position of supremacy in the mythology of the Middle Ages from obscure beginnings. In the last quarter of the 8th Century the chronicler Nennius, in his *History of the Britons*, records that Arthur, a war-leader (*dux bellorum*) resisted the Saxons together with the Kings of the Britons in 12 great battles. No further writings about King Arthur have survived between 800 and 1100. The chronicler William of Malmesbury mentioned Arthur in his writings and from the tone of his statements it seems likely that the stories told by the Britons were full of magical happenings and formed the source material for the Arthurian romances of Chrétien de Troyes.

queen has been taken can only be entered by one of two perilous bridges across a dangerous river; one is under water, and the other is made from the blade of a sword. Gawain, courteously given the choice by Lancelot, opts for the water bridge; Lancelot, crawling across the sword bridge on bare hands and knees, is badly wounded. He allows himself only one night to recover before battling with Maleagent, whom he defeats and would have killed if his father, King Bademagu, had not requested Guinevere to intercede for him. After disarming himself, Lancelot hurries to the queen who refuses to speak or look at him. Dumbfounded, he leaves the court to meet Gawain; musingly, he decides that the queen's reason for hating him must be that he rode in a cart, thus tainting her with his disgrace.

Meanwhile, a false report reached Guinevere that Lancelot had been killed. She reproached herself bitterly for her baseness and cruelty, and when Lancelot returned, greeted him with flattering warmth. She then informed him that her former cold behavior was a punishment, not for riding in the cart but for hesitating to get into it. He begged her forgiveness and she invited him to speak with her at her chamber window that night. The window was barred, a precaution by the noble King Bademagu to protect her from Meleagant. Inspired by love, Lancelot wrenched the bars from the window, badly cutting his fingers. He spent the night with the queen, leaving at dawn and replacing the bars. Unfortunately, his blood has stained the sheets and in the morning eagle-eyed Meleagant accused Guinevere of committing adultery with Sir Kay, who was sleeping in her room while recovering from wounds.

The accusation gave Lancelot an opportunity to defend Guinevere in trial by combat with Meleagant. Both men had sworn on holy relics of her innocence or guilt. Lancelot bested Meleagant and again Bademagu, who loved his base-natured son, begged the queen to intercede with Lancelot. Even though he had sworn on holy relics to have no mercy on Meleagant, Lancelot put up his sword on the queen's intercession not to strike a killing blow.

One more incident from the romance serves to demonstrate Sir Lancelot's absolute subjection to the whims of his beloved. The ladies of Arthur's court hold a tournament, with the intention of giving themselves in marriage to the knights who do best. Lancelot attends the tournament in disguise and, at first, performs wonders. The queen recognizes him and sends a message by a maiden that he is to "do his worst." Lancelot begins to miss his opponents, and eventually spends his time running away from them, and all the other knights despise him for a coward.

This lasts all day, and on the following day he receives the same message, and agrees to it with the same humility. This was the kind of paradox which the witty and well-educated lords and ladies of Marie of Champagne's court relished. The hero, instead of striving to win in order to please his lady and honor her with his high reputation, has to act completely against his normal character and do badly; a much keener test of his love for her, since it contradicts his self-love. Of course, it also gives Lancelot a splendid opportunity to come from behind. The queen eventually relents and bids him do his best, and he finishes the tournament as the acknowledged victor. More importantly, it completes the thematic exploration of love within the structure of the poem; Lancelot here atones for his earlier fault, when he hesitated at the cart to expose himself to shame and ridicule for Guinevere's sake.

CASTLES

MOST CASTLES MIGHT BE ACCURATELY DESCRIBED AS RESIDENTIAL FORTRESSES, YET THEIR MAJOR FUNCTION WAS AS A BASE FOR CONTROLLING SURROUNDING TERRITORY. THEY WERE MANNED BY KNIGHTS, LOYAL TO A SUPERIOR LORD OR KING TO WHOM THEY WERE TIED BY MILITARY SERVICE.

DEFENSE, DOMINATION, INTIMIDATION

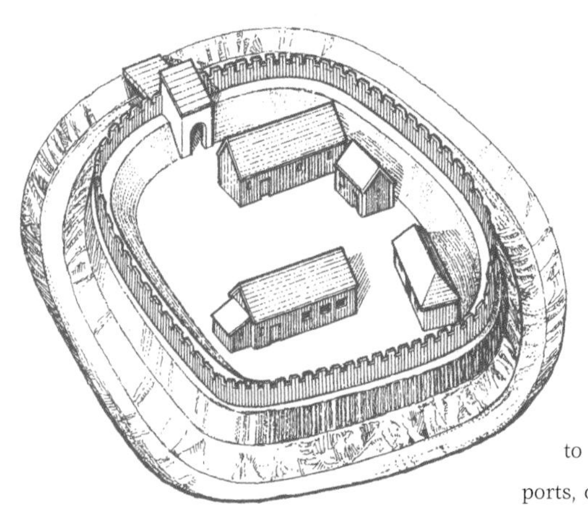

A representation of an early fortified site discovered in Lincolnshire, England, dating from about AD 900. This site revealed the signs of a simple earth and timber rampart surounding the chieftain's hall and ancillary buildings.

The origin of the word "castle" is the Latin word *castellum*, meaning little fort or refuge. A castle was a fortified feudal household, whether secular or ecclesiastical, but was sometimes a fortified manor house in late medieval times. Castles had two functions, domestic and military, being inhabited by a military élite or aristocracy as their defensible home and center of power. The term "donjon," or "dungeon"—the name of the great tower or innermost keep of a castle—originates with the Latin *dominium*, connoting lordship. Despite their military function, most castles were residential fortresses lived in but seldom subject to attack. Some were sited and constructed for purely military purposes near fords, ports, or places of strategic importance.

The main purpose of a medieval castle was offensive, as a base for military operations and raids into enemy territory. Raids were carried out to highlight an enemy's weakness, hoping to incite enemy nobles to turn on their lord. Sometimes raids destroyed crops or other resources, including people, to weaken the enemy as a whole by damaging the sources of revenue. Raids were occasionally pursued as instruments of political bargaining and negotiation, forcing an enemy to give concessions or be subject to even more raids: a form of political blackmail. Raiding was designed to weaken an enemy, show one's strength, or even force a battle. English raids in the

The Great Tower of the castle of St. Sauveur-le-Vicomte, in Normandy, France. The castle had been subjected to many sieges during the Middle Ages, notably being captured by the English in 1356, although it was retaken by the French in 1375.

Loches Castle, Indre-et-Loire, France, looking from the outer wall toward the central keep, which was constructed in the 11th Century.

Eltz Castle, Rheinland-Pfalz, Germany, was begun at the end of the 12th Century, making the best use of an elliptical rocky crag that forms the foundation of the whole castle. The castle structure continued to develop over the next 400 years.

Hundred Years' War sought to entice French armies into the field where English archers could winnow enemy ranks. Castles needed to be impregnable but seldom were. Their designs changed over the centuries to reflect prevailing military technology. Rectangular towers were replaced by round ones, since the former were prone to the corner stones being knocked out by battering rams.

Medieval castles were also spawned by the feudal system whereby a castle was held by the king or lord in return for loyalty and military service. Some of the earliest known castle sites date from the second half of the 10th Century in early feudal times, such as Longeais and Doué-la-Fontaine in France. Early Norman fortification in England can still be seen at Portchester, in Hampshire, where a castle was built on the site of a Roman fortification originally built as part of a defensive network against invading Saxons. Another ruin can be seen at Carisbrooke on the Isle of Wight, where William FitzOsbern likewise built on an old Roman site.

A castle was a reflection of a lord's power whether he was in residence or not. The imposing walls and towers displayed authority and the castle was a tool of local domination, being the seat of administration, justice, and military might. Often, a lord would not inhabit one castle but would move around several "eating" rents in kind: little money was in circulation, so rents were paid in agricultural or hunted produce. Courts and nobles traveled around their various properties consuming their rents. Normally, a small garrison under a constable would hold the castle, the soldiery sometimes being knights performing "knight service."

Castles could be enclosed within the walls of a town, such as Dinan or Carcassonne in France. A lord who could not defend his castles or towns lost more than the region they dominated. Reputation could be ruined. King John of England suffered such humiliation after the capture of his key Norman fortress at Château Gaillard in 1204. Likewise, a lord who could capture or destroy his enemies' fortresses displayed his power to everyone and might win over his enemy's vassals. The example of King John again shows this when his vassals in Normandy, Anjou, Maine, and Touraine seemed not to care that they were changing overlords.

There are many ways to categorize castles: concentric, ecclesiastical stronghold, enceinte, gatehouse, great tower, keep, motte and bailey, pele tower, ringwork, shell-keep and tower house. The two main types are the great tower within enclosing walls or an enclosure with a gatehouse and towers. All castles differ according to their sites or purposes but they all perform the same military function. Early castles could be built relatively quickly. William the Conqueror built an earth and timber fort at Dover, England, in 1066 and another at York, England, in 1069 in just eight days each. He cunningly used the Anglo-Saxon law of "burghwork," which laid down that all men could be required to build fortifications. Hence, campaigning after the Norman conquest meant that many castles could be little more than temporary defenses or staging posts, or supply centers when traversing enemy territory. More substantial stone castles, such as those built by King Edward I in Wales, brought in skilled workmen from all over England. Impressment meant that the English town of Chester, on the England–Wales border, became a gathering point for carpenters, diggers and masons from as far north as the counties of Cumberland and Northumberland, as far east as Norfolk and Suffolk, and as far south as Hampshire, Surrey, Sussex, and Kent. The latter county, in 1282–83, supplied 15 carpenters and 20 diggers. Woodcutters were another requirement and 1,600 of these were used in Edward's construction program.

Part of the defenses of the medieval town of Carcassonne in southern France. Carcassonne is one of the best preserved examples of defensive architecture still in existence. A clearer idea of the general appearance and dominance of this massive fortified town can be seen in the panoramic view of Carcassonne below.

MOTTE AND BAILEY

England and Wales saw large numbers of motte and bailey castles constructed to subjugate local populations while extending Norman colonization. The majority of these constructions were built in the 11th and 12th Centuries, their use falling rapidly in the 13th Century. These edifices rising above the locality demonstrated power, permanence, and legitimacy while terrorizing the locals.

The word "motte" originates with the Old French word *mote,* meaning mound, referring to the conical mound forming the site of a castle or camp. The mound was constructed while excavating a surrounding ditch (*fosse*). Mottes sometimes had their ditch filled with water to make a moat. The mound would have a flattened top upon which a wooden donjon or tower would be erected. The motte sometimes had its sides coated with clay and the bottom faced with timber or stone to strengthen it and make it difficult to climb. The bailey—from the Old French word *baile,* for palisade—was an enclosure with a rampart, or defensive wall, built from the spoil from a surrounding ditch. The rampart would be topped by a wooden fence, or palisade. The bailey was connected to the motte by a wooden bridge. A good example of a classic motte and bailey is Rayleigh Mount, Essex, England, which was raised around 1171.

Sometimes earlier defensive sites were used as the basis of a later motte and bailey. Robert of Mortain (c. 1031–90), for example, excavated the Iron Age earthworks at Montacute in Somerset, England. In other variations, a stone core would be built and the motte constructed around it. This would form foundations for a stone tower, such as at Farnham, Surrey, England, where a plinth was 51 feet (15.5 m) deep. These stone core mottes can be found at Lincoln, Aldingbourne, Saffron Walden,

A reconstruction of an early motte and bailey castle as it would have appeared in the 11th Century. The motte was a conical mound with a fortification on the top, the bailey a flattened area surrounded by a ditch and palisade. The two parts were connected by a protected timber stairway and a bridge over the surrounding ditch.

Medieval European Castles
Castle
Colours refer to period:
11th and 12th century
11th to 13th century
11th to 15th century
13th century
13th to 15th century
14th to 15th century
Fortified monastery/ bishop's palace
0 200 km
0 200 miles
N
SCOTLAND
IRELAND
WALES
ENGLAND
NORWAY
SWEDEN
DENMARK
NETH.
GERMANY
POLAND
CZECH REPUBLIC
SLOVAK
AUSTRIA
HUNGAR
SWITZ.
SLOVENIA
CROATIA
BOSNIA
FRANCE
ITALY
PORTUGAL
SPAIN
North Sea
Baltic Sea
ATLANTIC OCEAN
English Channel
Adriatic Sea
Mediterranean Sea
Africa
Corsica
Sardinia
Sicily
Majorca
Shannon
Elbe
Oder
Rhine
Saone
Danube
Ebro
Tagus
Guadalquivir
Stirling
Linlithgow
Borthwick
Ayton
Norham
Dunstanburgh
Alnwick
Warkworth
Belsay
Newcastle
Raby
Richmond
Durham
York
Carrickfergus
Lemaneagh
Blarney
Beaumaris
Caernarfon
Conisbrough
Lincoln
Harlech
Stokesay
Kenilworth
Longthorpe
Castle Rising
Norwich
Framlingham
Raglan
Chepstow
Caerphilly
Castle Hedingham
Orford
Little Wenham
Colchester
Rochester
London
Winchester
Dover
Corfe
Herstmonceux
Bodiam
Leyden
Muiden
The Hague
Brunswick
Goslar
Meissen
Cologne
Ghent
Marksburg
Pfalzgrafenstein
Eltz
Coburg
Cochem
Eltville
Prague
Karlstein
Trier
Rothenburg
Nuremberg
Trifels
Regensburg
Schönburg
Eger
Heidenreichstein
Rappottenstein
Salzburg
Habsburg
Chillon
Visby
Kalmar
Heilsberg
Marienburg
Mewe
Marienwerder
Rehden
Rambures
Chateau Gaillard
Gisors
Les Andelys
Coucy
Pierrefonds
La Forté-Milon
Vincennes
Mont-St-Michel
Caen
Houdan
Falaise
Dinan
Combourg
Dourdan
Paris
Provins
Étampes
Josselin
Fougères
Largoet
Châteaudun
Angers
Langeais
Saumur
Mehun-sur-Yèvre
Montreuil-Bellay
Loches
Chinon
Niort
Lesparre
St Georges d'Espéranche
Bordeaux
Roquetaillade
Bonaguil
Villandraut
Cahors
Najac
Villeneuve-lès-Avignon
Orthez
Puylaurens
Tarascon
Milan
Venice
Sarzanello
Canossa
Ferrara
Volterra
Todi
Tuscania
Rome
Tivoli
Lucera
Trani
Bari
Naples
Castel del Monte
Palermo
Messina
Catania
Fuensaldaña
Peñafiel
Medina del Campo
Soria
Coca
Loarre
Manzanares el Real
Barcelona
Lisbon
Amieira
Bellver

Right: Porchester Castle, Hampshire, England, is a fine example of a Great Tower that was built during the 12th Century.

and Totnes, England, and at Mont Glowne on the River Loire in France, built in AD 990. At Lincoln it is easy to see what domination means: the later stone castle and Lincoln Cathedral stand on a steep hill overlooking flat countryside and can be seen for miles around.

GREAT TOWER

The great tower, or donjon, built from stone could be up to six storeys high with tremendously thick stone walls, parapets with battlements, and a well protected entrance, often with a drawbridge. The totality was typically surrounded by a walled enclosure. A tower was sometimes built outside a city's walls, such as that constructed by Charles de Blois at Dinan, France, during the Wars of Breton Succession, beginning in 1341. A great tower could be any shape—square, triangular, rectangular, cylindrical, polygonal, or D-shaped—and built of wood, stone, or brick. The great tower was the last bastion to which defenders could retreat when the outer defenses of a castle were captured by besieging forces. Fine examples of great towers are Heddingham, England, and Provins, France.

Some historians prefer not to use the term "great tower," preferring "hall-keep" instead. These, however, are substantial buildings longer than they are high and used as residential buildings. The earliest example of this type of castle is William FitzOsbern's great tower at Chepstow Castle, England, (1067–75). This huge rectangular, two-storeyed hall-keep is entered at first floor level via an external stair way. Other hall-keeps worth mentioning are Middleham Castle in Yorkshire, England (1170)

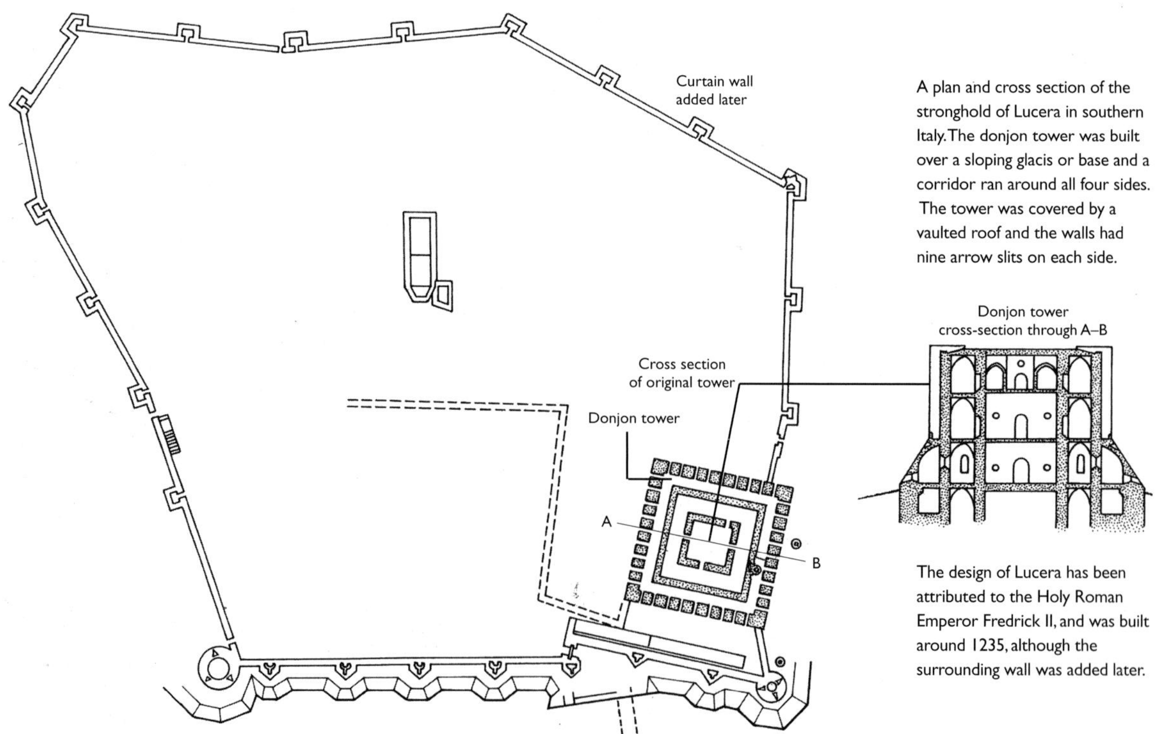

A plan and cross section of the stronghold of Lucera in southern Italy. The donjon tower was built over a sloping glacis or base and a corridor ran around all four sides. The tower was covered by a vaulted roof and the walls had nine arrow slits on each side.

The design of Lucera has been attributed to the Holy Roman Emperor Fredrick II, and was built around 1235, although the surrounding wall was added later.

Left: THE WHITE TOWER, PART OF THE TOWER OF LONDON
Below: DRAWING OF TOWER OF LONDON
Construction of the White Tower was started by William the Conqueror in 1078 and completed by his successors in 1087. In the 12th Century, King Richard, the Lionheart, constructed a curtain wall around the White Tower and dug a moat filled with water from the River Thames. The fortification was completed between 1275 and 1285 by King Edward I, who built an outer curtain wall, creating a magnificent concentric castle. Other buildings continued to be added in the years that followed.

Far right: Rochester Castle commanded the communications between London and Dover in the southeast of England. Constructed between 1086 and 1089, it was one of the earliest castles in England to be built in stone. It was probably built over a motte and bailey castle of timber and earth. One of Rochester's square towers was replaced by a more effective round tower after the siege of 1215.

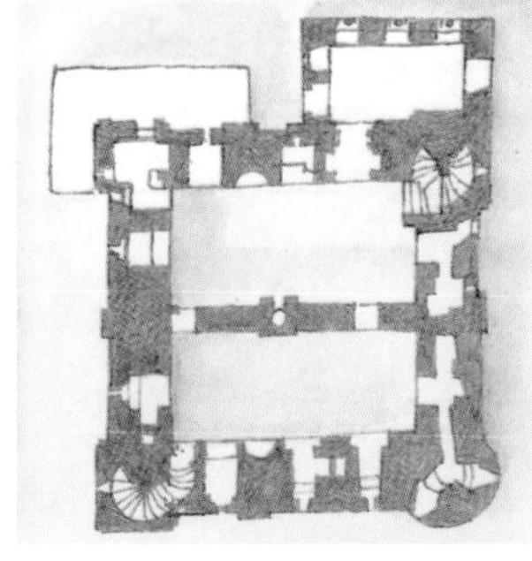

Above: A plan of Rochester Castle, England, showing the new round tower on the southeast corner.

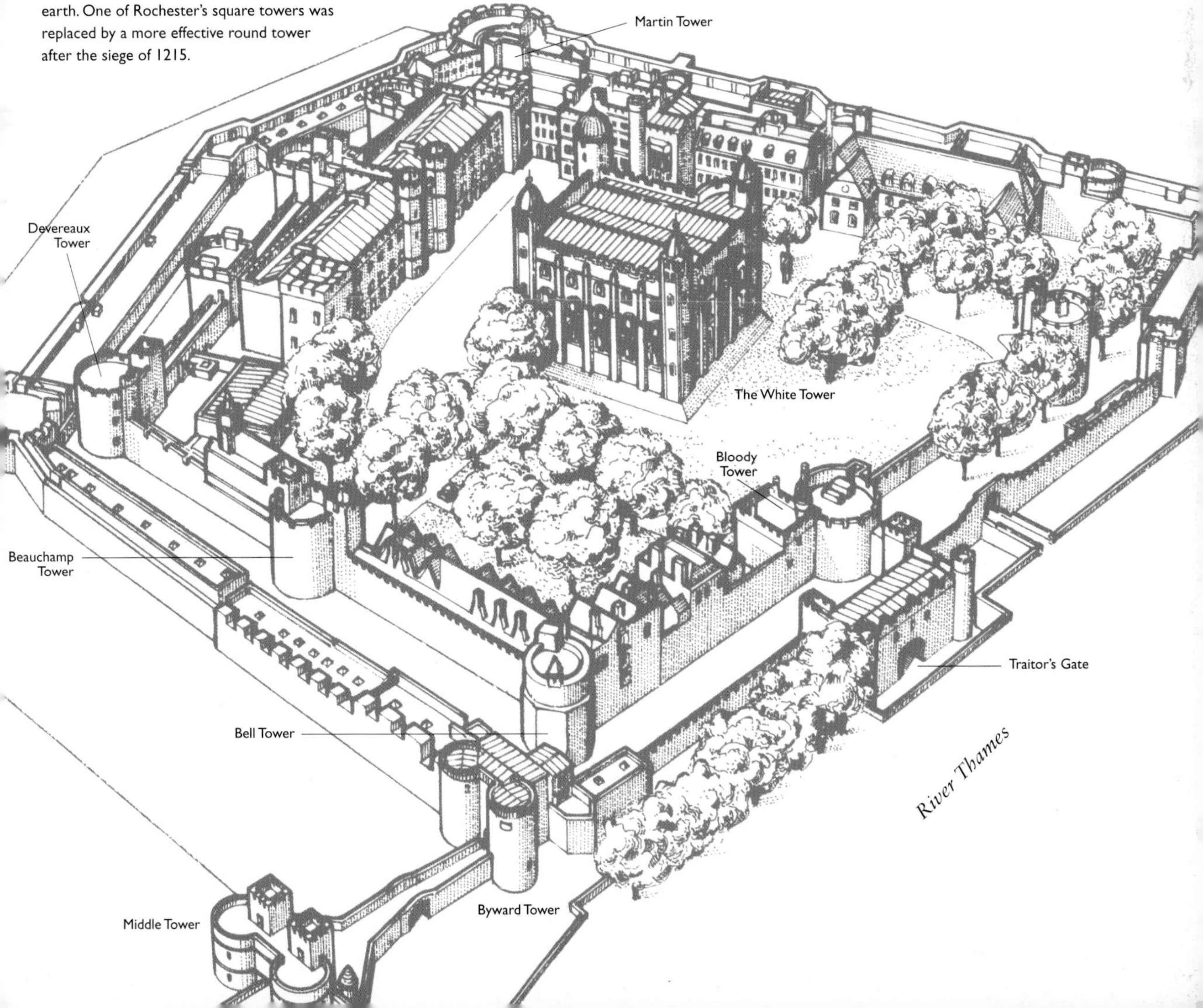

and Castle Rising in East Anglia (1138–40), the finest example of its type in England. A most famous great tower is the White Tower at the Tower of London, erected by William the Conqueror. Commenced in 1078 with a 20-year build, the psychologically dominating tower had walls 90 ft (27m) high and 15 ft (4.6m) thick.

SHELL-KEEP

Below: BODIAM CASTLE, Sussex, England.
A 14th-Century castle constructed in accordance with sound military principals in which round towers have replaced square towers. It was constructed by Sir Edward Dalyngrygg who received a license from the King to build the castle in 1385. By the time of its construction, however, it was more a home for a retired old soldier than a fortress that could have played any meaningful role in war.

Great Towers are massive and heavy, their weight sometimes causing subsidence and collapse. Another type of fortification with a more even weight distribution is a stone enclosure erected on a motte, circular or polygonal and cheaper to build. Residential buildings would be constructed against the inner wall, which was normally 8–10ft (2.5–3m) thick and 20–25 ft (6–7.5 m) high with an enclosure having a diameter some 40–100 ft (12–30m). Shell enclosures can be found with the later addition of a tower. At Tretower Castle, Powys, Wales, a large circular great tower was built in 1220–30 within a shell enclosure originally raised c. 1150. The irregular polygonal shell enclosure of Tamworth Castle, Staffordshire, England (c. 1110), had a variety of domestic buildings that were used into the 10th Century. Most of these buildings date from the period 1423–1688 when they were refurbished or rebuilt by the Ferrers family.

Right: RESTORMEL CASTLE, Cornwall, England. Its stone curtain wall crowns a motte and is often described as a shell-keep. The curtain wall was built around 1200 and internal living quarters added about 80 years later.

Below right: LEYDEN CASTLE, in the Netherlands. The flat terrain of the Low Countries offered few sites for natural defense and castles in this region were usually ring-forts, with fortified walls enclosing a courtyard. At Leyden a substantial central tower was added at a later date.

Bottom right: MARIENBURG CASTLE, the Prussian headquarters of the Order of Teutonic Knights, in east Prussia, now part of Poland and renamed Malbork. Constructed largely of brick, it is the largest brick-built castle in the world. Originally built as a functioning fortress, as the knights extended their territories it became a magnificent hotel for visiting European nobles, knights, and their followers who wished to participate in the Order's campaigns against the pagan Lithuanians.

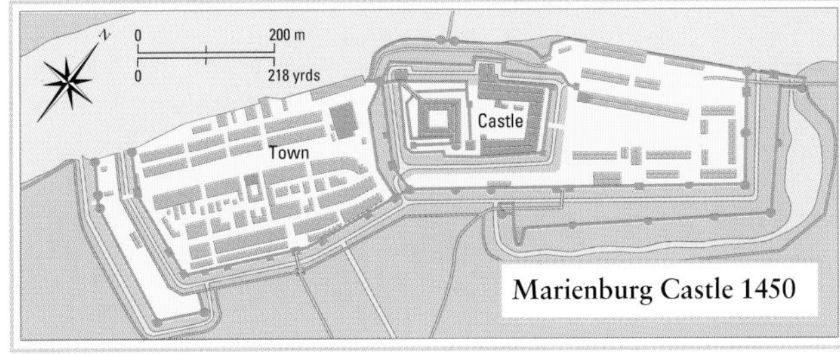

Above: KRAK DES CHEVALIERS, headquarters of the Knight Hospitaller in Syria and inspiration for many other concentric castles. It is located east of Tripoli on a 2,132-feet (650-meter) cliff along the route from Beirut to Antioch.

Below: SCOTS TOWER HOUSE. This type of simple, fortified structure was found along the unstable border zone between England and Scotland.

CONCENTRIC CASTLES

A concentric castle has no central strongpoint. It comprises an inner courtyard surrounded by concentric rings of walls, each higher than that outside, so inner and outer baileys can be defended at the same time. Each defense line is self-contained with the outer bailey being a killing ground should besiegers force their way in. The walls have flanking towers allowing enfilade fire from archers and crossbowmen. The idea of concentric castles came from the Crusader States. Gatehouses and towers had machicolations, holes through which boiling water or oil could be poured on to the heads of attackers below. There are no concentric castles in England but there are several in Wales, with Caerphilly Castle, erected 1268–71, the first to be built. Half of Edward I's Welsh castles are concentric: Aberystwyth (1277–89); Rhuddlan (1277–82); Harlech (1283–89). Beaumaris (1295–c. 1330), but never completed, has four concentric lines of defense, with massive curtain walls 36 ft (10.8m) high and 15ft 6in (4.65m) thick surrounding the inner ward. The outer ward is 60ft (18m) wide, a lower octagonal outer ward, curtain wall, and a water-filled moat.

SCOTS TOWER HOUSE

Scotland is home to numerous tower houses, which developed from the late 13th to the 16th Century. These private fortifications are square or rectangular buildings with thick walls, five or six storeys, battlements, and turrets. Good examples can be found at Borthwick (c. 1430), Elphinstone (1440), and Craigievar, completed in 1626 by William Forbes, brother of the Bishop of Aberdeen.

ARUNDEL CASTLE, Sussex, England, shows the development of the castle from earliest times with its central motte. The timber fort in the center was replaced by a stone building, then a masonry shell enclosure was added toward the end of the 12th Century. As the usefulness of the castle as a military structure declined, palatial residential buildings were added. This castle had transformed from a purely military structure into a luxurious palace.

Below: PLAN OF BEAUMARIS CASTLE, Anglesey, Wales.

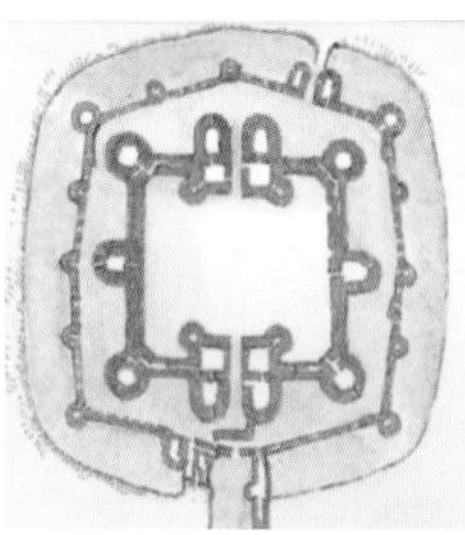

Above right: BEAUMARIS CASTLE, Anglesey, Wales. Begun in 1295, it was the last and largest of the castles to be built by King Edward I in Wales. Raised on an entirely new site, without any earlier buildings to fetter its designer's creative genius, it is widely considered to be the ultimate concentric castle. Built with an almost geometric symmetry, it is one of the most sophisticated examples of medieval military architecture in western Europe.

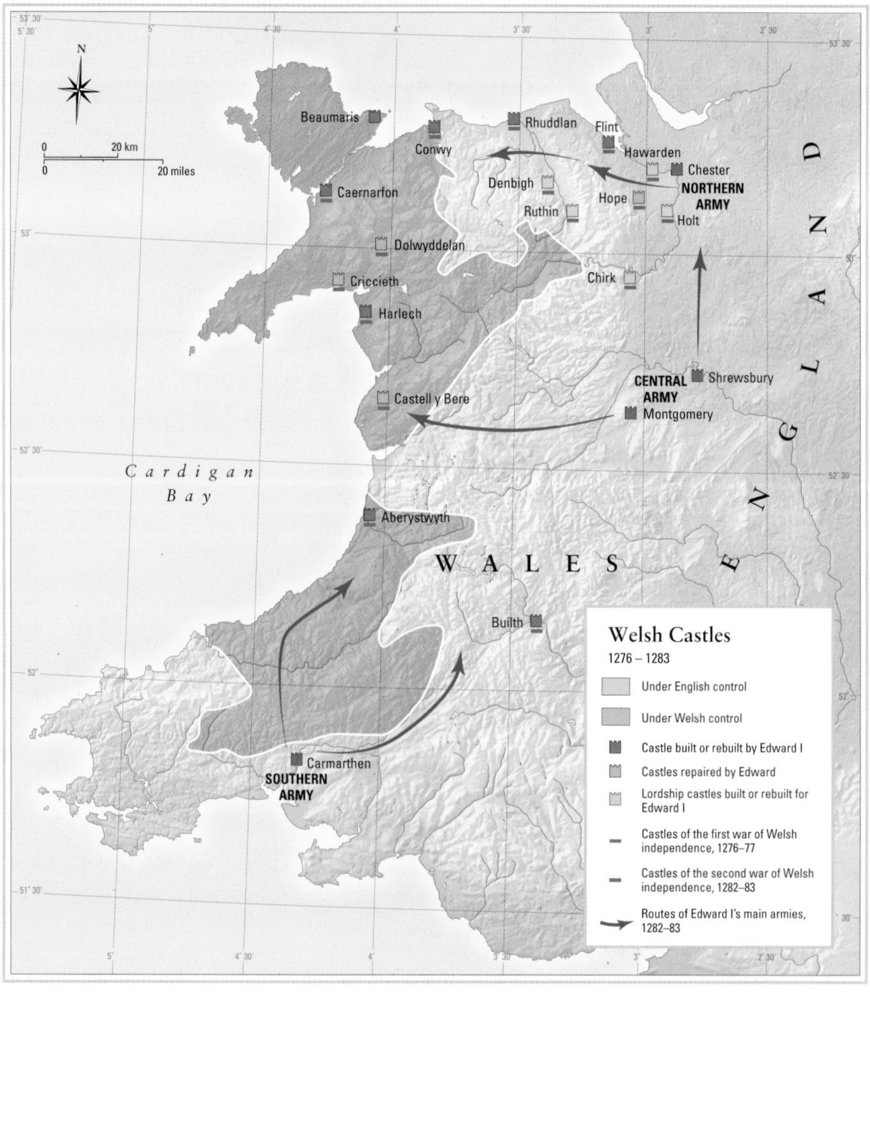

Welsh Castles
1276 – 1283

- Under English control
- Under Welsh control
- Castle built or rebuilt by Edward I
- Castles repaired by Edward
- Lordship castles built or rebuilt for Edward I
- Castles of the first war of Welsh independence, 1276–77
- Castles of the second war of Welsh independence, 1282–83
- Routes of Edward I's main armies, 1282–83

Beaumaris
Conwy
Rhuddlan
Flint
Hawarden
Chester
NORTHERN ARMY
Denbigh
Hope
Ruthin
Holt
Caernarfon
Dolwyddelan
Criccieth
Chirk
Harlech
CENTRAL ARMY
Shrewsbury
Montgomery
Castell y Bere
Cardigan Bay
Aberystwyth
WALES
ENGLAND
Builth
Carmarthen
SOUTHERN ARMY
0 20 km
0 20 miles
N

In 1429, English King Henry VI wanted small castles capable of defending the English Pale in Ireland, promising a £10 grant to anyone who would build one according to his specifications. Hence, there are a number of basic three-storey towers, 20ft (6m) long, 16ft (5m) wide, and 40ft (12m) high. A version of these residential fortifications was also favored by Irish chieftains, often being within a walled courtyard. A good example is Roodstown Castle in County Louth.

Smaller fortresses in Scotland are sometimes called Pele Towers, these being the tower-houses of the Border March. These towers originated in palisaded enclosures but the term pele applies to a small fortified tower-house, dating from mid-14th to the 17th Centuries. Whereas England and Wales were becoming more peaceful with a lesser need for fortresses, the Scottish Borders were notorious for *reiving*, raiding, often to rustle cattle, carried out by families both sides of the border. In the requirement for protection, these houses were generally built by the gentry and lesser nobility. Vicar's Pele at Corbridge, Northumberland, in the north of England (c. 1300) is a fine example, comprising a rectangular tower with very thick walls and tiny windows, entered by a flight of stone steps leading into the first floor. Older versions would use a ladder for entrance, which could be drawn inside in times of danger. Ground floors normally contained store rooms with a solar (upper chamber) above, further bedrooms above that, finally topped with an observation roof, sometimes with a corner tower. These tower-houses varied in design. Some possessed a walled courtyard (barmkin) to protect cattle from raiders. The state of border insecurity is evidenced by the 90 pele towers in Cumbria alone, the favored example being Sizergh Castle.

The Castle of Marksburg, near Braubach in Germany, is situated on the strategic waterway of the River Rhine. The central tower is Romanesque and the castle around it has grown by successive additions since the 13th Century. The illustration shows how the castle would have looked in the mid-15th Century. From 1479 it passed into the ownership of the Landgraves of Hesse who continued its fortification. Located around the triangular courtyard are three assymetrical wings. The south side, from which enemy attacks were expected, is well protected by the Kaiser Heinrich Tower. The central area contains the magnificent living quarters and the Knights' Hall on the upper floor. The Marksburg has a dominating view of the surrounding countryside and the strategic River Rhine.

CASTLES AND CONQUEST

The Anglo-Norman conquest of Wales was haphazard, with Norman and Welsh fortunes fluctuating over the years. Wales was united into a single Welsh political unit by Llywelyn ap Gruffudd, Prince of Gwynedd. His achievement was recognized by Henry III of England in the Treaty of Montgomery (1267) when Llywelyn's territorial gains and his self-claimed title "Prince of Wales" were confirmed. Later, this Prince allied with Simon de Montfort against Henry III, but eventually acknowledged the overlordship of the King. In 1273 Llywelyn refused to pay homage to the new King, Edward I, who implemented two devastating campaigns against Wales in 1277 and 1282–83. Gwynedd was overrun and the native Princes of Deheubarth were defeated or submitted. The third Welsh principality, Powys, was an English dependency and regarded as a virtual English barony. Llywelyn was forced to submit to humiliating terms, including the cession of part of his eastern lands to Edward and an annual acknowledgement of fealty. He rebelled in 1282 but was killed in battle. His brother, Dayydd ap Gruffud continued the fight, being captured and beheaded. Edward conquered the north and west of Wales by 1284 and initiated military government. By the Statute of Rhuddlan, Wales became an English principality, the new lands being turned into the English shires of Anglesey, Caernarfon, Meirionydd, Cardigan, Carmarthen, and Flint. To hold down Wales, Edward I had many new castles built and many old Welsh ones refurbished. Prominent amongst his castles were Harlech, Caernarfon, and Conway.

These castles were built rapidly, Conway taking only about four and a half years. Caernarfon

LOARRE CASTLE, in northern Spain. In the 11th Century this castle was a frontier fortress between the Pyrennian Christians and the Islamic rulers of Spain. It was from frontier fortresses like this that the Reconquest of Spain began.

THE CASTLE OF COCA, in Segovia, Spain, was built in the 15th Century by Don Alonso de Fonseca of Castile. Constructed of brick, it has an outer enclosure with polygonal towers at the corners and semi-circular towers on the walls. The building rises from a huge 40 foot (12 m) deep moat and adaptions were made for the castle to be defended by artillery.

was nearly completed by 1287, and Harlech by 1289. The totality of the Edwardian castles in Wales ringed the Welsh heartland in stone, subjugating and intimidating the people. The castles were also built using the latest technology and several had access to the sea. Rhuddlan Castle (1277–82) was erected on the site of earlier Norman fortification and, in order for it to be supplied by sea, Edward ordered that a two mile (3 km) long canal be dug from the sea to the castle with a fortified quay capable of docking a 40-ton craft. To fill the canal, the River Clydd was diverted. Estimates suggest that the digging would have required 75 men working six days a week for three years to achieve the feat. The dock was fortified and protected by a four-storey tower.

Harlech Castle (1283–89) was built on a rock with the sea below. A narrow flight of steps, the Way from the Sea, ascended the rock face from a dock with a water gate, drawbridge, and an earth rampart with a parapet wall. One hundred and eighteen steps ran from the water gate to a turret with a drawbridge carefully sited so that it in turn would be protected by the southwest tower of the castle. From this Upper Gate, 19 more steps lead to a gate at the foot of the northwest tower. Interestingly, platforms had been carved out of the rock into the cliff face in the outer ward to house siege engines and artillery to protect the water gate and sea access.

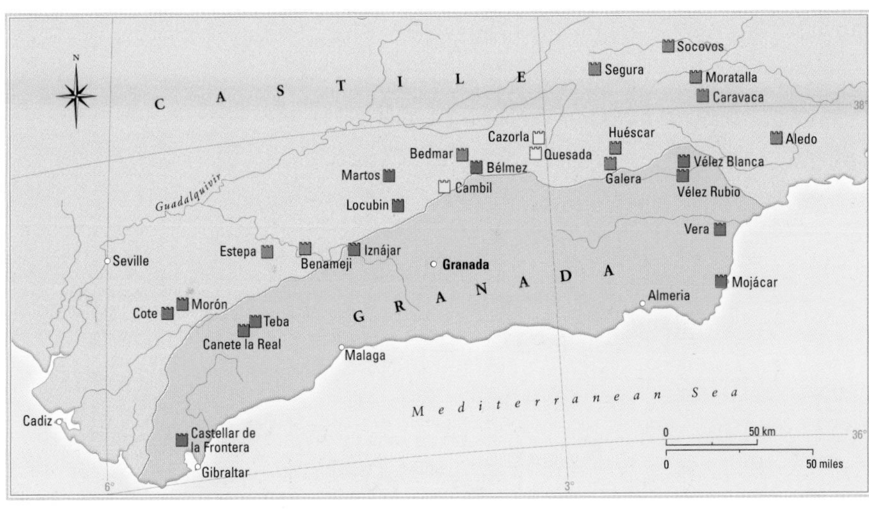

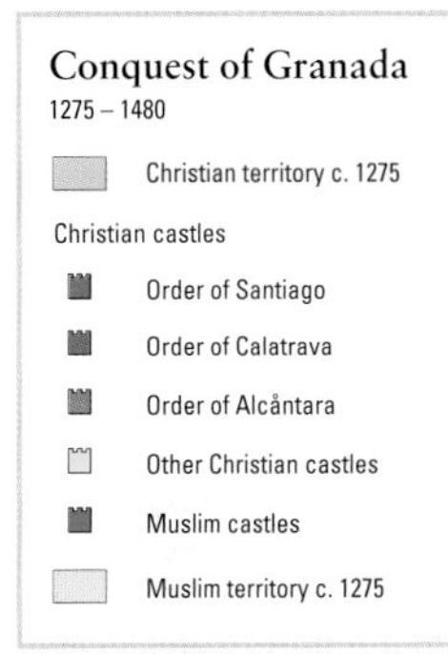

In Spain as the Reconquest moved intermittently southward castles would be captured and rebuilt or new castles constructed to defend newly aquired areas. In 1410 Castile captured Antequerra and twenty years later defeated the Sultan of Grenada at La Higuerela in 1431. Along the Castile-Granada border a string of castles were held by the Military Orders Calatrava and Santiago, these controlled the invasion routes in and out of Granada. In 1479 King Ferdinand V and Queen Isabella of Castile inherited the Kingdom of Aragon, their newly unified country, Spain now embarked on the final crusade on Iberian soil. The final conquest began in 1482 lauched from the Christian strongholds that now surrounded Granada. In 1492 the crusaders using both traditional tactics and now backed by the latest artillery available, captured the city of Granada itself, ending 800 years of Islamic rule in Spain.

SIEGE WARFARE

Right: The Turkish Siege of Malta. After all bombardments had done their work, the moment came to rush the walls, heading for any breach that may have been created before the defenders could effect repairs: this was a critical moment for most sieges.

Castles were more than bases for offensive actions; they were very important for concentrating troops so that an enemy invading a territory could not afford to leave it behind an advance because its occupants could make sorties and disrupt communications and logistics. Numerous castles in a province, all designed to resist siege, could delay an invader's incursions.

Sieges took place in both England and Europe. Wales witnessed a Welsh uprising by Madoc ap Llywelyn in 1294 and all Edwardian castles were able to resist because they were sited so that they could be provisioned by sea. However, in 1400–09, Owain Glyn Dwr's uprising saw the fall of Harlech and Aberystwyth castles because they were blockaded by a French fleet. The Hundred Years' War witnessed many sieges of fortified towns and castles, with Shakespeare's *Henry V* portraying the siege of Harfleur.

Any besieged town or castle could fall; provisions or water could run out or an attack succeed. Besiegers faced two military options: a direct assault or blockade and containment until a fortification's garrison was starving. However, a long siege could see sickness spread in the besiegers' camp resulting in a wasted campaign. Treachery might work or intimidation used to lower the morale of the besieged population. The heads of captives were sometimes catapulted over the walls. King Henry V captured Rouen by cutting off the city's water supply and polluted wells with dead animals. Plague took hold and the city eventually surrendered.

In this illustration of a siege in progress, a counterweight trebucket is brought into play, while occupants of the castle throw stones onto the attackers and crossbow fire is exchanged.

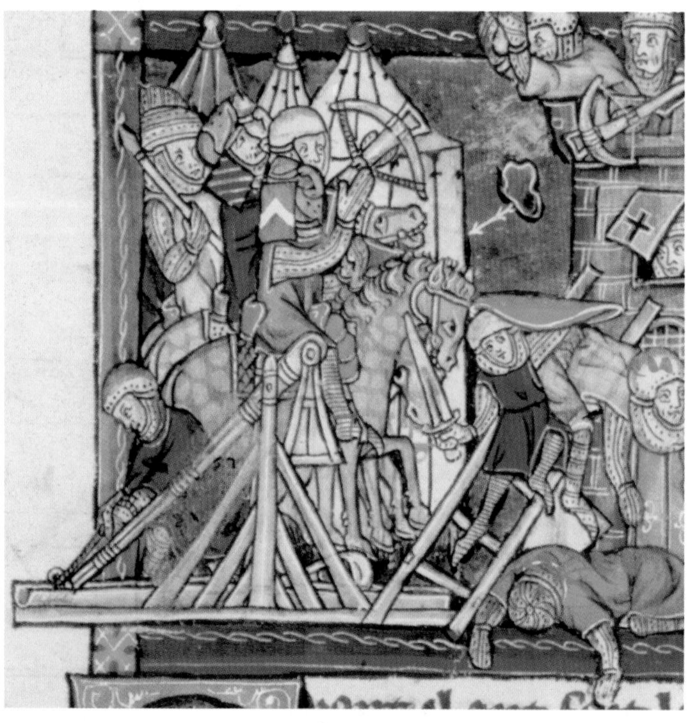

Methods of attack against a castle or fortification could involve bombardment, direct assault, or mining. Medieval artillery comprised a variety of stone-throwing machines seeking to smash a breach in a wall through which besiegers could attack. Often a gatehouse, regarded as a weak point, would receive concentrated attention. As time went on, gatehouses became heavily fortified and attackers turned their attention to the curtain walls. Eventually water defenses could keep siege engines at a distance or foil attempts at mining.

Stone-throwing machines were positioned on siege platforms or siege forts protected by mantlets, wooden shelters strengthened by leather. These engines could lob a rock from between 87 and 131 yards. The mangonel comprised a long arm with a cup or sling for a stone or other projectile at one end. The arm passed through ropes stretched between two posts; the ropes were twisted by windlasses (types of winch), the arm being dragged down by torsion until it was released. The trebuchet developed in the twelfth century: ammunition was fired like the mangonel from a revolving arm pivoting between two uprights with motive power

Far right: This 14th-Century manuscript shows the French army besieging a town using an early form of cannon. *Far right below:* Soldiers swarm up siege ladders in an attempt to capture a bastion.

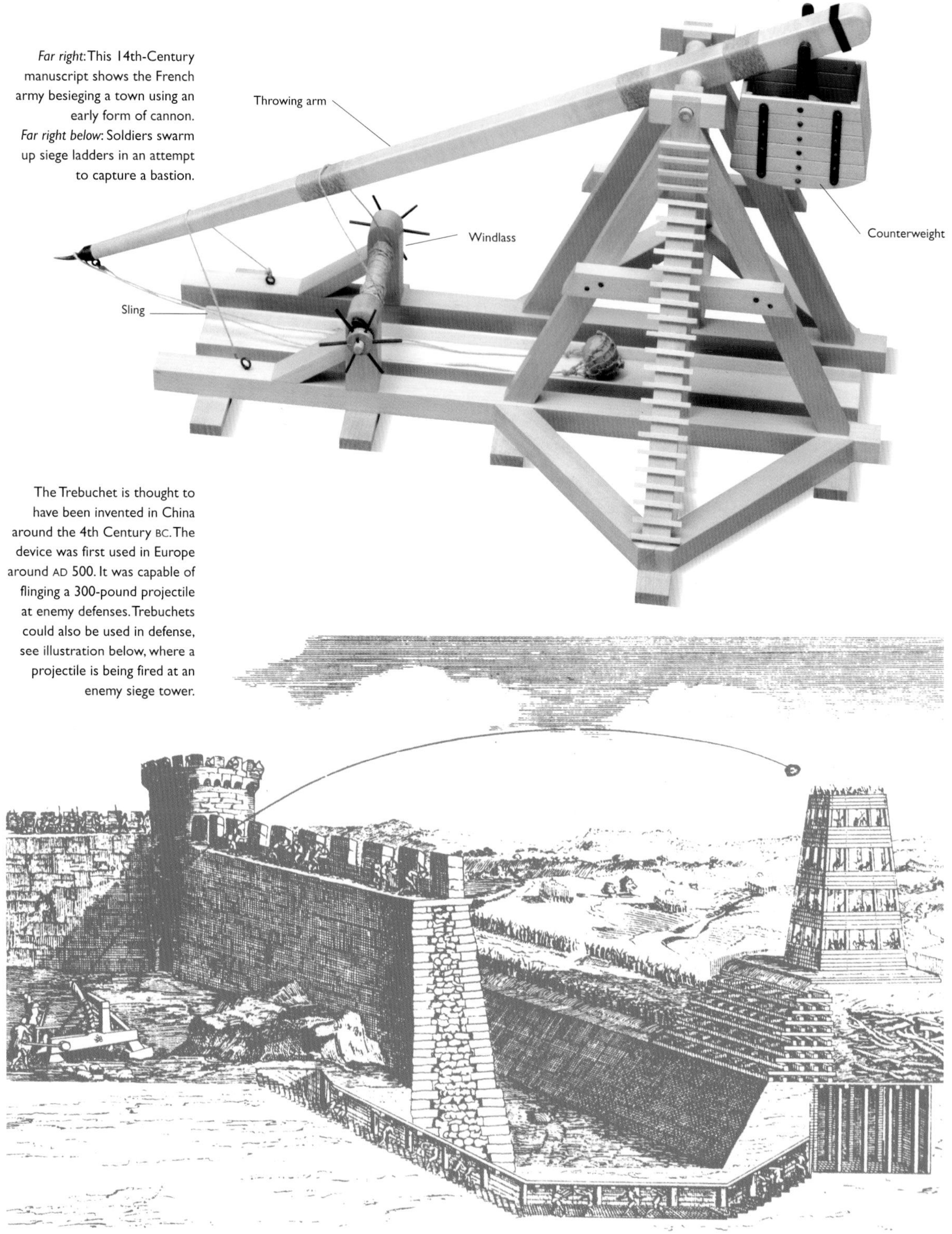

The Trebuchet is thought to have been invented in China around the 4th Century BC. The device was first used in Europe around AD 500. It was capable of flinging a 300-pound projectile at enemy defenses. Trebuchets could also be used in defense, see illustration below, where a projectile is being fired at an enemy siege tower.

SIEGE WEAPON TERMINOLOGY

Sieges involved various types of siege engines and techniques:

BALLISTA	Catapult built on a frame
BATTERING RAM	iron-capped tree trunk swung on ropes
BELFRY	mobile wooden tower
BOMBARD	cannon
BORE	iron-pointed ram
ENGINE TOWER	tower holding a siege engine
ESCALADE	scaling ladder
ESPRINGAL	frame-mounted arrow/bolt-shooting catapult
MANGONEL	stone-throwing engine, torsion powered
MANTLET	mobile shelter
PENTHOUSE	movable wooden shed
PERRIER	counterpoise stone-throwing engine
SAP	tunnel or trench
SIEGE PLATFORM	levelled base for siege engine
TESTUDO	tortoise, covering for ram or miners
TREBUCHET	stone-throwing engine, counterpoise
UNDERMINING	tunneling beneath a wall

supplied by a counterweight. Moving the counterweight along the arm could alter its range, making these machines quite accurate. These engines could chuck large stones or Greek Fire (a combustible compound). Disgusting ammunition was also used: the rotting entrails of animals, sacks of excrement, and the corpses of diseased animals, which would burst upon impact. Some engines were so vast that they required dismantling and numerous wagons to move them. Some were placed on the wall of a castle, or as engine towers allowing defenders to attack besiegers' machines. A third type of engine was the ballista, a generic term that included the espringal. This machine resembled an huge crossbow on which the string was drawn back by a winch. The torsion allowed bolts, stones or Greek Fire containers to be shot in horizontally over long distances.

Other machines used were for close quarter action. Battering rams would be suspended by ropes in a protective penthouse to attack gates or the corners of square towers. The pointed bore could be used to pick between masonry blocks to loosen them. Mining became an increasingly common method of attack. Tunnels would be dug beneath wall foundations with the ceiling held up by pit props. Any cavity made would be filled with inflammable material, which would then be burnt so that the wall could collapse into the cavity leaving a breach above ground. Within the beseiged castle, bowls of water placed in key places in a castle would ripple, suggesting underground activity. Counter-mines could then be dug to collapse the attackers' mine or to engage the enemy in underground combat.

A common, highly dangerous method of assault was the escalade by scaling ladders. A development of the escalade was the belfry, a tall, movable tower which could be rolled across a filled-in moat to reach the castle walls. A bridge would be lowered to allow besiegers to pour across to swamp defenses. The belfry would typically be protected by wet animal skins to lessen the risk that they could be set alight. Belfries were built with several fighting platforms at different levels connected by ladders and were generally constructed higher than the castle walls so that arrows could be fired downward at the defenders. Belfries could be used as observation platforms, mobile archer platforms, or even to entice a nighttime sortie where some of the defenders might be slaughtered or captured.

As the power of cannon-fire improved, the vulnerability of medieval curtain walls and towers increased. Thicker, heavier towers could be constructed but more immediately and quickly, defense could be provided by building artillery ditches and defenses beyond the walls, as shown in this illustration.

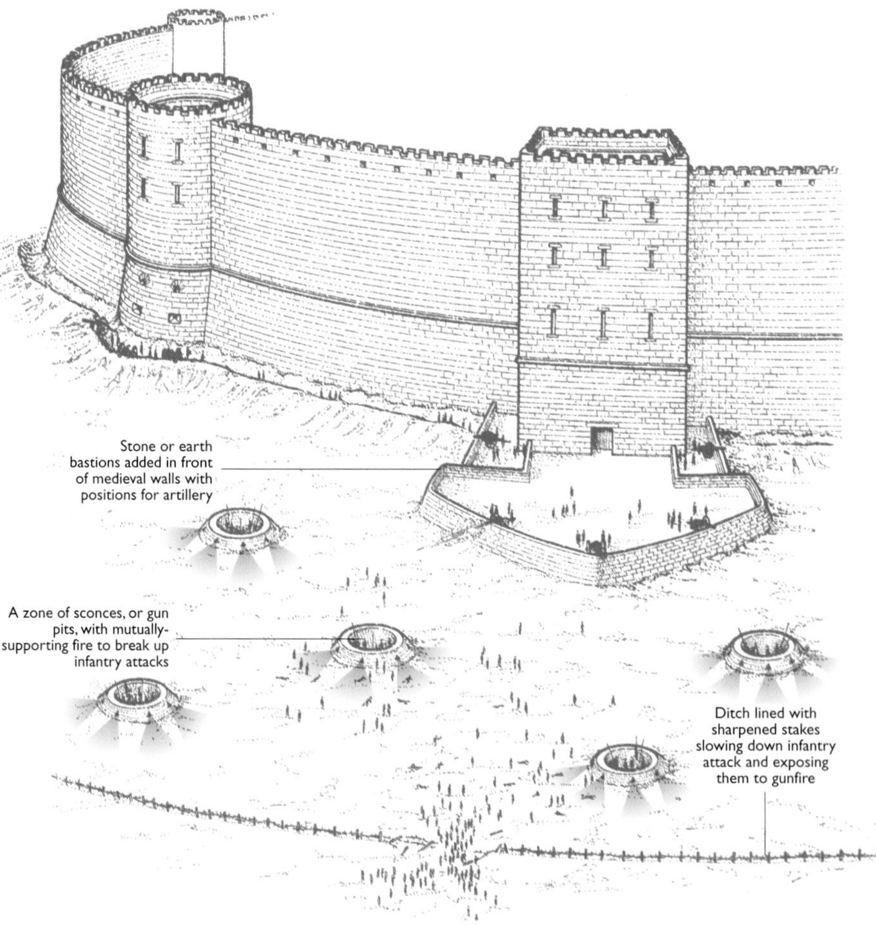

NUOVO CASTLE
The walls of this castle in Naples, Italy, were initially constructed in the late 13th Century. As artillery developed, huge, strong towers were added between 1442 and 1451. In the 1460s a low wall was added, built at the level of the top of the moat to provide a firing platform for defensive artillery.

THE CITY OF VIENNA (viewed from the north, looking south) Between 1500 and 1600 new styles of fortification developed and occasionally entire cities were defended with artillery-based defensive systems of angled bastions, giving the defenders the ability to create zones of cross fire as the enemy approached the walls. Here we can see the city besieged by the Ottoman army with lines of entrenchments approaching the southwest side of the city.

Above: CHÂTEAU-GAILLARD, Normandy, France. This castle sits on its rocky promontory overlooking the River Seine. It could only be approached by land at the point of the outer bailey and was thought to be impregnable in its day.

PORTRAIT OF A SIEGE: CHÂTEAU GAILLARD

Château Gaillard was King John of England's key castle in the defense of Normandy, France. Originally built by his brother, Richard I Lionheart, its constable—when besieged by King Philip II Augustus of France—was Roger de Lacy. Erected on a rock above the confluence of the Rivers Seine and Gambon, its outer approaches were protected by a ditch, backed up by a wooden palisade that prevented an enemy getting near the walls. The castle was built in three main sections. An outer enclosure protected a ward leading to an inner ward. Each ward was surrounded by powerful walls with towers. Each wall required a breach in turn with each wall being higher than the previous one, denying attackers any advantage. The final ward could only be entered by a narrow bridge of natural stone across a steep gully. De Lacy had a small force, this being normal since the task of a castle was for small forces to engage large numbers, preventing them from advancing across one's territory.

The French King was a solid tactician, not attacking Château Gaillard directly. Instead, he reduced neighboring castles until his prime target was isolated and his forces were not in immediate danger from local enemy forces. The English defenders had to sit out the siege but destroyed a nearby river bridge to stall French dispositions. The French forces filled the ditch and breached the wooden palisade that defended it thereby gaining access to the castle walls. Next a bridge of floating boats was built to allow French mobility. Towers were placed on some boats to defend against relief forces. King John's forces attempted a relief expedition comprising river and land forces. One force would destroy the bridge while the other attacked the besiegers. The land attempt failed and the river forces arrived late allowing the French to defeat each contingent in turn.

A nearby river island controlled by the English was attacked by Greek Fire and captured, totally isolating the castle. The French troops were housed in makeshift huts and trenches were dug to defend their camp. A road dug into a trench led toward the castle with protecting earth ramparts when the approach faced the castle walls directly. English archers had difficulty in attacking this communication system and the enemy engaging in siege works. Nearby hills had their tops leveled to provide platforms for siege artillery which pounded the walls with rocks, trying to batter the walls into rubble while ballistae shot bolts at the defenders. Meanwhile, de Lacy sent his noncombatants out of the gates because he did not want to feed them in an effort to make his provisions last longer. The French allowed some through but finally blocked them so the hungry people had to endure rocks and arrows flying in different directions above their heads. The French eventually relented and let these people through their lines.

King John attempted a distraction by raiding Brittany but Philip would not be drawn. Winter 1203–04 drained the castle's food supplies while the French were constantly reprovisioned as they built belfries and used battering rams and bores. By February 1204, the French were ready to attack.

Philip's assault was multipronged. Siege engines and archers attacked defenders on the walls while other engines attacked the walls directly covered by belfries. Miners dug under the walls hoping to eventually collapse the masonry after burning supporting pit props. The business was potentially dangerous with the possibility of tunnel collapse or countermining and fighting in the

Below: Siege Tower or Belfry, popular throughout the Middle Ages for attacking high curtain walls. It contained several floors and ladders through which attackers could reach the top level. Animal hides were draped on the front and side of the tower to protect the attackers from the defenders' missile fire.

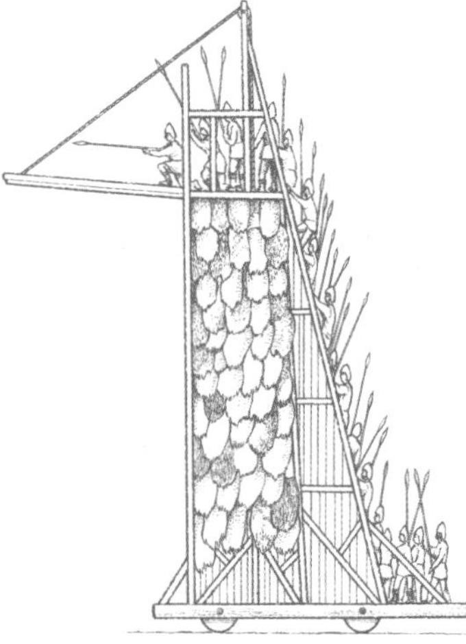

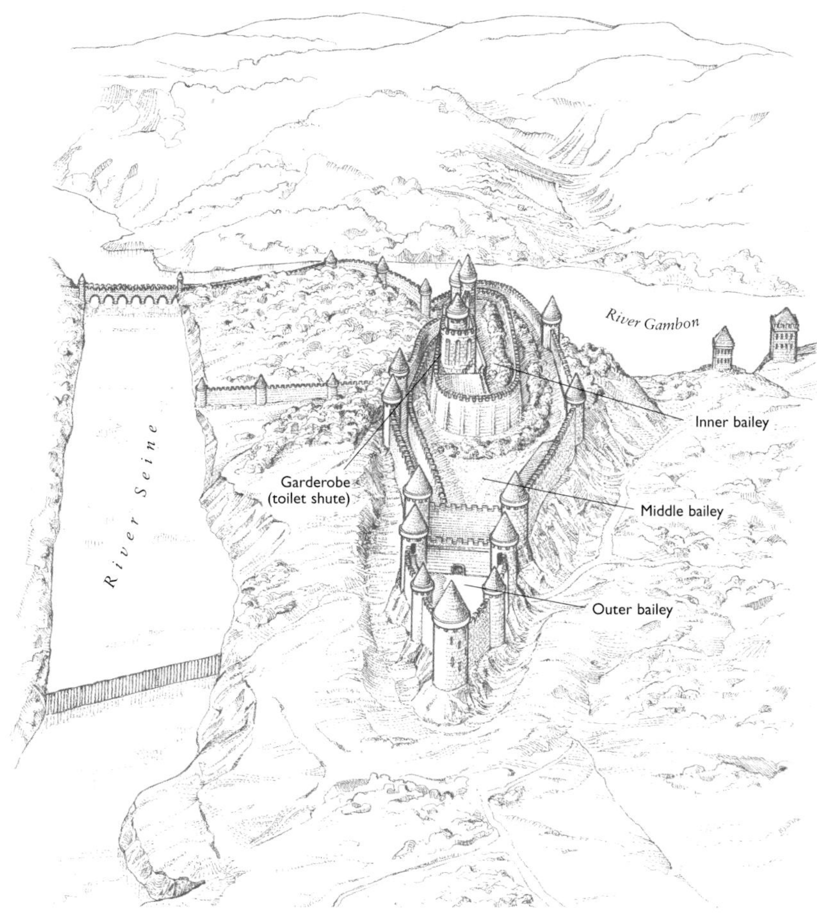

Left: CHÂTEAU-GAILLARD, Normandy, France.
This drawing shows the castle as it would have looked around 1204. It was an exceptionally strong fortress and proved extremely difficult to capture.

tunnels. A third assault method was escalade by ladders. Eventually this type of attack succeeded and the defenders were forced to retreat into the second bailey.

The second bailey fell in a most unusual manner. French soldiers discovered the chute of a garderobe, or toilet, and crawled up it to reach the second bailey's chapel. They set fire to the chapel door and, in the ensuing confusion, found the bailey's gate, opening it to allow the entry of a large assault force. Soon the middle bailey was a burnt ruin, the defenders now retreating to the third bailey and its keep.

The French faced suicide crossing the rock bridge while escalade was impossible and siege engines could not cross the gully, so mining commenced. The rock bridge sheltered the miners who forced entry into the inner bailey on 6 March 1204. Custom maintained that once a breach was passable with a good chance of success, further loss of life was pointless so surrender was honorable. If defenders surrendered, there was a reasonable chance they could walk away with their weapons, but if the fight continued with terrible loss of life, then the defenders could expect death. De Lacy gave up and returned to his home at Pontefact in England knowing he had fulfilled his duties as a soldier, acting in accordance with the best traditions of knighthood. Philip cleared the last English out of Normandy winning that Duchy plus Anjou, Maine, and Touraine. In England, John faced a fractious baronage that forced him to eventually sign the Magna Carta.

Below: The Battering Ram was used to attack, not only the wooden doorways of a castle but any perceived weak point in the walls.

Life of the Castle

THE CASTLE PROVIDED A HOME FOR A COMPLETE COMMUNITY OF LORDS, LADIES, THEIR KNIGHTS, SERVANTS, AND A PRIEST. THE BUILDING WAS A FORTRESS, HOME, A SCHOOL FOR SQUIRES, A TRAINING GROUND FOR MEN-AT-ARMS, AN ARMORY AND STABLES, THE VERY CENTER OF THE RURAL ESTATE.

DOMESTIC AFFAIRS

Besides being a fortress, a castle was the home of a lord and his family where the lord, but not his family, provided the focus and rationale for the castle's very existence. The accommodation arrangements reflected a lord's status in medieval society and his needs as the head of a sizable establishment and lands. The lord required a body of officials to implement and enforce his decisions and a secretariat to support them. The lord, his family, and officials were the inner household. Outside them were the mass of minor officials and servants who looked after the lord's personal needs and those of his family and guests. As the medieval period developed, the character and structure of the large *magnate* household, the *familia*, became more complex, as did the buildings within the bailey and the variety of departments it contained.

Members of the household severally and individually were duty bound to cater to the personal needs of the lord and his relations and guests. Additionally, they were required to administer his lands and in return gained his patronage. In times of war, they were required to fight for their lord in defense of his rights and lands. Sons of of the nobility and of knightly families were expected to serve in the households of superiors where they received a military and academic training, as well as education in manners. Even younger brothers of kings were expected to serve in a lord's household but obviously in a ducal household.

Right: The castle, as well as its military role, was also the center of administration for great feudal estates and was the home of its aristocratic lord.

Many magnates held a number of estates, traveling between them to consume produce as rents, or they spent time abroad at war or at estates in another country. Many lords held lands in both

France and England. When absent, the castles would be ruled by a constable or castellan with a residual garrison of soldiers, crossbowmen, and artisans such as smiths, carpenters, and masons for the upkeep and repair of the castle.

Surviving examples of European castles tend to have empty spaces in them because the courtyard buildings have vanished, since, made from timber or wattle and daub, they have decayed. These would have included a servants' hall, the kitchens, buttery, and other domestic offices with a smithy, armory, stables, and various other departments. Castles were bustling, noisy places with military training taking place, a smith or smiths shoeing horses or repairing armor, and servants moving food and provisions around, and orders constantly being shouted. The smells of the castle would have been varied: the odor of blood and offal from the slaughterhouse, the stench of pigs in the sty and horses in the stable, together with that of castle rubbish being tipped over the walls into a stinking heap in the castle ditch, a breeding ground for flies and disease.

This woodcut shows the huntsman taking his lord's hounds on the hunt.He carries a spear for protection against wild boar.The hunt was a major part of life on the feudal estate. As well as providing food for the table, the lord could show off his prowess with horse and lance.

Nowadays, castles are predominantly fractured remnants of their former glory, with little sense of their original interior layout. Generally, the more decorated a room in architectural terms or the more brightly painted, the higher the status of the owner. A room containing windows, perhaps with glass, a fireplace, chests, and access to a *garderobe* would belong to a lord or a high official. The great hall would be the center of castle life. Even when lords possessed their own suites of private rooms and a solar, living apart from the mass of the household, he would still take some meals in the hall to state the mutual commitment of the lord and his people; the hall would also be the seat of much estate business.

In the 12th Century, castle terminology developed in a sophisticated fashion. The *seneschal* (sometimes steward or dapifer looked after food and drink; interestingly, owing to pigs being such an important source of food, the term "steward" originates from sty-ward after the important pig man). The butler controlled the larder, the provisions store (especially meat), the pantry (bread), and the buttery (wine and ale), together with all the kitchen staff. The lord slept in a chamber whose contents were the responsibility of a chamberlain with a staff of door-keepers, janitors, and valets, tending the lord and keeping his clothes in order. During this period, the royal household appointed a chancellor to look after the royal chapel, and the monarch's written records. Henry II of England moved around his Angevin lands followed by many carts bursting with such records. Eventually, the Chancellor of the Exchequer had a permanent office in England at Westminster.

Lords would have household priests keeping records of dues owed to the castle such as: "wood-penny" for the right to collect firewood on the lord's land; "*agistment*" for the right to graze animals in the lord's forest; "*chiminage*" for the right to carry goods through the forest; "*bodel silver*" for the right to live in a house on the lord's land; "*foddercorn*," grain provided by a villain to feed the lord's horses; and "*heriot*," meaning a family upon a death had to give the lord the dead man's best animal. The aforementioned officers were the inner circle in the household. After them came the constable and marshal who were responsible for the castle's security, for overseeing and training the lord's troops, for garrisoning the lord's estates, and for ensuring the smooth running of the stables, and the mews where the hunting birds would be kept.

This French illustration, dating from the 15th Century, shows a party out hunting birds with dogs and a falcon. Falconry was a very popular form of hunting throughout the Middle Ages, a good, well-trained hunting bird could command a high price.

Household officials would be near their lord in status and as well as attending him, they would offer advice as individuals or in a council. Likewise, the King would consult his senior barons. Although democracy did not exist, a lord could do little if his vassals were in total disagreement so some type of consensus for action had to emerge.

A lord would tend to build comfortable quarters for his family in the bailey, the keep being kept as a final bastion in an attack. The garrison was stationed in the outer bailey. Thus, the majority of castles had two baileys with the heavily fortified inner bailey containing the lord's rooms, great hall, chapel, other lodgings, and domestic units, while the outer bailey housed all other departments and provided the environment for daily work of the garrison.

The 13th Century brought in changes in castle administration, especially in important households. The office of steward was split in two. The new steward was responsible for the estates and relations between the lord and his tenants, while the emergent treasurer looked after financial affairs. Now, too, there was a second domestic steward in control of stocking the castle with provisions and with their distribution. The cook, butler, and pantler were his responsibility. Another official was the marshal who looked after serving staff. However, the marshal was normally responsible for the lord's horses, soldiers, weapons, and military organization. A legacy here lies in some English private schools having a marshal to organize the transport bussing in pupils in the morning and out in the evening.

This century also witnessed a greater separation of rooms into different functions with a hierarchy of rooms reflecting status of those in greater proximity to the lord. As an occupant's status was lower on the social ladder, so would be the décor and size. The lord's chambers would tend to have aumbries, cupboards made in the walls. Carpets and tapestries may have been brought back from the Crusades. Magnates could be lucky enough to have a private garden with herbs and flowers such as lilies, lavender, marigolds, roses, and primroses. This may have been laid out as a knot garden. Architecturally, as enclosure castles developed, keep-gatehouses were built evolving into huge gatehouses where the constable would normally have his rooms and a lesser great hall for administrative purposes and the control of ingress and egress.

The 14th Century saw increased specialization in household tasks. The household steward was renamed the chamberlain, one of the lord's inner circle. A specialist clerk was placed in charge of the butler for buying in provisions. The lords increasingly separated themselves off from daily routines. Instead, the household developed into three carefully defined units: there was an inner core of household officers and their minions; a wide range of support staff managed the estates; and finally there were the vassals, necessary for war and ceremonies. A final element of the most powerful castle households was the council. This comprised senior household officials, lawyers, and senior vassals who joined together to advise their lord when summoned; its advice could be disregarded.

The 15th Century witnessed a very formalized official structure, the magnates modeling their households on the monarchy: the *seneschal* was the chief officer and lord's deputy controlling justice when the lord was away; the chamberlain was responsible for domestic affairs but eventually assumed a mainly financial role; the chancellor looked after administrative and legal affairs writing letters and issuing charters; the marshal cared for the horses, soldiers, and arms; and the steward ran the lord's estates. In the lord's absence the constable managed castle affairs but the administration was delegated to a receiver. There might also be an auditor, who would be responsible for monitoring financial matters, an almoner for dispensing charity, and sometimes a cofferer to administer diplomatic and war finances.

The title often became a surname passed down through the generations and many names were created by tasks associated with a castle and its environs. The name More referred to a mower of hay, while Hayward stored his product in the castle stables together with caring for all fences and hedges (*haies*). Farrier shoed horses but sometimes became a veterinary surgeon out of need. Leatherworking produced many names: Tanner, Barker, and Lister who could dye leather or cloth; Whitetayer or Whittier dressed leather with alum to produce white leather suitable for gloves. Thrower was a silk-winder and Harbisher made hauberks. Verderers, Hawkers, Falconers, Fishers, and Hunters were plentiful. The castle bailey produced Smith and Faber, who worked with armor; Bowyer and Fletcher concerned themselves with bows and arrows while Cooper and Hooper made barrels for storage. Archer, Fuller, and Salter were all jobs and the following jobs also became names. A biller made axes, a bolter sifted meal, a fuster or foster made saddle traces, and a loriner or lorimer made straps.

THE CASTLE CHAPEL

Every castle possessed at least one chapel, if only a private chapel near to the lord's chamber. There would be brightly painted walls, possibly a stained-glass window and a gold cross on the altar. When present, the lord and lady began each day by attending a short service. There might be a larger chapel for the garrison in the bailey, which sometimes served as a parish church.

A most impressive chapel is in the Tower of London where the apse of the Chapel of St. John projects from the east wall. Most castle chapels are basic structures. A simple rectangular room where a basin for holy water might have survived in the south wall, sometimes in a stone canopied niche. The altar would be at the eastern end, a liturgical requirement.

Religious ceremonies were performed by the castle priest who also said Grace before every meal. Priests were important for the castle administration since clerics were some of the few people who could read.

The castle chapel provided the lord with his private religious room of devotion.

PORTRAITS OF POWERFUL WOMEN

Aristocratic women were expected to marry and produce children, not fight in battle, nor to hold fiefs, or rule men: but they did. A stereotypical view of medieval women is that they were wives and mothers, put on a pedestal, or were evil seductresses or sexual objects. However, there were many women who took over men's roles out of necessity or paid to be left unmarried. Widows were expected to remarry—and the King could force this—but some paid fines to ensure their freedom, most noticeably, three times widowed Lucy, Countess of Chester.

Isabella de Fortibus best exemplifies the noblewoman who became a large-scale, feudal landowner through marriage and inheritance. She acted in a determined and tenacious fashion while extending her power to ensure her domains on the Isle of Wight, off the south coast of England, enjoyed a prosperity not seen again for 300 years.

Urraca, Queen of Aragon, ruled Leon-Castile in 1094 when her husband died. She remarried in 1098 and spent 13 years at war with her second husband, Alfonso the Battler, to protect the inheritance rights of her son by her first marriage.

In about 1100, Lady Isabel of Conches rode armed as a knight into battle and was regarded as daring and high-spirited but was she acting like a man? Another case is Petronella, Countess of Leicester, who like Matilda, Countess of Chester in 1141, was involved in military campaigns with her husband and was captured with him at the Battle of Fornham (1173–74) when he rebelled against Henry II of England. She was armed in a hauberk and carried a sword and shield. As a widow she granted charters in favor of religious houses in Normandy, France, and England. She held her own court, where her vassals made agreements that she witnessed. Jeanne de Danpierre, Countess of Montfort (c. 1300–74), held a besieged castle-town at Hennebont and strode the battlements in armor and rode a warhorse. She mobilized the townswomen to defend the ramparts with missiles. She broke out of the town with three horsemen during a French assault on the walls and fought her way to Brest. She returned with 600 additional men to reinforce the town. During the same year, she is reported to have taken part in a sea-skirmish off Guernsey, wearing a suit of armor and wielding a sword. The chronicler, Froisart describes Jeanne "with a very sharp sword to hand, fighting with great courage."

Margaret de Bohun was a woman of rank who controlled her own affairs and kept her independence as a widow by exercising the powers of a magnate. She was the daughter of Miles, Earl of Hereford, and his eventual heir. She married Humphrey de Bohun, a steward of Henry II, who died in 1177. Margaret ran her own court to manage the administration of her lands. As a great landholder, Margaret enfeoffed military followers, confirmed undertenants' charters, and granted 20 charters in favor of St. Mary's Priory, Llanthony Secunda.

These women wielded power and authority that was underpinned by their marital status, their female life cycle, and their social status and familial relationships. The 12th Century witnessed the wives and widows of powerful earls engaging in the affairs of an honor and the family, as well as public society. There roles were enhanced when they gained access to land in their own right, especially by widowhood. Women could hold public office if they had a claim through a patrilineal hereditary right. Nichola de la Haye was the eldest daughter and co-heir of Richard de la Haye, hereditary constable of Lincoln Castle and sheriff of Lincolnshire, England, and his wife, Matilda, the daughter of William of Vernon. She married twice, firstly to William of Erneis and then to Gerard de Camville, passing the office of constable to each of her husbands.

In August 1189, she and Gerard went to Barfleur to obtain a charter confirming her inheritance from King Richard. The paper confirmed to the two Nichola's inheritance and lands, the constableship of Lincoln Castle, plus lands at Poupeville and Varreville in the east Cotentin in Normandy. She was twice besieged in Lincoln Castle, once in 1191 with her second husband, and in 1217 as a widow.

While knights went on crusade, their wives remained behind to administer their estates and defend their castles. These women governed in their husbands' names, engaged in legal transactions, oversaw the estates and agricultural activities, collected money for ransoms, and raised the children. Strong women sometimes ruled as regents and kept kingdoms in being. The crusades provided economic resources allowing women to become patronesses of culture. Women were thus given an avenue where they could make their views heard. Eleanor of Aquitaine commissioned art in the Abbey of Fountevrault. Her daughters were patronesses of literature and culture all over Europe. Marie de Champagne was the patron of Chrétien de Troyes; her sister, Mathilda of Saxony, commissioned romances and introduced courtly poetry into the court of her husband, Henry the Lion; and, another sister, Leonor with her husband Alfonso of Castile welcomed minstrels and troubadours into their court.

Examples of really powerful and important women can be found in Anna Comnena of Byzantium, Melisende of Jerusalem, Eleanor of Aquitaine, Blanche of Castile, and Isabella de Fortibus of the Isle of Wight. Anna Comnena (1083–1148) was the daughter of the Emperor Alexius I Comnenus. Married to Nicephorus Bryennius, she joined her mother, Empress Irene, in a failed effort to persuade her father to disinherit his son John II Comnenus in favor of her husband. Later, she conspired to depose her brother but her husband would not become involved and the plot was discovered, leaving Anna to enter a convent. This failure in politics then gave her time to write the *Alexiad*, a history of the life and reign of her father, a book that became a valuable historical source as a pro-Byzantine slant on the early Crusades. Melisende was the daughter of the Crusader Kingdom of Jerusalem and ruled with her mother toward the end of his life. After she married Fulk V of Anjou, she coruled with him and when he died became regent for her 13-year-old son, Baldwin. After he gained his majority he warred with his mother, defeating her but after a reconciliation, she advised him until her death. She translated her greed for seizing political power into political influence.

Eleanor of Aquitaine (c.1122–1204) inherited her lands from her father, William X, Duke of Aquitaine, when aged 15 years. During her second marriage, to Henry II of England, she turned her ducal capital, Poitiers, into a major cultural center filled with poets and troubadours. When her sons rebelled against their father, she supported them militarily, for which she was placed under virtual house arrest until Henry died in 1189. She administered the Angevin Empire while her son, Richard I, was on crusade. She collected the ransom to release him from the Duke of Austria who had captured him while returning to England. When Richard was killed, Eleanor crossed the Pyrenees to take her granddaughter Blanche of Castile to marry her to the French King's son in the hope that he would leave the new King John of England alone. She defended Anjou and Aquitaine from French incursions and held Mirabeau against Arthur of Brittany until relieved. She was politically aware and tenacious and it is worth noting that when John lost his northern French territories to France in 1204, his mother's lands remained loyal. The nuns of Fontevrault who had benefited from her largesse described her as a queen "who surpassed almost all the Queens of the world."

Blanche of Castile (1188–1252) married Louis, the French royal heir, when she was 12 years old. She bore her husband 12 children and became Queen of France in 1229. Louis died on crusade leaving his wife as regent to her 13-year-old son, Louis IX. In her son's name, Blanche made alliances, led armies, laid siege to castles, and beat her enemies, especially Henry III of England and rebellious nobles. After her son gained his majority, she continued to advise him despite a falling out when he went crusading in 1248. In his absence, she consolidated French control over Toulouse, recently acquired through the Albigensian Crusade against the Cathars. She taxed France for crusade monies and built the port of Aigues-Mortes on the Mediterranean coast. She also collected the ransom for Louis after his capture in Egypt. Like her grandmother, Blanche was a marvel of wisdom and diplomacy and displayed sheer guts when confronting the dangers facing France.

Isabella was born in 1237 to Amicia de Clare and Baldwin III of the de Redvers noble dynasty. While still a girl she was married to William de Forbes, Count of Albemarle. She provided him with two sons, Thomas and William, and two daughters, Aveline and Cecilia. In 1260, aged 23 years, Isabella was widowed, inheriting William's lands and titles. Elsewhere, Isabella's brother, Baldwin IV, Lord of Wight, became involved in the conspiracies against Henry III's incompetence; he was poisoned with his coconspirator, the Earl of Gloucester. Baldwin's death meant Isabella inherited his Duchy of Devonshire and became the Lady of Wight. Then a young woman with immense estates, including her husband's in the north of England, she took up residence at Carisbrooke Castle from 1269, which she rebuilt over a period of 20 years. Included was a new kitchen 45 feet by 32 feet (14 by 10 metres) with a 16-foot (5 m) high ceiling, a connecting passage to a new Great Hall, new rooms for the constable and knights, a new chapel, new roofs, and repaired castle walls. A large fish tank lined with lead was constructed and a private garden developed. As well as having many tenants, Isabella ruled several manors directly such as Bowcombe, Brighstone, Carisbrroke, Freshwater, Niton, Pan, Thorley, Wellow, Westover, and Wroxall. She also owned the Forest of Parkhurst.

Isabella was fully aware of the need to create wealth. She gave a charter to the town of Newport, founded in the 12th Century by her family. The burghers were given their freehold, control of the river to the mouth of the Medina, Town Gate Mill, half of Ford Mill and unlimited pasturage in Parkhurst Forest. These burghers annually elected their own leaders and the town ruled and taxed itself. A virtual Queen, Isabella incurred the hostility of Edward I who was elsewhere smashing the independence of Wales and Scotland. As time went on, all Isabella's children died without issue. After having piloted her estates through the wars between Henry III and Simon de Montfort, her dynasty had died. While dying on pilgrimage to Canterbury on 6 November 1293, she sold the Isle of Wight to Edward for 6,000 marks. Apart from the island, all her possessions passed to distant relatives, the Courtney family.

THE CASTLE TOWN

Powerful lords, magnates, often allowed communities to grow near their castles or built their castles near to a town. Provisions could be more easily bought from a town's market and there would be increased trade and commerce with the possibility of occasional and profitable fairs. Walls could enclose the town making more extensive outwork fortification for the lord. In Wales, Edward I, who had seen *bastides* (fortified towns) in Gascony, created new towns or boroughs as part of his castle building program. These plantation towns were built adjacent to castles, their walls being integrated with those of the castle. The best examples of these can be found at Caernarfon and Conwy. Control of a town meant a measure of economic control of a region.

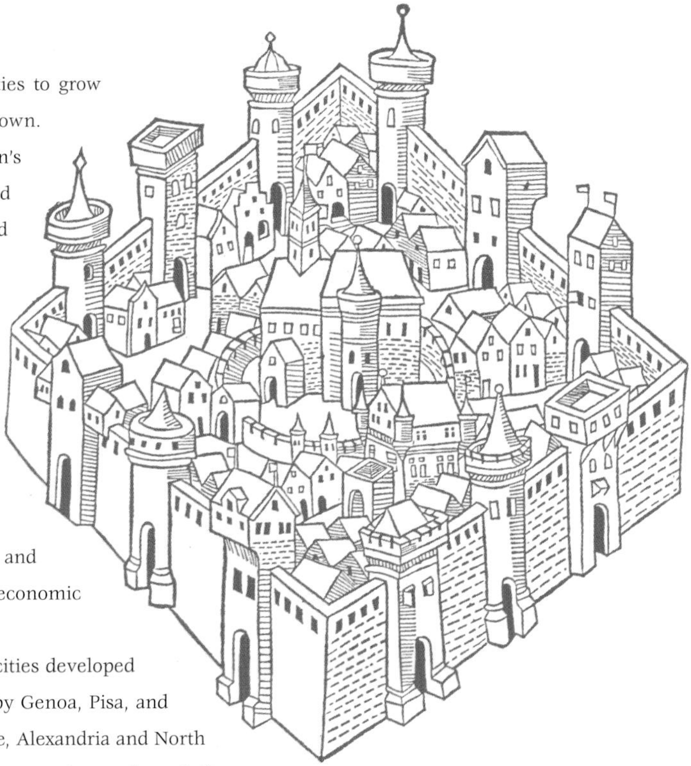

The earliest and biggest commercial towns and cities developed in northern Italy, especially Venice, soon followed by Genoa, Pisa, and then Naples. These ports traded with Constantinople, Alexandria and North Africa. Italian merchants dominated the Mediterranean and moved goods from the Muslim world over the Alps and so into France and Germany. More towns sprang up and nodal communication points. The sheer scale of trade was enormous: furs, slaves, metal, timber, silver, cloth, dyes, spices, cotton, and gold. Arab coins have been found by archaeologists in the north of England while the Flemish cities traded throughout France, the British Isles, the Rhineland, and the Baltic coasts. The Flemish textile industry imported much wool from England thereby becoming a factor in English foreign policy. Flemish wealth underpinned English economic development. Economic production became more specialized with regions exporting what they could produce most profitably. Hence, economies grew to be more interdependent with huge trading networks linking the fortunes of towns, particularly in Flanders and Italy. As merchants moved around, some formed leagues to ensure safer transport, to coerce trading privileges, and sometimes to attack competitors. The greatest of these economic concentrations was the Hanseatic League, focusing on the Baltic trade, with extra territoriality rights in their headquarters in foreign towns, like the Steelyard in London. Monarchs sometimes looked to the League to finance their own wars in return for trading rights. Here, the relationship between Swedish King Gustav Vasa and Lübeck is worth examining. All this trade oiled the medieval economy and it behoved lords to protect their towns. The increase in wealth financed crusading adventures, the construction of cathedrals, and the refurbishment of castles. The cash nexus meant that taxes need no longer be paid in goods; cash meant you could govern through salaried officials,

This woodcut shows a fortified town with the lord's home in the center. In fortified towns such as this, the great lords had a secure base from which they could oversee trade and collect taxes.

The castle town provided a market place for merchants to trade their goods during weekly or monthly markets. Occasionally major towns and cities would be granted an annual market, these would attract traders and merchants from across Europe.

and troops hired rather than relying on feudal levies. Specialist troops, such as Genoese crossbowmen, would only work for pay. If not paid, such mercenaries might take service with a lord's enemy.

The inhabitants of towns were wealthy peasants, ambitious land-hungry younger sons of the nobility, genuine merchants, runaway serfs, with more women than men. These towns were originally under the authority of the local lord whether he was lay or ecclesiastical, and subject to their tolls, taxes, and other exactions. To counter these burdens, the wealthiest inhabitants banded together to bring unity of purpose in the pursuit of business. These burghers wanted freedom of movement, from tolls at bridge and castle and to hold urban property without feudal or manorial dues and, especially, they wanted self management. Many lords, whether willingly or following revolts, granted charters to their towns giving them freedoms in return for an annual renewal fee. Huge sums were paid to obtain a charter, too. The economic and political benefits were large: the townspeople enforced their own laws in their own courts, decided their own way of collecting tax, and paid their fee to the lord in one lump sum, the earlier example of Newtown on the Isle of Wight, being an example. A model charter is that granted to the merchants of Newcastle-upon-Tyne, under Henry I of England and by Louis VI of France, to the commune of Lorris. Many lords recognized the benefits of chartering new towns, laying out streets on a grid plan with the enclosing protective wall. In Shropshire, England, Ludlow was built according to a 12th-Century grid plan with a wall pierced by seven gates, one of which remains. Partially surrounded by the River Teme as a first defensive line, this town on the Welsh border was protected by a magnificent castle and still retains some impressive ruins.

The growth of towns led to merchant oligarchies (small groups of people having control) administering local government, ruling over the remainder of the town. The environs also provided opportunities for female employment with women working in various enterprises as wives helping their husbands or working in an ancillary manner. A butcher's wife might run a sausage-making business. Widows were able to manage businesses as substitutes for their deceased husbands rather than as an independent businesswoman. The growth of trade in France and England was partially helped by Jews being welcomed into the land, where their knowledge of foreign parts, foreign languages, and overseas merchant communities could only benefit their host countries. The quality of merchanting was policed by craft guilds where their masters supervised apprentices and journeymen.

There are still some 40 English towns retaining sections of their medieval walls, some with the gate houses where visitors were held until their credentials could be checked out. The town walls ensured that law and order was effective and that unseemly elements did not spend the night inside. In the English boroughs constructed in Wales, the towns were for "the habitation of Englishmen" not for "mere Welshmen," an early example of racial exclusivity that caused much

Alqazar, in Spain, was provided with defensive walls in order to protect its valuable trade during the period of the Reconquest when both Christian and Muslim armies were likely to attack.

resentment and anger in the 14th Century. Fortified towns are exemplified by Carcassonne in the Languedoc region of France. When France acquired Roussillon province in 1659, Carcassonne lost its importance as a frontier town and started to decay. Reconstruction began in 1844 under the eye of medievalist and architect Viollet-le-Duc. In Brittany, Dinan occupies a plateau above the River Rance and one medieval street, Rue de Jerzual, drops down to its small port which the Rance links to St. Malo, a town with its own walls built by its bishops.

In England, York and Chester have magnificent walls that are still sttanding. By the 1300s, York's enclosed 263 acres, contained 40 churches, including a cathedral, nine chapels, four monasteries, four friaries, sixteen hospitals, and nine guild halls. Chester's walls are still nearly complete and run for two miles (3 km) being occasionally six feet wide (1.8 m), and rising forty feet (12 m) above street level; a wonderful sight, and a beautiful walk. Arguably, the finest surviving walled town is Conwy, in Wales, where the town is also divided by walls internally so that any section taken by an enemy could be sealed off. The circuit of the walls is 1,400 yards (1.3 km) with 22 towers and three twin-towered gateways. Additionally, a 60-yard spur wall (55 m) projects from the quay across the beach and into the waters of the Conwy estuary, ending in a tower. Conwy is also worth seeing for its suspension bridge built by Thomas Telford in 1826.

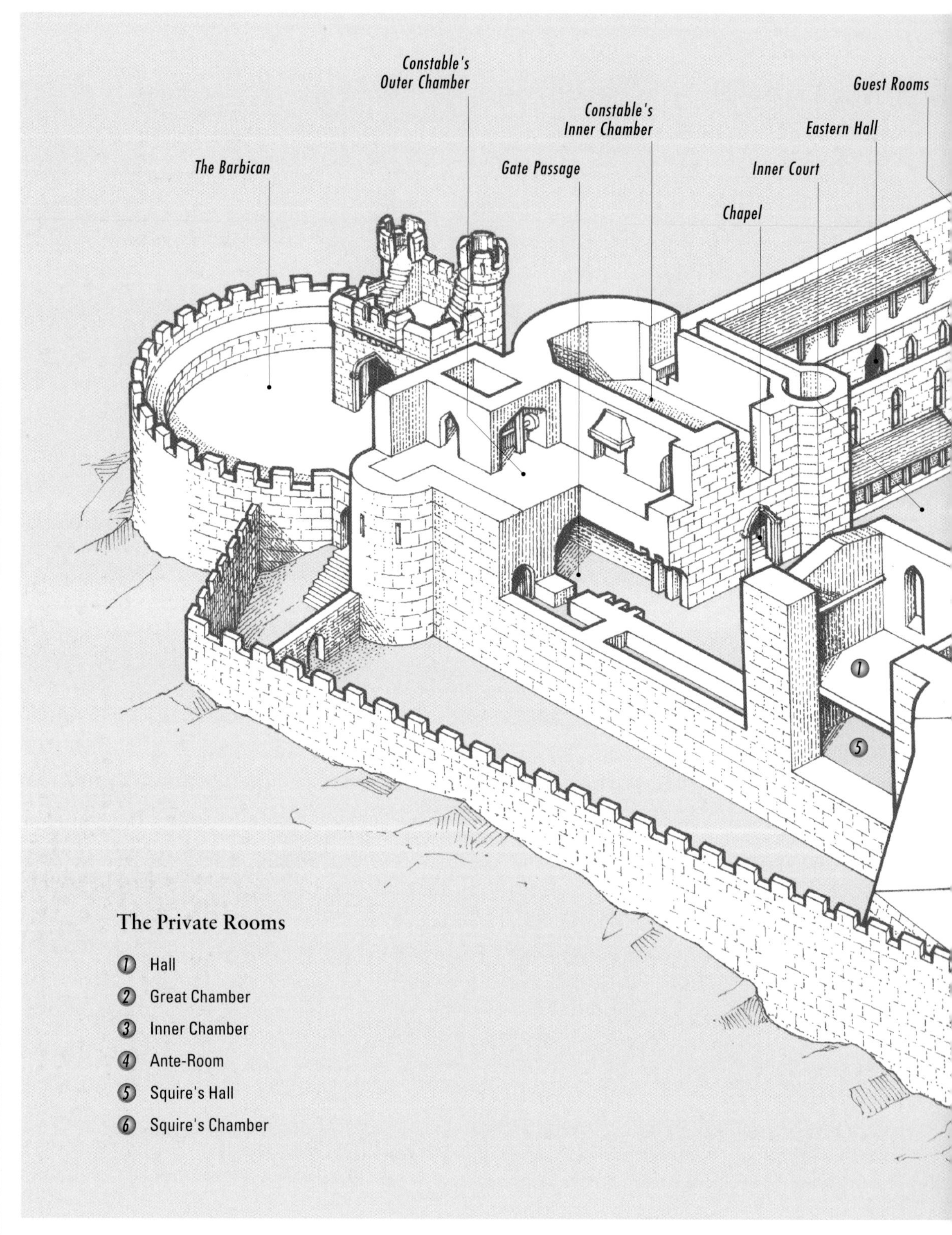

The Private Rooms

1. Hall
2. Great Chamber
3. Inner Chamber
4. Ante-Room
5. Squire's Hall
6. Squire's Chamber

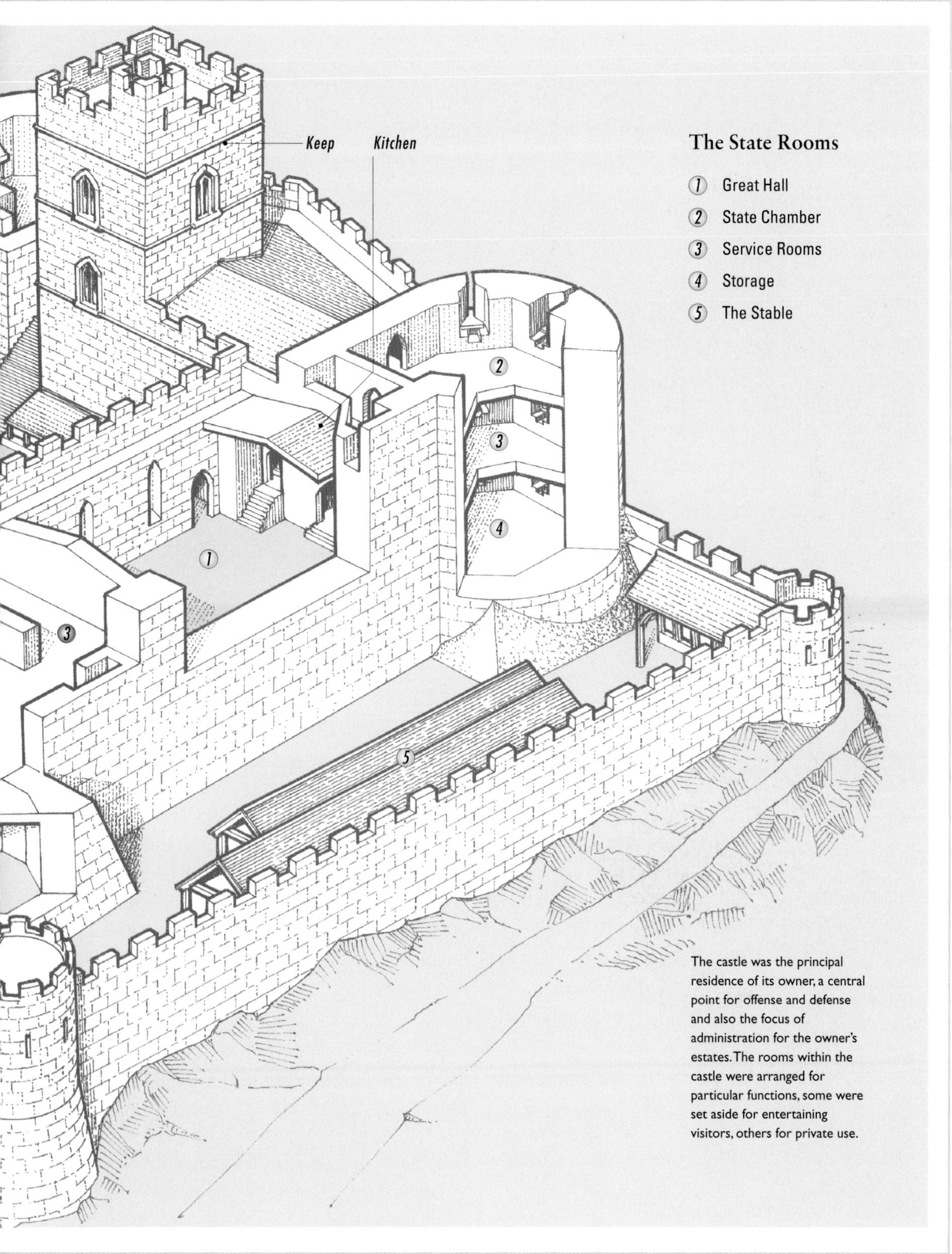

The State Rooms

1. Great Hall
2. State Chamber
3. Service Rooms
4. Storage
5. The Stable

The castle was the principal residence of its owner, a central point for offense and defense and also the focus of administration for the owner's estates. The rooms within the castle were arranged for particular functions, some were set aside for entertaining visitors, others for private use.

The Great Hall

THE CASTLE WAS NOT JUST A CENTER FOR DEFENSE AND OFFENSE BUT WAS ALSO A GREAT RESIDENCE FROM WHICH ITS OWNER ADMINISTERED HIS ESTATES AND DISPLAYED HIS SOCIAL STATUS AND POWER.

There were significant changes in everyday life in the medieval castle that came about as communities developed. One of the major changes was in the architecture of the early medieval Great Hall. Here, the lord and his household lived, ate, and slept together in one great open space. As the castle evolved, specific areas were devoted to different activities and, for the first time, there were individual chambers where people could be by themselves.

For the knight the castle was of crucial importance. Here the lord lived, and his wealth and prestige attracted to him as members of his household landless knights to form his retinue, clerics to administer his estate, and a host of servants needed to support his activities. The wealthier the lord, the more inclined he was to social display, and the more his household took on the character of a court, a center of wealth and patronage, attracting minstrels and men of letters, who celebrated in a new, sophisticated courtly literature the aristocratic values and activities of the lord and his associates.

The Great Hall had various functions, depending upon the type of castle. Usually, the hall would be the domestic heart of the castle, especially in small ones, such as Goltho in Lincolnshire, England. Yet, in the major castles of any country, particularly those owned by a monarch and wealthy lords, the hall was arguably not intended for daily domestic use but became the focal point for administration of the owner's estates and for justice. The hall would also be used for great occasions and festivals. However, since monarchs and lords moved between their various estates, inhabiting each for a short time, the hall, with the owner absent, could be used by the castle bailiff or steward. Many castles possessed separate private accommodation for the owner, constable, or steward. There might be a solar (upper chamber) off the hall or above it, a private room for the lord and his family, a bedroom and sitting room for the lady of the castle. Solars were often decorated with wall paintings, like those of saints in the pope's palace in Avignon, France. Some larger castles might have more than one hall, if more than one family or household inhabited the same building; certainly, there would be a series of family apartments.

Daily life would begin at dawn to make the most of daylight, there being no electricity in those days. Morning prayers were said, then trestle tables would be laid in the hall for breakfast, which generally comprised bread, cheese, and ale for the lord's retinue. This weak beer would be drunk in preference to water, since this might not be potable. The tables would be removed after the meal and castle business would commence, the hall becoming an office. Mid-morning there would be a break for the main meal of the day when the hall became a dining room once more. Supper was taken at sunset after which the hall became a dormitory with palliasses (straw-stuffed mattresses) used for bedding.

Different countries had different fashions regarding halls and chambers. In France, the lord's hall and chamber were typically on the first floor, and some English castles followed this fashion. In other countries, there was a hall on the ground floor with a private solar above, at one end of the hall. Norman kings followed this style as shown by the gigantic hall at Westminster, built by King William Rufus. Although located in a palace, not a castle, this hall was the largest in Europe at the time, measuring 250 by 79 feet (77 by 24 meters), divided into twelve bays with pilaster buttresses (projecting supports) on the outside. Altered by King Richard II, Westminster is famous for the installation of a hammer beam and arch-braced roof.

A German fashion built chambers on the first floor with a huge hall on the second floor. This is the design at Wartburg in the 20th Century and is seen at the castles of Bergen and Akerhus in Norway in the 13th and 14th Centuries respectively. However, this fashion is not specifically German since it can be found in the 12th Century Norman-Sicilian palace of Zisa at Palermo.

In this 15th-Century German illustration, the lord sits with his advisors and followers in the Great Hall. This was the domestic heart of the castle, particularly smaller halls, where the administration for the estate would be carried out in addition to being used by the occupants as an area to eat and sleep.

This woodcut shows a domestic servant bringing jugs of ale to his master's table.

TABLE SERVICE AND ETIQUETTE

When dining in the hall, the lord of the manor or castle would use a formal meal to demonstrate his status by sitting at the high table above the "salt," those of a lower social standing (originating from the custom of placing a large salt cellar in the middle of the table with the host at one end). The various household retainers would sit in their allotted places in a complicated social and occupational hierarchy. Everyone knew, more or less where they stood, or sat, in this case.

Medieval feasts in England, France, Norman Italy, the Germanies, and Scandinavia—certainly important ones—are better recorded than ordinary dinners but the latter would just have simplified versions of serving, seating arrangements, and menus. A long raised platform at one end of the hall would seat the lord and his family together with visitors of note. They all sat on one side of the table facing the room and musicians' gallery at the other end of the hall. The lord would sit in the middle. The main body of the hall would have tables set lengthwise with seats on each side to sit the household and guests of lesser rank. The table nearest to the lord's right was the most important and named the *rewarde* because it was served with dishes from the lord's table. The table opposite was called the *seconde messe*, and the rest were graded accordingly. It was not uncommon for the food of the lesser tables to be different and inferior to those at the higher tables.

Under the minstrel's gallery would be entrances to the kitchen (a fire risk and, therefore, sometimes in its own outside building), the buttery where wine and beer was stored and dispensed, cellar, and pantry. Near these were serving tables called *cubberdes* (cupboards). Nearby, would be a room with ewers and basins for washing hands before the meal.

The seating arrangements during a meal in the Great Hall reflected the social importance of the diner, with the head of the household at one end of the room and the lowest ranks furthest away from him.

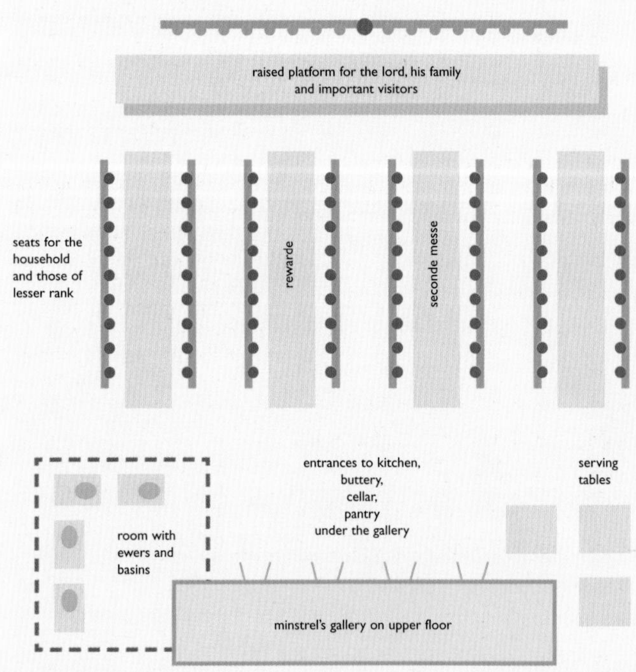

Trencher bread was used as plates; this was four-day-old brown bread, slightly hollowed out. After a banquet, they would be taken and given to the poor. Other common social features would be the exclusion of meat at least once a week, being replaced by fish. Since there was no refrigeration, the castle butcher had to take care lest he over kill and have leftovers that would rot.

Special groups of people needed different foods. Medical men, for example, dictated that children should not have red meat and fruit, believing it did them no good, but milk was allowed. The clerics themselves had an entirely separate menu, perhaps comprising fish four times a week. Any menu comprised two main courses, each containing a number of meat, poultry or fish dishes and several sweet ones. These were served at the high table but placed on the other tables for people to serve themselves. Each dish was portioned earlier into two or four to be served to a similar number of people sitting in a *messe*, either eating from a shared platter or by transferring bits to their trenchers.

FOOD

People in medieval Europe ate the same type of food whether they lived in the north or south. Most common people ate bread every day and a soupy stew called pottage. Country people baked their own bread but town dwellers bought bread from a baker or paid for a baker to cook their loaves in his bread oven. Scraps of dried meat, bacon, or dried fish were sometimes added to the pottage, which was cooked in an iron pot or cauldron over an open wood fire. The Bayeux Tapestry depicts ingredients being boiled in a cauldron and other food roasted on a spit. A meal of roast meat or fresh fish would be a novelty for most peasants.

Many households possessed a herb garden for preparation of medicines and for food flavoring. Honey was used to sweeten foods since sugar was virtually unknown, as were turkey, sweetcorn, chocolate, chilis, potatoes, tomatoes, and avocados: these would only reach Europe after the Americas were discovered in 1492.

Fresh meat was smoked and salted to preserve it. Those who controlled the Baltic herring trade were part of a lucrative business selling salt fish: this was needed so often in order to obey certain church dietary rules. Salt and pepper were used widely in households and spices were used for preserving and flavoring food; they were not, as is sometimes thought, used to hide rotting ingredients but more a fashionable dictate. Spices, since they were brought from abroad, were also a display of wealth and luxury. Venice was the great trading emporium for spices such as pepper and cinnamon. The people of Venice believed in trading with the Saracens rather than fighting them and therefore were able to secure goods from the Near East and Asia, particularly spices.

In this Italian Fresco dating from the 15th Century, a wealthy lord and his family is seen enjoying a meal in his garden. Spices were of great importance in the medieval world and a sign of wealth. These exotic flavors were usually attained by trading with Near East and Asian countries.

In northern Europe, people farmed livestock, mainly cattle and sheep, using dairy products in cooking such as milk, butter, and cheese, and buttermilk for the poor to drink. Apart from beer and ale, cider was made from apple and pears, while in the south grapes were used to make wine. In southern Europe, with its warmer climate, food varieties were greater in terms of vegetables, fruit, herbs, and olive oil was used instead of butter for cooking. Whereas most northern Europeans cooked on an open wood fire, boiling or spit-roasting food, using pots on trivets or baking in the ashes of a warm hearth, the southern Europeans used charcoal for quick cooking.

The nobility hunted throughout the year targeting deer, wild boar, and game birds; peasants occasionally poached. During winter, some livestock was killed off because there was not enough winter feed. Rich houses possessed a dovecote and maybe fish ponds. The peasants had only bacon or pickled pork during winter, since their pigs could forage in the woods and did not need winter fodder.

Hard cheese was a staple food for peasants but might be grated and served as macaroni cheese

SERVANTS AT A FEAST
There was an extensive list of staff engaged in the smooth running of a banquet or feast:
Steward, who ran the household.
Marshal, chief official at the feast.
Sewer, head waiter and taster.
Pantler (or panter), head of the pantry.
Butler, in charge of drinks.
Ewerer, responsible for hand-washing and linen.
Chief cook and helpers, *see drawing above*,
Carver Lord's cup-bearer
Various underlings, including waiters, assistant waiters, assistant cooks, scullions, spit-boys, pot-boys, and washers-up.

in richer houses in Europe. Sometimes grated cheese would be mixed with herbs and eggs to make *herbolace*, a cross between scrambled eggs and an omelette. Eggs were widely used in richer households for dishes such as custards. These were made from egg yolks and cream, colored with saffron and decorated with flower petals, such as violets and borage. Egg yolks, honey, wine, and bread crumbs were mixed together and heated to make *caudles*, a breakfast or bedtime drink.

Urban dwellers needed a road network to bring in food from the countryside but had a greater chance of obtaining imported foods through trade, such as sugar and spices. Merchants bought so many spices in bulk, *en gros* in French, that they became known as "grocers." Strict rules existed for selling food in most towns and cities. These related to quality and price and where meat and other foods could be prepared or sold. For instance, in 1345, a London law banned people from bringing in chickens and selling them in the lanes or in secret. In the 1400s, a king of France directed that all slaughter houses should be outside the city of Paris because the city stank of dead meat and the Seine was polluted with the blood and remains of dead animals.

Prepared food could be bought in inns. William Fitz-Stephen, writing before 1183, described roast, fried, and boiled birds and fish, and venison for the rich, being prepared on the Thames riverbank in London. Pictures depict tripe being prepared, cooked, and eaten in 14th Century Lombardy, France. Cook shops provided hot food to take away while inns provided drinks and hot meals. Descriptions exist of the population of Florence in the 14th Century consuming yearly: 4,000 oxen, 60,000 sheep, 20,000 goats, and 30,000 pigs.

THE BANQUET

In common with other opportunities for ceremonial display and pageantry, the banquet, either as a private celebration or as a great state occasion, became more and more stylized and elaborate as the Middle Ages progressed. Banqueting had always played an important part in the social life of knights, and even in the early Middle Ages was used to mark occasions, such as weddings, betrothals, comings-of-age, and tournaments. By the 14th and 15th Centuries even everyday dinner had become somewhat ritualized; the knight dined in his Hall with the entire household gathered.

Medieval banquets were great occasions, when the chef would stretch his ingenuity to the utmost to decorate, and even to disguise, the dishes served. Often there would be some form of entertainment for the guests with musicians in the minstrels' gallery. Sometimes there would be a jester in fanciful clothes who could sing rude songs or make bad jokes about those around him without fear of retribution. Nobody took the jester seriously because he was often mentally ill. Mummers were a favorite.

A feast might have three courses and at the end of each course a *sotelte*, a carved hard-sugar sculpture was presented to delight the guests; sometimes it was edible. New trenchers would be served before each course and there might be a procession to bring in a special dish, such as a decorated swan. The wealthiest lords had a steward who ran the household. Beneath him, the chief official at the feast was the marshal, followed by other ranks in charge of the various aspects of the meal: sewer (head waiter and taster); the pantler or panter (head of the pantry); the butler (in

MENU FOR A FRENCH ROYAL WEDDING BANQUET IN 1403

INSTRUCTIONS—Place first meat course side by side with first fish course and so on down the numbers.

I FIRST MEAT COURSE

- Head of wild boar, armed with tusks and decorated, served with a hot spicy gravy and a pudding of rice, spices, wine, and honey
- Cygnets, chickens, pheasants, herons
- Puddings
- A sotelte

I FIRST FISH COURSE

- Soup, salty fish, spiced lampreys
- Pyke, bream, roast salmon
- Fish pies
- Fritters
- A sotelte

II SECOND MEAT COURSE

- Venison cooked with frumenty and served with a jelly
- Stuffed piglets
- Rabbits, bitterns, stuffed chicken, partridge
- Bread and dried fruits, sliced and fried
- A sotelte

II SECOND FISH COURSE

- Porpoise with frumenty and a jelly
- Bream, salmon, eels, lampreys in batter, plaice
- Bread and dried fruits, sliced and fried
- A sotelte in the shape of a crowned panther

III THIRD MEAT COURSE

- Cream of almonds, pears in syrup
- Venison roasted Woodcock, plover, rabbits, quails, fieldfare pies
- A sotelte

III THIRD FISH COURSE

- Cream of almonds, pears in syrup
- Grilled tench, trout, fried flounders, perch
- Roast lampreys, sturgeon, crabs, and shrimps
- A sotelte in the shape of a crowned eagle

A lord enjoys his meal. Some recipes could be extremely complicated, such as the stuffing of one bird inside another, starting with a small songbird, then a pigeon followed by a chicken and ending with a goose. All cooked together with accompanying spices to create the final flavors.

This 15th-Century illustration depicts a feast in the Great Hall. The variety of food on offer to the guests was a clear indication of the social standing of the lord's household.

charge of drinks); the ewerer (in charge of hand-washing and linen), the chief cook, the carver, and the lord's cup-bearer (whose onerous task it was to taste the lord's drink in case it was poisoned). All these people had underlings except the last two: waiters, assistant waiters, assistant cooks, scullions and spit-boys and pot-boys and washers up. At an English state feast, the duties of the major household officials were carried out by noblemen, who would receive generous gifts for his service. The king or major lord holding the feast would be ritually served first with all his dishes being tasted, probably by the steward, for fear of poison. Only after the tastings could the guests sit down. The wine and ale tastings took place as the first roast was being served.

Medieval books of etiquette instructed guests to wash their hands properly, in order not to soil the tablecloth with fingermarks; not to drink from a shared cup if their mouth was full of food; not to slurp soup; pick their teeth with their knife; blow on their food; or wipe their mouth with the tablecloth. If a guest was sharing a dish, he should not stick his fingers in too deeply, or crumble bread into it in case he had sweaty fingers, or leave his dirty spoon in it. Belching and spitting were frowned upon, and so was scratching one's head at the table and gnawing or sucking on bones.

In the Middle Ages, a much broader range of animals, and particularly birds, was eaten. Swans and peacocks were popular for banquets, dressed as a magnificent centerpiece with a cured skin fitted over a wire frame on top of the roasted meat, so they appeared sitting upright; particularly effective with the gorgeous tail of a peacock displayed. Other birds included crane, heron, bustard, gull, egret, curlew, and, in smaller sizes, blackbird, lark, quail, plover, lapwing, thrush, snipe, and bittern, besides the more familiar game birds such as partridge and pheasant. Dishes full of tiny carcasses would be served, and formed an important element of any state banquet at which clergymen, who were forbidden to eat the meat of quadrupeds, would be present. In the later Middle Ages, the bird that formed the central dish of a banquet was often used as a symbol for the swearing of elaborate oaths, as in the poem *The Vows of the Heron*.

Contact with more sophisticated cultures through the Crusades and generally through trade led to widespread use of exotic imported foodstuffs, including spices, citrus fruits, dried fruits such as raisins and figs, almonds, and cane sugar. The use of spices in cooking for the wealthy probably resulted in more highly flavored food than modern palates would appreciate.

After-meal entertainment would be, in addition to jesters and mummers, jugglers, minstrels, actors, or mime artists. Often the entertainment would be enactments of scenes from famous romances or from great moments in history. In later medieval times, they became incredibly elaborate, as at the marriage feast of Charles the Bold, Duke of Burgundy, to Margaret of York in 1468. On that occasion, there were six days of jousting, followed by feasts at which various tableaux were presented, including the Twelve Labors of Hercules, a model of the Duke's new castle at Gorcum filled with singers dressed as wild animals, a collection of gardens containing golden trees with golden leaves and fruit, the event having been planned around a romance whose hero

SING A SONG OF SIXPENCE,

A POCKET FULL OF RYE,

FOUR AND TWENTY BLACKBIRDS,

BAKED IN A PIE;

WHEN THE PIE WAS OPENED,

THE BIRDS BEGAN TO SING;

WAS NOT THAT A DAINTY DISH

TO SET BEFORE THE KING?

A popular English children's rhyme believed to date from the Middle Ages.

Traveling players provided entertainment for the lord and his family and retainers as shown in this 14th-Century drawing.

RECIPES

The following recipes are a selection from various manuscripts in the British Museum, which were collected by the 18th Century 1st and 2nd Earls of Oxford. They were sold to parliament by the Countess of Oxford and her daughter, the Duchess of Portland in 1753. Written originally in old English, many of the recipes can still be followed today, once translated into the modern idiom.

SALAD

Salat: 'Take parsel, sawge, garlic, chibollas, oynons, leek, borage, myntes, porrectes, fenel, and ton tressis, rew, rosemarye, purslayne, lave, and waishe hem clene. Pike hem, pluk hem small with thyn hond and myng hem wel with rawe oile. Lay on vinegar and salt and serve it forth.' (John Russell's *Boke of Nurture*)

Use some or all of the following vegetables and herbs:

Spring onions, leeks, baby onions, large onions, fennel, garlic, purslane, parsley, sage, borage, mint, watercress, rue, rosemary

For the dressing:

Olive or walnut oil, white wine vinegar, salt

Wash and clean the vegetables and herbs.

Pick over, prepare and slice the vegetables thinly, and grate the garlic.

Shred the herbs by hand. Mix with enough oil to moisten. Sprinkle with vinegar and salt, and serve at once.

RASTONS

Rastons were small round loaves or large rolls, made of sweetened bread dough enriched with eggs, like a brioche paste. After baking, the tops were cut off 'in the maner of a crown', and the crumb was removed, leaving hollow shells. The crumb was finely chopped with a knife and mixed with clarified butter. It was then replaced in the hollowed bread crusts. The tops were replaced and the loaves or rolls were returned to the oven for a few moments to heat through. (Harleian MS 279)

Small rolls are more practical for modern meals.

Make a brioche paste, and bake it in deep bun tins.

When baked, cut off the tops, remove the crumb with a spoon, crumble and mix with just enough clarified butter to moisten.

Replace the tops and return to the oven for five to seven minutes.

HOT WINE BEVERAGE

A *caudle* was a hot wine drink thickened with eggs, which was drunk at breakfast or bedtime. This was a version for Lent or Fridays when, strictly, eggs were not allowed. (*The Forme of Cury*)

- 11 fl.oz. (275 ml) water
- 30 fl.oz. (850 ml) white wine
- 8 oz (225 g) ground almonds
- 1/2 tsp (2.5 ml) ground ginger
- 1 tsp (5 ml) clear honey or white sugar
- a good pinch of salt
- a good pinch of powdered saffron or a
- few drops of yellow food coloring

Bring the water and wine to the boil in a saucepan.

Tip in the almonds, and add the ginger, honey or sugar, and salt. Stir in the saffron or food coloring, and leave off the heat to steep for 15 to 30 minutes.

Bring back to the boil, and serve very hot, in small heatproof bowls.

LENTEN STEW

'*Soupes dorroy*' was listed as a pottage (soup-stew), so the original recipe can be interpreted as either a soup or a semisolid main dish for my lord's Lenten dinner, depending on how much liquid is used. From the way it is written, this version of the recipe (there are several) seems to be a main dish. (Harleian MS 279)

- 8 large onions
- 4 fl.oz. (125 ml) sunflower oil for frying
- 4 oz (100 g) ground almonds
- 1/2 tsp (2.5 ml) honey
- A pinch of salt
- 5 1/4 fl.oz. (150 ml) boiling water
- 5 1/4 fl.oz. (150 ml) white wine
- 8 rounds of "white" bread or brioche, crusts removed, about 1 in. (3 cm) thick

Slice the onions into rings, and simmer them in the oil, turning often, until soft and golden.

Put the almonds in a small saucepan. Mix the honey and salt into the water, and pour it over the almonds with half the wine. Leave to soak for 10 minutes, stirring occasionally.

Meanwhile toast the bread lightly on both sides. Lay the slices side by side in a shallow dish.

Add the remaining wine to the onions, and simmer until they are reheated through.

Heat the almond milk until steaming and pour it over the toast slices. Pile the onions on top.

SAUCE VERT

'Take percely, myntes, diteyne, peletre, a foil or ij of cost marye, a cloue of garleke. And take faire brede, and stepe it with vynegre and piper, and salt; and grynde al this to-gedre, and temper it up with wynegre, or with easel, and serve it for the.' (Ashmole MS 1439)

Suggested proportions:

Leaves of 10–12 sprigs parsley, mint and other fresh herbs

1 garlic clove

2 oz (50 g) of fine "white" bread crumbs

2 tbls (30 ml) cider vinegar

Freshly ground black pepper

Wine vinegar, and/or water as needed.

Chop the herbs finely. Parsley and mint should predominate. Squeeze the garlic over the herbs in a mortar.

Sprinkle the breadcrumbs with the cider vinegar and leave for 10 minutes.

Add to the herbs with salt and pepper. Pound until well blended. Then add enough wine vinegar or water, or a mixture, to give you a consistency rather like thickened mint sauce (or green bread sauce).

Serve with broiled or poached fish.

DATE SLICES WITH SPICED WINE

There are several old versions of this favorite medieval recipe: *leche lumbard.* This is an excellent dish for today since it keeps for 2–3 weeks in a refrigerator if left unsliced. (Harleian MS 4016)

$1^3/_4$ lb (800 g) stoneless black dates

$16^1/_2$ fl.oz. (425 ml) medium dry white wine

3 oz (75 g) light soft brown sugar

$^1/_2$ tsp (2.5 ml) cinnamon

$^1/_2$ tsp (2.5 ml) ground ginger

6 hardboiled egg yolks

about 6 oz (175 g) soft brown breadcrumbs (not wholemeal)

3–4 tbls (45–60 ml) Madeira heated with a pinch of mixed spice.

Break up the dates and simmer with wine and sugar until pulpy. Pound or put through a food processor until almost smooth. Mix in the spices and sieve or work in the egg yolks.

In a bowl, knead in enough breadcrumbs to make the mixture as stiff as marzipan. Form it into a 2 inch (5 cm) diameter roll, and chill until firm. Cut into $^1/_5$ inch (5 mm) slices.

Arrange in overlapping lines on a plate, and trickle a drop or two of cooled, spiced wine over each slice.

was Florimont, the Knight of the Golden Tree. To crown it all, on the final evening, guests were treated to the appearance of a large mechanical whale, which opened up to reveal sirens singing, accompanied by giants fighting a mock-battle against twelve knights. This was the kind of lavish spectacle that would develop into the masques of the 17th Century.

The cycle of farming on the lands of the manor, *above*, sowing wheat in the spring, *below*, threshing wheat in the late summer.

THE MANOR

When the Normans arrived in England, they introduced an administrative unit known as the 'manor', which was a holding of a feudal lord, being an economic, political, and judicial unit. The typical manor comprised a village, the lord's manor house, the arable, pasture, and meadows of the unfree and the free tenants, plus common land, woodland, and waste land. They often coincided with a parish. Ideally, the manor possessed 2,000 acres of arable land with the same amount of other lands, being a self-contained community. The holder of the lands was a fief holder. Several villages might be located on a manor but the peasants were the farmers producing the crops under the direction of the lord's overseer. They farmed the meat and draught oxen, paid taxes in services and were required as forced labor on the lord's lands and sometimes were expected to fight.

A large manor might have a water-driven mill for grinding grain, fish ponds, a bakery, orchards, herb and vegetable gardens, and skeps (wicker or straw beehives) for making honey. The sheep produced wool for yarn and clothes, while linen from flax could make finer clothing or be farmed for its oil. The peasants produced the ordinary food for the manor such as ducks, geese, pigeons, chickens, fish pork, beef, and mutton, as well as a range of vegetables such as carrots, turnips, cabbages, onions, and peas and beans (part of the staple diet of ordinary people). Fruit was grown, dairy products and alcohol produced. The manor would normally have a blacksmith, carpenter, and wheelwright who could make agricultural implements and carts.

The medieval manor was almost completely self sufficient and produced much of its own food, including keeping bees for collecting honey.

The manor operated a crop rotation system. Arable land was divided into fields: one for growing wheat or rye, sown in fall; a second sown in spring with barley, rye, oats, beans, or peas; a third left fallow. Fields were divided into strips without hedges or fences to separate them. Each male householding peasant would receive about 30 strips spread over good and bad land. He would work under the authority of the lord's overseer, but if he owned his own strips would follow village custom. The harvest would use all men, women, and children; the community's animals could forage on the fields afterwards. The lord's strips were also distributed through good and bad land and occasionally the parish priest might have his own strips that he farmed himself. The lord's needs were paramount and only about three days a week would be left for peasants to work their own strips and garden plots. Woodland held in common would produce wood and beech mast (the fruit of the tree used as pig food) and the animals were pastured on the village meadows. Food and agricultural surpluses would be sold at market.

Religion

MEDIEVAL CHURCHES WERE NOT ONLY PLACES OF WORSHIP, BUT ALSO THEY WERE COMMUNITY CENTERS PROVIDING A VENUE FOR SOCIAL, JUDICIAL, AND COMMERCIAL EVENTS. MANY WERE PROSPEROUS CULT CENTERS, WITH THE SHRINES OF SAINTS ATTRACTING PILGRIMS FROM ACROSS EUROPE.

A baptism, a detail from a German manuscript of the early 9th Century.

The triumph of the Christianity to which early knighthood adhered so strongly was not a guaranteed event. The nascent Church of the 4th Century witnessed the persecution of many Christians, the continued existence of paganism, the birth of different forms of competing Christianities, and a papacy beset by Byzantine control and competition with the Orthodox rite. However, the simple Christian message defeated pagan pantheons of gods and goddesses and its readily understood ethical and social message appealed so much that paganism was swiftly sidelined.

The organization of Christianity with its churches and bishops could match that of a state, and militant Christianity could convert with the sword. The Church was clever, too, in the use of saints and martyrs who superseded the mass of pagan deities together with religious festivals on pagan feast days. The first Christian state was Armenia, then Roman Emperor Constantine I (274–337) extended toleration to Christians in 313 by the Edict of Milan. He donated the Lateran Palace to the Bishop of Rome, converted to the faith, attacked paganism, turning the state Christian in 337.

The religion spread to the German peoples: the Burgundians, Lombards, and Vandals. These peoples turned to an alternative version of Christianity, Arianism, which possessed a deviant vision of the Holy Trinity. Was God the Father separate from God the Son as the Arians thought, or was one an aspect of the other, or were they both distinct and similar? The dispute was supposed to have been settled at a conference in Nicaea in 325 which made Arianism a heresy, while supporting Bishop Athanasius' view that Christ and God were the same substance, consubstantiability. However, strife over the subject continued until the reign of Theodosius.

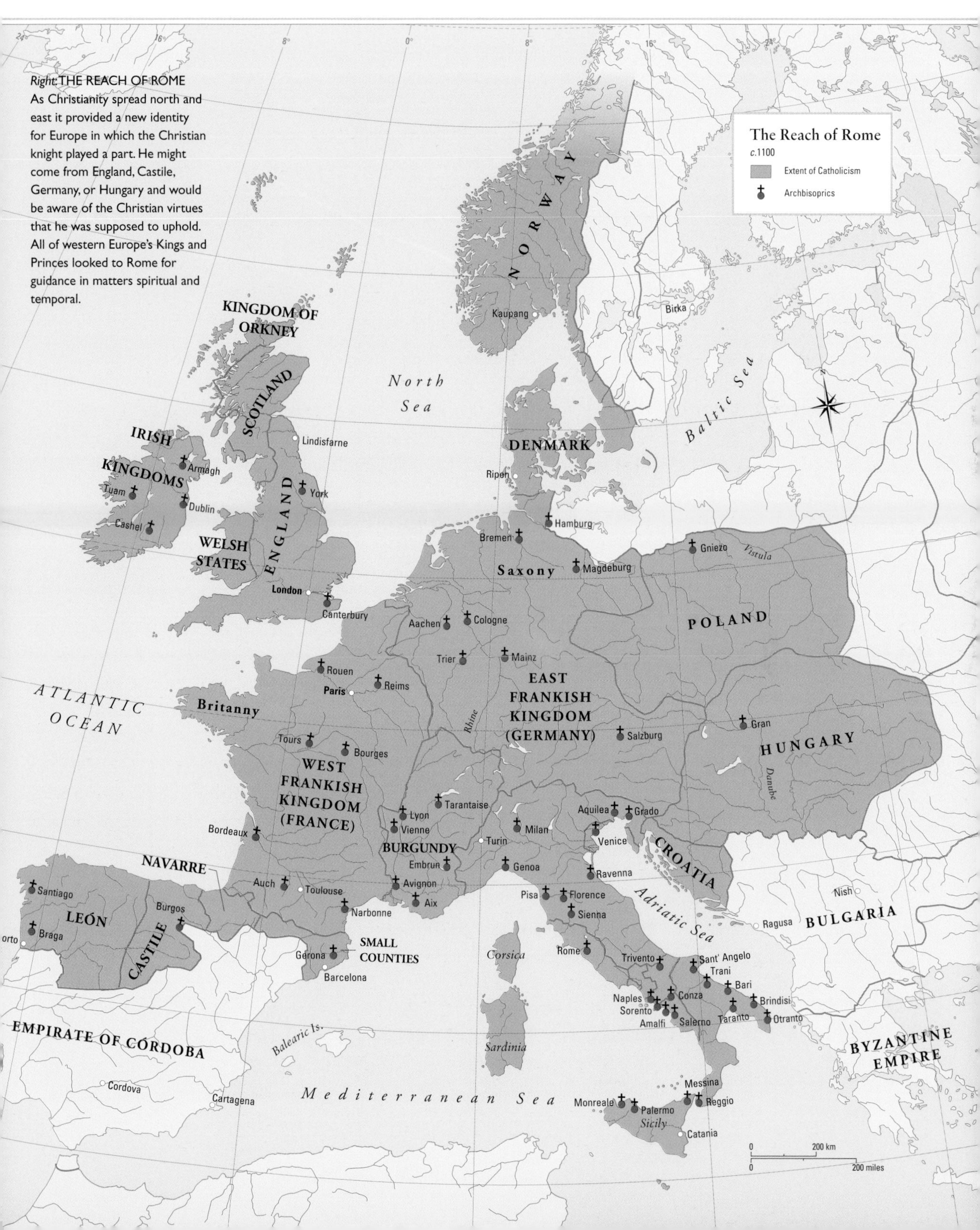

Right: THE REACH OF ROME
As Christianity spread north and east it provided a new identity for Europe in which the Christian knight played a part. He might come from England, Castile, Germany, or Hungary and would be aware of the Christian virtues that he was supposed to uphold. All of western Europe's Kings and Princes looked to Rome for guidance in matters spiritual and temporal.

This pope, believed to be Gregory VII, at Monte Cassino, c. 1087, is seen in an illustration from Exultet Rolls of southern Italy. The pope, who ruled the faithful from Rome, was seen as the absolute ruler of the Christian religion though there were arguments with secular authorities. The pope, however, invariably got his way.

Shortly after Nicaea, the Church was torn by the monophysite heresy whose doctrine was that Christ had a single nature. The orthodox doctrine that Christ combined divine and human qualities, was supported by Pope Leo of Rome at the Council of Chalcedon (451). The Bishops of Rome (papas) had by that time been called popes and the Bishop of Rome had become Supreme Bishop as other rival bishoprics passed into the hands of invading barbarians. The Eastern Emperors tended to be monophysite while the west supported Leo.

The importance of the heresies lies in their political nature. In early medieval times, discontent was not expressed in terms of national identity. However, minority peoples could oppose a central power by adopting a heresy as being a form of patriotism. Also, as German Arianists invaded ordinary Catholics, they kept their religious identity lest they be absorbed into the faith of the conquered, seeing that the Germans were a minority élite. However, the Franks under Clovis, adopted Catholicism, this helping him against the Arian Visigoths.

Meanwhile, the Roman Papacy was becoming the largest landowner in Italy as wealthy families donated land to the Church. The revenue from these patrimonies administered the Church, built religious edifices, equipped convents, paid the papal household, and supported the clergy. The papacy looked after poorhouses, hospitals, orphanages, and hospices for pilgrims, and fed Rome, thereby relieving the Emperor in the East of his obligations. These temporal tasks meant that the papacy became the champion of the poor and oppressed and when the Lombards invaded Italy the popes helped their Roman subjects become something other than Lombard or Byzantine, the beginning of that which became Italian as the West became isolated from Constantinople.

PAPAL STATES

As time progressed, the papacy became political in its work, a response to events elsewhere. The remaining Western emperors moved the capital to the more easily defensible Ravenna, eventually taken by Odoacer's Visigoths. When the Byzantines marched back in they established the Exarchate of Ravenna (today's Romagna), ruled by an exarch, a Byzantine viceroy.

Elsewhere, in Rome, the popes stood as a bastion against invaders with Leo I interceding with Attila the Hun (451) and Gelasius with Theodoric the Ostrogoth. Under Justinian, the papacy became a loyal supporter of Byzantine rule for 200 years against the encroachments of Lombards. The papacy also became a protector of Romans against Byzantine tax exactions generating the response of cities in central Italy building their own citizen's militias, backing and defending a papacy that they helped elect. When the Byzantine emperors attempted to smash this independent papacy, the Roman militia defended it. When Emperor Justinian II tried to kidnap Pope Sergius II, as had happened to Pope Martin I, the militias of Ravenna and of the Duchy of the Pentapolis (Rimini, Pesaro, Fano, Sinigaglia, Ancona, with Perugia, today's Marches) and kicked out the emperor's agents. Central Italy was developing a sense of unity and purpose, backed by the pope against any enemy. The papacy decided that the Eastern Empire with its religious iconoclasm developed by Emperor Leo III was no longer adequate protection against invading Lombards.

As the Lombards moved south in Italy, the old Byzantine duchy of Rome, Roman Tuscany north of the Tiber, and the Campagna south to Garigliano, and the Exarchate of Ravenna were linked geostrategically by the Duchy of Pentapolis, an obstacle to the Lombards, despite a temporary breakthrough when the Lombards managed to establish the Duchies of Spoleto and Benevento. Thus, Pentapolis was essential for the Rome-Ravenna axis but also for the northern and southern Lombard link. In 728, Lombard King Liutprand took the Castle of Sutri, which dominated the road to Perugia, but Pope Gregory II persuaded the religious king to hand it over as gift to the Apostles Peter and Paul, thereby strengthening the popular notion that Roman lands were defended by the Princes of the Church: the popes. However, Liutprand conquered the Lombard Duchy of Spoleto, ravaged the Duchy of Rome, besieged Rome, and seized important frontier fortresses. Pope Gregory III requested help from Charles Martel, mayor of the palace for the Merovingian Franks, but he was the Lombards' ally against the Saracens, and stuck to that alliance. The next pope, Zacharias, played off against each other Liutprand and the Lombard Duke Transamund and managed to save some lands from Lombard victories.

As the Christian Church expanded and grew rich on land ownership, major building projects were undertaken filling the landscape of Europe with major new stone buildings. This miniature by Girart de Roussillon, dates from around 1448 and shows stonemasons and builders at work.

In 751, Lombard King Aistulf conquered Ravenna laying open to seizure the entire exarchate and the Pentapolis. With these under his belt, and with Spoleto in his orbit, Aistulf turned all his energies against Rome. The new pope, Stephen II, would receive no help from Byzantium, so taking the advice of Emperor Constantine V, he made overtures to King Pepin of the Franks who had recently usurped (751) the Merovingian throne with Pope Zacharias' blessing. Pope Stephen crossed the Alps, reaching St. Denis near Paris where he anointed Pepin, his wife and sons, concluding an alliance whereby the Pope threatened to excommunicate anyone who failed to back the new Carolingian dynasty, while gifting Pepin with the title Patrician of the Romans, normally given to the ranking Byzantine official in Italy. Rome had now replaced their Byzantine protector.

In 754, Pepin, his army, and the pope marched into Italy forcing Aistulf to sue for peace. He promised to return the Exarchate and Pentapolis, which would be given by Pepin to the Church. However, when Pepin returned to France, the Lombard reneged on the agreement and besieged Rome. Pepin returned to Italy (756) trapping Aistulf in his capital at Pavia. The pope then received the Donation of 754: the Exarchate, the Pentapolis, and Commachio at the mouth of the River Po. These lands were now the temporal territory of the Holy See, being seized from the Lombards and crushing any idea of Byzantine sovereignty since the Greeks had not defended their Italian lands. These Papal States were the remnant of the Western Roman Empire, their existence guaranteeing papal independence and freedom from outside interference while linking the papacy to a new western civilization backed by Carolingian power and, when that empire collapsed, upon feudalism and nascent knightly strength.

When Pepin attacked the Lombards on behalf of the papacy, he ensured that the French home of European knighthood was firmly linked to the western concept of Christianity. He saw himself as defending the right belonging to St. Peter; he acted as an organ that righted a wrong inflicted by the Lombards on St. Peter and the papacy. From this point, the Franks were tied to the defense of Christian values. Pepin's son, Charlemagne, continued to support the papacy against the Lombards, capturing Lombardy and making himself king. A new territorial agreement was made in 781 based upon Pepin's Donation. The pope was to receive the Duchy of Rome, the Exarchate, Pentapolis plus

Far right: THE VATICAN CITY The Holy See's diplomatic history began in the 4th Century. However, the borders of the papacy's temporal power have moved over the centuries. Originally the popes ruled over a large portion of the Italian peninsula for over 1000 years. In the modern era, after the unification of Italy, the new Italian state, under Victor Emmanuel, seized the papal lands between 1860 and 1870 thus ending papal temporal power. Finally, three treaties resolved outstanding issues between the papacy and the Italian state in 1929, establishing the independent state of the Vatican City.

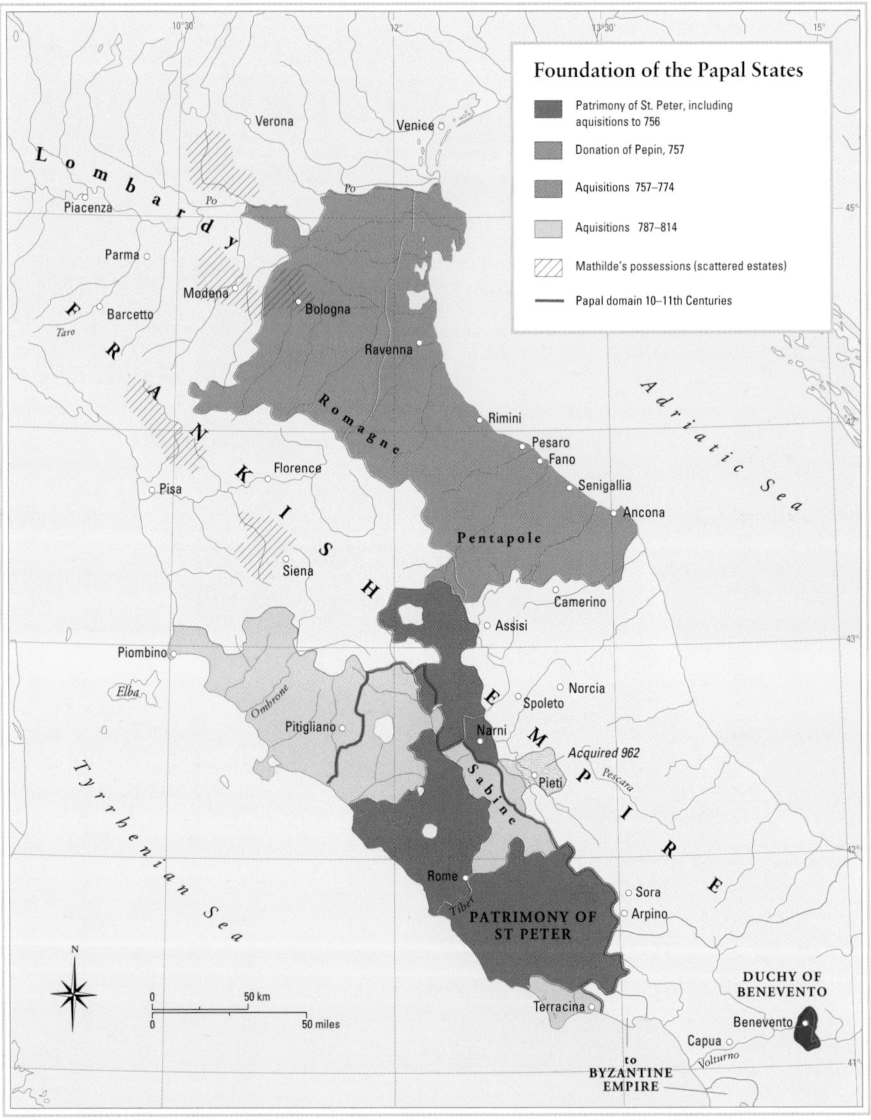

Foundation of the Papal States

- Patrimony of St. Peter, including aquisitions to 756
- Donation of Pepin, 757
- Aquisitions 757–774
- Aquisitions 787–814
- Mathilde's possessions (scattered estates)
- Papal domain 10–11th Centuries

The Castel Sant' Angelo. This commanding fortress overlooking the Tiber River, a little to the east of the Vatican City, was constructed over the remains of Emperor Hadrian's ruined family mausoleum. The medieval fortress was later modernized by Pope Alexander VI at the beginning of the 16th Century to include bastions for artillery. The popes were among the most progressive patrons of military architecture.

Imola, Bologna, Faenza, Ferrara, Osimo, and Umana. Patrimonies were also listed in the Sabine, in Spoleto, Benevento, Calabria, Tuscany, and Corsica. In 787, Charlemagne increased papal holdings with new gifts: Capua and some frontier cities of the Duchy of Benevento in addition to several cities in Lombardy and Tuscany, such as Populonia, Roselle, Sovana, Toscanella, Viterbo, Bagnorea, Orvieto, Ferento, Orchia, Marta, and Città di Castello. The relationship between Charlemagne and the papacy was substantiated when the pope crowned him emperor in 800. When Pope Stephen IV anointed Charlemagne's son, Louis, as western Emperor of the Romans in 816 at Rheims, a link was established between the emperor and God, officiated by the pope. This anointing distinguished

1. St. Peter's Basilica
2. Bernini's Bronze Doors
3. Bernini's Colonnade
4. St. Peter's Square (Piazza San Pietro)
5. Tower of Nicholas V
6. Apostolic Palace
7. Courtyard of San Damaso
8. Courtyard of the Marshal
9. Courtyard of the Parrot
10. Borgia Courtyard
11. Courtyard of the Sentinel
12. Sistine Chapel
13. Borgia Tower
14. Borgia Apartment
Collection of Modern Religious Art
Raphael Stanze (2nd floor)
15. St. Anne Gate
16. Church of St. Anne of the Palafrenieri
17. Vatican Printing Press
18. Vatican Post Office
19. Tapestry Workshop
20. Church of San Pellegrino
21. Offices of L'Osservatore Romano
22. Lapidary Gallery
23. Courtyard of the Belvedere
24. Vatican Library
Sacred Museum
Gallery of Maps (2nd floor)
25. Vatican Library
26. Courtyard of the Library
27. Tower of the Winds
28. Braccio Nuovo (New Arm)
29. Chiaramonto Museum
30. Courtyard of the Pine
31. Belvedere Niche
32. Vatican Library
Profane Museum
Gallery of the Tapastries
Gallery of the Candelabra (2nd floor)
33. Gregorian Egyptian Museum
Gregorian Etruscan Museum (2nd floor)
34. Pio-Clementine Museum
35. Octagonal Courtyard
36. Belvedere of Innocent VIII
37. Stairs of Bramante
38. Casina of Pius IV
39. Historical Museum (Underground)
40. Pinacoteca (Picture Gallery)
41. Gregorian Profane Museum
Pio-Christian Museum
Pontificial Missionary-Ethnology Museum
42. Entrance to the Vatican Museums
43. Vatican Gardens
44. Vatican Radio Station
45. Pontifical Ethiopian Museum
46. Palace of the Governorate of Vatican City
47. Floral arrangement in honor of the reigning Pontiff (displaying the Papal Coat of Arms)
48. Church of St. Stephen of the Abyssinians
49. Palace of the Tribunal
50. Mosaic Workshop
51. Railway Station
52. Tower of St. John
53. Palace of St. Charles
54. Sacristy and Treasury of St. Peter's
55. Piazza of the Protomartyrs
56. Arch of the Bells
57. Audience Hall (Aula)
58. Palace of the Congregation for the Doctrine of the Faith (Holy Office)
59. Holy Office Square
60. Church of San Martino degli Svizzeri (Church of the Swiss Guard)

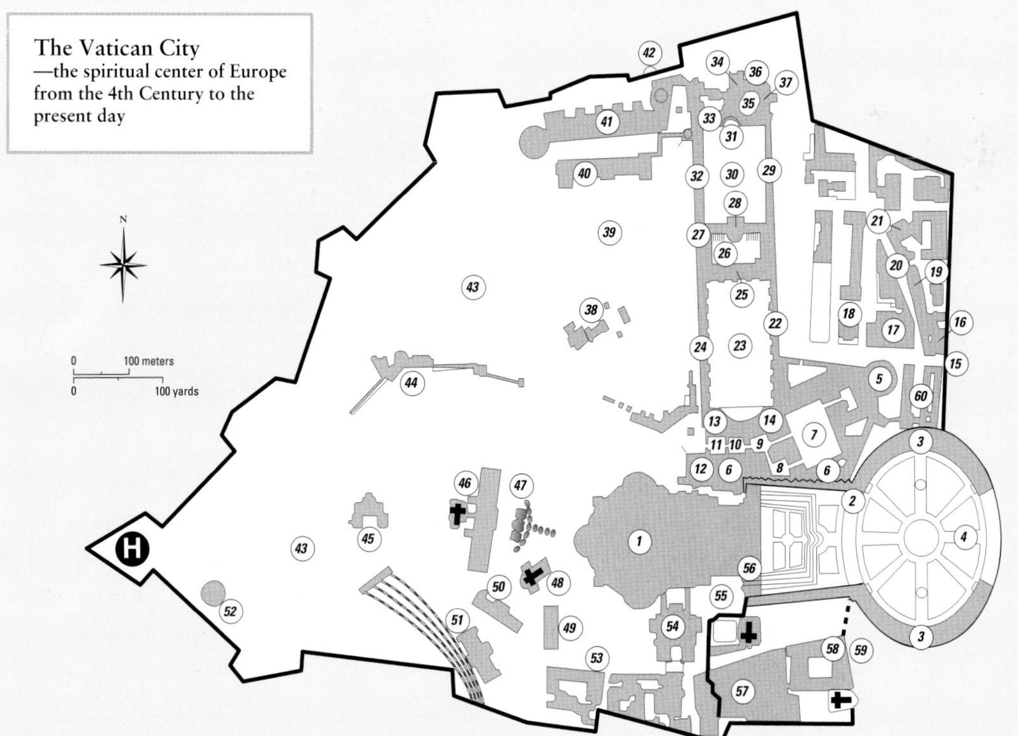

The Vatican City
—the spiritual center of Europe from the 4th Century to the present day

As the number of orders grew, they each had distinctive dress, above are the Franciscans. *Below left*: are Benedictines at prayer. There were seven regular services, starting from 2.30 am to 7.30 pm; they were Lauds, Prime, Tierce, Sext, None, Even Song, and Compline.

the imperial coronation in the west from that practiced in Constantinople. It was based upon the Old Testament; Stephen greeted Louis as "a second David." Thus, the pope intimated that Louis was a bastion of Rome against heresy and anything described as anti-Christ and the emperor's Christian knight service was the force to uphold the papacy. When the West Frankish king, Charles the Bald, was crowned emperor in 875, he gave new donations from Spoleto and Benevento.

The popes, sometimes puppets of local feudal lords, managed to maintain their sovereignty over lands throughout the Middle Ages, even acquiring the Duchy of Benevento in 1077. Even the dispute with the German Holy Roman Emperors that lasted from the mid-11th Century Investiture Controversy to the 14th Century failed to weaken papal control. Another problem occurred over the allodial lands (free of rent or service) of the Countess of Tuscany, donated to the papacy in 1102 but passing into Emperor Henry V's hands (1111). Papal sovereignty was often more notional than actual because many papal towns were ruled by local families. From the mid-15th Century, under the Renaissance popes, notably Julius II (1503–13), the Papal States reached their final boundaries, stretching from Parma and Bologna in the north, along the Adriatic coast, through Umbria, to the Campagna, south of Rome, but they were no longer a force in international politics.

RELIGIOUS ORDERS

Orders other than the Cistercians existed during the Middle Ages. Western monasticism is attributed to St. Benedict of Nursia, who regularized existing monasticism, stressing the coenobitic (monsastic) life under the authority of an abbot and the Benedictine Rule. Manual labor and prayer

Europe 1328
Holy Roman Empire
Border
Norwegian Sea
North Sea
Baltic Sea
ATLANTIC OCEAN
Mediterranean Sea
Adriatic Sea
NORWAY
SWEDEN
DENMARK
SCOTLAND
IRELAND
WALES
ENGLAND
FRANCE
SMALL STATES
TEUTONIC ORDER
LITHUANIA
MAZONIA
POLAND
BRANDENBURG
BOHEMIA
MORAVIA
AUSTRIA
STYRIA
HUNGARY
LUX.
Guienne
Gascony
VENAISSIN
ORANGE
NAVARRE
ANDORA
PORTUGAL
CASTILE
ARAGON
GRANADA
KINGDOM OF MALLORCA
REPUBLIC OF GENOA
VENETIAN REPUBLIC
PAPAL STATES
NAPLES
BOSNIA
SERBIA
BYZANTINE EMPIRE
Corsica
Sardinia
Sicily
Rhine
Vistula
Danube
Trondhjem
Bergen
Oslo
Stockholm
Åbo
Helsingfors
Reval
Riga
Aarhus
Roskilde
Königsberg
Danzig
Glasgow
Edinburgh
York
Dublin
Chester
Cork
Hereford
Oxford
Bristol
London
Hamburg
Stettin
Bremen
Amsterdam
Utrecht
Hanover
Poznan
Warsaw
Rotterdam
Dresden
Breslaw
Calais
Cologne
Cracow
Prague
Frankfurt
Mainz
Rouen
Rheims
Metz
Nuremberg
Brünn
Paris
Strasbourg
Vienna
Pozsony
Esztergom
Buda
Orléans
Munich
Salzburg
Nantes
Tours
Dijon
Zurich
Innsbruck
Graz
Szeged
Bern
Pécs
Limoges
Geneva
Trieste
Zágráb
Temesvár
Lyon
Milan
Verona
Bordeaux
Turin
Venice
Belgrade
Genoa
Bologna
Corunna
Oviedo
Bayonne
Toulouse
Zara
Spalato
Nish
Bilbao
Avignon
Pisa
Montpellier
Nice
Florence
Mostar
Marseille
Oporto
Rome
Saragossa
Salamanca
Barcelona
Bari
Naples
Toledo
Taranto
Lisbon
Valencia
Cagliari
Córdova
Saville
Granada
Cartagena
Palermo
Messina
Cadiz
Malaga
Catania
Tangier
Algiers
Tunis
16°
8°
0°
24°
56°
52°
48°
44°
40°
36°
N

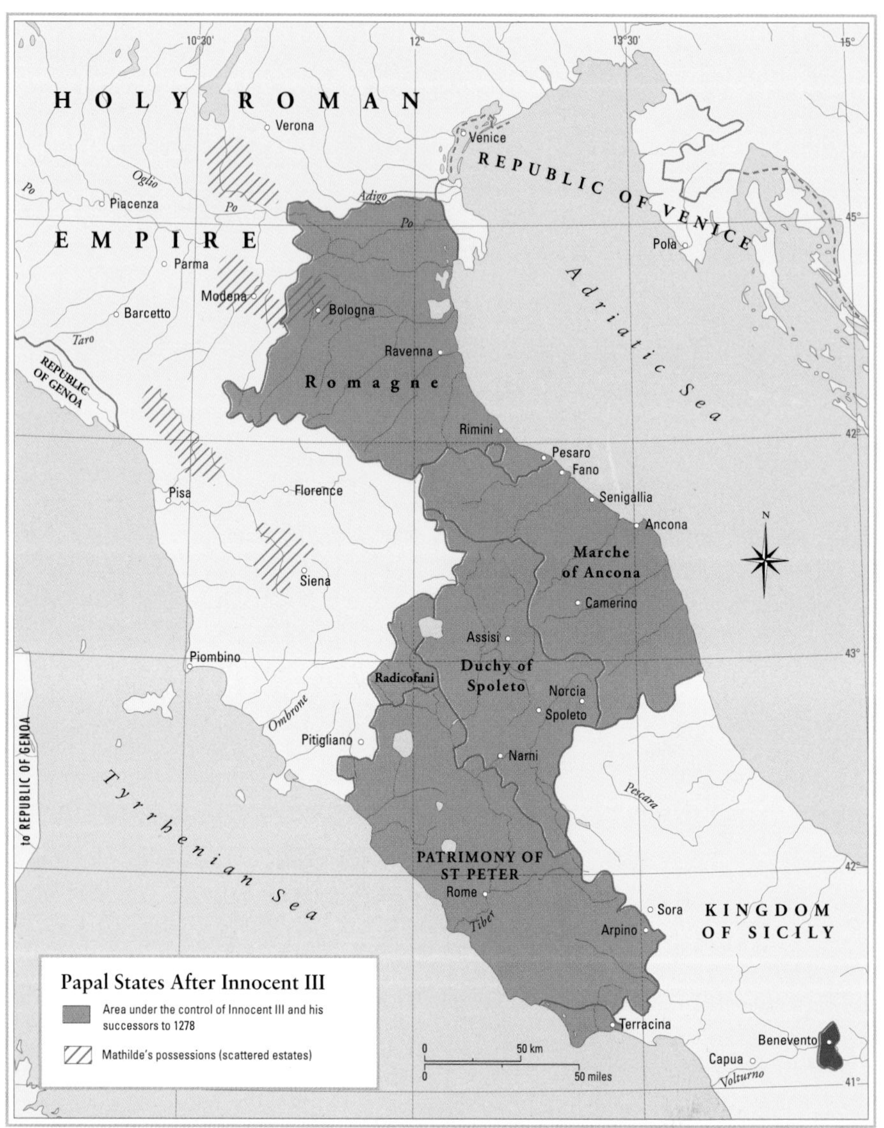

constituted the focus of monastic life and was reflected in the Benedictine motto, *Ora et Labora*. Manual labor was interpreted to include academic life.

Benedictines

The first 15 monasteries were founded at Subiaco, near Rome, by Benedict, in the 6th Century. Benedict later founded Monte Cassino. The Benedictine Rule did not impose harsh conditions on its monks who were well-clothed, fed, and housed. They engaged in devotional activities for four hours a day, slept for seven to eight hours, the remainder of the day being put aside for mainly

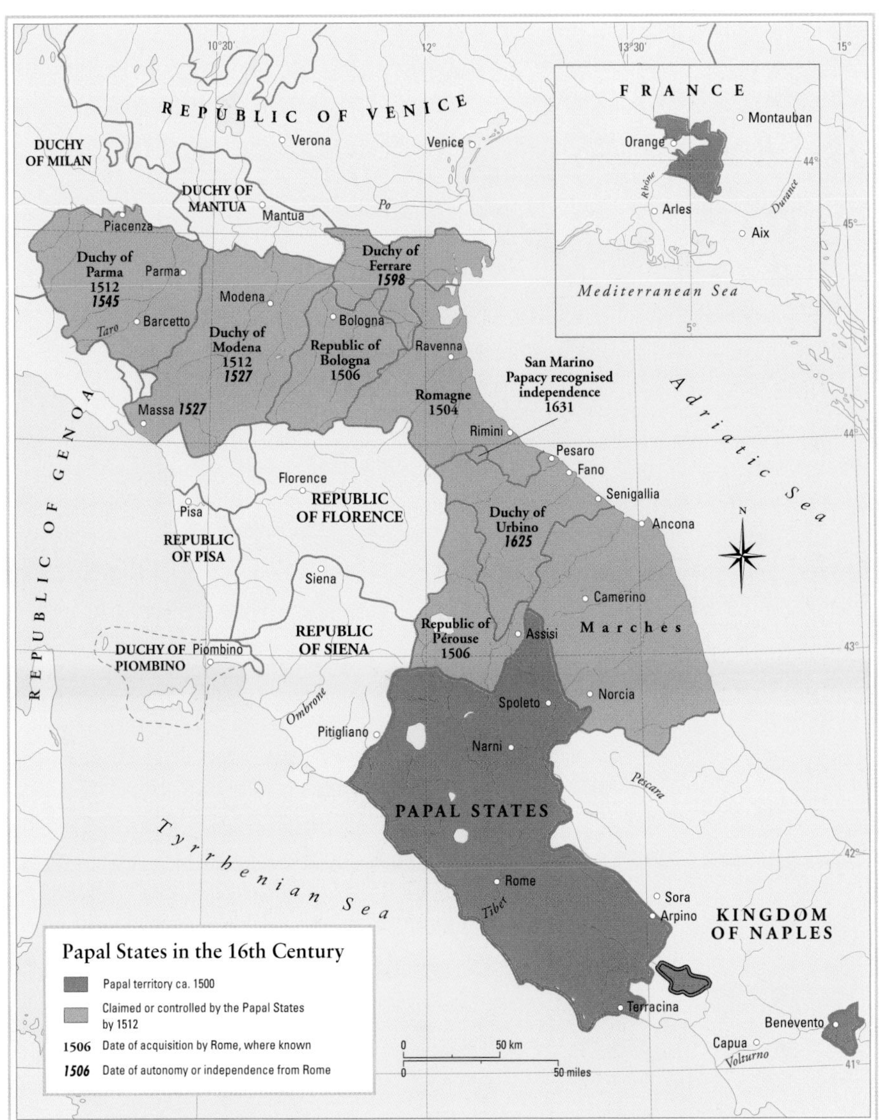

agricultural work, religious reading, and study. The Order became the most important in Europe until the 11th Century. Pope Gregory I was the first of 50 Benedictines who have been pope and many have been Archbishop of Canterbury in England. Many English cathedrals were originally Benedictine abbeys including Canterbury, Ely, Norwich, Winchester, and Durham.

Augustinians

The Augustinians followed the precepts of St. Augustine of Hippo. The Roman Synods of 1059 and 1063 wanted the clergy to adopt common rules with an active life in the lay community while following the monastic vows of poverty, chastity, and obedience. Many canons throughout Christendom gave up property and established quasimonastic groups that became the order of Augustinian Canons, their rule being endorsed by the pope at the Fourth Lateran Council.

Carthusians

Founded in 1084 by St. Bruno in the valley of Chartreuse near Grenoble, France, he and six companions wore poor clothing and lived on bread and vegetables. Each monk lived in a cell comprising a bed, library, raw materials room, and tool room. There was normally unbroken silence and the monks only left their cells on festivals, funerals, and a weekly communal meal. An order of Carthusian nuns was founded at Salette c. 1229. The Order is now famous for producing two liqueurs, green and yellow Chartreuse; the recipes are very old and no one knows when they were first created.

Dominicans

The Dominicans were founded in 1214 by St. Dominic at Toulouse, recognized by Pope Honorius III in 1216. They were granted the right to preach, educate, and hear confessions anywhere without permission. Dominic insisted on this policy after his experiences attempting to convert the Cathar about 1205. The Order was mendicant and by 1300 had 50 friaries housing these Black Friars in France, Spain, England, Scotland, Ireland, Italy, Bohemia, Russia, Greece, and Greenland.

Franciscans

Probably founded in 1208 by St. Francis of Assisi with Pope Innocent III's approval, Francis preached while espousing poverty and with some companions used a chapel of Santa Maria degli Angeli, living nearby in huts built from branches. Copying Christ, they became itinerant preachers, while practicing poverty. In 1223, Pope Honorius III made them into a formal order.

Premonstratensians

Otherwise known as Norbertines and in England as the White Canons, the Premonstratensians were founded by St. Norbert of Xanten at Prémontré, near Laon, France. They followed an austere version of the Rule of St. Augustine, place special devotion upon the Holy Eucharist and follow the monastic and apostolic life. By the 14th Century they had several hundred houses throughout Europe. Their churches, like the Cistercians, were dedicated to Our Lady.

Gilbertine

Founded by Gilbert of Sempringham in Lincolnshire, England, this was a community of men and women but kept separately.

Béguines

Although some women joined Holy Orders others acted more informally, many joining the *béguine* movement. These pious women first appeared in the Low Countries and the Rhineland in the early 13th Century and then spread through France, Switzerland, and central Europe. Many adherents were

CATHOLICISM AND ORTHODOXY c. 1000
Christianity had spread north from the Mediterranean basin with Catholicism spreading largely in the west and central Europe and Orthodox rite Christianity spreading through the Balkans and what was to become Russia.

members of the new affluent bourgeoisie and some lived in small houses and others in a large Béguinage within an enclosure. The members renounced worldly goods, adopted poverty, became celibate, and lived by working in hospitals or cloth manufacturing, and occasionally begging. The Béguines were often mystic and experienced visions. A Béguinage was established in Paris in 1264 with King Louis IX of France acting as a patron. Some male clerics suspected them of heresy. So, in 1310, Marguerite Porète was condemned and burnt, together with her mystical work, *The Mirror of Simple Souls.*

The Crusades

Crusading allowed violent, brutal land-hungry knights to become soldiers of Christ fighting the heathen. Knighthood became a holy vocation whereby knights could achieve salvation through the exercise of their martial skills.

During the 10th and 11th Centuries, the Church initiated two campaigns to reform and control the behavior of knights across Europe by ecclesiastical legislation known as the Peace of God and the Truce of God. Enacted between 990 and 1049, these laws were made in response to social conditions that threatened the peace and stability of the community at large, including the Church. The main source of disruption was the constant petty wars between rival lords, mainly conducted as a series of guerrilla raids on the territories of their enemies, destroying villages and their male populations if resistance was met, while stealing and slaughtering livestock. Robber barons carried this to excess by using strongly fortified castles from which they could extort goods from the local community and travelers. The civil war in England between Stephen of Blois and the Empress Matilda (1135–54) witnessed the civilian population being plundered for 19 years. Local lords were known to levy a tax, called the *tenserie,* a form of protection money.

The Peace of God and the Truce of God were designed to counteract such abuses. The Peace of God was supposed to protect noncombatants, and the Truce of God was to prevent hostilities at certain times. In 989 the Council of Charroux, at the abbey in La Marche on the borders of Aquitaine, pronounced that anyone who robbed churches or attacked an unarmed member of the clergy or stole from peasants would be excommunicated. The order was soon extended to include merchants and, in addition, prohibited certain acts such as destroying vineyards or mills. The Truce of God began modestly by reviving one of the capitularies of Charlemagne, which had forbidden the prosecution of blood-feuds on Sundays. By the time the Council of Nice sat in 1041, this had been extended to include Easter and other feast days, and war-making and plundering were forbidden from Thursday to Sunday. Most lords ignored such interference but the Church was boldly attempting to subject knights to its authority, bypassing secular authorities and its law enforcement. The Church was trying to assert ultimate temporal as well as spiritual authority in Christendom and was increasingly involved in the struggle for political power.

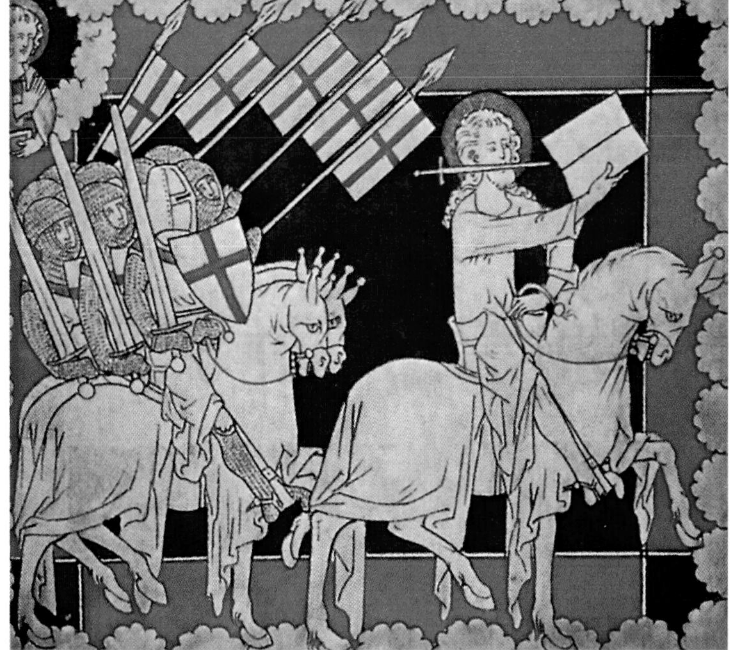

A 14th Century depiction of Christ himself leading English crusaders to Jerusalem. In liberating the most holy place in Christendom, the knights thought that they might pave their way into heaven or, at least, earn forgiveness for their past sins.

The revolutionary Pope Gregory VII said that laymen, peasants, and monarchs were subject to central authority of the papacy and must serve its interests in all aspects of life; in this scenario, knights were the "vassals of St. Peter." This pope completed the transformation of ecclesiastical pacifism to militancy. Earlier popes, such as Pope Leo IV in 853, had appealed for military support against the Saracens, the enemies of God and the Church. Gregory envisaged leading an army in person to the aid of the Christians of the Eastern Empire against the Turks, and to liberate Jerusalem. Instead, he became embroiled in a bitter quarrel with Emperor Henry IV over who should control the investiture of bishops in the German Empire. He excommunicated Henry and invited other applicants for the post of emperor. Henry retaliated by declaring Gregory deposed and created an alternative pope, Clement III, a 16-year-old relative. With the Imperial army at his command, Henry captured Rome in order to install Clement. Gregory, meanwhile, retreated behind the walls of the fortress of Sant' Angelo and summoned to his aid the army of Robert Guiscard, the Norman adventurer who had conquered southern Italy and Sicily. Robert repulsed Henry and released the pope. Eventually a compromise over investitures was reached, and the pope triumphed. However, he had achieved more than that; he claimed that knights fighting for him against the emperor would be rewarded with St. Peter's blessing "in this life and life to come." Now, this evangelical militancy might be aimed at other targets, noticeably in the Crusades.

The various crusades from 1099 to the crusades of French King, St. Louis IX, ending in 1270 ostensibly centered upon the control of the holy sites between Muslims and Christians. They led to deep enmity between the two faiths right into the 13th Century. Interpretation of the crusades has normally involved a western perspective: militant Christian pilgrims defeated Muslims and rescued Christian Holy places. This ignores the victories of Saladin and that the crusade front was just one more Muslim war against enemies including Byzantium and Persia. Thus, the hegemonic myth that Islam was an enemy of civilization has induced a stereotypical view in many western historians. Today, this hostility continues towards Islam, a faith that has unfortunately been associated with the term "Islamic fundamentalism." This western viewpoint sees the Europeans as the great educators of

The Byzantine Emperor Alexius Comnenus. His timely intervention against the invading Turks held the Christian frontier in Asia Minor.

the "oriental" others, bringing them democracy and political freedoms as opposed to the abhorrence of eastern slavery and serfdom. The reality was in fact quite the reverse, since so much cultural, medical, mathematical, and scientific knowledge flowed from East to West.

BYZANTIUM AND THE SELJUK TURKS

The Seljuk Turks, originally a nomadic tribe of Oghuz Turkmen that had converted to the Sunni variant of Islam, migrated in the tenth century from central Asia and southeast Asia into the Middle East, where they settled in the lands of the Abbasid caliphate. The Caliph awarded their leader, Tughril Beg, the title of Sultan. They occupied Persia imposing a military sultanate over the caliphate, occupying Baghdad in 1055. They then attacked the eastern Anatolian provinces of the Byzantine Empire, in eastern and central Asia Minor. After this, they turned to the south against the Fatamids in Egypt.

In 1043, Basil II, Emperor of Byzantium, acquired Armenia through careful diplomacy; however, within a period of 20 years, Armenia was conquered by the Seljuk leaders, Alp-Arslan, Tughril's nephew, and Malik Shah, along with the annexation of Mesopotamia, Syria, and Palestine. Their conquests led to a series of systematic raids that resulted in the conquest of Asia Minor, which was so important to the security of the Byzantine Empire.

Constantinople was frightened, and the new emperor, Romanus IV Diogenes, organized a vast army and drove back the invaders from Asia Minor and Syria, then took the offensive himself. His political position was unsafe. He had married the widowed Empress Eudoxia on the death of her husband, Emperor Constantine X Dukas. When Seljuk raids continued, he advanced with a large but motley army into Armenia, confronting the disciplined Seljuk forces at Manzikert, north of Lake Van (1071). The Seljuks defeated the Byzantines at the Battle of Manzikert, capturing the emperor in the process and then establishing themselves in Nicea. The Byzantine defeat was facilitated when the Emperor was deserted by Andronicus Dukas and other Byzantine magnates.

Romanus was released by the Turks and he attempted to regain his throne but was defeated and blinded by his opponents, dying soon after. Various pretenders sought the Byzantine throne, the Seljuks often supplying mercenary troops to one side or the other, spreading themselves over most of Anatolia in the process. Threatened on all frontiers, the Byzantine cause was temporarily saved and secured on its eastern frontier by the intervention of Emperor Alexius Comnenus, a general bent on feathering his own nest, who, on his coronation in April 1081, negotiated with the Seljuks and diplomatically recognized their claims in Asia Minor, so that he would be free to turn his attentions to other quarters.

The year 1081 witnessed a war against the Normans under Robert Guiscard and later his son, Bohemund. Their Balkan project was ultimately defeated by an alliance between Alexius and Venice, and the judicious use of Seljuk cavalry and the guerrilla tactics of the Balkan peoples who hated the heretical Latins. In 1086 there was a revolt of the Bogomils in Thrace and Bulgaria. These heretics were supported by Patzinaks and Cumans who defeated Alexius at the Battle of Drystra (1087). After the Cumans ravaged the entire eastern Balkans, Alexius took them into his service and smashed the

Patzinaks at the Battle of Leburnion (1091). Further trouble occurred in 1094 when Constantine Diogenes, a pretender to the throne, crossed the River Danube with an army of Cumans, not Alexius', and besieged Adrianople, but was defeated in the Battle of Taurocomon.

The Seljuk conquest of the Middle East signified the beginning of Turkish power in that region and the Seljuks would make a strong impression upon Islam in both a political and a religious sense, as witnessed by the building of mosques and madrasahs in which religious scholars and state administrators could be educated and trained. However, despite their impact upon Islam and the Middle East, the Seljuks soon began to quarrel among themselves. Factionalism was also caused by the Seljuk custom of dividing up provinces equally among the male successors of each deceased ruler. In 1072, Alp Arslan was murdered in Turkestan, being succeeded by his son, Malik Shah who left the western Seljuk advances in the hands of subordinate generals. Atziz commanded in Syria and Palestine, capturing Jerusalem in 1071 and Damascus in 1075; in 1079, he was succeeded by Malik Shah's brother, Tutush. The Fatamites were almost expelled from Palestine.

In 1094, Malik Shah died occasioning a civil war in Mesopotamia amongst the various claimants, including Tutush, to the throne. The Seljuk leaders in Syria and Asia Minor were left to themselves. Tutush was killed in Mesopotamia and the Egyptian Fatamites took the opportunity to regain Jerusalem during the First Crusade. When the First Crusade commenced, Syria and north Palestine were occupied by Seljuk emirs, acknowledging the caliph in Baghdad and the authority of their Sultan. In reality, however, they acted unilaterally and received scant assistance from the Sultan. South Palestine and Jerusalem were controlled by Egyptian Fatamite forces, under the authority of their Caliph in Cairo. The two Muslim groups hated each other, just as they hated crusaders.

THE FIRST CRUSADE AND ITS ORIGINS

Pilgrims had traveled to Jerusalem to worship at the scenes of Christ's life and death for centuries, and they continued to do so long after Jerusalem had been captured by the Arabs. A Christian community was permitted to remain in Jerusalem; Harun-al-Rashid, the famous Caliph of Baghdad featured in *The Thousand and One Nights*, acknowledged the right of Christians to maintain the Church of the Holy Sepulchre and made it over to Charlemagne, with whom he conducted a long and amiable correspondence. The status quo was disrupted, however, on the appearance of the Seljuk Turks in the 11th Century.

After the Battle of Manzikert, Christian pilgrims to the Holy Places might be arrested, imprisoned, or even sold as slaves. It was reports of these abuses that inspired Pope Gregory VII in his desire to lead a Christian army to the rescue of Jerusalem.

In the event, a more roundabout route led to the First Crusade. The Byzantine Emperor, Alexius Comnenus, who had ascended the throne in 1081, was determined to recover the lost provinces from the Seljuks but found his resources unequal to the task. During the 1080s and 1090s, he wrote to the pope and to numerous great lords and princes of the west, requesting them to raise armies and come to Constantinople. The Byzantine Empire, he argued, must be preserved against the inroads of the Turks, to protect the objects and places that were sacred to eastern and western Christians alike.

One of his letters, written in 1093 to Count Robert of Flanders, has survived. It contains an extraordinary mixture of enticements and appeals. He begins by describing in detail some of the atrocities committed by the Turks:

> *"I shall merely describe a very few of them... the enemy has the habit of circumsizing young Christians and babies above the baptismal font... Then they are forced to urinate into the font... Those who refuse are tortured and put to death. They carry off noble matrons and their daughters and abuse them like animals... Then, too, the Turks shamelessly commit the sin of sodomy on our men of all ages and all ranks... and, O misery, something that has never been seen or heard before, on bishops..."*

He explains that Constantinople itself is not threatened by the evil Turks, and that it must never fall into the hands of the pagans because of all the important relics in the city.

> *"It would be better that Constantinople falls into your hands than into the hands of the pagans,"* he remarks, and adds that besides the holy relics the city is crammed with gold and treasures. *"In your coming you will find your reward in heaven,"* he tells Robert, *"and if you do not come, god will condemn you".*

Alexius thought of the Franks as little better than Barbarians, however, as is clear from his parting injunction:

> *"If all this glory is not sufficient for you, remember that you will find all those treasures and also the most beautiful women of the East. The incomparable beauty of Greek women would seem to be a sufficient reason to attract the armies of the Franks to the plains of Thrace."*

After his initial success at Clermont, Pope Urban II set off on a tour of France and the Low Countries to gather international support for his crusade. Here he preaches to a packed congregation at one of the great cathedrals of France.

Pope Urban II, learning of the contents of the letter, was moved and saw that the threatened destruction of the Christian Byzantine Empire would be an appalling disaster. He was concerned about the atrocities perpetrated by the Turks, but equally he was concerned about the depredations of Christian knights in their own countries. He therefore sought to unite the quarreling lords behind one great cause, under the leadership and authority of the Church. He determined to carry out his predecessor's plan to provide military aid to the beleaguered Christians of the East, and set in motion one of the most extraordinary events in the history of western Europe.

Texts of his main speech and news of his intentions had been circulated through the courts of Europe, and advance notice was given of his visit to Clermont, in November 1095. This was a council of bishops and other prelates, at which Church business was conducted. Urban confirmed yet again the Peace of God and the Truce of God. On 17 November he addressed himself directly and to the people. Such a large crowd had gathered that his address had to be made outside the city in a field. He began by enlisting the sympathies of his audience, exciting their sense of outrage by giving grisly details of the atrocities committed by the Turks against Christians, and their contempt for, and defilement of, the holiest shrines of Christianity. Urban was a Frenchman, and according to Robert the Monk, chronicler of the First Crusade, his message was aimed at the Franks:

> *"Who shall avenge these wrongs, who shall recover these lands if not you? You are the race upon whom God had bestowed glory in arms, greatness of spirit, physical energy, and the courage of humble the proud locks of those who resist you... O most valiant knights, descendants of unconquerable ancestors, remember the courage of your forefathers and do not dishonor them!"*

According to another chronicler, Balderic, the inspired Pope did indeed address himself especially to the knights, but in a somewhat less complimentary style:

> *"You, girt about with the badge of knighthood, are arrogant with great pride; you rage against your brothers and cut each other in pieces. The true soldiery of Christ does not rend asunder the sheepfold of the Redeemer... you, the oppressors of orphans, the plunderers of widows; you guilty of homicide, of sacrilege, robbers of others' rights; you who await the pay of thieves for shedding of Christian blood—as vultures smell fetid corpses, so do you sense battles from afar and rush to them eagerly."*

But the knights had a chance to redeem themselves; the Truce of God in the west could be observed by fighting a holy war in the east. And at this point Urban gave full expression to the concept of the crusading indulgence: those who fall in the battle against the heathen will have earned a heavenly reward. In the enthusiasm of the moment, huge numbers of people, knights and peasants, princes, and men at arms, "took the cross." It was no trivial matter for a knight to go on crusade. To pay for the journey, the equipment, the horses, the provisions, and the staff to get him to the Holy Land, many a knight had to mortgage or sell his estates. Duke Robert of Normandy raised a loan of 10,000 silver marks from his younger brother, William Rufus, the King of England, using his duchy as a pledge.

There were some advantages to going on crusade. Every knight who took the cross made a vow that he would pray at the Church of the Holy Sepulchre in Jerusalem. This was very like—and indeed it was called at the time—going on pilgrimage, and meant that crusaders were granted certain privileges. They had temporary clerical status, so were subject only to ecclestiastical jurisdiction. They did not have to pay any taxes, or pay off any debts, or incur any interest on their debts, or perform any ordinary feudal military service, while they were away on crusade. The Church also promised to protect a crusader's property and family against usurping claimants.

The five armies of the official crusade, under the leadership of Count

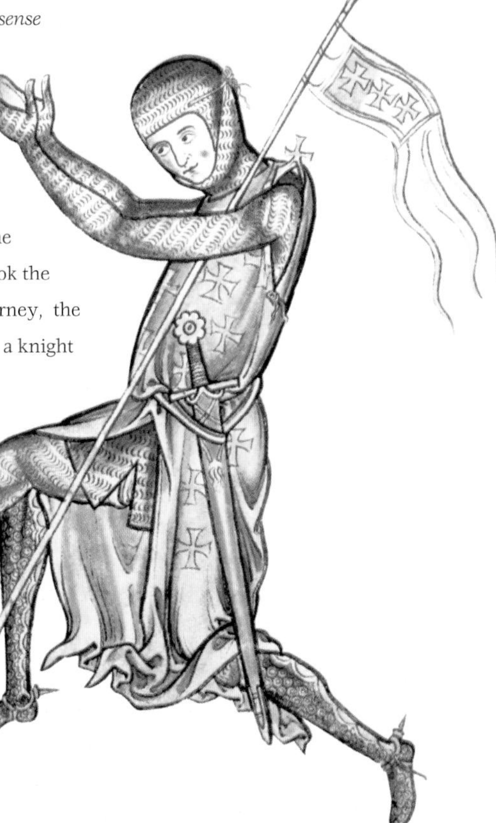

A crusader knight wearing holy crosses on his tunic at prayer and seeking the Lord's blessing before setting off on crusade. This illustration comes from a 13th Century English psalter, a copy of the biblical Psalms.

The Crusades
1096–1204
Religion:
Latin (Catholic) Christian
Greek (Orthodox) Christian
Armenian Christian
Muslim
Route of Crusades:
First Crusade, 1096–99
Second Crusade, 1146–48
Third Crusade, 1189–92
Fourth Crusade, 1202–04
Borders shown c. 1200
NORWAY
SCOTLAND
North Sea
IRELAND
ENGLAND
WELSH STATES
London
Hamburg
Bremen
Berlin
Kingdom of German
Cologne
Frankfurt
Regensburg
Rheims
Paris
Stuttgart
Munich
HOLY ROMAN EMPI
Nantes
FRANCE
Bern
Geneva
Lyon
Milan
Venice
ATLANTIC OCEAN
Genoa
Kingdom of Italy
Bordeaux
Avignon
Aigue-Morte
Marseilles
Pisa
PISA
Florence
NAVARRE
Corsica
Corunna
LEON
ARAGON
Rome
PAPAL STATES
Barcelona
Saragossa
Naples
CASTILLE
Sardinia
Oporto
Balearic Islands
PORTUGAL
Toledo
Balansiyah
Cagliari
Lisbon
Palermo
Messina
Sicily
Cartagena
Tunis
Silves
Ishbiliyah
Algiers
EMPIRE OF THE ALMOHADS
Malta
Oran
Fez
Tripoli
0°

POMERALIA
LITHUANIANS
PRUSSIANS
GREAT POLAND
Poznam
MOZOVIA
Liegnitz
Breslau
LITTLE POLAND
Cracow
Olmutz
POLOTSK
Minsk
TUROV-PINSK
VOLHYNIA
CHERNIGOV
MUROM
RYAZAN
PEREYASLAVL
Kiev
Galich
KIEV
GALICH
Volga
Don
CUMANS
Buda
HUNGARY
Pécs
Olech
to Kiev
Belgrade
Bucharest
Cherson
to Byzantine
Tmutarakan
to Byzantine
to Kiev
Serbia
Odessus
ALANS
Croatia
Black Sea
Philippopolis
Greater Bulgaria
Constantinople
Epirus
BYZANTINE EMPIRE
Bari
Taranto
Salonica
Nicaea
RUM (ICONIUM)
GEORGIA
Aegean Sea
Smyrna
Athens
KINGDOM OF ARMENIA
Antioch
Crete
Cyprus
Limassol
Tripoli
Beirut
Damascus
Mediterranean Sea
Acre
Jerusalem
Alexandra
Damiette
Cairo
Egypt

Godfrey of Bouillon, brother of the French king, is seen in this French illustration leading his men in the attack and capture of Jerusalem in July 1099.

Raymond of Toulouse, Count Godfrey of Bouillon, Count High of Vermandois (brother of the French king), Duke Robert of Normandy (brother of the English king), and Bohemond of Otranto (son of Robert Guiscard), set off late in the summer of 1096 for the Holy Land. It is difficult to estimate the actual numbers, as the accounts left by the chroniclers are exaggerated, but it seems there was a total of about 35,000 crusaders, of which between 3,000 and 4,000 were knights. Some knights and soldiers took their wives and families with them, and the chroniclers report stories of great bravery from these women in support of their menfolk.

Pope Urban had nominated his legate, Bishop Adhemar of Le Puy, as the leader of the expedition, in the hope of retaining control on behalf of the papacy. But, though the response to the call to arms had been truly astounding, the knights were not so ready to espouse the authority of the Church over their own business.

This did not mean that the knights were not motivated by religious zeal; it is clear that many were. Though historians often suggest that going on crusade was a splendid opportunity for landless younger sons to make their fortunes and settle down with new estates carved out in the East, in practice the majority of the crusaders returned home not long after the capture of Jerusalem. Some of the leaders were more devout than others. Raymond of Toulouse and Godfrey of Bouillon, for example, were noted for their piety. The Prince of Otranto, however, was known as a wild and godless adventurer, who only a few years before had invaded the western edge of the Byzantine Empire, to whose aid he was, in theory, now coming. He and Baldwin of Boulogne were certainly more interested in acquiring new territories for themselves than fighting a purely religious war. After Baldwin had established the first Christian state at Edessa (1098–1291), and Bohemond had become the Prince of Antioch (1098–1268), they both stayed in their new cities and left the deliverance of Jerusalem to the others.

Right: THE SIEGE AND CAPTURE OF JERUSALEM June–July 1099. After previous assaults had failed, siege towers were built and deployed against the northeast walls of the city. A breach was made and once the crusaders had entered the city almost every inhabitant was killed; the Holy City was in Christian hands again.

The dedication and religious fervor that had launched the knights on the crusade were sorely tested by the harsh conditions they encountered on the campaign. Burning heat and thirst, contaminated water and bad food, led to constant outbreaks of illness among the troops. When the armies eventually reached Jerusalem they found that all the trees had been cut down and the wells poisoned for miles around. The soldiers became maddened by thirst.

Earlier, when they had finally taken the city of Antioch after a grueling seven-month siege, the crusaders were dismayed to learn that a huge Turkish army was close behind them, ready to recapture the city. The soldiers were exhausted and weakened by illness and starvation but at this low point in their fortunes their morale was restored by the miraculous discovery of the Holy Lance beneath an altar in the city. Bishop Adhemar, who had seen one of those already in

Constantinople, remained sceptical about the find but he was already sick with the fever that was to end his life and could do nothing to stem the exaltation of the soldiers. Raymond of Toulouse, too, was ill; it was Bohemond who organized a desperate sortie from the city and, carrying the Holy Lance in their midst (this spear was widely considered to have been used by a Roman soldier to pierce Christ's side when he was on the cross), the starving Christians defeated and put to flight a much larger Turkish army. This victory seemed little short of miraculous and was wholly attributed to the presence of the Holy Lance, and probably without the faith and hope it had inspired they would not have succeeded.

A less acceptable face of the crusaders' religious zeal was shown at the capture of Jerusalem, when they indulged in a terrible frenzy of slaughter and massacred almost the whole population, Muslim and Jew. A Latin state of Jerusalem was established in 1100, lasting until 1291, while the county of Tripoli existed from 1102 to 1289.

The Siege and Capture of Jerusalem
June–July 1099

- Deployment of Crusader forces
- Crusader attacks on the city walls
- Crusader advances within city
- Muslim force and population retreat

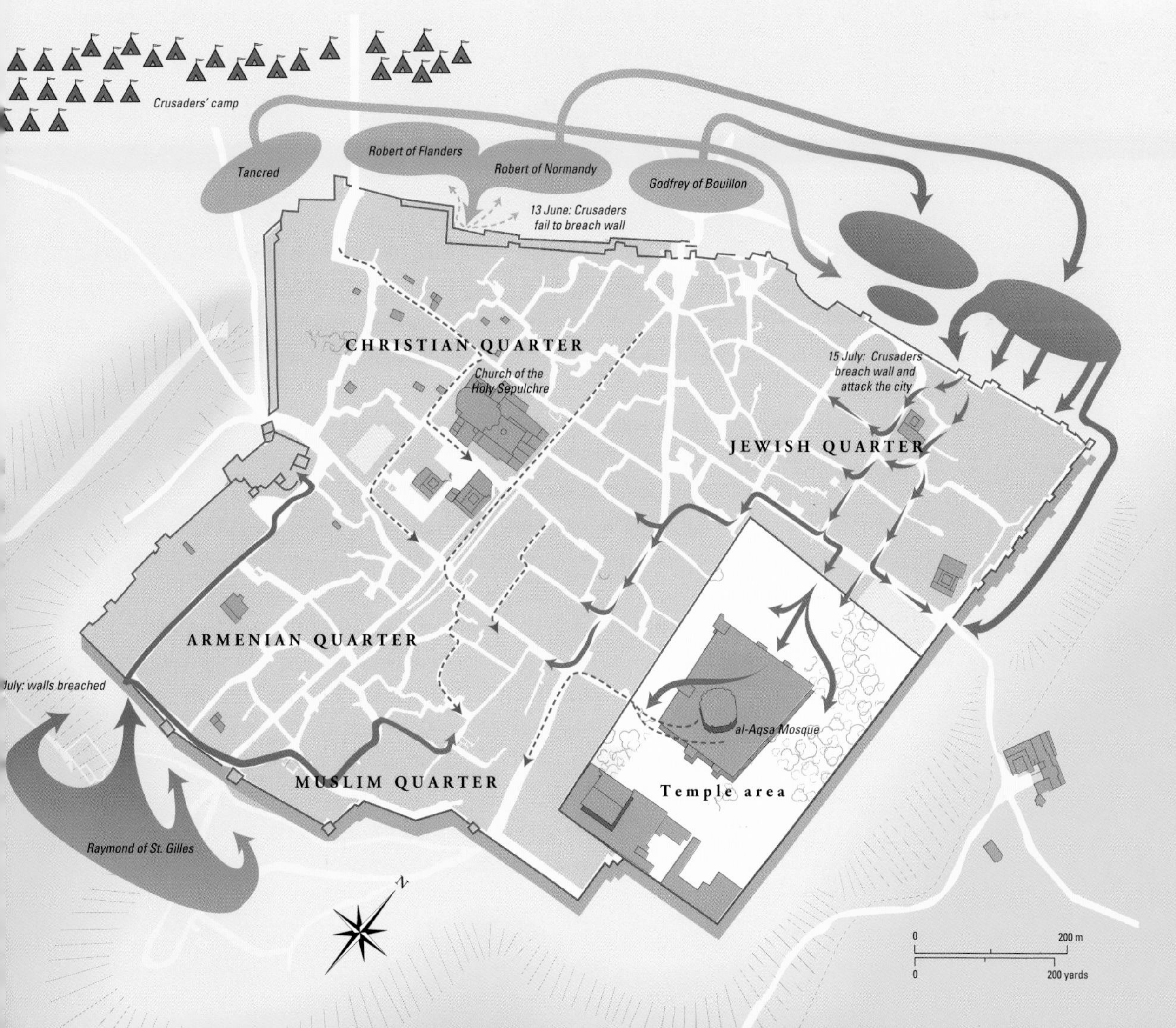

LATER CRUSADES

Other expeditions followed helping to capture ports, plains, and increase the size of Outremer's (the French Crusader States') hinterland. Examples are the endeavours of King Sigurd of Norway (1109–10), Fulk V of Anjou (1120 and 1128), and the Doge of Venice (1123–24).

In 1144, Edessa fell to the Turks resulting in the Second Crusade, led by King Louis VII of France and Emperor Conrad III. When their forces, numbering 50,000, arrived in Syria, instead of retaking Edessa they laid siege to Damascus in 114, but failed to take it, and with the ensuing defeat, accusations flew in all directions, bringing a low ebb to relations between Europe and the Crusader States.

Crusaders attack a city in the Near East using a trebuchet loaded with the severed heads of their enemies.

Saladin, the Muslim Sultan of Egypt, Syria, Yemen, and Palestine was the founder of the Ayyubid dynasty. In 1169, aged 32 years, he had been appointed both commander of the Syrian forces and vizier of Egypt. Later, he used his wealthy agricultural possessions in Egypt to finance his control of Syria, which he controlled with a small but well-disciplined army. By 1186, he acquired northern Mesopotamia too. Saladin developed an elite force of askaris (soldiers), a regular force of bodyguards, and mounted archers, some 8,000 men who were backed up by feudal levies.

Saladin ended the internecine strife of previous Muslim leaders, which had hindered their resistance to Christian crusaders. A determined and virtuous ruler with a reputation for firmness and fairness, he implemented the concept of *jihad* (holy war), the Muslim equivalent of the Christian Crusade.

In 1187, Saladin destroyed a crusader army at Hattin near Tiberias in northern Palestine and then overran most of the kingdom of Jerusalem. Most of the 15,000 crusader army was killed on the battlefield but Saladin spared the life of Guy of Lusignan, King of Jerusalem: he regarded Guy as a "real king" like himself and considered that kings did not kill each other. Within three months, Acre, Toron, Beirut, Sidon, Nazareth, Caesarea, Nablus, Jaffa and Ascalon had fallen to the Muslim armies, and at the beginning of October 1187, Jerusalem, Holy City to both Christian and Muslim alike, fell to Saladin after 88 years in Frankish hands.

Unlike the earlier Christian conquest of Jerusalem, which had been marked by its ruthless barbarity, the Holy City was occupied by Muslim troops in a more civilized fashion. The cause of the crusaders had been dealt a serious blow and they now only controlled three cities on the Levantine coast, of which Tyre became the rallying point of the Christian cause.

This disaster prompted Pope Gregory VII to call a Third Crusade led by the Kings of France and England, who traveled by sea, joining Emperor Frederick II, who had taken the land route. During his voyage King Richard I Lionheart of England captured Cyprus, which remained in Christian hands until

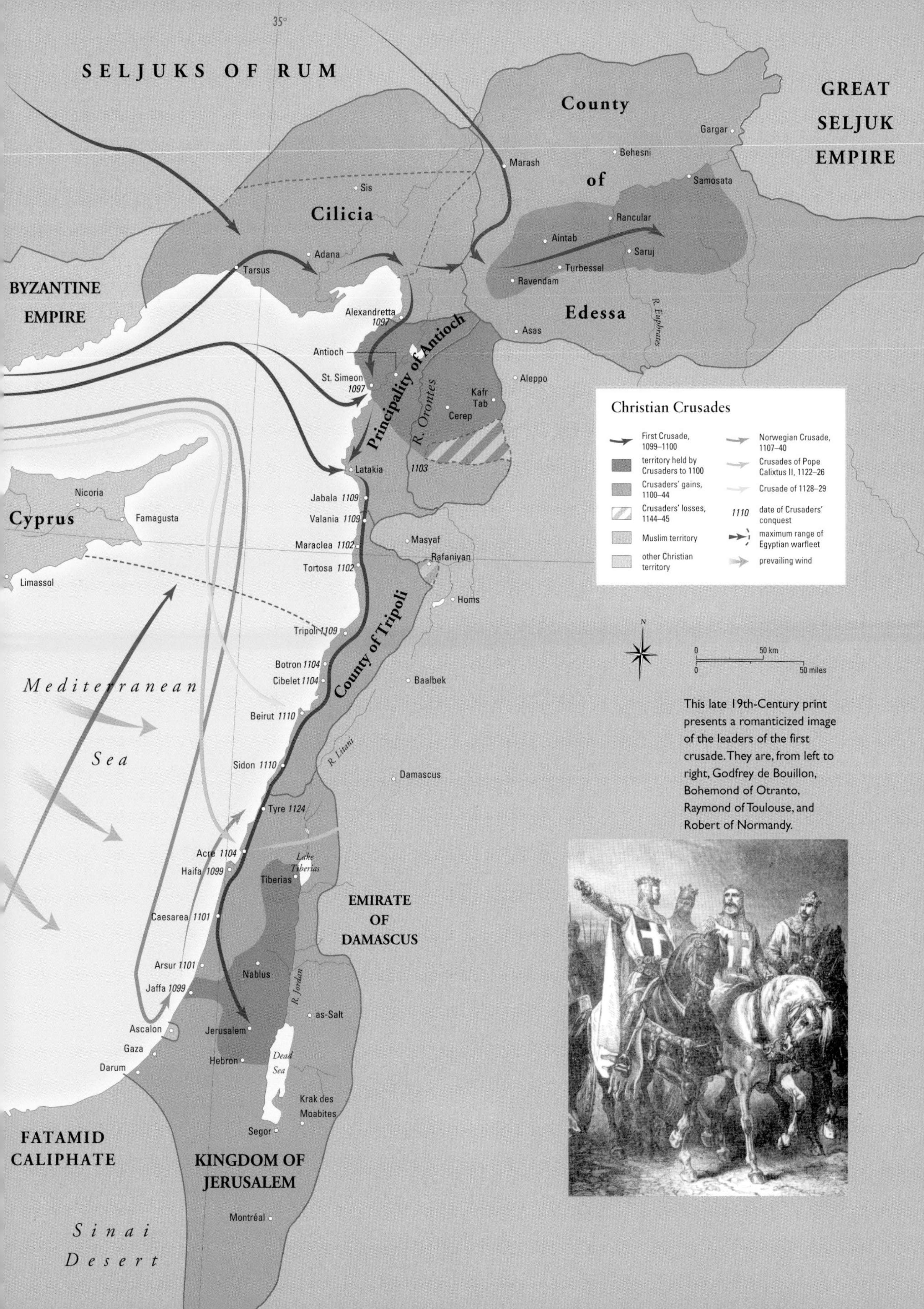

This late 19th-Century print presents a romanticized image of the leaders of the first crusade. They are, from left to right, Godfrey de Bouillon, Bohemond of Otranto, Raymond of Toulouse, and Robert of Normandy.

The Crusades
1218–1270
Religion:
Latin (Catholic) Christian
Greek (Orthodox) Christian
Armenian Christian
Muslim
Route of Crusades:
Fifth Crusade, 1218–21
Sixth Crusade, 1248–54
Seventh Crusade, 1270
Borders shown c. 1300
NORWAY
DENMARK
North Sea
SCOTLAND
IRELAND
WELSH STATES
ENGLAND
London
Hamburg
Bremen
Berlin
Cologne
Frankfurt
to Castile
Rheims
Regensburg
Stuttgart
Normandy
Paris
Munich
HOLY ROMAN EMPIRE
Nanjou
Innsbruck
Nantes
Bern
FRANCE
Geneva
Lyon
Milan
Venice
ATLANTIC OCEAN
Genoa
Bordeaux
English controlled
Pisa
PISA
Florence
Aigue-Morte
Avignon
Marseilles
PAPAL STATES
Corsica
Rome
NAVARRE
Corunna
ARAGON
Naples
Barcelona
Saragossa
Sardinia
Oporto
CASTILLE
Balearic Islands
KINGDOM OF SICILY
PORTUGAL
Toledo
Valencia
Cagliari
Messina
Palermo
Sicily
Lisbon
Cartagena to Aragon
Tunis
Seville
GRANADA
Algiers
Malta
Oran
HAFSIDS
ZAYYANIDS
Fez
MARINIDS
Tripoli
0°

SWEDEN
Konigsburg
LITHUANIA
POLOTSK
Moscow
GREAT POLAND
Poznan
MOZOVIA
TUROV-PINSK
SILESIA
Liegnitz
LITTLE POLAND
Breslau
Cracow
ingdom of Bohemia
Olmutz
Kiev
Galich
THE GOLDEN HORDE
Volga
Don
Vienna
Buda
HUNGARY
Pécs
Belgrade
Bosnia
Bucharest
Caffa
to Genoa
Serbia
Bulgaria
Odessus
ALANS
Black Sea
Philippopolis
Constantinople
Epirus
BYZANTINE EMPIRE
Bari
Taranto
Salonica
Nicaea
TREBIZOND
GEORG
RUM (ICONIUM)
Aegean Sea
Smyrna
Athens
ILKHANE EMPIRE
Antioch
Crete
Cyprus
Limassol
Tripoli
Beirut
Mediterranean Sea
Damascus
Acre
Jerusalem
Alexandra
Damiette
Egypt
Cairo
MAMLUKS
20°
40°

1571. Richard took Acre but failed to reach Jerusalem despite his victory at Arsuf. Eventually the Treaty of Jaffa (2 September 1192) gave the crusaders control of the coast from Acre to Jaffa and allowed access to Jerusalem for pilgrims and freedom of movement between Christian and Muslim lands.

The Fourth Crusade was launched by Pope Innocent III to retake Egypt, but it was diverted when the crusaders took the town of Zara on the Dalmatian coast for the Venetians, despite the port belonging to King Emeric of Hungary, a fellow crusader. When the crusaders arrived in Constantinople in 1204, they captured the Byzantine capital and in league with the Venetians founded the Latin Empire of Constantinople, which lasted for 60 years and weakened the Byzantine Empire, thus ending any possible reconciliation between the Orthodox and Latin churches.

In 1215, the King of Hungary set out for Acre, launching the Fifth Crusade. In 1218, the King of Jerusalem, Jean de Brienne, invaded Egypt and put the port of Damietta to siege; however, his subsequent march on Cairo ended in disaster in 1221. The Sixth Crusade was launched in 1223 by Pope Honorius III in support of an expedition led by Emperor Frederick II, later excommunicated for his procrastination. The Sultan eventually gave up Jerusalem, Bethlehem, and Nazareth to Frederick and signed a ten-year truce.

The Seventh Crusade, originated in 1239, was led by the King of Navarre and the Duke of Burgundy. Nevertheless, Jerusalem once again fell to Muslim forces. Louis of France then led a campaign against Egypt; he captured Damietta in 1249 and marched on and captured Cairo in 1250. Antioch fell in 1268, which resulted in an Eighth Crusade, led by the King of France, who attacked Tunis but died during the siege in 1270, his army subsequently being forced into retreat. Other anarchic crusades followed, even into the 15th Century, but achieved nothing.

LATINS AND CATALANS IN GREECE

The seizure of Constantinople in 1204 by crusader forces occasioned the partition of much of the Byzantine Empire. Rump Byzantine states existed in the Empire of Nicaea and the Despotate of Epirus. Elsewhere, Latin Emperors from the houses of Flanders and Courtenay controlled lands around the city on both sides of the Bosporus. The Latin Kingdom of Thessalonica stretched from these around the northern Aegean Sea to the Duchy of Athens and its overlord the Principality of Achaea, run by Geoffrey of Villehardouin.

Despite owing fealty to the Emperor in Constantinople, the Villehardouin family were virtually autonomous administering their lands according to feudal customs as seen in the kingdom of Jerusalem. In the Morea, their baronage included the Templars, Teutonic Knights, and the Hospitallers, together with the Archbishop of Patras. The Latin knighthood was ensconced in castles, chiefly in the towns and on the coasts. Latin settlement had little to do with the locals who were exploited feudally and by Latin ecclesiastical institutions.

The Prince of Achaea was the liege lord of Latin rulers such as the lords of Thebes and Athens, the Dukes of Archipelago (the Cyclades), and several of the Ionian islands. The island territories were held by Venetians such as the Orsini family in Cephalonia. The Latin hold on Greece was tenuous. The Venetians demanded concessions for their role in the Fourth Crusade and they controlled the

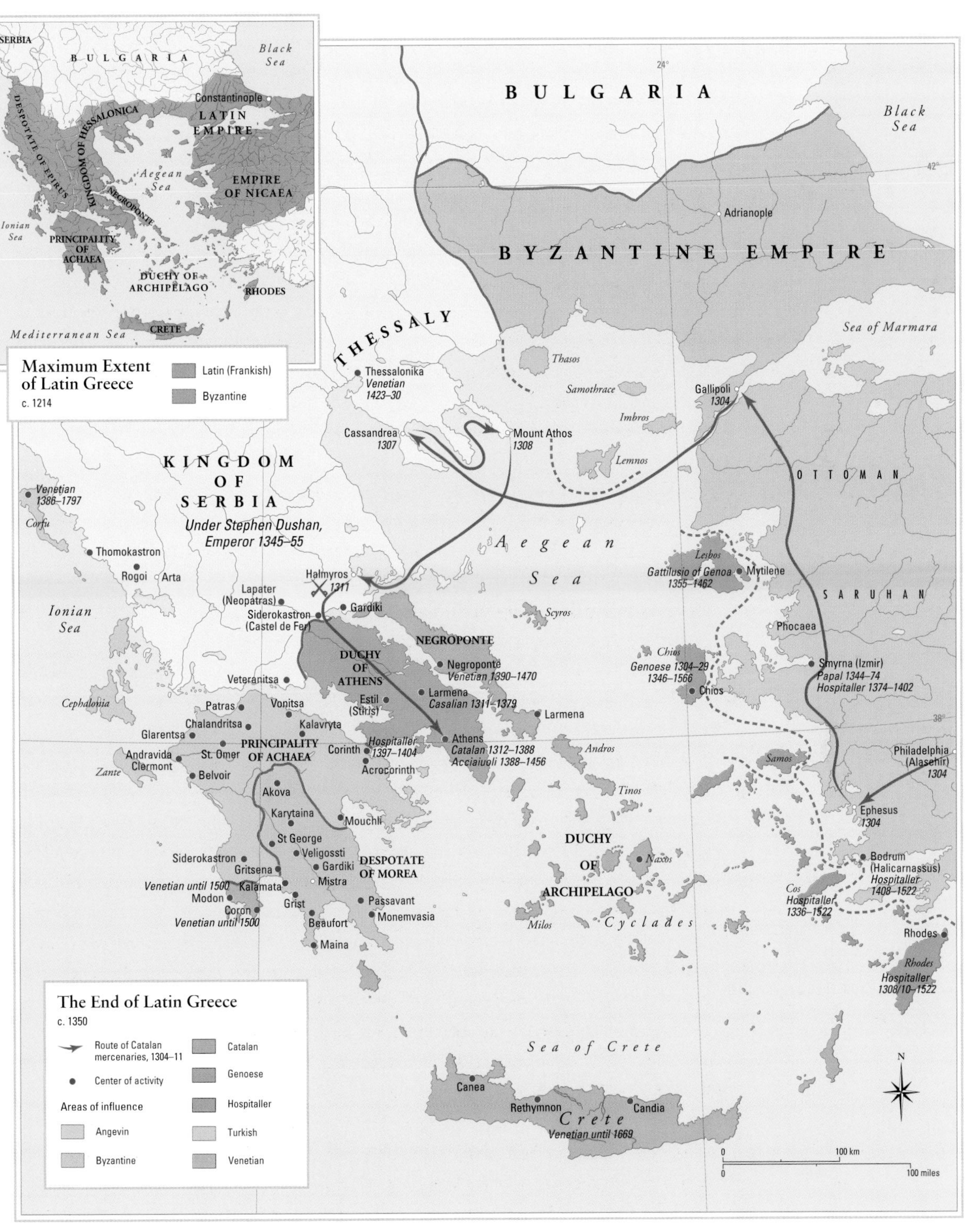

Maximum Extent of Latin Greece
c. 1214
Latin (Frankish)
Byzantine
SERBIA
BULGARIA
Black Sea
Constantinople
LATIN EMPIRE
EMPIRE OF NICAEA
KINGDOM OF THESSALONICA
DESPOTATE OF EPIRUS
NEGROPONTE
Aegean Sea
Ionian Sea
PRINCIPALITY OF ACHAEA
DUCHY OF ARCHIPELAGO
RHODES
CRETE
Mediterranean Sea
BULGARIA
Black Sea
BYZANTINE EMPIRE
Adrianople
Sea of Marmara
THESSALY
Thessalonika
Venetian 1423–30
Thasos
Samothrace
Imbros
Gallipoli 1304
Cassandrea 1307
Mount Athos 1308
Lemnos
KINGDOM OF SERBIA
Under Stephen Dushan, Emperor 1345–55
OTTOMAN
Venetian 1386–1797
Corfu
Thomokastron
Rogoi
Arta
Aegean Sea
Lesbos
Gattilusio of Genoa 1355–1462
Mytilene
Halmyros 1311
Lapater (Neopatras)
Siderokastron (Castel de Fer)
Gardiki
Scyros
SARUHAN
Ionian Sea
NEGROPONTE
Phocaea
DUCHY OF ATHENS
Negroponte
Venetian 1390–1470
Chios
Genoese 1304–29 1346–1566
Chios
Smyrna (Izmir)
Papal 1344–74
Hospitaller 1374–1402
Veteranitsa
Larmena
Casalian 1311–1379
Larmena
Cephalonia
Patras
Vonitsa
Estil (Stiris)
Chalandritsa
Kalavryta
Glarentsa
PRINCIPALITY OF ACHAEA
Hospitaller 1397–1404
Athens
Catalan 1312–1388
Acciaiuoli 1388–1456
Andros
Samos
Philadelphia (Alasehir) 1304
Andravida
Clermont
St. Omer
Corinth
Acrocorinth
Zante
Belvoir
Tinos
Akova
Ephesus 1304
Karytaina
Mouchli
St George
DUCHY OF ARCHIPELAGO
Naxos
Bodrum (Halicarnassus)
Hospitaller 1408–1522
Siderokastron
Veligossti
Gritsena
Gardiki
DESPOTATE OF MOREA
Mistra
Venetian until 1500
Kalamata
Modon
Grist
Passavant
Cos
Hospitaller 1336–1522
Coron
Venetian until 1500
Beaufort
Monemvasia
Milos
Cyclades
Rhodes
Maina
Rhodes
Hospitaller 1308/10–1522
The End of Latin Greece
c. 1350
Route of Catalan mercenaries, 1304–11
Center of activity
Areas of influence
Angevin
Byzantine
Catalan
Genoese
Hospitaller
Turkish
Venetian
Sea of Crete
Canea
Rethymnon
Candia
Crete
Venetian until 1669
N
0
100 km
0
100 miles
24°
42°
38°

seaways with bases at Modon and Coron. Additionally, the Venetians had their own compounds in Constantinople and they developed the island of Crete into a colony with Italian settlers., and had a dual overlordship in Negroponte.

Lurking in the background were the angry Byzantines in Nicaea and Epirus. The Epirot despot, Michael Angelus Comnenus, conquered Latin Thessalonika in 1224. Relations with the Bulgars were stormy. Under Kaloyan, they had defeated Emperor Baldwin and Doge Dandalo near Adrianople in 1205, overrunning much of Thrace and Macedonia, exterminating a large part of the Greek population. In 1230, they took Thessalonika, keeping part of it while the remainder and Thessaly was passed to Manuel, brother of Theodore of Epirus. By 1246, these lands were swallowed by Nicaea, which captured all Latin-held lands in Asia Minor by 1235. In 1259, a new Nicaean Emperor, Michael VIII Paleologus, defeated a coalition of Michael II of Epirus, William of Villehardouin of Achaea and the King of Sicily, at the Battle of Pelagonia, thereby ending their attack on Thessalonika. The Prince of Achaea was captured with many Latin lords and in 1261 was forced to disgorge Monemvasia, Maina, and Mistra as part of his ransom. The same year saw an alliance between Michael Paleolous and the Bulgarians, and the Treaty of Nymphaion with Genoa, promising the Genoese all the privileges enjoyed by the Venetians. On 25 July, in the absence of the Venetian fleet, a Greek army, led by Alexius Stragopulos, crossed the Bosporus Sea retaking Constantinople and ending the Latin Empire. Baldwin II fled. The Byzantine Empire was reestablished. The principality of Achaea remained but, on Villehardouin's death in 1275, passed to his son-in-law Philip of Anjou, son of Charles I of Naples. Achaea was then ruled from Italy.

Into this scenario marched the Catalan Company comprising the aggressive Light Infantry Almogovars. These specialist troops wore open-work iron helmets, a sleeveless sheepskin jacket, and light but tough sandals. They carried a short spear (*azcona*), javelins that could penetrate armor, and a knife (*colltell*) much like a butcher's cleaver with a sharp point. They were trained to fight cavalry, enjoying a fierce reputation fighting for Aragon against Angevin-French Sicily. At the end of his Italian campaign in 1302, the Byzantine emperor, Andronicus II, hired them to fight the Turks. Under Roger de Flor, they repulsed a Turkish attack on Philadelphia. When the Byzantines failed to pay them, they attacked Constantinople and ravaged Thrace and Macedonia. In 1311, the Company was hired by the Duke of Athens but fell out with him. He led a army of 6,000 knights and 8,000 infantry against them. Despite being outnumbered, the Catalans decided to give battle at Kephissos. They dammed a river to turn their front into a marsh, breaking a Frankish charge. Then the Almogavars attacked filtering amongst the enemy ranks; being lightly armed they danced on the marsh and butchered the knights. The Catalans established their own power base in Athens. Meanwhile, they had given their allegiance for Athens to Aragon, turning Greece into yet one more battleground between Anjou and Aragon. In 1388, Catalan power was removed by Nerio Acciaiuoli, the Florentine lord of Corinth, whose heirs were crushed by the Ottoman advance in 1456.

Elsewhere, Achaea was gained by the Byzantine despot of Mistra in 1432, Genoa, for some time ruled Lesbos, Chios, and Samos, the Hospitallers held Rhodes and Cos until 1522, while the Venetians remained in Crete until 1669.

Right: THE TEMPLAR AND THE HOSPITALLER, c. 1250.
The Templar (left figure) is wearing a padded arming cap on which his helm will rest. His main hauberk is now worn over a padded undercoat called a gambeson and under the surcoat of the Order—white with a red cross on the breast. This loose, knee-length garment is split to the waist at the front and back for ease when riding. He has mail leggings and prick spurs.

The Hospitaller (right figure) wears the black surcoat with white cross, which was adopted by the Order in 1248. In 1259 this was changed to a red surcoat with white cross. He wears a simple round helmet over his mail coif. Shields have, by the time, grown shorter and more triangular in shape. The mail leggings are laced behind the knight's calves.

Padded arming cap
Round helmet over mail coif
Helm
Gambeson
Surcoat
Triangular shield
Mail leggings
Prick spurs

A Hospitaller Knight is seen here among the defenders of Acre. The fall of Acre in 1291 marked a major defeat of the Christian armies in the Near East after two centuries of bloody warfare.

THE MILITARY ORDERS

That thousands of knights and men at arms should mount an expedition overseas at the express bidding of the Church was remarkable enough, but out of this strange wedding between warriors and churchmen came an even stranger offspring: the military orders, knights who were also monks. They lived under a monastic rule, which included the usual injunctions to poverty, chastity, and obedience. This separated them from the dynastic concerns, which preoccupied so many of their secular counterparts and, though many of the military orders became wealthy, they were prohibited from participating in the more frivolous activities of knightly life, such as tournaments or dancing. In that sense they were out of the mainstream of knighthood but they developed its military aspects to a high degree, particularly in training and discipline, the construction and defense of castles, and the tactics of siege warfare.

THE KNIGHTS TEMPLAR

For several years before the recapture of Jerusalem in 1099, a group of knights had acted as guides and protectors to Christian pilgrims traveling through the lands of the hostile Seljuks. At the time of the First Crusade they lived in a hostel near the Temple of Solomon in Jerusalem, and when Hugues de Payns and Geoffrey de St. Omer had the idea of formally incorporating the knights as a religious order in 1119, they took the name of the Poor Knights of the Temple of Solomon, or the Knights Templar. The Order was formally recognized by the Church at the Council of Troyes in 1128, and St. Bernard of Clairvaux, the most influential Churchman of the day, was commissioned to write the Rule by which they should live. St Bernard embraced the cause of the Templars enthusiastically and, at the request of Hugues de Payns, who had become the Order's first Grand Master, followed by the Rule with *De laude novae militiae* (In Praise of the New Chivalry) in which he forcibly contrasted the noble austerity of the Templars with the luxury, vanity, greed, and violence of the secular knights.

The idea of the military monk-knights was received with great enthusiasm. A group of Templars toured France and England to recruit members, and also to solicit gifts of money and property so that the Order could support its military activities in the Holy Land. The gifts, especially grants of estates, poured in and soon there was a Templar Commandery in every province and in most major towns and cities, where the knights were recruited and trained, the estates administered and religious services sung in the Templars' characteristic round churches.

Their record of service defending the Christian kingdom of Jerusalem was distinguished, though somewhat marred by their relations with their great rivals, the Hospitallers, which by the 1240s had deteriorated to the extent that knights from each Order were fighting openly in the streets of Acre. Because the great majority of knights on the eight crusades to the Holy Land returned home as soon as the military campaign was over, the task of keeping the kingdom against the Turks, and later the Egyptians, fell to the Templars and Hospitallers. They invested huge sums of money in the construction of a chain of massively fortified castles, some of which were never captured by the enemy but were abandoned when the knights withdrew from Palestine in 1291. They were famous for the ferocity of their fighting. After the disastrous Battle of Hattin in 1187, Saladin took prisoner about two hundred Templars and Hospitallers, including both Grand Masters and ordered them all to be executed, on the grounds that they were "the firebrands of the Franks."

Both the Templars and the Hospitallers entered into diplomatic negotiations with various Muslim leaders over the years. Because they had to live permanently in the Holy Land, they often had a different perspective from that of the crusaders who appeared periodically in pursuit of short term military objectives. The Third Crusade came nearest to recapturing Jerusalem, which had fallen to Saladin after the Battle of Hattin. But when Richard the Lionheart and his armies were encamped before the city in 1192, the Grand Master of the Templars persuaded him not to attack; and again, in 1228, they were opposed to a negotiated return of the city on the grounds that they could not defend it successfully with the resources available to them.

The Castle of the Knights of St. John, located on the Greek island of Rhodes. After the loss of Acre, the Knights of St. John's main stronghold in the eastern Mediterranean was their castle at Rhodes. The buildings included the Palace of the Grand Master, a cathedral and the eight hotels representing each nation of the Order. The major influences in the architecture are French and Spanish.

After the capture of Acre in 1291, the last outpost of the kingdom of Jerusalem had fallen. The Templars withdrew to their European estates. They had lost many of their best knights in the last desperate days of the siege and were demoralized by their failure and by the fact that with the loss of the kingdom they had lost their *raison d'être*. Over the years they had become heavily involved in banking and diplomacy; what had originally begun as a financial facility for pilgrims had grown to an international business that lent large sums of money to kings and governments. The Templars were perceived to be wealthy and corrupt, and they became unpopular.

Their wealth was untouchable because over the years they had won many privileges, including exemption from the payment of taxes and tithes. They were not subject to secular law, and were answerable only to the pope himself. This made them a law unto themselves in the countries of western Europe where they held lands, and they were very powerful. In 1307, however, King Philip the Fair of France thought of a way to unlock that vast wealth. He and his chancellor, Guillaume de Nogaret, hit on the idea of accusing the Templars of heresy and having the Order abolished. This was done; in 1307 all the Templars in France were arrested (only 13 escaped) and "interrogated." Under torture, or the threat of torture, the knights confessed to a fascinating variety of crimes, ranging from spitting or urinating on the crucifix to sodomy. Later many knights retracted their confessions but it was too late; the damage to their reputation was irreversible. In 1312 Pope Clement V reluctantly agreed to issue a papal bull (edict) suppressing the Order and Philip had its Grand Master and two senior officers burnt at the stake. The pope ordered the Templars' properties to be handed over to the Hospitallers but, though this was done in Germany, in France and England most of it went to the crown. In Spain and Portugal the Order was simply refounded under new names.

THE KNIGHTS OF ST. JOHN AND THE HOSPITAL

The Hospitallers, as their name implies, had been a charitable group that cared for sick and weary pilgrims in the Hospital of St. John in Jerusalem. When they had been incorporated as a military order not long after the Templars, they continued to run hospitals, which may explain why they remained popular and respected. Their service in the East was parallel to that of the Templars, and the largest and most famous of the crusader castles—Krak des Chevaliers—was built by them.

After the fall of Acre, they retreated briefly to Cyprus, but they had already made plans for their new role. For some years they had built and run a fleet of ships, which provided the Christian kingdom with supplies and trade, and also kept down the pirates in the eastern Mediterranean. In 1307 they bought the island of Rhodes and made their headquarters there. They continued their naval operations, fortified the town and harbor of Rhodes, built a fortress for the Grand Master and a large hospital for the sick. They also reorganized themselves so that the knights of each different nationality were grouped together, each in their own "Inn," and each having responsibility for a section of the town and for defending a stretch of the wall.

For most of the 14th Century they were unmolested, but the Muslims were less than happy to have such a strong Christian power base securely settled in the eastern Mediterranean. In 1435 Rhodes was attacked by the army of Sultan Baybards, but after a month's siege of the town the knights came out unexpectedly and put them to flight. The power of the Byzantine Empire was shattered—rather an own goal on the part of the crusaders who had sacked Constantinople on the Fourth Crusade in 1204, irrevocably weakening the Empire—and, when the Turks finally took Constantinople in 1453, the Hospitallers on Rhodes were the only Christian outpost left in the East. In 1480 a huge army of Turks, under Palaeologos Pasha, landed and prepared to capture the town by pounding the walls with massive cannon. Thanks to the inspired leadership and careful planning of the Grand Master, D'Aubusson, this attack was also repulsed by the knights, though almost half of their number lost their lives in the defense of their city.

The next attempt came in 1522, with the vast armies of Suleiman the Magnificent under the command of his Grand Vizier, Pir Mahomet Pasha. After six months of heroic resistance, the knights surrendered and were allowed to leave the island, having won the admiration of their enemies and of the western world.

Emperor Charles V, who had been moved by their courage though unable to send them help, donated their next home: Malta. In 1565 they were attacked once again by the forces of Sulieman the Magnificent, now an old man of 70 years. The story of how the knights resisted the siege of Malta, under the leadership of their Grand Master, Jean de la Valette, is one of the most thrilling and inspiring of the age. The tiny force, of perhaps 700 knights and 1,500 men at arms, managed to defeat the full might of the Turkish Empire by meticulous preparation and outstanding courage.

The crusades seriously damaged the Byzantine Empire and ironically strengthened Muslim power in the Middle East. The construction of Crusader States caused the Muslim leaders to reorganize and unify their military efforts against the Christians, finally driving them out in 1291. The crusades also strengthened papal power as popes united so many Christian leaders in a concerted effort against a

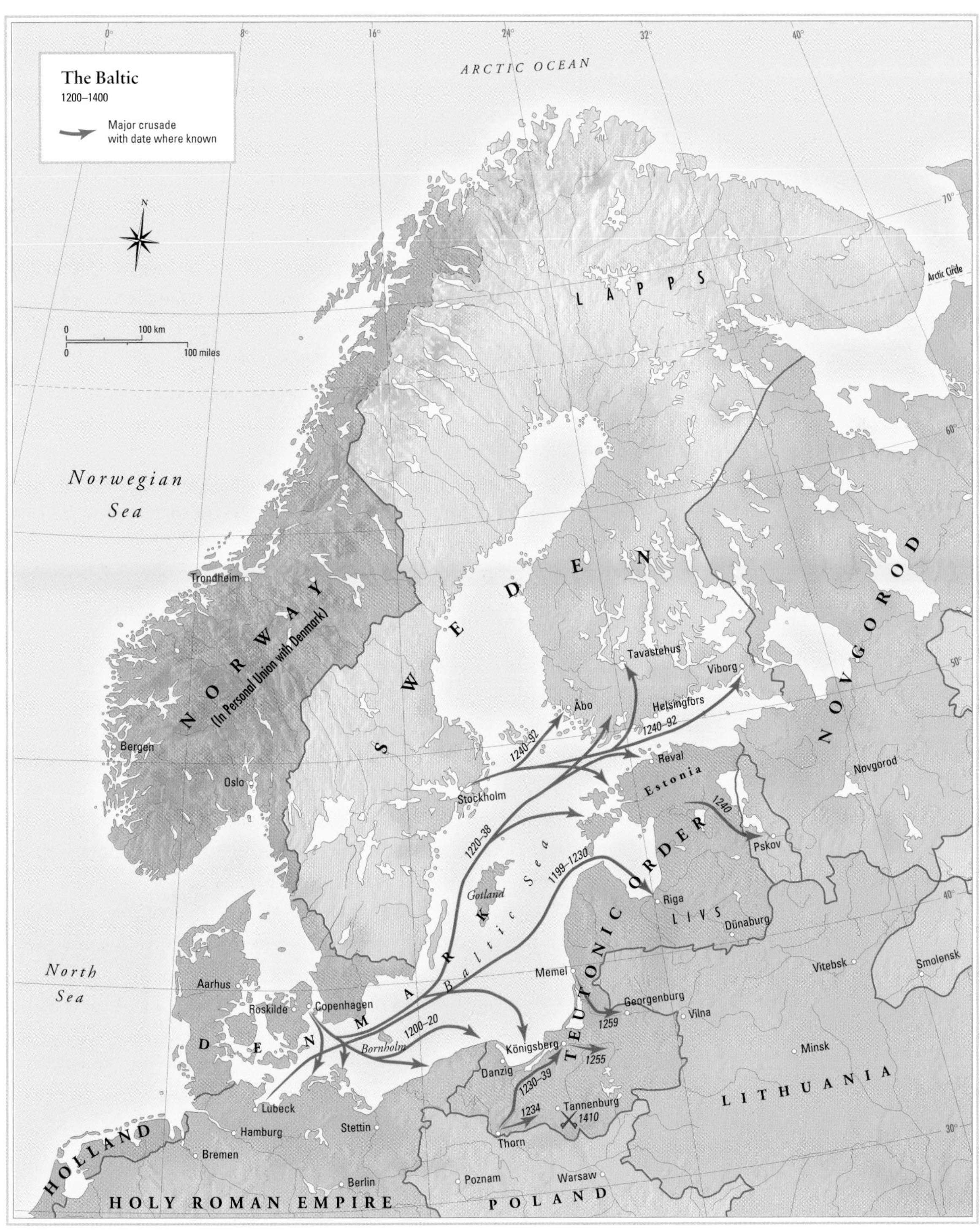
The Baltic
1200–1400
Major crusade with date where known
ARCTIC OCEAN
Norwegian Sea
North Sea
LAPPS
NORWAY
(In Personal Union with Denmark)
SWEDEN
NOVGOROD
DENMARK
TEUTONIC ORDER
Estonia
LIVS
LITHUANIA
HOLLAND
HOLY ROMAN EMPIRE
POLAND
Baltic Sea
Gotland
Bornholm
Trondheim
Bergen
Oslo
Stockholm
Åbo
Tavastehus
Helsingfors
Viborg
Reval
Novgorod
Pskov
Riga
Dünaburg
Memel
Georgenburg
Vilna
Vitebsk
Smolensk
Minsk
Königsberg
Danzig
Tannenburg
Thorn
Warsaw
Poznam
Berlin
Stettin
Lubeck
Hamburg
Bremen
Copenhagen
Roskilde
Aarhus
1240–92
1220–38
1199–1230
1200–20
1230–39
1234
1255
1259
1240
1410
Arctic Circle
100 km
100 miles

THE BATTLE OF TANNENBURG, 1410
The final conversion of the Lithuanians to Catholicism and their union with Poland, seriously undermined the power of the Teutonic Order. In 1410, the combined Polish and Lithuanian forces crushed the Teutonic Knights at the Battle of Tannenburg. Almost all of the senior knights and over 400 other knight-brothers were killed. The victors imposed a vast war indemnity on the Teutonic Knights; this seriously curtailed their program of bringing German-Christian settlers to their Prussian lands. With few heathens left to fight, the Order seems to have lost its vitality. When war was renewed with Poland in the 1450s, it ended with the loss of the Order's properous west Prussian territories to Poland. The Grand Master himself became a vassal of the Polish King. The Order's vast headquarters at Marienburg Castle was also sold to the Polish King to settle the unpaid wages of mercenaries who had fought for the Order.

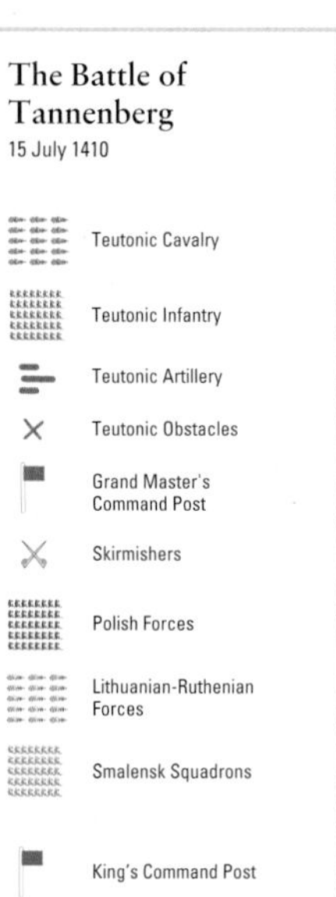

perceived common enemy. Benefits accrued from crusading activities. Western trade penetrated the eastern Mediterranean and flowed into the Black Sea. This trade continued after 1291, chiefly through the activities of Venetian and Genoese traders. Very important, too, was the western study of Arabic when Arab translations of Greek and Roman classic writings were restored to European libraries to be studied again after being translated into Latin.

TEUTONIC KNIGHTS

The Teutonic Knights began as a charitable order looking after German pilgrims in Jerusalem and then running a hospital for wounded German knights outside the city of Acre during its siege by Richard the Lionheart in 1191. When incorporated as the Teutonic Knights of the Hospital of St. Mary the Virgin, they continued to care for the sick and wounded as well as fighting the Turks.

The Order contained knights, sergeants (skilled men at arms who were not knights) and priests; the knights had to be legitimate, German and of knightly descent. They continued to fight in Palestine and Teutonic Knights were killed alongside the Templars and Hospitallers in the heroic last stand at Acre in 1291. However, they had already begun to fight the Holy War on a new front: the Baltic states of northeastern Europe. The King of Hungary and the Duke of Masovia had been struggling against ferocious Prussian tribesmen and appealed to the Teutonic Knights for help. The Grand Master of the Knights, Hermann von Salza, agreed to fight in exchange for the grant of a territory for the knights where they could station themselves and build secure fortifications. The King of Hungary gave them part of his frontier in Transylvania but expelled the knights for attempting to build their own state within his.

THE NORTHERN CRUSADES

The Northern Crusades began when Scandinavian and German rulers considered their neighbors in a new religious light, just as other Europeans had come to regard the Muslims of Spain and Palestine. The Baltic region was seen as a Christian frontier held by armies of the true Holy Church against a hostile, wicked outer world of paganism and a schismatic orthodox Church.

Other motives were present too. Crusaders and rulers wanted to capture trade routes, win land for those who needed it, to augment revenues and reputations of egotistical monarchs and priests, to acquire larger shares of resources, and to grab booty. However, the northern lands were not rich like the Middle East so crusaders might have been less inspired by a profit motive. Northern crusades were decreed by the pope and the Teutonic Knights were commissioned by Rome to wage perpetual Holy War.

The Northern Crusades really began in the 1190s when Popes Celestine III and Innocent III decided to support missionary activity and a church amongst the pagan Livs around the lower reaches of the River Dvina. The fact that German merchants from Lübeck and Bremen were

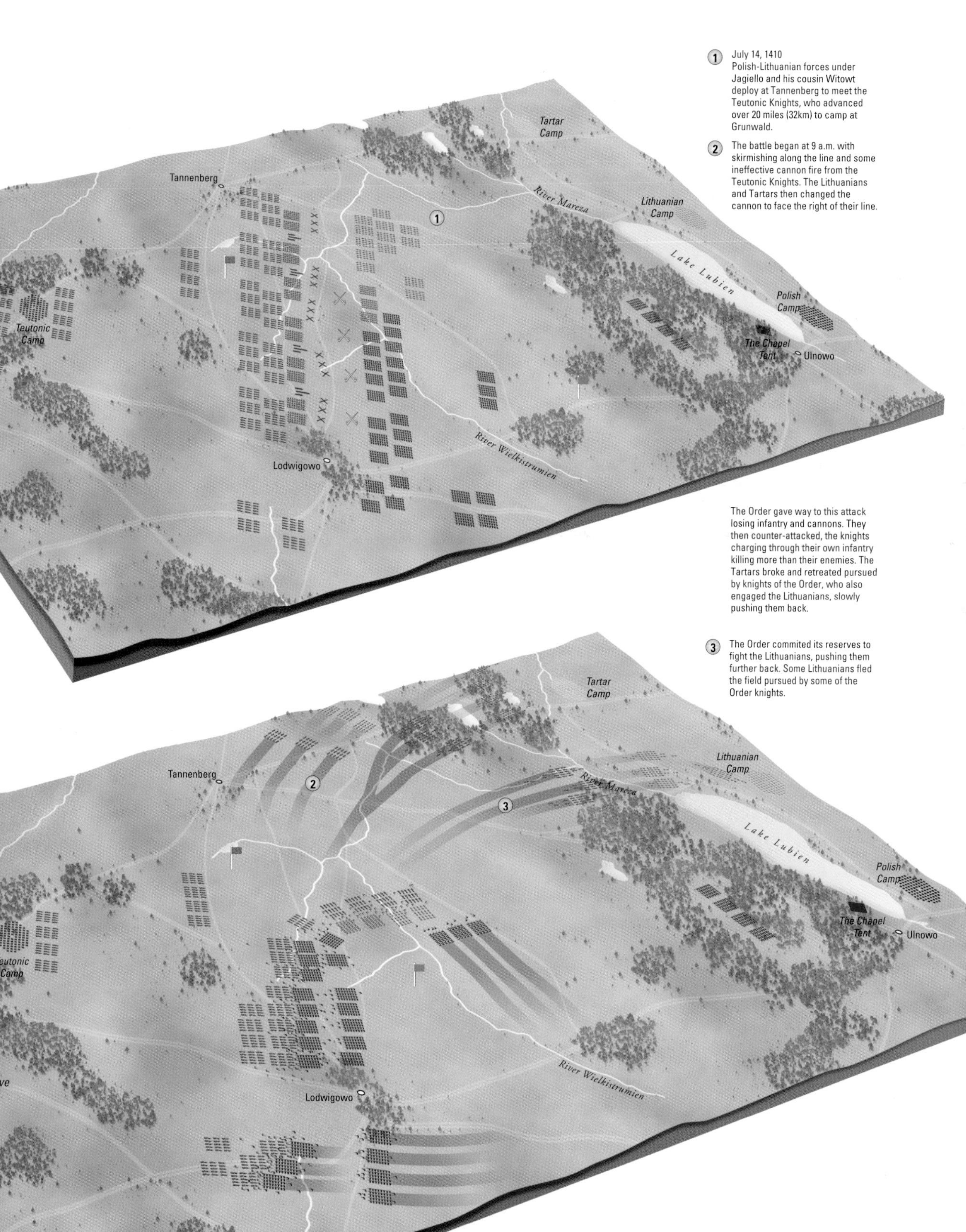
1 July 14, 1410
Polish-Lithuanian forces under Jagiello and his cousin Witowt deploy at Tannenberg to meet the Teutonic Knights, who advanced over 20 miles (32km) to camp at Grunwald.
2 The battle began at 9 a.m. with skirmishing along the line and some ineffective cannon fire from the Teutonic Knights. The Lithuanians and Tartars then changed the cannon to face the right of their line.
The Order gave way to this attack losing infantry and cannons. They then counter-attacked, the knights charging through their own infantry killing more than their enemies. The Tartars broke and retreated pursued by knights of the Order, who also engaged the Lithuanians, slowly pushing them back.
3 The Order commited its reserves to fight the Lithuanians, pushing them further back. Some Lithuanians fled the field pursued by some of the Order knights.
Tartar Camp
Tannenberg
River Mareza
Lithuanian Camp
Lake Lubien
Polish Camp
The Chapel Tent
Ulnowo
Teutonic Camp
River Wielkistrumien
Lodwigowo
1
Tartar Camp
Tannenberg
2
Lithuanian Camp
River Mareza
3
Lake Lubien
Polish Camp
The Chapel Tent
Ulnowo
Teutonic Camp
River Wielkistrumien
Lodwigowo

trading there was probably the trigger for this move. Trade was so important that merchants needed protection. So, in 1202, Bishop of Livonia, Albert von Buxhoevden, founded the Order of the Brothers of the Sword, with papal permission, as a permanent military unit in Livonia to protect the Church's conquests and to forcibly convert pagan tribes and protect trading interests. The Order is also known as the Knights of the Sword, Livonian Order, or Livonian Knights. By 1206, the Order became the dominant power in the territories of the Livs and by 1217 it had conquered the neighboring Latvian tribes north of the Dvina and also southern Estonia. The Order then commenced advances into lands south of the Dvina but the native Curonians and Semigallens put up fierce resistance. In September 1236, the Order's army, overladen with loot from a raid in Lithuanian Samogitia, were attacked by combined forces of Semigallian and Samogitia, being beaten and destroyed as a military force at the Battle of Saule. Grand Master Volquin was killed and the Order was forced, by the pope, to disband and become part of the Teutonic Order (1237). The Pope and the Holy Roman Emperor were concerned that the Order used brutal tactics more to establish a feudal domain than gaining converts to the faith.

Elsewhere, between 1200–1220, the Danes attacked the Pomeranian coast from Lübeck to Danzig, Finland, Prussia, Dagö, and Ösel before capturing northern Estonia in 1220. Further north the Swedes joined the crusading scene with attacks on Finland, but an excursion into Leal in Estonia saw them pushed out by the Danes and the Sword Brothers. Various Swedish crusades were mounted between 1240 and 1292. The latter year witnessed King Birger attacking the Karelians, as disturbers of Christianized Finns. This raid appeared to achieve little; however, in 1295, the King announced to traders from Lübeck, and other Hanseatic towns, that he had converted the Karelians, erecting a castle at Viborg to protect his domains together with travelers and merchants. He hoped to become the protector of the main northeast trade route, thereby making himself indispensable to German merchants and Russians. He could deal with a strong hand to Hanseatic merchants in Swedish towns and with Russo-Karelian fur traders in the Arctic north.

Finland became a home in its southern new land, or Nyland, for small freeholders who wished to avoid Swedish seigneurial impositions. Most profit went to the knights, bishops, and landed magnates. Tithes, conversions, and rents benefited a political élite while the expense of annexation was borne by the peasants. After 1292, papal rhetoric translated Novgorodian raids into the border regions as onslaughts against the Christian faith: knightly and religious values were upheld by fighting Russians. South of Livonia was more pagan territory. A missionary bishop, Christian, a Cisterican, tried to convert the Prussians on the lower Vistula River, with help from a military order known as the Knights of Dobrzyn. Their failure caused Duke Conrad of Masovia to call in the Teutonic Knights.

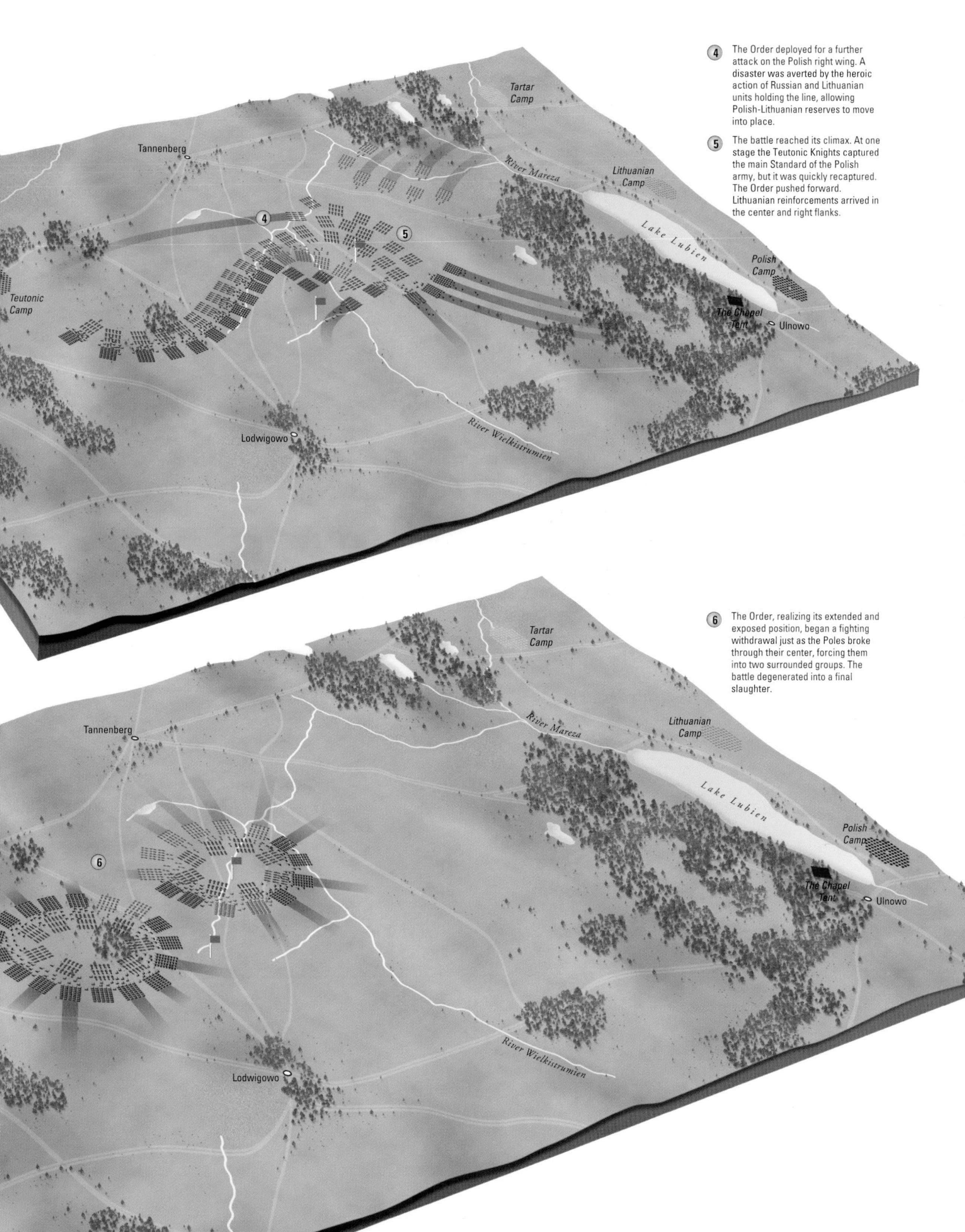
4 The Order deployed for a further attack on the Polish right wing. A disaster was averted by the heroic action of Russian and Lithuanian units holding the line, allowing Polish-Lithuanian reserves to move into place.
5 The battle reached its climax. At one stage the Teutonic Knights captured the main Standard of the Polish army, but it was quickly recaptured. The Order pushed forward. Lithuanian reinforcements arrived in the center and right flanks.
Tartar Camp
Tannenberg
River Mareza
Lithuanian Camp
Lake Lubien
Polish Camp
Teutonic Camp
The Chapel Tent
Ulnowo
River Wielkistrumien
Lodwigowo
6 The Order, realizing its extended and exposed position, began a fighting withdrawal just as the Poles broke through their center, forcing them into two surrounded groups. The battle degenerated into a final slaughter.
Tartar Camp
Tannenberg
River Mareza
Lithuanian Camp
Lake Lubien
Polish Camp
The Chapel Tent
Ulnowo
River Wielkistrumien
Lodwigowo

RECONQUISTA

THE CAPTURE OF GRANADA IN 1492 SIGNALED CHRISTIANIZATION OF THE COMBINED KINGDOMS OF CASTILE AND ARAGON, FROM WHICH WAS EMERGING WHAT WE TODAY CALL SPAIN. THE "RECONQUISTA" USHERED IN FORCED RELIGION CONVERSIONS, ETHNIC CLEANSING, AND THE NOTORIOUS SPANISH INQUISITION.

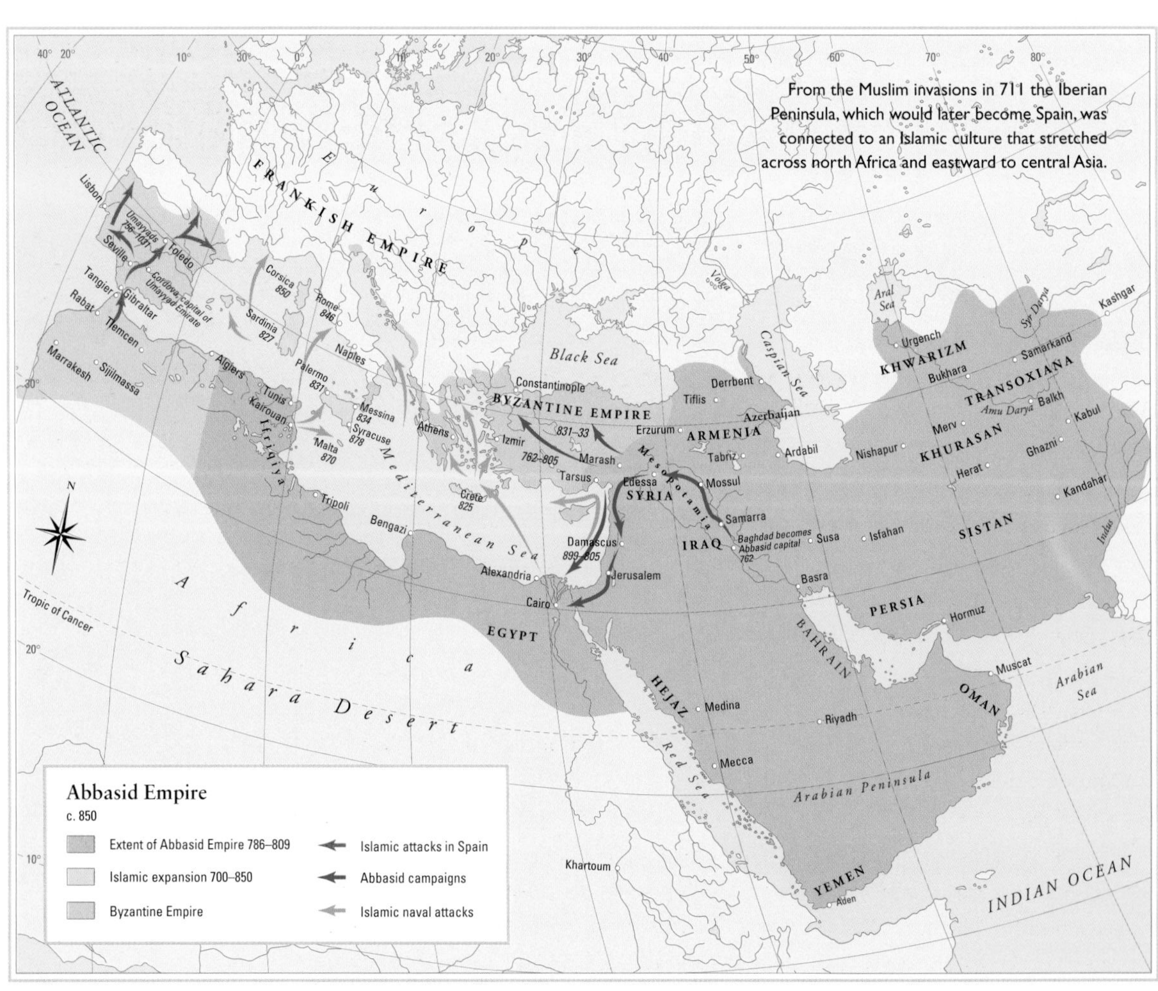

From the Muslim invasions in 711 the Iberian Peninsula, which would later become Spain, was connected to an Islamic culture that stretched across north Africa and eastward to central Asia.

THE FIRST COLD WAR

In the year 711, the Muslim governor of Tangier, Tariq, led a force of Berbers across the Straits of Gibraltar to southern Spain, landing at a rocky promontory still bearing the leader's name, Jabal Tariq (Gibraltar). He moved inland and that year reputedly defeated the Visigothic forces of King Roderic, before occupying Cordoba and Toledo. Shortly after, the Arab governor of Ifriqiya (North Africa), Musa ibn Nusayr, took reinforcement to Spain. He captured Seville, Merida, and Zaragoza, thereby bringing the Ebro Valley under his control. His son, 'Abd al-'Aziz, continued the conquest, bringing almost the whole peninsula under his control except for the mountainous areas of the western and central Pyrenees. The Muslim territory in Spain would be known as al-Andalus, with Córdoba as the center of government.

Al-Andalus was torn by internal dissension. An Arab elite of landowners, military governors, and civil servants reduced the Berbers to a second class rural proletariat who rebelled. Syrian troops were sent by Caliph Hisham to quell the disorder. Defeated by Maghrab Berbers, the Syrian remnants crossed to Spain and pacified the Andalusi Berbers, receiving lands in payment in 742. Thus was introduced to the peninsula an intertribal hostility: the original Arab settlers were descended from a Yemeni federation of tribes whose traditional enemies were the Qaysis, the Syrians being part of the latter confederation. Andalusi politics were bedeviled by this feud for generations. The Berber insurrection had another outcome. Muslim garrisons north of the Douro were withdrawn to fight in the south, allowing the Christians of the Asturias, who rebelled in 718–722 against Muslim rule, to consolidate their independence.

A Christian warrior and a Muslim warrior play chess, in this symbolic 12th-Century illustration, reflecting the fact that al-Andalus, Cordoba, and Granada were once home to a rich cultural mix, and that an uneasy peace existed prior to the Reconquest by crusading knights.

In 756, a grandson of Caliph Hisham, after surviving an Abbasid purge of his family, seized Córdoba, proclaiming himself emir or prince of an independent Andalus. The country was divided into three Marches: the Lower based on Merida; the Middle, centered in Toledo; and the Upper in the Ebro Valley with a capital in Zaragoza. Power remained with local Berber tribes with an admixture of lordly Arab families, and muwallad (mixed ancestry) families of Visigothic descent who had converted to Islam, such as the Banu Qasi family. Al-Andalus was constantly rent by inter-ethnic rivalries leading to semi-independent princes who began to fortify their residences. The majority Christian and Jewish communities, "People of the Book" according to Islam, sometimes converted to Islam in order to integrate themselves in Muslim society to enhance career prospects and have access to wealth and power. Although not embracing Islam, most Christians became increasingly Arabized, being known as Mozarabs, from the Arabic *musta'rib*, meaning Arabized. Thus, al-Andalus was a polity (organized society) of great diversity but a real problem was growing. In 854, Paulus Alvarus of Córdoba bemoaned the fact that Christian youth preferred Arabic and Muslim learning to their own. Some Christians objected so much to Islam that they publicly denounced the faith, incurring the death penalty. Forty eight Christians were executed, including Bishop Eulogius of Toledo. Religious divisions would also develop with the other Spains in the northern mountains. The confrontation developing was to become known as a "cold war," the term coined in the 14th Century by Don Juan Manuel during the "Reconquista," the reconquest of Spain. He depicted a religious-ideological struggle between totally different life and culture styles.

To go back, Christian resistance had defeated the Arabs in 722 at Covadonga, leading to the establishment of the Christian in the Asturias under King Pelayo. His heirs grabbed Cantabria and Galicia, savaging and ravaging the Duro Valley, creating an empty buffer zone between Christians and Muslims. Other resistance centers sprang up in Pamplona and Aragon, while the Carolingians captured Gerona in 785 and Barcelona in 801, creating a Spanish March against the Muslims, also being a buffer for the Carolingian Empire.

After 929, the Emir at Córdoba elevated himself to the rank of Caliph. Independent al-Andalus had commenced a southward march into the Duro Valley creating a new border with this resettlement, being defended for a century by fortresses such as Simancas and by warrior settlers organized by abbeys like Sahagún. The next Christian surge took place after 1002, the caliphate of Córdoba having disintegrated into some 36 statelets, known as the Taifa Kingdoms. Disunited, Muslim power collapsed, the taifa paying tribute to the Christians until 1085 when Alfonso VI of

León came to power. Further Christian attacks appeared imminent so the Muslims pleaded for aid from the Almoravid rulers of northwest Africa, who defeated Alfonso in 1086 at Sagrajas, annexing Muslim Spain to their own empire. All the taifa rulers fell from power and the Almoravid advance was only stopped by Rodrigo Díaz de Bivar (El Cid) in Valencia. In 1102, three years after his death, his widow, Jimena, evacuated the city and region, leaving it to be overrun by the Almoravids.

Elsewhere, in Aragon, crusading commenced when, with papal help, King Sancho Ramírez recruited thousands of French mercenaries, all hungry for land and imbued with religious feelings. He and his heirs conquered the Muslim Kingdom of Saragoza, uniting it with Aragon and Catalonia creating a new state, a rival to both Léon and the Almoravids. Most Almoravid Berber attacks were aimed at Toledo and this bastion sapped their strength. Kings Alfonso VI and VII of León, also with papal help, reconstructed their kingdom with Europeanizing policies such as adopting the Roman liturgy instead of the Mozarabic one, and replacing Visigothic with Carolingian script. The state's religious, military, and demographic resources were developed and when the Almoravid Empire collapsed in 1140, Alfonso VII managed to extend Christian power to the Tagus Valley, allowing the Muslims to retain the southern part of Spain.

ARAGON AND CASTILE

The year of 1140 ushered in deep-seated changes in the political geography of Muslim and Christian Spain. The Almoravids were overthrown and replaced by the puritanical Almohad sect from northwest Berber Africa, their leader claiming to be a *mahdí*, a promised messianic figure. Meanwhile the large Leonese kingdom separated into three: Portugal, Castile, and León. All three kingdoms attempted expansion south along the old Roman roads such as the Camino de la Plata from León to Seville, ensuring conflict with the Almohads.

This Reconquest is an example of crusading, despite the fact that the Spanish Christians received little help from other countries. Nevertheless, the crusading spirit and technique was spreading with military orders, Santiago and Calatrava and others, being established to defend the borders. King Alfonso VIII of Castile captured Cuenca in 1177 and marched southwest to Plasencia and Trujillo. Defeated at Alarcos by the Caliph in 1195, he waged a successful campaign to thoroughly smash the Almohads at Las Navas de Tolosa in 1212, where he led the allied armies of Castile, Navarre, and Aragon, with some crusaders. However, the Christians derived little benefit from this victory. Peter II of Aragon became involved in the Albigensian Crusade in France and was killed in battle by Simon de Montfort; Aragon was left with five year old James I as king being fought over by a fractious baronage. In 1214, Caliph Mohammad and Alfonso VIII died, pushing Aragon and Castile to reach a truce with the Muslims. Portugal witnessed the death of Sancho I who left his inexperienced son, Alfonso II, to achieve little, except a fleet of German crusaders bound for Egypt captured Alcacer do Sol in 1217. Political infighting elsewhere eventually allowed the reuniting of the kingdoms of Castile and León.

The Almohad state saw various contenders vying for the caliphate, often using Christian

In this 13th Century illustration the results of close quarter battle can clearly be seen. In the excavation of burials at battle sites, most combatants died of head and neck wounds.

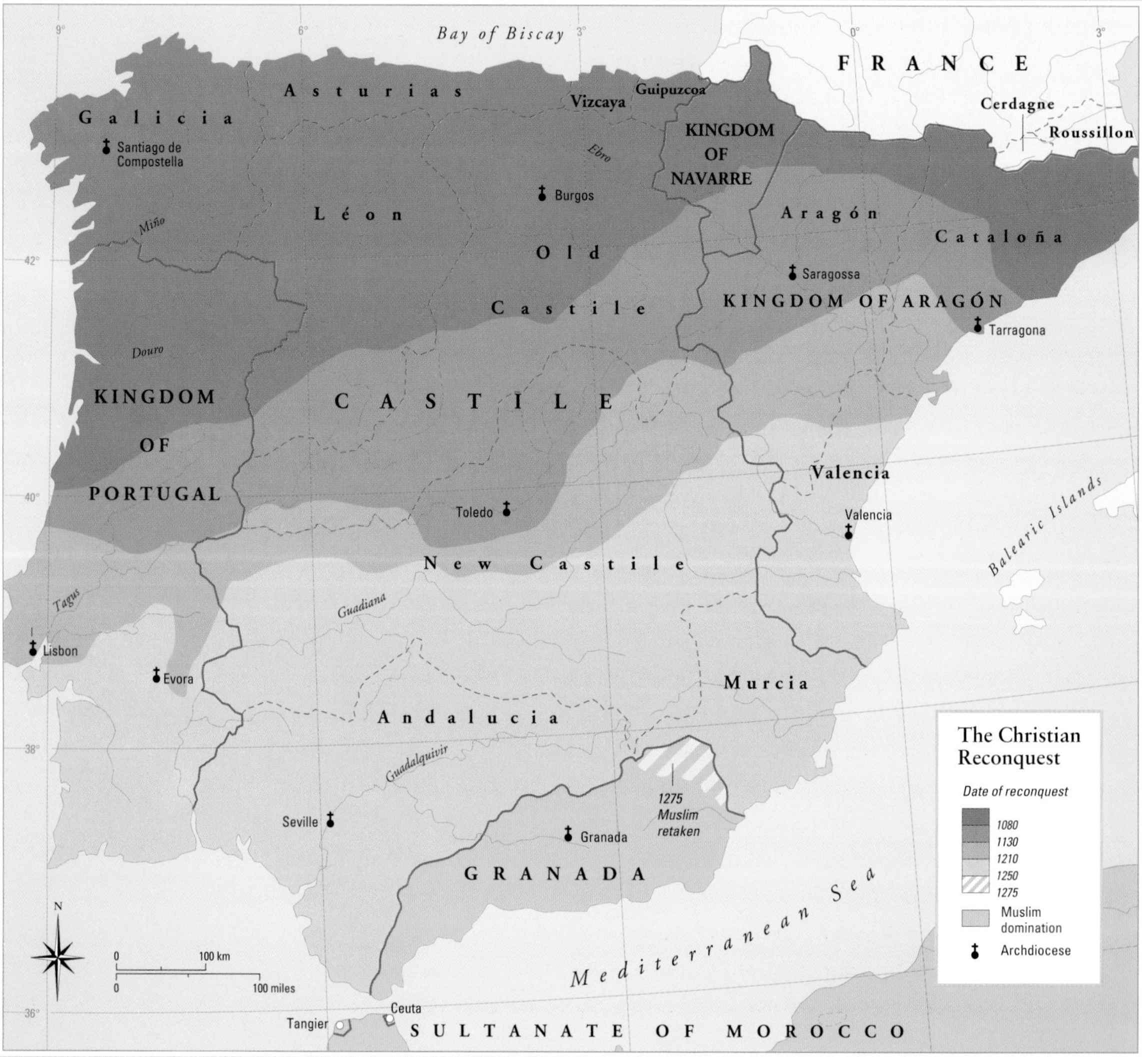

Bay of Biscay

FRANCE

Asturias

Vizcaya

Guipuzcoa

Galicia

Santiago de Compostella

KINGDOM OF NAVARRE

Cerdagne

Roussillon

Ebro

Burgos

Léon

Aragón

Cataloña

Miño

Old Castile

Saragossa

KINGDOM OF ARAGÓN

Tarragona

Douro

KINGDOM OF PORTUGAL

CASTILE

Valencia

Valencia

Toledo

Balearic Islands

New Castile

Tagus

Guadiana

Lisbon

Evora

Murcia

Andalucia

Guadalquivir

1275 Muslim retaken

Seville

Granada

GRANADA

Mediterranean Sea

0 100 km

0 100 miles

N

Tangier

Ceuta

SULTANATE OF MOROCCO

The Christian Reconquest

Date of reconquest

1080

1130

1210

1250

1275

Muslim domination

Archdiocese

mercenaries. One claimant was defeated by Alfonso IX of León at Alange in 1230 allowing Alfonso to take Badajoz and its hinterland. One of the new taifa rulers was Muhammad ibn a'-Ahmar (1237–72) who, in 1237, created the new state of Granada that lasted until the 15th Century. The Christian kingdoms were facing a much weakened and divided Muslim Spain and soon sought to expand their territories at Muslim expense. The pope offered crusading indulgences and the Spanish kingdoms advanced. James I of Aragon captured Majorca and the Balearic islands (1229–33), and then invaded the *taifa* (independent Muslim-ruled principality) of Valencia (1232–45), the city itself being captured in 1238. Majorca and Valencia became separate kingdoms in the dynastic union known as the Crown of Aragon. James expelled the Muslims from the cities and turned them into virtual serfdom in the countryside under a new landowning nobility from Aragon and Catalonia. In the east, Alfonso IX of León marched south into current Spanish Extramadura, gaining Cáceres in 1227 and Mérida. Ferdinand III of Castile advanced down the Guadalquiver Valley, winning Córdoba in 1236, Jaén in 1246, and Seville in 1248. His grandson, Alfonso X, expelled all Muslims from Catilian Andalucia repopulating the area with thousands of Christians. The Murcian taifa was captured by Castile in 1243–44. By 1249, the Portuguese, ruled by Alfonso III (1248–79), ended their campaigns by capturing the southernmost regions of the Algarve. Landlocked Navarre failed to benefit from the Muslim collapse. By the mid-13th Century Muslim Spain had been reduced to the new, small kingdom of Granada and a few enclaves on the Atlantic coast. The Muslims were in despair over the collapse of their power.

The poet, Abu al-Baqa' al-Rundi, from Ronda, wrote a poem in 1267, *Lament for the Fall of Seville*, in the hope of getting aid from north African Muslims to contain the Christian threat.

> *'Where is Córdoba, the home of the sciences, and many a scholar whose rank was once lofty in it?*
> *Where is Seville and the pleasure it contains, as well as its sweet river overflowing and brimming full?*
> *[They are] capitals which were the pillars of the land, yet when the pillars are gone, it may no longer endure!*
> *The tap of the white ablution fount weeps in despair, like a passionate lover weeping at the departure of the beloved'*
> *Over dwellings emptied of Islam that were first vacated and are now inhabited by unbelief;*
> *In which the mosques have become churches wherein only bells and crosses may be found....*
> *Are there no heroic souls with lofty ambitions; are there no helpers and defenders of righteousness?*
> *O, who will redress the humiliation of a people who were once powerful, a people whose condition injustice and tyrants have changed?*
> *Yesterday they were kings in their own homes, but today they are slaves in the land of the infidel.'*

FERDINAND AND ISABELLA

The remaining two centuries of the Reconquest involved occasional warfare. Granada continued to survive by paying tribute, and it was further protected by its mountainous nature, the many fortresses and castles that had been built, and a large population and the diplomatic skill of its rulers maintaining its independence until 1492. Meanwhile, Morocco was ruled by the Marinids, another orthodox tribe decided to wage jihad against Christian Spain. The Emir of Granada gave the Moroccans a base on the Straits of Gibraltar from where they could raid the Guadalquiver Valley. They failed to capture any cities but they drew the attention of Castile, thereby allowing Granada to continue consolidating its position. Moroccan volunteers helped protect Granada's borders and even recapture some towns that had been taken by the Christians. Aragon and Portugal had almost given up the Reconquest until, in 1340, Alfonso IV of Portugal helped Alfonso XI of Castile to defeat the Muslims by the River Salado, which lead to the capture of Algeciras in 1344, ending Moroccan adventures in Spain.

MONZON CASTLE
One of the Templar strongholds in Spain. The Templar Order was closely associated with the Reconquest of Spain. Northern Spain, the center for pilgrimages to the shrine of St. James of Compostela, was liberally dotted with Templar castles. These defended Christian Spain from Moorish incursions; however, the wealth and power of the Templars made them an object of envy and suspicion. The French King, Philip IV, ordered the arrest of the leaders of the Order on charges of heresy in 1307. Later the Templar's Spanish property was granted to other military orders.

Civil wars in Castile gave a breathing space to Granada from 1350, allowing it to to capture and sack several cities. After 1388, the Castilian Kings restored themselves and were able to capture Antequerra in 1410 and were victorious at La Higueruela in 1431. From that date until 1480, Granada and Castile were rent by civil wars, leaving local lords to engage in intermittent border skirmishes. The military orders of Calatrava and Santiago's castles protected roads and trade routes and guarded Castilian borders. Some Spanish clans such as the Guzmáns and Fajardos raided Granada seizing castles, slaves, and loot. Foreign crusaders sometimes helped but occasionally cooperated with the enemy to hinder cross-border crime.

In 1479, King Ferdinand V and Queen Isabella of Castile inherited Aragon, unifying Christian Spain and imbuing it with a crusading spirit with the intent of capturing Granada. A *casus belli* was provided in December 1481 when Muslims attacked the frontier town of Zahara. The Christians immediately seized Alhambra the following February and made preparations for all out war. A ten-year war followed. The Castilian nobility provided troops as did town militias; a largely Swiss mercenary force was hired. The papacy offered spiritual indulgences for foreign volunteers. The pope granted the monarchs 10 percent of the revenues of the Spanish Church for war expenses as well as other grants, providing vast quantities of gold to Ferdinand and Isabella.

The Christians were helped by another Granadan civil war. Seizing the opportunity, Christian armies with their enormous financial backing and a sizable artillery train reduced Granadan castles and cities: Ronda fell in 1485; Málaga in1487; and Muhammad XIII surrendered Guadix and the port of Almería in 1489. Granada was besieged in 1491 and terms of surrender were negotiated in 1491. In January 1492, Ferdinand and Isabella entered the city in triumph. Approximately 200,000 Muslims moved to North Africa. Those remaining were guaranteed their property, laws,

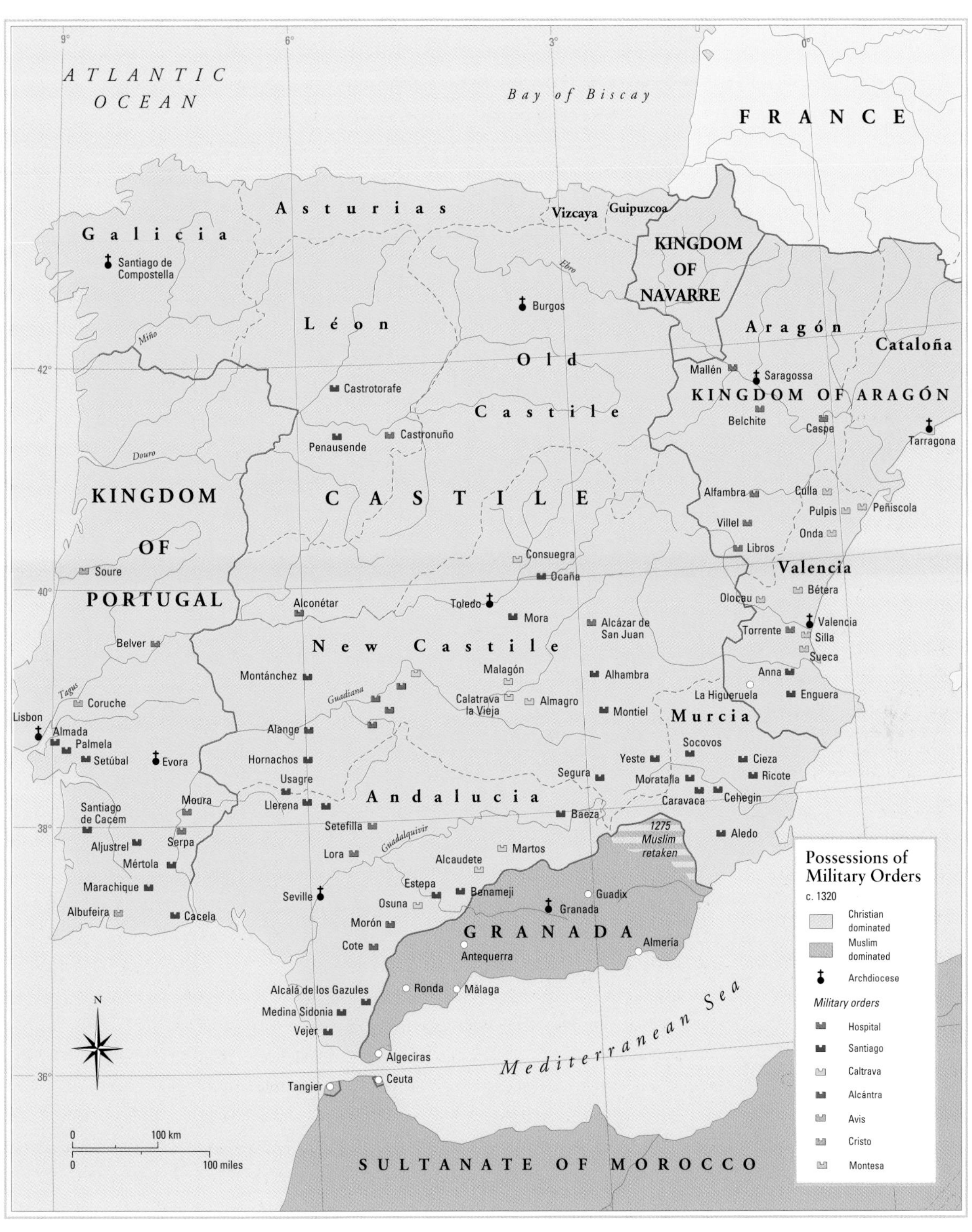
ATLANTIC OCEAN
Bay of Biscay
FRANCE
Asturias
Vizcaya
Guipuzcoa
Galicia
Santiago de Compostella
KINGDOM OF NAVARRE
Burgos
León
Aragón
Cataloña
Old Castile
Mallén
Saragossa
KINGDOM OF ARAGÓN
Castrotorafe
Castile
Belchite
Caspe
Tarragona
Castronuño
Penausende
KINGDOM OF PORTUGAL
CASTILE
Alfambra
Culla
Pulpis
Peñiscola
Villel
Onda
Libros
Consuegra
Soure
Ocaña
Valencia
Bétera
Alconétar
Toledo
Olocau
Mora
Alcázar de San Juan
Valencia
Belver
Torrente
Silla
New Castile
Sueca
Malagón
Alhambra
Anna
Montánchez
Coruche
Calatrava la Vieja
Almagro
La Higueruela
Enguera
Lisbon
Montiel
Murcia
Almada
Alange
Palmela
Socovos
Setúbal
Evora
Hornachos
Yeste
Cieza
Usagre
Segura
Moratalla
Ricote
Moura
Llerena
Andalucia
Caravaca
Cehegin
Santiago de Cacem
Baeza
1275 Muslim retaken
Setefilla
Aledo
Aljustrel
Serpa
Lora
Martos
Mértola
Alcaudete
Marachique
Estepa
Benameji
Guadix
Seville
Osuna
Granada
Albufeira
Cacela
Morón
GRANADA
Almería
Cote
Antequerra
Alcalá de los Gazules
Ronda
Màlaga
Medina Sidonia
Vejer
Algeciras
Mediterranean Sea
Ceuta
Tangier
0 100 km
0 100 miles
SULTANATE OF MOROCCO
Possessions of Military Orders
c. 1320
Christian dominated
Muslim dominated
Archdiocese
Military orders
Hospital
Santiago
Caltrava
Alcántra
Avis
Cristo
Montesa

customs and religion, in addition to their own judges and officials. The conquest of Granada was followed by the expulsion of Jews and Moriscos, Muslims baptized into Christianity, in a burst of religious intolerance. The guarantees of 1492 were soon ended and the Inquisition, instigated in 1478, continued its brutal work in rooting out heretics. Arabic books were burnt, traditional Arab dress was banned and bath-houses were outlawed. Spain turned in on itself and lost some very productive citizens as religious refugees.

AL-ANDALUS

Al-Andalus, the name for Muslim Spain, benefited from the wider Muslim civilization of which it was part. Despite civil wars and border skirmishing, al-Andalus drew from the knowledge of all Muslim conquered nations that the Arabs digested and refined. Philosophers read and provided commentaries on Plato and Aristotle while doctors read medical treatises of Galen and other Greek medical men, developing new cures and drugs. Astronomers built on Ptolemy's work and gave stars Arabic names that are still used today. Mathematics was developed using the Arabic numeral system, borrowed from the Hindus, including the number 0, so fundamental for the growth of European mathematics. In this brilliant culture, cities developed and none was more resplendent than Córdoba.

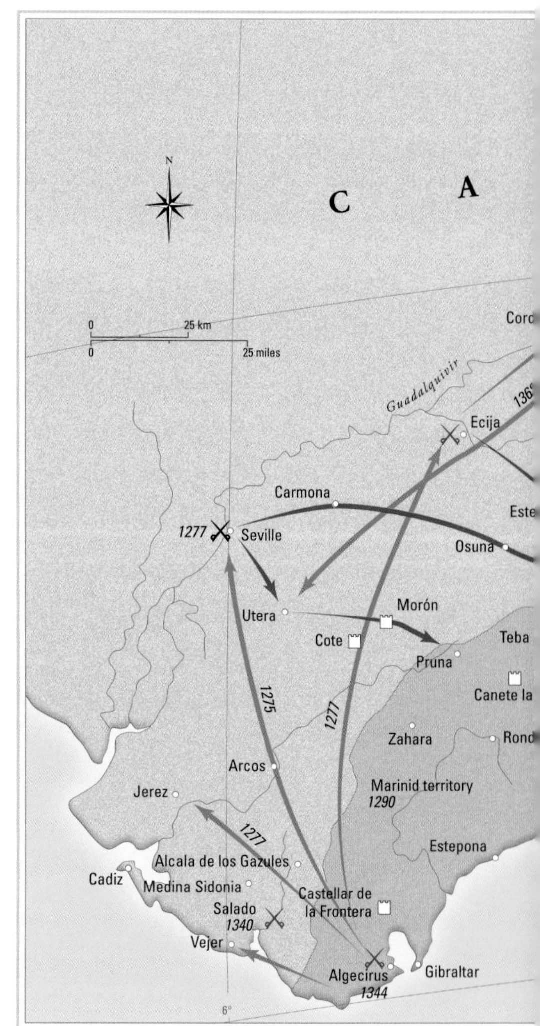

Córdoba was renowned for its one million population, 300 mosques, 60,000 palaces and great buildings, for its university, 80 free schools, and 300 public baths. The city possessed an efficient police force, sanitation service and street lighting. Muslim travelers in Christian Europe would comment on the dirty bodies, the clothes that were never washed, and the general lack of hygiene. Roswitha, a German religious woman and poetess from Saxony called Córdoba "a splendid jewel." A Frankish monk, Gerbert of Aurillac (c. 945–1003) went to Córdoba to learn mathematics and astronomy. Scholars traveled there to use its libraries to read ancient preserved texts and to read newer Islamic works. The medical texts of philisopher and physician Ibn Sina (980–1037), who was known as Avicenna, became major exponents of the healing arts and the rationalist philosophy of Ibd Rushd (1126–1198), who was known as Averroes, laid the foundations for a school of intellectual thought in 13th Century Paris.

This rich Andalusi culture was underpinned by agricultural surpluses, a green revolution, which allowed urban centers to expand and produce goods for internal consumption and export. New vegetables were introduced such as aubergines and asparagus with staple crops like rice, cotton, and sugar-cane. With these, irrigation systems were established with the help of the *noria* or water

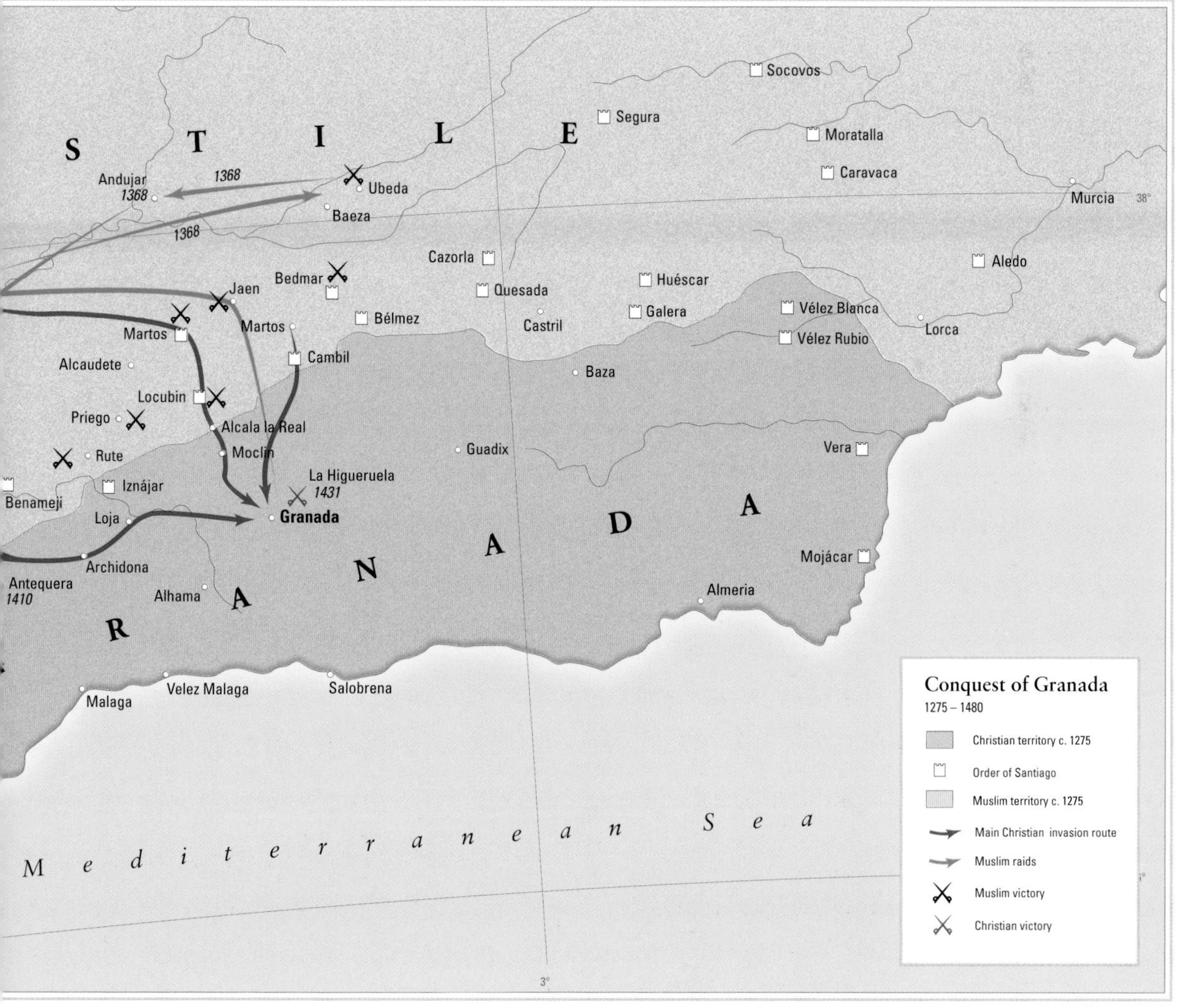

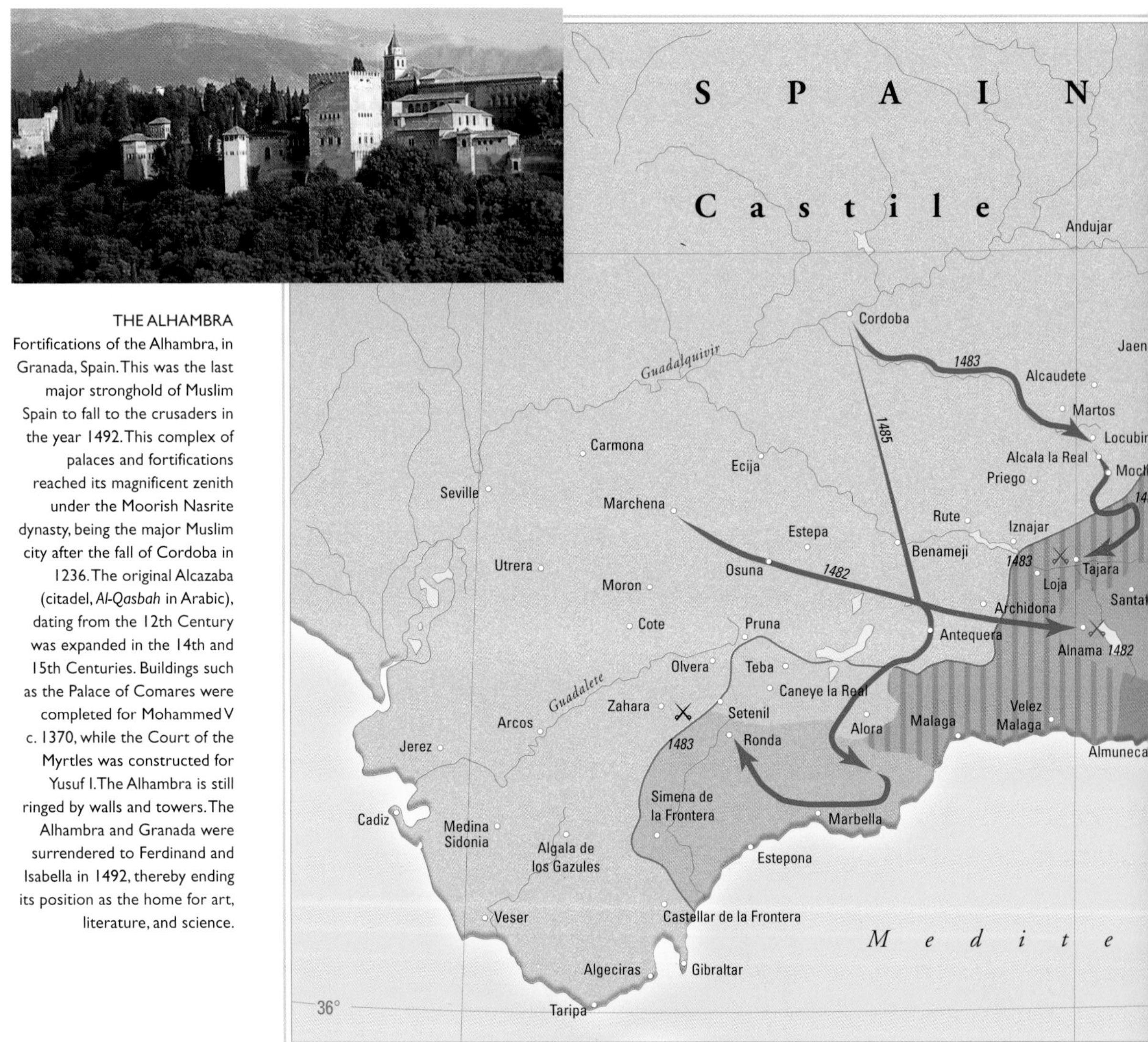

THE ALHAMBRA
Fortifications of the Alhambra, in Granada, Spain. This was the last major stronghold of Muslim Spain to fall to the crusaders in the year 1492. This complex of palaces and fortifications reached its magnificent zenith under the Moorish Nasrite dynasty, being the major Muslim city after the fall of Cordoba in 1236. The original Alcazaba (citadel, *Al-Qasbah* in Arabic), dating from the 12th Century was expanded in the 14th and 15th Centuries. Buildings such as the Palace of Comares were completed for Mohammed V c. 1370, while the Court of the Myrtles was constructed for Yusuf I. The Alhambra is still ringed by walls and towers. The Alhambra and Granada were surrendered to Ferdinand and Isabella in 1492, thereby ending its position as the home for art, literature, and science.

wheel, which scooped bucket after bucket of water into a basin that fed irrigation channels. The laws governing water distribution survived into the Christian period, these laws having originated in Syria and the Yemen. Legend says that Mu'tamid of Seville planted hills with almond trees so blossom could please his queen with the effect of snow. Linens, cottons, silks, metals, ceramics, glassware, leather, paper, dried fruit, and olive oil linked into Europe, the Mediterranean, and the entire Islamic world. Andalusi textiles went to Egypt and maybe India; Málaga figs were eaten in Baghdad while imports included spices, flax, raw wool, perfumes, and precious stones. The country acted as a transit station rerouting furs from northern Europe, Russia, and Central Asia, gold from the western Sudan, and slaves from Christian Spain and Eastern Europe. The latter saqaliba Slav

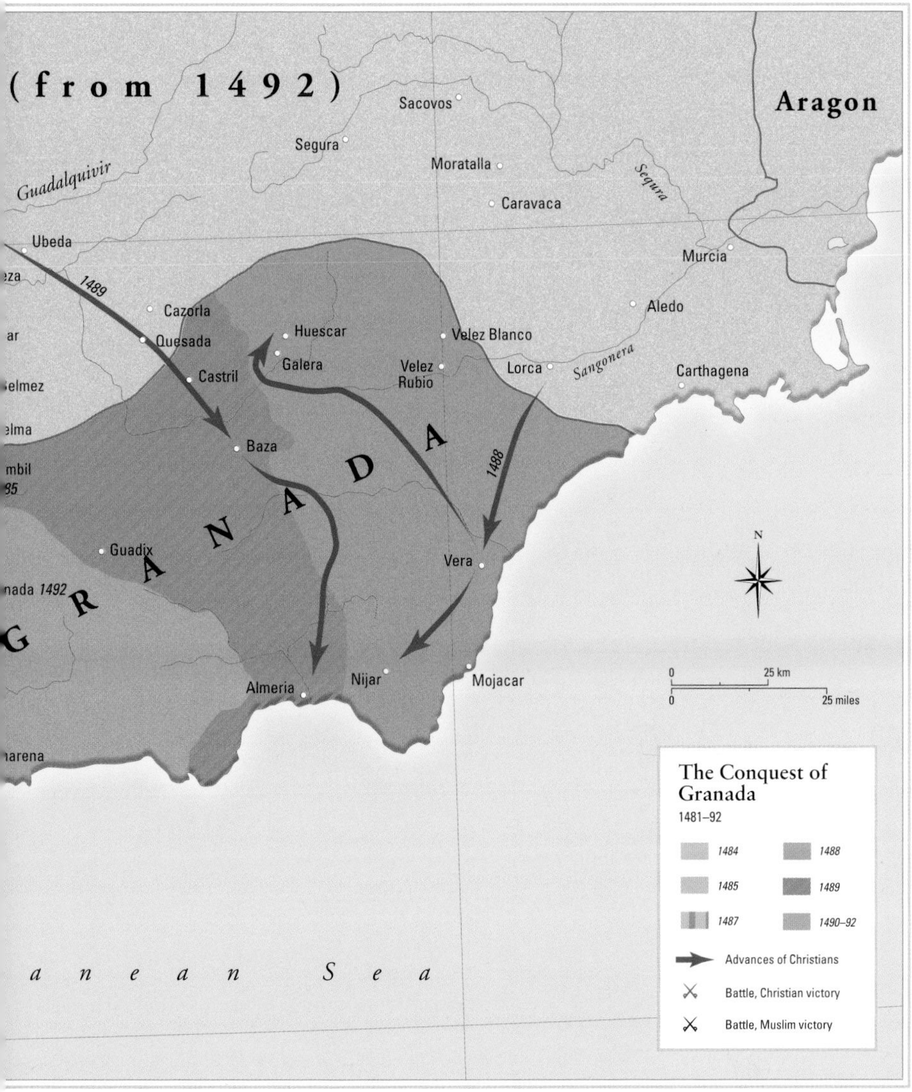

The Conquest of Granada
1481–92

1484 · 1485 · 1487 · 1488 · 1489 · 1490–92

Advances of Christians

Battle, Christian victory

Battle, Muslim victory

An interior of the Alhambra Palace. Its Muslim architecture left a permanent mark on the new Spain, its features would occur in Christian buildings built after the conquest. A noticeable example is the *Alcázar* (Arabic for castle) in Seville. Also, Seville Cathedral, begun in 1402, is built on the site of a mosque, a fact reflected in its broad, rectangular floor plan. Indeed, some features of colonial Spanish architecture in the New World show clear Muslim influence.

and north Europeans were used as mercenaries and to people the civil service. Umayyad rulers patronised culture, 'Abd al-Rahman II embracing the cultural influences of the eastern Islamic world. An exiled Persian scholar and musician, Ziryab, became the judge of good taste in Córdoban high society. He brought in new fashions in hairstyles, clothes, and cuisine, as well as the guitar, toothpaste, and underarm deodorants, albeit not in tubes nor aerosols. The rule of 'Abd al-Rahman III and his son and heir, al-Hakam II (961–976) saw an explosion of works in science, geography, history, philosophy, and grammar.

Under the Almoravid rulers, the regime became immensely rich with Andalusian workmanship appearing on tombstones in the neighborhood of Gao on the Niger, with Ghanian gold flowing

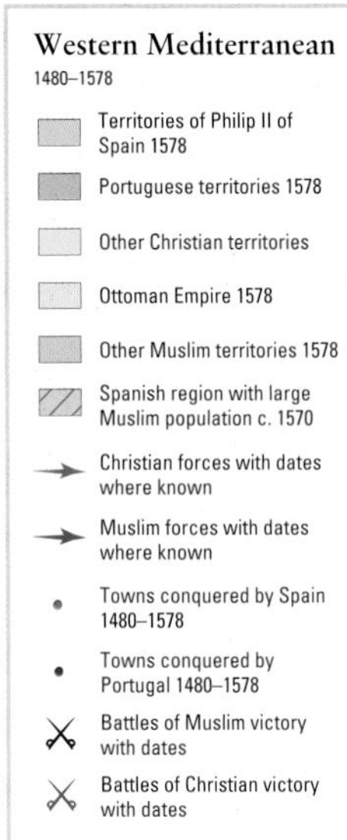

northward to Marrakesh and onward. Almoravid gold dinars swamped the silver dirham, which was the standard currency of the Maghreb. Such wealth brought power to be used in the strangest fashions; Catalans were used as a police force in North Africa for many years.

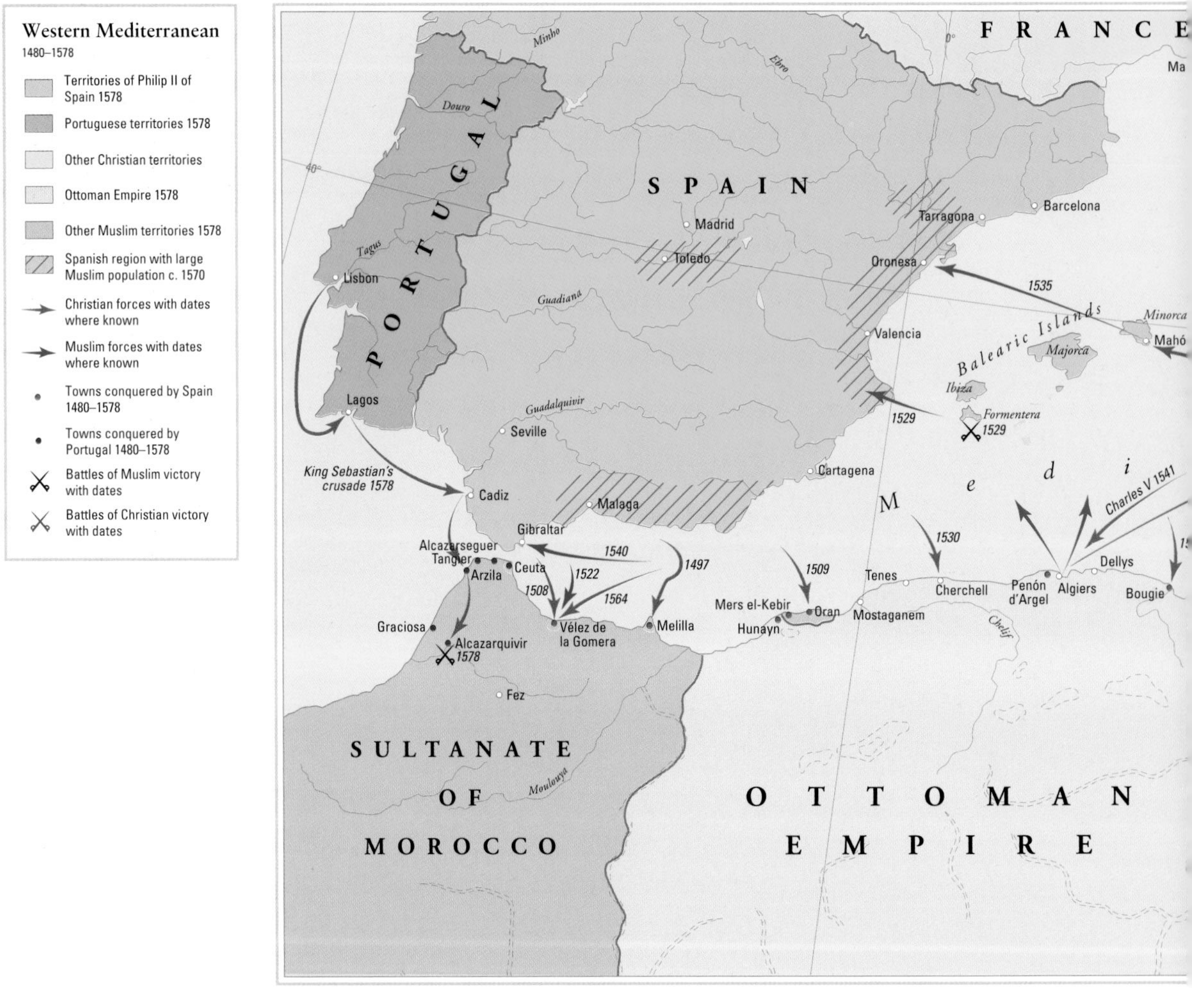

When unitary political power in al-Andalus disintegrated into the taifa states, new rulers sought to mirror the glory of the Umayyads with huge building projects such as the Aljafería Palace at Zaragoza. Cuenca witnessed a school of ivory carving under the patronage of the Dhu'l Nunids of Toledo. Important writers were the astronomer Ibn al-Zarqiyal whose readership extended all over Europe and Ibn Hazm of Cordoba who wrote a treatise on love, *The Ring of the Dove*.

A cultural bridge existed between Christian and Muslim Spain. As the Christians advanced southward, they digested Islamic styles of architecture and decoration, using brick, plaster, and wood instead of stone. The Chapel of La Asuncíon, built in the royal nunnery of Las Huelgas in Burgos in the late 12th Century is definitely influenced by Almohad and Arab craftsmen. Likewise,

An early drawing of the coat of arms of the United Kingdom of Spain, showing the arms of Castile quartered with those of Aragon. The pomegranate and leaf motifs at the bottom of the shield ae intended to represent the newly conquered Kingdom of Granada.

the frescoes decorating the ceiling of the Sala de los Reyes in the Alhambra Palace-complex in Granada—much of the work implemented under Nasrid patronage in the 14th Century—might have been carried out by Christian artists.

This, then, was the culture that held much of Spain in thrall for so long until it was "rescued" by chivalrous Christian knights on crusade. But, each side has its knight as revealed in the poem *The Sweet Smell of the Bough of Andalus the Fresh and Tender*, by Al-Maqqari, the last great historian of Muslim Spain.

"For God the knights have let their pennants fly
As hawks upon your highness' foemen bent;
Their spears shall dot the I's their swords inscribe,
dust dry the ink, and blood the paper scent..."

New Threats

THE MONGOLS WERE A MAJOR MENACE TO RUSSIA AND EUROPE, WHERE STATES LINKED TO ROMAN CATHOLICISM WERE BEING ESTABLISHED. THE MONGOLS CAMPAIGNED IN WINTER, USING FROZEN RIVERS AS HIGHWAYS. RUSSIAN PRINCIPALITIES WERE PLACED UNDER THE TATAR YOKE BEFORE ATTACKS WERE MADE UPON EASTERN AND CENTRAL EUROPE AND THE BALKANS, DEPOPULATING AREAS AND BURNING TOWNS AND CITIES.

EUROPE ON THE EVE OF THE MONGOL INVASIONS c. 1220
In the west, France was engaged in lengthy wars with England, in Spain the Reconquista had gathered pace opening the way into Muslim territory. The Holy Roman Empire, while impressive on the map, was a lose amalgam of petty states owing allegiance to the Emperor. Each state may or may not obey his call to arms. In the east, the Byzantine Empire had been severely weakened by the fourth crusade attacking and capturing Constantinople, fracturing its political cohesiveness. Hungary had grown in power but still looked to its restless eastern and southern borderlands. There was no power or unity through which Europe could face any external new threat.

The major monarchs of the late 15th Century began to organize centralization policies in finance and administrative reform, building a foundation for the emergence of the nation-states of Europe: England, France, and Spain. However, the Christian states were facing new threats around their borders while within Europe the faith was being questioned by heretics, the precursors of the Reformation and religious wars between Protestant and Roman Catholic.

To the north, Denmark became increasingly powerful in the Baltic. Queen Margaret of Denmark (1353–1412) became Regent of Norway and Sweden, the latter because rebellious nobles wanted to oust their King, Albert of Mecklenburg. Margaret attacked Albert's forces, defeating and capturing him, with Stockholm being acquired in 1388. Margaret's political manipulation secured the succession of all three Scandinavian crowns for her sister's grandson, Erik of Pomerania who was thrice crowned at Kalmar. The Union of Kalmar (1397–1523) created a potentially powerful northern state. Margaret laid the foundation by reducing noble privileges, raising taxes that paid off state debts, reclaiming pawned areas and buying Gotland from the Teutonic Knights. Although Sweden broke away from the Union, the unity of Denmark and Norway lasted into the 19th Century when 1814 witnessed a Swedish land grab after Napoleon I was defeated at Leipzig.

The nascent states in Russia saw Vladimir I (c. 980–1015) converting to Eastern Orthodoxy after

Europe on the Eve of Mongol Invasion

c. 1220

The Holy Roman Empire

Arctic Circle
LAPPS
ICELAND
Norwegian Sea
NORWAY
SWEDEN
FINNS
NOVGOROD
(to NORWAY)
Bergen
Oslo
Kaupang
Stockholm
Birka
Helsingfors
Reval
(to DENMARK)
ESTONIANS
ORDER OF THE SWORD BROTHERS
Novgorod
Pskov
KINGDOM OF MAN (to NORWAY)
SCOTLAND
Glasgow
Edinburgh
Lindisfarne
North Sea
Baltic Sea
CURONIANS
LITHUANIANS
SMOLENSK
Polotsk
Vitebsk
Smolensk
POLOTSK
Minsk
Dnieper
CHERNIGOV
IRELAND
Dublin
Cork
York
WALES
ENGLAND
London
Bristol
DENMARK
Ripen
Hedeby
Hamburg
PRUSSIANS
POMERLLIA
CUJAVIA
MAZOVIA
Vistula
TUROV-PINSK
Bremen
Hanover
GREAT POLAND
LITTLE POLAND
Wroclaw
SILESIA
VOLHYNIA
KIEV
Kiev
KINGDOM OF GERMANY
Cologne
Rhine
Calais
Aachen
Meissen
Cracow
Mainz
Frankfurt
Prague
KINGDOM OF BOHEMIA
Brunn
Galich
GALICH
Dniester
Paris
Metz
Strasbourg
Munich
Vienna
ATLANTIC OCEAN
Nantes
Tours
Orleans
Dijon
Zurich
Salzburg
Esztergom
Buda
Kolozsvar
HUNGARY
FRANCE
Limoges
Geneva
Lyon
KINGDOM OF BURGUNDY (ARLES)
Graz
Pecs
Danube
Szeged
Temesvar
Brasso
Zagrab
KINGDOM OF ITALY
Milan
Venice
Turin
Genoa
Belgrade
Bordeaux
(to ENGLAND)
Gascony
BOSNIA
Varna
Bayonne
Toulouse
Montpellier
PROVENCE
Marseille
MARSEILLE
Florence
PISA
Ravenna
VENETIAN REPUBLIC
Spalato
Nish
BULGARIA
SERBIA
Serdica
Oviedo
LEON
NAVARRE
Adriatic Sea
PAPAL STATES
Ragusa
Scupi
Philippopolis
Adrianople
LATIN EMPIRE
Constantinople
Oporto
PORTUGAL
CASTILE
Salamanca
Saragossa
ARAGON
Corsica
Rome
KINGDOM OF SALONICA
Salonica
Barcelona
Bari
DESPOTATE OF EPIRUS
ROMANIA
Toledo
Balearic Is.
(Genoese influence in part)
Sardinia
Naples
Taranto
Otranto
Aegean Sea
EMPIRE OF NICAEA
Balansiyah
Janina
Smyrna
Las Navas de Tolosa
KINGDOM OF SICILY
Athens
Qurtubah (Córdova)
Granada
Cartagena
Malagah
PRINCIPALITY OF ACHAIA
VENETIAN REPUBLIC
Panormus
Messina
Sicily
Catania
Mediterranean Sea
TO VENICE
Algiers
Tunis
Crete
EMPIRE OF THE ALMOHADS
Fez

visiting the Hagia Sophia Church, bringing his Kievan subjects into the Christian fold. The new religion took hold despite the collapse of Kiev through civil war. This spread of Byzantine civilization helped the development of Russian culture as did the response to the Tatar-Mongol invasions when the Russian principalities were made tributary for the Golden Horde in the 13th Century. The Mongols were a recently confederated number of tribes united from the 1190s by Ghengis Khan. His expansionist plans absorbed non-Mongol peoples as he extended his power over Central Asia and China. His successors attacked the Middle East and Europe. Alexander Nevsky of Novgorod (c. 1220–1263) cooperated with the Mongols, they granting him the title of Grand Prince. Eventually, Moscow's Grand Princes worked with their overlords, becoming the sole collectors of tribute, even helping their Mongol masters to put down rebellions of other Russian Princes. Anti-Mongol resistance was eventually led by Ivan III who rejected Mongol authority and abolished the tribute system. After the fall of Constantinople in 1453, he viewed himself as the heir of the Byzantine Empire, espousing a Byzantine Princess, dubbing himself Tsar (or Caesar). He annexed many other Russian principalities including Novgorod in 1478 and Tver in 1485. Ivan III ruled unfettered by national assemblies, developing the notion of autocracy while desiring territorial expansion as seen in his invasion of Poland-Lithuania, which was a threat to his growing state. Muscovy, a latent force, was poised for adventure but was regarded as a barbaric, rude country by western European peoples.

A European Knight armed and equipped ready for battle. The Mongol army, however, was a new and unfamiliar threat and used new tactics, including fast-moving mounted archers.

Islam and the Ottoman Empire were recognized as dangerous with the crushing of the Balkan peninsula. Their further advances were halted by long supply lines and the fact that their enemies kept the art of fortification alive, essential to hold up cavalry armies. However, western Europe knew that the fall of Constantinople was a shattering event because victory was attained largely by artillery: the age of gunpowder had begun. The siege witnessed the use of a monster cannon. Its barrel measured 26ft 8in (8.1m) in length, had a calibre of 8 in (20 cm), required a crew of 700, and could fire a cannonball weighing one ton over one mile (1.6 km). However, it could only be fired seven times a day. The Ottoman Empire was the major threat to the Mediterranean, Habsburg domains, and Hungary.

Other parts of Europe were not threats owing to their disunity but could be theaters for war as more powerful rulers sought expansion. The Habsburg retained loose control over a cornucopia of more than 100 cities, counties, duchies, and principalities in the Holy Roman Empire. Its constitution was laid down in the 1356 Golden Bull, instigated by the pope but confirmed by the Empire's parliament (the Diet). Imperial succession was decided by the seven electors: the archbishops of Mainz, Trier, and Cologne; the Count Palatine of the Rhine; the Duke of Saxony; the Margrave of Brandenburg; and the King of Bohemia. The imperial tile resided with the Luxembourg family between 1346 and 1437 and the Habsburg family after 1438. However, no King could guarantee that his heir would inherit the imperial title. Little power was held by the Emperor owing to few resources. Most lands were usurped during the 13th Century and imperial towns often mortgaged. Royal rights over the mess of church and secular principalities were reduced by granting immunities in return for political support, or through neglect. The Emperor could not become the focus for political unity and the Germanies remained fragmented until Napoleon I changed their political geography.

THE COURT OF THE GREAT GENGHIS KHAN
Genghis Khan ruled over the largest contiguous Empire ever recorded in world history. It was this empire that was about to impact on Europe and its chivalric armies.

Italy was a fragmented patchwork of puny states that was important in constructing a rationalized balance of power concept discussed in some major literary works. Poland-Lithuania became a vast

country stretching from the Baltic to the Black Sea but its size meant it was difficult to defend, subject to Russian and Ottoman incursions, and misruled owing to weak political institutions, a selfish nobility, and lack of skilled administrators. Interestingly, language politics was an issue in the state. Belarussian was the language used for official documents until 1569 when the Polish nobility demanded the supremacy of their language.

In this western impression the heavily-armored Christian knights, wearing their great iron helmets, struggle with the Mongols, represented here in their pointed caps. In the end it was the lightly-armored Mongols mounted on their small but extremely tough horses that carried the day.

THE MONGOLS

The nomadic Mongols (or Tatars) originated in the area of today's Mongolia. These various tribes were united by Temujin, better known as Genghis Khan. The first Mongol onslaught against Europe came in 1221 when their armies passed northward through the mountains between the Black and Caspian Seas. Russia was attacked for three years making the Mongols rich with loot as they returned to the central steppes after their longest march in history. Temujin's grandson, Batu Khan, led a winter cavalry blitzkrieg through the northern Russian principalities with a large force in 1237, thereby impacting upon the histories of Russia and Europe. The Rus and their neighbors were defeated and placed under the Tatar yoke. Only Novgorod survived as an independent state.

Initially, they defeated the Volga Bulgars, then rode into Vladimir Suzdal, ravaging its wealthy towns. In 1239, owing to internal dissension between the various principalities, the lack of a united front against the Mongols meant that the nomads could overrun southwest Rus. Kiev was sacked and hundreds of settlements were destroyed. The Mongols then moved to a tented city in the Don basin while their leaders rested and amused themselves with drinking games.

In 1240, the Mongols advanced deep into the heart of Russia, destroying Kiev. They wintered near Przemsyl near the current border between the Ukraine and Poland. The head General Subedei had contrived a daring and complex military plan. Three *touman* (a cavalry division of 10,000 men) would occupy and hold down Russia, while another ten touman would advance on a 621-mile wide front moving west between the Black Sea and the Baltic. Two touman, commanded by Baidar and Kadan would scythe northwest into Poland and Lithuania in a diversionary raid moving south in support of the main drive. Another touman under Siban would move along the northern edge of the Carpathians and enter Hungary, the chief target, from the north. Batu with perhaps four touman would use the

Mongol campaigns in Russia
1223–40
Russian principalities
Mongol raids, 1223 and 1230
Battle
REPUBLIC OF NOVGOROD
SWEDEN
Finns
Baltic Sea
Gulf of Finland
Lake Ladoga
Lake Onega
Onega
Pinega
Dvina
Velikiy Ustiug
to Rostov
Vyatka
Tallinn
to Denmark
Narva
Ests
ROSTOV
Vologda
ORDER OF THE SWORD BROTHERS (combined with Teutonic Knights 1237)
Novgorod
Riga
Pskov
Curonians
Lithuanians
Sit River 4 March 1238
Yaroslavl
VLADIMIR SUZDAL
Torzhok
Rostov
YURIEV
Nizhniy Novgorod
Volga
PEREYASLAVL
1238
Suzdal
Vladimir
Kazan'
TEUTONIC KNIGHTS
Prussians
Polotsk
SMOLENSK
Moscow
Bulgar
POLOTSK
Smolensk
Tula
1236
Niemen
Minsk
Riazan
VOLGA BULGARS
MAZOVIA
Kozelsk 1238
TUROV-PINSK
CHERNIGOV
MUROM RIAZAN
1230
LITTLE POLAND
Pinsk
Pripyat'
Desna
VOLYNIA
NOVGOROD-SEVERSK
1223
Kiev
Dec. 1240 taken by Tartars
1240
PEREIASLAV
1238
Don
Ural
Dniester
KIEV
Cumans
GALICH
Donets
1239
Volga
Emba
HUNGARY
Dnieper
Tunai
Kalka River 31 May 1223
Sarai
Astrakhan
to Kiev
to Kiev
1223
Danube
Kaffa
Sudak
Alans
to Venice
BULGARIA
Varna
Black Sea
Caspian Sea
SERBIA
LATIN EMPIRE (ROMANIA)
to Venice
Constantinople
Tbilisi
EMPIRE OF NICAEA
Trebizond
EMPIRE OF TREBIZOND
GEORGIA
1221
RUM (ICONIUM)
Eastern Euphrates
LESSER ARMENIA
AYYUBIDS
EMPIRE OF THE KHAWAZARAM SHAH
200 km
200 miles

Novgorod, the oldest and the greatest of the Russian trading cities, was massively fortified by walls and towers. It was not the strength of its fortifications that saved the city but the spring thaw in 1238, when the ice melted on the rivers surrounding the city and robbed the Mongols of their maneuverability, forcing them in to retreat. They renewed their campaign in 1239–40, heading westward for Poland and Hungary.

Transylvanian passes to enter Hungary from the east. Elsewhere, Subedei would march along the River Danube appearing from the south. If the opposition appeared too strong to confront the combined eight touman, they would retreat until the northern force attacked the enemy's rear.

The northern force was designed to draw out the Hungarian armies on to the south Russian steppes. Lublin, Zawichos, and Sandomir were taken but the Hungarians were slow to move. Batu savaged Wallachia on the northwestern shore of the Black Sea. Seizing three passes through the Carpathian Mountains allowing the Danube and Tizsa river corridors to channel the Mongols toward Pest. King Bela of Hungary allowed the Cumans, refugees from the Mongols, to enter Hungary, while he attempted to fortify his borders. Bela summoned his nobility and armed forces but the baronage wanted the Cumans expelled, bickering while the Mongols were advancing. The Hungarian nobility murdered the Cuman lords and the Cumans rode off killing and plundering as they went. The events are surprising since Bela's son was married to a Cuman Princess to win over the refugees. Meanwhile, in the north, the Mongols touched Crakow then retreated. The Polish governor and his forces left the city in pursuit, falling foul of a feigned retreat, being killed to a man in the Mongol arrow storm.

By the end of March 1241, the Mongols reached the gates of Pest and then withdrew enticing Bela and his 100,000-strong army on to the banks of the River Sajo at Mohi. Wagons were chained together encircling the army as a defense or even a prison as it materialized. Batu's and Subedei's combined six touman used catapults to throw flammable liquid at the river bridges and turn the camp into an inferno. Seventy thousand Hungarians died and Bela was forced to flee 300 miles to an Adriatic island

Mongol campaigns in Europe
1240–45
Main attack
Flank attack
Reconnaissance and minor raids
Battle site
SWEDEN
Stockholm
Reval
Estonians
ORDER OF THE SWORD BROTHERS
Novgorod
NOVGOROD
Pskov
ROSTOV
YURIEV
PEREYASLAVL
Moscow
MUROM-RYAZAN
Riga
Curonians
Lithuanians
SMOLENSK
Smolensk
Tula
Polotsk
Vitebsk
Lund
Baltic Sea
DENMARK
Prussians
POLOTSK
Minsk
CHERNIGOV
Don
Hamburg
Bremen
Stettin
TUROVPINSK
NOVOGOROD-SEVERSK
Hanover
GREAT POLAND
Poznan
MAZOVIA
KINGDOM OF GERMANY
Liegnitz
Wrotizla
Meissen
Vistula
SILESIA
LITTLE POLAND
1241
Vladimir
VOLHYNIA
KIEV
Kiev
PEREYASLAVL
1239
1240
Frankfurt
Oder
Prague
KINGDOM OF BOHEMIA
Cracow
Przemysl
Nuremberg
Brunn
1241
Mongol army concentrates here January 1241
Galich
GALICH
Dniester
Cumans
Mohi
Munich
Pozsony
Danube
Zurich
Salzburg
Viennea
Esztergom
Buda
1243
to Kiev
Graz
HUNGARY
Kolozsvár
Milan
Szeged
Pécs
Brassó
Zágráb
Temesvár
to Venice
KINGDOM OF ITALY
1241
Bologna
Belgrade
VENETIAN REPUBLIC
Pisa
PISA
Florence
Zara
BOSNIA
1242–43
Black Sea
Spalato
Danube
Varna
BULGARIA
Nish
PAPAL STATES
SERBIA
Serdica
1242
Philippopolis
Rome
Scrupi
Adrianople
LATIN EMPIRE (ROMANIA)
Constantinople
DESPOTATE OF EPIRUS
KINGDOM OF SALONICA
Salonica
Angora
Bari
Naples
Taranto
KINGDOM OF SICILY
EMPIRE OF NICEA
Janina
N
DUCHY OF ATHENS
Palermo
Athens
Messina
PRINCIPALITY OF ACHAIA
Catania
0
200 km
0
200 miles
VENETIAN REPUBLIC
Mediterranean Sea
KINGDOM OF CYPRUS

A typical western knight of the mid-13th Century as portrayed in this French bronze cast. The knight wears a sheet-metal helmet and a coat of chain mail under his surcoat. From the position of the figure's arm, the knight would originally have carried a lance. A fully armored knight required a large, strong horse to carry such an enormous weight into battle.

while evading Mongol pursuit. Meanwhile, Hungary was so ravaged that half its population died in the Mongol invasion.

In the north, the Mongols found Crakow deserted and torched it. They then advanced on Breslau finding the city burnt by its inhabitants sheltering in its castle. Meanwhile, Henry of Silesia had summoned a large army and waited at Leignitz for King Wenceslas of Bohemia, who was marching with a 50,000-strong army. Baidar sent this news to Kadan and Batu and raced to prevent the juncture of these two armies.

The forces confronting each other were entirely different. Henry's army contained Silesians, Teutonic Knights, Templars, Hospitallers, and Germans from villages in Lithuania and survivors from Crakow. These 25,000 knights, men-at-arms and infantry were poorly trained apart from the Holy Orders. The Mongols, totaled some 20,000 men

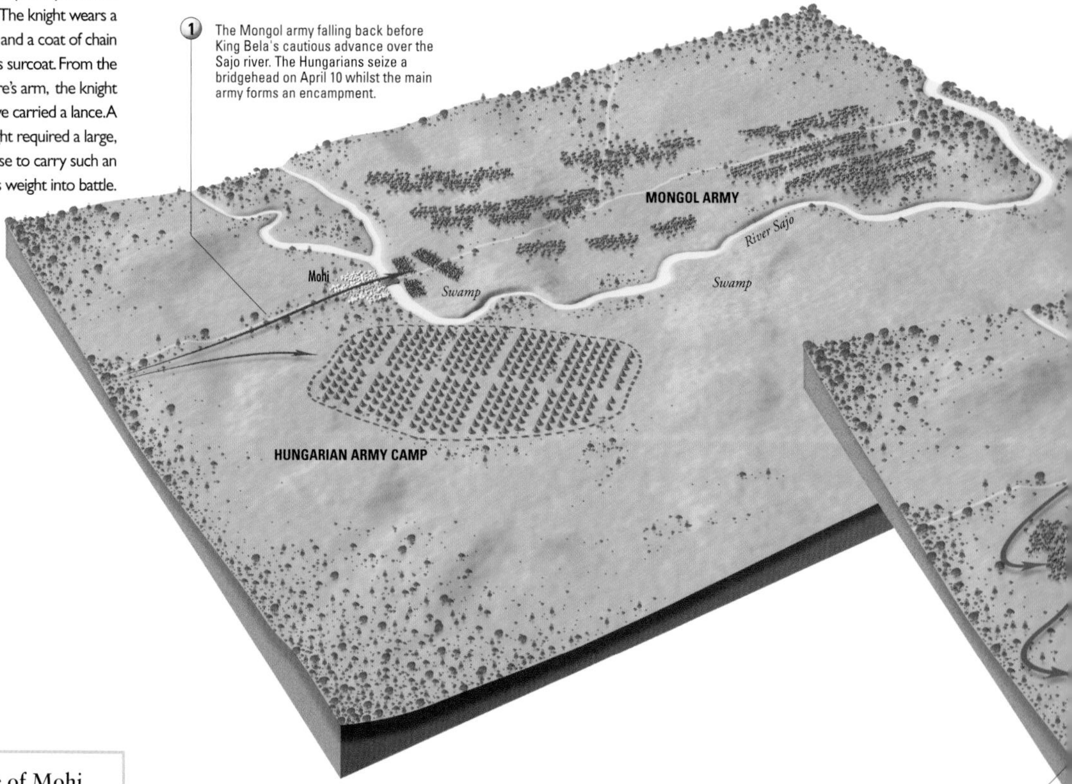

1 The Mongol army falling back before King Bela's cautious advance over the Sajo river. The Hungarians seize a bridgehead on April 10 whilst the main army forms an encampment.

MONGOL ARMY

River Sajo

Mohi

Swamp

Swamp

HUNGARIAN ARMY CAMP

The Battle of Mohi
1241

Hungarian advance
Mongol advance
Hungarian retreat

Some Hungarians begin to slip away through a gap in the Mongol lines. This becomes a route, the Mongols close in slaughtering many of the fleeing troops. 4

comprising 1,000 Mangudai cavalry, 11,000 horse archers, and 8,000 heavy cavalry. The Mangudai light cavalry, trained in feigned retreat, were sent forward but Henry's Silesian cavalry fled so the Polish cavalry and Teutonic Knights were advanced and pushed back the Mongol light forces, which then ran away. The knights charged forward when the Mongol archers closed on the flanks, pouring in arrow fire. A smokescreen was also prepared in the path, being ignited after the knights had ridden over it. The remaining Christian infantry could not see the fate of their cavalry as they were routed by the Mongol heavy cavalry. The infantry fled but the westerners were pursued by faster horses; the carnage was terrible and the army wiped out. In

By contrast to the western knight, the Mongol horseman is unhampered by heavy armor. A small, sturdy horse characteristic of those found on the Asian steppe provided his mount. This, combined with a powerful bow, meant that he could out-maneuver the heavily-equipped European knights he was to meet in combat.

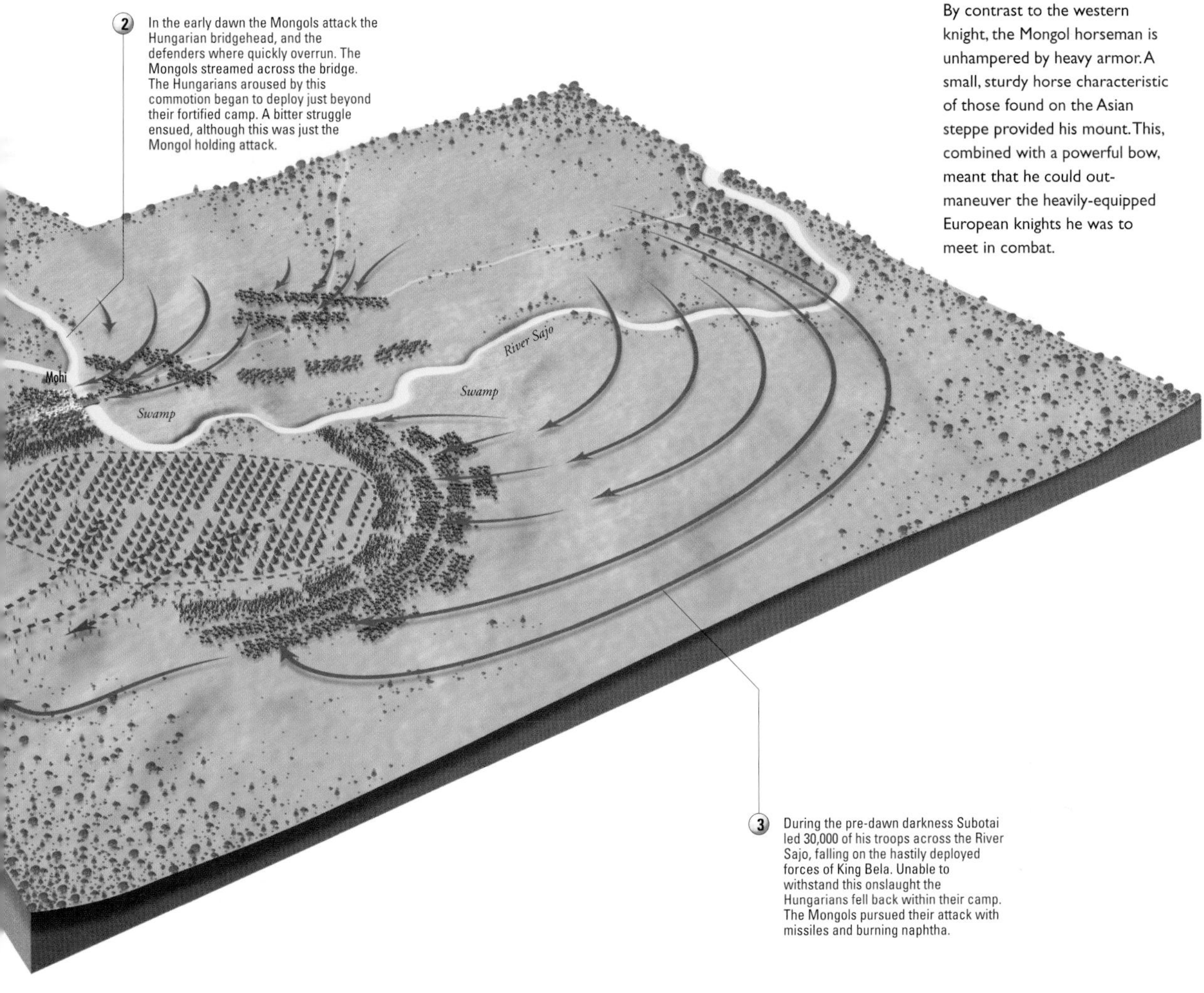

2 In the early dawn the Mongols attack the Hungarian bridgehead, and the defenders where quickly overrun. The Mongols streamed across the bridge. The Hungarians aroused by this commotion began to deploy just beyond their fortified camp. A bitter struggle ensued, although this was just the Mongol holding attack.

Mohi

Swamp

River Sajo

Swamp

3 During the pre-dawn darkness Subotai led 30,000 of his troops across the River Sajo, falling on the hastily deployed forces of King Bela. Unable to withstand this onslaught the Hungarians fell back within their camp. The Mongols pursued their attack with missiles and burning naphtha.

half a week the Mongols had killed three armies of some 150,000 men leaving Europe wide open.

The Polish population along the River Oder was nearly exterminated. Pest was burned and, when the Danube froze in winter, Batu crossed on Christmas Day and destroyed what today is the city of Esztergom, while Kadan did likewise to Buda and Zagred. Mongol scouts reached the outskirts of Vienna and Venice, although a Croatian army beat them back at Grobnok, 50 miles from Trieste.

Deliverance came to Europe in two ways. The great Khan Ogedai, son of Temujin, died in 1241 and all Mongol princes had to return to a *kuriltai* (political and military council) at Karakorum, 3,500 miles away in Mongolia. The Mongols retreated and left Europe, but they exacted tribute for years. The new Khan Kuyuk decided to attack the Muslim world but the Mamluk forces of Egypt soundly defeated the Mongols at Ain Jalut in 1281.

EXPANSION OF THE OTTOMAN TURKS AND THE FALL OF CONSTANTINOPLE

This painting shows Sultan Mehmet II "the conqueror" leading his troops into Constantinople in 1453. This spelt the end of the old Christian order in the Near East. The Ottomans were now poised to strike deep into the Balkan Christian heartlands.

The growth of Turkish Ottoman power lay in their internal unification by the Osmanli dynasty and the weakness of neighboring empires, especially the wounding of Byzantium by the Fourth Crusade of 1204, which aided and abetted Ottoman expeditions into southeastern Europe throughout the 14th Century. Furthermore, the Ottoman quest for power was aided by the defeat of the Seljuks at the Battle of Kösedagh by the Mongols in 1423, which caused the break up of their empire in Anatolia creating a power vacuum there and in Persia. The Ottoman state steadily expanded under Orkhan (c. 1324–1362), Sultan Murad (1360–1389) and Bayezid I (1389–1402). This was the era of continuous Ottoman expansion, achieved through warfare, alliance, and territorial purchases.

In 1326, the Ottomans made Bursa their capital, the later acquisition of the Karasi Emirate bringing them to the shores of the Dardanelles. Led by Osman's son, Orkhan, they crossed to Gallipoli in 1355 winning a bridgehead in Europe. The growth of Ottoman power sufficiently worried the Mongol leader, Timur Lenk, known as Tamerlane to those in the West, that he paused in his campaigns in India, seeking to defend his western frontier by defeating Bayezid I at Ankara in 1402. This apparent catastrophe was short lived because Timur failed to consolidate his victories and soon died leading an expedition against China.

Meanwhile, in Europe, Thrace was captured and in the 1370s Adrianople and the northern parts of Greece and Macedonia were occupied. The roads to central Europe lay open. Later, the Serbian aristocracy, led by Prince Lazar, was hammered at the Battle of Kosovo Polje (The Field of Blackbirds) on 28 June 1389, thereby providing a feature of modern Serb nationalism.

Ottoman expansion parallels certain aspects of the Crusades, especially the notion of Holy War, as implemented by Saladin. In Muslim theory, Holy War is embodied in the idea of *jihad*, the duty to fight for the faith. This struggle can occur against physical enemies but also within oneself for

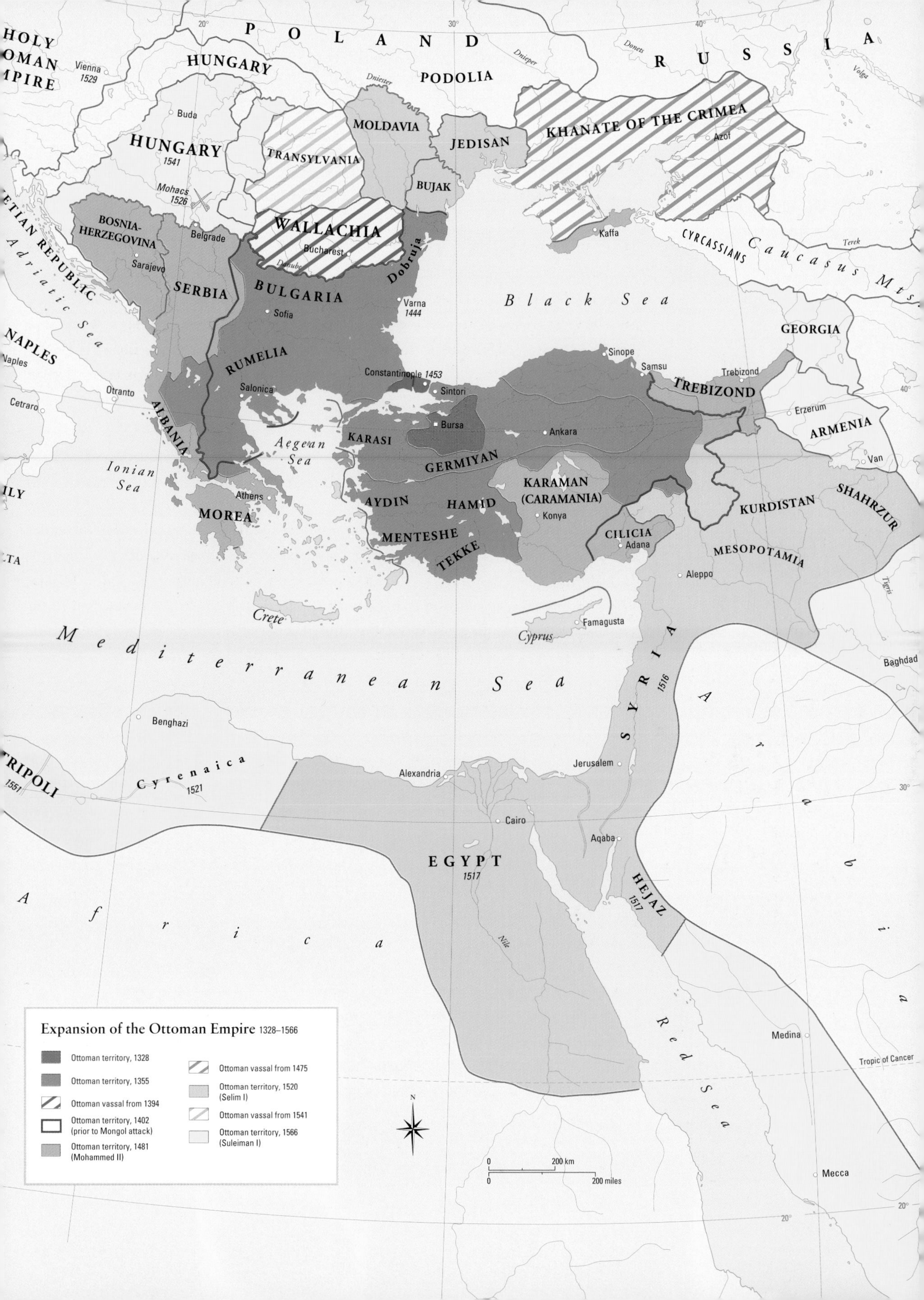
Expansion of the Ottoman Empire 1328–1566
Ottoman territory, 1328
Ottoman territory, 1355
Ottoman vassal from 1394
Ottoman territory, 1402 (prior to Mongol attack)
Ottoman territory, 1481 (Mohammed II)
Ottoman vassal from 1475
Ottoman territory, 1520 (Selim I)
Ottoman vassal from 1541
Ottoman territory, 1566 (Suleiman I)
HOLY ROMAN EMPIRE
POLAND
RUSSIA
HUNGARY
Vienna 1529
PODOLIA
Buda
HUNGARY 1541
MOLDAVIA
TRANSYLVANIA
JEDISAN
KHANATE OF THE CRIMEA
Azof
BUJAK
Mohacs 1526
WALLACHIA
Bucharest
BOSNIA-HERZEGOVINA
Belgrade
Sarajevo
SERBIA
BULGARIA
Dobruja
Varna 1444
Sofia
Kaffa
CYRCASSIANS
Caucasus Mts.
Black Sea
GEORGIA
VENETIAN REPUBLIC
Adriatic Sea
NAPLES
Naples
RUMELIA
Constantinople 1453
Sinope
Samsu
Trebizond
TREBIZOND
Otranto
Cetraro
Salonica
Sintori
Bursa
Ankara
Erzerum
ARMENIA
ALBANIA
Aegean Sea
KARASI
GERMIYAN
Van
Ionian Sea
Athens
MOREA
AYDIN
HAMID
KARAMAN (CARAMANIA)
Konya
KURDISTAN
SHAHRZUR
MENTESHE
TEKKE
CILICIA
Adana
MESOPOTAMIA
Aleppo
Crete
Cyprus
Famagusta
Mediterranean Sea
Baghdad
SYRIA 1516
Arabia
Benghazi
TRIPOLI 1551
Cyrenaica 1521
Alexandria
Jerusalem
Cairo
Aqaba
EGYPT 1517
HEJAZ 1517
Africa
Nile
Red Sea
Medina
Tropic of Cancer
Mecca
Dniester
Dnieper
Donets
Volga
Terek
Danube
Tigris
0 200 km
0 200 miles

the perfection of faith. The Holy War itself, the *ghaza*, is carried out by *ghazis*, the warriors for the faith. Was the Ottoman Empire a ghazi state? Similar to the crusader states in the Near East, the Ottoman conquests in Europe led to the political administration, both politically and in religious terms, of a minority élite. However, whereas the crusades were long-distance expeditions dependent on control of the seaways with long, vulnerable logistic supply lines, the Ottoman Empire expanded over land, making conquests more secure than those of the crusaders. Sultan Mehmet II, ascending the throne aged 19 years, decided to capture Constantinople, the capital of the reduced Byzantine territories. The city fell in May 1453, followed by the Morea, Trebizond, Bosnia, Albania, and the Crimea. Crusader armies were defeated at Varna in 1444. Ottoman expansion continued under Selim I (1512–1520), who defeated the Mamelukes in 1517, thereby acquiring Syria, Palestine, Egypt, and Algeria. The surge into Europe was halted in the Mediterranean at the Battle of Lepanto in October 1571.

The siege of Constantinople and its aftermath were traumatic events for Christian Europe with its crusading heritage. Mehmet II, a drunken and belligerent person who died from overindulgence when aged 49, desired Constantinople to be the capital of an Ottoman universal empire that would bestride the world. He cheekily called himself the "Shadow of God upon Earth." The siege was marked by Mehmet's brutality. A Venetian ship attempting to reach the city was sunk, its crew butchered, and its captain, Antonio Rizzo, impaled, his body being left to rot as a warning. The 12,000 defenders, Byzantines, Catalans, Italians, and Turks, led by Prince Orhan, an enemy of Mehmet, faced 120,000–150,000 Ottoman forces but they had the wonderfully fortified city with three defensive walls and a moat. The fortresses at Therapia and Studius capitulated and the seventy-six defenders were impaled. A third fort on the island of Prinkipo witnessed its garrison burning itself to death rather than surrender to a terrible fate. A constant artillery bombardment and incessant night attacks weakened the defenses, while part of the Ottoman fleet was moved on rollers overland to the Golden Horn, threatening Constantinople from the north.

Finally, expecting a grand assault, the defenders attended mass where Orthodox and Catholic prayed to God for deliverance. Venetians and Genoese, always hostile to each other, Catalans, Castilians, and Byzantine Greeks took Holy Communion together from their respective clergies. The assault was launched when a small gate was found open, allowing Ottoman *janissaries* (infantry) to rush in, open the main gates, and swamp the defenders. Emperor Constantine XI died fighting as did Orhan's Turks and the Catalans, fighting to the last man. The Turks killed, looted, and raped their way throughout the city. Fifty thousand Byzantines were enslaved while 4,000 fell in battle.

The fall of the Byzantine capital was an horrific event for the Christian world, which saw the beginning of the end of their faith. The Ottomans brought in members of Sufi brotherhoods from central Asia and their blend of Sunni and Shi'ite beliefs married to Christian practices and beliefs enabled the conversion of Greek- and Armenian-speaking Christians. The Turks excluded bishops from their sees and Christian Orthodox hospitals, schools, orphanages, and monasteries were replaced by Muslim institutions with Arab and Persian scholars. By the 15th Century 90 percent of the Anatolian populations had converted to Islam.

THE HUSSITES

During the 14th Century, Bohemia became the administrative center of the Holy Roman Empire. The King of Bohemia was an elector of the Emperor. Charles IV, Emperor and King of Bohemia, made Prague into a Gothic city architecturally and founded what became the oldest university in Europe in 1348. Bohemia was a prosperous region where gold and silver were mined providing Europe with a basic supply of precious metals. The transport system linked Italy to the Baltic. Charles IV of Luxemburg was the son of King Ottokar II's granddaughter, he being a 13th-Century Bohemian King with expansionist aims.

The university became an unruly hotbed of religious dissent, the heretical university professor Jan Hus demanding reform of the corrupt religious establishment. Hus combined religious dissent with Czech nationalism, his post provided a powerful platform for his religious visions, which were heavily influenced by the radical English reformer, John Wycliffe. The times were right for ferment because the new Bohemian King, Wenceslas IV, was a weak ruler and the Catholic Church was still reeling after the 1378 Schism. Wenceslas was deposed from the Imperial throne in 1400 and the Decree of Kutná Hora in 1409 gave the Czechs a controlling majority in the university's administration against German elements.

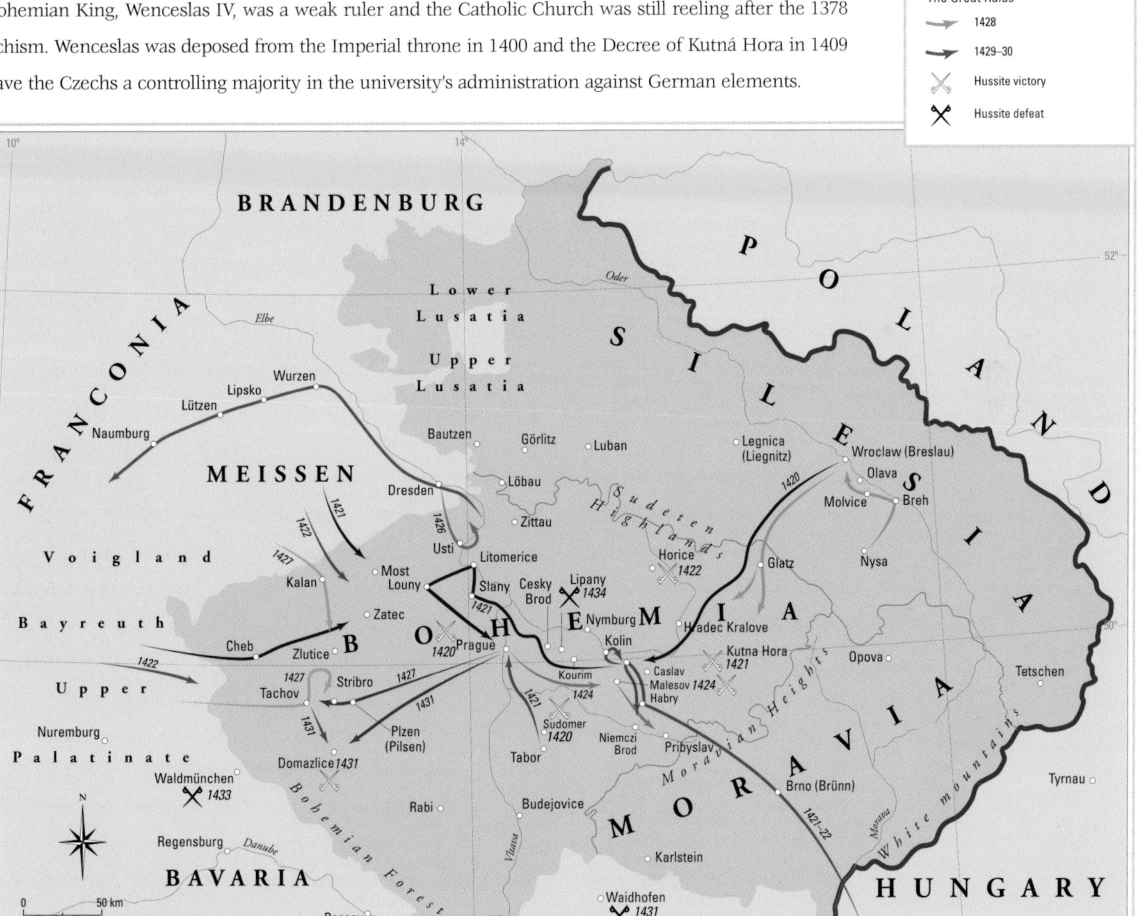

Hussite war wagons deployed for battle. The Hussite armies developed a mobile fortress based on wagons equipped with cannon and crossbows. This mobile fortress proved itself successful many times during the Hussite crusades.

Hus was burned as a heretic in 1415 and the Hussites, lately condemned by the Council of Constance, demanded clerical reform in the Four Articles of Prague (1420): free preaching of the Word of God; communion in both kinds; the confiscation of the secular property of the clergy; and the punishment of public sin. The movement split into several sects: the right-wing were Utraquists who demanded the right to receive communion in both kinds (wine and bread); the center followed the moderate teachings of Jakoubek of Stribro; while on the left were the Taborites, who pursued chiliastic (millenarian) views; and, on the extreme left were the Adamites, a sect preaching nudity and who denied the doctrine of the Real Presence (the actual presence of Christ's body and blood in the Eucharistic elements).

Hussite support was rooted in Prague, where Hus and his followers had preached at the Bethelem Chapel, northwest, west, and south Bohemia. Moravia and Slovakia remained Catholic throughout the Hussite wars (the conflict within the Roman Catholic Church, 1419–36). After arrests followed, open rebellion followed in 1419 when some of the king's councillors were thrown from an upper window, falling to their deaths in the first defenestration of Prague. The Taborites founded the community of Tábor in 1420, comprising gentry and peasants who abolished feudalism while constructing a municipal form of government. The sect's vision spread to the five towns of Plzen, Slany, Zatec, Louny, and Klatovy, which the movement regarded as the final bastion of the elect against the Antichrist in Rome.

In 1420, Wenceslas died leaving the throne to his brother, Sigismund, King of Hungary and Emperor-elect. He marched into Bohemia, laid siege to Prague, crowned himself king, leading the first crusade against the Hussites. The Hussites elected four military commanders, one being Jan Zizka who, in 1419, defeated a 2,000-strong royal force at Nekmer using small cannon mounted on seven wagons to repel their assault. Zizka's military experience in Bohemian civil war and against the Teutonic Knights at Tannenberg was enhanced when Catholic forces attacked his 400 men on the way to Tabor when his force defeated 2,000 dismounted Catholic men-at-arms with each side receiving heavy casualties.

At Prague, the Hussites held a hill outside the city on the Ridge of Vitkov where there was an old tower. Attacked by the Imperialists, Zizka mounted a counterattack causing Sigismund's mainly mercenary troops to flee, which later became a rout. The Imperialists suffered about 1,000 casualties. The Imperial siege faltered in the hot summer sun, money ran out to pay the troops, and disease broke out. Sigismund lifted the siege hoping to use his remaining troops to relieve a Hussite siege of Wyschrad, where he was defeated again.

Zizka used the gold and silver mined near Kutná Hora and iron and quicksilver near Prague to acquire wealth to purchase hand guns that could be fired from the Hussite wagons. A dozen victories were won in this fashion. Next year, Zizka was wounded and died in 1424. Hussites were turning on their more militant elements, therefore showing the moderation of the majority; so, they were no longer anathema and could be approached diplomatically. Hus' immediate supporters, the Utraquists (Orebites) commenced calling themselves the Orphans, and these moderates allied with Catholics via the Compacta of Basel entered a civil war with their radical coreligionists resulting in the Battle of Lipany, in 1434, when the extremists were defeated. Negotiations were now possible with the king and he agreed to a new archbishop being appointed from the Utraquist faction. In 1436, the Compacta was ratified at Jihlava and Sigismund returned to Prague as king. This event secured peace between Hussites and Catholics until the loss of Czech independence in 1620.

In total there were five anti-Hussite crusades, the major one lasting from 1464 to 1471. Hussite wagon armies were again successful, some of the wagons being crewed by as many as eighteen mercenaries.

POLAND-LITHUANIA

Poland grew in power under Casimir III the Great (1333–1370). Diplomatically, John I of Luxemburg, King of Bohemia, was persuaded to give up his claims to the Polish crown but himself was forced to relinquish claims to Silesia, acquired by John during a period of Bohemian expansion, thereby losing a well-populated and wealthy region. Despite abandoning all claims to Eastern Pomerania, benefiting the Teutonic Knights, for a while, he forced the Piast Dukes of Mazovia to consent to his overlordship, despite him seizing some of their lands. Some lands annexed by Brandenburg were regained and the period 1340–52 saw the acquisition of Red Ruthenia with its cities of Przemysl, Lvov, and Halicz. In 1366, he exerted his rule over the Ruthenian principalities of Chelm, Belz, Wlodzimierz, and Podolia. Casimir died without issue but his successor and nephew, Louis I of Hungary (1370–82), kept the Polish kingdom intact but considered Poland to be less significant than Hungary, ruling the state by a governor. However, the succession was only achieved by granting privileges to the nobility.

During the reigns of these two monarchs many new cities, castles, fortifications, town halls, and merchant dwellings were founded. Courts of justice were created but, despite the growth of a bourgeoisie and merchant class, the aristocracy remained the most important political group. Spiritually, Dominican, Franciscan, and Augustine religious orders built 80 monasteries and secured a powerful position for the Roman Catholic Church. Poland differed from other European countries by tolerating other Christian traditions within its borders. The Othodox tradition created a Halicz-Lvov metropolitanate while an Eastern Orthodox metropolitanate was established in Halicz, and later Lvov. An Armenian bishopric of Lvov was founded. These strains of Christianity lived side by side for 200 years before the Reformation. Under Casimir, Jews were protected, the kingdom receiving many Jewish refugees fleeing German pogroms of the mid-14th Century, bringing with them a language later known as Yiddish, a form of German. Thus, Poland became a multireligious state and a cosmopolitan empire comprising: Poles, Germans, Ruthenians, Flemings, Walachians, Armenian, Jews, Tatars, and Karaites, a Jewish subgroup. The religious and ethnic tolerance was underpinned by the foundation (1364) of the University of Cracow, which had an outstanding law faculty and the second oldest university in east and central Europe after Prague.

The death of Louis sundered the union between Hungary and Poland. The Hungarian nobility chose his eldest daughter, Maria, to be their queen while the Polish preferred the younger, Jadwiga, thereby developing the concept of an elective Polish monarchy. The Polish aristocracy had another agenda. They aimed at a union with Lithuania that could restore Red Ruthenia and Podolia to Poland after their loss during Louis' reign. The year 1385 saw the marriage of Jadwiga to Jagiello, the pagan Grand Duke of Lithuania. He converted to Christianity and took the reign name of Wladyslaw II Jagiello in 1386, thereby establishing a dynasty for the next 183 years. The Polish-Lithuania

Eastern Europe
c.1460
Holy Roman Empire
Lithuania-Poland
Ottoman Empire
0 150 km
0 150 miles
N
Abo
Helsingfors
Reval
NOVGOROD
Novgorod
MUSCOVY
Kazan
ROSTOV
Nizhniy Novgorod
Volga
Pskov
TVER
Riga
TEUTONIC ORDER
Moscow
KHANATE OF KAZAN
Dünaburg
Malmo
DENMARK
Ryazan
Tula
Wilno
Vitebsk
Smolensk
Königsberg
SMALL PRINCIP-ALITIES
RYAZAN
Gdarisk
Minsk
Stettin
Don
Berlin
Poznan
Vistula
Kursk
Warsaw
GREAT KHANATE (GOLDEN HORDE)
LITHUANIA
Breslau
LANDS OF THE BOHEMIAN CROWN
POLAND
Kharkov
Prague
Kiev
Cracow
Lwow
Brünn
Dnieper
Kassa
AUSTRIA
Pozsony
Vienna
Dniester
Buda
Debrecen
Suceava
KHANATE OF CRIMEA
Graz
STYRIA
HUNGARY
Jassy
Kolozsvar
MOLDAVIA
(to Genoa)
Szeged
Pecs
Zagrab
Temesvar
Brasso
(to Genoa)
Caffa
Danube
Tergovist
Belgrade
Zara
WALLACHIA
Bucharest
Bosna Seray
HERZEGOVINA
Black Sea
Ruschuk
Mostar
Nish
Varna
GEORGIA
REPUBLIC OF RAGUSA
Sofia
VENETIAN REPUBLIC
Trebizond
Uskub
Philippopolis
Adrianople
NAPLES
Local rulers
Bari
Constantinople
OTTOMAN EMPIRE
Taranto
Salonica
Angora
Janina
DULKADIR
KARA KOYUNLU
Smyrna
(to Genoa)
Athens
RAMAZAN
KNIGHTS OF ST JOHN
Morea
Mediterranean Sea
MAMELUKES

established a bishopric of Wilno to convert Lithuanians to the Roman Church. The union incorporated vast Lithuanian landholdings, much uninhabited steppe country, with only notional Lithuanian sovereignty. However, the Polish annexation defended the eastern boundaries of Poland from Mongol and Tatar attacks and from Muscovy, then under the Mongol yoke. On the down side, Poland needed to defend Lithuania from the Teutonic Knights. Via a Lithuanian success in 1366, Kiev came under the union's control and Poland was able to reincorporate Red Ruthenia and Podolia under its rule. Authority was asserted over Moldavia (1387–1497), part of contemporary Romania. This access to the south allowed Eastern trade to flow into Poland through the cities of Kaffa in the Crimea and Akkerman. Urban life was stimulated along the Silesian Oder and Vistula Rivers while Cistercian influence in rural areas helped develop agriculture.

Polish-Lithuania borders ebbed and flowed. In 1398, Samogitia was lost to the Teutonic Knights in return for the end of all hostilities, linking the Order's lands in Prussia and Courland. In 1410, Poland and Lithuania, the latter being governed by Jagiello's cousin, Vytautas (Witold), fought the Order at Tannenberg, inflicting a massive defeat. The 1411 Treaty of Torun returned Samogitia to Lithuania. Jagiello supported the Hussites in order to weaken neighboring Bohemia, sponsoring a pro-Hussite confederation of Polish nobility, while demanding that they were not infected by this heresy. Earlier, in 1412, the king obtained 16 mainly German cities in the High Tatra Mountains in the Spicz region. Later wars waged by Casimir IV (1447–92), created a Lithuania-Russia border 90 miles west of Moscow. Conflict with the Teutonic Knights secured the Prussian-Eastern Pomeranian lands (1454) and the 1466 Treaty of Torun regained Eastern Pomerania, now known as Royal Prussia together with the bishopric of Ermland. The remainder of the Order's territory came under the authority of Poland.

The territorial expansion and consolidation of Poland-Lithuania did little to strengthen the state internally. Attempts at unions with Bohemia and Hungary sapped political energy while the great threats of the Ottoman Empire and Muscovy were poised on the borders. Additionally, aristocratic power was bolstered between 1422 and 1433: the right to a political say in political matters; exemption from taxation; and habeas corpus. Thus, the state was damaged by the rich grain lands not generating revenue, an elective kingship, religious divisions with the nobility, and eventually slave raids by the Crimean Tatars under the auspices of the Ottomans, who acquired the commercial cities of Kaffa, Kilia, and Akkerman from Poland. There were too many enemies around a state with indefensible borders and self-interested nobility.

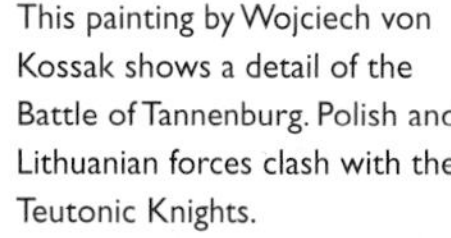

This painting by Wojciech von Kossak shows a detail of the Battle of Tannenburg. Polish and Lithuanian forces clash with the Teutonic Knights.

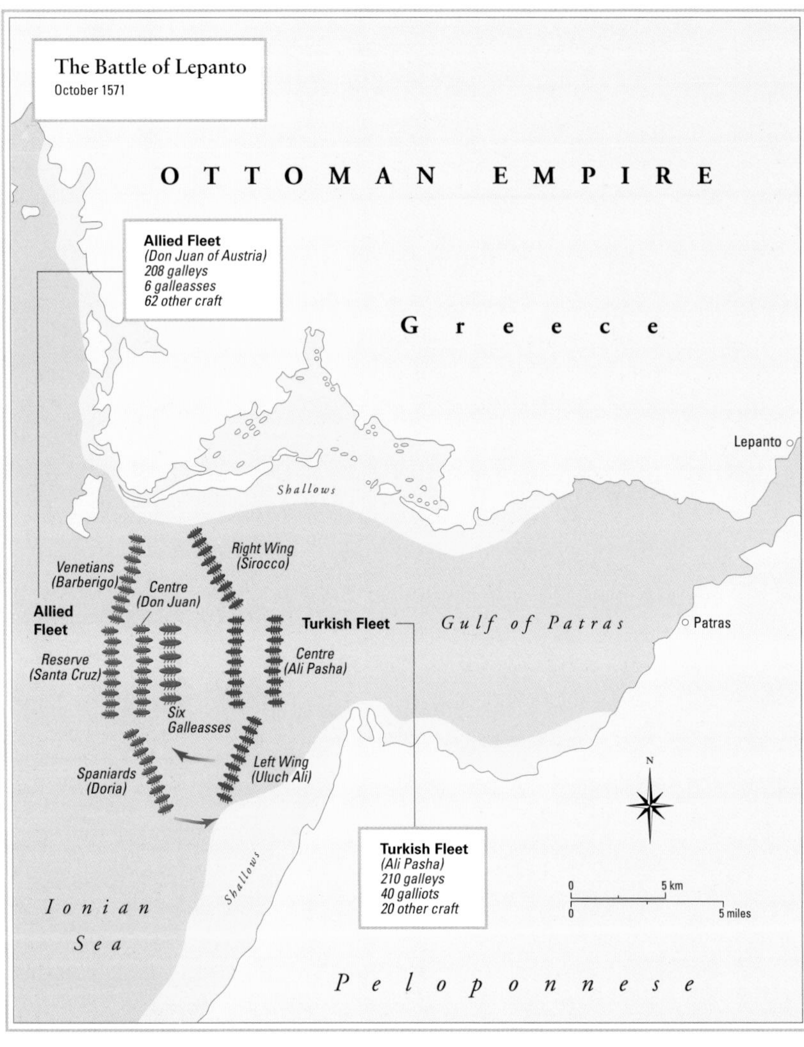

RHODES, MALTA, AND LEPANTO

In 1291, after the fall of Acre, the Hospitallers decamped to Cyprus, then captured Rhodes and adjacent islands from the Byzantines. The Rhodian headquarters was fortified and the Hospitallers' western lands and possessions provided human and financial resources, brethren or mercenaries, to defend the island and wage sea warfare with its galleys driving many Muslim squadrons from the seas. The capture of Smyrna provided an Anatolian toehold for the Christian, the Latin from 1344–74, then the Hospitaller from 1374–1402, being replaced by Bodrum 1408–1523 after Smyrna fell to the Mongols under Timur Lenk.

Several expeditions were launched against Rhodes in 1440 and 1444 by the Mamluks (slave-soldiers who converted to Islam and achieved high office in Egypt, becoming Sultans), followed by an onslaught by the Ottomans was repulsed in 1480. Despite the walls of the city of Rhodes being strengthened to withstand Ottoman artillery, a renewed assault by Sultan Suleiman I was so powerful that the courageous Hospitaller defense ended in defeat; the Order surrendered in December 1522.

The surviving Hospitallers sailed to Italy and eight years later, Emperor Charles V offered them Malta and Gozo and Tripoli as a bastion of his Mediterranean empire. The castle of St. Angelo in Malta's Grand harbor became the Orders home with the adjacent town of Birgu. The holdings were badly fortified and the Turks ravaged Gozo and recaptured Tripoli in 1551. By 1565, Birgu and Senglea, together with St. Elmo's fort, an outpost across the waters of Grand harbor, were fortified in time to withstand an Ottoman siege. Master Jean de Valette, survivor of the Rhodes siege, commanded the defense of Malta during a massive Ottoman siege in 1565. The summer heat sapped the will of the besiegers whose supply lines were too long. The Turks left in the face of a Spanish relief fleet under García de Toledo, the viceroy at Palermo. The fight at St. Elmo had cost the Order some 1,500 men, of whom 150 were brethren; the Turks lost 8,000 in the fort's capture. Overall, the Maltese garrison numbered 9,000 when the siege commenced, being reduced to about 600 capable of fighting at the end, with nearly 250 Knights of St. John dying. The Ottomans lost 30,000 men.

The knights were committed to Malta, seen in the construction of the city of Valetta and lines of fortification, the Cottonera around Birgu and Senglea. Their fleet was expanded and used against Turkish shipping in a form of legalized piracy that brough in huge profits while turning Malta in a trading center. Commerce developed and the Maltese population grew while the Order was corrupted by wealth. The Order participated in the allied victory over the Turks at Lepanto.

On 7 October 1571 in the seas dividing Thessaly from the Mora, the fleet of the Holy League of Spain, the Papacy and Venice, under the command of Don Juan of Austria, defeated the main battle fleet of the Turks under Ali Pasha. Lepanto, together with success at the siege of Malta, ensured that the Mediterranean would never become a Muslim sea. Don Juan was the son of Emperor Charles V and half-brother to Philip II of Spain. Amongst his sub-commanders were Santa Cruz of Spain; Andrea Dorea, leading a Genoese squadron; and Marco Antonio Colonna commanding Papal forces.

In this detail from a contemporary illustration of the Battle of Lepanto, a Venetian galley flying the golden lion flag can be seen being attacked by Ottoman galleys flying their crescent moon flags.

The League's forces were brought together to check Ottoman advances by sea and to diminish the raids and piracy of the African Barbary states of Algiers, Tunis, and Tripoli. The allied fleet comprised 300 ships, 66 percent being royal galleys propelled by rowers with 100 soldiers on board. The Venetians possessed heavily armored galeasses, high-sided ship-rigged galleys with a round forecastle taking eight heavy artillery pieces and many smaller guns mounted on swivels on the rails. Pictures of the Lepanto ships depict three masts rigged with lateen sails. The allies meeting at Messina numbered some 80,000 with 50,000 at the oars.

At Lepanto, Ali Pasha had been reinforced by Algerian corsair Uluch Ali. Don Juan planned tactics with his commanders: six galleasses were towed into forward positions to engage at long range. The aim of the opposing commanders was to lay their ships against each other so a land battle could begin on the decks. Don Juan thought that Spanish arquebusiers (men armed with portable guns) could thin out the Turkish ranks. He engaged the Turkish flagship which could not get its guns to bear while Don Juan's guns emplaced at a low level could pour shot below the Turkish waterline. The Turkish ship was boarded and the poop taken. Ali Pasha's head was cut off, mounted on a pike and held up in the air to sap Turkish morale on other ships. Resistance soon ended, the Ottoman standard, a sacred icon inscribed with the name of Allah 29,000 times, was captured and can still be seen at the Doge's Palace in Venice.

The battle devoured 8,000 of Spain and Italy's chivalry with 16,000 wounded. The Turks lost three times as many with some 20,000 Christian galley slaves being rescued. Both sides were courageous but the better leadership of Don Juan, the galeasse, and superior weapons gained the upper hand. The Ottomans might seize Crete and Cyprus in their part of the eastern Mediterranean and the advance westward was stopped.

THE KNIGHT IN LITERATURE AND ART

ALTHOUGH THE SUBJECT OF KNIGHTS, THEIR HISTORICAL AND FICTIONAL DEEDS, AND THEIR CODE OF CHIVALRY, CONTINUED TO INSPIRE THE SCHOLARS AND CREATIVE WRITERS OF EUROPE AFTER THE 15TH CENTURY, IT BECAME INCREASINGLY DIFFICULT FOR ANYONE TO UNDERSTAND WHAT IT HAD BEEN LIKE TO BE A MEDIEVAL KNIGHT. SINCE THE MIDDLE AGES, NO OTHER GROUP IN ANY EUROPEAN SOCIETY HAS ATTAINED SUCH A POSITION OF MILITARY, SOCIAL, AND CULTURAL DOMINANCE, LET ALONE THE KIND OF INTERNATIONAL DOMINANCE SHOWN IN THIS BOOK.

The major figure whose personality has imbued popular culture with a cult, knightly figure is King Arthur with his Knights of the Round Table. This semilegendary King of the Britons allegedly lived during the 6th Century and earned great respect for fighting against the invading Anglo-Saxons. Despite historians considering Arthur a mythological king, he is depicted as a warrior, son of King Uther Pendragon, himself the brother of King Ambrosius Aurelianus. Other sources claim the historical background surrounding the British leader, Vortigern who invited Saxons into Britain to aid in the defense against invading Picts from Scotland. These mercenaries found Britain a pleasant land and stayed with their wives and raised families. Other Anglo-Saxons followed and these migrants came into conflict with native Britons who were torn by internal rivalry as petty king sought power over petty king. In this period marked by violence, looting, and raping can be found the legends of Arthur, a king or powerful military leader.

The first reference to Arthur is in the Welsh poem *Y Gododdin* (c. 600), followed by another allusion in the *Historia Britonum* written by Welsh historian and cleric Nennius (c. 800). This book was edited in the 10th Century by Mark the Hermit and the document was found in the library of the Vatican Palace, in Rome, Italy.

"Arthur fought against the Saxons alongside the kings of the Britons but he himself was the leader in the battles (*dux bellorum*). The first battle was at the mouth of the river which is called Glein. The next four were on the banks of another river, which is called Dubglas and is in the region of Linnuis ... The Twelfth was on Mount Badon, in which—on that one day —there fell in one onslaught of Arthur's nine hundred and sixty men; and none slew them but he alone, and in all battles he remained victor."

Apparently, the twelve defeats of the Anglo-Saxons held them in check for several years. A 10th-Century work, the *Annales Cambriae* mentions Arthur offering 537 as the date of his death. The fully developed tales and legends of Arthur appear in the *Historia Regum Britanniae* (c. 1139) of the English historian Geoffrey of Monmouth but numbers of tales had appeared in several languages. The Welsh collection of stories, *The Mabinogion* (c. 1100) told stories of Arthur's wife Guinevere and the knights, Kay, Bedivere, and Gawain.

The Arthurian tradition developed in Europe, possibly passed on by the Celts, many of who migrated from Britain to Brittany in France in the 5th and 6th Centuries. By 1100 the romances surrounding Arthur were known in Italy. These were inspired by notions of chivalry and courtly love and are generally concerned with the deeds of Arthur's knights. In France, the Arthurian romances were written in a series of poems by Chrétien de Troyes. Taken together, all the written sources show Arthur and his Queen, Guinevere, keeping a court at the legendary castle Camelot, which may have been the great hill fort at South Cadbury in Somerset, England. Archaeological excavations at the hill show that this pre-Roman fort was refortified at the end of the 5th and the beginning of the 6th Centuries and the remains of other hill-forts do not exhibit the scale of rebuilding at Cadbury where the refortification comprised a 16-foot (4.8 m) thick unmortared stone wall with blocks of Roman masonry on top of it, plus a surrounding earth bank, an internal dry-stone wall and a gate tower with two entrances. The 18-acre site could have housed 1,000 men; this does not mean that Arthur was there but its use fits the right period of history.

In legend, Arthur's wars and victories include campaigns against the forces of the Roman Empire in continental Europe, after which he faces internal rebellion at home at the hands of his traitor nephew Mordred. In a final battle at Camlan, Arthur and Mordred wound each other but Arthur is spirited away to the mythical Island of Avalon, thought to be Glastonbury Tor, where he would be healed.

Chrétien de Troyes wrote five romances and introduced into Arthurian legend, the Grail, the chalice that Christ used at the Last Supper according to one story. His poems pursued the themes of

Perhaps the archetypal Knight in Shining Armor, complete with white charger, a beautiful and sensitive image of Sir Galahad painted in 1864 by George Frederick Watts.
Sir Galahad was a late addition to the world of late medieval romance (the original hero of the story of the Holy Grail was in fact Sir Percival), but he appealed to late 18th-Century readers who preferred his absolute purity and integrity to the more flawed and human character of his father Sir Lancelot, by far the more popular figure in the Middle Ages.

The Knights of the Round Table were the men awarded the highest order of chivalry at the Court of King Arthur. The shape of the table—without head or foot—represents the equality of the members. In the legends of King Arthur the knights numbered between 12 and more than 150. In this French 15th-Century illustration an assembly of named knights witness a vision of the Holy Grail, which appears in the center of the table before them.

This photograph taken in 1874 by Julia Cameron, sets the scene for 19th-Century interpretations of the Arthurian legends.

finding the Grail and the adulterous love story of the French knight Lancelot and Guinevere. Lancelot becomes an important figure because he can never see into the Grail since he has sinned with his queen while his son, Galahad, is portrayed as the pure knight who achieved the vision of the Grail. Another aspect of the Arthurian legend is the verse romance written by Robert de Boron in the early 13th Century. This Merlin narrates the story of Arthur's birth and childhood upbringing and the winning of his crown by pulling a magic sword from a stone.

Arthur's knights are judged to be equal and hence the Round Table at Camelot demonstrated this but when the knights rode off on adventure to find the Grail, the fellowship was sundered, the kingdom falling into eventual disarray. The final work adding to the legend is the anonymously written Sir Gawain and the Green Knight (c. 1370). Eventually, a number of these stories were

"... my heart was never so heavy as it is now, and much more I am sorrier for my good knights' loss than for the loss of my fair queen; for queens I might have enough, but such a fellowship of good knights shall never be together in no company."

The heroes of medieval romance did not allow scruples to deflect the physical consummation of their love. Here Sir Lancelot is tricked into sleeping with the daughter of the King of Norgalles, believing her to be his true love Queen Guinevere (the wife of his overlord King Arthur). This was how Sir Galahad was conceived; his illegitimacy brought no stain upon his knightly perfection.

offered in England in English prose in Sir Thomas Malory's *Morte d'Arthur.*

In 1759, at the height of the Age of Reason, the great scholar, J. B. de la Curne de Sainte Palaye, published his *Memoires sur l'ancienne chevalrie*. It contained extracts from many medieval French romances, in which the author had immersed himself, and, together with his next book, *Histoire littéraire des troubadours*, stimulated a revival of interest in the art and, more especially, the literature of the Middle Ages.

In late 18th- and early 19th-Century England, "Gothic" became a popular and fashionable style in architecture and novels contributing to the development of Romantic poetry. Tennyson's *Idylls of the King* explores the Arthurian legend that has fascinated the minds of poets, writers, and people of all eras since its telling by Chrétien de Troyes, who said that the best of tales was the Grail legend. This legend in which knights search for a treasure difficult to attain with ultimate deliverance from a magic spell is fundamental to Christians since it weaves a fairy-tale into the Christian legend.

The Grail legend has found its way in to German, English, Welsh, Spanish, and the northern languages. Wagner's *Parsifal* is a particularly brilliant rendition of the story. Scholars have researched the legend in great depth and one school of thought

believes that the Grail legend is a Christianized, no longer understood, remnant of an old Near Eastern Phoenician or Syrian vegetation ritual. Other scholars have looked to Persia and Vedic India to find the Oriental origins of the Grail, which have since been wedded to Celtic influences. The legend has been linked to the Cathars and their treasure, to the Templars, and in particular to the tales known as the *Contes Bretons*, a series of stories centered on the part-historical, semi-legendary person of King Arthur of Britain while recounting the deeds of his knights. The Round Tables, in these lays, is a type of school of knightly training. Part of the story is that Joseph of Arimathea is supposed to have brought the Grail to England landing at Glastonbury, the Isle of Avalon, where King Arthur and

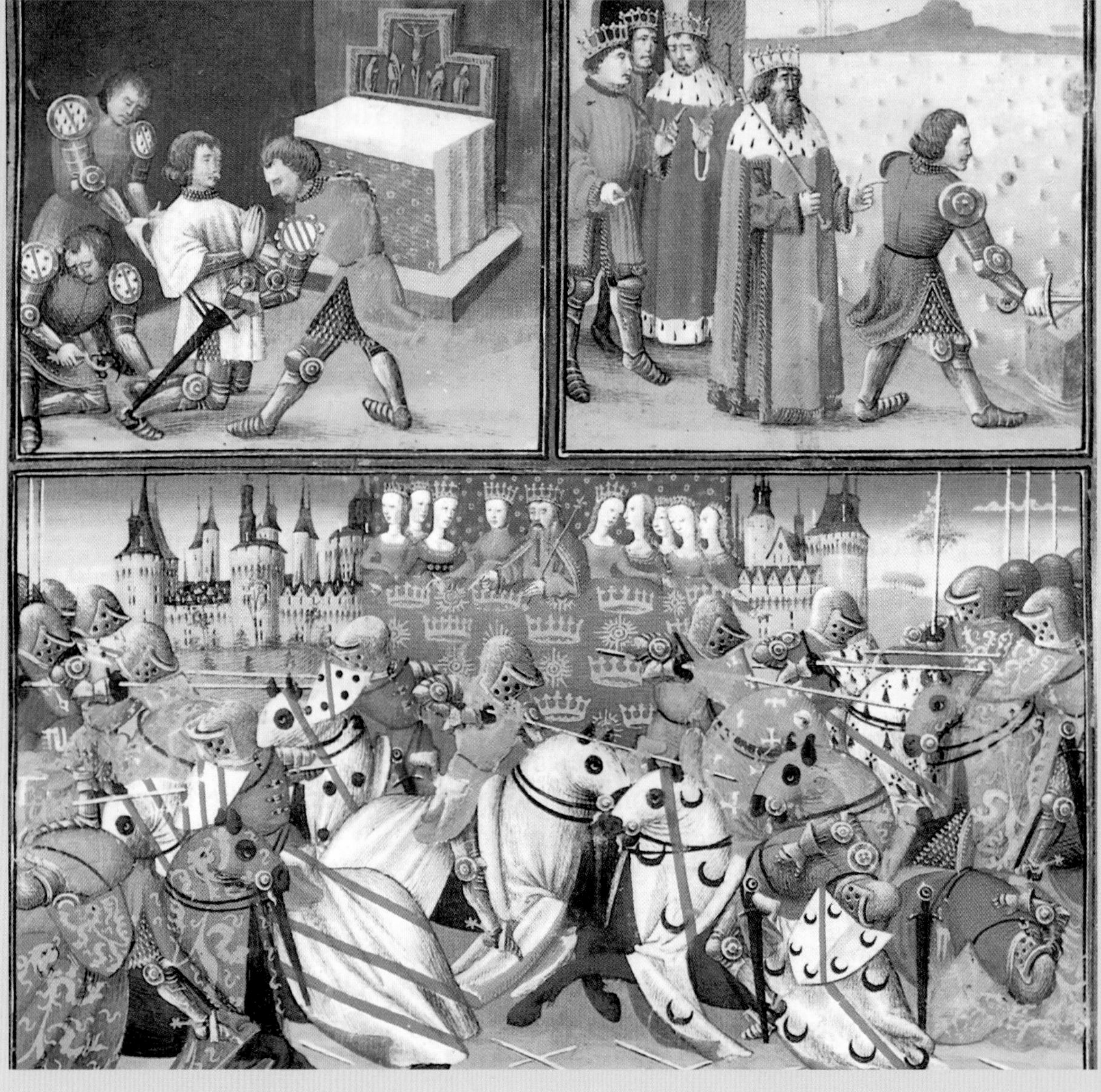

Scenes from the life of Sir Galahad, son of Sir Lancelot. At the top left Sir Galahad is knighted in a chapel; top right, he draws his sword from a magical floating stone before Camelot; bottom, he takes part in a tournament *Melee* in the presence of King Arthur and Queen Guinevere.

Alfred, Lord Tennyson photographed in 1874 dressed as King Arthur. Many artists and writers of the period were inspired by Arthurian legends and the chivalric knightly culture of the middle ages.

On the tomb of many Knights an attempt was made to live up to Knightly traditions and Christian chivalric values in their lives. They often failed miserably in this ideal but when faced with the Almighty and eternity sought to create their best face.

his wife are buried. The importance of the Grail and Arthurian legends is that they are not like ordinary fairy tales, since they have been shaped by a range of specific poets over time. They therefore include certain archetypal features but are specific to an age and its attitude of mind. The poems allow ordinary people to touch the Middle Ages' mentality, through troubadours, and this in turn focuses upon problems of the Christian era that are psychologically important for people today: the search for the unachievable ideal.

In the 19th Century, Sir Walter Scott's novels on knights were well received and he expounded his theories on chivalry in an essay in the 1818 edition of the *Encyclopaedia Britannica*. In common with the other great 19th-Century apologists of chivalry, he made it something much more moral and ideal than it had ever been in the Middle Ages. A genuine belief existed that the code of chivalry had force and relevance for 19th-Century Britain, but the key concepts for the Victorians were purity, nobility, high moral seriousness, and that excessive gallantry and tenderness towards women. This is rather nauseating and anachronistic to people today in the 21st Century. The favorite hero of the Victorian medievalists was the pure but rather empty Sir Galahad, rather than Sir Lancelot, whose knightly character was tainted by his guilty rather than courtly love for Queen Guinevere. Tennyson's *Idylls of the King* probably expressed this consciousness of moral chivalry best. Tennyson developed a theme that was already strongly expressed in Malory's *Morte d'Arthur*. In this work the tensions generated by Lancelot's adulterous love affair with the queen become unbearable and are obviously going to destroy the fellowship of the Round Table because the idealistic comradeship is warped by a lie and the kingdom is built on truth so Arthur's realm will die. At this point King Arthur says:

"... my heart was never so heavy as it is now, and much more I am sorrier for my good knights' loss than for the loss of my fair queen; for queens I might have enough, but such a fellowship of good knights shall never be together in no company."

Likewise for Tennyson, the noble ideals of the Round Table are brought down by the corruption and evil generated by the guilty love affair. According to Tennyson's son, his father had said of the *Idylls*. "My meaning was spiritual. I only took the legendary stories of the Round Table as illustrations. Arthur was allegorical to me. I intended him to represent the Ideal in the Soul of Man coming into contact with the warring elements of the flesh." King Arthur explains the impact of her behavior to Guinevere when the destruction of the Round Table appears inevitable. His summing up of his aims in forming the Fellowship are perhaps the clearest expression of the Victorian understanding of chivalry:

"I made them lay their hands in mine and swear
To reverence the King, as if he were
Their conscience, and their conscience as their King,
To break the heathen and uphold the Christ,
To ride abroad addressing human wrongs,
To speak no slander, no, nor listen to it,

To honour his own word as if his God's,
To lead sweet lives in purest chastity,
To love one maiden only, cleave to her
And worship her by years of noble deeds,
Until they won her; for indeed I knew
Of no more subtle master under heaven
Than is the maiden passion for a maid,
Not only to keep down the base in man,
But teach high thought, and amiable words
And courtliness, and the desire of fame,
And love of truth, and all that makes a man."

This is both more and less than the ideals of real medieval knights who certainly admitted the power of love to inspire them to noble deeds and the desire for fame, but would probably have been less impressed with the idea of purest chastity; and who consistently maintained a sturdy independence of spirit and the subordination of moral purpose to secular goals such as the attainment of wealth and the enjoyment of power. King Arthur continues to Guinevere:

"And all this throve before I wedded thee,
Believing, 'Lo mine helpmate, one to feel
My purpose and rejoicing in my joy.'
Then came this thy shameful sin with Lancelot;
Then came the sin of Tristan and Isolt;
Then others, following these my mightiest knights,
And drawing foul ensample from fair names,
Sinn'd also, till the loathsome opposite
Of all my heart had destined did obtain,
And all thro' thee!"

Tennyson's neighbor on the Isle of Wight, off the south coast of England, was the photographic artist, Julia Margaret Cameron (1815–79)—allegedly the mother of the soft-focus technique—who a number of sitters to construct pictures of the *Idylls*. She created her ideal representations of Tennyson's work, which itself was representative of legendary subjects. Her work pre-dated the Pre-Raphaelites, men who she knew, and they carried on more detailed representations in their painting or tapestry work.

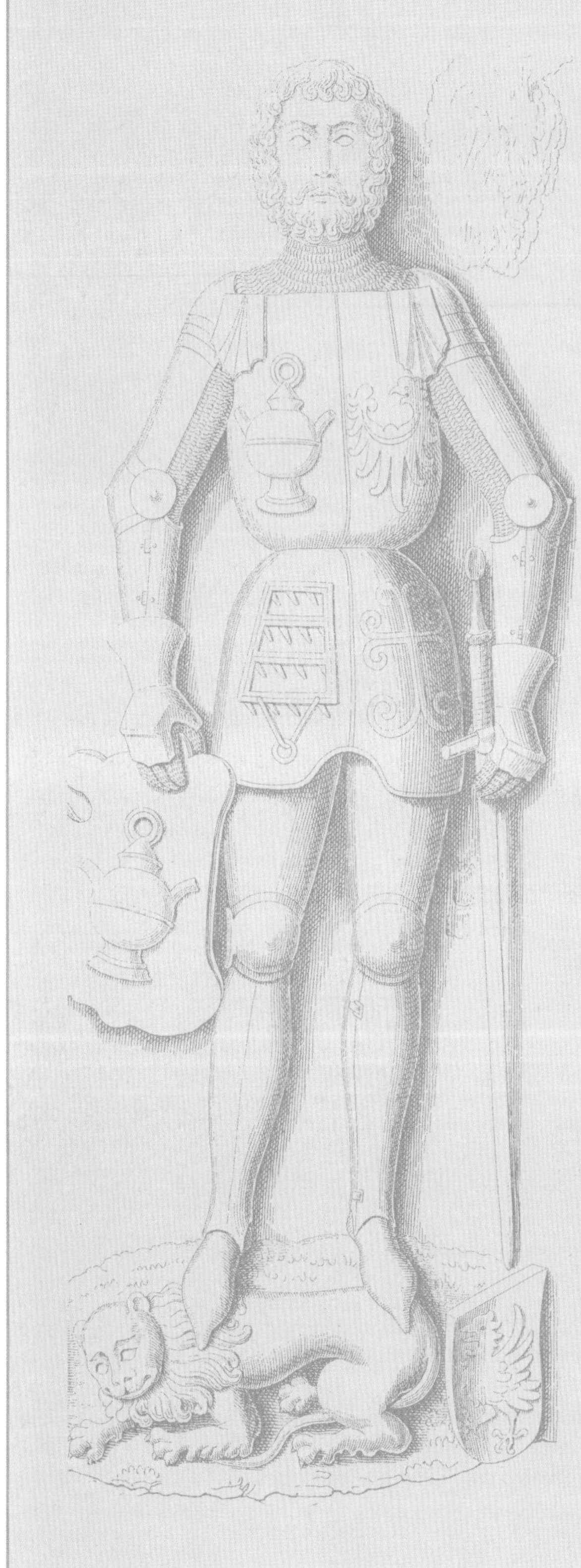

Advances in historical research into the Middle Ages have touched off a certain cyncism about the very lofty and pure standards of behavior supposed to have been held by medieval knights. The grim and brutish reality of medieval life for the majority seemed to sit ill with the high civilization of the ideal and almost vulgar displays of wealth, which often accompanied it in later medieval chivalry. The romantic glow cast by Scott and Tennyson over the figures of real or fictional medieval knights has inescapably colored everyone's perceptions of the subject and has been transmitted in a less subtle form by Hollywood epics of medieval heroes. Much criticism has been made by historians who are convinced that the knights gradually lost touch with their original purpose and forgot the ideals, founded on loyal service and the upholding of justice, in pursuit of rich, vain self-glorification. Perhaps chivalry was a moral code only applied by the lucky few in their behavior toward each other, in a huge extravagant, fantastical game that took the knights, particularly of the later period, even further and further from the "harsh realities" of the period. This view is connected with the modern obsession of what is fact. In the Middle Ages, as any study of medieval historians will demonstrate, fact was not nearly so important as meaning. It was an age of symbols, and the deeds of arms achieved at some richly decorated tournament could and did stand for the same values as those achieved in battle or siege. Doubtless, from the 12th Century onward, knights were in love with their own image; but some facets of that image have proved to be of genuine and lasting worth, and have certainly made a major contribution to the ethos and culture of Western Europe. As Jane Austen said, "Respect for right conduct is felt by everyone."

The importance of the Arthurian legends is that they have become a fictionalized part of British history. The tales have also excited many writers who have adapted the stories of Arthur and his knights. Edmund Spenser used Arthur as the perfect knight in *The Faerie Queene* (1590–99), his allegory of Elizabethan society. Mark Twain's *A Connecticut Yankee at King Arthur's Court* (1880) compares New England society with the medieval, while T.H. White's *The Once and Future King* (4 vols. 1939–58) provide a modern version of the legend that is widely read.

In a detail from a series of tapestries designed between 1890 and 1893 by Sir Edward Coley-Burn Jones, William Morris and John Henry Dearle, Sir Galahad attains a vision of the Holy Grail, while on the Grail quest.

Asian Knighthood

THOUGH MANY SOCIETIES HAVE PRODUCED WARRIOR ELITES, THE SAMURAI WERE THE CLOSEST IN ALMOST EVERY WAY TO THE KNIGHTS OF MEDIEVAL EUROPE. FROM PURELY MILITARY BEGINNINGS THEY DEVELOPED AN ETHOS BASED ON TRADITIONS OF SERVICE AND HONOR.

The *samurai* warrior, who many people incorrectly believe was a swordsman, began as a highly trained, deadly-accurate mounted bowman. This Japanese knight was protected from retaliation by an elaborate suit of armor quite different in appearance and manufacture to that of his somewhat cumbersome European counterpart.

JAPAN IN THE MIDDLE AGES

By the 9th Century, Japan was unified under the Yamato court. The emperors began to withdraw from state affairs to concentrate upon the Shinto faith and ceremonial duties. Power was delegated and eventually fell into the hands of the Fujiwara clan who divided up the land, giving it to nobles as tax-free payment for their administrative tasks, or gifting land to Buddhist monasteries. By 1028, Fujiwara power declined and the Kyoto court sucked in the nobility who left their estates to be run by retainers, the *samurai* (the powerful military caste). As lawlessness spread through the provinces, estate managers developed a feudalistic society by concentrating lesser samurai on the estates in a lord-vassal relationship.

Eventually two families came to determine events in Japan: the Minamoto in the east, and the Taira in the southwest. They conflicted as each sought control over all Japan and the Kyoto court. In 1156, a civil war known as the Hogen Disturbance broke in a succession dispute within the Fujiwara clan. A second war followed, the Heiji Disturbance (1159–60), wherein the Taira crushed the Minamoto and ousted the Fujiwara. A surviving Minamoto, Yoritomo, raised the flag of rebellion in 1180 and after a five-year-long war, the Taira were wiped out in 1185 at the naval Battle of Dannoura. Thus ended what were known as the Gempei Wars (1180–85); from this moment there was a military government in Japan for the next 700 years.

Yoritomo ran Japan from Kamakura utilizing his field headquarters, the *bakafu*, as the focus of a new administration. Japanese feudalism spiraled as Yoritomo appointed retainers to run provinces

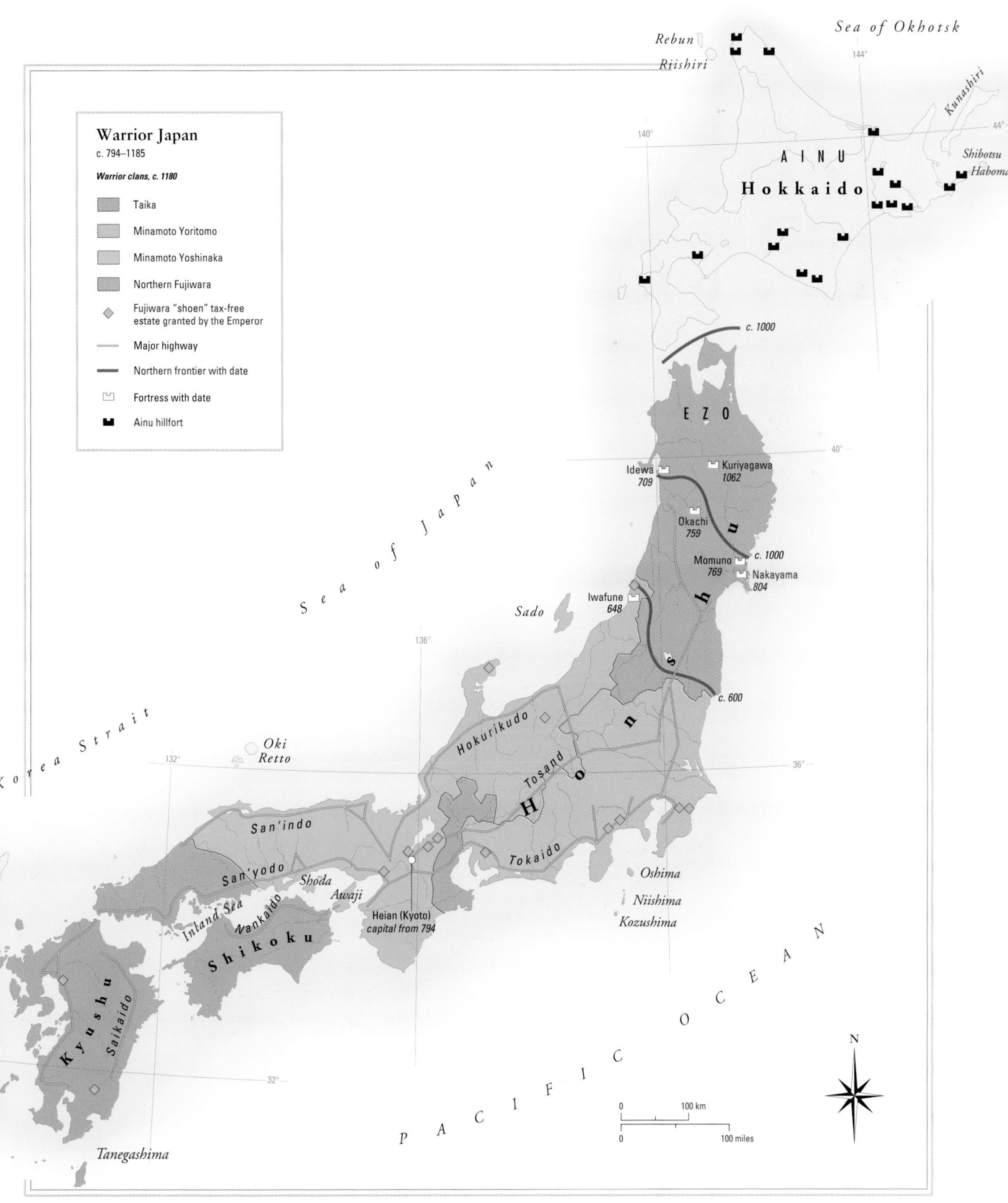
Warrior Japan
c. 794–1185
Warrior clans, c. 1180
Taika
Minamoto Yoritomo
Minamoto Yoshinaka
Northern Fujiwara
Fujiwara "shoen" tax-free estate granted by the Emperor
Major highway
Northern frontier with date
Fortress with date
Ainu hillfort
Sea of Okhotsk
Rebun
Riishiri
Kunashiri
Shibotsu
Habomai I.
AINU
Hokkaido
c. 1000
EZO
Idewa 709
Kuriyagawa 1062
Okachi 759
Momuno 769
c. 1000
Nakayama 804
Iwafune 648
Sado
Sea of Japan
c. 600
Honshu
Hokurikudo
Tosando
Oki Retto
Korea Strait
San'indo
San'yodo
Tokaido
Shoda
Awaji
Inland Sea
Nankaido
Heian (Kyoto) capital from 794
Oshima
Niishima
Kozushima
Shikoku
Kyushu
Saikaido
Tanegashima
PACIFIC OCEAN
N
0 100 km
0 100 miles

and landed estates in paralel with official governors or owners. In 1192, he was given the title of *Seiitaishogun* (barbarian-subduing great general) normally shortened to *shogun*. The Kyoto court became merely titular and powerless.

In 1219, the Hojo family eradicated Minamoto rule and ran Japan for about 100 years, replacing Minamoto administrators with their own men. After two failed Mongol invasions of Japan disaffected daimyô, great lords, vassals of the shogun (1333), led by Takauji Ashikaga ousted the Hojo. The Ashikaga became shogun in 1338. However, this shogunate never fully controlled Japan and Buddhist monasteries became political centers whose warrior-monks and their lay brethren became important in military campaigns often being a deciding factor in obtaining victory.

The Omin Wars (1467–1477) erupted when two powerful daimyô families, the Hosokawa and Yamana, took opposing sides during an Ashikaga succession dispute. Kyoto was destroyed, the traditional daimyô families weakened. Ashikaga authority was destroyed and there was no winner in the wars. Warring daimyô jockeyed for power in a period of intense hostility known as the Period of Warring States. Usurpations occurred and Japan decentralized into various daimyô-controlled provinces. During this period, the Portuguese arrived bringing with them the arquebus. The presence of this early firearm changed the nature of samurai warfare, which had previously relied upon the bow and arrow, and the sword.

Into this ferment came Oda Nobunaga, a native of Oswari province, near today's Nagoya. In 1560, a warlord, Imagawa, invaded Oswari with an army of 25,000 men but was ambushed in a narrow gorge by Nobunaga with his 3,000 men. Imagawa and his forces were annihilated and Nobunaga marched on Kyoto, taking the city in 1568. He later met his enemies in the decisive Battle of Nagashino in 1575. Nobunaga's peasant arquebusiers mowed down the enemy cavalry rendering it obsolete. In 1582, Oda Nobunaga was when a subordinate general, Akechi Mitsuhide, turned traitor and assailed him in the temple of Honnoji in Kyoto. Another general showed his loyalty to his dead master; Toyotomi Hideyoshi (1536–98) hurried back from campaigning and defeated Mitsuhide at the Battle of Yamazaki.

Seeking to plug the power vacuum left by Obunaga's death, Hideyoshi carried out a series of campaigns over five years eliminating or neutralizing his enemies—including Nobunaga's sons and brothers—unifying Japan by 1591. Hideyoshi made two attempts at conquering Korea. Hideyoshi's general, Konishi Yukinaga, was extremely successful marching to the Imjin River, ambushing Koreans, and reaching Pinying. Meanwhile, a Korean admiral named Yi-san constructed a number of "tortoise" ships, oared galleys protected by iron sheeting and armed with underwater rams. These vessels together with numerous normal warships attacked a fleet carrying Japanese reinforcements, sinking 47 and capturing 12 Japanese vessels in a battle near Han-san island, causing the sea to run red with the blood of the 9,000 Japanese killed. In 1594, the Japanese evacuated Korea after the Chinese crossed the Yalu River to help the Koreans. A second invasion in 1597 was more successful but Hideyoshi's death put an end to the Korean adventure.

Japan looked ready to slip into anarchy again since Hideyoshi's son and heir was only five years old but nevertheless was supported by Ishida Mitsunari and many other daimyô. War broke out and various contenders for the shogunate finally came to battle at Sekigahara in 1600. The victor was

Warrior monks of the Ikko-ikki in action against the forces of Oda Nobunaga. They were amongst his fiercest opponents and are portrayed here fighting a group of Nobunaga's samurai.

Tokugawa Ieyasu (1542–1616), aided by Kobayakawa Hideaki treacherously changing sides with some 15,000 men during the battle, thereby ending Hideyoshi political pretensions. The Tokugawa Shogunate began in 1603. The remnants of Toyotomi Hideyoshi were defeated at the Siege of Osaka Castle in 1614–15. Despite an uprising in the Shimabara Rebellion of 1637–38, the Age of the Warring States was finished. Ieyasu managed to establish stability by ensuring that the estates of former enemies were surrounded by the fiefs of loyal daimyô. The Tokugawa shogunate lasted until 1868.

DIAMYÔ, SAMURAI, AND BUSHIDO CODE

Samurai were governed by the concepts of honor, personal integrity, and loyalty to their daimyô. These warriors served their lords not only through tending their estates and fiefs but fighting for their masters on the battlefield. The most serious duty was seeking death on the battlefield and even committing suicide if their lord fell. *Bushido*, the code of the samurai, is best expressed in the *Hagakure*, a collection of the sayings of the samurai Tsunetomo Yamamoto (1659–1719) written down by his friend, fellow samurai Tsuramoto Tashiro. The opening paragraph says much of the samurai view of the world:

> *"I have found the essence of Bushido: to die! In other words, when you have a choice between life and death, then always choose death: this is all that you must remember. It is neither troublesome nor difficult. You only have to go on with a clenched stomach."*

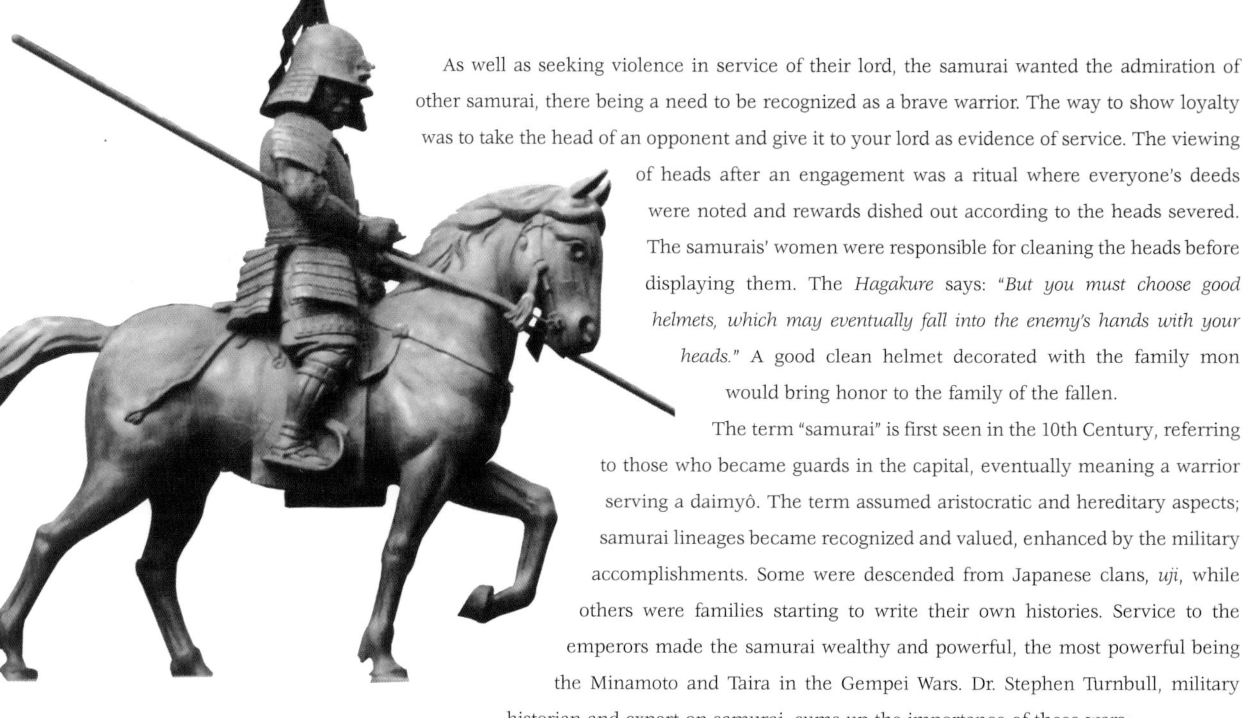

This modern bronze equestrian statue shows Yamaucho Kazutoyo, the *daimyo* of Kochi, and stands near Kochi Castle. He is equipped with full armor and is carrying a lance.

As well as seeking violence in service of their lord, the samurai wanted the admiration of other samurai, there being a need to be recognized as a brave warrior. The way to show loyalty was to take the head of an opponent and give it to your lord as evidence of service. The viewing of heads after an engagement was a ritual where everyone's deeds were noted and rewards dished out according to the heads severed. The samurais' women were responsible for cleaning the heads before displaying them. The *Hagakure* says: *"But you must choose good helmets, which may eventually fall into the enemy's hands with your heads."* A good clean helmet decorated with the family mon would bring honor to the family of the fallen.

The term "samurai" is first seen in the 10th Century, referring to those who became guards in the capital, eventually meaning a warrior serving a daimyô. The term assumed aristocratic and hereditary aspects; samurai lineages became recognized and valued, enhanced by the military accomplishments. Some were descended from Japanese clans, *uji*, while others were families starting to write their own histories. Service to the emperors made the samurai wealthy and powerful, the most powerful being the Minamoto and Taira in the Gempei Wars. Dr. Stephen Turnbull, military historian and expert on samurai, sums up the importance of these wars:

"First, the battles that took place such as Ichi no tani, Yashima and Dan no Ura created benchmarks for samurai excellence that were to last for the whole of samurai history. Heroic tales and works of art logged the incidents in the Gempei War as a verbal and visual catalog of heroism that would show future generations the most noble, brave, and correct ways of being a samurai. Nearly all the factors that were to become indelible parts of samurai culture have a reference point somewhere within the Gempei War. Prowess at archery and hand-to-hand fighting, the juxtaposition of art, poetry, and violence, undying loyalty to one's lord and the tremendous tradition of ritual suicide, all have key passages and proof texts in the tales of the Gempei War."

RITUAL SUICIDE

Much mention has been made of ritual suicide—*hara kiri* or *seppuku*. Warriors sometimes chose to disembowel themselves rather than be captured. At the Battle of Uji in 1180 Minamoto Yorimasa made this choice on his defeat. Some samurai who faced a degrading execution for not performing their duty were ordered to commit suicide to wipe the shame from themselves and their families. When Reizei Motomitsu was killed at Ulsan, his three closest retainers who had become separated from him, on learning of his death, committed suicide.

Traditionally, the suicide would stab himself in the lower left-belly draw the blade to the right and then pull the knife upwards. This painful practice would release the samurai's spirit, enhance his

This illustration shows the legendary archer Minamoto Tametomo. He was the first named samurai mentioned in the War Chronicles to commit *hara kiri*, ritual suicide, after boats carrying Taira samurai approached his island of exile. It is said that Tametomo sank one of the invading boats with a well-aimed arrow before meeting death at his own hand.

reputation, and show his admirable behavior. Occasionally, the suicide would have a second, a *kaishaku*, who would use his sword to behead the dying suicide to prevent too much agony. Minamoto Yorimasa committed suicide on the battlefield while his sons held the enemy at bay without using a second, and even managed to write a poem on his war. In 1582, Akechi Mitsutoshi committed seppuku and wrote a poem on a door using a brush and his blood. Another method of suicide was *junshi* where warriors followed their lord into death. In 1333, when Kamakura Castle was captured, the lord killed himself whereupon his retainers, 20 in number, rushed into the bailey of the burning castle, told the garrison of the event, then lined up and committed seppuku. Three hundred others did likewise.

A form of heraldry was used by Japanese samurai to identify warriors in battle, as were coats of arms in the West. This illustration depicts Nawa Nagatoshi (d. 1336) wearing a *sashimono* flag attached to the back of his armor. The "ship on the water" *mon*, or crest, shows his allegiance to his lord, Kusunoki Massahige.

Some samurai became *ronin*, 'men of the waves', a warrior who had lost his lord and was available for new employment. Such were the *Seven Samurai* in Akira Kurosawa's 1954 epic film, hired by farmers to defend their village from attacking bandits. In 1703, a samurai named Asano was ordered to arrange an elaborate ceremony at the shogunate. He sought the help of a courtier, Kira. Asano did not offer him enough for his services so Kira gave him bad advice. Arriving at court, Asano realized he had been tricked, drew his sword and wounded Kira. This was an unpardonable offense in the shogun's palace, so Asano went home and committed seppuku. Asano's samurai became ronin seeking revenge. They fell into a life of debauchery, divorcing their wives, and disowning their children, so they seemed no threat. In December 1703, Asano's 47 ronin seized Kira's palace and found Kira cowering in an outhouse. The ronins' leader, Oishi, ordered Kira to commit suicide. When he failed to do this, Oishi beheaded him with his dead master's sword. The ronin went to their lord's grave, placed the severed head upon it, then all committed seppuku. The ronin were buried with high honors and thousands traveled to their burial place to pay tribute to their loyalty and courage.

Nabeshima Naoshige (1537–1619), retainer of the Ryuzoji clan, and a respected general, once said of the bushido code:

> *"The Bushido signifies desperate death. Several tons of sane samurais could not kill a single samurai who burns with this mad death... To the Bushido, loyalty and filial duty will naturally follow from your madness. Because in this desperate death, both of these qualities dwell in your actions."*

SAMURAI HERALDRY

Samurai heraldry is a complicated area. The mon, badge, or family crest, was normally depicted in white on black or black on white. Another form of identification in battle was the use of the *sashimono*, a small flag being fastened to the back of a samurai's armor using two brackets. As the 16th Century developed so did heraldry and the use of flags and standards.

JAPANESE CASTLES

The earliest Japanese castles were Yamashiro mountain castles relying on natural topography to provide defenses and wood from the forests to build palisades and towers. Sometimes, a series of hilltops would be linked together by footpaths and ridges, each succeeding mountain top being another bailey. These castles continued to be constructed even after stone castles were developed. They were designed to keep an enemy force restricted to a certain area where it could be observed and attacked by arrows. The hilltops would be flattened to allow space for building towers and a palisade enclosure. When attacked, the garrison would fire arrows through arrow slits in the walls or make sorties. The attackers had no siege engines because Japanese cities had no walls so fighting was by missiles or hand to hand.

HIMEJI CASTLE
This castle overlooks the city of Hemeji in Hyogo Prefecture in Japan. Constructed in the 14th Century and set on a low hill, the castle is made up of an intricate system of compounds and gates and is surrounded by a moat.

The Yamashiro castles developed into the Sengoku Yamashiro. These castles involved using the topography even more creatively by excavating and sculpting hillsides and mountain tops turning them into inner and outer baileys, each overlooking the one below. Different baileys on neighboring hilltops could develop interlocking field of fire for bows and crossbows in series of earth fortifications

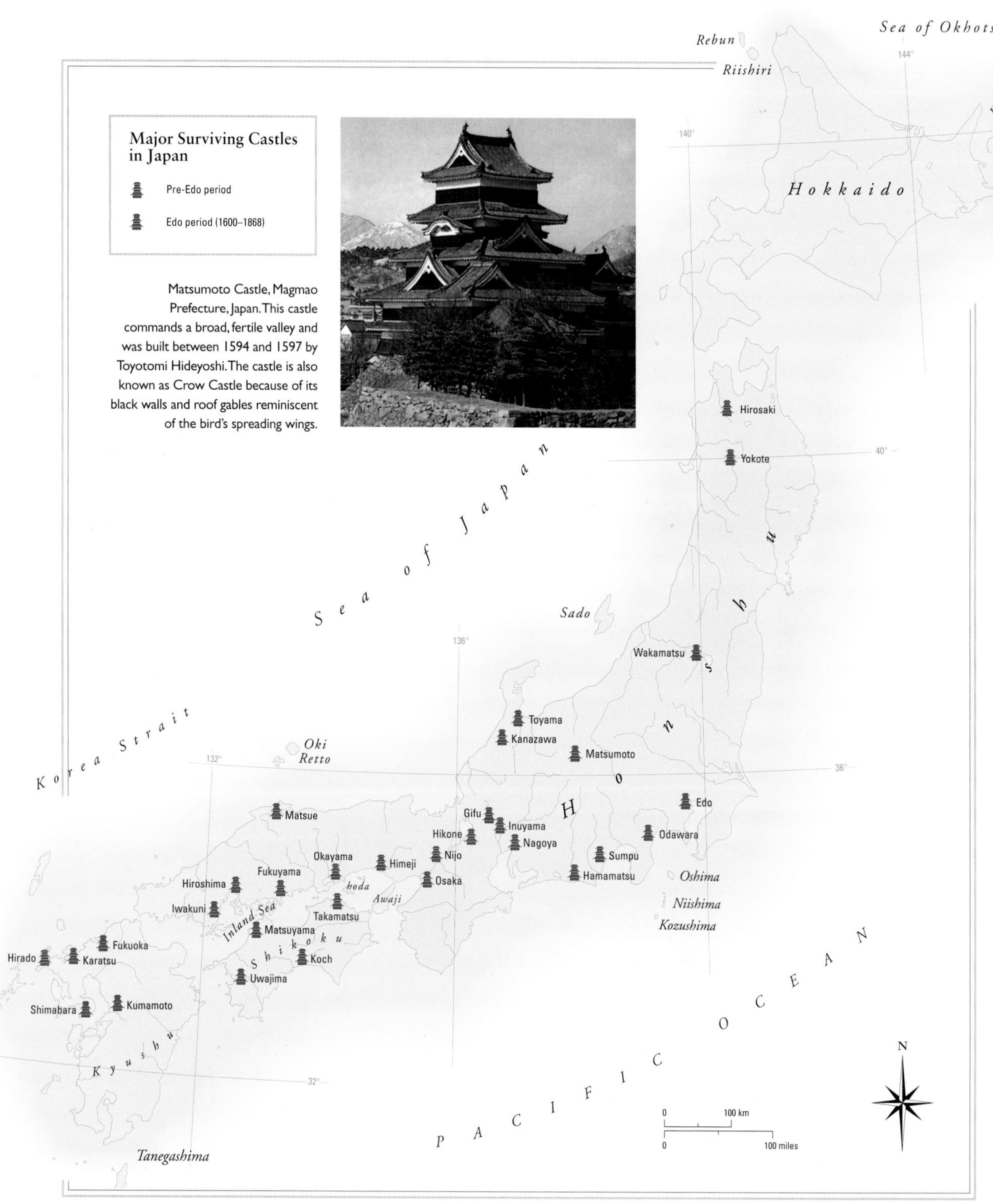

Matsumoto Castle, Magmao Prefecture, Japan. This castle commands a broad, fertile valley and was built between 1594 and 1597 by Toyotomi Hideyoshi. The castle is also known as Crow Castle because of its black walls and roof gables reminiscent of the bird's spreading wings.

topped by wooden walls. The Sengoku Yamashiro castles are exemplified by that at Shikizan, built in 1550. Here, mountain streams were diverted to create moats while the wattle and daub walls were strengthened with wooden buttresses inside the fortifications and had arrow slits cut through. The walls were topped with shingles to keep out rain and protect the walls from the elements.

The mountain castles with a sculpted motte or hillside had a basic weakness. Once forests had been cut down to eradicate cover for attackers, the hillside became less stable and the weight of towers caused many to collapse. Therefore, the Japanese came up with a solution. They moved castle building down to flatter areas and built strong stone bases by cladding carved earth mounds with huge rocks. These edifices would also withstand earthquakes. Few daimyô possessed just one castle and may own a main castle, *honjô*, supplemented by a number of supporting, satellite castles, *shijô*. Another key development in castle construction was the tower keep, designed for both defense, intimidation, and as an expression of a daimyô's power. The castle at Osaka is an example of a concentric castle with rings of huge stone walls cladding earth cores with multiple layers of defense, all dominated by the central keep.

Castle designers used natural water obstacles for defensive purposes, whether lakes, rivers, or the sea. The castles had a keep at the highest point surrounded by a series of interlocking baileys, not necessarily at the same level. The main bailey housed the keep. The defenses of Himeji Castle, built 1611, were defended by a difficult access route. Any attacker hoping to reach the keep would need to fight through a maze of walls, gates, and baileys in a circuitous route traveling in a spiral, through 21 ordinary gates including five water gates.

Castle walls were sometimes dry stone with an outward curve adding compactness or strength. The wedge shaped stone base could sometimes support walls 130 feet high and the bases linked together in a self-supporting, overlapping defense system. Small walls inside the baileys could be made of plaster and ground rock and would be pierced for guns (triangular holes), and archers (rectangular holes). Behind the walls would be planted rows of trees proving a shield against arrows and bullets and within the outer walls would be trees to shroud troop movements. The keep, *tenshu kaku* (high heavenly protector), had several functions: to provide a viewing point; to be the final defensive bastion; to be a symbol of power; and to provide a storage unit.

During a castle siege, defensive and offensive weapons would be bows and arquebuses, the use of cannon a great rarity. Assaults would be direct,

The main building of Himeji Castle is five stories high on the outside with seven floors in the interior. Himeji Castle served largely as a fortress and garrison but it also provided a residence for the ruling élite.

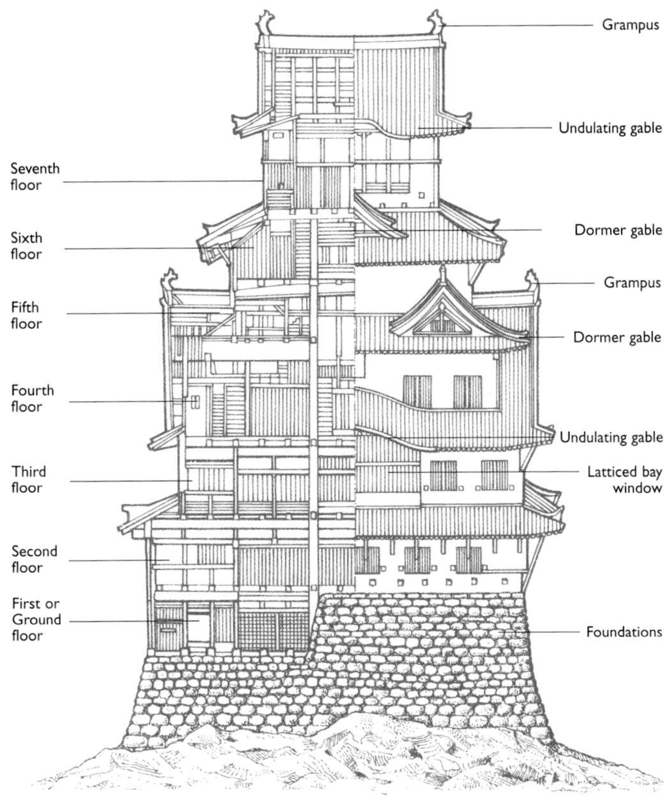

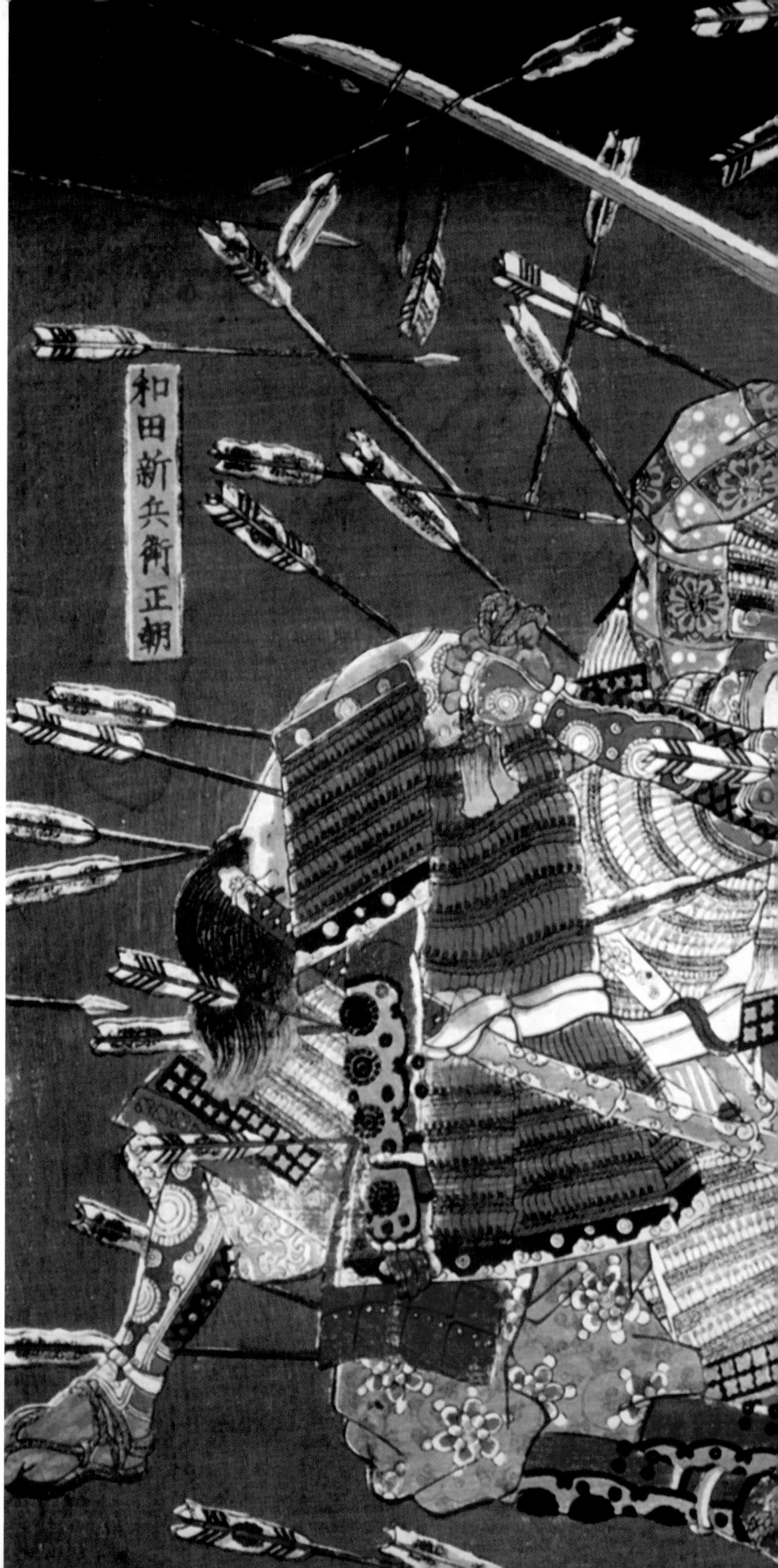

The Battle of Shijo-Nawate in 1348, was one of the fiercest battles of the Nanbokuchô wars. This print depicts the savage fighting in what became known as the last stand of the Kunosoki Family.

一勇斎國芳画

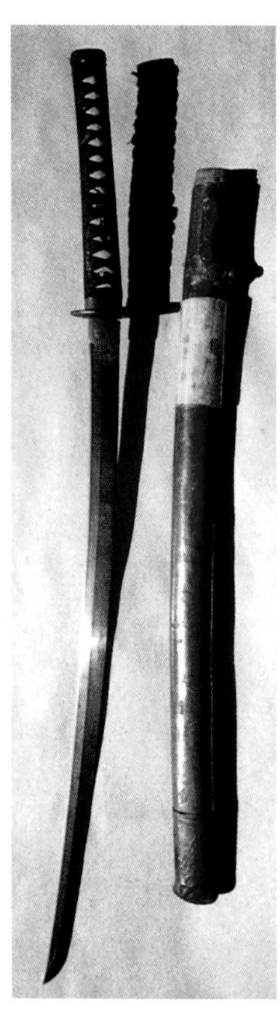

The Japanese sword blade, forged by master swordsmiths in a solemn ritual, became a prized possession, 'the soul of the Samurai'.

although mining might be used. However, there is no evidence that countermining was used. Siege engines were few but Chinese-style traction trebuchet were used by both offense and defense, occasionally throwing soft-cased exploding bombs against defenders, a primitive form of grenade.

Several castles remain in Japan, some originals, and some rebuilt from the original plans. Edo was the seat of the Tokugawa shogun and is now the Imperial Palace in Tokyo. Himeji is a jewel of a castle, the keep having been rebuilt in 1601 by Ikeda Terumasa. Macchiolations still survive and tourists can walk the route through the many gates and visualize an attacker's problems. Kakegawa castle is the result of a modern rebuild using the plans and exact materials of the past. Osaka Castle is built on the site of the fortress cathedral, Ishiyama Honganji, home of the Ikko-ikki Buddhist sect. The new build by Toyotomi took place in 1586. Other significant castles are Hikone, Inuyama (still owned by the original Naruse daimyô family), Kumamoto, Matsumoto, and Nijo castle's palace, an architectural gem.

SAMURAI WEAPONS

Originally, samurai were horse archers, the bow, *yumi*, being a weapon of choice. Bow lengths varied as did the types of wood used in their construction. Normally, the length ranged from five-and-a-half to seven feet (167–213 cm). One major historical figure was the giant Tametomo (1139–1170) who used a bow nearly nine feet (274 cm) in length and is reputed to have sunk a boat with a single heavy arrow. Archery practice took place in buildings 128 yards (117 m) long. One later famous archer, Tsuruta Masatoki, between 7.00 pm on 19 May and 3.00 pm on 20 May, 1852, fired 10,050 arrows at a rate of nearly nine shafts a minute. Of these, 5,383 snaked through the air burying themselves in the targets. A warrior's prowess was judged by his skill on firing from a horse. The technique developed the martial art called *yabusame* in which mounted archers try to hit wooden targets while galloping. Only when the arrows were spent did a samurai become a swordsman.

Eventually, Ashigaru Infantry were armed with the bow thereby destroying the picture of an élite mounted samurai archer. The bow was composite in nature and a cross-section will show that between two strips of bamboo forming the back and belly of the bow are set three more strips of bamboo, thicker than the outer ones, being set edgewise to give greater strength. Outside these and forming the outer edges of the bow would be two strips of hazelwood, the totality being secured with fish-glue, lacquered overall and bound at intervals with rattan. The deerskin grip would be set two-thirds of the way down the bow. The bow would be drawn behind the ear with longer arrows than a European type. Arrows were fledged with feathers from eagles, pheasants, and cranes with wedge-shaped heads or razor sharp barbed points for enemies. Woodblock prints depict dying samurai with many arrows sticking out of his body while crawling from the battlefield. Artistic license, perhaps, but during the Nanbokuchô Wars (1336–92), Imagawa Yorikuni was reputed to have needed no less than 20 arrows to kill him.

Much mythology surrounds the samurai sword. The *katana* was paired with a short sword, the *wazizashi*, the two together being called *daisho*. The razor-sharp cutting edge of the sword is legendary, all samurai expecting that they could take an enemy head with one blow. The strength and sharpness of the blade comes from a soft iron core being enclosed by harder metal. The metals

The Samurai warrior originally viewed himself as a mounted archer. However, the development of fine sword blades would mean a cultural shift in arms, equipment, and method of warfare.

were welded together to form a rectangular ingot, some six inches long, two inches wide and half-an-inch thick (15 by 5 by 1.2 cm). This was reheated, folded back on itself and hammered out again, this process being repeated as many as 18 times. Other ingots could be added during the process, the final bar comprising countless layers. The bar was beaten into shape, the final result being patterned like wood grain. Tempering required that a clayey material was applied to the entire blade apart from the edge. The totality was heated and then plunged into cold water. The exposed metal cooled instantly becoming very hard while that part encased in its clay sheath cooled slowly remaining relatively soft. The edge would then be ground and perhaps tested on the bodies of dead criminals to show a purchaser its virtues.

Swords were sometimes signed by a renowned swordsmith. They were typically decorated with sword furniture, such as *tsuba*, sword guard, and the hilts covered in fish- or giant ray skin and flat, often silk, braid. The *katana* averaged 2 ft 2 in (65 cm) in length, but some warriors wielded a *nagatachi* that measured anything from five to seven feet (151.5 to 213.5 cm). The samurai never used shields, the sword serving that purpose. The sword's resilience allowed it to absorb and knock aside an enemy blow before counterattacking. Not all swords were well made, and there were many reports of broken blades. The sword sometimes stuck in the body of a dead enemy putting a samurai at a

distinct disadvantage. Nevertheless, samurai and sword go together in the imagination, the *katana* being the "soul of the samurai."

Two more weapons saw much use. The *yari* was a straight-headed, double-edged spear or pike, three to 20 ft (1–6 m) long. The longer, *omi no yari*, was used by infantry and the shorter, *tae yari*, by cavalry. The wars of the 16th Century saw much use of this weapon. The more formidable *naginata* (glaive) was a pole-arm, its shaft being as long as the wielder's body, topped by a long curved blade one to three feet long. The Sohei monk warriors used it, especially in the Gempei Wars, finding it good for dismounting cavalry, arguably forcing the development of the armored shin guards, *sune-ate*. The naginata was often used by samurai wives because they were expected to defend the home while the man was away. One, Itagaki, renowned for her naginata skills, reputedly led 3,000 warriors from a Taira stronghold against 10,000 Hojo clansmen but was captured after being wounded by an arrow, taken to the Minamoto shogun and married off to Asari Yoshito.

SAMURAI ARMOR

The earliest forms of samurai armor have been excavated from dolmen burial chambers. One variety comprises a leather brigandine, fastening at the front, with metal plates laced upon it; another consisted of a plated and riveted cuirass of metal, which fits around the body. Clay figures in the same burial sites depict a wide, protective skirt, probably of leather, reaching to the knee. The helmets are carefully constructed with ear pieces and neck protectors.

During the 5th to 7th Century, armor made of small plates, laced together and overlapping, was introduced. This style became the norm, with embelishments. The lamellar plates were lacquered to prevent rust, and being fastened to each other by rawhide cords in horizontal sections, which were combined vertically by silk suspensory cords.

The great harness, *yoroi*, utilized various combinations of plates to create the suit of armor. Firstly, there is body armor (*do*) from which hangs a row of tassets (*kusazuri*) making an armored skirt. Sleeve armor (*kote*) was worn, as were larger

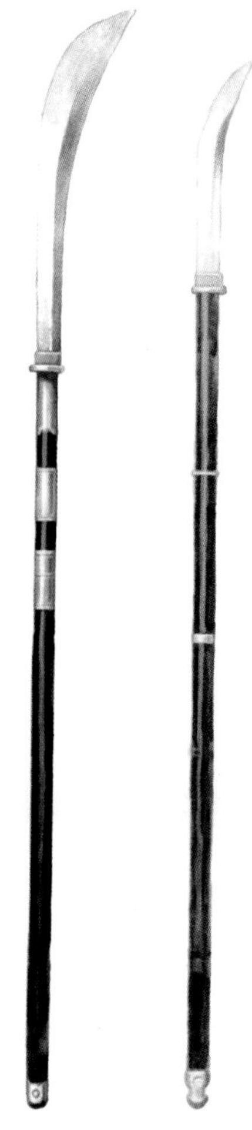

Top left: This print by Kuniyoshi, shows the samurai Sakurai Kiyokazu in battle using a *naginata*, a spear with a curved blade; two examples of which can be seen above. They were usually around 6 feet in length (c. 2 meters).

shoulder plates (*sode*) and a throat protector (*nodowa*). Beneath the body armor, thigh guards (*haidate*) and shin guards (*suneate*) protected the legs. A facemask (*mempo*) of plate metal was worn above the neck, decorated with horsehair and features not only to protect but also to terrify the enemy, provided an anchor point for the iron helmet (*kabuto*). A lamellar neck guard (*shikoro*) hung from the helmet's rim while the helmet was decorated with horns, or other displays. The use of *mon* became general in the 15th and 16th Centuries, being incorporated in the décor of armor.

Samurai armor retained the same characteristics for hundreds of years, the only major development being to make armor bullet proof after the introduction of the arquebus by the Portuguese in 1543. Solid breastplates were introduced for the *do* and solid irons plates for the horizontal sections of skirts and shoulder guards. These centuries saw the rise to celebrity status of families of armorers such as the Myochin and Satome.

The firearms introduced by the Portuguese are interesting in that the samurai never used the wheel lock, snaphaunce, or flintlock but moved directly from the matchlock to percussion and pinfire, such was the mechanical skill of Japanese gun makers.

Far left: During the Tokugawa (Edo) period (1603–1867) armor tended to become more decorative and ceremonial. This suit of red-laced armor with decorative sleeves is of the *domaru* type. The helmet, resplendent with its symbolic horns, echoes previous periods in Japanese armor design.

NINJA

Ninja or *shinobi* were special warriors, adept at secret intelligence gathering and assassination. Their underhand modus operandi was anathema to the more straightforward samurai but their uses were legion, especially as scouts. The mid-15th Century sees the first references to *ninja* activities, their major operational bases being the Iga and Koga areas of central Japan. The ninja were employed by daimyô families as mercenaries in their wars against each other.

Spying was the main ninja task and they were masters of disguise, sometimes traveling as *komuso*, wandering flute-playing Zen mendicant monks; *yamabushi*, ascetic mountain monks, or strolling players such as puppeteers and *saragaku* dancers. Disguises could enable access to castles, to the keep to provide entertainment, or general intelligence gathering in an enemy countryside. During the Age of Warring States, ninja were also used as *kisho*, surprise attackers, and *koran*, agitators. The ninja of the Iga and Koga regions were professionals, developing strong links with Shogun Tokugawa Ieyasu, who, when given Hojo lands by Toyotomi Hideyoshi, created his capital at Edo (eventually called Tokyo) where he had an Iga and Koga ninja unit as guards.

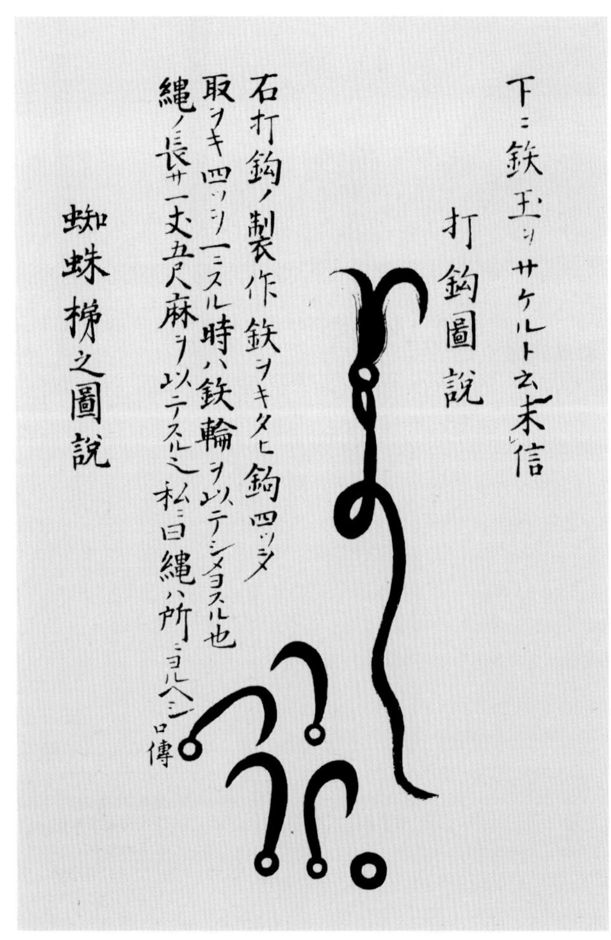

This chart shows the equipment that the Ninja could use in their secretive style of warfare. The rope with a hook could be used in scaling defensive walls on specialized assassination missions.

Ninja are renowned for reputedly tight-fitting black clothing, hooded with their face masked with a cloth. Their equipment comprises a shorter, straighter *katana*, heavy iron knuckle-dusters, *tekagi*, and a hooked rope, *kaginawa*, for climbing. A favored weapon was the *kusari gama*, a sickle connected to a chain. The weighted chain would be swung to catch an opponent's sword arm or leg, to render them off balance, when they would be killed by the sickle. *Shuriken*, throwing stars are well-known but not the but ninja also used *caltrops*—four or more sharp nails arranged so one always points upwards from a stable base—that could be scattered as an obstacle to pursuers. Specialized tools were sometimes used for crossing moats, while the use of rope and bamboo ladders have been recorded. When a ninja had climbed the base of a stone castle, he might pierce the wattle and daub wall with a *kunai*, a knife-type tool suitable for gouging. Also used was the *hamagari*, a long, thin saw bolted to a long handle so it could be used like a penknife and would serve as a weapon too. A ninja would be conversant with Chinese explosives: one type was soft-cased, designed to let out smoke or stun by noise or containing fragments of pottery or metal to act like a small grenade; and the second comprised hard-cased bombs, made of pottery or iron, a fragmentation device capable of delivering terrible wounds or destroying parts of buildings.

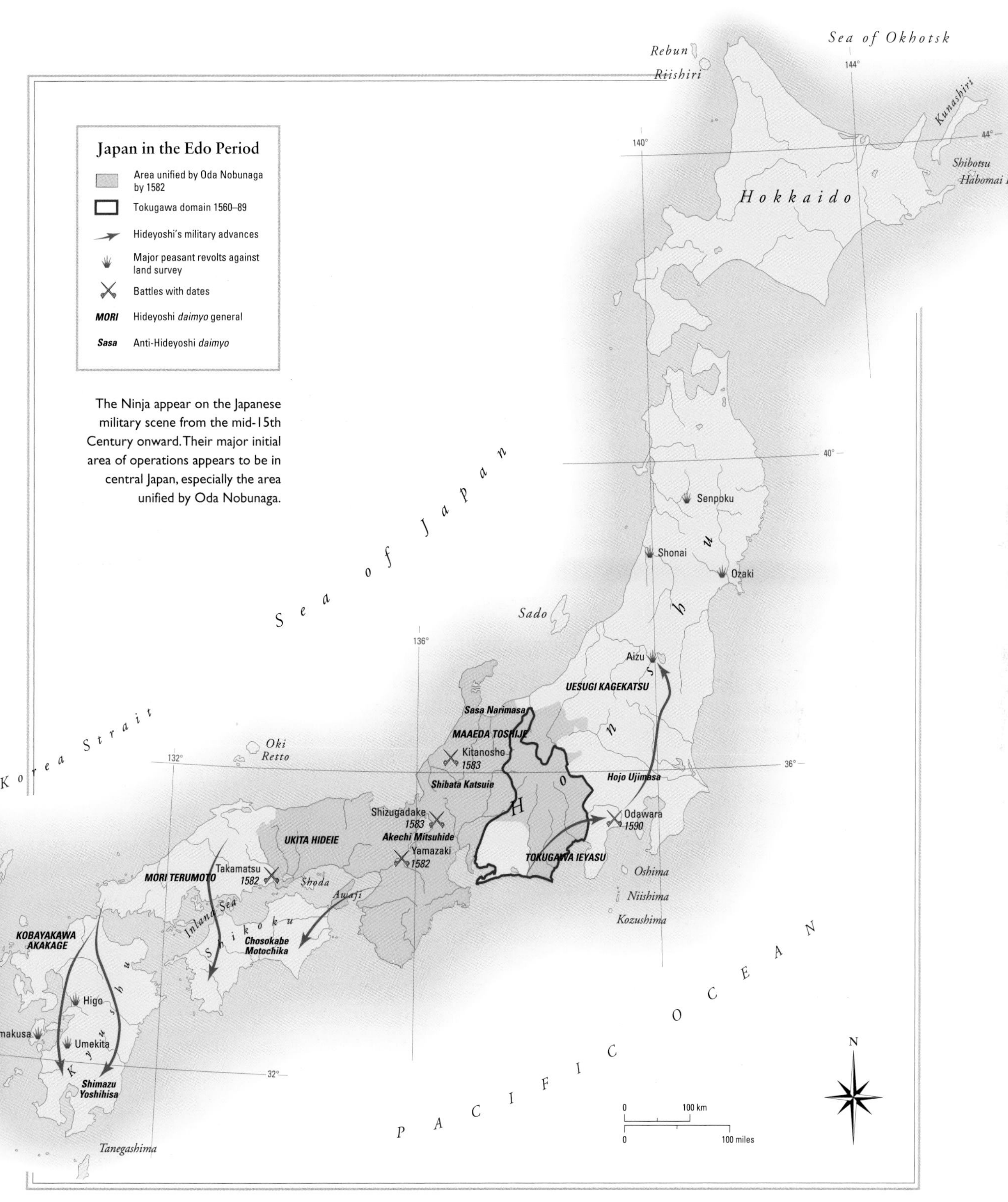

The Ninja appear on the Japanese military scene from the mid-15th Century onward. Their major initial area of operations appears to be in central Japan, especially the area unified by Oda Nobunaga.

Ninja might be hired for a specific task or for a campaign. A frequent task would be to secretly enter a castle and engage in arson. One example occurred in 1540 when Kizawa Nagamasa's territory was invaded by Miyoshi Chokei. Kizawa Nagamasa holed up in Kasagi Castle. Miyoshi's ally, Tsutsui Junsho, attacked the castle and used Iga ninja to enter the castle, set fire to the priests' quarters and several outbuildings, and to capture two baileys. Assassination was another ninja task, leading to defensive measures being taken to make houses ninja-proof. The ninja Ishikawa Goemon is supposed to have attempted Oda Nobunaga's life by dripping poison down a thread into Nobunaga's mouth while he slept. A well known assassination story concerns Uesugi Kenshin, who was murdered in his toilet when a ninja concealed in the sewage pit thrust a spear or sword up Kenshin's anus.

When at war, ninja might gather intelligence before an attack but might be used for more extreme situations. In 1558, Rokkaku Yoshikata launched a campaign against a disaffected vassal, Dodo, who hid himself away in Sawayama Castle. Yoshikata's siege was proving ineffective so he decided to use

This is the earliest known drawing of a ninja in action and it shows the crossing of a moat using the special hooked rope shown in the previous illustration. The ninja had no known equivalent in the medieval western order of battle.

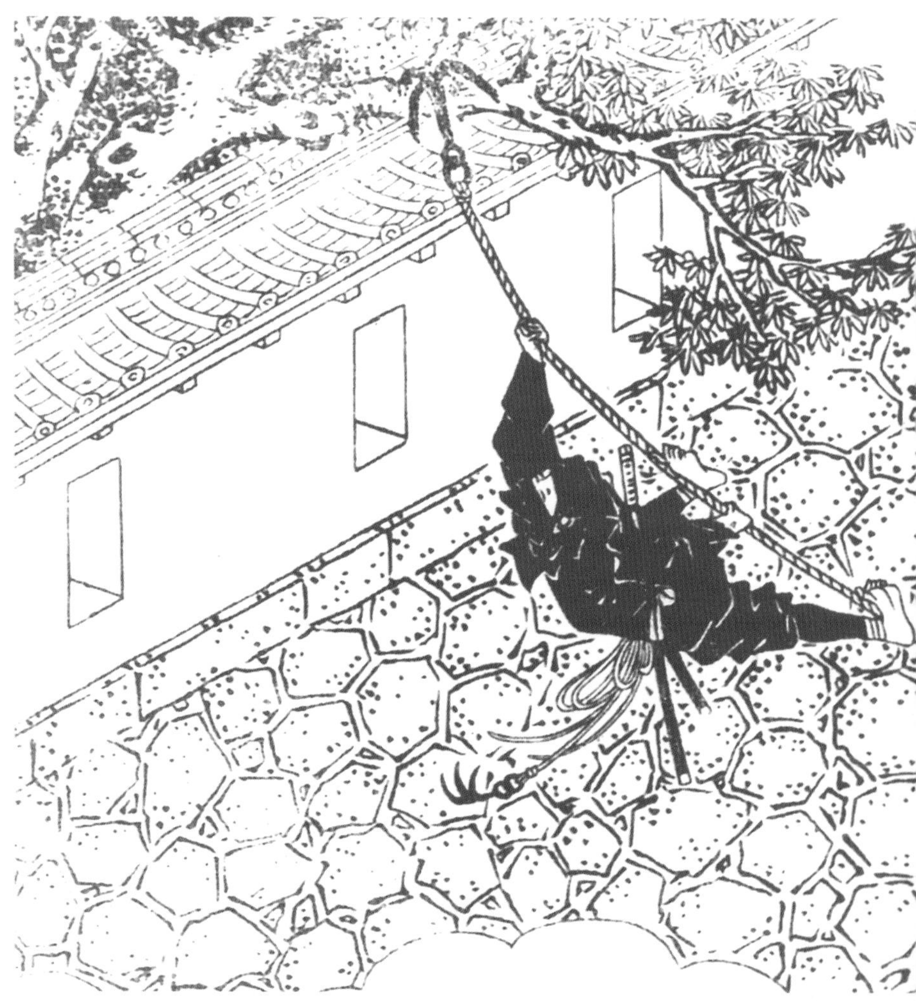

a ninja from Iga, called Tateoka Doshun. The latter, mid-ranking ninja, a *chunin*, brought a 48-strong ninja team. He decided to use *bakemono-jutsu*, a disguise operation. Doshun stole a paper lantern bearing Dodo's mon, then replicated a mass of them. Doshun and his men walked through the castle gate and set fire to the castle causing Dodo's garrison to think traitors were at work. The fire engendered panic and Yoshikata launched a successful final assault.

The last time that ninja were used in battle was at Shimabara in 1638. Insurgents against the Tokugawa shogunate and a local daimyô, Matsukura Shigemasa, fortified themselves in an old castle of Hara on the Shimabara peninsula beating off all attacks against them. Ninja were used to survey the depth of the moat and search for loopholes. A raid stole some of the castle's food supplies. Some ninja entered the castle and stole a banner, returning with it as a souvenir. Toward the end of the siege a Koga ninja unit under Matsudaira Nobutsuna captured two baileys remaining inside the castle and joining in the fighting in the final attack. After this, ninja enter the world of myth and legend.

The Passing of an Age

Knights gradually became a redundant anachronism. The cost of armor and warhorses, the development of disciplined infantry, artillery, and the arquebus all proved that the medieval knight was no longer able to command the battlefield.

This German woodcut shows a gunner loading a bronze cannon. The improvement in gun technology began to dominate the battlefield and made the expensively armored and equipped mounted knight increasingly redundant.

A curious phenomenon occurred in some parts of medieval Europe in the 14th and 15th Centuries: the refusal or reluctance of men who were by birth and fortune eligible for knighthood to take it up. In part, this can be accounted for by the sheer expense involved in maintaining the equipment a knight needed if he were called to perform his military obligations. The highly developed plate armor of these centuries, ever more refined, heavy, and strong, had to be manufactured by specialists. Northern Italy, Austria, and Germany were the homes of the most skilled and expensive armorers. A suit of plate armor had to be fitted to the contours of its owner. It had to be strong enough to protect its wearer from the weapons he was like to encounter in battle or tournament. War-horses, too, were expensive.

With the increased weight of body and horse armor, a war-horse had to be specially bred for the power and stamina necessary to carry such heavy burdens for hours at a time. They also needed extensive training to perform under the stress of combat. Such beasts were worth perhaps 15 or 20 ordinary horses, and a knight, who had to have several horses in case—as often happened—they were killed under him in battle, might have to invest the equivalent of several years' income in his horses alone, and perhaps half as much again for his armour.

For knights who were not particularly prominent or wealthy, to risk such valuable articles, not to mention their own persons, in military service was a severe financial burden. Not surprisingly, many knights, who were simply country gentlemen, preferred to stay at home and manage their estates. Their value in the musters of their overlords were overshadowed by the prospect of their own ruin. Laws were made enforcing gentlemen who owned property yielding an income of a certain fixed

KNIGHT OF EMPEROR MAXIMILIAN, 1518

The knight wears a magnificently decorated harness with a close-helmet, crested with colored plumes. His shoulders are now protected by heavy pauldrons with a raised collar to ward off blows at the neck. His gauntlets are of a mitten form. For the purposes of a parade, the knight has put on a velvet, fluted skirt typical of this period. His sabatons are now square-shaped at the toe rather than pointed. His horse, too, is armored; he wears a decorated chanfron to protect his face and a mail crinet over his neck.

The caparison is now shorter and beautifully worked with gold wire brocade. Under it the horse might also be carrying further armor plates: a peytral for his breast, flauchards for his flanks, and a crupper for his hindquarters.

amount or more to become knights (in England from 1292 onward this was £40 per year); failure to do so made them liable to pay a fine, which was equally valuable to the king because he could buy the services of mercenaries with it. North Anglian gentleman John Paston I paid his fine to avoid being knighted in 1457, though his son John was knighted at the age of 21 years.

At the same time as the traditional source of knights was declining, knights were being made in greater numbers from less illustrious parts of society. Knighthoods began to be handed out as rewards to successful burghers whose services had been financial rather than military and, at the other end of the scale, to professional soldiers of lowly birth, who could be dubbed on the battlefield. There was in practice no monopoly on who could dub knights, though numerous medieval rulers attempted to confine it exclusively to royalty; tradition in this case was more attended to, and traditionally knighthood could be conferred by anyone who was already a knight. Nobles, lords, and lesser knights all indulged in the practice of knighting their own squires and other members of their retinues.

The strict ideas of previous centuries about the duties, obligations, and moral fitness of candidates for knighthood were not attended to. There was no longer a universal assumption that any nobly-born young man would serve his apprenticeship in arms and then be knighted; some even conferred knighthood on their children while they were still far too young to have much idea of what it meant, or the ability to discharge its more practical obligations.

In addition, the knights who did serve on campaigns began to be less distinguished from other, lower ranks of soldiers. Squires, sergeants, and men-at-arms all wore armor, though not as much as a knight; some monarchs even provided horses for their archers so that they could achieve the necessary speed and mobility while conducting raids in enemy territory. Knights themselves, as mounted warriors, were of less value than formerly in the military formation of an army, and were increasingly deployed to fight on foot, side-by-side with the common soldiers.

All these factors combined to make knighthood less desirable than in previous centuries, and its decline was regarded with dismay by rulers and commentators alike. Medieval kings and princes still regarded knights as necessary in their armies as well as in their civil administrations but, apart from the view of knights as a valuable source of military manpower, there were other equally important social and cultural factors to consider. The later Middle Ages were moving rapidly toward the economic conditions prevailing in modern times. The world turned increasingly by means of commerce rather than by other ethics of feudal loyalty and personal ties. This was so in the spheres of trade, law, medicine, the arts and, equally so, in the military sphere. Yet, here in particular, loyalty was an essential element in what was increasingly a professional relationship. Kings and princes and lesser lords sought to maintain and reinforce the loyalty of their own retainers by stressing the honor of their service and rewarding it with displays of largesse,

A superb 16th-Century tournament suit of armor of German manufacture. Surfaces which were once smooth and polished to deflect missiles are here decoratively fluted.

intended not as financial recompense so much as to boost their knights' sense of worth and self-esteem. In the 14th and 15th Centuries this often took fanciful and theatrical forms; the burgeoning of secular orders was merely one sign of a conscious cultural revival of the ancient forms and values of chivalry. Even though extravagant and flamboyant feasts and tourneys and vowing ceremonies derived their inspiration largely from romance and legend, they were still quite clearly related to the sturdy tradition of a lord rewarding his followers with gifts and praise, a practice that had been central to the evolution of knighthood from the days of the early Middle Ages and was still vital in its late flowering.

URBAN POWER

Towns became increasingly important in the late Middle Ages, assuming political roles and initiating their own foreign policies. Trade in northern Europe was conducted by various German towns, disputes between them transferred to courts at Lübeck, which, during the second half of the 13th Century, had assumed the leadership of the League of Towns known as the *Hanse*. By 1300, Lübeck's laws were enforced in 19 autonomous towns. Lübeck had been founded in 1143, receiving an imperial privilege in 1226. The adoption of its laws at Hamburg in 1232 gave it primacy within the Hanseatic League, despite the city having no desire for political dominance. The Hanse laws reached the towns of Livonia in 1254 and Riga in 1270. The burghers of the major towns in the Baltic agreed to cooperate in enforcing common codes of commercial law, combining against piracy and other enemies of trade. A key factor explaining this political cooperation was the absence in the region of any effective royal ruler in whose name laws might be enforced.

The Hanse operated in a region where there were numerous small principalities, many fighting against pagans. In this milieu cities like Lübeck and Hamburg could hold their own with their own military forces. Hence, the League was able to engage in its own political activities. The Hanse needed access to the port of Flanders as filters for their trade into the North Sea. Denmark could close the Kattegat. After Danish King Waldemat IV (1340–75) seized Scania and sacked Visby, the Hanse allied with the Swedes and imposed the peace of Stralsund (1367) on Denmark, giving the League the monopoly of the Scania herring industry, liberties for the Confederation of Cologne Merchants. Erik of Pomerania brought all three Scandinavian kingdoms under one crown in 1397 under the influence of Queen Margaret, his great-aunt, who kept this Kalmar Union in her hands until her death in 1412.

Then, the League, fearing the autocratic tendencies of Erik, reorganized itself with a supreme assembly or Hansetage, representing almost 100 members, meeting at Lübeck when required. This new federation managed to blockade Denmark, which stimulated a movement for Swedish independence. Despite its success, the Hanse's position was weakened. Events elsewhere hurt the League as the King of Poland defeated the Teutonic Knights and recovered the coastal Polish towns closing off part of the Baltic to their commerce, at least not on its terms. In the Low Countries, the Duke of Burgundy backed Dutch maritime enterprises until they decided to challenge the Hanse in the Baltic, with the support of Denmark.

The experiences of the Hanse show that at some future date economic and social communities

The Baltic
c. 1400–1500
Lands of the Jagellons
Church Lands (Baltic States)
Principal towns of the Hanseatic League
Holy Roman Empire
Boundaries as in 1396
Internal boundary
Principal trade routes
Arctic Circle
0 100 km
0 100 miles
N
Barents Sea
Kola Peninsula
White Sea
Lappland
Norwegian Sea
KINGDOM OF NORWAY
Jemtland
Trondheim
KINGDOM OF SWEDEN
Finland
Vasa
Gulf of Bothnia
Karelia
RUSSIA
Lake Onega
Lake Ladoga
Vyborg
Abo
Helsingfors
Gulf of Finland
Aland
INGRIA
Wessenberg
Reval
Narva
Ivangorod
Novgorod
ESTHONIA
Bergen
Oslo
Uppsala
Karlstad
Stockholm
Norrköping
LIVONIA
Pskov
Alvsborg (Gothenburg)
Visby
Gotland
Windau
Velikiye Luki
to Western Europe
KURLAND
Riga
Varberg
Libau
Oland
SAMOGITIA
KNIGHTS
Polotsk
Smolensk
KINGDOM OF DENMARK
Copenhagen
Funen
Zeeland
Baltic Sea
North Sea
Bornholm
Königsberg
Danzig
Elbing
Stralsund
Rostock
Greifswald
Lübeck
Wismar
Stettin
TEUTONIC
GRAND DUCHY OF LITHUANIA
Hamburg
Thorn
Bremen
HOLY ROMAN EMPIRE
NEUMARK (Teutonic Knights) 1402–1455
KINGDOM OF POLAND
Warsaw
Brunswick
Magdeburg

with legal autonomy would necessarily have to finance the military cost of independence. In a rural society, towns depended on the countryside for their resources and were outnumbered by rural populations. Independence could be won and kept by becoming small states with their own territories and rural populations, meaning that urban governments became imperialists in their rural rule. In Germany, imperial free cities existed side-by-side with hundreds of tiny principalities with no one large state willing or able to change the political environment. In the Low Countries, the dream of city-state status by Bruges or Ghent was swamped by the jealousy of their many small neighbors and by the Counts of Flanders and Dukes of Burgundy who were determined to enforce their rule on the towns. In the Swiss regions, Berne was able to build up its territory but Zurich failed.

Italy was the success story where some small towns—Milan, Florence, Venice, Genoa, and Pisa—managed to create viable states from the original city. The Italian geopolitical jigsaw maintained its own balance of power but the confusing series of wars meant that urban capitalism, the most advanced in Europe, needed to finance mercenary armies to supplement town militias in an attempt to keep independence, as Milan digested smaller towns while the pope constantly sought to increase the size of the Papal States.

ITALIAN CONDOTTIERI AND ITALIAN CITY STATES

The 13th to 16th Centuries witnessed an increase in wealth of Italian city states such as Venice, Florence, and Genoa as they traded with the Near East. These city states required armed forces to protect them and the city rulers turned to mercenaries as a solution to their security needs. The *condottieri* was the leader of a mercenary company and he signed a *condotta* (contract) putting himself and troops at a city's service. The initial mercenary companies comprised foreigners. The earliest (1303) was the Catalan Company who had fought in the dynastic wars in the south, being taken there by King Pedro III of Aragon in 1282. In 1333, mercenaries with John of Bohemia served Perugia against Arezzo, the group being known as Compagnia della Colomba, Dove Company. In the mid-14th Century, the Grand Company comprising mainly Germans and Hungarians savaged the country, severely damaging Romagna, Umbria, and Tuscany. These well-organized Free Companies were commanded by Duke Werner of Urslingen and Count Conrad von Landau. Their units had a strict code of discipline and rules to share out loot. A famous English captain was Sir John Hawkwood, who went to Italy during a lull in the Hundred Years' War, and led the White Company for the next 30 years.

By the end of the 14th Century, Italians raised mercenary armies and soon condottieri were conquering principalities for themselves. Their organization became sophisticated in the 15th Century under Muzio Attendolo Sforza, in the service of Naples, and his archrival Braccio da Montone, who served Perugia. Muzio's son Francesco Sforza seized control of Milan in 1450, becoming duke after marrying the daughter of Duke Filippo Maria Visconti. The condottieri became notorious for their fickleness. They often switched sides for a better pay rate, sometimes during a battle. Their services were so valuable that their monopoly of military power allowed them to dictate terms to prospective employers. The mercenaries tended to be old fashioned because they retained armored knights and medieval weapons and tactics after the rest of Europe was experimenting with pikemen and arquebusiers.

Some condottieri came to a poor end. Francesco Bussone da Carmagnola initially served the Visconti of Milan but moved into the service of Venice against Milan. The Venetian doges feared possible treachery and executed him in front of the Palace of St. Mark in 1432. Cola di Renzo had Werner of Urslingen executed in Rome in 1347, leaving the Great Company in von Landau's hands. Von Landau was betrayed by his Hungarian allies and was defeated in 1362 by Albert Sterz and Hawkwood's White Company, which used better tactics and formations and had archers.

From the 15th Century, the condottieri were mainly Italian, often aristocrats who had failed with their estates, choosing fighting as a living. The most famous was Giovanni dale Bande Nere from Forli, son of Caterina Sforza, his son being Cosimo I de' Medici, Grand Duke of Tuscany. The pay rates for a condotta were so high that some lords became condottieri for a while just to increase their revenues. Amongst these were Sigismondo Malatesta, Lord of Rimini, and Federico da Montefeltro, Duke of Urbino. In 1448, Guglielmo of Monferrato received 6,600 florins a month from Francesco Sforza of Milan. His troops' pay was just half this amount. Ultimately, the condottieri became totally immersed in their financial interests and sought to prevent armed conflict by bribes or accepting money not to join someone's else's forces and remain neutral. Self-preservation of themselves and their condotta became the prime object in order not to waste an asset.

The age of the condottieri passed when King Charles VIII's French national army of gendarmes proved too powerful for the small divided Italian states with their much smaller condotta forces. The French also used an artillery train that proved too much for the Italians. Some condottieri decided to work for foreign powers. Gian Giacomo Trivulzio left Milan for France and Andrea Doria entered the service of King Francis I of France. Eventually, the well-trained foreign troops, Swiss pikemen, Spanish *tercios* (mixed infantry formation of pikemen and musketeers), German *landsknechte* (pikemen and foot soldiers), and French cavalry drove them into history.

The lavish funeral monument to the great mercenary captain Sir John Hawkwood (known to the Italians as Giovanni Acuto) commissioned from Paolo Uccello by the grateful citizens of Florence.

MERCENARIES: SIR JOHN HAWKWOOD AND THE WHITE COMPANY

Sir John Hawkwood's origins are unclear. Born in Sible Hedingham, Essex, England, he was either a London apprentice or a tailor before he became a soldier. He fought in Edward III's armies during the Hundred Years' War and might have been at the Battles of Crécy or Poitiers, although there is no evidence. Myth suggests that he was knighted by the King or the Black Prince but this is not recorded. However, commoners were sometimes raised to the knighthood for excellent battlefield service. The Treaty of Brétigny ended his servive and he moved to Burgundy, fighting for France, later joining the Great Company that fought papal troops near Avignon. By the beginning of the 1360s he had joined the White Company in the service of Pisa, later being elected its leader.

In 1369, the White Company fought for Perugua against papal forces and in 1370 he joined the Visconti in their war against an alliance of cities including Pisa and Florence. In 1372, he fought for the Visconti against a former master, the Marquis of Monferrato. He then moved his company into

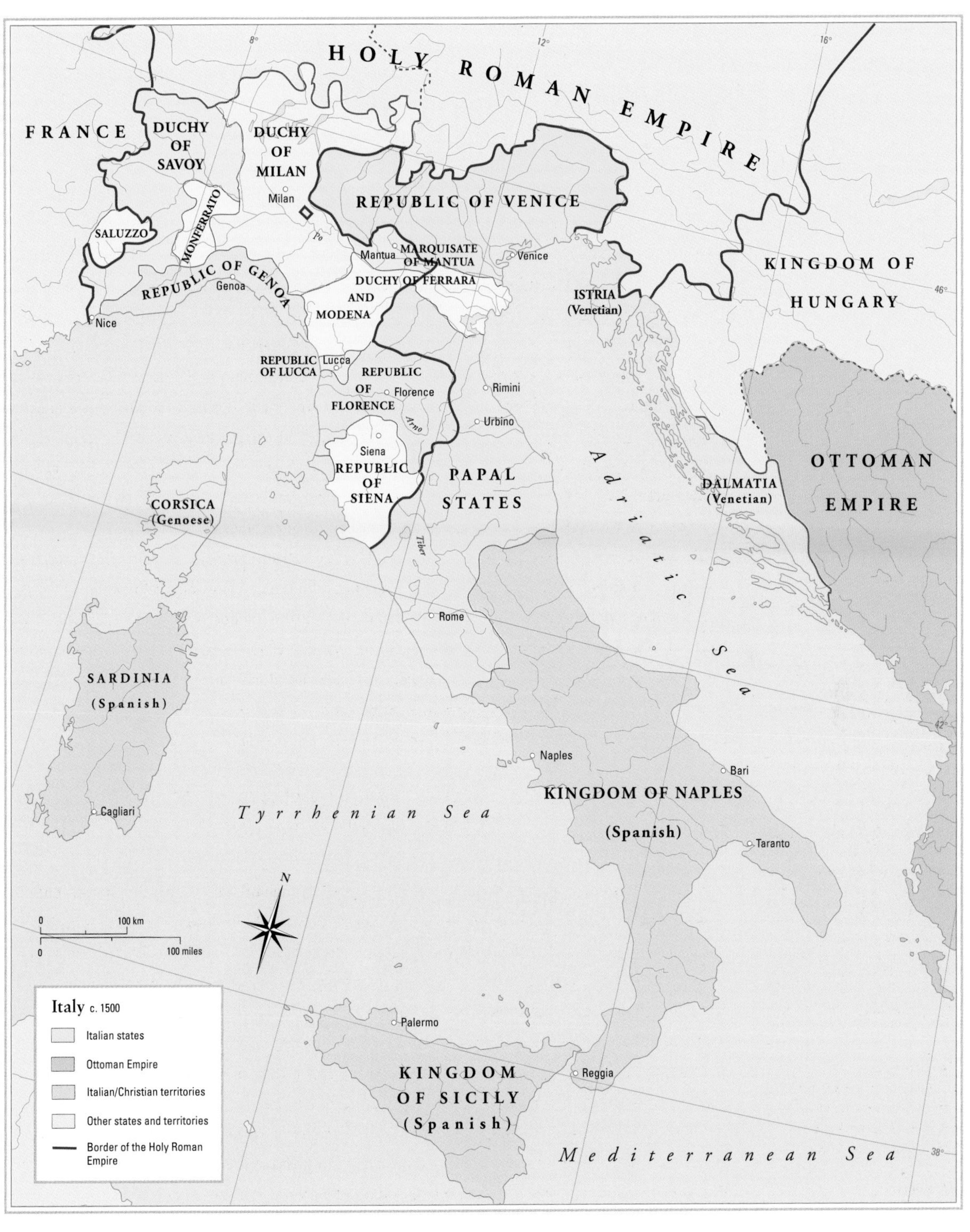
HOLY ROMAN EMPIRE
FRANCE
DUCHY OF SAVOY
DUCHY OF MILAN
Milan
SALUZZO
MONFERRATO
REPUBLIC OF VENICE
REPUBLIC OF GENOA
Genoa
Nice
Po
Mantua
MARQUISATE OF MANTUA
DUCHY OF FERRARA
AND MODENA
Venice
ISTRIA (Venetian)
KINGDOM OF HUNGARY
REPUBLIC OF LUCCA
Lucca
REPUBLIC OF FLORENCE
Florence
Arno
Rimini
Urbino
Siena
REPUBLIC OF SIENA
PAPAL STATES
Adriatic Sea
DALMATIA (Venetian)
OTTOMAN EMPIRE
CORSICA (Genoese)
Tiber
Rome
SARDINIA (Spanish)
Naples
Bari
KINGDOM OF NAPLES (Spanish)
Cagliari
Tyrrhenian Sea
Taranto
N
0 100 km
0 100 miles
Palermo
KINGDOM OF SICILY (Spanish)
Reggia
Mediterranean Sea
8°
12°
16°
46°
42°
38°
Italy c. 1500
Italian states
Ottoman Empire
Italian/Christian territories
Other states and territories
Border of the Holy Roman Empire

papal service. In 1375, when the White Company was fighting for the pope against Florence, that city negotiated an agreement with him, paying him not to attack for three months. He was renowned for his acute business tricks, such as threatening employers with desertion or looting their lands. His wealth grew and he bought estates in Romagna and Tuscany with a castle at Montecchio Vesponi.

In 1377, Hawkwood led the destruction of Cesena by mercenary armies while working for Pope Gregory XI. Over 2,000 of its citizens were slaughtered, allegedly on the orders of a cardinal. He soon left for antipapal service and married Donnia Visconti, the illegitimate daughter of Bernabò Visconti,

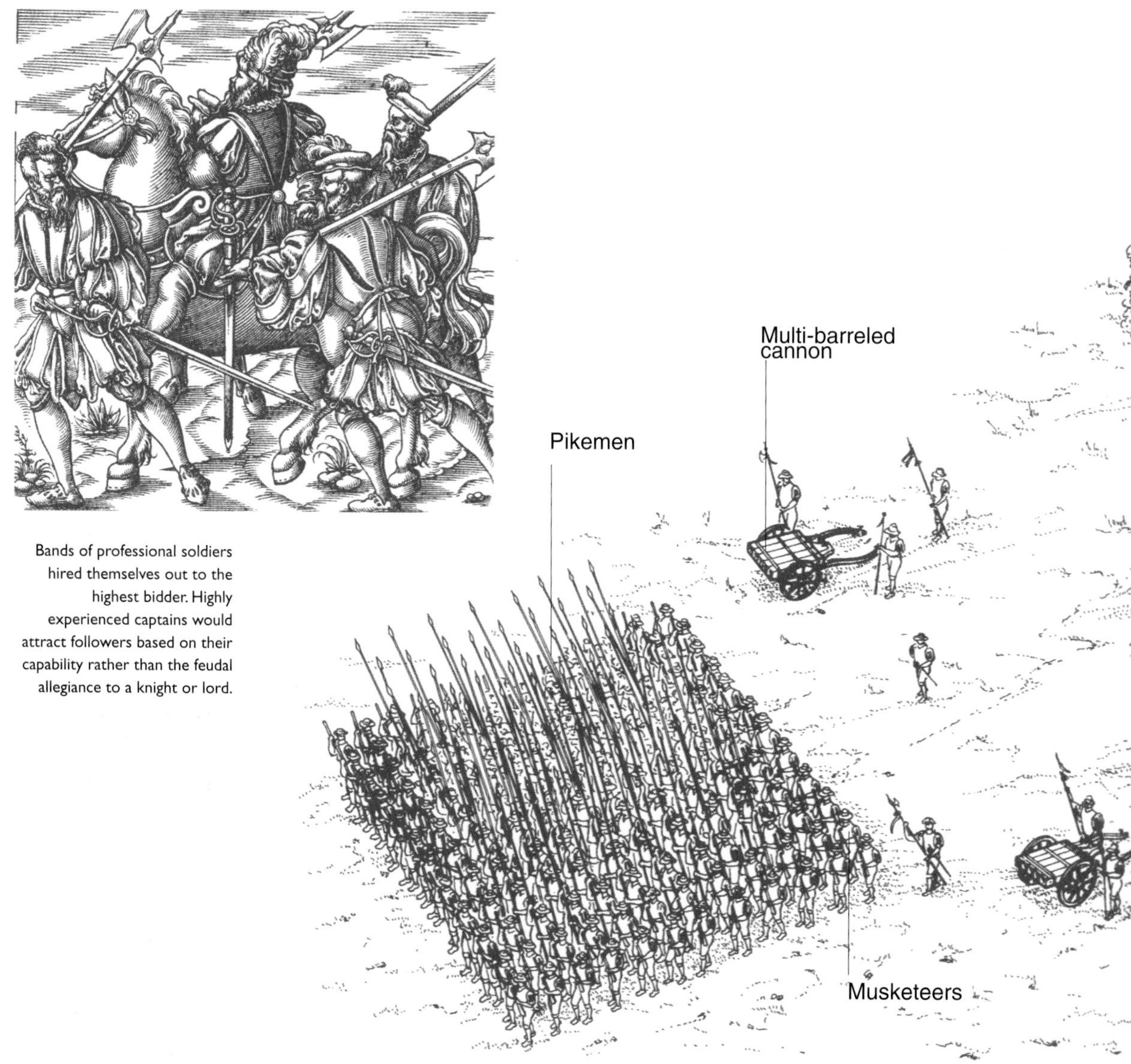

Bands of professional soldiers hired themselves out to the highest bidder. Highly experienced captains would attract followers based on their capability rather than the feudal allegiance to a knight or lord.

Duke of Milan. Falling out with that family, he switched to a contract with Florence. In 1381, Richard II of England appointed him ambassador to the Roman court. In 1387, he fought for Padua and defeated Giovanni Ordelaffi from Forli, who led Veronese troops. Hawkwood won the Battle of Castagnaro against him. In 1390, being commander-in-chief of Florentine forces, he invaded Milanese territory trying to stop Milanese expansion. He was forced to retreat but later defeated the Milanese forces under Jacapo dal Verme outside Florence forcing the Visconti to sue for peace.

Florence realized that Hawkwood had defended their independence and made him a citizen, also

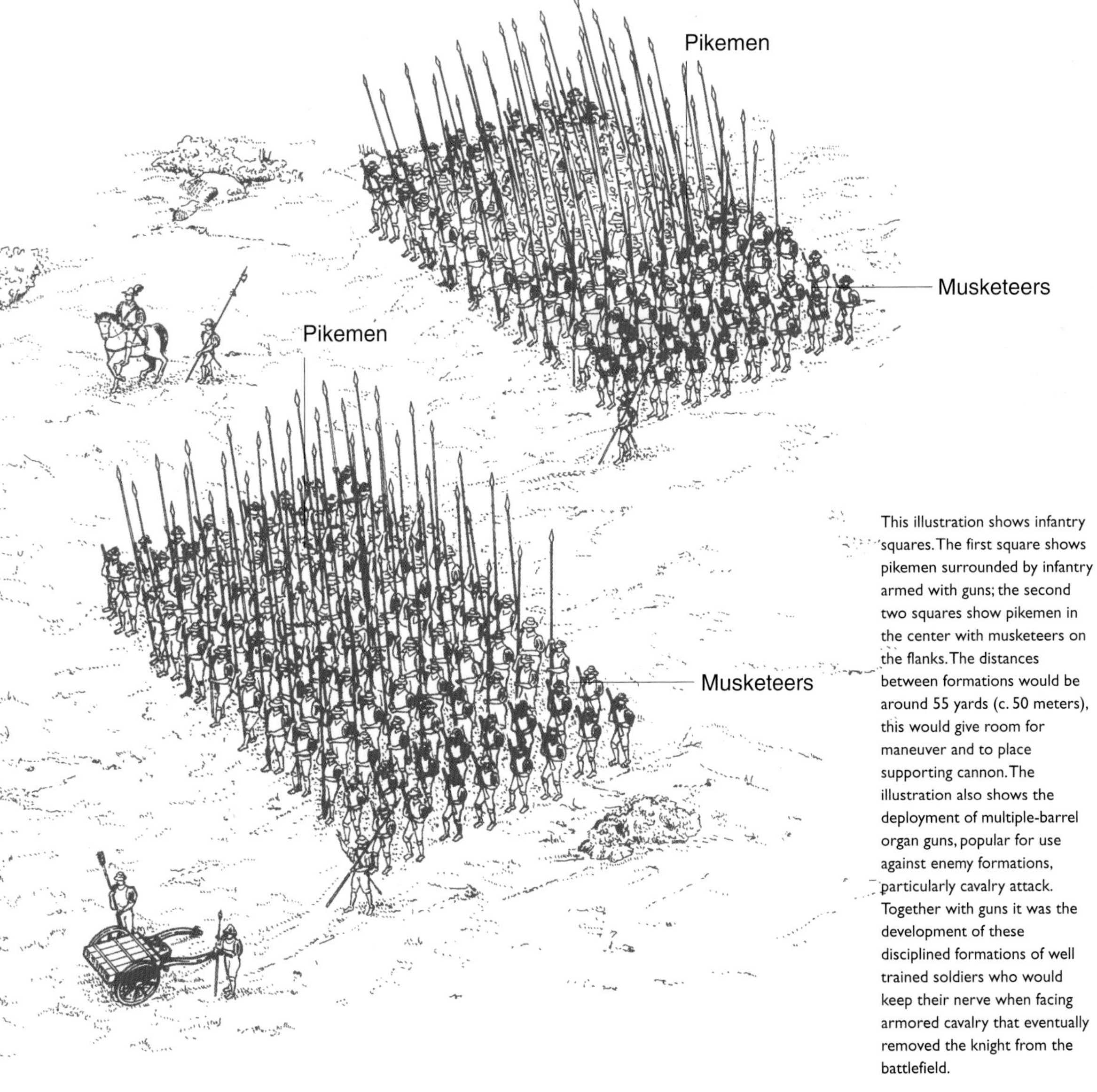

This illustration shows infantry squares. The first square shows pikemen surrounded by infantry armed with guns; the second two squares show pikemen in the center with musketeers on the flanks. The distances between formations would be around 55 yards (c. 50 meters), this would give room for maneuver and to place supporting cannon. The illustration also shows the deployment of multiple-barrel organ guns, popular for use against enemy formations, particularly cavalry attack. Together with guns it was the development of these disciplined formations of well trained soldiers who would keep their nerve when facing armored cavalry that eventually removed the knight from the battlefield.

The knight meets his nemesis. This reconstruction created by the Royal Armouries, Leeds, England, using armor and equipment of the period, shows the knight meeting professional infantry armed with guns and pikes.

Below: BATTLE OF PAVIA, 1525
Lannoy, the Imperial commander, organized a night march and a dawn attack on the French camp at Pavia. This bold, tactical move completely reversed the fortunes of the campaign. To date King Francis I of France was on the verge of consolidating his power in northern Italy. However, after his defeat at Pavia, he found himself the prisoner of his archrival, Charles V of Spain.

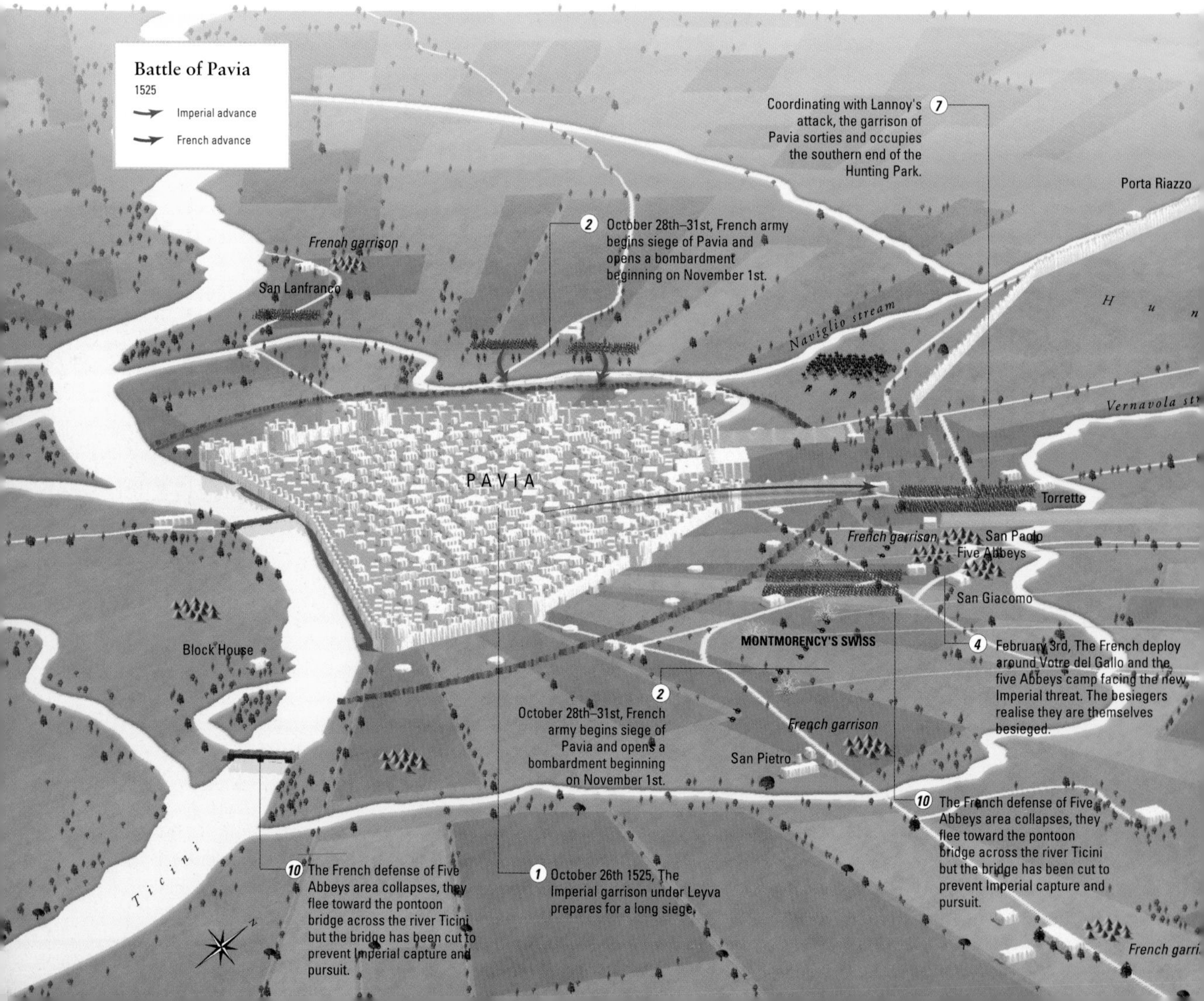

Battle of Pavia
1525

Imperial advance
French advance

7 Coordinating with Lannoy's attack, the garrison of Pavia sorties and occupies the southern end of the Hunting Park.

Porta Riazzo

2 October 28th–31st, French army begins siege of Pavia and opens a bombardment beginning on November 1st.

French garrison

San Lanfranco

Naviglio stream

H u n

Vernavola st

PAVIA

Torrette

French garrison

San Paolo

Five Abbeys

San Giacomo

MONTMORENCY'S SWISS

4 February 3rd, The French deploy around Votre del Gallo and the five Abbeys camp facing the new Imperial threat. The besiegers realise they are themselves besieged.

Block House

2 October 28th–31st, French army begins siege of Pavia and opens a bombardment beginning on November 1st.

French garrison

San Pietro

10 The French defense of Five Abbeys area collapses, they flee toward the pontoon bridge across the river Ticini but the bridge has been cut to prevent Imperial capture and pursuit.

Ticini

10 The French defense of Five Abbeys area collapses, they flee toward the pontoon bridge across the river Ticini but the bridge has been cut to prevent Imperial capture and pursuit.

1 October 26th 1525, The Imperial garrison under Leyva prepares for a long siege.

French garri

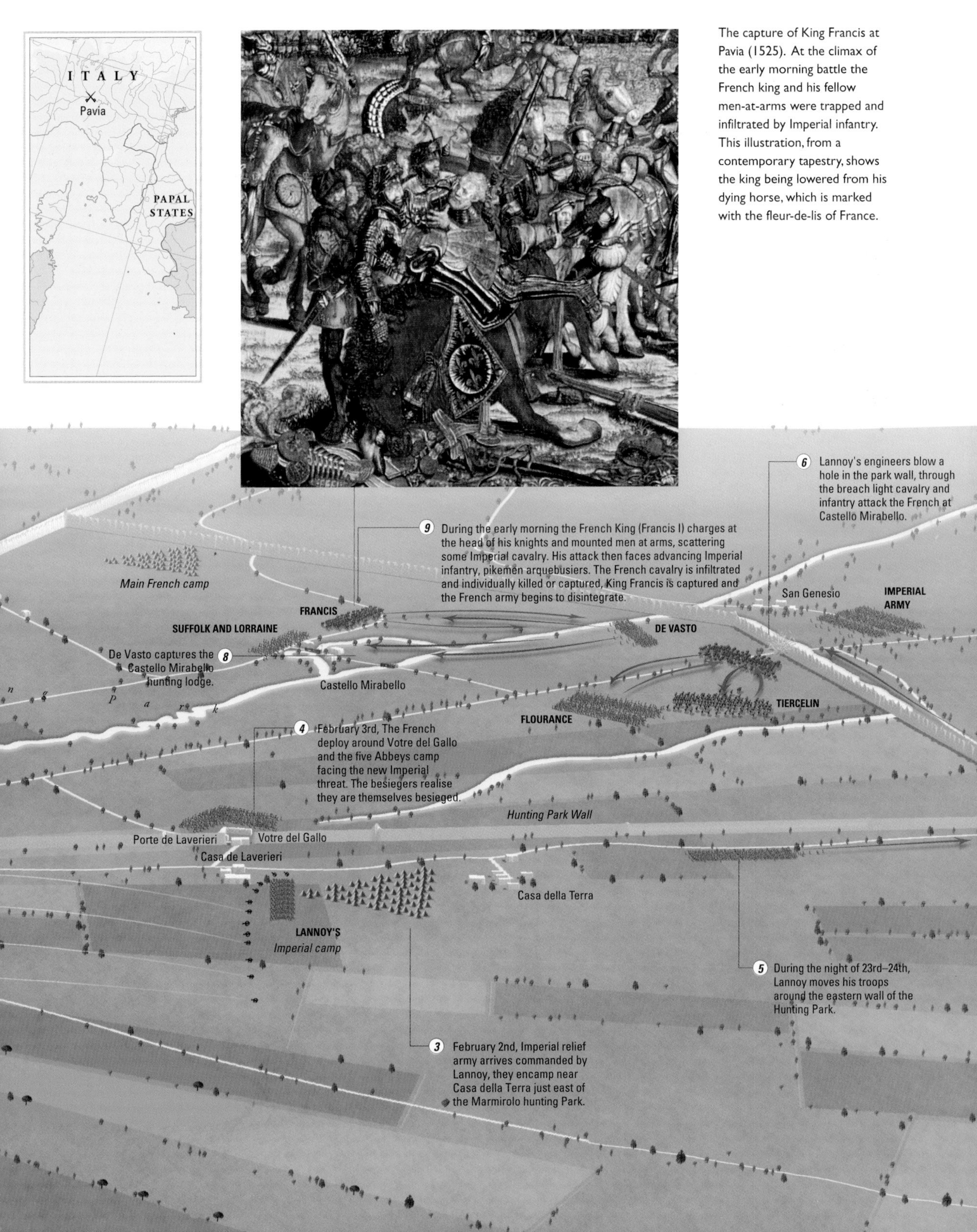

The capture of King Francis at Pavia (1525). At the climax of the early morning battle the French king and his fellow men-at-arms were trapped and infiltrated by Imperial infantry. This illustration, from a contemporary tapestry, shows the king being lowered from his dying horse, which is marked with the fleur-de-lis of France.

giving him a pension. He spent the rest of his life in a villa near Florence, dying aged 74 years in 1394. His reputation is based on the speed of his military movements, he had lighter armor and equipment than most to aid that rapidity, his archers, his skillful use of infantry, and the discipline of his troops. His memory is honored in Florence where there is a fresco depicting him in the Duomo (cathedral).

HENRY VIII, FRANCIS I, AND THE FIELD OF THE CLOTH OF GOLD

King Henry VIII of England and King Francis I of France shared many characteristics, both in character and position, and both monarchs were enthusiastic devotees of the tournament. In his youth, Henry had designed his own tourneying armor, later importing specialist German armorers with the permission of another royal tourneying enthusiast, Emperor Maximilian I of Germany, and establishing his own armory at Greenwich. He maintained permanent tiltyards at Greenwich, Westminster, and Hampton Court, and loved to celebrate great occasions, such as his accession to the throne, with lavish tournaments. Francis I was also an eager practitioner, anxious for a great chivalric reputation. He had requested to be dubbed to knighthood by the Chevalier Bayard, the most famous knight of the age, *sans peur et sans repoche*.

When they met outside Calais in the June of 1520, the occasion was primarily a diplomatic one, intended to forge peaceful and amicable relations between their two countries (they were at war within two years, however). The political aspects of the meeting were kept very low-key, however, and the splendid tournaments, jousts, and feasts that accompanied it appeared in the eyes of contemporary observers to take precedence over everything else. The arrangements for this great display of chivalric arts had taken months to prepare; the tents pitched in the field sparkled and shone with gold thread and embroidered gems, giving the occasion its popular name of the "Field of the Cloth of Gold."

The dimensions and construction of the tiltyard were the subject of lengthy correspondence between the household officers of each court. These had survived, together with a "panoramic view" of the scene at Hampton Court, which, however, employs a certain degree of artistic license. In the traditional style of the great 15th-Century *pas d'armes*, a tree was erected from which the three shields signifying combat with sword, axe, or lance were hung. Challengers touched the shields to indicate their preferred type of joust.

Each of the two kings led his own team of seven knights in the contests that followed, and bands of knights who had come as "challengers" in response to the proclamations that had been made in France, England, and the Low Countries, joined their chosen team. This was not difficult, as all the challengers were either English or French. The kings were, of course, vying to outdo one another in their splendor and magnificence; Francis's horse wore purple satin trimmed with gold and embroidered with black plumes, Henry's wore cloth of gold fringed with damask. The liveries of the two teams reflected this theme: French knights wore cloth of silver trimmed with purple velvet, English knights cloth of gold and russet velvet. The kings themselves appeared in a succession of sumptuous costumes, bearing chivalrous or patriotic mottoes. The kings jousted against each other and each other's knights (Henry rode one of his horses so hard in the jousting that it died later than night). Knights, within teams, jousted against each other as well as against their opponents. More than 300 spears were broken in these jousts and, unhappily, a French knight was fatally wounded after jousting against his own brother.

The jousts were followed by tourneying, but this consisted of knights fighting one another, two against two, instead of the traditional mêlée. Games of skill on horseback took place between the bouts, and other, less traditional sporting contests, were added, such as archery, in which Henry excelled. He also attempted to introduce an impromptu wrestling match, as one chronicler records:

> *"The King of England and the King of France retired together to a pavilion and drank together, and then the King of England took the King of France by the collar and said to him 'My brother, I want to wrestle with you,' and gave him one or two falls. And the King of France, who is strong and a good wrestler, gave him a 'Breton turn' and threw him on the ground... and the King of England wanted to go on wrestling, but it was broken off and they had to go to supper."*

Panorama of the *Field of the Cloth of Gold* (now at Hampton Court Palace). The artist has used some license; the field was actually further inland from Calais than it appears here, and it would not have been possible to see London in the distance.

Largesse was used almost as a weapon; if one king admired the other's horse, he was obliged to make a present of it, and several gifts exchanged hands in this way during the post-tournament drinking and feasting that concluded most days. At the end of the week's festivities, prizes were awarded, with both kings heading the list of prizewinners.

THE END OF THE KNIGHT

The French Army of King Louis XII approaches the defenses of Genoa in 1507. Amongst his forces was a gorgeously-equipped company of noble mounted men-at-arms; an impressive sight to all who witnessed it. This glory was not cheap: a fully-equipped knight needed a beautifully crafted suit of armor, yards of expensive fabric, and a full suite of personal equipment including a sword, shield, and axe, all of which was expensive to purchase and almost as expensive to maintain.

History has proved that well-led, disciplined infantry can always defeat cavalry. At Hastings or Senlac, the Anglo-Saxon shield wall held against repeated charges until some soldiers were lured from it after a feigned retreat. At Bannockburn, Robert the Bruce, with schiltrons armed with pikes, pushed the English knights into the banks of a stream and marshy ground where they were pinned down and slaughtered. The Scots army was a people's army fighting to preserve Scotland's independence, and national motivation gives will power to stand firm against an enemy. Likewise, the people's armies of Flanders and Switzerland proved that infantry can take on horse soldiers. The Swiss relied on pikemen but they required other troops to get the pikemen in range of the enemy. They used crossbowmen and handguns to counter the enemy's missile fire and used halberdiers for flank attacks while cavalry were trying to get into the pike block (formation). Charles the Bold of Burgundy, Duke of Burgundy from 1463, sought to link together his disparate lands. His army comprised Italian condottieri cavalry, English mounted longbowmen, and Flemish pikemen plus 500 artillery pieces. He intended to integrate all arms in mutual support but this was difficult to achieve.

In 1476, Charles took the Swiss-held town of Grandson but was forced to retreat after an initial success against a pike block when the main body of Swiss arrived. At Mürten, his fortified camp was overrun when the Swiss attacked him at lunchtime, pinning the Burgundian troops against a lake where they could be killed. At Nancy, Charles was again defeated, being killed in the rout of his forces. The determined Swiss became the best mercenary pikemen in Europe until other leaders upgraded their troops to include pikes.

The English archers, the bane of French chivalry, were expensive to train as was the construction of bows. The development of artillery changed the face of the battlefield. The Flemings developed the *ribaudequin*, a multibarreled gun mounted on a wheeled cart. This weapon was deployed at Beverhoutsfeld in 1382, enabling the men of Ghent to hold off a Brugeois attack until they turned the enemy flank with infantry. The Hussite gun-wagons proved effective against their enemies. The 1525 Battle of Pavia demonstrated the value of the Imperial arquebusiers against French cavalry. In England, it took so long to train an archer that when handguns became available it was cheaper to make a gun than a bow and anyone could use them. Artillery power made castles redundant. In France, castles became residences of pleasure. In England, Henry VII of England, at the end of the Wars of the Roses, made sure he controlled all the major castles and prevented noblemen from having large retinues in their livery, thereby diminishing noble power. His son's fortifications were basically gun battery platforms to protect English ports.

Essentially, the expense of armor and horses and novel means of firepower ensured that cavalry in the medieval knightly form was militarily redundant.

LEGACY OF THE KNIGHT

THE IMAGE OF THE KNIGHT IN SHINING ARMOUR DEFENDING HIS LADY AND SLAYING DRAGONS IS LARGELY A MYTH. YET, THE LEGEND LIVES ON AS AN IDEAL OF MILITARY, CHRISTIAN, COMRADELY AND COURTLY VIRTUES. THE CODE OF CHIVALRY IS NOT YET DEAD.

A poster for the 1952 film *Ivanhoe*. A spectacular MGM production which portrayed the life of the medieval knight in true Hollywood style.

FILM KNIGHT

The world is full of medieval images despite the period ending several hundred years ago. Each century has produced its own unique images of the knight in a variety of media: painting, architecture, poetry, music and the novel. The Elizabethan humanist, scholar, Roger Ascham (1515–1568) condemned Sir Thomas Malory's *Le Morte d'Arthur*:

> *"...the whole pleasure of which booke standeth in two speciall points, in open mans slaughter and bold bawdrye: In which booke these be counted the noblest Knightes, that do kill most men without any quarrel, and commit foulest adulteries by subtlest shiftes."*

In succeeding centuries, the knights' most lasting and powerful legacy was their literature, in particular the best of the medieval romances and chivalrous treatises, and the histories and chronicles of writers such as Froissart and theorists such as Geoffrey de Chargny and Ramon Lull. For centuries, knights were see by scholars of antiquity through the romantically tinted medium of chivalrous literature, gaining great insight into the ethos of an era, but not its lives. In the 18th and 19th Centuries poets, such as Keats, Coleridge, Browning and Tennyson were fascinated by the idea of the Middle Ages, in turn inspiring Pre-Raphaelite painters.

Arguably, 19th Century industrial society saw a revival in 'Chivalry' as a concept when ancient honour and its code offered a psychological need and escape for those increasingly pressurised by the transformation of England into an industrial, mechanical, commercial and urban society which could lose its traditional values and beliefs. In 1790, the conservative politician, Edmund Burke, said of the death of Marie Antoinette in the French revolution:

> *"Little did I dream that I should have lived to see disasters fallen upon her in a nation of gallant men, a nation of men of honour, and of cavaliers. I thought ten thousand swords must have leapt from their scabbards to avenge even a look that threatened her with insult. But the age of chivalry is gone. That of sophisters, economists, and calculators, has succeeded; and the glory of Europe is extinguished for ever."*

In the 20th and 21st Centuries, film has defined medieval history more so than any other medium and people's conceptions of the Middle Ages are coloured by the strong stories and images of film. Hollywood films have reached a wide audience with big budget productions. Romanticism moved to the screen in influential works like *Ivanhoe* (1952), based on Sir Walter Scott's 1819 novel of the same name, and *El Cid* (1961). There have been many others ranging from the 1954 *Black Shield of Falworth*, *The Lion in Winter* (1968), *Caedfael* (1994), and the *Kingdom of Heaven* (2005). So great is medieval subject matter on film that some university courses teach the area, such as Georgia College and State University's HIST 4950 Medieval World in Film. Europe has produced Fritz Lange's two-film series *Die Nibelungen: Siegfrieds Tod* and *Die Nibelungen: Kriemhilds Rache* (1924), Sergei Eisenstein's *Alexander Nevsky* (1938), and Ingmar Bergman's *The Seventh Seal* (1957). And, 1954 witnessed a tale of Asian knighthood in Akira Kurusawa's *Seven Samurai*.

The most recent film portrayal of the knights' ethos can be found in the Jedi, the noble monastic peace-keeping organisation portrayed in the *Star Wars* series. Exemplified by Obi-Wan Kenobi, Yoda

Russian film maker Eisenstein produced *Alexander Nevsky*, a dramatisation of Russia's struggle against an invading army of Teutonic Knights, released in 1939. By 1941, Russia's struggle had become all too real.

In the best traditions of the medieval knightly orders, the Jedi Knights from *Star Wars* fight evil in all its forms seeking no personal reward. The trusty sword has been replaced by the light sabre, here wielded by Obi-Wan Kenobi (above). In the imaginary battlefields on distant worlds of the future, body armour has made a comeback, as shown on this well-armed mercenary warrior (below).

and Luke Skywalker, these warriors wield their lightsabres or sometimes two, and occasionally double-handed weapons. The analogies with old chivalry are clear. The Jedi Order uses the Ashla or good side of the Force to combat evil in an unselfish manner to benefit society. The force can be understood in terms of Christianity's mystical side, of Chine qi, Japanese *Ki* or Indian *prana*, or the experiences felt in the *latihan* prayer of *Susila Budhi Dharma*. Thus, the Jedi principles resemble some world religions and the series touch people.

The Jedi live a life of simplicity, adhering to the code with no material possessions. They train their *padawan* (apprentices/squire) who can be given the accolade of knight after fulfilling severe physical tests while displaying skill, knowledge and dedication to the Code. In their wars against the Sith, a cult using the dark side of the Force, the Order appeared to be the last bastion of civilization against an alien ideology as they had been in earlier times when their headquarters temple on planet Coruscant was destroyed. One can draw parallels between the Jedi and certain crusading Orders such as the Teutonic knights against pagans, and the Templars, Hospitallers and those of Calatrava in wars against Islam, not always successful ones. There are themes in the Jedi redolent of the Japanese *sohei*. These priest-monks, akin to the Teutonic warrior-monks, were dedicated Buddhists linked to a particular monastery in their thousands, such as the communities at Mount Hiei and the Shingon sect at Negoroji in Kii Province. The fortified Buddhist 'cathedrals' at Nagashima and Ishiyama Honganji rivalled any samurai castle or crusader bastion. Like the Jedi, the Teutonic knights and *sohei* are bound together by zeal for their particular beliefs and faiths making their armies a match for anyone. No wonder the cinema audiences are attracted to the old themes when portrayed in science fiction: the ethos of chivalry still excites.

LATE MEDIEVAL SECULAR ORDERS

The secular orders of knighthood which became so popular in the 14th and 15th Centuries had little in common with their religious predecessors, the military religious orders. The latter were indeed religious, in the sense of committing their members to a way of life cut off from secular concerns, such as the pursuit of worldly honour and loyalty to individual secular lords, and governed by monastic rule. The secular orders, on the contrary, were very much concerned with the rewards and celebrations of worldly honour and most of their statutes enforced specific loyalties, to their founding lord and his heirs, and, more commonly, to each other, so that a member had to do everything possible to help other members and their disputes were his disputes. In part, this can be understood as an attempt to breathe new life into the ideology of knighthood: to recreate closer bonds to loyalty and brotherhood between knights who acknowledged specific objectives in a world in which the old-fashioned values of chivalry were becoming increasingly difficult to maintain. The secular orders were formed for less idealistic reasons, such as the reinforcement of privileges and the exclusive status of the knightly class, and the creation of useful alliances in the pursuit of diplomatic and political ends.

The orders were, of course, religious in the usual knightly sense; they sought to emphasis that piety and respectful religious observance were essential qualities of true chivalry. Many associated

In this 15th-Century French illustration, the king founds the Order of the Star and can be seen wearing its regalia. The new orders stated principal aim was to honour and glorify the traditions of French knighthood. Its real reason may have been to attract the nobility of France to his person and his rule; in this hope the order failed.

themselves with specific saints, St. George being the most popular, or feast days, concerning themselves with the establishment of charitable foundations, endowing chantry chapels and paying for masses; and all had ordinances for religious services before or after their meetings.

These orders were many and varied. Some were founded by kings or great lords, such as the Order of the Band, founded in about 1330 by King Alfonso XI of Castile, the Order of the Garter, founded in 1351 by King John of France whereas the English version was created by King Edward III in 1348. The Order of the Knot was founded in 1352 by King Louis of Naples, and the Order of the Buckle was founded in 1355 by Emperor Charles. IV. There were many others. Some were temporary societies in which members were bound together by particular oaths that they had sworn, such as the Order of the Dame Blanche a l'Escu Vert (the White Lady of the Green Shield) of Marshall Jean de Boucicaut. Others were basically associations of like-minded knights, calling themselves 'confraternities' or 'brotherhoods', as well as Orders. These were particularly common in Germany, where many knightly brotherhoods were formed along lines of tourneying societies, which had been in existence form some time.

Certain characters were shared by all orders and confraternities. They all had constitutions and regulations laid down in statutes, defining the objectives of the association and the rules governing eligibility for membership, and conduct of members. All held meetings or 'chapters' regularly, once a year or more frequently, to outline activities, celebrate achievements, initiate new members or discipline existing ones. All were exclusive about the social status of people who could be invited to join (the sole exception being the Order of the Ermine in Naples, which admitted men who had been knighted as a reward for their deeds, even if they were not of noble birth). All selected some members to act as officials, each of whom had specific duties to perform. All had special robes or insignia, which could be worn only by members.

Noble birth, though in most cases a prerequisite for membership of a secular Order, was by no means the only one. Most Orders and confraternities would only admit members possessing a good reputation and were *sans reproche*. Robber knights, the impious who had been repeatedly excommunicated, and any knight who spoke ill of women were all excluded from membership by the constitutions of some German Orders. For example, almost all had provisions for judging and punishing any members guilty of misconduct, which could range from showing cowardice in battle, to behaving discourteously towards ladies. The majority of Orders were exclusive to men, but some admitted ladies as well, such as the Order of the Dragon of the Count of Foix, the Order of St. Anthony of the Counts of Hainault, and, at least in its early days, the Order of the Garter. Whether they admitted ladies to membership or not, the service to ladies was an important element of most constitutions. The Castilian Order of the Band defined the two principal objectives of its members as the preservation of chivalric honour, and of loyalty, a value on which much store was set:

> *"Loyalty is one of the greatest virtues that there can be in any person, and especially in a knight, who ought to keep himself loyal in many ways. But the principal ways are two: first to keep loyalty to his lord, and secondly to love truly her in whom he has placed his heart."*

This illustration, from the 1890s, shows a member of the Knightly Order of the Grand Cross. It was fashionable at the time to imitate the dress of the late Middle Ages.

Members of Marshal Boucicaut's Order of the White Lady of the Green Shield swore an oath to serve ladies for five years. This service included taking the part of widows or women without menfolk of their own in legal disputes as well as the more obvious aspects of physical protection. The honour and service of ladies was only one aspect of the avowed chivalric aims of secular orders which had been influenced by romance literature. The Round Table of King Arthur was said to have inspired Edward III in his creation of the Order of the Gartar.

The king in the nobility of his heart resolved that he would rebuild Windsor Castle, which Arthur first constructed and where the Round Table was first established, an account of the prowess of the knights who were there then, who had served him as well that he held them so worthy and noble that their peers could not be found in any kingdom; and it seemed to him that he could not honour them too much, so much did he love them.

Other orders, too, were influenced by romances, such as the *Roman de Troie* or the 14th Century French romance, *Perceforest*. The prestige which was associated with membership of an order such as these, in which membership was only open to those who had the most distinguished records of character and service, was a major factor in their success. The secular orders represent an important, new and vigorous growth of later medieval chivalry, in which practical aims were combined with a genuine respect for values of chivalry and an attempt to revive those values in a valid and contemporary context. In this sense, they were a transition into contemporary chivalric orders where service is again stressed.

CONTEMPORARY ORDERS OF KNIGHTHOOD

The more recent monarchical orders are honorific, designed as a reward for personal services to the sovereign or state or as a means to confer prestige and distinction, and entailing no real commitment to any course of action, or loyalty to the sovereign beyond the normal citizen's call of duty. Some high ranking orders seemed to be given to any head of state like army rations and appear to be fairly meaningless. The distinction between an order and 'decoration' is now rather arbitrary. Some orders created in the 17th and 18th Centuries were given for military merit without noble rank, no limited membership, no chapter, no laid down activities. Examples are legion: a few with fascinating names are given here: Precious Blood (Mantua, 1608), Amarantha (Sweden, 1645); Elephant (Denmark, 1693 revival); White Eagle (Poland, 1713); and Fidelity (Baden, 1715). A few well-known orders include:

This 15th Century illustration shows the Arms of England, lower left, and the Arms of France, lower right, together with the Arms of the Order of the Garter, together with the word, Concordia.

Order of the Garter

When Edward III founded the Order of the Garter in 1344 he used the chapel of St. George as its centre with a small group of 26 knights, each of whom would have a stall in the chapel. The name of the Order is said to have referred to when the Countess of Salisbury lost her garter at a court ball in Calais, reprimanding those who mocked her with the words which came to be the motto of the Order: *Honi soit qui mal y pense*, shame on him who thinks evil of it. Apparently, the king used the words to mean his claim to the throne of France. Making somebody a member of the order is in the gift of the sovereign.

Order of the Bath

The Order of the Bath was founded by George I, the name being derived from the bath of purification needed before being dubbed a knight. Awarding membership to the Order was used by Prime Minister Walpole at that time as one of a system of awards which would bind people to him in Parliament: the buying of favours. The Chapel of the Order is the Henry VII Lady Chapel in Westminster Abbey.

Order of the Rising Sun

Conferred in Japan on men only, the Order of the Rising Sun is awarded for military or civil affairs. Women can be awarded the Order of the Precious Crown instead. The award, unlike in Europe, can be given posthumously.

Supreme Order of the Chrysanthemum

The highest Japanese Order, its Grand Cordon is the highest honour for a Japanese citizen. Apart from the imperial household, only three grand cordons have been given to living citizens and eleven posthumously.

Order of Malta

After the Hospitallers were banished from Malta by Napoleon I, they were not allowed to return when Britain gained the island. The Order of Malta, as it is now, moved to Messina, Catania, and Ferrara before settling in Rome in 1834, where it owns two properties with extraterritoriality rights. The Order has 12,000 members as well as 80,000 trained volunteers and 11,000 employees and is heavily engaged in medical and humanitarian activities. Most volunteers work in the ambulance corps. It has hospitals in Germany, France, Belgium, England and Italy and carries out much work with the terminally ill. Its French Association runs medical facilities in West Africa, and in Senegal and Cambodia the Order runs hospitals for lepers. Much work is carried out around the world for disabled people and for the old. The Order runs institutions for the homeless in Belgium, France, Switzerland, Hungary, Germany, Italy and the U.S.A. In Germany and Portugal, the Order handles drug addicts and a rehabilitation centre in the latter. Whenever there is a refugee problem from a natural disaster, the Orders workers will be there, such as earthquake relief in Armenia in 1989 and in the Czech Republic in 2002 after serious flooding after summer storms.

Windsor Castle, King Henry VII Gate, the main entrance to the largest inhabited castle in the world and the oldest in continuous occupation.

WINDSOR CASTLE: TOURISM

In Saxon times there was a royal residence at Windsor but William the Conqueror constructed a motte and bailey castle there in 1070, with successive kings building in stone, and Edward II building a chapel to be the centre of his Order of the Garter. The castle now comprises two sets of quadrilateral-shaped building complexes that are separated by the huge Round Tower. The court west of the tower is the lower ward, that to the east is the upper ward. The lower ward contains St. George's Chapel and the Albert Memorial Chapel. The castle is open to tourists to see the chapels, some private rooms, and various collections. The town fills with tourists in summer with other attractions being Eton College and river trips on the Thames.

BELVOIR CASTLE: FAMILY HOME

Belvoir Castle is a home in Leicestershire, England, built on the site of an old Norman castle. During the English Civil War it was a royalist stronghold Its façade was rebuilt after a fire in the 19th Century.

BELVOIR CASTLE, Leicestershire, England. This castle has been occupied continuously as a family home since the 11th Century.

The central tower looks like that at Windsor Castle.

The castle is a home and working castle. Inhabited by David, 11th Duke of Rutland and Marquess of Granby and his duchess, Emma, with their five children their life replicates many ordinary people with the chores of school runs and running the family business, albeit in a large castle. The castle has estates to run, the land to maintain, and the castle can be hired for conferences and weddings, in a variety of rooms with fine-sounding names: Guard Room, Ball Room, State Dining Room, Picture Gallery, Old Kitchen, Old Servants Hall, Stewards Room, and the Old Library. The family also owns and runs the Manners Arms public house in Knipton. Additionally, visitors are allowed and there is and associated business which produces an interesting range of cordials: elderflower, ginger, blackcurrant, blueberry and cranberry.

FAIRYTALE CASTLES: NEUSCHWANSTEIN

Schloss Neuschwanstein castle or New Swan Stone Castle is a late 19th-Century castle near Hohenschwangau and Füssen in southwest Bavaria. The build commenced on the orders of King

Ludwig II of Bavaria, being inspired by the Swan Knight, Lohengrin, in his friend's, Wagner's opera. Built by Christian Jank, the castle is near the older schloss of Hohenschwangau which had been restored by his father, Maxmillian II of Bavaria, and where Ludwig was born.

Ludwig lived in a fantasy world sleeping during the day and waking at night. He increasingly identified himself with Parsifal, the legendary Grail Knight, who through his purity saved his uncle, a notorious sinner. Ludwig was obsessed by the conflict between good and evil. The schloss was intended to be a monument to the *minnesingers* (German knight, troubadour and poet) of Medieval times, but Ludwig saw it as the Castle of the Holy Grail, the Throne Room being redesigned as the Hall of the Holy Grail, dedicated to the salvation of mankind. In 1886, Ludwig was legally deposed according to the Bavarian constitution after being declared mad. The next day, his body was discovered drowned in Lake Starnberg together with the psychiatrist who had certified him.

Tapestries and paintings in the castle rooms show scenes from Wagner's operas. Ludwig's concept of purity was unusual; he thought the prose of his mother's, Marie of Prussia, desecrated Hohenschwahgau, and the gods would leave, fleeing to Neuschwanstein to breathe the air of heaven.

SCHLOSS NEUSCHWANSTEIN in Bavaria, Germany. King Ludwig II of Bavaria indulged his infatuation with all things medieval in constructing the fantasy castle of Neuschwanstein in 1868. It is said to have been inspirational for numerous film makers and cartoonists even since.

Neuschwanstein has appeared in television programmes such as *The Amazing Race* and Grimm's Fairy Tale Classics. The schloss is shown in several films including *Chitty Chitty Bang Bang, The Timekeeper, Ludwig* and *Spaceballs*. It also inspired the Sleeping Beauty Castle at Disneyland.

CASTLE DROGO: ENGLAND'S LAST CASTLE

Castle Drogo can be found at Drewsteignton, Devon, not far from Okehampton and Exeter. This country house was built in the 1920s and 1930s for Julius Drewe (1856–1931), a millionaire and self-made businessman and founder of the Home and Colonial Stores. Drewe commenced researching his ancestry after retiring from the tea and retail trades. His findings produced a discernable link to a Norman baron called Drogo (or Dru) de Teigne, whose family had given their name to the Devon's parish of Drewsteignton on the River Teigne.

Wanting an unique and splendid stately home in this wild part of Devon, he employed the renowned architect, Edwin Lutyens. The build commenced in 1910 and lasted 20 years. The stately home is a granite pseudo-castle overlooking the Teign gorge, borrowing style from the medieval and Tudor periods. The defensive characteristics are pure decoration. An interesting feature of the castle is the encasement of a service staircase around which the main staircase climbs. The castle possesses an excellent garden, designed by Lutyens with Gertrude Jekyll in charge of planting, which contrasts with the wildness of the edge of Dartmoor. Among the estate's oak tress are mounds where timber is burnt to make charcoal. The building was handed over to the English National Trust in 1974, being the first 20th Century building the charity had acquired.

HEARST CASTLE

Hearst Castle is the palatial estate built by newspaper tycoon William Randolph Hearst (1863–1951). Built on a hill overlooking the Pacific Ocean, it is located at San Simeon halfway between Los Angeles and San Francisco. Named La Cuesta Encantada, the Enchanted Hill, it was donated to the state of California in 1957 by the Hearst Corporation.

HEARST CASTLE, San Simeon, California, United States of America. This castle was built on a 40,000 acre estate originally purchased by George Hearst in 1865 and inherited by Randolph, by which time the estate had grown to 250,000 acres. Construction began in 1919 and continued until 1947.

The castle is a mixture of architectural styles viewed by Hearst on his European travels. San Francisco architect, Julia Morgan, designed almost all of the buildings, though Hearst himself was an inveterate tinkerer. He would have structures demolished and re-built at a whim, and the castle was never completed in his lifetime. The castle is reputed to contain 56 bedrooms, 61 bathrooms and 19 sitting rooms. Hearst furnished this vast space with art and antiques, even complete decorated ceilings that he had acquired from Europe and Egypt. Outside there were 127 acres of manicured gardens, tennis courts, a theatre, an airfield and the world's largest private zoo. The main house looks like a 16th-Century Spanish Cathedral while the outdoor pool sports an ancient Roman temple front transported from Europe and reconstructed on site. Hearst's chief guests came from the worlds of cinema and politics, including Charlie Chaplin and Winston Churchill. One scion of the house is Patty Hearst known for her flirtation with the Symbionese Liberation Front. The castle is truly a palace, the dream of a potentate, a mish-mash of styles, much like some European architecture.

The Death of King Arthur is an evocative picture of mystical beauty captured by the Scottish painter James Archer who, in 1859 began to paint a series of Arthurian subjects. Arthur's death is shrouded in mystery. In Archer's painting the king, wounded during the Last Battle of Camlann, knew he was to die and asked his trusted knight Sir Bedivere to toss his magic sword Excalibur back into the lake from which he had received it. Shortly afterwards, while Arthur lay dying, watched over by his half-sister Morgan Le Fay, three queens arrived. The Queen of the Waste Lands, the Queen of Northgales, and the Lady of the Lake transported Arthur to the island of Avalon to be cured. The ghostly appearance of an angel bearing the Holy Grail perhaps indicates the king's eventual fate and death.

Bibliography

The author readily acknowledges the work of many scholars and published works that have been consulted in preparation of this atlas. Amongst this selected bibliography are books recommended for further reading and study of knights, castles, and chivalry.

Alexander, Jonathan and Binski, Paul, *Age of Chivalry: Art in Plantagenet England, 1200–1400*, London: Royal Academy of Arts with London: Weidenfeld and Nicolson, 1987

Anderson, Roberta and Bellinger, Dominic, *Medieval Religion. A Sourcebook*, London: Routledge, 2006

Arnold, Benjamin, *Power and Property in Medieval Germany. Economic and Social Change, c.900–1300*, Oxford: Oxford University Press, 2004

Barron, Caroline M., *London in the Later Middle Ages. Government and People, 1200–1500*, Oxford: Oxford University, 2005

Bennet, Judith M. and Warren Hollister, C., *Medieval Europe. A Short History*, New York: McGraw Hill, 2006

Berkhofer, Robert F. III, Cooper, Alan, Kosto, Adam J. (eds), *The Experience of Power in Medieval Europe, 950–1350*, Aldershot: Ashgate, 2005

Boas, Adrian, *Archaeology of the Military Orders*, London: Routledge, 2006

Bradbury, Jim, *The Routledge Companion to Medieval Warfare*, London: Routledge 2004

Brears, Peter, et al., *A Taste of History. 10,000 Years of Food in Britain*, London: English Heritage, 1994

Brooke, Christopher, *The Saxon and Norman Kings*, Oxford: Blackwell Publishing, 2001

Brown, Warren C. and Górecki, Piotr, *Conflict in Medieval Europe*, Aldershot: Ashgate, 2003

Caille, Jacqueline, *Medieval Narbonne. A City at the Heart of the Troubadour World*, Aldershot: Ashgate, 2005

Cameron, Averil, *The Byzantines*, Oxford: Blackwell Publishing, 2006

Cardini, Franco, *Europe and Islam*, Oxford: Blackwell Publishing, 2001

Castleden, Rodney, *King Arthur*, London: Routledge, 2003

Chibnall, M., *The Normans*, Oxford: Blackwell Publishing, 2006

Christiansen, Eric, *The Norsemen in the Viking Age*, Oxford: Blackwell Publishing, 2001

Christiansen, Eric, *The Northern Crusades. The Baltic and the Catholic Frontier 1100–1525*, London: Macmillan Press Ltd., 1980

Clanchy, M. T., *England and its Rulers, 1066–1307*, Oxford: Blackwell Publishing, 2006

Cohn, Samuel K., Jr., *The Black Death Transformed*, London: Hodder and Stoughton, 2003

Collins, Roger, *The Arab Conquest of Spain, 710–797*, Oxford: Blackwell Publishing, 1994

Contamine, Philippe, *War in the Middle Ages*, Oxford: Blackwell Publishing, 1986

Costen, Michael, *The Cathars and the Albigensian Crusade*, Manchester: Manchester University Press, 1997

Coulson, Charles, *Castles in Medieval Society. Fortresses in England, France and Ireland in the Central Middle Ages*, Oxford: Oxford University Press, 2004

Crouch, David, *The Birth of Nobility: Constructing Aristocracy in England and France, 900–1300*, London: Longman, 2005

Crouch, David, William Marshal: *Knighthood, War, and Chivalry, 1147–1219*, London: Longman, 2002

Cushing, Kathleen, G., *Reform and the Papacy in the Eleventh Century*, Manchester: Manchester University Press, 2005

Devries, Kelly et al., *Battles of the Medieval World 1000–1500*, London: Amber Books Ltd., 2006

Donner, Fred M., *The Early Islamic Conquests*, New Jersey, Princeton: Princeton University Press, 2005

Duby, Georges, *France in the Middle Ages, 987–1460*, Oxford: Blackwell Publishing, 1993

Duggan, A., *Thomas Becket*, London: Hodder and Stoughton, 2004

Earenfight, Theresa, *Queenship and Political Power in Medieval and Early Modern Spain*, Aldershot: Ashgate, 2005

Edwards, John, *The Spain of the Catholic Monarchs, 1474–1520*, Oxford: Blackwell Publishing, 2001

Foster, Roy F., *The Oxford Illustrated History of Ireland*, Oxford: Oxford University Press, 1989

Fowler, Kenneth, *Medieval Mercenaries, Vol. I: The Great Companies*, Oxford: Blackwell Publishing, 2001

Fowler, Kenneth, *Medieval Mercenaries, Vol. II: Sir John Hawkwood and the English Condottieri in Italy*, Oxford: Blackwell Publishing, 2007

France, John, *Medieval Warfare, 1000–1300*, Aldershot: Ashgate, 2006

France, John, *The Crusades and the Expansion of Catholic Christendom*,

1000–1714, London: Routledge, 2005

Friar, Stephen and Ferguson, John, *Basic Heraldry*, London: A & C Black, 1999

Friday, Karl, *Samurai, Warfare, and the State in Early Medieval Japan*, London: Routledge, 2003

Gillingham, John, *The Angevin Empire*, Hodder and Stoughton, 2000

Given-Wilson, Chris, *The English Nobility in the Late Middle Ages*, London: Routledge, 1996

Haldon, John, *Warfare, State and Society in the Byzantine World*, London: Routledge, 1999

Hamilton, Bernard, *Religion in the Medieval West*, London: Hodder and Stoughton, 2003

Harriss, Gerald, *Shaping the Nations. England, 1360–1461*, Oxford: Oxford University Press, 2005

Herlihy, David, *Medieval Households*, London: Harvard University Press, 1985

Holmes, George, *Europe: Hierarchy and Revolt, 1320–1450*, Oxford: Blackwell Publishing, 2000

Holt, R. and Rosser, G., *The Medieval Town in England, 1200–1540*, London: Longman, 1990

Hopkins, Andrea, *Knights. The Complete Story of the Age of Chivalry, from Historical Fact to Tales of Romance and Poetry*, Edison, New Jersey: Chartwell Books, Inc., 2001

Houben, Hubert, *Roger II of Sicily*, Cambridge: Cambridge University Press, 2002

Howell, Margaret, *Eleanor of Provence*, Oxford: Blackwell Publishing, 2001

Huscroft, Richard, *Ruling England, 1042–1217*, London: Longman, 2005

Jackson, Peter, *The Mongols and the West, 1221–1410*, London: Longman, 2005

Jacoby, David, *Commercial Exchange across the Mediterranean. Byzantium, the Crusader Levant, Egypt and Italy*, Aldershot: Ashgate, 2005

Jaspert, Nikolas, *The Crusades*, London: Routledge, 2006

Johns, Susan M., *Noblewomen, Aristocracy and Power in the Twelfth-Century Anglo-Norman Realms,* Manchester: Manchester University Press, 2003

Johnson, Matthew, *Behind the Castle Gate*, London: Routledge, 2002

Jung, Emma & Von Franz, Marie-Louise, *The Grail Legend, New Jersey*, Princeton: Princeton University Press, 1970

Keen, Maurice H., *England in the Later Middle Ages*, London: Routledge, 2003

Kennedy, Hugh, *The Armies of the Caliphs*, London: Routledge, 2001

Lambert, M. D., *Medieval Heresy*, Oxford: Blackwell Publishing, 2002

Laynesmith, J. L., *The Last Medieval Queens. English Queenship, 1445–1503*, Oxford: Oxford University Press, 2005

Lawrence, C. H., *Medieval Monasticism: Forms of Religious Life in Western Europe in the Middle Ages*, London: Longman, 2000

Le Goff, Jacques, *Medieval Civilization, 400–1500*, Oxford: Blackwell Publishing, 1990

Le Goff, Jacques, *The Birth of Europe*, Oxford: Blackwell Publishing, 2006

Le Roy Ladurie, Emmanuel, Montailliou. *Cathars and Catholics in a French Village, 1294–1324*, London: Scolar Press, 1978

Lock, Peter, *The Routledge Companion to the Crusades*, London: Routledge, 2006

Lupack, Alan, *The Oxford Guide to Arthurian Literature and Legend*, Oxford: Oxford University Press, 2005

Mackay, Angus with Ditchburn, David, *Atlas of Medieval Europe*, London: Routledge, 1997

McLynn, Frank, *1066. The Year of Three Battles*, London: Pimlico, 1999

Najemy, John M., *Italy in the Age of the Renaissance, 1300–1550*, Oxford: Oxford University Press, 2004

Neillands, Robin, *The Hundred Years' War*, London: Routledge, 2001

Noble, Thomas F. X., *From Roman Provinces to Medieval Kingdoms*, London: Routledge, 2006

Oldenbourg, Zoé, *Massacre at Montségur. A History of the Albigensian Crusade*, London: Phoenix Press, 2000

Pearsall, Derek, *Arthurian Romance*, Oxford: Blackwell Publishing, 2003

Petit-Dutaillis, C., *The Feudal Monarchy in France and England*, London: Routledge, 1997

Power, Daniel, *The Central Middle Ages, 950–1320*, Oxford: Oxford University Press, 2006

Power, Daniel, *The Norman Frontier in the Twelfth and Early Thirteenth Centuries*, Cambridge: Cambridge University Press, 2004

Prestwich, Michael, *Plantagenet England, 1225–1360*, Oxford: Oxford University Press, 2005

Raban, Sandra, *England under Edward I and Edward II*, Oxford: Blackwell Publishing, 2000

Reichert, Michelle, *Between Courtly Literature and Al-Andalus. Oriental Symbolism and Influences in the Romances of Chrétien de Troyes*, London: Routledge, 2006

Reilly, Bernard, *The Contest of Christian and Muslim Spain*, Oxford: Blackwell Publishing, 1995

Rose, Susan, *Medieval Naval Warfare*, London: Routledge, 2001

Riley-Smith, Jonathan (ed.), *The Atlas of the Crusades*, New York: Facts on File, Inc., 1991

Story, Joanna (ed)., *Charlemagne. Empire and Society*, Manchester: Manchester University Press, 2005

Thomas, Hugh M., *The English and the Normans. Ethnic Hostility, Assimilation, and Identity, 1066-c.1220*, Oxford: Oxford University Press, 2005

Thompson, Michael, *The Medieval Hall. The Basis of Secular Domestic Life, 600–1600 AD*, Aldershot: Scolar Press, 1995

Turnbull, Stephen, *Samurai: The World of the Warrior*, Wellingborough: Osprey Publishing, 2005

Turnbull, Stephen and McBride, Angus, *Japanese Heraldry*, Wellingborough: Osprey Publishing, 2002

Turner, Ralph V. and Heiser, Richard R., *The Reign of Richard Lionheart: Ruler of the Angevin Empire, 1189–1199*, London: Longmsn, 2000

Ullman, Walter, *A Short History of the Papacy in the Middle Ages*, London: Routledge, 2002

Villalon, L. J. Andrew and Kagay, Donald J., *Crusaders, Condottieri, and Cannon: Medieval Warfare in Societies around the Mediterranean*, The Netherlands, Leiden: Brill, 2002

Walvin, James, *Atlas of Slavery*, Harlow: Pearson Education Ltd., 2006

White, Stephen D., *Feuding and Peace-making in Eleventh Century France*, Aldershot: Ashgate, 2005

White, Stephen D., *Rethinking Kinship and Feudalism in Early Medieval Europe*, Aldershot: Ashgate, 2006

Winks, Robin W. and Ruiz, Teofilo F., *Medieval Europe and the World. From Late Antiquity to Modernity, 400–1500*, Oxford: Oxford University Press, 2005

Wood, Charles T., *The French Apanages and the Capetian Monarchy, 1224–1328*, London: Harvard University Press, 1966

Index

Figures in *italics* refer to illustrations.

A

B

F

G

H

I

J

K

L

M

P

R

S

T

U

W

Z

ACKNOWLEDGMENTS

For Cartographica Press
Design, Maps and Typesetting: Jeanne Radford, P A B Smith, Alexander Swanston, Malcolm Swanston and Jonathan Young

The publishers would like to thank the following picture libraries for their kind permission to use their pictures and illustrations:

Red Lion: pp. 10, 14, 15, 23, 29, 32, 37, 58,79, 101, 140, 170, 183, 184, 193, 202, 203, 205, 206, 208, 211, 217, 224, 225, 226, 227, 234, 240, 268, 276, 305, 342, 347, 353, 367
Dover Publications: pp. 11, 18, 44, 45, 48, 50, 56, 76, 82, 83, 98, 101, 105, 115, 146, 148, 149, 150, 156, 157, 160, 161, 164, 165, 167, 171, 174, 176, 177, 178, 179, 187, 188, 194, 196, 197, 230, 233, 237, 238, 244, 246, 247, 249, 250, 251, 252, 253, 308, 358, 366
Private Collection: 12, 21, 26, 34, 72, 78, 80, 195, 204, 209, 277, 284, 293, 330, 331, 333, 338, 341, 343, 344, 348, 351, 353, 354, 356, 364, 38, 381, 382
e.t.archives: 13, 24, 49, 68, 135, 158, 337
Historishes Museum, Bern: 16
Bibliotheque Nationale, Paris: 27, 134, 260, 274, 373, 377
Rheinischer Landesmuseum, Bonn: 30
Quarto Publishing Group: 31, 57, 97, 147, 151, 152, 153, 181, 185, 186, 189, 211, 283, 350, 359
John Haywood: 36
National Film Board, Norway: 38
Spanish Tourism Board: 41, 218, 239, 298, 302, 303
Pierpont Morgan Library/Art Resource, New York: 52
Peter Newark's Historical Pictures: 54, 81, 114, 270
Bayeux Tapestry: 60, 62, 64
British Museum: 61, 128, 210
Scottish Tourist Board 70
Alari: 83, 85
Bryan Byron: 86
Michael Holford: 88
British Library: 89, 99, 118, 124, 127, 129, 136, 166, 201, 220, 221, 260, 267, 271, 325, 384
Cathedral Treasury, Hereford: 93
Getty Archive: 96, 168
Internet sources: 111, 375, 378, 383
Trustees of the Wallace Collection: 113
Giraudon: 116
University Library, Heidelburg: 117
Mareanne Marjarus: 132
Musée Condé, Chantilly: 138, 229
Durham Cathedral Library: 141
Royal Armouries, Leeds: 142, 143, 145, 154, 155, 162, 163, 222, 360, 368
House of Lords: 175
Fernand Nathan: 190
Christopher Page: 198
Sussex Tourist Board: 212
English Heritage: 213
Colin Baxter: 214
Skyscan: 215
Jean Williamson: 216
Sonia Halliday: 218
The Art Archive: 223
Osterreichische Nationalbibliothek: 235, 257
Bayerische Staatsbibliotheke: 254
Greek Tourist Board: 285
Bodliean Library: 320, 332, 379
Wojeiech von Kossak: 323
Japanese Tourist Board: 345, 346, 352
MGM: 374
Lucasfilm: 376

Every effort has been made to contact the copyright holders for images reproduced in this book. The publishers would welcome any errors or omissions being brought to their attention.